Endorsements

"*'From Zion to a City of Hope: A Journey of Faith'* is well written, and it appropriately gives all credit to God. I agree that God calls us in many different ways and that listening is key."
— Eric Newhouse, *Pulitzer-Prize-winning Journalist, and Author*

"*'From Zion to a City of Hope: A Journey of Faith'* is a touching and honest personal story of a man facing a life-threatening illness. Henry intimately integrates all aspects of healing; the physical, the emotional, and the spiritual with candid honesty about the importance of community in bringing all of these aspects together."
— Laura Wending, *LMFT, Former Program Director, Cancer Support Community Pasadena*

Advance Praise for Henry and Vanessa Dotson's
FROM ZION TO A CITY OF HOPE

"This is an inspirational story for anyone who is struggling and looking for ways to find light in darkness. The story takes one on a spiritual journey and describes miracles that happened which cannot be explained in human terms. The power of faith and God's grace is the only explanation. For the reader, this book may initially feel like an overwhelming amount of text to read. But the narrative manages to capture the reader to engage more deeply and takes one on the roller coaster ride of a faith journey that begins with an initial diagnosis of a pulled muscle to overcoming a deadly cancer, Multiple Myeloma. For me, it became a page-turner."
— Ruth S. Johnson, *Ed.D., Professor, Author, Consultant*

"When I first read the manuscript, it was as if Henry and Vanessa were holding my hands as they walked me through the darkest valley of their lives in their fight against cancer. With captivating details, their journey testified to the grace, goodness, and power of the Almighty God in overcoming incredible odds against the invisible enemy. God answered the prayers of their family members and friends in restoring Henry to good health and preserving and strengthening their marriage. Now they are telling their story to encourage those who are on a similar journey. But this book is also for those who are not on the same journey. You will gain valuable insights and develop empathy toward those who are suffering. I commend everyone to read it. It will bless your heart, and nourish your soul."
— Alvin Low, *Th.D., Ph.D., Minister, Author, Speaker*

"When readers look closely at the story of the life of Henry B. Dotson, III, they will discover a man who is a believer, a Christian who preached to others, and believes in the "power of prayer." Henry suffered a physical injury for which he sought standard medical care but was diagnosed with a cancer that he was told had no "cure." Henry prayed for guidance and, in this book, explains the prayer pathway he followed when he turned himself over completely to God's word. The story of his journey is also told in the book through the eyes of his JPL colleague and ultimate wife and caregiver, Vanessa, and will keep the reader turning the pages of their co-written and compelling story of how love, faith, and prayer combined. Their constant and unwavering day-to-day diary of what Henry and Vanessa went through together is more than a love story or one challenged by cancer of the worst kind and a surgery that could have ended his mobility. It is a treatise on how God has plans that, when heard and followed, can and do result in miracles."
— Julie Davey, *College Writing Professor; Cancer Survivor; Author, "Writing for Wellness"*

The Authors

Henry B. Dotson, III

Henry was born and raised in Los Angeles, California as the middle child by both parents and his two siblings. Henry developed an interest in writing because of his mother. She loved to read, and she wrote letters regularly to family members. As a result, he developed a love of reading all types of books, and writing about what he was doing, thinking, and feeling. Henry is an extrovert and has many close short-term and long-term relationships with family and friends on both the east and west coasts.

Henry became a Christian at the age of seven.

He received all his education in Southern California. He has degrees in electrical engineering and mechanical engineering from Cal Poly, Pomona, and is a registered Professional Electrical Engineer. Currently, he is a consultant to the electric utility industry.

Henry began his writing journey after college as one of his job responsibilities. This came about because his managers discovered he could write well, despite the fact that he was an engineer.

Henry had been in good to excellent health almost his entire life up until his cancer diagnosis.

Henry considers himself an "unexpected" author because writing a book was never on his bucket list. Henry is driven by his curiosity about "how" and "why," and has the ability to connect the dots between seemingly unrelated information.

Henry became an author out of obedience to God. Henry was informed in his spirit that one of the reasons God spared his life was for him to tell his story of miraculous healing. Henry believes his testimony will be an encouragement to readers and a reminder that God is still in the miracle-making business.

Henry B. Dotson, III is available for select readings and speaking engagements. To inquire about a possible appearance, please contact The VanBern Group at **speakers@thevbgrp.com**.

Vanessa Foster-Dotson

Vanessa was born in Philadelphia, Pennsylvania, where she spent the first nine years of her life with her parents as an only child. At that time, her family moved to Franklinville, New Jersey, where her sister was born. Vanessa is an introvert with a few close friends and almost all her family living on the east coast. She is task-oriented and very committed to family and close friends.

After graduating from high school, she earned a degree in Computer Science from Virginia Tech and a Master's degree in Telecommunications Management from Claremont College in California. Currently, she is a technical sales consultant for IBM.

Vanessa has been a Christian since the 1990s. She describes her life as one spared from any significant drama or traumatic experiences until Henry's diagnosis. She considers herself blessed not to have gone through what many others she knows have gone through.

Vanessa became an "unexpected" author when her Facebook posts became the basis for this book.

From Zion to a City of Hope:
A Journey of Faith

From Zion to a City of Hope: A Journey of Faith

Copyright ©2020, Henry Bernard Dotson, III

All rights reserved under International and Pan American Copyright Conventions. No part of this book may be reproduced, stored in a retrieval system, or transcribed, in any form or by any means – graphic, electronic, mechanical, including photocopying, recording, taping or by any information storage retrieval system or otherwise – without the publisher's prior written permission except in the case of brief quotations embodied in the text. Send requests to: **permissions@thevbgrp.com**.

Permissions acknowledgments for previously published material can be found beginning on page 567.

This book may be ordered through booksellers or by contacting: www.hbdotson3.com

Because of the dynamic nature of the internet, any web addresses or links contained in this book may have changed since publication and may no longer be valid.

The authors of this book do not dispense medical advice or prescribe the use of any technique as a form of treatment for physical, emotional, or medical problems without the advice of a physician, either directly or indirectly. The intent of the authors is only to offer information of a general nature to help you in your quest for emotional and spiritual well-being. In the event you use any of the information in this book for yourself, which is your constitutional right, the authors and the publisher assume no responsibility for your actions.

FACEBOOK® ("F" box icon, thumbs-up icon): Fair Use of Trademark – The commentary and/or visual reference(s) to trademarked material is for **educational purposes only** and not an endorsement by or of the holder of the mark.

Line Editor: Julie Davey

Technical Editor: Laura Seiler

Proofread by: Hazel Clayton Harrison, Angela Clayton / Jah Light Media

Book Cover/Inside Production Designer: Vincent Williams

Back Cover Headshot Photographs by: Alfred Haymond / Observational Photography

HENRY B. DOTSON, III & VANESSA FOSTER DOTSON
FROM ZION TO A CITY OF HOPE: A JOURNEY OF FAITH

Hardback ISBN: 978-1-7375609-3-7

Paperback ISBN: 978-1-7375609-2-0

EPUB ISBN: 978-1-7375609-1-3

Kindle ISBN: 978-1-7375609-0-6

Registration Number: TXu 2-253-727

Printed in the United States of America

From Zion to a City of Hope: A Journey of Faith

To my parents, who instilled in me the faith that carried me through this journey.

To Valenda and our Facebook Prayer Team, without whom my journey may have had a different end.

To Annie and James Foster, aka Mom and Dad.
Thank you for being such wonderful role models.

You provided an excellent example of what it means to have a loving and functioning marriage. I learned the value of being faithful, dedicated, resourceful, caring, long-suffering, and appreciative from both of you.

Thank you for all of the positive qualities that you nurtured in me throughout my life. Until we meet again, Rest In Heavenly Peace.

To Rosalind McCoy Gardner, my best friend forever.
You were my big sister...always sharing life lessons. You provided strength as I struggled to support Henry during his cancer battle. You did not want to tell me that your cancer had returned.

Your spirit is in this book.

Thank you for being such an important part of my life.

"Man is wise and constantly in quest of more wisdom; but the ultimate wisdom, which deals with beginnings, remains locked in a seed. There it lies, the simplest fact of the universe and at the same time the one which calls forth <u>faith</u>, rather than reason."

— Hal Borland

Table Of Contents

Foreword 1
Preface 3
Introduction 7

Part 1: Providential Beginnings 9

  What's Up Doc? 11
    A Preliminary Diagnosis 12
    I am Blessed 14
    Fear Not 15
    Peace 15
    God Is Good 15
  Orchestrating My Circumstances (Prologue) ... 17
    Crushing Blows 17
    Blow #1 18
    Blow #2 19
    Blow #3 21
    Blow #4 23
    Valenda 24
  The Move 28
    Jezreel 28
    Costa Mesa, CA 29
    Dad's Final Months: Los Angeles, CA ... 30
    Homegoing, Part I 32
    Mission to South Africa 33
    Homegoing, Part II 34
    My Injury 35
  Oh, My Aching Back! 37
    Letting Go of the Familiar 38
    Last Physical at Kaiser 39
    My Colonoscopy 40
    Hello PPO 42
    Preliminary Examination 43
    More Than What Meets the Eyes 45
    Testing 1, 2, 3 45
  Following the Shepherd's Voice 46
    Margaret 48

    Close Encounter of the Fifth Kind: Contact with CTCA   53
Breaking the News. 55
    My Siblings 55
    Our Children 61
    My Cousins 63
    My Friends. 67
Beware! The Enemy is Near! 77
    Making Plans 77
    Trip to LAX. 77
    The Thief Strikes 80
    A Fitful Night 82
Last Leg to CTCA. 84
    Bus Ride to CTCA. 84
    Arrival at CTCA 85

Part 2: Zion. **87**

Confirmation 89
    The Mother Standard of Care 90
    The Diagnosis 92
Let the Battle Begin 94
    Disease Triage 95
Flesh of My Flesh. 100
    Vanessa. 100
    1st Bone Marrow Biopsy 105
    A Short Report 107
Delirium 110
    Flushing the Pipes 112
    Saints: 1, Satan: 0. 112
    A Closer Look 113
Push 'Em Back, Push 'Em Back, Way Back! 115
    Saints: 2, Satan: 0. 116
    VRD. 116
A Call to Arms 117
    Facebook Prayer Team 118
    Chief Among Them 122
Fighting the Good Fight 123
Visits From Home 146

GoFundMe 153
The Empire Strikes Back 157
The Force Is With Us. 175
Night Angel 178
An Outpatient in Zion. 183
You're Free to Go. 201
Return to Cali. 203

Part 3: Middle Passage **211**

The Middle Passage 213
Check-In at COH. 215
One Last Assault 227
Turning Back the Tide 241
Ironman. 247
Battle on the Homefront 250
Don't Sweat the Small Stuff 258
Taking Care of Business 262
A Little Help Around the House. 269
Let's Get Physical 278
Welcome To The Community 284
Another Trip Around the Sun 294
A Birthday to Remember. 298
Decisions, Decisions! 311
Open to Options 316
Should I Stay or Should I Go? 320

Part 4: A City of Hope **325**

City of Hope. 326
Time to Give Thanks. 326
Time To Collect. 332
Unforeseen Delay 335
Trying to Get Blood out of a Turnip 344
Full Stem Ahead 353
Dem Bones 360
Happy New Birthday To Me! 361
Battlefield of the Mind 369

Back To The Future 373
Pre-Op Prayer Request 380
The Bionic Man. 389
Here Comes The Bride 390
Going On Trial 401
Putting In The Work. 403
Staying On Track. 407
Happy Anniversary!. 409
One Year Into the Journey 413

Part 5: Dawn of a New Day **417**

Celebrate Good Times Come On! 418
A Dotson Celebration. 422
Some Words of Thanks 425
I Got The Victory. 428
A Father's Blessing. 435
    Rites of Passage. 435
Under The Microscope 444
    MRD Test. 444
Walk For Hope 446
Go Tell It On The Mountain 447
    I've Been Restored 449
Happy Thanksgiving. 455
What's Left 463

Part 6: Epilogue. **465**

The Genesis of This Book. 466
    Friday Late-Night Prayer Meeting. 466
    Praise Reports. 467
    A Word From God 467
Time with the Community. 468
Return to Work. 469
Health Challenges 469
    One More Miracle 470
    Great Is Thy Faithfulness 473
    One More Thing 477
    COVID-19 480

HomeGoings 481
New Additions 483
Celebrations 484
    60th Birthday 484
    20th Wedding Anniversary 485
Multiple Myeloma Milestones 487
The Facebook Prayer Team 487
    Be Not Discouraged 488

Part 7: A Journey of Faith **491**

Looking Back 495
    Providential Beginnings. 495
    Zion 500
    Middle Passage 501
    A City Of Hope 503
    Dawn of a New Day 503
In Retrospect 505
    Seek Help From Others 505
    Do Not Be Afraid to Help 506
    God's In Control 507
    Mustard Seed Faith 507
    Follow By Faith 508
    Stay In Line With God's Will 508
    It's Not About Me. 508
Moving Forward 526
    The New Normal 533
    I've Got More To Do 538
    Final Thoughts 540

Appendices **541**

About Zion 542
About CTCA, Chicago. 546
About City of Hope 548
About Cancer Support Community Pasadena. 551
Citations. 552
Topical Index 559
Scripture Index. 563

Quotation Index 565
Permissions and Acknowledgements 567
    Acknowledgements 570
    Our Facebook Prayer Team. 572

Foreword

If you enjoy true stories that keep you engaged, with twists and turns, leaving you wondering how could this be possible, this journey of faith is for you. This book is about the love between a husband and wife, struggling daily to overcome certain death, daring to look nonstop for a solution, even enlisting the help of their faith community of friends to help save Henry Dotson's life.

God has a history of working through people who face certain death and hopelessness, but somehow, they rise above the dark stormy clouds to see greater possibilities, even working along with medical doctors, demonstrating that Jesus is still a healer.

I've known Henry Dotson for many years as his pastor and friend. When I learned he was suffering from a deadly form of cancer, Multiple Myeloma, his life had already taken a turn for the worst, leaving him and his wife, Vanessa, fighting for his life.

This book is not only about how a disease can disrupt everything in your life but how enlisting the prayers and support of a faith community can produce unimaginable results.

This journey of faith reveals how God will work through the people in our lives, even strangers, to become instruments in His hands. While this book walks you through the rollercoaster ride of faith experienced by Henry and Vanessa Dotson, it's much more than that. It is a true story of what faith in God can do in the lives of ordinary people, unselfishly giving of themselves to focus their attention to literally help save another human's life.

This journey of faith resonates with me because I am a minister of the Gospel who has ministered to the sick for over thirty years with many wonderful results. Yet, in Henry Dotson's case, God chose a different path to get to the same results. This is important to point out because the way God does things cannot be put in a box or conform to a cookie-cutter approach. He is still the almighty God.

This story of faith, love, mercy, grace, and healing is about God, the creator of heaven and earth, demonstrating again and again that He cares about every one of his creations, made in His image. If you ever wondered if God is real? If God is Alive? If God cares about you? This book is a must-read.

As founding pastor of Zoe Christian Fellowship in Whittier, California, for thirty years, I've seen the power of faith in God do miracles in the lives of many committed followers of Christ, but also in people who were seekers. If you, a loved one, or a friend, are in need of God's miracle healing power and provision, this book, you will want to read.

You will discover God has not left you alone or helpless. God will show up in ways you least expect it, but you will know it only happened because of God through His son Jesus Christ.

May you experience the promise of two Bible passages dear to my heart:

Psalms 91:16 — *"With long life will I satisfy him and show him my salvation."*

St. John 3:16 — *"For God so loved the world, that he gave his only begotten Son, that whosoever believeth in him should not perish, but have everlasting life."*

Edward A. Smith, *Presiding Bishop*
    Zoe Association International

Preface

We all need encouragement and inspiration when facing dire situations. It is my sincerest hope you will find a healthy dose of both as you read this book. This is a true story about faith, hope, and love in the face of a late-stage cancer diagnosis, kidney failure, and a surgery that could have ended in paralysis or death. It is also a story about the transformative power of corporate prayer.

I also believe that after reading this book, you will be equipped to be a source of encouragement and support to others facing dire situations.

Lastly, I believe you will learn something about cancer, cancer treatments, and the cancer support community.

When I sat down to write this book, I began as I always do when writing something of any significance. I asked myself:

Why am I writing this?
What message am I trying to communicate?
With whom am I trying to communicate?

This exercise helps me to keep the end goal in mind and not to stray too far off-topic. So, there is nothing unusual for me in this approach to writing. But when I contemplated the question, *"What message am I trying to communicate?"* it became equally important for me to answer another more personal question: *"How did I get here?"*

How did I get to the point where I am compelled to write this book in the first place? I knew the answer to this question, coupled with the answer to the first question, *"Why am I writing this?"* would be the lynchpin upon which the tone, tenor, and purpose of the whole book hang.

I had to ask myself these questions because everyone has a story they can tell. Everyone has experienced something in their life that, if shared, would make a difference in the lives of others. My story centers around my bout with Multiple Myeloma – a form of bone cancer.

Inspiring books, movies, and plays about people overcoming tragedies abound. Millions of people around the world exemplify how the human spirit continues to overcome in the face of tremendous adversity. I have seen and spoken to many people whose stories are just as impactful as mine, if not more so.

So, what compelled me to write this book? Writing a book about my journey through this crisis was no small undertaking. If it were to have significant value to others, I would have to examine my life and ask hard, probing questions. I would have to honestly and willingly share my innermost thoughts and feelings, courageously making myself vulnerable to others to connect with their humanity and hearts.

Many writers compare this process to giving birth – the mental, emotional, and spiritual labor it demands and the overwhelming love one has for the precious child who comes forth as a result. I found it wise, therefore, to thoroughly consider the cost before committing pen to paper and hands to keyboard.

And after giving it much thought, I realized that I got here, and I am writing this book to give glory and honor to God.

For you see, since the age of seven, I have been a Christian. And as a Christian, I have a biblical worldview that drives everything I do and is the lens through which I view the world and tell this story.

"How did I get here?" is the question that resonated in my spirit due to my biblical worldview, and as such, it became an integral part of the book. Communicating to you how I got here is as essential a part of this story as the journey itself.

The Bible says:

> *"And we know that all things work together for good to them that love God, to them who are the called according to his purpose."*
> — Romans 8:28, King James Version

This scripture says all things, not just the enjoyable and pleasant things, but <u>all things</u> work together for good. It tells me what appears to be a bad thing – something painful, a setback, a loss, a crisis, etc. – works together with everything else affecting my life for my good. I may not understand it while I am going through it, but I believe in my heart that when I am able to view my circumstances in the "big picture" (and sometimes this only happens in hindsight), I will see what I perceived as bad has worked out for my good.

I believe I got here because God navigated the circumstances both in and affecting my life, for the good of bringing me through the valley of the shadow of death for His divine purposes and glory.

"Why am I writing this book?" God spoke to my spirit and said my journey with cancer is not about me; it is for the benefit of others as a testimony to give Him the glory. God then spoke to my mind and said He blessed me by saving my life from cancer so that I may become a blessing to others by sharing my story. I received confirmation from many people – family, friends, acquaintances, and even strangers – who all told me, "You should write a book about your story. It would be a great testimony."

> God said to Abraham: *"...I will bless you...and you will be a blessing to others."*
> — Genesis 12:2, New Living Translation

and He said to Zechariah: *"I will save you that you may become a blessing."*
— Zechariah 8:13, New American Standard

I am humbled, grateful, and so thankful that God decided to use me in this way to help fulfill His purposes. I have been blessed in so many ways from this experience that I cannot count the blessings.

As you will see, this journey was shared by many, and we all have been encouraged, inspired, and transformed by what we believe God has done. I hope this book will bless you as you continue on your life's journey.

— *Henry B. Dotson, III*

My parents were excellent role models for how a husband and wife should relate. Who knew that the traits that I learned from them would be so important as I supported Henry during his battle with cancer?

Without question, I would be with Henry throughout his battle! Yes, it was extremely hard to be by Henry's side and hear his doctors express the dire state of his condition. However, Henry's attitude was always positive, and his light gave me strength.

As I found myself alone and scared in Zion, Illinois, during our six-day evaluation that turned into 33 days of suspense, fear, and anxiousness, I used my technology background to bridge the gap.

My Facebook posts about Henry's condition provided a means for me to share his status. However, it also was a way for me to somewhat overcome my loneliness, connect with others and often gather much-needed medical advice.

What was it like for me to make lifesaving decisions without having a medical background? What was it like for me to be a caregiver? What was it like for me to be a loving wife? What was it like for us to walk an unknown path and face fear head-on?

It was all about faith (Matthew 17:20).

My posts were a therapeutic outlet for me in many ways. In time I learned that my posts gave others hope and belief in the possible.

As this book takes you through our cancer journey, it is my prayer that my posts give you hope as well and that they provide an inside glimpse of what it was like for us to battle Henry's cancer…together.

I thank God that He chose me to be His child and that He gave me the ability to express myself in writing.

May this book be a blessing to you and everyone that you share it with.

— *Vanessa Foster-Dotson*

Introduction

"In July 2015, I was diagnosed with Stage III Multiple Myeloma, a form of bone cancer. 90% of my marrow was cancerous, my kidneys had failed, and I was anemic. The admitting oncologist told me it was a miracle I even survived the flight from Los Angeles to Chicago to get to the hospital."

It was indeed a miracle, but it was in no way the first, and there were many more yet to come.

What do you do when you, a loved one, or a friend face a life-threatening situation with very little chance of survival? How do you react? In what or whom do you trust? In what or whom do you place your faith?

In this book, we describe the roller coaster journey of faith we experienced along with everyone who decided to support us through prayer and in other tangible ways.

Readers will learn about the power of corporate prayer, how God ministers to His people miraculously and through others, and what to do when facing similar circumstances. Readers will gain insight into the cancer support community and what cancer patients and their families experience during their bouts with the disease.

This book is based mainly on Vanessa's posts on a Facebook page she created to communicate with family and friends about my status during our cancer journey. Her posts are an excellent account from her perspective of the events that occurred from the time we received my diagnosis in July 2015 through my entering into remission in November 2016.

I placed my account of what occurred leading up to my cancer diagnosis at the beginning of the book. We then inserted both Vanessa's postings and some responses (Comments) from Facebook group members.

I then added my thoughts and my account of my experiences during the journey, coinciding with each of Vanessa's posts. My version includes conversations I had with Vanessa and others. The quoted conversation text may not be verbatim but represents my recollection of what was said.

The book also includes the personal testimonies of key individuals who not only invested their prayers and comments but served as God's hands, feet, and voice to minister to Vanessa and me in our times of need. Their testimonies are presented as answers to specific questions I asked them as I prepared to write this book. The intent is to give readers an account of the journey from their perspective.

Lastly, I added an epilogue and finished with my perspective on my journey of faith as a retrospective look back in hindsight.

I very much enjoy a good story. A good story to me has a meaningful message and is told well. The intent of storytelling is for you, the reader, to be either informed, encouraged, entertained, or all of the above. I enjoy all genres of storytelling – books, movies, live performances, podcasts, etc. There have been many scenes and lines from stories that I have found memorable and sometimes quite profound. As part of my effort to tell a good story about this cancer journey, I have included references to other good stories in the form of quotes and my recollection of scenes from movies when applicable. I hope you find these references helpful in you seeing the journey from my point of view.

PART ONE:
PROVIDENTIAL BEGINNINGS
1941 - July 16, 2015

"For I know the plans that I have for you," declares the LORD, "plans for welfare and not for calamity to give you a future and a hope. Then you will call upon Me and come and pray to Me, and I will listen to you."

— Jeremiah 29:11-12, New American Standard

What's Up, Doc?

Huntington Family Medical, Pasadena, CA
July 8th, 2015, 3 p.m.

———————————

THE PET SCAN[1] WAS THE LAST STRAW. Vanessa and I were beginning to ask ourselves why there were so many tests, exams, scans, whatever, and no new diagnosis. Dr. Mahmoud had already diagnosed that I had seriously pulled the muscles in my lower back, and it would take about three months to heal. However, I was getting more tired and uncomfortable with each passing day.

"We need to schedule an appointment with Dr. Mahmoud just to find out what is going on," I had said to Vanessa a few days earlier.

I called our doctor's office that day, and we were able to get an appointment on Wednesday, 08-Jul-2015, to see Dr. Mahmoud.

"We need to get to the bottom of this!" Vanessa said.

We arrived at the doctor's office on time and determined. The nurse took us back to the same windowless examination room where we had met with Dr. Mahmoud on all of our previous visits. The same two chairs, along with an examination table, were its only furnishings. There was a built-in base cabinet and overhead cabinets containing various medical supplies and equipment.

On the walls were posters about the human body and different ailments one should be aware of. On one of the walls was a plastic rack containing brochures on everything from coping with depression to how to do a breast examination. A model of the human spine and pelvis sat on the floor suspended by a hook that was part of a display fixture. I looked around at the familiar surroundings and thought to myself; *I will not leave without something more to go on.*

Vanessa sat down in the chair at the back of the room, facing the door. She always likes to be seated where she can see everything going on, both inside and outside. I sat down in the chair next to the examination table across from the cabinets and waited for Dr. Mahmoud.

A few moments later, Dr. Mahmoud came in. She greeted us, leaned up against the examination table, and asked us what we wanted to know.

"We want to know why you have been ordering all of these tests," Vanessa replied firmly. She especially did not understand what a urine test had to do with pulled muscles.

"I want to know why you are ordering tests that have nothing to do with soft tissue, nothing to do with pulled muscles," I added.

"I saw something on your x-rays that was not normal, so I wanted to have more tests done to confirm my suspicions," she said.

"Well, do you know what it is?" I asked.

"I think I know what it is, but I am not 100 percent sure," she replied.

I sensed she did not want to share her opinion without being absolutely sure of her diagnosis.

"How sure are you?" I continued to press.

"Well, I'm about 75 percent sure," she answered slowly.

"Okay," I said slowly. Now I had something to work with. I was determined to get a diagnosis, even if it was not a certainty.

"We won't hold you to it, but if your 75 percent is correct, what would you say it is?" I asked. I waited for her reply with great anticipation.

After a brief pause, she said, "I think you have Multiple Myeloma" flatly.

I had never heard of Multiple Myeloma. I had no real sense of what it was. I vaguely recalled that diseases ending in "oh-ma" were typically not good in the back of my mind.

"What is that?" I asked inquisitively.

A Preliminary Diagnosis

"I'm afraid you have bone cancer, my friend," she finally said.

The next second and a half seemed to last for at least 60 seconds. I just had a head-on collision with the "C" word. Several thoughts raced through my mind in that scant 1.5 seconds.

The first thing that happened was my thinking became extremely narrowly focused. Whatever was the most important, pressing concern in my life just the moment before became absolutely, unequivocally, unimportant and insignificant, almost forgotten. Cancer had just barged into my life and had taken hostage my complete and undivided attention. It was all that mattered.

Next, what came to my mind was several separate memories all at once. Three similar sermons from different pastors melded together in my mind into one message.

"It is easy to sing praises and be joyful while we sit in our pews on Sunday and all is well. But how will you react when you receive that report from the doctor you were not expecting? Will you ask, 'Why me?' Will fear grip you? Will you worry? Will you get angry? Will you sink into despair? Or will you trust in God and His word? Will you praise Him anyhow? Will you trust His Word when it says:

> "Be anxious for nothing, but in everything, by prayer and petition, with thanksgiving, present your requests to God. And the peace of God, which surpasses all understanding, will guard your hearts and your minds in Christ Jesus."
> — Philippians 4:6-7, Berean Study Bible

Or when it says,
> "When my anxious thoughts multiply within me, Your consolations delight my soul." — Psalm 94:19, New American Standard

Whatever happens in your life is no surprise to God. He says in His word:

> "For I know the plans I have for you," declares the LORD," plans to prosper you and not to harm you, plans to give you a future and a hope." — Jeremiah 29:11, Berean Study Bible

"He knows the number of days of your life. Nothing happens that is outside the authority and Will of God."

"So, at the end of the day, it comes down to this. Every challenge you face in life is a challenge to your faith. Do you truly believe what you profess to believe? If you were accused of being a Christian, would there be enough evidence to convict you of the charge? In whom or what do you place your trust? When faced with a crisis in your life, what are you going to do? How are you going to react?"

Then I thought to myself, Wow, I am experiencing that moment now! I could feel my heartbeat quicken.

However, I did not react negatively, nor did I expect I would. I had learned long ago from scriptures and my own life experiences that Christians are not guaranteed a life without trouble just because they are Christians. The scriptures say:

> "He causes His sun to rise on the evil and the good, and sends rain on the righteous and the unrighteous."
> — Matthew 5:45, New American Standard

They also say,

> "Count it all joy, my brothers, when you meet trials of various kinds..."
> — James 1:2, English Standard Version

I did not ask myself the question, *Why me?* Instead, I asked myself, *Why not me?* I did not expect to be spared the trials of life but for the power of the Holy Spirit to give me the strength to bear what was put before me. So, the feelings of fear, worry, anger, and despair never rose in me.

What occurred next caught me totally by surprise. I felt an overwhelming sense of gratitude. It was a spontaneous emotional reaction. I would never have guessed I would feel that way when given such a report; I was thankful. It was a relief to know what I was dealing with and not have to guess what my trial would be about.

I am Blessed

The next thought that came to my mind was, *I am so blessed to have my God and a support network to see me through this trial, just as they have been there to see me through all the other trials and tribulations in my life.* I then began to think about the people who make up my support network:

He Blessed Me With Family

God truly blessed me by placing me in a God-centered biological family, both my immediate and extended family, both my father's people and my mother's people. They have shared the good times as well as the bad.

God blessed me with church family members. Our relationships go beyond once-a-week conversations after Sunday church service.

God blessed me with Bible teaching pastors and other clergypersons that had enriched my life with their God-inspired messages and their genuine concern for my spiritual well-being.

He Blessed Me With Friends

As with family, God blessed me with an abundance of wonderful friends with whom I have close relationships. We talk about things that matter. The important issues we are dealing with in our personal lives. God uses us to minister to one another as trusted confidants. We also share our joys and sorrows.

He Blessed Me With Vanessa

> *"He who finds a wife finds a good thing, And obtains favor from the Lord."* — Proverbs 18:22, New King James Version

Vanessa is my "good thing." God brought her to me to be my helpmate. I knew she would be there in sickness and in health.

Fear Not

I then understood why Dr. Mahmoud was reluctant to deliver a cancer diagnosis without being 100 percent certain. It would be terrible to frighten a patient with the prospect of facing cancer if you are not convinced that you have the correct diagnosis.

Dr. Mahmoud did not know that I am a Christian who believes the Bible when it says "be not afraid" and "fear not" 103 times in the King James Version of the good book. At that moment, I chose to place my trust in God and "fear not."

Peace

I then experienced the kind of peace the Bible talks about – God's peace. The peace,

> *"...which surpasses all understanding, will guard your hearts and your minds in Christ Jesus."*
> — Philippians 4:7, Christian Standard Bible

All this in about 1.5 seconds. I almost looked forward to seeing what God was going to do.

"What will it take to be 100 percent sure?" I asked calmly.

"You need to see an oncologist," Dr. Mahmoud said. "An oncologist will be able to determine whether or not you have Multiple Myeloma."

"How soon will I be able to see an oncologist?" I continued.

"I will refer you to City of Hope. They will be able to make that determination," she said. "I will call you tonight and let you know when they will be able to see you," she continued.

"Okay," I said, finally convinced we had done all we could at the moment. We thanked Dr. Mahmoud and left her office.

God Is Good

Isn't God good? I thought. City of Hope's main campus is located in Duarte, California, only 10 miles away from our home. I had heard good things about the place.

Vanessa and I returned to the house and awaited the call. We said a little prayer and asked God to give us the strength to make it through this new trial before us. We did not pray for God to remove the trial but to provide us with the strength to make it through the trial. We prayed for a good report from City of Hope, not for a report that said this was a false alarm or that this was not cancer. A good report to me was an accurate one. To me, God was running this show. I just wanted to know what was going on.

Vanessa started looking up Multiple Myeloma online. She wanted to know what it was and what the survival rate was. After a while, Vanessa stopped looking online because the information was dire. She realized it was important to note when the information was published. There is a lot of historical information online that does not reflect the current state of the disease.

After doing all we could, we found ourselves with a partial Multiple Myeloma cancer diagnosis and awaiting confirmation of the diagnosis from an oncologist from City of Hope. We needed a word from God.

I had a moment to reflect on just how I got to this health crisis. My first thought was, *Oh yes; it was The Move.* But upon further consideration, I realized The Move was no surprise to God. He was not surprised by the report I was receiving from my doctor. He had already orchestrated my circumstances before I was knitted in my mother's womb to bring me to this point in my life.

---

1. Positron emission tomography scan (PET scan). Positron emission tomography (PET) is a nuclear imaging technique that creates detailed, computerized pictures of organs and tissues inside the body. A PET scan reveals how the body is functioning and uncovers areas of abnormal metabolic activity.

Orchestrating My Circumstances (Prologue)

"For you created my inmost being; you knit me together in my mother's womb. I praise you because I am fearfully and wonderfully made; your works are wonderful, I know that full well. My frame was not hidden from you when I was made in the secret place, when I was woven together in the depths of the earth. Your eyes saw my unformed body; all the days ordained for me were written in your book before one of them came to be."
— Psalm 139:13-16, New International Version

WHEN I LOOK BACK ON THE CIRCUMSTANCES OF MY LIFE that brought me to this point looking for a good report from the doctors on my health situation, I recognize that God has been orchestrating the circumstances of my life from the very beginning. None of the events in my life are a surprise to Him; He has been a lamp to my path from before I was born. As long as I listen for His voice and follow where He leads, I will stay safe in His arms.

This is not spiritual mumbo jumbo or a philosophical discussion held in an ivory tower with academia or self-enlightenment. This comes from examining the evidence of the facts of my life and seeing how God's hand has played a role in preparing me for a time such as this. This preparation has come both through difficult times and when receiving God's favor. Regardless of the situation, God was orchestrating my circumstances.

Crushing Blows

Blows that wound cleanse away evil; strokes make clean the innermost parts. — Proverbs 20:30, English Standard Version

"There are two types of Pain in this world: Pain that hurts you, and Pain that changes you!" — Jim Rohn

If one lives long enough (and sometimes that is not long at all), one experiences in his or her life what I call a "crushing blow," something that is profoundly devastating. It goes beyond physical pain – it wounds your heart and crushes your spirit. It is something you will never forget. You know your life will never be the same after the experience. It typically takes a long time for you to heal and recover. Most people experience more than one crushing blow in their lives.

The Word of God says:

> *"And we know that all things work together for good to them that love God, to them who are the called according to his purpose."*
> — Romans 8:28, King James Version

Not just the enjoyable things, but in all things. This must therefore include crushing blows.

When I look back, I can see four crushing blows in my family story that worked together for my good, according to Romans 8:28. In hindsight, I can see God's faithfulness where four times He redeemed the worst and turned it to the good. God set the stage for my Multiple Myeloma journey through these crushing blows.

I share them now for your consideration.

Blow #1
Vicksburg, MS
1941

My father, Henry B. Dotson, Jr., was the first to receive a crushing blow in the chronology of my family story. At nine years of age, my father went off to school as usual. When he returned home, where he expected to see his paternal grandmother and older sister, he made a devastating discovery. His grandmother and sister had packed up and moved! He had no idea where they went and was left behind to fend for himself from that point on. He never told us why they abandoned him.

He chose to trust in God and to do what he could with what he had. He managed to survive on the kindness of others and doing odd jobs. I was told that it was not uncommon to find young children in the city living on their own and fending for themselves at that time in our nation's history. Word would spread through the community, and families would allow these children to share a family meal or spend the night now and again. My father found work as a caddy at the local golf club. It was one of the few jobs a "negro child" could get without too much trouble or notice. Despite support from the community and a job, my father experienced many days of struggle because of a lack of food and a place to stay. He would eventually outgrow his clothes and often did not have the money to buy clothes that fit. He had to make do with what he had.

Because of his difficult childhood due to his crushing blow, he made some critical decisions in his life that have impacted me. First, it was to trust in God. Second, it was to do what you can with what you have. Third, he committed himself to provide food, shelter, and clothing to his children so they would have more than he did as a child. He also was committed to staying in his marriage and not abandoning his children.

Because he had to work, he graduated one year later from high school than his peers. After graduation from high school, he joined the army because there were no good job prospects for a young black man in Vicksburg, Mississippi, in 1952. He served during the Korean War and spent some of his time in Korea as a radio communications operator. After serving in the army, he was honorably discharged in Mississippi in 1955.

Job prospects were no better in Mississippi in 1955 than they were when he left three years beforehand. He decided to relocate to Los Angeles, where his mother, younger brother, and younger sister were living. He later told me first on his list of things to do upon arriving in Los Angeles was: 1) join a church; 2) register to vote; and 3) join the NAACP.

Blow #2
Riverside, CA
1955

My mother, Eunice W. Dotson, had her life all planned. She planned to graduate from Virginia Union with a degree in English and then marry her longtime sweetheart, who had joined the Air Force. They would settle down somewhere in Richmond, Virginia, after completing his military service and live happily ever after. She would teach elementary school children how to read – this was one of her life's purposes – and be a good wife and mother. She had completed steps one and two: she had graduated from Virginia Union with a degree in English and earned her teaching credential in Virginia. As soon as her fiancé returned from service, it would be time to marry. Life was going to plan.

There is a saying that men make plans, and God laughs. My mother received disturbing news from her fiancé. He wrote her a letter and said he thought it would be best if they stopped seeing one another and not get married! He gave no explanation. He was stationed at March Air Force Base in Riverside, California, at the time.

My mother was not about to take this news lying down without a fight. She decided to go to California and find out what was going on, determined to straighten things out and get back on plan. She decided to enroll in the Masters of English program at UCLA to be close to her fiancé and make sure things stayed on plan.

Again, my mother had things going to plan. She was accepted to UCLA and moved to California. She then went to March Air Force Base to confront her fiancé and get to the bottom of things. When she arrived, she met with her fiancé's commanding officer. Much to her surprise, he suggested that she follow the advice in the letter and return to Virginia. Despair and confusion set in as she walked back to her car. Just at that moment, she saw her soon-to-be ex-fiancé walking across the base.

It was at that moment my mother received her crushing blow. She saw her fiancé walking across the base hand in hand with another man! She instantly knew that it was all over. Her plans were simply not to be. She had to decide what to do next. She had already been accepted at UCLA and had all her belongings moved out to California. She called her parents and explained the situation and asked if she should come home. She told me her mother said, "You made your bed; now you have to lie in it."

They were not in favor of her committing to move across the country before knowing what was going on. She had no family in California, so she would be on her own, at least until her fiancé was out of the service, if she could straighten things out. Her parents advised her to at least stay at UCLA and complete her studies.

So what did she do? She put her trust in God and decided to stay on the West Coast, 3,000 miles away from her family, finish her education, and see what would happen next. She also made one more crucial life-altering decision, though not recognized as being such at the time. She knew that if she stayed in Los Angeles, she would need to find a church home.

When faced with a devastating situation, my mother chose to trust in God and tough it out as a stranger in a strange land. Most blacks who migrated from the South followed after relatives or close friends so they would have support so far away from home. This was not the case for my mother. She looked to establish close relationships in church.

Working for Good in My Life

My parents joined Second Baptist Church in Los Angeles, CA, on the same day. These two individuals, whose meeting each other was highly unlikely just a few weeks before, met during an altar call at church (God's house), and the rest is marital history. From this union came three children, me being the middle child flanked by an older brother and younger sister.

I learned the value of nurturing relationships from my mother. She would write home to her family on the east coast every week and send birthday cards to everyone. I remember her going to the bank to get $2 bills to put in the birthday cards of her nieces and nephews. She never forgot a birthday or anniversary. She taught by example that the most important things in life are not things; they are people.

I learned from my father what it meant to be responsible and committed to his marriage and family. I learned how to be a critical thinker and to push through in times of adversity. What I learned was mostly caught, not taught. It was observing him in how he carried himself as a man that I learned what men do.

God took what looked at first as a bad situation and created a family unit that: 1) trusted in Him; 2) had a father thoroughly committed to being the material provider for his family; and 3) had a mother that nurtured her children the way she was nurtured as a child, which helped to fill in the gaps that my father had when it came to being emotionally available as a parent – something he never experienced as a child. "You can't get blood out of a turnip," as the saying goes.

So, these two crushing blows in my parents' lives worked together for my good and to help fulfill God's purpose on the earth.

Blow #3
Upland, CA
1992

It was Tuesday, May 5th, 1992. I got off from work at JPL and went to a parenting class I had signed up for at the YWCA close to work in Pasadena, CA. I wanted to be a better father to my two children. I was concerned that I had become a workaholic and was not spending quality time at home. I was particularly excited this evening on the way home from the class because I had learned something that night that I thought would make a significant difference in our relationship.

When I got home, I rushed in to talk to my first wife about what I had learned. It was a little after 9 p.m., so the children (age 5 and 3) were already asleep in bed. We sat down at the dining room table, and I enthusiastically recounted my evening in class. I was so excited that my first wife could not get a word in edgewise.

After I had finished my ramblings, my first wife said she too had something she wanted to talk about. I was eager to hear what she had to say because it had been a while since we had found the time to talk. I was coming home so late and leaving so early that we rarely spent time together. I thought this was the beginning of us getting back into sync with each other.

Okay, I told myself, *you just need to keep your mouth shut and listen intently to what she is saying.* That was part of what I learned in class that evening. I needed to be present and engaged with my first wife and children when I was with them.

She began by saying she had not been happy for some time. She had gone to see a counselor and felt much better after a few visits. *This is good,* I thought. *We can begin to figure out how to move forward and get unstuck from this rut.*

Then things began to get confusing. It was time for me to receive my first crushing blow. My wife started talking about major problems in our marriage, things I knew nothing about, and then said she wanted a divorce! It was so unexpected that when she said it was time to go, I asked her, "Where are we going?"

When what she was saying finally sunk in, I went into shock. I saw her mouth moving, and that sound was coming out, but I did not hear one word. I remember thinking, *I'm so glad that my breathing and keeping my heart beating are involuntary body functions. If I had to keep them going consciously, I would be dead now.* I sat in a daze as she continued to talk.

When she finished talking, she went upstairs, seemingly happy to have gotten what troubled her off her chest. I sat at the dining-room table, still in shock for what seemed to be hours. I finally managed to summon enough strength to drag myself from the table to the living-room sofa, where I collapsed.

I remained in shock for many, many hours. I did not move from the sofa for three days. I got very little sleep and had no appetite. My heart was deeply troubled, and my spirit was crushed. It was as if I was in the Twilight Zone in a terrible dream. Everything was surreal, and I was disoriented. There was great pain and sorrow, but I was too stunned to weep. I did not even have the presence of mind to cry out to God, even though that was when I needed Him the most.

But early on the third day, as the morning light from the sun began to creep across the living room floor through the window facing east, Jesus sought after me for my resurrection. I heard what seemed to be an audible voice saying,

"Henry, you need to get up. People depend on you. You cannot lie here any longer."

I felt the restoration of a small portion of my strength. I wondered how Lazarus must have felt when he was raised from the dead. In the scriptures, it says:

> *"...Jesus called out in a loud voice, "Lazarus, come out!"*
> — John 11:43, New International Version

So even though it was difficult and painful, I managed to get to my feet. I then heard what I knew to be the voice of my Savior say, *"All right. Now that you have had the faith to be obedient, heed my voice and take the first step, everything will be all right. It may not turn out the way you would like or think it should be, but it will be all right."*

Even though I had no idea how things would turn out, that peace that passes all understanding came over me. God raised me from the depths of my despair. Love lifted me.

That crushing blow began a 26-month long divorce case that severely wounded me and caused great moments of disappointment and despair. But through it all,

I knew that God had never left me nor forsaken me. I knew that I came out of that valley of the shadow of death a better person; spiritually, emotionally, and mentally. I was prepared to move forward and not get stuck in a rut.

Working for Good in My Life

My divorce forced me to grow exponentially in terms of my spiritual and emotional maturity. It also taught me how to be more patient while things worked themselves out in God's infallible timing. It taught me to trust in God for my everything and to know that in Him I could trust.

Most importantly, going through my divorce allowed Vanessa to witness my growth firsthand. Unbeknownst to me at the time, she came to truly respect me and began to see me as a man of good character and integrity. Traits that only show themselves in times of adversity. This caused her heart to turn towards me and ultimately led to our becoming husband and wife. She was to become the life partner I would need to make this journey I now write about by my side. More to come about my bride later. I will put a pin in it for now.

One last thing. I thought I needed God to be a reconciler – to restore my first marriage. But His thoughts were not my thoughts, neither were my ways His ways. He knew I did not need a reconciler. He knew what I needed was a mailman – someone to *deliver me* from a troubled marriage that was not according to His Will, and place me where He wanted me to be. He knew there was someone else I would need by my side when it came time for my Multiple Myeloma journey to begin. But, again, let me not get ahead of myself.

Blow #4
Pasadena, CA
December 17th, 2006

On December 17th, 2006, I received a call from one of my closest friend's mother. It was a call that I was not looking forward to taking.

"She's gone," her mom told me. "She said she was ready to go, and I said it was okay. I was in bed with her, holding her as she took her last breath."

My heart broke. I knew her passing was inevitable, but I was not prepared for the devastating pain. My heart had just had a part of it torn away, and my body shook from the reality that my dear friend of 28 years, all of her adult life, was gone. All I could do was weep. I believe I began to go into a mild depression, but I managed to keep from sinking into total despair.

VALENDA
Pomona, CA
September 1978

Valenda rushed into my life in September 1978, with all the enthusiasm of a bright and confident 18-year-old high school graduate ready to take on the world, starting with college – pursuing a degree in engineering. The world was at her fingertips, just waiting for her to explode on the scene and demonstrate what she could do. And she was ready to tell us all how things should be done.

Being three years her senior and a Black engineering student at a predominantly white university whose views on affirmative action were not at all welcoming, I knew she would soon have a reality check. All of us upper-class Black engineering students (perhaps 15 at most) knew that it was our responsibility to look out for our underclass brothers and sisters. We needed to give them a fighting chance against an administration and faculty that mostly thought we did not deserve to be there. We upperclassmen had already faced both the covert and overt racism in the School of Engineering along with the challenging curriculum and had managed to survive (some of us quite well, I might add).

Each of the upperclassmen was informally assigned an underclassman to look out for. I was given the responsibility to look out for Valenda. We jokingly called her the "black lollipop" because of her large afro and slender frame. It did not take long before she was like a younger sister to me.

Pomona, CA
August 1980

It was a warm sunny day in the mid-'80s with a slight breeze in mid-August 1980 at Cal Poly Pomona when I first caught sight of her on the Quad in the middle of campus. I called out to her, and we greeted each other with a big hug. I was so glad to see her. It was the first time I had seen her since the spring term ended, and everyone went on summer break. We sat on the grass under a tree to catch up.

We began talking about what we did over the summer months. I had worked full-time at a local aerospace firm as an intern. I had been working there since December of 1978, so there was not much new for me to talk about. On the other hand, during the summer between her sophomore and junior year, Valenda went to North Carolina for ROTC training and came back a changed woman. She had built up her muscle mass and tone to the point where she could no longer be called the "black lollipop." She told me stories about boot camp and going out for training in the woods. She was in the middle of describing her experiences when she said:

"The training was hard, and I was doing pretty good, but then I got this bump on my shin."

She rolled up her pant leg and showed me a noticeable lump on her shin a little below the knee. I touched it, and it was surprisingly hard.

"You'd better get that checked out," I said. "It could be cancer."

I did not seriously think that it was cancer, but I thought she would be motivated to get medical attention as soon as possible by saying this.

She looked at me and said in a low voice, "It is cancer."

I was dumbstruck with shock and guilt! I never expected her to say anything like that. I immediately was drawn to her as a friend and committed to stand by her come what may.

My fierce commitment to Valenda bonded me in a way that I had never bonded to anyone before. My brother and I went to the hospital to pray over her shortly after the surgery to remove the tumor. We kept in constant contact during her recovery, and I would visit her at her father's home. I was not deterred when her father eyed me suspiciously every time I visited, wondering what my intentions were with his daughter.

While recovering at her father's house, Valenda met her brother's college roommate, who had tagged along when her brother visited her one day. When they met, sparks flew, and her brother's college roommate eventually became Valenda's husband.

Valenda recovered from surgery, and her cancer went into remission. I had several long talks with her fiancé by phone to learn about this man marrying my little sister from another mister. He came across as a humble young man with an earnest desire to be a good husband and provider for his family.

He checked out with me, and I let Valenda know (not that it would have made much difference, in my humble opinion). They married in August 1982, and I attended the wedding as a guest. Her old Cal Poly friends wished them well later that evening as they prepared for their honeymoon.

Valenda and her husband eventually had four children – Jezreel, Kadesh, Jeremy, and Ethan – one daughter and three sons.

She and I stayed in touch over the years, but we mainly focused on raising our families. Her eldest son and my son were born the same year. Her second son and my daughter were born the same year. I worked as an engineer at the Jet Propulsion Laboratory (JPL) in Pasadena, which was a little more than a stone's throw from Valenda's house. She became a stay-at-home mom homeschooling the children, so I would stop by to visit sometimes on my way home.

While I was going through my divorce, I stopped by Valenda's house more often. I did not look forward to the long drive home to an empty house, and I missed my children. I would spend time talking with Valenda and playing with her children. I would wrestle with the boys and tickle all of them unmercifully, Jezreel included. That was something I used to do with my children. Child's play helped me to deal with the pain I was going through.

Unfortunately, Valenda's marriage deteriorated, and she found herself separated with four children to raise mainly on her own. Her husband became a fireman a few years after they married and spent a lot of time at the firehouse. What started with so much hope and promise fell victim to the many vulnerabilities and threats to a marriage.

We found ourselves raising our children as single parents (mine on a part-time basis). We remained close through this traumatic period in our lives. I would sometimes go to family court with Valenda when she had to appear for a hearing.

Throughout their pre-teen years, my children grew up playing with her children often. We would celebrate birthdays together, take the children on play dates, and visit museums. I considered her children my niece and nephews. They all call me "Uncle Henry."

Valenda's cancer returned with a vengeance after 20 years in remission. She ultimately returned to Detroit, where her mother was her primary caregiver. Vanessa and I visited her in Detroit, and I continued to call her as often as possible. We talked about many things and what our children would become when they grew up.

When Valenda passed away, I attended her memorial service in Detroit. I was privileged to speak when it came time for reflections. As I gave my remarks, I looked at her children. I could sense my commitment to Valenda transferring to them. I could think of no better way to honor her than to strive to be a positive influence in her children's lives. I knew I would be there for them in whatever way that I could.

It was a time of sorrow and heartbreak, but I knew I would rise from this crushing blow with God's help, for He had helped me through the crushing blow of my divorce. He put Valenda in my life during a time when we could help each other go through the valley of despair.

Working for Good in My Life

The good that would come from this final crushing blow would not manifest for eight and a half years. And its manifestation would in itself first appear to be something that was not good. Again, let me not get ahead of myself.

I believe that crushing blows introduce crises in our lives. How we respond in a crisis, how we come out of a crisis, and what we do moving forward after a crisis is based on where we have placed our faith; in what or in whom we believe.

My faith in God is not a mere conjuring of theoretical ideas but one founded in the crucible of my own life's experiences. How I came out of each crisis – the condition of my heart and spirit – was predicated on what I believe.

The Move

"Let us not become weary in doing good, for at the proper time we will reap a harvest if we do not give up. Therefore, as we have opportunity, let us do good to all people, especially to those who belong to the family of believers."
— Galatians 6:9-10, New International Version

Jezreel

Jezreel (aka "Jez," pronounced "*Jazz*") is Valenda's eldest child and is like a niece to Vanessa and me. I have watched her and her three brothers grow up alongside our two children. When they were small, I would visit Valenda's home often to check in on all of them and to play with the children, especially the boys. We would get together to celebrate a birthday or go on an outing to some local venue that catered to children.

Once Jezreel and her siblings got older, I would either call or meet each one to recognize and celebrate their birthdays. Our get-togethers would often be over a meal, where I would continue to nurture our relationships.

In 2009, Vanessa and I started celebrating Thanksgiving with our extended family the Saturday after Thanksgiving. All of Valenda's children had a standing invitation. Jezreel showed up most often compared to her siblings, and sometime during the gathering, I made it a point to pull her aside to have a heart-to-heart talk about what was going on with her. I made sure our conversations would always end with me asking Jazz what Vanessa and I could do to help her and tell her that I loved her.

Jezreel married in 2009 and had two boys, four years apart. When she visited during the Thanksgiving holidays, she would bring the boys along, and now there were grandnephews to play with. It reminded me of the times I spent with her brothers when they were children.

Sadly, Jezreel's marriage deteriorated, and she separated from her husband in 2012. Life got tough for Jazz and the boys as she struggled to manage as a single parent. Despite her difficulties, she seemed always to manage to appear for our annual Thanksgiving extended family gathering. Jazz and I continued to have our "talks," and I let her know Vanessa and I were there for her if she needed us, and I constantly reminded her that I loved her.

Her life had been in turmoil for several months as she was going through difficult times with her estranged husband. She had constantly moved from women's shelter to women's shelter, seeking privacy and protection from her abusive spouse. This move was the latest in a series of moves that we hoped would bring to her very young family that most sought-after place of being - stability. Her situation reminded me so much of what Valenda went through those many years ago. I wanted to be there for Jezreel just as I was for Valenda.

One day in May of 2015, Jez decided to take us up on our offer to help. She called us to let us know she and the boys were moving to a city in Orange County, some 35 miles away from Los Angeles, and she needed help with the move. Jez had some belongings in storage in downtown Los Angeles that she wanted to take with her to Orange County. She planned on getting help from her brothers and possibly other friends to be part of a group helping with the move.

I did not hesitate to help out, but I told her that I would need to make sure I was available when she planned on moving. She said the apartment would be ready for her to move in the first weekend in June. I checked my schedule, and fortunately, I was available Sunday, June 7th, which happened to be my father's birthday.

Everything was set, and I began to prepare for the move. It felt good to know that I would be able to help someone I loved in their time of need. I loved Jazz, and I was looking forward to demonstrating that love in service to meet her needs.

Costa Mesa, CA
June 7, 2015 – 8:00am

Today would be my father's 83rd birthday if he were alive, I thought. The sun was bright this Sunday morning. I had just picked up a U-Haul truck from one of their service locations in Costa Mesa and began making my way to a downtown Los Angeles Public Storage facility to meet with Valenda's sons.

I paused a moment to reflect on my father's impact on my life and the circumstances of his passing almost five years before. My father had adopted a "do the best you can with what you have" attitude from when he was a child. His self-reliance and dealing with adversity in his formative years culminated in a man who did many things alone but was always willing to help those in need. He was doggedly loyal to his family, making sure we had a roof over our heads, clothes on our backs, and food in our stomachs—something he did not have as a child.

He was very active in community service. In the late 1960s and early 70s, he was the president of the Southwest Los Angeles Branch of the NAACP. He was active in local politics, helping to launch the careers of many Los Angeles County-based African American politicians in federal, state, and local elected offices. Recently, he taught boys and girls in South Los Angeles how to play golf. He found this pastime less demanding than his work with Habitat for Humanity, building affordable homes for economically disadvantaged families in his community.

My father did not have many close friends, just a few golfing buddies and one or two men from church. His best friend was his brother, my Uncle Ted (short for Thomas Earl Dotson – he did not want to be called "Uncle Tom"). In their 30's and 40's, they played ping pong and golf. As they got older, golf was the activity that remained. My father did not seek help from others. He always wanted to be the one to help and to make it on his own. He lived his life this way until the very end.

Dad's Final Months
Los Angeles, CA
May 2010

At this stage of his life, my father was a 77-year-old widower, approaching the first anniversary of my mother's passing. He lived on his own in the house my siblings and I grew up in and was self-sufficient. On a Thursday morning, he woke with a severe headache. He made it through the day, but the headache persisted. The next day he woke with the same nagging headache. He was determined not to allow the headache to keep him from getting on with his day. He had some errands to run, so he got in his car to take care of things.

While driving north on Figueroa Street next to the USC campus, north of Exposition Blvd., my father realized he needed to get on the northbound 110 (Harbor) freeway. He was not in the right turn lane but needed to be. He wanted to make a right turn onto eastbound Jefferson Blvd. so he could get on the northbound Harbor freeway on-ramp at Jefferson Blvd.

My father did not notice the vehicle to his right as he made his move to get into the right-turn lane. This oversight resulted in a minor accident as my father's car sideswiped the car to his right. My father and the other driver pulled their cars out of traffic next to the Felix Chevrolet dealership on Figueroa Street, just north of Jefferson Blvd.

The driver of the other vehicle got out of his car and went to check on my father. He asked my father if he was alright. My father said he was okay, but upon further conversation, he said he thought he was in Oakland, California. At that point, the other driver thought my father had sustained injuries during the accident. Perhaps a concussion.

The police had not been called, but a tow truck had been summoned to the accident to tow my father's car. When the tow truck driver realized my father had a mental problem, he hooked up my father's car and then drove my father to Emergency at Kaiser Permanente West Los Angeles Hospital on Cadillac Avenue. The driver found my brother's phone number in my father's cell phone and called my brother while en route to the hospital. He informed my brother of our father's accident and said someone should meet him at the hospital.

My brother called me, and I left work immediately. I arrived at the hospital before the tow truck driver arrived with my father. That was quite a feat since I worked 27 miles away from the hospital, and the accident occurred only seven miles away from the hospital. I believe this may have happened because the tow truck driver dropped off my father's car before proceeding to the hospital.

When my father exited the tow truck, I immediately knew something was very wrong. It was not just the fact that he looked dazed and disoriented. My father was wearing his pajama top, a pair of jeans, and a bathrobe. He would never leave the house looking like that under normal circumstances. He was known as being a well-dressed man no matter what he was wearing. It came from years of having to wear clothes he had long outgrown when he was a child. I knew something had happened to him before he left the house that morning.

Stroke

His initial examination and tests revealed that my father had suffered a major (not massive) stroke. The stroke was the cause of his headache. The area of the brain affected by the stroke did not affect his motor skills. That is why it went undetected. It did, however, affect his higher-level brain function, including situational awareness, critical thinking, and information processing.

My father's stroke marked the beginning of the end for him. He was admitted immediately to the Intensive Care Unit for observation. If he could survive the next 48 hours with no swelling of the brain, he had a fighting chance. Unfortunately, on Sunday, the doctors detected brain swelling. He was given a tracheotomy as a precaution and never spoke again. A nurse placed mittens on his hands so he would not be able to remove his breathing tube. He needed to be restrained at times to keep him from attempting to remove the tube, even with the mittens. That was my father. He was trying to regain his independence and meet this challenge on his terms. He did not want others to have to look after him.

Los Angeles, CA
August 3, 2010

His condition improved over time, and he was transferred to an acute care facility. The family was planning our next move to get him into a sub-acute care facility when we received a call late Monday night, August 3rd, 2010. The acute care facility called to say he was found not breathing and unresponsive by the night nurse doing rounds. The facility went on to say they had called an ambulance and we should get to the hospital as soon as possible. Vanessa and I arrived at the hospital only to find he was just pronounced dead after several minutes of trying to resuscitate him.

Vanessa and I had just visited him two days before on Sunday. He was alert, but I am not sure he recognized us. He raised his hands and motioned for us to remove his mittens. He seemed disheartened because he could not do anything for himself with his mittens on. We sang hymns to him since it was Sunday and he was not in church. His eyes lit up, and he focused on us as if he knew who we were. I am sure he recognized the songs. They seemed to give him some degree of comfort.

My father passed away late at night. His death certificate says August 4th, 2010, but I believe he had already passed away when they found him at the acute-care facility. He died 13 months to the day after my mother passed away (July 3rd, 2009). When I thought about his passing, I realized how merciful God is. My father never wanted to be a burden on his family and wanted to depart on his terms. I believe God bestowed His mercy on my father by not allowing him to suffer a long disabling illness where he would have to rely on others' long-term care. One day my father was okay and self-sufficient. The next he was in intensive care. A short three months later, he was home with the Lord.

My father taught me mostly by example. He instilled in my siblings and me a sense of right and wrong and a sense of responsibility for ourselves. Just as importantly, he instilled in me a sense of responsibility to others. I have an obligation to my family first and then to the community at large. My father always went about his business without fanfare and did not seek notoriety or attention. He demonstrated his love and commitment through his actions.

That was the man I knew to be my father, and those were the values I learned from him. My goal became to follow his example and make a difference in the lives of others. I learned to strive to leave the people and places I encounter a little bit better than when they were before our paths crossed.

It is out of the compassion in my heart for others that I express my love towards them. That is who I am. That is what my Heavenly Father taught me through my earthly father.

HomeGoing, Part I
Second Baptist Church, Los Angeles, CA
August 11, 2010

My father's homegoing service was a testament to his service to the community. Besides family, friends, and church members, many people attended that he had helped in their careers and political aspirations. When my father was president of the Southwest Los Angeles branch of the NAACP, he worked with many state and local elected officials. The takeaway for me from the service was how important it was to him to be of service to others. Here is part of what I shared on that day:

> *"I discovered a man with feet of clay and a tender heart. I discovered a man who learned to live with disappointment and still do what needed to be done. You once told me, 'There is a debt you owe for the space you occupy. You were not put here to be served, but to be a service to others.' It is how you lived your life to the best of your ability, how you never gave up, how you expressed your love by your actions, that I discovered you had never left me. I have been truly blessed to have my hero restored."*

Mission to South Africa
Pasadena, CA
August 12, 2010

In addition to grieving over my father's passing, Vanessa and I were responsible for leading a team of missionaries to South Africa for a 14-day trip scheduled to leave the following day, Thursday, August 12th. We considered not going and letting someone else lead the team. I prayed about it and asked God what we should do.

That familiar small, still voice responded and said we should go. I was reminded again of what my father had said, *"do what you can with what you have."* I believed he would have wanted us to go. So, while still mourning over his passing, Vanessa and I led the team to South Africa.

When we arrived in Tzaneen, South Africa, on the eastern side of the country, local church leaders we would be working with greeted us. Together, we had planned the trip in the months leading up to our arrival. We had our itinerary set, and we wanted to make the best use of the limited time we would be there.

Our hosts had received the news of my father's passing before we left the United States. They were quick to offer their condolences in person, as they had already done in their emails. One of the pastors then made a very unusual request. One of the young people we had met on a previous trip had just recently passed away. Her homegoing services were to be held later that week in Julesburg, a small town about two hours southeast from Tzaneen. The pastor said they had requested that I deliver the eulogy at her homegoing memorial service.

I was not prepared in any way, shape, or form. Again, I remembered what my father had said. I also remembered that small still voice saying I should go on the trip. With those thoughts in mind, I agreed to give the eulogy for the young teen.

HomeGoing, Part II
Julesburg, South Africa
August 14, 2010

During the trip from Tzaneen, I continued to think about what I was going to say. I know I had met the young teen on the trip the previous year, but I was having difficulty finding something that I could reference to help me make a better connection in my mind. I wanted to speak words of comfort to the family and encourage those who would be in attendance. I decided to stop thinking about it and let the Holy Spirit take charge and say what He had to say.

It was a cool Saturday evening in Julesburg. It was wintertime in South Africa, and it does get very cold in the evening. We arrived around 8 p.m. at the small church. I recognized the red porch at the front of the building from my last visit a little less than a year ago. The service was already in progress, and the congregation was singing. I came in and took my seat. I put my Bible down and prayed quietly to myself.

Once the song was over, Pastor Thomas got up to introduce me. He told the congregation I had come all the way from the United States to speak to them this evening. He also let them know that my father had passed away a little more than a week before. He told them that God had something special for them to hear that evening. He then called me up to the podium to speak.

When Pastor Thomas said I had come all this way to speak to them because God had something special for them to hear, it became clear to me what I was going to say! I remembered that the young teen was active in the church. That she showed up to all the events the last time we were there. I thought about serving the community. That night I gave a eulogy for her and my father.

I spoke about the importance of using your time here on earth to do good for others. To trust in God to put you in situations where you can minister to others in need. I shared how we will be the closest thing they see of God for many people we meet on earth. That we are His hands and feet called to do His Will. To show people that there is a living and loving God, I shared what my father would say to me about the debt we all owe for the space we occupy. I said we should not just mourn the loss of our loved ones; we should also celebrate that they were here.

My words resonated with the congregation. Afterward, many came up to greet me. They thanked me for the eulogy and said it was exactly what they needed to hear to help them through their time of sorrow. I knew then that this was a big part of the reason I was on this mission trip.

I was there to help when called upon to do so.

My Injury
Los Angeles, CA
June 7, 2015 – 9 a.m.

As I concluded these reflections on my father and my trip to South Africa, I realized that I was just completing the journey from Costa Mesa to the downtown Los Angeles Public Storage facility. There I met Jezreel, two of her brothers (Kadesh and Jeremy), and Kadesh's wife, Angella. Our task was easy to grasp: 1) pick up the pieces Jezreel identified and move them into her apartment in Costa Mesa; 2) return the U-Haul truck before closing. The question was whether we had enough time given the number of people available to help with the move. After sizing up the situation, I realized I would need to be involved with the physical labor aspects of the task more so than I had initially planned. Jezreel had recruited more help, but more help did not come.

The move was going fairly smoothly. Angella turned out to be quite an asset. She helped organize the moving activities in the facility on the third floor while I orchestrated packing the truck in the parking lot. However, I became concerned when I took time to figure out how long the move would take, given our current efficiency. I realized that we would need to pick up the pace to get the U-Haul truck back in time. I decided I needed to shift some of my time from supervision to actual physical labor.

I felt somewhat prepared to help with the physical parts of the task. After all, hadn't Vanessa and I recently returned to the fitness club and were back on an exercise routine? I was confident that a little physical labor would not be a problem. Everything was going fine until the incident. We should never underestimate how quickly our lives can change significantly in the twinkle of an eye.

I was pulling a load of boxes up the ramp to the U-Haul truck when the load shifted, and the hand truck I was pulling began to tip. As I struggled to regain control of the hand truck, I felt a pain shoot through my lower back. I managed to steady the hand truck, but something was definitely wrong with my lower back. I continued to work, hoping I could either work out the stiffness or at least help complete the move if I were careful.

Once we loaded the truck, we headed off to Kadesh and Angella's house to pick up some more things. I did not assist with moving those items. I was saving myself for Costa Mesa. We made it out of Los Angeles at a reasonable time, but I knew we would have to hurry along with the move in order to return the truck in time not to incur additional fees.

Fortunately, we made good time traveling to Costa Mesa, and someone at the apartment complex was willing to help us get the items off of the truck into the play area outside the apartment building. I did not need to help yet; I just needed to get the truck back in time. Thanks be to God we made it with a few minutes to spare.

The challenge appeared when I realized Jezreel's new apartment was on the second floor of the apartment building, and there was no elevator. The only help available to get the furniture into the apartment was Jeremy and me.

There was a narrow, steep staircase with concrete steps and a wrought iron handrail leading up to Jezreel's apartment. There was a small landing at the top of the stairs with Jezreel's apartment on the right. We would have to maneuver the larger pieces of furniture around the railing to get them into the apartment. Moving in the sofa was going to take a fair bit of manipulation.

Jeremy and I took the sofa up the stairs. I was at the bottom pushing, and Jeremy was at the top pulling. Somewhere on the way up, I took on most of the weight of the sofa. Something in my back made a crunching sound, and I tweaked my lower back muscles once again. I knew I had done something serious to my lower back that caused further damage. I persevered and helped with the rest of the move. I believed that I needed to see this through; finish what I had started. Jezreel needed my help, and I was determined not to let her down.

I managed to get the U-Haul truck back to the Costa Mesa location before the end of the day. I drove back to Pasadena in severe pain but satisfied that I had kept my commitment to helping Jezreel in her time of need.

Oh, My Aching Back!

"When you feel pain, you know you're alive." — Criss Angel

Pasadena, CA
June 7, 2015 – 8:00pm

WHEN I GOT HOME THAT EVENING, I told Vanessa that I injured my lower back during the move.

"What happened?" she asked.

I proceeded to give her the long version of the day's events. She was a little more patient with my pontification than usual.

"How bad do you feel now?" she continued.

"Oh, I'm pretty sore," I said. "But I think I need to take it easy for a few days and see how it goes."

It had been a long time since I had suffered any significant injury. I could not remember the last time I had been injured this badly. For the most part, I have lived a fairly injury-free life as an adult. In my youth and through college, I managed to break my feet six (6) times. On one occasion, I even managed to break both feet at the same time. Those injuries have not resulted in any complications like chronic foot pain or the onset of early arthritis through God's grace. My feet do not start to ache when the weather starts to change or when it gets colder. So, the pulled muscles in my lower back just reminded me that I was not as young as I used to be.

"My days of moving heavy loads are over," I told Vanessa. "From now on, I will be taking a supervisory role in all such endeavors." She nodded in agreement.

My lower back did not get any better over the next couple of days; it felt worse. I had continued to wear the back brace but to no avail. Warm towels, a heating pad, medicated patches, and ice provided no relief. I was hurting so much that I took some over-the-counter pain medication and muscle relaxants, which I rarely do.

I avoided taking any medication unless it was absolutely necessary. I have been blessed with a reasonably high tolerance for pain and discomfort. Therefore, I would much rather deal with the pain and discomfort of injury than put something in my body to help me cope. I knew I would feel better if I took something, but I was more concerned about the long-term effects on my liver, kidneys, and other organs from taking over-the-counter medications. So, to get to the point where I was willing to take something for my lower back pain was a significant indicator to Vanessa that I should seek medical attention.

"Henry," Vanessa finally stated after seeing me hobble around the house for a few more days, "I think you need to go to the doctor as soon as possible."

There was something in her tone of voice that told me there was no use in me trying to make a case for me not to see a doctor. Besides, I was hurting. I had tried all of the home remedies, including over-the-counter medications, and things were not getting any better. Logically, it made sense for me to go. But there was also something in the tone of her voice that *compelled* me to go. I sensed it then, but I did not think much about it at the time.

This would be the first time I received medical care for an injury under Vanessa's medical plan. I had been a member with Kaiser since before I could remember. My mother and father went to Kaiser from the 1960s until they passed away forty-plus years later. As children, my siblings and I would go to Kaiser for our annual physicals and immunizations like clockwork while on summer vacation. I would find myself at either the Inglewood Kaiser facility or the one on Sunset Blvd. in Los Angeles whenever I had some childhood bump, scrape, or injury. I remember going to Kaiser to be treated for ringworm when I was in elementary school. I even had a few visits to Kaiser urgent-care facilities while I was in college. When it came time for me to select a medical plan at work during the open enrollment period each year, it was a no-brainer. I followed the "family tradition." I added our children to my Kaiser healthcare plan before they could crawl. We were a legacy Kaiser Family, and I was happy with the level of care up to this point.

Letting Go of the Familiar
Los Angeles, CA
January 2015

THINGS WOULD BE DIFFERENT THIS YEAR. I was let go by my employer (Southern California Edison) in October of 2014. Vanessa and I decided the best thing for us to do was add me to her plan from her employer during the open-enrollment period in November of the same year. Vanessa has never been interested in HMO plans, preferring the benefits and flexibility provided in PPO plans. I kept my Kaiser medical plan under COBRA[2] so our daughter Talia would continue to be covered until she turned 26 in January of 2015. After that, I planned on dropping my coverage at the end of March 2015. From then on, I would be in unfamiliar waters in our nation's healthcare system. Mind you, I was not concerned; I just knew this year things would be...different.

Before leaving Kaiser, I thought it would be good to get a final thorough check-up. One for the road, I thought. I wanted to take full advantage of everything Kaiser had to offer before saying goodbye to my lifelong healthcare provider. It was like saying goodbye to an old family friend. So, I scheduled a complete physical examination and a colonoscopy for the first time in my life.

I was not concerned at all about the physical exam. I felt I was in pretty good shape for my age. I was, however, somewhat concerned about going in for the colonoscopy. I remember taking my mother to Kaiser for her first colonoscopy. When I picked her up after the procedure, I asked her how things went. She looked at me as if she was wronged and said, "They hadn't ought treat people that way."

That was all she had to say about it. I chuckled a little at her remark, but it planted some seeds of anxiety in my mind about the procedure. I remember taking Vanessa to a colonoscopy appointment. She didn't have any problems or complaints; she just seemed a little loopy afterward as the anesthesia wore off. So, I associated that loopy feeling with being a part of having the procedure done. I don't drink and have never experimented with drugs, so the thought of me feeling that way was not something I wanted to experience.

Last Physical at Kaiser
Los Angeles, CA
February 2015

I had not had a physical in a while, and I had just changed my primary care hospital from Kaiser's Baldwin Park facility in Baldwin Park, CA, to their Sunset Blvd. facility in Los Angeles, CA. This change also required me to change to a Kaiser doctor that worked out of the Sunset facility. After asking a close family friend who worked at Kaiser most of her career as a nurse and project manager, I selected Dr. Park from a roster of doctors listed at the Kaiser Sunset facility to be my family doctor. Dr. Park was a young man (in his early to mid-30s) with a reportedly reasonable bedside manner.

After having my blood drawn when I first arrived, I met with Dr. Park to go over my physical exam and lab work results. He said I checked out okay based on my physical results except for my reported sleep apnea. I had self-reported to him about the condition, so he prescribed a new sleep apnea machine.

"They are much smaller and more efficient than the one you currently have," he said

I took the prescription and made a mental note to get it filled at the same place I got my original prescription filled several years ago.

He proceeded to say my lab work was okay except for my creatinine level.

"What does that mean?" I asked.

"Your kidneys were not functioning at 100 percent," he said.

"How bad is it?" I continued with my questioning.

"Well," he said rather casually, "they really are not too bad."

I sensed he did not want to give me a reason to be alarmed.

"Do you want to find out now, or do you want to wait for the other shoe to drop?"

I was not sure exactly what he meant...'wait for the other shoe to drop.' I needed to process what he was saying. My mother died of kidney failure because she decided to stop receiving dialysis. But her kidneys were not functioning at all, and she had been on dialysis for three years. Before that, her kidney function slowly decreased over several months until it got down to about 5 percent. Then she went on dialysis. Based on my mother's condition, I thought my doctor's comment might mean I had a reasonable amount of time to figure out how bad things were before 'the other shoe dropped.'

I then remembered seeing a documentary on television where a doctor informed a female patient that her kidneys had failed and would have to go on dialysis. The news came as a total shock to her, and she broke down into tears. It seemed as if everything was fine before the news, and all of a sudden, she was in a crisis. Based on this recollection, I thought I might not have as much time as my mother did before 'the other shoe dropped.'

These recollections flashed through my mind in a matter of moments. They did not help me to come up with a reply to Dr. Park's question. I was not prepared at that moment to let Dr. Park know what I would like to do next. In reality, I did not even know what options I had as far as how to proceed.

"I'll think about it," I said. So, I left the appointment with no plan of action. I continued the conversation with Dr. Park through a series of emails over the next few days, trying to understand what the creatinine numbers meant, but that did not result in a plan either. Finally, I decided to take up the matter after I switched to Vanessa's medical plan. Dr. Park did not exhibit any sense of urgency, I reasoned, so neither will I. My interpretation of his comment, therefore, leaned more towards my mother's scenario.

I learned later when I was diagnosed with Multiple Myeloma that decreased kidney function is one of the most common symptoms.

My Colonoscopy
Los Angeles, CA
February 2015

When the time came, my brother, Ira drove me to my colonoscopy appointment. He waited with me until a nurse called my name. He then left to run some errands. Ira said he would return once he received a call from the hospital letting him know

> **What are C.R.A.B. Symptoms of Multiple Myeloma?** [3]
>
> We often hear of the term C.R.A.B. in myeloma, but what does that mean? CRAB is the acronym for the most common symptoms of Multiple Myeloma:
>
> **C = Calcium (elevated) - hypercalcemia:** Myeloma attacks the bone, and as bone is broken down, it causes high calcium levels in the blood. This can cause a variety of symptoms, including excessive thirst, nausea, constipation, loss of appetite, and confusion.
>
> **R = Renal failure:** The most common cause of kidney failure in the myeloma patient is due to the proteins secreted by the malignant cells. Myeloma cells produce abnormally high levels of abnormal proteins in the blood. Depending on the size of these proteins, they may be excreted through the kidneys, which can cause damage. Additionally, increased bone loss leads to hypercalcemia, which can also contribute to kidney failure.
>
> **A = Anemia:** Anemia caused by myeloma results from the replacement of normal bone marrow by infiltrating tumor cells and inhibition of normal red blood cell production. Anemia can cause exhaustion, weakness, mental fatigue, and forgetfulness.
>
> **B = Bone lesions (bone pain):** Bone pain affects a majority of myeloma patients, usually in the spine and ribs. Bone fractures and spinal cord compression is also common. The breakdown of bone also leads to the release of calcium in the blood, leading to hypercalcemia. It is common for bone problems to cause pain, breaks, and spinal problems.

I was ready to be picked up.

When the nurses came to prep me, I let them know that this was my first colonoscopy.

"Don't worry," one said. "We do over 1,000 colonoscopies a year here."

"You will be sedated with propofol and won't feel a thing," another said.

"Isn't that the medication that killed Michael Jackson?" I asked.

"Yes, but there will be an anesthesiologist monitoring you all the time," she replied.

"Wasn't there a doctor nearby when he died?" I asked.

"You really don't have anything to worry about," she said.

When the nurse said the word "worry," a recollection came to my mind that I found great comfort in. I remembered my pastor saying during one of his sermons, "The Bible says, 'Be anxious for nothing.'" Then I remembered that God was with me. From that point on, I was confident it would all work out. Maybe not the way I anticipated, but it would all work out.

Once I was prepped, I was wheeled into the operating room. The nurses then busied themselves hooking me up to all the monitoring equipment. When all was ready, the anesthesiologist placed a mask over my nose and mouth and said to me,

"Now, I want you to count backward from 100. We will be all done before you know it."

I obediently began my countdown to unconsciousness. "100, 99, 98, 97, ..."

The next thing I knew, I was in the pre-op/post-op room with other post-op patients, each in our area separated by curtains. I had never felt so rested after awakening from sleep. I thought to myself, *No wonder Michael Jackson said he wanted 'the milk' to help him sleep. I feel great!*

I did feel a little dizzy, so I lay still for a few moments to collect myself. I got up slowly and dressed to leave. A staff member observed me while in recovery and placed a call to my brother when they saw that I was getting up.

After hanging up, she said, "We've called you brother, and he said he is on his way. It should be about 10 to 15 minutes."

I waited patiently for his arrival. In the meantime, I thanked God for an uneventful procedure.

When Ira came back to take me home, we stopped and had an early dinner at a restaurant I had recently discovered near the hospital. I had to fast 24 hours before the procedure, so I was looking forward to my next meal. I told Ira how I felt under the influence of propofol while we ate.

"I have no problems with pain medication," he said between bites of the dinner special. "That's the only way I get by with my chronic back pain. Better life through chemistry, if you ask me."

The results came back from the colonoscopy a few days later. My doctor said everything was normal. I remember saying a little prayer of thanksgiving when I received the good report. Again God's Word proved true.

"Be anxious for nothing, but in everything, by prayer and petition, with thanksgiving, present your requests to God."

— Philippians 4:6, Berean Study Bible

Hello PPO
Huntington Family Medical, Pasadena, CA
June 16, 2015

Once my benefits under Vanessa's PPO plan took effect in January 2015, we called the office of Dr. Mattai, Vanessa's doctor, to see if she could take me on as a patient. Dr. Mattai is very good and has a wonderful bedside manner. I've observed, over the years, how well she has cared for Vanessa. Vanessa had commented that she was pleased with Dr. Mattai and had no intentions of ever-changing doctors. Doctor

Mattai's patient list was full, so I was assigned to her colleague, Dr. Mahmoud. Dr. Mahmoud was new to the practice, so we were trusting on Dr. Mattai's referral. The first time we went to see Dr. Mahmoud was to see about my sore back from the move.

Preliminary Examination

After checking in, Vanessa and I sat down in the waiting area for a little while before the nurse called us. I wondered to myself how Dr. Mahmoud would compare to Dr. Mattai. Vanessa had seen only one or two other doctors besides Dr. Mattai, so there wasn't much to go on in terms of what to expect. As I thought about it a little more, I reasoned that it didn't really matter because it was probably just your typical weekend warrior injury that any competent doctor could take care of.

When the nurse called my name, she took us back to a windowless examination room to wait for Dr. Mahmoud. I thought it would have been nicer to wait in an examination room on the other side of the hall with windows to let in sunlight.

As we waited for Dr. Mahmoud, I took inventory of our surroundings. *Two chairs and an examination table to sit on,* I thought to myself: *a built-in base cabinet and overhead cabinets containing various medical supplies and equipment.* My gaze moved on to the walls. There were posters about the human body and different ailments one should be aware of.

On one of the walls was a plastic rack containing brochures on everything from coping with depression to how to do a breast examination. "I don't see anything here that talks about an aching back," I thought as I felt a shooting pain in my lower back. I then glanced at the floor in one corner of the room. A model of the human spine and pelvis sat on the floor suspended by a hook that was part of a display fixture. *Dem bones, dem bones, dem dry bones, now hear the Word of the Lord,* I sang to myself in my mind.

After a short while, Dr. Mahmoud came into the examination room. I guessed she was in her late 30's, early to mid-'40s. She appeared to be of Indian descent.

"Hi, I'm Dr. Mahmoud. I understand you hurt your back," she said. "Tell me what you were doing at the time of the injury."

She had a slight accent and spoke with an air of confidence without any hint of arrogance. That helped to put me at ease. I gave her the abbreviated version of the move (I did not expect her to be as patient with my pontifications as Vanessa).

"Let's take a look," she said. "Please remove your clothes from the waist up."

I removed my clothes cautiously, trying not to aggravate my back any further, and Dr. Mahmoud examined my lower back.

"I do see some swelling," she said. "I am going to order some x-rays just to see if there's more to your injury than just soft tissue damage."

"Okay," I said as I gingerly put my clothes back on.

I picked up the prescription from the office staff and went to the imaging center down the street straight away. I wanted to get everything I could get done in one trip so I could go home and lie down. I needed pain relief as soon as possible.

I checked in at the front desk of the imaging center after a tortured walk from the parking structure to the facility. It was only about 40 yards, but it was difficult. I felt some relief as I sat down in the airconditioned waiting area in their comfortable seating. The medical building was less than ten years old, and the imaging center had all the trappings of a sleek design that gave it a nice ambiance.

A female x-ray technician came out and called my name after a short wait. She led me to a small changing room and again asked me to remove my clothes from the waist up. She asked me to put on a gown before going to the x-ray room. Again, I tried not to cause myself any more pain while doing as instructed.

I made my way to the x-ray room, and after a few quick clicks, it was over.

"How soon will the x-rays be available?" I asked the x-ray technician.

"Oh, it will only take a few minutes, and then we will send them to your doctor," she said. "Dr. Mahmoud will contact you to go over your results."

"Great," I said. I went back to the changing room, got dressed, and hobbled to the car. I then made a beeline to the house for some much-needed rest.

We received a call from Dr. Mahmoud later asking us to return the next day to go over the results. Vanessa and I found ourselves back in the same examination room the next day, waiting on the doctor.

Dr. Mahmoud came in and said, "Well, you certainly pulled the muscles in your lower back. It looks like it's going to take about three months for you to heal."

I was surprised that it would take so long for my recovery. I was hurting badly, and I began to contemplate how soon the pain would subside if it were going to take three months to heal.

"I am going to prescribe ibuprofen for the pain," she said. "You should continue to wear the back brace for support and apply heat to relax your muscles."

"Okay," I said. "I will do that."

I then began to wonder how this would affect my work. As a consultant, I travel a good portion of the time. I need to be in good shape so the wear and tear of travel do not become problematic. *This will make travel difficult. Maybe I should only take contracts where I can work from home,* I thought. I was grateful that I could choose what assignments I took without worrying about how my employer would perceive me.

More Than What Meets the Eyes

"But I think there is something else going on here, so I want you to get an ultrasound," Dr. Mahmoud said.

Her words brought my attention back from my inner thoughts. "Okay," I said without much thought and no worries. I just wanted to get everything taken care of so we wouldn't have to come back later for something we could handle now.

Testing 1, 2, 3
Huntington Medical Imaging Center, Pasadena, CA
June 18, 2015

Dr. Mahmoud wrote the prescription, and I was back at the imaging center in just a couple of days. The ultrasound began a series of various imaging procedures, none of which had anything to do with muscle tissue. Each time she got results, she would order another imaging procedure: CT scan, MRI, PET scan. Dr. Mahmoud even referred me to an orthopedic doctor for a second opinion. All the while, I was getting progressively worse. It was getting harder and harder to get out of bed. The back brace provided some relief, but each morning when I arose, I felt stiffer. Still, we had no diagnosis from Dr. Mahmoud.

That was when Vanessa and I were motivated to get some answers proactively. That was when we both wanted to know, "What's Up, Doc?" That is why we pressed for a diagnosis. After all, something was better than nothing.

---

2. The Consolidated Omnibus Budget Reconciliation Act of 1985 (or COBRA) is a law passed by the U.S. Congress on a reconciliation basis and signed by President Ronald Reagan that, among other things, mandates an insurance program which gives some employees the ability to continue health insurance coverage after leaving employment.

3. Lizzy Smith | Posted Feb 22nd, 2016 - https://www.myelomacrowd.org/myeloma-101-c-r-a-b-symptoms-of-multiple-myeloma/

Following the Shepherd's Voice

*"I am the good shepherd. I know My sheep and my sheep know Me...
and they will listen to My voice..."*

— John 10:14, 16, Berean Study Bible

Pasadena, CA
July 8, 2015, 8:30 p.m.

As promised, Dr. Mahmoud called around 8:30 that evening. Vanessa and I picked up and listened together on the speakerphone.

"I checked with City of Hope to see who would be able to take you on as a patient," Dr. Mahmoud began. "There doesn't seem to be an oncologist that can take you on as a patient at this time. I may be able to arrange for one of their oncologists at their South Pasadena outpatient facility to see you in about twelve days."

Something in my spirit said *You don't have 12 days to wait for just the possibility of being seen by an oncologist.*

I had heard God's voice.

"Is there any way I can be seen sooner?" I asked.

"That is the best I can do at the moment," she said. "I will continue to look to see if I can get an earlier appointment, but that is the earliest available time."

"We appreciate whatever you can do to move up the appointment," I said.

We hung up the phone, disappointed. With its outstanding reputation as a top cancer research center, I was looking forward to getting my diagnosis from City of Hope. I wanted to know for sure what I was dealing with and not be misdiagnosed. I had heard of many cancer cases where the patient died because it took too long to be correctly diagnosed. They had been initially misdiagnosed and by the time they received the correct diagnosis, cancer had spread to the point where doctors could not successfully treat it. I did not want to be another one of those types of patients.

It seems as though God has something else planned for us, I thought.

"We've got to find another way to be seen sooner," I said to Vanessa. We said a prayer and went to bed, waiting to see what the next day would bring.

Pasadena, CA
July 9, 2015, 10 a.m.

The following day I had my weekly conference call with my colleagues to work collaboratively on a project. Since I was unsure about my health condition, I thought it was the right thing to do to let them know that I may not be available in the coming weeks to work on anything, depending on a diagnosis from an oncologist. I did not want to alarm anyone, but I thought it was best if I shared some of what was going on so they would understand my situation. After the usual few minutes of greetings, I wanted to get right to the point.

"Before we get into today's agenda, I want to share some news with you all," I began. "There is a possibility that I have Multiple Myeloma, a form of bone cancer. I am trying to get a confirming diagnosis from an oncologist, but I am not having much luck getting in to see someone quickly. In any case, I just wanted you all to know that you should not plan on me being available to work on the project for the foreseeable future."

Suddenly, the conference line got quiet. There was a pregnant pause before anyone spoke up.

"Gee, I'm really sorry to hear that," said one colleague. "I had a bout with prostate cancer, and I want to wish you the best."

I was a little surprised with how quickly my colleague was willing to share some of his health challenges. I thought most people don't just share that kind of private information with others. Keeping personal things private was an assumption I must have concluded from what I had seen in the past.

"What seems to be the problem with getting a diagnosis?" another colleague asked.

"Well, my family doctor said the earliest she would be able to get me in to see a specialist would be 12 days at best," I replied.

The next thing I heard was a familiar voice with an equally familiar Texas drawl.

"Henry, if you want to find out what's going on in a hurry, then you need to go see the folks at the Cancer Treatment Centers of America in Chicago. That's where I am going for my ovarian cancer. They don't mess around when figuring out what 'cha got and how to fix it. They got a whole program and everything for people from all over the world to get treated. I will send you the contact information you will need to get the ball rolling right after this call."

It was my mentor in utility industry consulting, Margaret.

Margaret
Palo Alto, CA
2012

I first met Margaret at a working group meeting in Palo Alto, California, in 2012. It was not a momentous occasion. She was there to take care of the group's business, and she had a personal agenda that she voiced which did not exactly match the official agenda. That was my first meeting with this group, and I was there as a guest representing my employer (Southern California Edison). I was the technical lead on a company project that had submitted its work to the group for adoption, and I was there to answer questions when the topic came up on the official agenda. I, too, had a personal agenda, which I did not voice, and that was to observe the proceedings to help me decide if this was a professional organization I would want to join and become an active member.

By the end of the three-day meeting, Margaret had made certain all agenda items were addressed. I am not sure if she was the one who organized and called the meeting, but she took charge when a leader was needed. The main takeaway from the meeting for me concerning Margaret was that she was passionate about the work being done by the organization because it benefited the entire utility industry, and she was willing to help anyone who wanted to get involved. Her commitment and willingness to help others for a worthy cause helped me decide that I would indeed become involved.

I became an active member, and as I attended more of these types of meetings over the next couple of years, I learned that Margaret was one of the founding leaders and drivers of the organization. As we worked on various technical issues, we developed a mutual respect. I thought very highly of this very determined, committed individual. She really knew her stuff and was a 'Don't mess with Texas' native! You never had to wonder what her opinion was, or if she disagreed with you, or a proposed course of action. She made that clear in no uncertain terms. At the same time, it was always for the good of the organization. Her motivation was never for personal gain, and she was one of the hardest working members of this volunteer group of technical experts.

Orange County, CA
November 2014

A turning point for me professionally came in November of 2014. Southern California Edison laid me off in October 2014. I was thinking about what I wanted to do next in my career. I knew I did not want to work for a large company where I would have to start building relationships and dealing with office politics to earn trust. I also knew I wanted to continue working in the utility industry, perhaps doing contract work with a large consulting firm or work as an independent utility industry consultant. I was confident that I had the knowledge and skills to do contract work, but I was not sure I was ready to strike out on my own as a consultant.

Vanessa and I talked about the possibilities. She said she knew that I always wanted to have a business of my own, and this could be the time to make a go of it. Vanessa said whatever I decided to do; she had my back. She had total faith in me and was there to support me.

> *"He who finds a wife finds a good thing and obtains favor from the LORD."*
>
> — Proverbs 18:22

> *"Who can find a wife of noble character? She is far more precious than rubies."*
>
> — Proverbs 31:10

Knowing that I had Vanessa's support was essential. Without it, I would have removed the option of becoming an independent consultant from my list of possibilities. But I knew I also needed endorsements from my peers, especially those doing what I wanted to do.

To that end, I reached out to my peers, managers, and internal clients at Southern California Edison and asked them to write endorsements for me and post them on my LinkedIn page. They provided terrific endorsements for me and my work as a coworker, which was great, but not as a technical expert in the area I wanted to move into. And frankly speaking, they were not qualified to give me that type of endorsement. I needed endorsement from my peers in the professional working group I was involved with.

I wanted to ask for endorsements from my peers in the professional working group face to face. All of the group meetings I had attended to this point required domestic air travel and incurred travel expenses, all of which had been covered by Southern California Edison. I did not want to spend a lot of my own money to attend such a meeting, so I needed some favor from the Lord. I prayed for His favor and left the rest up to Him. True to His word, He did not fail me nor forsake me. The next face-to-face group meeting was scheduled to take place in November in Orange County, California, close enough for me to drive, so I could afford to go. Isn't God good?

Margaret attended the meeting, and I asked her what she thought about me hanging up my shingle as a consultant. She said, "I'm sure you can do it. I've seen you in our meetings, and you have what it takes to be successful" (paraphrased). I heard the Shepherd's voice. That was God speaking to me through her to give me the confirmation I was looking for. I followed the Shepherd's voice with Vanessa's blessing and endorsement, and I started my own consulting business in January 2015. Margaret did more than give me her endorsement. She was instrumental in me getting my first contract only two months after I started my business.

Branson, MO
May 2015

A turning point in my personal relationship with Margaret occurred when I attended another one of these three-day group meetings in Branson, MO, in May 2015. The meeting was held in Branson because Margaret was returning to the group for the first time since she was diagnosed with stage 4 ovarian cancer in late 2014. She lives in Missouri, so the only way she could attend a meeting would be to travel by car according to her doctor's orders.

She was late for the first meeting she had planned to attend. When she entered the room, all conversation stopped, and everyone watched a frail Margaret make her way to her seat. She was noticeably thinner, and everyone could tell she was making a huge effort just to be there. Everyone gave her a hearty welcome. Although she was weak and did not stay for the entire meeting, her fighting spirit was still present, albeit toned down, as she participated as best as she could.

I was able to spend some time with her during the breaks and at mealtimes. I had the opportunity to see a different side of her. Margaret was humble and candid about her battle with cancer. I discovered that she was a Christian, and she spent her early years growing up in Mexico because her father was a full-time missionary. She came back to the United States to live because she was beginning to lose her ability to speak her native language of English.

Margaret talked about her faith in God and how she asks Him to lead her in what to do for that day. Our talks increased my respect for her, and I rejoiced inside because she was part of the family of believers.

Pasadena, CA
July 9, 2015, 11 a.m.

True to her word, I received an email from Margaret shortly after the call was over. I asked her what was going through her mind as I prepared to write this book.

In the meantime, Vanessa posted a message on her Facebook page requesting prayer. She did not want to alarm anyone since we did not know what we were up against, but she did want others to start praying. So, she wrote:

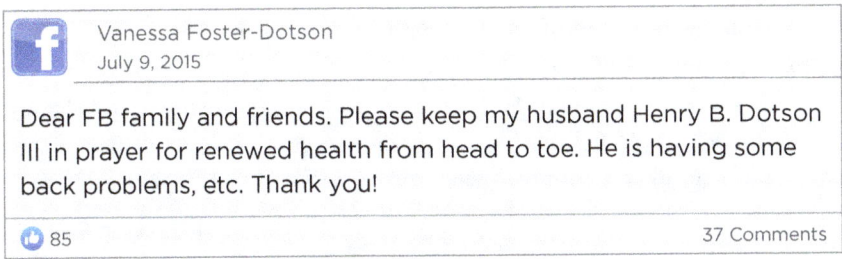

Within a few hours, she received 37 comments from friends who said they would begin to pray and 85 "Likes" from others.

Q: Had you heard of multiple myeloma before hearing about my diagnosis?

MARGARET: Not exactly. I first thought you had Bone Marrow cancer, and I now do not believe that is the same thing that you had/have, but I could be wrong. However, when you told me what you had, I knew it was extremely serious because ALL cancer is extremely serious. I had a feeling that yours was deadly and that you were close to death. I don't know why I felt this way, but right after you told me about your condition, I felt an extreme urgency for you to get to a treatment facility that would MOVE quickly.

Q: How did you feel when you learned of my diagnosis?

MARGARET: I knew it would be close and that it would depend on whether you received the treatment as quickly as possible – I had learned through my cancer that speed and thorough examinations were the keys. It is not just that cancer kills you. It is what cancer causes to happen in your body. If you do not act quickly to locate all the cancer cells and the side effects of cancer, you will not survive. I was very concerned about your ability to get that treatment in time to catch not only the cancer cells but the side effects of that cancer. I immediately began to pray daily for your recovery and for your doctors. Everything must fall into place if one is to survive any cancer and especially your cancer at the stage you were at. I just felt that you needed immediate care and a team that would cover all the bases.

I looked up CTCA Chicago online. I found that there were five centers located around the country. CTCA Chicago is their Midwest Regional Medical Center and the original center of the five. This center was the Mothership of the treatment centers.

After my quick navigation of their website, I felt a sense of peace come over me. In my mind, I reasoned, *If you have to take this journey to a place you've never been before, then you should follow the path of someone who has received the kind of outcome you want to receive.*

It was not my mind's reasoning; it was God's small still voice speaking in my ear.

Pasadena, CA
July 10, 2015

The next thing I did was to go into the next room to talk with Vanessa.

"We are going to the Cancer Treatment Centers of America in Chicago to get a diagnosis," I said.

"Why do we have to go all the way to Chicago? There are other places around here like USC or UCLA?" Vanessa replied.

"I think I heard from God that we are supposed to go to Chicago," I said.

"Oh," she said. And without a moment's hesitation or further push back, Vanessa said, "Well, I guess we're going to Chicago." I told Vanessa about my conversation with Margaret. I told her that she had sent me the contact information I would need, and we should call them right away. Vanessa agreed. I called, and the receptionist said the intake nurse was not available for the rest of the day but to call first thing in the morning. The receptionist said I should be prepared with my diagnosis so she would be able to set things up accordingly.

Something did not seem right. I was looking to get a diagnosis from CTCA, not treatment. I did not understand how this was going to work. It seemed like the chicken-and-the-egg problem to me. Do I need a diagnosis to be seen, or do I go to get a diagnosis? Which comes first? I was unsure how it would work out, but I knew that I had heard from God that this is where I was to go. So, I just trusted that God would work it all out according to His plan. We would just have to wait and see what the intake nurse would say.

Vanessa and I again said a prayer and waited to make the call the next day.

Close Encounter of the Fifth Kind: Contact with CTCA
Pasadena, CA
July 10, 2015, 8 a.m.

Vanessa and I got on the speakerphone together and placed the call. I recall the conversation going like this:

"Hi, my name is Henry Dotson. I was given your name by one of your current patients to call to see about getting checked out for Multiple Myeloma."

"Okay, sounds good. When did you receive your diagnosis?"

"Well, I don't have a diagnosis," I began. "I thought you would be able to confirm whether or not I have Multiple Myeloma."

"Hmmm. I'm sorry, that is not how our program works. We work with patients that have already been diagnosed with some form of cancer."

Undaunted, not willing to take the first no as my final answer, I decided to explain my situation further.

"Well, I have a partial diagnosis from my family doctor," I said.

I then explained The Move, being examined by my family doctor, the x-rays, ultrasounds, CT and PET scans, etc.

After telling the "Cliff Notes" version of my story, the intake nurse said, "Well, I'm glad you gave me the background story to your situation. I think there is sufficient evidence that something is going on, and we should be able to take a look to find out what that is."

I felt a sense of relief when I heard that CTCA would take a look. I was reminded of some of the lyrics of Donnie McClurkin's song, "Stand." Sometimes you just have to stand and watch what the Lord will do after you have done whatever you can do.

The intake nurse continued, "We have a six-day evaluation program where we will fly you and a caregiver here to CTCA, provide lodging for your stay, and meal vouchers from our cafeteria while we determine what is going on. There is no cost to you for this program. I just need to get the paperwork started so that we can make your travel reservations. Will that work for you?"

That floored me! I had never heard of such a thing in all my experience with our nation's healthcare system. I asked the intake nurse one question. "How is all this possible?"

"Well," she began. "We see people from all over the world, and they come here for cancer treatment. Cancer treatment is all we do. So, we have some generous donors that contribute to a fund to make this program available to anyone we think needs our help."

My heart was full. All I could think was, "Look at God! Look at what the Lord can do! Thank you, Jesus!"

Later on that day, Vanessa and I were contacted by CTCA's travel department. We made reservations to arrive in Chicago on Wednesday, 15 July 2015, and see the doctors at CTCA the next day on Thursday, 16 July 2015.

So instead of waiting for a possible meeting with a doctor from City of Hope on 20 July 2015, the Lord made a way for me to be seen at least four days earlier halfway across the country. Little did I know how important those four days would be. God's timing is always on time.

Vanessa and I said a prayer of thanksgiving for God making a way out of no way.

> *"I have heard your prayer, I have seen your tears; behold, I will heal you. On the third day you shall go up to the house of the LORD."*
> — 2 Kings 20:6, New American Standard

Providential Beginnings

Breaking the News

"Though it be honest, it is never good to bring bad news."
—William Shakespeare, *Antony and Cleopatra*, Act II, Scene 5

Pasadena, CA
July 10, 2015

I DID NOT WANT TO UPSET ANYONE, but I knew I had to break the news to the rest of my family and close friends. That was not something Vanessa could do for me. At best, she could be with me when I shared this troublesome message. I knew I had to tell my siblings - my brother Ira (and his wife Cris), and my sister Pat; our children - our son, Bart, and our daughter, Talia; and my close cousins Beryl and Kathy. These were my closest family members after Vanessa. I also had to tell several close friends, and I had to let them all know as soon as possible, even though I knew it would be hard to take.

In preparation for this book, I asked each of them to share what was going through their minds and what they felt in their hearts when I broke the news to them. I have included their replies in the following passages:

MY SIBLINGS

"No matter where you live, brothers are brothers and sisters are sisters. The bonds that keep family close are the same no matter where you are."
— Takayuki Ikkaku, Arisa Hosaka and Toshihiro Kawabata, *Animal Crossing: Wild World*, 2005

"Do you know what friendship is... it is to be brother and sister; two souls which touch without mingling, two fingers on one hand."
— Victor Hugo, *The Hunchback of Notre Dame*

I grew up the middle child in a family of three children. I have an older brother - Ira, and a younger sister - Patricia (Pat) . We grew up very close. We are close in age and grew to have very similar Christian worldviews.

My parents had the three of us in just shy of 24 months. My brother was born October 31, I was born the following year, October 28, and Pat was born the next year, October 11. I often wondered what was going on in January with my parents besides New Year's celebrations.

From my perspective, it seemed as if we grew up as a unit. Most everything we did, we did together. Our parents gave one birthday party for the three of us and another childhood friend because we were all born within 30 days of each other. I believe I was three or four years old. It was our first birthday party. The party was so overwhelming to my mother that we never had another birthday party again.

Because we were evenly spaced approximately one year apart, our family went through nine consecutive years of graduation – from elementary school through high school. Every year someone was graduating from somewhere. For nine years, it was a family tradition in June to attend a graduation ceremony and then have a family meal at a restaurant to celebrate afterward.

We all took music lessons. We each had the choice of which instrument we would play, but we were all going to learn to play something. Ira played the trumpet, I played the saxophone, and Pat played the piano. We tried to play a song or two together, but we sounded more like a cacophony than a symphony.

Our parents instilled in us the value of education and how to be critical thinkers. Our mother taught elementary school in the Los Angeles Unified School District for over 30 years. Our father was interested in law and ultimately became an arbitrator for the California State Employees Association, the labor union for state employees. He would represent state employees in arbitration hearings before an arbitration judge. Our parents saw to it that we attended some of the best junior and senior high schools in the district by participating in a voluntary busing program that was part of the history of desegregating the schools in Los Angeles. We banded together with the other African American students bussed from South Central LA to West LA.

Most of our father's people lived in South Central and Southwest Los Angeles. They had migrated from Vicksburg, Mississippi, to Southern California. We would spend most holidays at some family member's house with our cousins. There were about a dozen of us running around someone's house. Our mother's people live on the east coast. Once every three years, we would go back to Richmond, Virginia, and down to Winston Salem, North Carolina, to spend the summer with our grandparents, aunts, uncles, and cousins.

We were involved in church activities throughout our childhood. Later on, we added high-school sports. Ira ran track and played football his senior year. I was on the gymnastics team, and Pat played softball. Everyone at church and school knew of the Dotson children. One year our church voted us Family of the Year. In school, both Ira and I competed for city honors in our respective sports. Through it all, we were taught to be there for one another.

We lived in the same three-bedroom house in Southwest LA from when we were in preschool/kindergarten until we graduated from high school. After my father passed away, my sister moved back into the house and lives there today. Ira and I shared the bedroom in the back, and Pat had a room to herself towards the front of the house. Our parents' bedroom was situated between our bedrooms and directly across the hall from the bathroom.

We grew up in a home with no divorce and two hard-working, God-loving parents. It certainly was not a Norman Rockwell family or the type of family depicted on television in the 1950s and 1960s. We had challenges and struggles, as most families do. We saw our parents argue, but not often. We saw their imperfections, but we saw them work through them because of their commitment to each other. It was from those beginnings that we learned to love God, aspire to make the most out of our natural gifts and talents, and care for one another.

Ira and Cris

After graduating from high school, Ira went to Howard University. He wanted to study film. He completed his first year at Howard and then transferred to the University of California at Santa Barbara to continue his studies. After his sophomore year, Ira left college and moved to Maui, Hawaii. He stayed in Hawaii for a couple of years before returning to Los Angeles, California.

Shortly after returning to Los Angeles, Ira felt the call to ministry and became involved in domestic missionary work. It was at his church where he met and married his wife, Cris. He has been in ministry since 1979.

I was Ira's best man at his wedding, and he was my best man at both of my weddings. We've always stayed close either by phone or by face-to-face visits. We discuss current events and our family members. Many times, we discuss the Bible and what it says about living in our times. We confide in each other and have a very close brotherly bond.

Q: How did you hear about my diagnosis?

IRA: I am not sure when I heard about the diagnosis from a chronological perspective. I remember that you contacted me approximately three to five days after you received your diagnosis.

CRIS: Your brother Ira told me.

Q: Had you heard of multiple myeloma before hearing of my diagnosis?

IRA: I had heard of Multiple Myeloma before. A close friend of mine was diagnosed with the disease. She spent several years fighting the illness, but I did not understand what her ailment entailed. When you told me about the disorder and your subsequent fight, it was clear to me the severity of the disease. Afterward, I contacted my friend, and we discussed her treatment and her remission. She is a Multiple Myeloma survivor.

CRIS: No.

Q: How did you feel when you learned of my diagnosis?

IRA: My initial reaction was being in shock. Between the three of us, you had experienced the best health of us all. Our sister, Pat, suffered from a debilitating disease starting in her late twenties. I have had back problems since my late twenties, and as I approached my fifties, I suffered three heart attacks. As far as any of us knew, we could not recall any major medical problems you ever suffered. So, being in shock was my first reaction.

After the initial shock, I had a sense of despair. I only knew that you had some type of bone cancer. Although I am not a health care professional, I understood that our blood is created within the marrow of our bones. If you had bone cancer, then it was serious. Also, I believe you said you were in the final stage of this disease. The information left me feeling uncertain about your future and the future of the remaining members of our family.

CRIS: Shocked, stunned, concerned, but also hopeful that everything was going to be okay.

Q: When did you understand how serious my condition was?

IRA: The only understanding I had regarding your diagnosis was it was final-stage cancer. That did not leave much room for optimism.

CRIS: When you went to Cancer Treatment Centers of America in Chicago.

Q: Did you ever seriously question my survival?

IRA: I had a serious concern regarding your survival. However, I went to church that week and our church has what we call "small group prayer." It is a time during our service where we will break up into groups of two or three and share a prayer request. As one of the elders in the church, I rarely participate in this part of our service. The issues I was praying about were not something I felt comfortable sharing with any of the members of our church. It was not so much that I was better than them, but there were a number of confidential situations within our church that I was praying behind.

Nevertheless, I felt that I needed to pray about your diagnosis. I found another elder in our church, and I shared your situation. Another member of his family had cancer, and I believe he succumbed to the disease (This was another reason why I shared with him. I wanted someone who would not respond with fear but was willing to stand in faith with me through this situation).

As we began to pray for you, the anointing of God poured over me. I am not sharing this as a person that looks for spiritual phenomenon whenever I pray. Over the course of my life, I have probably had less than ten times when I felt God's anointing in a tangible way. This was one of those times.

It felt as if there was a cauldron above my head. As we prayed, I could see the cauldron above me begin to tilt and pour the substance within it over me. It felt like a fresh spring shower that covered my entire body. Not only did I feel refreshed in my spirit, but the joy of the Lord encompassed me. Even though we were praying about a serious situation, I knew at that moment that you were going to survive this illness. I did not know how or when, but God's Presence was so strong that I knew it was His confirmation of your outcome.

As far as I was concerned, you were healed. I did not share your illness with many people because I did not want to hear their fear or doubt regarding your outcome. I shared it with my wife, and we began to talk about how we anticipated your return to full health.

CRIS: I never really seriously questioned your survival because, deep down, I knew you would make it.

Pat

Pat enlisted in the army after graduating from high school. She had to wait until October (when she turned 18) before she could take the oath. She became a veterinary technician, studying at Walter Reed Hospital in Washington DC, and then was stationed in Germany, Alabama, and Central California. Pat was forced to leave the army in 1986 due to an automobile accident. She could no longer satisfy the physical fitness requirements because of the injuries she sustained in the accident.

Pat moved to Los Angeles at the end of August 2008 to help our father take care of our mother as her health declined. In September of 2008, Pat was diagnosed with breast cancer. Instead of taking care of our mother, Pat found herself in need of care.

Pat moved in with Vanessa and me while she received treatment. We took her to her appointments and became her primary caregivers. Pat went into remission and has remained in remission ever since.

Pat returned to Central California after completing her cancer treatments. She returned to Los Angeles in 2010 when our father suffered his stroke. Once back, Pat became involved with a small neighborhood church. After the pastor passed away, Pat was called to the ministry and took over the church's leadership. Pat faithfully ministers to her congregation every day. Her call is to the poor and disenfranchised of her community.

Q: How did you hear about my diagnosis?

PAT: IN JULY 2015, I RECEIVED THE MOST DEVASTATING PHONE CALL OF MY LIFE. I knew something was up; something was weird... you asked me if I had time and if I was sitting down. And what made it even stranger, Vanessa was also on the phone.

If anyone knows you, they know that when you have to tell them anything, you've got to tell them the whole thing! So, you patiently, from the beginning, started telling me how you helped a friend move and hurt your back. I already knew about your hurt back because we had talked about it sometime before. You told me again how it did not seem to be getting better, so you went to the doctor to find out what was going on. When you started to tell the whole thing again, I thought to myself, **BERNARD CAN TALK!!!**

Q: Had you heard of multiple myeloma before hearing of my diagnosis?

PAT: So, as I sat there listening and listening with words beginning to run together. Then I heard the words, Multiple Myeloma! Now that got my attention! I wasn't exactly sure of it all, but one thing I did know was that it was cancer!

Q: How did you feel when you learned of my diagnosis?

PAT: I felt like someone had to hit me with a ton of bricks! Your words began to ramble on while I was dazed by what I was hearing. I was trying to concentrate on what was being said, but all I could think about was, "My brother has cancer! No! Not Bernard!" I immediately went into a selfish mode. I kept saying, "Not my brother! Not my Nardy!" I could not imagine my life without my brother!

Being a cancer survivor myself, I knew that usually, if cancer is caught early enough, there really isn't a lot of pain in cases I know about. So, in the back of my head, I'm thinking that if you're in that kind of pain, you may not have caught it early. Somewhere in the mix, I hear you say bone cancer! We had relatives who were currently dealing with Multiple Myeloma, and the reports we heard were not that encouraging. **THIS CAN'T BE HAPPENING!**

Q: When did you understand how serious my condition was?

PAT: When you and Vanessa were on your way to Cancer Treatment Centers of America in Chicago. **THIS IS SERIOUS!**

My mind was reeling! I almost felt physically sick. To my knowledge, you had never been truly sick in your life. Hearing that you had, or possibly had, bone cancer was more than my mind could handle at the time.

Q: Did you ever seriously question my survival?

PAT: I truly believe that God is a healer! There is nothing that He can't do! The question that I kept having was, would He? My brother is an amazing human being. To know you is to love you. God has used you in the lives of so many people that I guess I was questioning if God was ready for you to come home, questioning if your mission here on earth was complete. My faith and my belief in God's healing power was truly tested. I have seen God's miracle-working power on other people that had stage four cancer, who were blind, and even like myself, were raised from a wheelchair.

THIS IS PERSONAL!! This was my Nardy!! I could not begin to imagine my life without you here.

OUR CHILDREN

"God sends children for another purpose than merely to keep up the race - to enlarge our hearts."
— Mary Howitt

"Children are the hands by which we take hold of heaven."
— Henry Ward Beecher

Bart

Bart is our eldest child. We named him Henry Bernard Dotson, IV, but we called him Bart from the beginning so we could distinguish him from the other three living Henry Bernard Dotsons in the family. He was living and working in Phoenix, Arizona, when he received the news. Bart went to Arizona after graduating from high school to attend Arizona State University (ASU). Bart decided to make Arizona his home once he left ASU. Bart joined a local church and became very active as a layperson in the congregation.

Q: How did you feel when you learned of my diagnosis?
BART: Two years before the diagnosis, I had a prophetic dream that you had been diagnosed with cancer. I remember it very clearly. In the dream, it wasn't clear whether or not you would survive, simply that you were diagnosed. When I woke up, I spent a few months grieving. When I learned of your diagnosis, the emotional impact was greatly lessened.

Q: Had you heard of multiple myeloma before hearing of my diagnosis?
BART: I had not heard of Multiple Myeloma before your diagnosis.

Q: When did you understand how serious my condition was?
BART: I didn't understand how serious the condition was until I was face-to-face with you in Chicago.

Q: What did you do immediately after you hung up from learning of my diagnosis?
Bart: After I learned of your diagnosis, I began to pray for you.

Talia

Talia is our second and youngest child. I like to tell her she is my favorite daughter. She is quick to remind me that she is my only daughter. She was living and working in Rancho Cucamonga, California, when she received the news. Talia attended Pitzer College of the Claremont Colleges in Claremont. Talia remained in the area after graduation and became involved in social issues in the local African American community.

Q: How did you feel when you learned of my diagnosis?
TALIA: I was a little in shock. I knew something was wrong, so I think hearing the actual diagnosis, I was preparing to absorb whatever it was; when I heard the news, I went sort of numb.

Q: Had you heard of multiple myeloma before hearing of my diagnosis?
TALIA: Not really.

Q: When did you understand how serious my condition was?
TALIA: When Vanessa told me on the phone that you were in a specialized treatment facility.

Q: What did you do immediately after you hung up from learning of my diagnosis?
TALIA: I was in Northern California running hospitality for a music festival, so I hung up the phone, prayed for my dad, and went to set up.

MY COUSINS

"Call it a clan, call it a network, call it a tribe, call it a family. Whatever you call it, whoever you are, you need one."
— Jane Howard, Families

I am very close to my East Coast extended family. It was through those summer visits and subsequent family visits that my family ties with them grew strong.

During my divorce, it was my family that helped me through those very difficult days. Family members on both sides came alongside me to support me as I struggled to cope. Several family members came to my side during my cancer journey, but there were two members in particular that I leaned on quite a bit; my cousin Beryl and cousin Kathy, both on the East Coast.

Beryl

My cousin Beryl holds an extra special place in my heart. We share a bond that is hard to explain. It goes beyond kinship. We pray together every time we speak on the phone. We challenge and encourage each other to be what God has purposed each of us to be. We always talk about the things that matter the most to us – our loved ones and what God is doing in our lives.

I reached out to Beryl to tell her about my partial diagnosis as soon as I could. Unfortunately, I could not reach her directly on the phone, and I did not want to leave a message. I spoke with my Aunt Zenobia, mother's sister, Beryl's mother, notifying other family members. Aunt Z spread the news to her children (my cousins), except for Beryl. She was also unable to reach her directly by phone (Beryl is a busy woman).

Q: How did you hear about my diagnosis?
BERYL: I heard about your diagnosis in July 2015. My sister, Phyllis, told me that my mother had contacted her and told her that you had been diagnosed with cancer, and you were going to the Cancer Treatment Centers of America in Chicago. I told my sister that my mother must have gotten the information wrong. I had just spoken to you 2-3 weeks ago, and you had said nothing to me about cancer. I knew that you were having problems with your back as a result of an injury sustained while helping a friend move.

I followed up with my mother who had left me a message to call her. She stated that she had actually spoken to you, and the information that she shared was accurate.

Q: Had you heard of multiple myeloma before hearing of my diagnosis?
BERYL: I had never heard of Multiple Myeloma before.

Q: What did you think when you first heard about my diagnosis?
BERYL: I was confused. There were no symptoms. How could this be? Then, a thought flashed into my mind. I recalled your having an unexplained cough when you attended Uncle Ray's homegoing. Approximately a year earlier, I had had an insurance agent who also was a friend who had an unexplained cough and was later diagnosed with throat cancer. When I heard you coughing, I didn't want to overreact, but I did check with you to see if you had followed up regarding your cough, and you had.

Admittedly, when I first heard about your going to CTCA, I wondered if the cough was a warning, and perhaps if I had said something then, you would not find yourself seeking treatment at CTCA. In my mind, CTCA was a last resort for people who have tried to utilize local resources.

Q: How did you feel when you learned of my diagnosis?
BERYL: Were you going to die? Will I ever see/talk to you again? I didn't want to experience the pain I felt when my sister, Sharon, died. Life without Cousin Bernard? I felt so powerless. The thoughts were overwhelming, so I immediately went into denial.

However, hearing that you had been admitted to CTCA, there was no denying that you were receiving treatment for cancer.

When I heard of your specific diagnosis, I immediately went to the internet to get a better understanding of the disease. From what I had read, this form of cancer was treatable but not curable.

I also specifically recalled Grandpa Winfrey having bone cancer and wondered if you had the same disease. So many deaths due to cancer or cancer-related. Is it in our genes? I then experienced feelings of depression. I was fatigued, had difficulty sleeping, and isolated myself. I had been in this place of despair before. I had no strength, so I did the only thing I knew to do. I cried out to the Lord. "Please don't let my cousin die!"

Q: When did you understand how serious my condition was?

BERYL: I thought it was serious by virtue of the fact that you apparently had been diagnosed quickly and immediately saw a need to go to CTCA. I really learned how serious it was from reading Vanessa's updates and later talking with you.

You sounded weak, but you were "yet holding on." I recall you saying that when you got the diagnosis, one of your initial thoughts was that you had family and friends who would support you.

I gained so much strength from the brief conversation we had. Your words and tone of voice indicated no signs of fear, doubt, or anxiety. Here I was, the person who is "healthy," gaining strength from the one who was experiencing massive doses of chemotherapy. I thought even in this condition, Bernard is still ministering. That's not Bernard. That's God. God's got him.

Q: Did you ever seriously question my survival?

BERYL: Upon hearing a diagnosis of cancer, I did question your survival, especially since it appeared to me that the diagnosis was made so quickly, and you were immediately going to CTCA for treatment.

I remember the Lord asking me, "Who said Bernard is going to die?" The Lord reminded me that your diagnosis and treatment at CTCA had not caught Him by surprise. He is sovereign – in absolute control of all things. He then reminded me of how much He loved us, and just His presence in the CTCA hospital room or in my bedroom gives us a peace that passes all understanding.

I heard the Lord say,

> "Just pray My will be done, and whatever happens to Bernard will fall out for the furtherance of the Gospel. That's what Bernard would want you to pray."

He brought to my mind His love for you and me and the importance of trusting Him; "Just pray My will be done."

So, I began praying just that. And every time I thought of you, no matter what time of the day or night, I did what you physically did to me. I would give you a big bear hug, lift you up, gently kiss your forehead and tell you that I love you.

Kathy

My cousin Kathy and I have kept in regular contact over the years, mostly through birthday phone calls. Whenever I was on the East Coast in her vicinity, I would make an effort to get by to see her and her family. Kathy is the eldest of two siblings (she and her brother George Allan are the children of my Aunt Dorothea, mother's eldest sister), a widow, and the mother of two daughters.

I truly appreciate Kathy because underneath her outer calm in difficult situations is a fiercely loving, loyal, compassionate mother, sister, cousin, and friend. I believe we resonate with each other because she is also very analytical – wanting to know all the details. Something that causes most of my friends' eyes to glaze over when I go down the rabbit hole. She was there for me during my divorce with encouraging words whenever we spoke.

We also share a unique indirect family connection: Vanessa and Kathy's husband Roger were classmates and friends in college. Vanessa and Roger met in college five years before I met Vanessa and over 3,000 miles away. The four of us first met together while attending a backyard pool party while Vanessa and I were back East visiting family. Vanessa and Roger had not seen each other in over 15 years. I find it interesting when you discover the closeness of the circles in which we travel.

Q: When did you hear about my diagnosis?
KATHY: July 2015

Q: How did you hear about my diagnosis?
KATHY: You, via telephone.

Q: Had you heard of multiple myeloma before hearing of my diagnosis?
KATHY: Yes.

Q: How did you feel when you learned of my diagnosis?
KATHY: I was distraught and scared. Everything seemed so dire, and

I wondered whether it was caught in time. My neighbor, living with MM, was also alerted by persistent back pain. She suffered kidney failure as a result. My former, longtime, family dentist lost his battle with MM after treatment and remission. I also spent a lot of time at the doctor's office for about a year afterward, thinking that any little pain would reveal some kind of hidden diagnosis. The thought that something could be raging in your body while you're thinking it's nothing was frightening. I became a little obsessed.

Q: When did you understand how serious my condition was?

KATHY: After research online medical books I had at home and talking to others.

Q: Did you ever seriously question my survival?

KATHY: Yes. Again, everything that I'd read talked about short-term survival, if at all. It was not a very optimistic picture, and after knowing how close to the edge it was, it was a very shaky feeling.

MY FRIENDS

"A real friend is one who takes the hand of his friend in time of distress and helplessness." — Afghan Proverb

"When someone allows you to bear his burdens, you have found deep friendship." — Gordon Atkinson, RealLivePreacher.com

Norman and Ruth

Norman has been my best friend for over 40 years. He and Ruth live in San Diego County. We talk with each other every two weeks and occasionally get together during the year.

I met Norman our first term in college. We were both freshmen in the School of Engineering, and we were in the same Calculus class. Not only were we in the same Calculus class, but we also lived in the same on-campus dormitory.

My first roommate was a senior, and after the first term, he moved off-campus. Norman heard it through the grapevine that I needed a roommate, so he approached me. I was a little surprised and caught off guard when he asked if I would consider becoming his roommate. We did not know each other well, but I thought it could work out.

In my arrogance, I thought there would be more upside benefit for Norman than there would be for me in this pairing. After all, I was the somewhat popular, more gregarious one. I thought I would not have as much of a challenge finding a roommate as Norman would. I had a smug posture, at least in my mind, if not also in my body language.

Nonetheless, I thought it might be an interesting pairing. If it didn't work out, I could make a change later. So, after a few moments, I agreed to be Norman's roommate. Unbeknownst to me at the time, it was one of the best decisions I ever made in my life.

In a nutshell, we clicked very well. Our personalities were well suited for each other. Norman was outgoing in his own way. Different than my way, but at its essence, inclusive and engaging. Norman is Jewish, and I went to predominantly White and Jewish junior high and high schools. My junior high school would get days off for Jewish holidays. One time, I went to synagogue with my high-school friends for high holiday services. Consequently, I had a lot of Jewish friends from my public education days.

We both were curious to figure out how things work. We both would look for ways to solve problems and then act to fix the problems. Over the summer between our freshman and sophomore years, I went to Norman's parent's house to design and build a loft for our dorm room so we would have more floor space.

I learned a lot from Norman while in college. He unknowingly taught me how to drive a manual transmission car by letting me drive his Datsun B-210 hatchback. He modeled for me how to devise plans and to put those plans into action. His drive to accomplish his goals encouraged me to double down on pursuing my own. Since we were both electrical engineering students, we would work together on lab assignments and discuss our lab reports.

We exposed each other to experiences that we would have never otherwise experienced. I learned about car rallying, and he learned the words to Sugar Hill Gang's "Rapper's Delight." I helped him set up stereo equipment when he was the DJ for dorm parties, and I would tell Norman what it was like to be a Black student bussed to predominantly White and Jewish schools.

More than anything, Norman is a man of integrity, a true friend, and someone I want to spend time with. He would not hesitate to challenge authority about situations that asked him to compromise his integrity. We have had many conversations about work situations where he refused to take part in actions that went against his values and integrity, even at the risk of not being considered for future career opportunities.

Norman and I have been integral parts of each other's lives since college. I celebrated with his family when he received his MBA. I left the defense industry in part because it was not my passion but also because he asked me if I would come and work with him at a start-up company. I always wanted to work with him professionally, and it was an opportunity to do so.

We had done a summer internship together one year, but this was much more than simply working at the same company. We worked with each other closely to develop a product. While we were successful in developing the product, the company was not a successful business venture. It eventually folded, and I never had another opportunity to work with Norman professionally again. I still imagine how much fun it would have been even today.

When I was at my lowest point, when my first wife dropped the bombshell that she wanted a divorce, I needed to leave the house for three months if there was to be even a ghost of a chance of reconciliation. Norman was there for my children and me in a big way.

Upland, CA
May 1992

Norman called me up a few days after my first wife's ultimatum. He was just checking in on me to see how things were going. He had no idea what had happened. I recall the conversation went like this:

"Hey Mr. D, how are things with you?"

"Not so good."

"Really? What's going on?"

"A few days ago, XXX said she wants a divorce."

"What!?" He said incredulously. "Wait a minute, what the #!?<'s going on!?"

I recounted the events of the evening of May 5th, 1992. It still seemed surreal to me even as I spoke the words. I ended the devastating tale by saying, "She says I have to move out for three months if there is to be any chance of us working things out."

"So, what are you going to do?" Norman asked in a less excited tone.

"I've got no choice. I have to move out," I said. There was a heaviness to my words.

"Do you know where you are going to go?" Norman asked inquisitively.

"Not really," I said. "I thought about renting a room in a motel somewhere close by, but I don't think that would be a good place for the kids. They will be with me every other weekend."

My mind began to drift off as I thought about what the near-term future would look like for the children and me. It was not a pretty picture, far from what I had ever envisioned for myself and my family. After a few moments, Norman broke the silence.

"You can stay with me," he said calmly. Norman's problem-solving skills and pragmatism had gone to work on my behalf.

"What?!" I said in wonderment, taken almost as entirely by surprise as Norman was when I shared my unexpected news. The thought had never crossed my mind.

"I know it's been a while since we last roomed together," he said light-heartedly, "but this time, I've got a couple of spare rooms, so you won't keep me awake at night with your snoring or wake me up too soon with your habit of getting up so early!"

I could tell he was trying to lighten the mood with some humor.

"When it's your weekend with the kids," he continued, "they can stay in the other bedroom."

I was dumbstruck. I was sharing my troubles with Norman because he was my trusted best friend. He was the second closest person in my life (after Vanessa) that I shared the news with. I had not even told any of my family members yet.

Instead of just being there to listen, Norman opened up his home to my children and me in my time of trouble. His was to be my earthly refuge where I would weather the worst stormfront of the coming season of despair in my life.

I was immediately aware of the magnitude of Norman's generosity. I was also immediately aware of God's presence in my time of need. I knew then that God placed Norman in my life over 15 years beforehand for a time such as this. Not for his sake, but for mine.

My thoughts rushed back to when Norman and I first met and how I thought he would be the greater benefactor of our relationship. I was ashamed, humbled, and blessed at the same time. Ashamed because of my arrogance in thinking that I was "All that and a bag of chips." Humbled because of Norman's sacrifice and God's grace and mercy that He so lavishly bestowed on me in my time of need. I was blessed beyond measure despite my faults and frailties.

Upland, CA
December 1992

When I was struggling to get through the divorce process, Norman called me and asked me to be his navigator on a car Rallye he participated in every year. His other close friend was no longer able to do so because of other commitments. I was hesitant at first because it was difficult going through my trials and tribulations. But I decided to go ahead with it because he needed a navigator, and I wanted to help him out. He had done so much for the kids that I wanted to do something for him in return and me.

The car Rallye he had registered us for what is known as a Time, Speed, Distance (TSD) Rallye. In TSD Rallying, a team consists of at least one driver and one navigator. The goal is to finish each leg of the Rallye precisely on time – down to the one-hundredth of a minute – on every leg.

It was not the team that finished first that wins, but the team that completed most of the legs of the Rallye on time who won. A team was penalized if it finished the leg early or late. This TSD Rallye had anywhere from 10 to 14 legs on a 14-hour course that started in Santa Barbara, CA and ended in Las Vegas, NV. The team with the least penalties won. So, the goal was to finish the Rallye with zero penalty points. The navigator's job was to direct the Driver to arrive at each leg's checkpoint on time.

A TSD Rallye was indeed a nerd's playground. It required math and navigation skills, strategic and critical thinking skills, driving and communication skills. A good team had to be able to work well together and figure things out in real-time.

Once again, what I thought was a generous gesture on my part, God used to be the best thing for me at the time.

The navigator's role required a tremendous amount of focus. I had to calculate average speeds, tell Norman when he was approaching turns, and instruct him on which direction he should turn. Once we arrived within 100 yards of the checkpoint, I had to direct him so our front tires would cross the rubber hose that marked the leg's checkpoint precisely on time.

The TSD Rallye was very hectic and sometimes chaotic.

It forced me to concentrate intensely on what was happening at the moment. That took my mind off of my family crisis. After we completed a leg, we would get our score from one of the checkpoint workers and figure out the next leg. There was no time to discuss or worry about the score we just received; we had to move on to the next leg. I had to get focused on the next thing.

After a couple of legs where we did not do so well, I realized that the Rallye was an analogy of my life at that moment. I did not have time to lament over the latest frustration I had experienced in my trials. I had to stay focused and move on to the next thing.

The car Rallye brought me out of my funk and changed my attitude. After the Rallye, I was able to move on to the next thing I had to deal with in my divorce and not get stuck spending too much time thinking about the last thing.

Norman's goal was to win a trophy at the car Rallye. We did not come close. On the way back home, we talked about what went right, what went wrong, and what we could have done better. Norman asked me if I would do it again the following year. I said I would for two reasons: 1) I could help Norman do something he truly enjoyed, and 2) I would have bonding time with him at least once a year.

We were teammates for 10 years. The last year we participated in the Rallye was the last year the Rallye was held. And in our tenth year, we finally won a trophy. I had never seen Norman so excited. He wanted to know if I wanted to have shared custody of the trophy. I told him he could keep the trophy.

My reward was spending time with him over the years. That was worth more to me than any trophy. Even if we had won every year, I was also thankful that I could do something for him that meant so much to him. He had done so much for my family and me. I don't think I can ever thank him enough.

Norman was a groomsman at both of my weddings. When I married Vanessa, he and all of my groomsmen traveled from California to Pennsylvania to be a part of the ceremony.

I was a groomsman at his wedding to Ruth. I was a Chupa holder and recited the Sheheckianu in Hebrew at his wedding reception.

Vanessa and I, along with my children, attended the bat mitzvah and bar mitzvah of both of Norman's children. We traveled from Pasadena, CA, to San Diego, CA, for the affairs. At Joel's bar mitzvah, I recited one of the prayers during the service in Hebrew.

Q: When did you hear about my diagnosis?
NORMAN: About two weeks before you headed to Cancer Treatment Centers of America in Chicago. Possibly a little earlier, but the diagnosis was not yet confirmed.
RUTH: I don't remember.

Q: How did you hear about my diagnosis?
NORMAN: We spoke about it on the phone.
RUTH: Through Norman.

Q: Had you heard of multiple myeloma before hearing of my diagnosis?
NORMAN: Yes. A friend at work's dad had it and died. Actually, come to think it, I know another person that has/had it. We have not been in contact with that person in quite some time... However, I think someone we know has recently spoken with her.
RUTH: Yes.

Q: How did you feel when you learned of my diagnosis?
NORMAN: Shocked. Worried. I always viewed you as having healthier habits than me. Very worried because of the late diagnosis.
RUTH: Profound sadness and fear.

Q: When did you understand how serious my condition was?

NORMAN: When I started reading about the disease, and I heard you speak about your kidneys (so you were at CTCA), I knew things were not good. I was unsure of the early outcome, and that was troubling. It was troubling to ponder the possible passing of someone with whom I have shared so many life experiences, almost 42 years worth Ð graduation, weddings, kids, home improvement, the aging and passing of parents, joys, sadness, depression, work problems. And, this kind of stuff acts as personal mileposts also. There is less road ahead; most of the road is behind us.

RUTH: When I heard the words "stage 3," and when you flew to Chicago for your first round of treatment.

Q: How did you feel about my situation after we spoke for the first time after my diagnosis?

NORMAN: The local diagnosis did not get me too worked up. It was the reports from Chicago that I found so troubling. There was much more data that highlighted the serious nature of the situation.

RUTH: Afraid. Convinced this was soon to be fatal.

Q: Did you ever seriously question my survival?

NORMAN: Certainly, the initial reports from Chicago were disconcerting. I did wonder what the prognosis would be Afterward. Actually, at one point, perhaps my question was if there would be a prognosis. They were not happy thoughts. It was saddening.

RUTH: Yes, early on, especially the first time Norman and I came to see you at home with your back brace and significant 40-pound weight loss.

Lois and Michael

Lois and Michael are part of my church family. Vanessa and I have known them for over a decade, maybe as early as 2002. They are close friends for a couple of reasons. First, we live in the same city and are part of the same home-based Bible study group that Lois and Michael lead. We meet with the group every two weeks. Secondly, we have gotten together socially with them on several occasions. We went on an Alaskan cruise together with them and other church family members in 2008. We have socialized during other church activities. We have attended couples' ministry events.

Through all of these interactions, we have developed a special relationship. Most importantly, Lois and Michael made themselves available whenever Vanessa and I needed personal assistance along this journey. They took me to doctor visits. They ran errands. They sat with me when Vanessa was not able to. They came to visit me in the hospital. They would call just to check on us.

Q: When did you hear about my diagnosis?
LOIS: I was one of the first, so it must have been July 2015.
MICHAEL: July 2015.

Q: How did you hear about my diagnosis?
LOIS: You told us about the diagnosis.
MICHAEL: I don't recall. I think it was you.

Q: Had you heard of multiple myeloma before hearing of my diagnosis?
LOIS: Yes, I had heard of Multiple Myeloma prior to your diagnosis.
MICHAEL: No.

Q: How did you feel when you learned of my diagnosis?
LOIS: I have to admit it gave me a sinking feeling in the pit of my stomach because a cancer diagnosis is one of those that strikes fear and dread into the thoughts of people who care about the person diagnosed.
MICHAEL: He knows the Word.

Q: When did you understand how serious my condition was?
LOIS: I knew immediately that the diagnosis was serious because of my nursing background. I have to say I was not familiar with all that the diagnosis entailed, but I knew the seriousness of it.
MICHAEL: At the time you told us.

Q: Did you ever seriously question my survival?
LOIS: Yes, I did silently question your survival. How could I not since I had this bit of nursing knowledge. Of course, I KNOW God can heal, I knew Henry and Vanessa would pray and believe God for healing, and I knew our Life Group would support him with prayer as well as the church. While I know about healing, one never knows how the ill person is believing or praying or whether they have sin or unbelief in their heart

to obstruct healing, so I really didn't know what the outcome would be. I've not ever been this close to a person ill with cancer.

MICHAEL: No.

Cecily

I met Cecily in our freshman year of college while we both were taking a gymnastics class. We just clicked for some reason. Her family lived close to campus, and I met many family members when I visited her at her parents' home.

After college, we remained close. I attended both of her weddings, and we kept in touch through annual family letters at Christmas time. She moved to Northern California and would come down occasionally to visit family and for required continuing education training for nurses. Vanessa and I would sometimes meet her at her parents' house when she came down, and I would meet her for dinner when she was in town for training. I would send birthday cards and gifts to her daughters and call her and her husband on their birthdays.

Cecily played a critical role at the very beginning of this journey. There were so many medical terms and things that Vanessa didn't know that she was overwhelmed. When Vanessa shared this with the Prayer Team, Cecily jumped in. She became Vanessa's medical advisor, telling her everything she needed to do and to check on as my primary caregiver. Some of those early decisions would have long-term consequences, so it was important to deal with them soon and get it right the first time. God put Cecily in the right place at the right time.

Q: When did you hear about my diagnosis?

CECILY: I am not sure exactly when I heard of your diagnosis. I think it was July 2015, as it was soon after your diagnosis because I assisted with your journey to Illinois.

Q: How did you hear about my diagnosis?

CECILY: You called me to tell me of your symptoms and the lack of good quality health care. You were trying to make decisions by being active in your illness because of the lack of availability at City Hope.

Q: Had you heard of multiple myeloma before hearing of my diagnosis?

CECILY: I had heard of it but did not know the specifics of the illness, symptoms, how to diagnose it, and the prognosis.

Q: How did you feel when you learned of my diagnosis?
CECILY: I felt heartbroken. I cried. I felt I was losing one of my oldest and dearest friends.

Q: When did you understand how serious my condition was?
CECILY: When you flew to Illinois and when you got a high fever and low Hbg/HCT.

Q: Did you ever seriously question my survival?
CECILY: There were a number of times when you were in Illinois I thought I would never see you again. When Vanessa would call and discuss your case, there were times when it was grim. But one factor she would always say is, 'Henry has the strongest faith, and he believes he will be saved/healed.'

Q: How did you feel about helping Vanessa through the early medical decisions she had to make?
CECILY: I was comfortable with Vanessa asking me questions. I had to look up specific things, and some things were not in my field of family practice but were in oncology, a specialty. I had always had a close friendship with you and felt Vanessa and I became closer friends because we had something in common; our love for you and your survival. We became closer to one another – Soul Sisters.

Beware! The Enemy is Near!

"... take up the full armor of God, so that when the day of evil comes, you will be able to stand your ground, and having done everything, to stand." — Ephesians 6:13, Berean Study Bible

"Be sober-minded and alert. Your adversary the devil prowls around like a roaring lion, seeking someone to devour. Resist him, standing firm in your faith and in the knowledge that your brothers throughout the world are undergoing the same kinds of suffering. And after you have suffered for a little while, the God of all grace, who has called you to His eternal glory in Christ, will Himself restore you, secure you, strengthen you, and establish you. To Him be the power forever and ever, Amen." — 1 Peter 5:9 - 11, Berean Study Bible

Making Plans
Pasadena, CA
July 11 – 15, 2015

We still had five days before the flight, and I was getting progressively worse. I felt more tired, and it was getting more difficult for me to get up each morning and get around. Vanessa noticed that I was slowing down. She began to realize that much of the physical effort to prepare for the journey would fall on her. For my part, I was just trying to do whatever I could with what energy I could muster. Each day I would wake up and remember what my father had sown into my life. "Just do the best you can with what you've got."

Over the next few days, we arranged for our dog to be looked after and for one of our neighbors to look after the house. We put a hold on our mail and got help from a family friend that lived near LAX to take us to the airport from his house and let us leave our car with him to avoid long-term parking fees.

Trip to LAX
Pasadena, CA
July 15, 2015

We were scheduled to depart LAX on American Airlines flight 1307 on July 15th at 1:15 p.m., arriving in Chicago at O'Hare International Airport approximately 4 hours and 30 minutes later at 7:45 p.m.

We were running late. All of the packing was left to Vanessa just as she had anticipated. Vanessa was worried that we might miss our flight. I just wanted to get to Chicago and get some rest. I got into the driver's seat and drove us from Pasadena to LAX. I drove because my car had room for all of our luggage, and it had a manual transmission. Vanessa does not like to drive my car, and I prefer that she does not.

We made good time on the 210 Freeway traversing Pasadena from east to west. We got off the 210 freeway at Orange Grove and headed south to the 110 Freeway on-ramp. As we began to wind our way through the Arroyo Seco towards downtown LA, we started to see some mid-day traffic.

Vanessa later told me that she started thinking to herself, *Let's just get there!* I was not too concerned. I knew if we could just get through downtown, past the 10 Freeway, we would probably get to LAX with time to spare. After all, we had the MTA transponder in my car that would allow us to take the HOV lane to the 105 Freeway.

As we shot past the Vernon exit, my mind automatically went to familiar thoughts of, *This is where I was born. Right here on the Harbor Freeway.* I then began to recount how my birth story was told to me by my mother when I was a young boy.

Los Angeles, CA
Early morning, October 28, 1957

My mother shook my father while in bed to wake him up.

"Henry, I think it's time to go to the hospital. I just had some sharp labor pains."

My father got up slowly at first, trying to shake off the grogginess that lingered from a night of too little sleep. "Are you sure?" he asked. *The baby isn't due until November,* he thought to himself.

But this was their second child, and second children are known to arrive early.

"Yes, let's go. We've got to get to the hospital," she insisted.

So, my father jumped up, pulled a few things together, and they headed out in their 1954 Hudson in the Monday morning commuting hours to drive north to LA County Hospital, where most African American children were born in Los Angeles at the time.

Traffic seems to have always been a problem in Los Angeles. As they approached the northbound Vernon exit, traffic slowed to a crawl. My mother's labor pains were getting stronger and more frequent.

"Henry, I think I have to have a bowel movement!" my mother said.

"Well, just do it right here, and we will worry about it later!"

My father was intent on being with my mother when his second child was born.

Just a year earlier, my father missed the birth of his first child, a son. When he found out he had missed the delivery, my mother said he went outside of the hospital, sat down on the sidewalk, and cried.

My mother pulled down her pants and pushed. Instead of a bowel movement, their second son entered the world!

As the scene unfolded, everything seemed to become surreal. My father was able to pull off the freeway at the northbound Vernon Avenue exit. He stopped at a Sherwin-Williams paint store and got some rags. They called for an ambulance. My mother and I were whisked away with sirens blaring to the county hospital.

There was quite a commotion when we arrived at the hospital. It was rare for a baby to be born outside of the hospital under such unsanitary conditions. We were placed in isolation so as not to contaminate the other hospital-born babies.

In the meantime, my father was still on Vernon Avenue trying to clean out the front passenger footwell of the car. My mother said he could never get the smell out of the car, and they had to sell their pink 1954 Hudson.

At least he was there to witness the birth of his second child. God is merciful indeed.

Just as I entered the world by hitting the floor, wriggling, and shaking my hips, Elvis Presley was also scheduled to make his Los Angeles debut at the Pan Pacific Auditorium in Hollywood later that evening doing the same. The *Los Angeles Examiner* printed articles about both events the following day.

I know firsthand that God has a sense of humor and impeccable timing.

Los Angeles International Airport, Los Angeles, CA
July 15, 2015

My thoughts returned to the present as we approached American Airlines at Terminal 4. I must have been on autopilot while thinking about my birth. We had already transitioned from the 110 Freeway south, past the 10 Freeway, onto the 105 Freeway west, exited at Sepulveda Blvd, and were into LAX. Everything seemed to be going according to plan. It looked as if Vanessa and I would just make it before the end of boarding since we both had TSA-Pre-Check status. All we had to do was to get on the plane and get to Chicago. My help would soon be coming after that.

Our TSA Pre-Check status got us to the front of the line and through the body scanners in just a few moments. Vanessa was moving faster than I was, so she got through the body scanner first. She picked up one of her two carry-ons from the conveyor belt and then turned to me.

"Henry, get my other bag and I will run ahead to the gate and let them know we are on our way."

"Okay," I said. I was still waiting for my one carry-on.

The Thief Strikes

"The thief comes only to steal and kill and destroy. I have come that they may have life, and have it in all its fullness."
— John 10:10, Berean Study Bible

Vanessa hurried ahead, and I waited for the bags. I picked up one bag from off of the conveyor belt. For some reason, the second bag was not on the conveyor belt. I spotted it on the floor at the end of the conveyor belt, so I bent over to pick it up. When I attempted to stand up, there was an audible cracking sound that I heard coming from my back. At the same instant, a crippling pain shot up my spine. I could not stand up, so I sank to my knees. An airport worker helped me to a chair and said he would call for a wheelchair.

For a moment, there was nothing but chaos. Vanessa did not know why I was not right behind her, ready to get on board. I was sitting in a chair in pain, waiting for a wheelchair. The airport worker was getting frustrated because the wheelchair was not coming fast enough.

For Vanessa, the chaotic moment became one of panic. She knew instinctively I was in trouble, and she began to worry that something had happened to me. She was also worried about us missing our flight.

But panic only motivated Vanessa into taking action. She quickly explained the situation to the gate attendants and got them to hold the plane at the gate until she returned. She then returned to the security area and found me. By that time, a wheelchair was only moments away. Once the wheelchair arrived, we raced to the gate (which happened to be at the last gate at the very end of the terminal) and were the last ones to board the plane.

Once on the plane, the battle shifted from the ground to the air. It was a test to see what shape I would be in by the time we landed in Chicago. The four-hour-and-thirty-minute flight became an endurance test. I could feel myself getting more tired with each passing minute. I began to focus on just getting there. By God's grace, I endured the flight.

O'Hare International Airport, Chicago, IL
July 15, 2015, 7:45 p.m.

When we arrived in Chicago, there was a wheelchair waiting for me because the flight attendants had already called ahead to the airport to let them know I would need assistance once I disembarked the plane. To not hold up everyone else, Vanessa and I had to wait until all of the other passengers disembarked as I struggled to make it to the exit.

It was a relief to see the wheelchair in the jetway when I got off the plane. I immediately plunked down to take the weight off of my feet. The short trip from my passenger's seat to the wheelchair seemed to have sapped all of my strength.

A ground attendant took charge of the wheelchair as Vanessa and I made our way to baggage claim. The attendant tried to make idle talk, but I was not very engaged. Vanessa did her best to chat, but it was clear to me that she just wanted to get settled in the hotel. Once Vanessa collected our baggage, we made our way to the exit designated for people going to CTCA. The limousine driver greeted us, took our luggage, and placed it in the huge trunk of the long black stretch limousine. Vanessa tipped the ground attendant and steered my wheelchair towards the limousine.

When our travel plans were put in place by CTCA, we were told there would be a limousine waiting to take us to our hotel. It had been quite a while since I had been in a limo, and I had forgotten how low the seats are. It was getting dark, but I could see that this was not going to be easy.

I was in so much pain that I needed to be helped into the vehicle by the limo driver. It seemed as though every bone in my back creaked as I struggled to get in. After getting settled, my breathing was a little heavy. The limo was well stocked with bottled water and various fruit juices. Normally I would have grabbed a bottle of water, but I did not dare move because of the pain.

Another couple in the limo greeted Vanessa and me. They were on a return visit to CTCA for a follow-up appointment. I could tell by the look on their faces that I did not look well. Despite that, they were very encouraging.

"CTCA is a wonderful place," they said. "They are one of the best cancer centers in the country," they continued. "You're going to love it."

At that point, I just wanted to lie down.

"How long will it take to get to the hotel?" I asked.

"Oh, about 40 minutes," the limo driver said. "The hotel is actually in Prairie, Wisconsin."

Wisconsin? I thought. I was so tired that I couldn't think about anything but lying down. Contemplating the geography of Illinois and Wisconsin and the relationship between Chicago and Prairie was beyond my limited mental faculties. Instead, I conceded it was going to be a long ride and just focused on getting there. I remained silent, just taking in the view. Vanessa may have tried to make small talk, but I really couldn't say for sure.

The limo made its way north on I-294 until it turned into I-94. The limo slowed momentarily as the driver made his way through to the toll booth as I-94 became part of the Tri-State Tollway. We continued north, and I caught a glimpse of Six Flags Great America on my right. The sky darkened as the sun set, so I stopped peering out the window and tried to get comfortable for the remainder of the ride. That proved to be impossible as my body began to ache more with each passing mile.

> *"Come to me, all you who are weary and burdened, and I will give you rest."* — Matthew 11:28, New International Version Bible

Radisson Hotel and Conference Center-Kenosha, Prairie, WI
July 15, 2015, 8:45 p.m.

When we arrived at the hotel, I needed help getting out of the limo. I was exhausted, and most of my strength was gone. The limo driver pulled me up out of the low seats and helped steady me. I held on to him as we made our way inside. Vanessa went to the front desk to check us in and get help with our baggage.

The first thing I needed to do in the hotel was to relieve myself in the restroom. I was so weak that the limo driver had to help me into the restroom. Once inside, he guided me to one of the urinals. He released me, and I swayed a little while I fumbled with my zipper. He then stood behind me while I used the urinal, just in case I lost my balance. I felt a little better when I was done, so I made my way to the sink on my own and washed my hands. The limo driver handed me a paper towel so I wouldn't have to make my way to the dispenser. After I tossed the paper towel in the waste bin, the limo driver took my arm and helped me back to the front desk.

Vanessa thanked the limo driver and tipped him. She took my arm and told me our room number and that we had to take the elevator to get there. With Vanessa's help, I made it into the elevator and leaned against the wall once inside. I experienced a little pain when the elevator jerked slightly as it came to a halt on our floor. The bellhop had taken our baggage to the room, so Vanessa and I made our way to the room with me leaning heavily on her arm.

A Fitful Night

When Vanessa and I got to the room, I collapsed onto the bed. As soon as I lay down, I knew that I would never be able to get up in the morning because my back hurt so much. I knew I would not have the strength come daylight to rise. So, I got back up and decided I would have to sleep in the chair. I unceremoniously plopped down, not taking off anything but my shoes, and tried to get comfortable. I reclined the chair to get my feet off the ground. Vanessa put a blanket over me. Weariness mercifully took over, and I quickly drifted off to sleep.

Although I was to have a fitful night of sleep, the battle this day was over. I would live to see and fight another day. The long day had finally come to an end.

> *"Through You we will push back our adversaries; Through Your name we will trample down those who rise up against us. For I will not trust in my bow, Nor will my sword save me."* — Psalm 44: 5-6

Last Leg to CTCA

"Blessed are those whose strength is in you, in whose heart are the highways to Zion." — Psalm 84:5, English Standard Version Bible

---

Radisson Hotel and Conference Center-Kenosha, Prairie, WI
July 16, 2015

THE MORNING CAME EARLY TO ME IN PRAIRIE, WI. That was a good thing because of the fitful sleep I had the night before. Despite all that, I did get some rest, and I felt better than I did when I first settled in the chair. I was looking forward to getting an official diagnosis.

I moved slowly as I got dressed, and Vanessa fussed over me to make sure I looked my best. She learned the night before that there was a shuttle service every 30 minutes to and from the hospital.

"CTCA told us to get there early this morning so we can go through all the paperwork involved with the check-in process before our lab appointment," she said.

Bus Ride to CTCA

Vanessa and I caught the first morning shuttle from the hotel to the hospital. I was in quite some pain, and it was challenging for me to board the shuttle bus. I may have even required assistance from the driver to get to my seat. There were a few other passengers headed for CTCA from the hotel. They were all very calm and understanding of my difficulty boarding the bus.

It was a 10 – 12-minute drive from the hotel to the hospital. We had to make a stop along the way at another hotel to pick up more patients. We were on our way after the driver had collected everyone. Some passengers were on return visits as outpatients from out of town. You could tell because they were more upbeat, talkative, and encouraging.

"Is this your first trip here?" one asked.

"This is a fabulous place," another chimed in.

We newbies were also easy to identify. Most had already had their diagnosis confirmed and were thinking about what lay ahead. Although I was not 100% sure at this time that I had Multiple Myeloma, I knew I would find out later that day. We were more somber, not sure what to expect. I could see the concern on their faces. I could not always figure out who was the patient and who was the caregiver. Both travelers looked as if they were going to be the ones receiving treatment.

"What type of cancer do you have?" seemed to be the question of the day on the shuttle ride. Everyone was perfectly willing to share their diagnosis when asked. Prostate, lung, breast, and ovarian seemed to have the majority. There was no one else on the trip diagnosed with Multiple Myeloma.

I was somewhat surprised at the candor with which each one shared their stories. I had not spent any time with cancer patients, and I found it refreshing to talk so openly about what we all were facing. I would find out much later in this journey that this is an integral part of the recovery process. But let me not get ahead of myself.

> **Caregiver**
>
> When one is a cancer patient, it is extremely important to have a caregiver. The cancer caregiver role is defined as the person who most often helps the person with cancer and is not paid to do so.[4] The caregiver goes with the patient to their appointments and sits in on all the conversations with the doctors. The caregiver typically has been legally empowered by the patient to make decisions on the patient's behalf regarding their healthcare and medical treatment. This authority is activated when the patient is unable to make decisions or consciously communicate their intentions regarding treatments. This crucial step of empowerment occurs when the patient signs a legal form called the **Healthcare Power of Attorney (HCPA)**, designating (typically) the caregiver as the empowered individual.
>
> The caregiver role is crucial. The caregiver takes the burden of dealing with administrative tasks off the patient. The caregiver is intimately aware of the patient's health status and can be the point of contact for anyone concerned about the patient's condition. The caregiver is the primary advocate for the patient. This allows the patient to only focus on fighting the good fight.

Arrival at CTCA

"This is the gate of the LORD; The righteous will enter through it. I shall give thanks to You, for You have answered me, And You have become my salvation." —Psalm 118:20-21, New American Standard

As we approached the hospital, I remembered the long ride from the airport to the hotel and that we were staying in Prairie, Wisconsin, not Chicago.

"Exactly where is CTCA?" I asked. "I thought it was in Chicago," I continued.

The driver told me, "CTCA Midwest Regional Medical Center is actually located in Zion, Illinois. The brand name is CTCA Chicago because most people don't know where Zion, Illinois, is, and Chicago is the closest major city."[5]

For the first time, I fully realized the magnitude of what was going on from my Biblical worldview:

> *"I will lead the blind by a way they do not know; In paths they do not know I will guide them. I will make darkness into light before them; and rugged places into plains. These are the things I will do, and I will not leave them undone."*
>
> —Isaiah 42:16, New American Standard

I had come to Zion to receive my healing!!

---

4. American Cancer Society, https://www.cancer.org/treatment/caregivers/what-a-caregiver-does/who-and-what-are-caregivers.html

5. While CTCA identifies major US cities as the locations of their hospitals in their advertisements and branding, some of the hospitals are in fact located in neighboring smaller cities. The CTCA Atlanta location, also known as the Southeast Regional Medical Center, is located in Newnan, GA. The CTCA Philadelphia location also known as the East Regional Medical Center is located in Philadelphia, PA. The CTCA Phoenix location also known as the Western Regional Medical Center is located in Goodyear, AZ. The CTCA Tulsa location also known as the Southwestern Regional Medical Center is located in Tulsa, OK. The CTCA Chicago location also known as the Midwest Regional Medical Center is located in Zion, IL.

PART TWO:
ZION
July 16, 2015 – August 17, 2015

"...you have come to Mount Zion, to the city of the living God, the heavenly Jerusalem. You have come to thousands upon thousands of angels in joyful assembly, to the church of the firstborn, whose names are written in heaven. You have come to God, the Judge of all, to the spirits of the righteous made perfect..."

— Hebrews 12:22-23, New International Version Bible

"Then you will know that I am the LORD your God, Dwelling in Zion, My holy mountain."

— Joel 3:17, New American Standard

"What's in a name? That which we call a rose by any other name would smell as sweet."

— William Shakespeare, Romeo and Juliet

Confirmation

"Okay, Houston, we've had a problem here."
— John L. "Jack" Swigert, Apollo 13 Command Module Pilot

Cancer Treatment Centers of America, Zion, IL
July 16, 2015

THE BUS SLOWLY PULLED UP to the northwest entrance of the hospital after the 20-minute ride from the hotel. I gazed at my surroundings, but I didn't know what I was looking at. Directly west of the hospital was Shiloh Park. The beautiful park with its three large ponds was designed and built as the center of the city. On July 14, 1900, it was there that the city was dedicated to God by its founder, the Reverend Dr. John Alexander Dowie, a Scottish-born minister with extraordinary powers of healing. To the north was the historic Shiloh House, the former residence of Dr. Dowie.

Vanessa and I were some of the last to exit the bus. I was weak but excited, knowing I would finally get a verifiable diagnosis. It still had not quite sunk in that I really might have cancer. It was the "might" that suspended my full mental engagement in the journey. As an engineer, I needed substantiated evidence before focusing all my resources, both tangible and intangible, on this situation with this huge unknown. I needed to hear from an oncologist with 100% certainty that I indeed had cancer despite how bad I felt.

It was a little bit of a struggle to make it up the half dozen or so stairs that led to the entry door. There was ramp access for patients in wheelchairs or with other physical limitations, but the thought never occurred to me to use it. After all, I was not in a wheelchair. Besides, it was a personal challenge for me to conquer the stairs, thus satisfying my drive to do all I could with what I had to work with.

We entered the lobby and were greeted warmly by the receptionist. After checking in, we sat in the lobby, awaiting the start of the intake process.

While waiting, it occurred to me that I had been admitted to a hospital only one other time in my entire life that I could recall. When I was about five years old, I went in to be circumcised. I am not sure why they waited so long for the procedure to be done. My mother told me simply that it needed to be done. I don't know if it was done because of religious beliefs, family notions of tradition, or hygiene. I just recall being forewarned by my mother that, "It might hurt a bit."

I was admitted to the hospital after I was born on the freeway. My mother told me I was also admitted to the hospital when I was a baby because I'd had an asthma attack. I was placed under an oxygen tent for three days. She said the doctors wanted me to stay longer, but she said I looked so sad that she couldn't bear for me to stay. She said she sneaked me out of the hospital without the doctor's permission. I have no recollection of those hospital stays.

The Mother Standard of Care

After about 20 minutes, a woman called our names to begin the intake process. We were led to a small office near the lobby and greeted by a charming woman. She pulled out an intake packet of forms that we needed to fill out. There were a lot of papers in that packet. The pile seemed to be more than an inch thick. I remembered something my friend Cedric said about his bout with prostate cancer:

> *"There's only two things you need to defeat cancer – God and good health insurance."*

What I observed was that there were two questions that one must answer before anything would happen. One was, "What's your name?" The other was, "What's the name of your medical insurance carrier?"; and I'm not sure which question was asked first. While both names are important, it became clear to Vanessa and me along the journey that my name was not the most important one. But let me not get ahead of myself.

We went up to a second-floor waiting room after we completed all the paperwork. We waited for a nurse to call my name for my initial blood draw. What struck me while I was waiting was how different the waiting room was furnished compared to all other hospital waiting rooms I had been in before. It was more like a parlor or a lobby. It was incredibly open, and there were a lot of very comfortable chairs. It was well lit and quiet. It almost seemed a little homey. Everyone there, including the patients, appeared to have a welcoming spirit – something I had not noticed or experienced at other hospitals or doctors' offices.

The atmosphere and culture at CTCA did not happen by accident. I learned later that the mission of CTCA is to take care of patients to the "Mother Standard of Care." That means everyone at CTCA treats patients the way they would want their mother treated if she had cancer; to treat every patient as if they were a member of their family.

We had some wait time before my blood draw. I felt slightly tired, and I was hungry. I could not eat beforehand, so Vanessa and I planned to go to the cafeteria afterward. I was just glad that the chairs were comfortable. I was not really focused on why I was there.

The one thing I recall about my blood being drawn was how much was taken. It seemed like quite a bit to me. I am not squeamish about getting stuck with a needle, so the blood draw did not bother me. Vanessa, on the other hand, does not like needles. She told me, "Better you than me," as she witnessed the procedure.

Vanessa has a very expressive face. It is not hard to figure out what is going through her mind if you observe her facial expressions. She would not make a good poker player. She was most certainly more uncomfortable about the whole experience than I was.

We had food vouchers, so we did not have to come out of pocket for our meals. The cafeteria was large, in my opinion. There was a wide variety of food to choose from. The dining area had not only tables but booths to sit in. It looked more like a restaurant than it did a hospital cafeteria.

Vanessa and I chose to sit at a table. There were quite a few people in the cafeteria at the time because it was around lunchtime. Vanessa and I noticed that most of the people in the cafeteria, not just the employees but the patients and their caregivers, were all very positive. Strangers greeted us with smiles and words of encouragement. We didn't feel alone.

"This is the best place you can be," one would say.

"The people here are fantastic," commented another.

We sat next to a couple there for an outpatient visit. They initiated a conversation and began to share their story about their cancer journey. They were candid and also very positive.

"God brought you to the right place," the caregiver said. "He is doing miraculous things here. You will be alright; you just wait and see."

All around us, there seemed to be people bringing God into our situation. Vanessa and I could feel His presence.

We lingered around the cafeteria for a while before heading back upstairs to get our lab results. The nurses told us to come back after lunch for the results, but I think we lost track of time with all the positive energy we were getting in the cafeteria. I felt good about where I was.

When we returned to the lobby where we had waited for the blood draw, a nurse spotted us and approached us quickly.

"We have been looking for you," she said. "We have your lab results, and the doctor is waiting to see you. Please come with me."

I detected a sense of urgency in her voice. I think that was the first time that my pulse quickened because I knew I was going to get the information I was waiting for. Finally, I was going to receive an answer.

The Diagnosis

We were escorted into the doctor's office and asked to wait until a staff member had notified the doctor that we had returned. It was a pleasant office, not an examination room. There was a nice-sized desk and a couple of comfortable chairs for visitors. The doctor's chair was not as plush, more like the typical office desk chair one would expect. There were medical posters on the wall of various types of cancers. There was a bookshelf with many books. Some looked like textbooks, others like medical journals. It seemed as if this was the office of a well-read and very experienced individual.

After a while, the doctor came in. He was an older man with a calm demeanor. He walked in with a manila folder under his arm. He graciously introduced himself and let us know that he was the admitting oncologist on duty. He told us that he had been at CTCA since almost its beginning. After his brief introduction, he got straight to the point.

"We have your lab results back, and we have positively diagnosed that you have Multiple Myeloma. It appears on the Lambda light chain protein of your blood plasma cells."

I was not familiar with the term "Lambda light chain protein," but I did understand that I had a confirmed Multiple Myeloma (MM) diagnosis. The following conversation ensued:

"Well, it is good to finally know for sure," I said. I was not alarmed, but I began to contemplate what would be coming next. I began to wonder what the six-day evaluation entails. More tests? Time as an inpatient? Something else?

"But I must tell you, Mr. Dotson, you are a very sick man."

"I am?" I said. I was caught off guard by what I had just heard. Partly because I was a little lost in my train of thought, but primarily because of the tone of the doctor's voice. It was heavy and ominous. I certainly was not feeling my best. I was extremely tired, and my lower back was aching because of the move. Despite my not being up to par, I did not feel like I was "a very sick man."

"Ninety percent (90%) of your bone marrow is cancerous," he continued. "Your kidneys have failed, and you are anemic. It is a miracle that you survived the trip here. You could have had a heart attack, stroke, or simply died of kidney failure before we even had a chance to draw your blood. You could have easily died somewhere along the way due to the added stress of airline travel on your body, and we would have never had the chance to reach this diagnosis."

I was trying to get my head around what he was telling me because I simply did not feel as bad as I would imagine one would feel if they were as sick as he was reporting me to be. His expression was serious and somber. He had delivered his diagnosis in a very deliberate and measured tone. He did not mince his words to try to sugarcoat the message. It appeared as if he were trying to be as frank as possible to convey the magnitude and seriousness of the situation and yet keep from saying I was near death even as we spoke.

"It sounds as if I am as close to death's door as you can be and not be on the other side," I said.

"As a doctor, I would not choose those words to inform my patients of their condition, but I would say that it is a fair assessment," he replied.

Before I had a chance to ponder what he just told me, he went on to say,

"So, we are not going to do the six-day evaluation as originally planned. We are going to admit you immediately and begin an aggressive chemotherapy treatment plan in response to this very aggressive case of Multiple Myeloma you have. We will get you into a room as soon as we make one ready."

Vanessa took it all in in silence. She later told me she was in disbelief. She was thinking to herself; *He's not talking about my husband!*

The doctor rose and exited the room leaving Vanessa and me there to process what we had just heard.

I was somewhat stunned – not the same response I had when I heard the partial diagnosis from Dr. Mahmoud. I still was not afraid or anxious; it was just a lot of information that I was trying to process.

"Wow," I said. "This is pretty serious." That was about all I could manage to say.

Vanessa sat still in silence.

Before she could speak, a nurse came in with a lot more paperwork to sign as part of the admitting process and told us there was a room available for me.

An orderly came in shortly after that and pushed my wheelchair out of the office and down the hall to the elevators to take Vanessa and me upstairs to the patient floors of the hospital. I remained silent, still trying to process the information. *Ninety percent cancerous* kept going through my mind. *Complete kidney failure... anemic...miraculous plane trip...high risk for heart attack and stroke...near-death...* A lot to take in all at once.

But at least I finally had my diagnosis.

Let the Battle Begin

"The tribe of Zebulun supplied 50,000 experienced troops, trained in the use of every kind of war weapon, in order to help David with undivided loyalty."

— 1 Chronicles 12:33 – International Standard Version

Cancer Treatment Centers of America, Zion, IL
July 16, 2015

WHEN I SETTLED IN MY HOSPITAL ROOM, the admitting oncologist told me directly, "You have a very aggressive case of Multiple Myeloma, so we will take equally aggressive measures to fight it. We will start you out on a Hyper-CVAD regimen."

More words I did not understand. I soon discovered that when you enter into a fight with cancer, you will first confront what seems like a whole new language, one used to describe the type of cancer you have, the types of treatment that are available to treat your cancer, and the known side effects of both. Hyper-CVAD was just the first of many new words both Vanessa and I would need to become familiar with in order to be active participants in my care.

There would soon appear a host of doctors, nurses, therapists, certified nurse's assistants, technicians, and others to wage the fight for my life. They would come equipped with knowledge, skill, equipment, medications, procedures, and much more. They would bring every kind of weapon used in the war against Multiple Myeloma to the fight to care for me. Hyper-CVAD was just the beginning.

Of course, Vanessa and I did not know this when they asked me to sign the consent form for treatment. As a rule, Vanessa will not sign anything until she has read it thoroughly and understands what she is signing. In this instance, however, we both knew we were way out of our depth, so the previous rule did not apply.

The only thing we understood before they presented us with the form was that they could not treat me unless they had my consent. After scanning the document, we understood two things. First, healthcare providers are legally required to disclose all known side effects of medication. Second, there is all manner of unpleasant known side effects possible from the Hyper-CVAD regimen up to and including death.

After reading the part about death being one of the possible side effects, I remember thinking, *This would be very concerning if it were not for the fact that the doctor said I am already at death's door. So, I've got nothing to lose.* But even more so than my logical reasoning about the risks of moving forward, I had a peace about me that came from knowing that God was in control. So, I signed the consent form without a moment's hesitation.

Disease Triage

The Oxford dictionary defines 'triage' as "The process of determining the most important people or things from amongst a large number that require attention." In my situation, the large number of "things" that required attention were Multiple Myeloma, kidney failure, a crushed T7 vertebra, small stress fractures in both legs, anemia, and dehydration. The doctor handling my case would have to determine what to focus on first.

One of the nurses told me Dr. Sayed Abutalib, Assistant Director of the Stem Cell Transplant and Cell Therapy Program, Hematologist, and Medical Oncologist was assigned to be in charge of my case.

"He's the best doctor we have in the treatment of Multiple Myeloma," she told us. "His personality is a little different than most doctors you meet," she continued.

I wasn't sure what she was hinting at, so I asked, "What do you mean?" skeptically.

"Oh, you'll like him," she said assuredly. "You'll see."

At that moment, as if on cue, the door to my room swung open quickly. Dr. Abutalib bounded into the room. He was energetic and animated. "I'm Dr. Abutalib. I will be overseeing your case," he said as he smiled broadly. "You've got a lot going on, Mr. Dotson!"

Before I could say anything, he continued.

"The first thing we have to do is to deal with your kidneys. If we don't get control of your kidneys, we won't have to worry about the Multiple Myeloma."

I knew exactly what he meant. My mother died of kidney failure. My mind flashed back to her last days and played the movie over again in my head.

Kaiser Hospital, Bellflower, CA
June 23, 2009

"I can't do it anymore!" my mother cried out.

She had been on dialysis for about three years and decided the treatment was just too difficult to bear. She was receiving treatments three days a week. She had small veins and didn't like needles. After the four-hour treatment, she would be very weak. The day after treatment, she would regain her strength slowly and spend the day worrying about her subsequent treatment the following day.

Eventually, she would refuse to go for treatment, and my father would not insist that she do so. She would get dehydrated and faint; my father would call an ambulance; she would be rushed to the hospital, where they would give her fluids and dialysis and send her home after a day in the hospital. The cycle repeated several times. There was no quality of life for her.

We were in the hospital phase of the cycle after re-hydration when she refused dialysis. All of the times before, she had consented to the dialysis treatments while in the hospital. This time was different.

The attending physician led the family outside of her room to talk.

"We cannot force a patient to take dialysis," the doctor said. "She has a right to refuse treatment," he continued.

My brother and I looked at my father. We could see he was at a loss for words. I turned to the doctor and asked, "What is your prognosis?"

"She will die of kidney failure," he said flatly. "The longest anyone has survived with failed kidneys and no dialysis treatment is 21 days."

I believe the doctor interpreted our body language and facial expressions to mean we were concerned that our loved one would suffer in her last days. I say this because he offered this insight into kidney failure.

"You shouldn't worry about your mom's suffering. If you asked any doctor if they had a choice on how they would die, all would choose kidney failure because it is painless. First, you get tired. Then you get sleepy and fall asleep. While asleep, you may get a little fever, maybe not. Once asleep, you never wake up."

We respected our mother's right of refusal and took her to a hospice facility in Torrance, CA. Just as the doctor said, my mother got tired, then sleepy, and eventually fell asleep. Ten days later, on July 3, 2009, we received a call from the hospice facility late that night saying she had passed away.

HOMEGOING
Second Baptist Church, Los Angeles, CA
July 11, 2009

My mother's homegoing service was a testament to her love of family and dedication to teaching. The takeaway for me from the service was how important it was to her to be of service to others. I was filled with gratitude for her being the kind of mother she was to me. Here is what I shared on that day:

ZION

"A Grateful Heart
For your patience with an overactive and curious boy.
For your nurturing that taught me to have compassion for others.
For sharing your faith that led me to my own personal relationship with God through Jesus Christ.
For your encouragement for me to be the best me I can be.
For instilling in me a love of learning and more importantly a love of giving back to others from what I have learned.
For your encouragement and support in my most desperate times of need.
For being my mother first, and then my friend.
For all the love and care you poured over me as no one else could do.
I am blessed with a grateful heart for having you in my life forever, for always.
Henry Bernard Dotson, III July 2009"

When my mother passed, I thought about God's mercy. My mother had always been afraid of dying. She told us so even when we were children. She did not want to suffer, and she worried about feeling suffocated when they closed the casket.

We knew she did not have to worry about suffocation, but we could not look into the future to tell her she did not have to worry about suffering. But God, in His mercy, spared my mother from suffering as she transitioned into heaven.

We serve a loving God!

My mother's homegoing was very difficult for my father. He was spent emotionally and physically after 53 years of marriage and three years of being her sole caregiver at home. He broke down after the family got into the hearse to drive from the church to the cemetery.

My Aunt Zenobia, who had traveled from Baltimore to attend her younger sister's funeral services, said to my father,

"Henry! You know we didn't come here to stay! Everything will be alright."

My father stopped crying, looked up at her, and said, *"You know,...you're right."*

My father was then able to regain his composure and maintain it for the rest of the day.

My father, brother, sister, and I remained at the gravesite once the interment services were over and most of the attendees had left. We all just looked at the open grave in silence. My parents had purchased a funeral plot designed to accommodate two stacked caskets. My Uncle Ted, my father's brother, came over to join us. After a few more moments of silence, he said,

"Well, Henry, at least you know that you will end up on top."

I am unsure if my uncle was trying to lighten the mood, but his remark, in a curious way, eased my heartache briefly, and everyone seemed to breathe more easily. God comforts us by whatever means He so chooses.

Cancer Treatment Centers of America, Zion, IL
July 16, 2015

It did not take long for the movie to re-play in my head; it was just a split second.

I knew from my mother's passing that the first sign of your body shutting down due to kidney failure was getting tired. I was feeling more tired with each passing day starting two or three days before. Since my kidneys had already failed, there was no telling when they had shut down. I was already in the 21-day window. The only indication we had was the results from my creatinine blood test.

> **Creatinine**
> Creatinine is a by-product of normal muscle contractions, which becomes a chemical waste product filtered from the blood through the kidneys. High levels of creatinine in the bloodstream indicate abnormal kidney function.

The normal range for the marker indicating how much creatinine is in the bloodstream is from 0.7 to 1.3. My creatinine blood test results found the level of creatinine in my bloodstream was 8.84.

"We are going to give you saline solution to try to get your kidneys functioning again," Dr. Abutalib continued. "This will also address your dehydration."

"How will hydration help my kidneys?" I asked.

"Kidney failure is a side effect from your Multiple Myeloma," Dr. Abutalib replied. "You see, Multiple Myeloma draws the calcium out of your bones. That is why Multiple Myeloma patients break bones easily. The kidneys filter the calcium from the blood. The calcium coming from your bones is clogging your kidneys. Now your kidneys cannot filter out the toxins in your blood. When your kidneys are not doing their job, we call that kidney failure."

It was beginning to make sense to me.

"If we can flush the calcium out of your body, then your kidneys may start to function again, and you will not have to go on dialysis. We will have to wait and see."

Dr. Abutalib continued explaining his treatment plan. "While we are hydrating you, we will also begin the Hyper-CVAD. Okay, I will check in on you later."

With a disease triage plan in place, he left the room as dramatically as he had entered.

Shortly after that, nurses came in and began to hook me up with IVs to administer the saline solution and the Hyper-CVAD. Unlike my mother, I am not afraid of needles, and my veins are relatively large. I could not recall if I had ever had an IV, so this was a new experience. I found it fairly painless – just a quick poke. I had experienced worse pain getting a splinter of wood under a fingernail. When the bags of saline solution and Hyper-CVAD arrived, the nurse hung them from the tree of hooks and set up the pumps to dispense the fluids at the correct flow rate.

In addition to the saline solution and the Hyper-CVAD, Dr. Abutalib ordered a bone marrow biopsy, a PET scan, and an MRI. These procedures would give the doctors a closer look at my condition to know how to proceed with my treatment plan.

Once I was connected to several IV lines and bags, I looked over at the pumps and saw the numbers blinking and the drip, drip, drip from the bags. It was at that moment that I knew the battle had truly begun.

The Hyper-CVAD kicked in before the procedures started, and I began to fade out. I do not remember the procedures ever taking place.

But Vanessa does.

Flesh of My Flesh

"So the LORD God caused a deep sleep to fall upon the man, and he slept; then He took one of his ribs and closed up the flesh at that place. The LORD God fashioned into a woman the rib which He had taken from the man, and brought her to the man. The man said, 'This is now bone of my bones, and flesh of my flesh; She shall be called Woman, Because she was taken out of Man.'"
— Genesis 2:21-23, New American Standard

"'For this reason a man will leave his father and mother and be united to his wife, and the two will become one flesh.' So they are no longer two, but one flesh." — Mark 10:7-8, Berean Study Bible

"A wife of noble character who can find? She is worth far more than rubies. Her husband has full confidence in her and lacks nothing of value. She brings him good, not harm, all the days of her life...Her children arise and call her blessed; her husband also, and he praises her: 'Many women do noble things, but you surpass them all.'"
— Proverbs 31:10-12, 28-29, New International Version

Vanessa
Los Angeles, CA, 1988

VANESSA AND I MET UNDER CIRCUMSTANCES THAT WERE SEEMINGLY INCONSEQUENTIAL AT THE TIME. We both were attending the regularly scheduled monthly meeting of the Los Angeles Council of Black Professional Engineers. I was the Recording Secretary of the organization. Vanessa and her best friend Rosalind were attending as first-time visitors.

One of my responsibilities as Recording Secretary was to meet and greet first-time visitors after the meeting. The purpose was to collect contact information and to get some additional background information from the visitors. The organization was interested in why first-time visitors decided to attend, their first impressions, and any possible future benefit the organization could offer.

I found out that Vanessa and Rosalind met at work and quickly became friends. Rosalind had initiated their meeting.

"Hi. My name is Rosalind. What's yours?"

That is how Rosalind said that they met. They found out that they both were from back East and had come to California because of job opportunities in the aerospace industry. They clicked right away because of their East Coast vibe. They were both from Pennsylvania; Rosalind grew up in Bristol, and Vanessa in Philadelphia for nine years.

Rosalind was two years Vanessa's senior, and they soon got along like sisters. So much so that they bought a condo together in Pasadena and were housemates. They both had degrees in Computer Science, and they had come to the meeting to do some networking.

I collected their information and took notes. I would include the key details in next month's meeting minutes as usual. There were no sparks or even interest when we first met. I was happily married with a one-year-old son. I was simply fulfilling my duties as Recording Secretary. Vanessa also says there was nothing special about our meeting. She even contends that this did not count as our first meeting. She was just working the room.

But, a few weeks later, I received a call from Vanessa while at work. The conversation went something like this:

"Hi, this is Henry Dotson."

"Hi, my name is Vanessa Foster. I met you at last month's council meeting. Do you remember me?"

I was a little surprised to get a call at work from someone other than a coworker. I worked at NASA's Jet Propulsion Laboratory (JPL) as a contract engineer in their Deep Space Communications Network organization. I usually did not receive calls at work about the council, so it took me a moment to recall who Vanessa was. I remembered her name, but I could not remember what she looked like. I did remember that she came with her roommate.

"Oh yeah, I think I do remember you," I said after a brief pause.

"Great. The reason I'm calling you is that I am looking at a job opportunity at JPL, and I was wondering if you would write me a recommendation."

I paused and thought for a moment. *I don't know this person well enough to say I will make a recommendation straight away just because she asked me. I need to learn more about her professionally before I can commit to fulfilling her request.* When you recommend someone, you are putting your reputation, your political capital on the line. *That is not something one should do without careful consideration,* I thought to myself.

"Tell me something about your education and work experience," I replied.

"Well, I have a degree in computer science from Virginia Tech, and I currently work for company X." I can send you a copy of my resume with all the rest of my information."

"Okay. That sounds good. Let me take a look, and I can let you know once I've had a chance to think about it."

"Okay. I will send you my resume to your email address. Thanks, goodbye."

"Goodbye."

That was my first encounter with what I have come to know and appreciate about how Vanessa operates. Almost everything she does is planned and deliberate. While I was just performing my duties as Recording Secretary, Vanessa had already decided before she and Rosalind came to the meeting to network with people working at JPL so she could get recommendations for a position she was applying for at the company. She knew recommendations from current employees would have a much greater impact than those coming from outside the organization.

I later discovered her decision to seek employment at JPL was planned and deliberate as well. A position at JPL would allow her to meet the objectives she had established for herself concerning her quality of life, professional pursuits, and educational goals:

1. Vanessa had decided earlier that she did not want to spend a lot of time commuting to work. She would not even consider working somewhere that was more than 15 minutes away from where she lived. "Life is too short to spend hours in traffic," Vanessa would later tell me. When she and Rosalind purchased the condo in Pasadena, Vanessa knew that she would change jobs. She was working in Pico Rivera, a good 45-minute commute. That would have to change.

2. Working for a company that was known for its technical excellence would improve her marketability. The Jet Propulsion Laboratory is known worldwide for conducting unmanned space exploration for the United States. The Voyager mission to explore all the planets in our solar system and other planetary missions made JPL a great place to have on one's resume if working in a technical field.

3. She wanted to work for a company that would pay for her to pursue advanced degrees. Vanessa wanted to obtain at least a master's degree like her mom. Her mother inspired her because she was the first black woman to receive a master's degree in nursing from the University of Pennsylvania. She also knew this would make her stand out and give her more opportunities in her career.

But she also had the courage to ask for a favor from someone she did not know. Whether she knew it or not, she was operating on a biblical principle that Jesus taught in a parable.

> "I tell you, even though he will not get up to provide for him because of his friendship, yet because of the man's persistence, he will get up and give him as much as he needs. So I tell you: Ask, and it will be given to you; seek and you will find; knock, and the door will be opened to you. For everyone who asks receives; he who seeks finds; and to him who knocks, the door will be opened."
>
> — Luke 11:8-10, The Berean Study Bible

Our phone conversation was just one of many tasks she needed to get done to move forward with her personal agenda. If I had said I was unwilling to give her a recommendation at that moment, I am certain that she would have simply crossed the phone call off of her To-Do list and moved on to the next person on her list of JPL contacts. Our future interaction probably would not have ever amounted to more than a mere acquaintanceship at best. Vanessa was focused on achieving her goal; she was not looking to make a new friend.

But God had other plans in mind.

After receiving and reviewing her resume, I felt comfortable giving her a recommendation for employment at JPL. Something about her being so proactive in pursuing her goals informed me of her determination and ambition. That was something she would need if she were to be successful at JPL.

According to Vanessa, the first time we formally met was when she came to JPL for her first interview. It turned out that my immediate supervisor posted the job she was interviewing for. God moves in mysterious ways. My manager brought her to my building to say hello since I recommended her, and I worked for him. I remember our second encounter.

"Henry, I've got someone here I think you would like to say hi to," my manager said.

I turned to see my manager and Vanessa enter the room. I did not work in the same building as my manager, and he came with Vanessa unannounced. I recognized her right away from the council meeting.

"Oh, hi Vanessa! It's a surprise to see you!"

"Hi Henry. It's good to see you again!"

She smiled, and we greeted each other with a quick hug. I think we both instinctively knew that we had to make it appear as if we had known each other for a while to lend credibility to my recommendation.

"Vanessa is a pretty bright lady," my manager said. "She is going to be working for me over in our main building."

"That's great!" I said. "I guess I will see you around then."

"I think so," she replied.

After some small talk, Vanessa and my manager left the building.

That was the first I knew that she was going to be a coworker. *Hmm,* I thought. *I'd better keep an eye on her to make sure everything goes as smoothly as possible. My reputation is really on the line now.*

Jet Propulsion Laboratory, Pasadena, CA
Summer 1988

At first, I did not see Vanessa very much at work. Our offices were in different buildings, and we worked on different projects. I would stop in to say hi every couple of weeks when I had to turn in my time card or attend a meeting. My main purpose was to see how things were going on her projects. It was a little self-serving because I wanted to know if I had done the right thing by making a recommendation for her. I soon found out I had nothing to worry about. Vanessa had things well in hand.

After about four months, my project ended. I was reassigned to a new project that moved me to Vanessa's same building and floor. Our supervisor started having weekly staff meetings to collect status reports from his team so that I would see Vanessa at least once a week in those meetings.

I was notorious for falling asleep in these meetings, and Vanessa would kick me under the table to wake me up (something she still does today). When I would ask her later after the meeting why she was kicking me, she said, "It's rude to fall asleep, and we have to represent." She was concerned about how my sleeping would affect the opinion others had about blacks working in this high-tech environment. I also like to think that was when she started looking out for me.

She was always on me about spending too much time on the job. I was a bit of a workaholic, and she was always telling me, "You spend too much time here at work. You should be home with your family!" She would harp on me around Valentine's Day and Mother's Day to make sure I recognized the days and that I had cards and gifts for my first wife. I later discovered how important gift-giving is to Vanessa's family. It is one of her love languages.

She had always been an advocate for my first wife. She was genuinely concerned about me doing the right thing by having a healthy work-life balance. By this time, Vanessa had become a family friend. We lived about 30 miles apart, so we did not visit socially often. Once or twice my first wife and I and our son visited Vanessa at her condo. There was one visit when Vanessa came to our house to braid my first wife's hair while she was pregnant with our daughter Talia. My family attended Vanessa and Rosalind's graduation from grad school, and we went to their condo for the graduation celebration party.

At work, Vanessa and I would go out to lunch now and again. Sometimes she would ask me questions about why men do the things they do. Throughout our friendship, she was in a couple of relationships and wanted my opinion to help her understand why her significant other was behaving badly. I did the best I could to provide answers, but I never considered myself having a deep understanding of affairs of the heart. I truly wanted to be a supportive friend. I've always considered it a privilege when someone trusted me enough to share things in their lives that matter. I wanted to be there when she asked for trusted advice.

Cancer Treatment Centers of America, Zion, IL
July 16, 2015

I WAS RUDELY AWAKENED BY A SUDDEN AND STRONG URGE TO PEE. I managed to make my way to my private bathroom before I lost control of my bladder. I was being given 1 liter of saline solution at a rate of almost 250 mL per hour. Like clockwork, about every hour and a half, I was up out of bed to the bathroom to put out about 250 mL of urine. That went on for about 4 hours.

When it got more difficult to get in, and out of bed, I let the nurse and PCA know that it was becoming too much for me to manage. That is when I discovered the most wonderful item ever invented – the urinal!

From then on, I did not have to get out of bed every time I had to "Do a number 1." The only thing I had to worry about was making sure the PCA kept fresh urinals available. I told the PCA on duty to make sure there were two or three empties hung on my IV tree so I would not have to wait for one in the middle of the night.

It was difficult getting a full night's sleep because I would wake up to use the urinal. Sometimes I would be so groggy that my aim was not so good, and I would have to get my sheets changed. Most of the time, I found myself roused to a semi-conscious state, just enough to do the right thing. I would imagine myself the captain of a ship receiving a command from some unknown voice saying, "Make it hap'n, Cap'n!" That went on for five straight days.

1st BONE MARROW BIOPSY
Cancer Treatment Centers of America, Zion, IL
July 17, 2015

The next day, Dr. Abutalib came into my room and informed Vanessa that he would perform a bone marrow biopsy to determine exactly what was going on in my marrow. He explained the procedure to her and had her sign a consent form.

She read and signed the form but did not really understand exactly what was about to happen. It wasn't that she did not comprehend the words on the page and was uninformed. She understood the risks stated and that the procedure was necessary for the doctors to help get me better. She just did not understand the detailed steps involved in extracting marrow from my bones.

Bone Marrow Biopsy

A bone marrow biopsy is a procedure that can sample the spongy tissue deep within the bone structure. It is considered one of the more sophisticated procedures in medical terms. Doctors do not recommend it unless it is important. Usually, a doctor specializing in blood disorders or cancer, such as a hematologist or a trained healthcare worker, will perform the procedure. The actual biopsy itself takes about 10 minutes.

The practitioner applies a local anesthetic to numb the area. The bone marrow biopsy is most commonly taken from the ridge of the rear hipbone or the chest bone.

The practitioner will then make a small incision so a hollow needle can easily pass through the skin.

The practitioner then inserts the needle into the bone and pushes it through the hard bone tissue until it reaches the marrow in the middle of the bone. If conscious, the patient may feel a dull pain or discomfort as the needle passes through the hard portion of the bone.

The hollow needle is attached to an empty syringe with its plunger fully compressed. The practitioner pulls back on the plunger, and the bone marrow is drawn into the barrel of the syringe through the hollow needle.

After the procedure, the practitioner will apply pressure to the area to stop any bleeding and then bandage the incision.

When Vanessa saw the long hollow needle, she was shocked and thought, *Oh my God, what are they going to do?!*

Vanessa could not envision what was about to happen, even though the doctor explained the procedure beforehand. Vanessa is a very visual person. She does not get a picture of something physical in her mind's eye when presented verbally or in written form. She has to see it to comprehend it fully. When I asked her later on why she was so surprised when they had told her what they were going to do, she said, "But they could have told me anything, and I wouldn't know what it was until I saw it."

When Vanessa saw Dr. Abutalib start inserting the needle, she started to get squeamish and looked away. The next thing she did when the reality of the crisis hit her was to pray.

She then pulled out her cell phone and started texting a close friend. She asked her to start praying. She looked up periodically and texted her friend a blow-by-blow explanation of what was going on. That helped her keep from losing her composure through the procedure.

The next thing she did was send out text messages to key people asking them to pray. She knew the power of prayer, and she wanted some real prayer warriors to start praying for both her and me. She did not go into much detail but made it clear that she needed prayer at that very instant.

She began receiving responses in a matter of minutes. All she could do as she received the responses was to continue to send out the simple message to pray for her husband, Henry. Soon her phone was blowing up with replies to her plea for help. People were coming into agreement with her for God to show up and show out at that very moment. Words of encouragement, passages of scripture, expressions of love for the two of us all came pouring in.

All of these messages helped Vanessa maintain a calm appearance. Internally, although she was really struggling, she did not feel alone. She felt God's presence through the prayers of others. That gave her a small measure of much-needed peace.

After the procedure was over, Dr. Abutalib said inserting the needle through my bone was like going through butter. Vanessa asked the doctor what that meant. He said it meant my bones were fragile. The Multiple Myeloma had softened them. Dr. Abutalib then instructed the nurse to send the bone marrow samples to the lab, and he left my room.

The procedure was much more difficult for Vanessa than it was for me. I was oblivious to my surroundings due to the Hyper-CVAD. After it was over, Vanessa steadied herself by focusing on the thought, *We need to do whatever it takes to get him better.* She found strength by thinking, *We will be closer to the information we need when we get the results of the bone marrow biopsy.*

A SHORT REPORT

"...the most valuable of all talents, that of never using two words where one will do..."
— Thomas Jefferson

Cancer Treatment Centers of America, Zion, IL
July 18, 2015

Vanessa arrived at the hospital early the following day. The bone marrow biopsy had been quite an ordeal for her. Not only was it difficult to watch, she knew we were in for the long haul. She began to think about how our lives would be affected by an extended hospital stay so far away from home.

Later, she told me the first thing she thought about was our lodging accommodations. So she sent an email to the travel department within CTCA to find out how much it would cost if we had to stay 21+ days. Next, she wanted to know more about the disease itself. So, she started doing more research online to get more information.

While waiting in my hospital room, Vanessa received the results of the bone marrow biopsy. It confirmed that I had Stage III "IgG Lambda Multiple Myeloma."

Multiple Myeloma

There is one main type of myeloma. It is cancer of the plasma cells in the blood. The cancerous plasma cells make different antibodies in different people. The antibodies are called immunoglobulins.

Each immunoglobulin is made up of 2 long protein chains (called heavy chains) and two shorter protein chains (called light chains). Immunoglobulins can be classified into one of 5 types depending on their heavy chains. These are A, G, M, D, and E.

In each case of myeloma, only one type of immunoglobulin (Ig) is overproduced. This varies from person to person. In myeloma, IgG is the most common. IgM, IgD, and IgE are very rare. All these types of myeloma are treated in the same way.

About 20% of people with myeloma do not produce complete immunoglobulins. They only produce the light chain. There are two types of light chains - called kappa and lambda.

Stage III is the full, active form of myeloma. The number of plasma cells in the bone marrow is generally more elevated; anemia (a decrease in the total amount of red blood cells in the blood) is present; there is a depression of normal immunoglobulin levels; there is a lower level of calcium in the bones, and there is the presence of bone lesions.

I had all of the Stage III diagnosis:

1. The number of plasma cells in my bone marrow was elevated - the normal count of plasma cells in the marrow ranges from 750 to 1500. My count was 13,000;

2. I was diagnosed with anemia;

3. There was a depression of normal immunoglobulin levels in my marrow - my marrow was 90% cancerous;

4. I had bone lesions in my legs and a collapsed T7 vertebrae.

Vanessa took a deep breath. That was a lot to absorb all at once. She knew I was not well. But this was the corroborating evidence that just made it all the more real.

The closer look brought her face-to-face with the not-so-good, the bad, and the ugly. Vanessa knew she had to tell the rest of the family what the doctors had found. However, she did not want to do an email blast with the devastating news, so she sent an email to my brother with a short message:

> *Hi Ira,*
> *Here is Henry's medical info:*
> *Diagnosis: "IgG Lambda Multiple Myeloma"*
> *Doctor's Info: http://www.cancercenter.com/midwestern/doctors-and-clinicians/syed-abutalib/*
> *Love You Brother!*

Although cryptic, she knew Ira would get the underlying message. She knew he would probably start looking online for more information. That would at least help to spread the news.

In the meantime, Vanessa was beginning to receive emails and replies on her Facebook page from family and friends wanting to know more details about my condition. People had read her July 9th post and were more than a little concerned.

She knew the inquiries would continue, and more people would start asking about my health status. She could see that this could become a job in itself and quite overwhelming. That was something she knew she would have to address eventually. But not right now. She had enough on her hands to keep up with my care and make sure she understood the medical treatment options available to us. Staying in touch was a problem for another day.

Delirium

"Toto, I don't think we're in Kansas anymore."
— Dorothy Gale, The Wizard of Oz

Cancer Treatment Centers of America, Zion, IL
July 18, 2015

MY MIND HAD TURNED TO MUSH THE DAY BEFORE. I was disoriented, often incoherent, dazed, and confused. I could not keep a thought in my head, let alone put together a decent sentence. I would have had trouble keeping up in a conversation with a two-year-old, and the two-year-old would probably appear to be the much wiser one in the exchange. I was fading in and out of consciousness, not always sure where I was or what time it was.

In my brief moments of lucidity, I found myself asking the same question over and over again, "How did I get here?" Each time I raised the question, I would get another piece of the puzzle, and I tried to fit the pieces together to make sense of it all. At times, I put a couple of pieces together before I lapsed back into a stupor. Other times, I was only able to grab a new puzzle piece. Each puzzle piece was one fragment of memory belonging to a string of events that ultimately brought me to this point. It was as if I had amnesia like Jason Bourne[6] and saw only flashes of past events. What I did not know at the time was that I was suffering from what is known as "Chemo Brain."

Chemo Brain

Chemotherapy (chemo) is the use of any drug to treat any disease. But to most people, including me, the word chemotherapy means drugs used for cancer treatment. The goal of chemo is to stop or slow the growth of cancer cells. Chemo medications are formulated to attack rapidly growing cancer cells of a specific type (depending on the type of cancer being treated), but they also affect healthy cells that produce rapidly. In most cases, the nerve cells in patients receiving chemotherapy are also affected. It turns out nerve cells are healthy cells that grow rapidly and absorb the chemo faster than other healthy cells. As a result, they too are killed by the chemo medications at a high rate.

continued

> The brain is made up of mostly nerve cells, so millions of them are killed when chemotherapy is used. Some of the brain cells that get destroyed are the ones that allow you to concentrate and put thoughts together, the ones that allow you to think. A hospital staffer told me if a person signs a legal document while receiving strong chemotherapy, the document may not hold up in court. It could be argued that the individual could not make sound decisions when the document was executed (signed).

Hyper CVAD

I vaguely remembered a doctor saying, "You have a very aggressive case of Multiple Myeloma, so we will take equally aggressive measures to fight it. We will start you out on a Hyper-CVAD regimen."

Later on (much later on), I discovered Hyper-CVAD is the term used in oncology to specify both a treatment method and a suite of chemotherapy drugs administered to fight Multiple Myeloma. The "Hyper" part of the term simply meant I would be receiving smaller (hyper-fractionalized) doses of chemotherapy drugs (the "CVAD" part of the term) more than once a day. That is not the standard protocol for administering chemotherapy medications. Typically, you receive one dose per week of a chemo drug due to the side effects. However, the doctors wanted to get as much chemo in me as possible due to my Multiple Myeloma's aggressive nature while minimizing the side effects as much as possible. A Hyper-CVAD regimen is prescribed in cases like mine.

My case of Multiple Myeloma was considered aggressive based on the results of one of my blood tests. Multiple Myeloma is a form of bone cancer in which ill-formed blood plasma cells start growing at an uncontrolled rate. These ill-formed cells do not function properly and are ineffective. Everyone has ill-formed plasma cells in their blood, but the body eliminates them, and they do not get out of control. The normal range for the Multiple Myeloma marker in the bloodstream is from 750 to 1500. My Multiple Myeloma marker was 13,000.

Some of the more likely side effects of a Hyper-CVAD regimen result in the patient becoming extremely tired and very weak, not to mention "Chemo-Brain." I experienced all three. As I strained to keep the movie in my mind going to recall what got me here, the effects of Hyper-CVAD kicked in, and I found myself fading back into an uneasy unconsciousness before I could grab another piece of the puzzle. As I was drifting off, I remembered the scene in The Wizard of Oz when Dorothy said, "Toto, I don't think we're in Kansas anymore."

FLUSHING THE PIPES
Cancer Treatment Centers of America, Zion, IL
July 19, 2015

I was not aware of how important it was to get my kidney situation under control. By this time, I was into Day 4 of my hydration treatment. I had gotten quite proficient at using the urinal. It was a no-brainer during the day, and the nights were not so bad. I did not know how long I would receive hydration, but since it was no longer challenging to manage, I did not put more thought into it. It is amazing how quickly you can get used to something.

Saints: 1, Satan: 0

Later that day, Dr. Abutalib came bursting through my hospital room door.

"We've saved your kidneys!" he exclaimed. He had a big smile on his face and continued with the good news.

"Your creatinine numbers are coming down, which means your kidneys are beginning to function once again. You came in with a creatinine count of 8.84. It is now down below 3.00. You will not have to go on dialysis now or in the future because of your Multiple Myeloma."

I felt relieved! The hydration procedure had flushed the calcium out of my kidneys, and they were responding on their own. God had spared my kidneys and was restoring them to be fully functional.

> **Multiple Myeloma and Kidney Failure**
>
> Renal impairment is a frequent complication in patients with Multiple Myeloma (MM) with an important impact on survival. It is found in 20-40% of cases at diagnosis and in almost 50% in the disease course. Ten percent of MM patients will require renal replacement therapy support. The complete recovery of renal function is associated with better overall survival. Also, the achievement of dialysis independence is linked to better survival. *(M Laforet, 2016)*

Just to be sure, the doctor prescribed the hydration procedure for one more day. He wanted to make sure my pipes were as clear as possible before stopping the treatment. By this time, I had gotten used to the procedure and was an expert with the urinals. *One less hill to climb,* I thought to myself – *one less hill to climb.*

A Closer Look

"If you want to uncover problems you don't know about, take a few moments and look closely at the areas you haven't examined for a while. I guarantee you problems will be there." — Bob Parsons

Cancer Treatment Centers of America, Zion, IL
July 20, 2015

Today, I had a PET scan and an MRI. Vanessa was not stressed about these procedures because she knew they were non-invasive and completely painless. I had had these procedures done in California when my family doctor was trying to diagnose the problem. Besides, I was still out of it due to the Hyper-CVAD. Sometime later, an orderly came and took me to the imaging center where the PET scan took place.

PET Scan

Positron Emission Tomography – Computed Tomography (PET/CT) scan is a type of nuclear medicine imaging. It uses small amounts of radioactive materials called radiotracers, a special camera, and a computer to help evaluate organ and tissue functions.

The radiotracer is either injected into the body in a dye, is swallowed, or inhaled as a gas. It eventually accumulates in the organ or area of the body under examination.

A special camera detects radioactive emissions from the radiotracer.

A PET scan produces 3-D color images of the functional processes within the human body and provides molecular information.

Later that day, the results of the PET scan came back. Here is an excerpt from the report:

Exam: PET CT WHOLE BODY
Date of Exam: July 20, 2015
Reason For Exam: MM;
Visit Reason: Multiple Myeloma;
FINDINGS: There is diffuse mild increased metabolic activities throughout the marrow cavities of the skeletal structures, which include the cervical, thoracic, lumbar spine, pelvic bones, sacrum, manubrium, sternum, both clavicles scapulae humeri, including both femurs consistent with the clinical diagnosis of Multiple Myeloma.

IMPRESSION: Increased activity is throughout the marrow cavity of the skeletal structures consistent with the clinical diagnosis of Multiple Myeloma.

Nothing new or unexpected here, Vanessa remembers thinking. *Just further confirmation of what we already know.*

Next came the results of the MRI.

Vanessa was starting to get the hang of the medical terminology. She still was not confident in her ability to navigate through all of the medical mumbo-jumbo, but it was not as daunting as before.

---

6. Created by author Robert Ludlum, the Bourne films are a series of action spy thriller films based on the character Jason Bourne (Matt Damon), a CIA assassin suffering from extreme memory loss who must figure out who he is.

Push 'Em Back, Push 'Em Back, Way Back!

"You are my King and my God, who decrees victories for Jacob. Through you we push back our enemies; through your name we trample our foes. I put no trust in my bow, my sword does not bring me victory; but you give us victory over our enemies, you put our adversaries to shame. In God we make our boast all day long, and we will praise your name forever."

— Psalm 44:4-8, New International Version Bible

July 21, 2015

THE AGGRESSIVE PHASE OF MY TREATMENT PLAN WAS COMING TO AN END TODAY. I had five days of continuous Hyper CVAD infusions and more than 30 liters of saline solution pumped through me during the same period. It had been a storm that I had no idea was coming until moments before it was upon me. It was a storm that had buffeted me with lightning, winds, and fierce rain in this first weather front, and it would certainly not be the last front to roll through.

I was happy that this phase was coming to an end. I could not sleep on my own because of the hourly activity going on to administer medication, draw blood, or check my vital signs. I would occasionally lapse in and out of unconsciousness due to the side effects of the chemotherapy, but I would not call that sleep.

I focused on the goodness of God through it all to persevere. I knew there was nothing else for me to do. I could not come up with my treatment plan. I could not make my body respond to the treatments favorably. I could not do anything that would sway my lab results. All I could do was concentrate on being in the moment. Moments became seconds, seconds became minutes, minutes became hours, and hours became days. Ultimately the first five critical days had come and gone, and I was still here. Still (metaphorically) standing.

When I was in this first storm, a lot of pushing was going on—pushing from the weather conditions of the storm (my situation and circumstances), pushing from the enemy, and pushing from God. That is why the scriptures say it is our job just to stand. We stand by being obedient to the Word of God and by trusting in what He says He will do in His Word.

"The purpose of problems is to push you toward obedience to God's laws, which are exact and cannot be changed. We have the free

will to obey them or disobey them. Obedience will bring harmony, disobedience will bring you more problems."
— Peace Pilgrim, Steps Toward Inner Peace

Saints: 2, Satan: 0

After five days of Hyper CVAD, the myeloma indicators in my blood dropped significantly. I had gone from being grievously ill to being critically ill. My situation had improved, and I was no longer in imminent danger of losing my life. I still had a long way to go, but things had turned around. To God be the Glory!

Dr. Abutalib delivered the good news. He said we no longer needed to continue the Hyper CVAD treatments, and we could switch to a VRD regime. Again, I was unsure what the treatment was, but I understood that it was a more conventional one. This change in treatment was critical. It was essential to determine whether or not I would respond to this first-line protocol for treating the disease.

VRD

Medications used in chemotherapy treatments are formulated to treat specific cancers. Each type of cancer (breast, prostate, lung, etc.) has its own unique set of medications used to combat that form of the disease. These "chemo cocktails" are referred to as treatment "protocols."

VRD is an acronym that stands for "Velcade," "Revlimid," and "Dexamethasone." Velcade and Revlimid are brand names for bortezomib and lenalidomide, respectively. Dexamethasone (Dex) is a steroid (It is easy to see why most patients and healthcare providers simply call it VRD). This chemo cocktail is one of the standard (first line) protocols used to treat Multiple Myeloma.

In my chemo-brain induced vivid imagination, these three medications were like the Three Musketeers, intended to work together with a fourth Musketeer to stop an evil plot. The fourth Musketeer was the team of healthcare providers at CTCA. The evil plot was the plot of the devil to take my life.

All for one, and one for all, I thought. To me, "All for one" meant the VRD and the team were the "all," and I was the "one." The "one for all" meant God was "the one," and He was overseeing us "all." The mind can come up with some interesting thoughts when under the influence of drugs.

The VRD was administered to me intravenously. We would have to see over time how well this protocol would work. I was not concerned. That was not because I had the best care available.

Even in my altered state of mind, I knew God was in control.

A Call to Arms

"When he arrived in the hill country of Ephraim, Ehud sounded a call to arms. Then he led a band of Israelites down from the hills."
— Judges 3:27, New Living Translation

"There will be a day when watchmen cry out on the hills of Ephraim, 'Come, let us go up to Zion, to the LORD our God.'"
— Jeremiah 31:16, New Living Translation

Radisson Hotel and Conference Center-Kenosha, Prairie, WI
July 21, 2015

BY THIS TIME, VANESSA HAD BEEN ABLE TO ABSORB THE SHOCK, and the numbness had worn off. Now that she was away from the hospital, she collected herself, and her mind began to get back in gear. She knew she had a significant problem on her hands. Her first reaction was to pray. Shortly after that, her natural ability to organize and apply logic kicked in.

Based on the number of messages she had already received, Vanessa knew she had to figure out a manageable way to keep the people who made up her support system informed. She knew it was vitally important. She needed their support, but she had to contend with the following challenges to make it work:

1. **She had limited time.** She knew she could not spend a lot of time communicating directly with people individually. Her husband had too many friends and family members who would want to know what was going on for her to keep them informed one on one. She knew she would need to spend most of her time caring for her husband, not giving status reports.

2. **She hated repeating herself.** First of all, this was a tremendous waste of time for her, and she **highly** valued her time. Secondly, she knew she could not repeat the story consistently. She would invariably forget to tell someone something crucial that she had previously shared with others as she repeatedly shared the details.

3. **She was not a phone person.** She did not like to talk, talk, talk, talk, talk. While she enjoyed meaningful conversation, she was not a person who truly enjoys talking for extended periods (like her husband). She was much more task-oriented, focused on action, and about getting things done. Being an

introvert, she felt drained after long conversations, while extroverts (like her husband) felt energized after lengthy conversations.

Given these challenges, she had to work her way through to a solution logically. That is how she operates. She first identifies the problem and then works it out in her mind. Sometimes the solution comes quickly, and sometimes it comes slowly. A viable solution always comes in time to execute a plan of action. She gives herself a time limit to develop a solution and makes sure she comes up with something (even if it is just a partial solution) by her self-imposed deadline. If it is a partial solution, then she repeats the process to work on the remaining issues.

As she thought about how much she did not like to talk, she concluded, *I'm not a big Facebook person either. I mean, I may read things others post, but I don't want all of my information out there for the world to see on my wall.*

But the word "Facebook" triggered a thought that gave her an idea. *There must be a way to use Facebook to post messages to a select group of people,* she reasoned. *This is probably a common problem, and someone has already figured out how to solve it,* she continued.

After some research, Vanessa found out that Facebook allowed users to create a "Secret" Facebook Group. The user that creates the group has complete control over who gets added as a "member" to view the Facebook page.

Facebook Prayer Team

She immediately went about creating the page. The page needed a name, and Vanessa knew immediately what that should be. She named the page "Prayer Team for Henry "Bernard" Dotson, III."

It was "On and Crackin'" now! Below is the official description of the page:

 Vanessa Foster-Dotson
July 23, 2015

Prayer Team for Henry "Bernard" Dotson, III The purpose of this page is to create a prayer team for my husband, Henry Dotson. The doctors are saying that he has aggressive Multiple Myeloma...bone marrow cancer. As a result, Henry's treatment plan is also aggressive. The intensive portion of the treatment plan started on Tuesday, 07/21, and will continue through Saturday, 07/25.

So we are asking that the members of this team come together in prayer as Henry fights the cancer disease... especially during this

continued

> intense portion of his plan. This group will also be used as a way to provide status updates as Henry progresses. We are claiming victory and are asking for your support as we cry out to God. Thank you in advance!
>
> 85   37 Comments

One of the side benefits of using a Facebook page to post what was happening was that Facebook automatically keeps track of how many members view the page and allows members to reply to the posts with comments or a response icon. Below is a sample of the replies to Vanessa's post:

> **PJ**   I'm thinking about you, Bernard! My prayers go up continually! I can't wait to hear the next praise report!
>
> **RH**   I know God has your back through all this, Henry. Just know that he will heal all that is wrong. Just know family is here.

She also sent out this text message to a few more close friends:

> "Not sure if you were aware that Henry had hurt his back. Well, as it turns out, there has been a bit more going on than just his back. So please give him a call at xxx-xxx-xxxx so that he can fill in the details.
>
> Meanwhile, Henry was wondering if you would mind being part of his support team. He is asking team members to either be willing to 1) pray, 2) be available as needed, or 3) be willing to execute something if needed. Let us know if you are OK with being a member. If so, could you please text me your middle name? Thank you! Love You!"

Vanessa had taken my cell phone with her when she took my clothes back to the hotel. If anyone called my number, she would know that it was about my condition. She did not want people calling her cell phone unless it was for work or indeed for her.

She had found a solution! Facebook fit perfectly because it resolved all of her challenges. She could look after me while simultaneously communicating with the people that mattered the most to her and me. In retrospect, this is something she had been doing for me almost from the beginning.

Jet Propulsion Laboratory, Pasadena, CA
May 1992

THE DEVASTATING BLOW OF MY DIVORCE WAS THE BEGINNING OF THE CHANGE IN MY RELATIONSHIP WITH VANESSA. I was in a state of shock for three days after my first wife announced that she wanted a divorce. I could not move from the sofa in our living room for the next three days. I managed to call in sick at work, but that was all that I could do.

When I finally returned to work, Vanessa was one of the first people I saw. When she saw me, she came up to me quickly and asked,

"Where have you been?"

I could see the look of concern on her face. She knew I never missed a day of work, let alone three. I took her aside and told her quietly,

"My wife wants a divorce. She said she has not been happy for a long time."

The look on Vanessa's face was one of shock and dismay. She was just as surprised as I was when I heard the words three days before. After three years of advising/warning me of maintaining a healthy work-life balance, I found myself telling Vanessa of the precise family crisis she had been concerned about.

I was humbled and ashamed. I did not have the answers to why this was happening, but I knew that I had my share of the blame. Relationships are not one-sided. Relationship dynamics result from how both parties interact with each other, not what one party does to the other. Whatever I did or did not do, know, or did not understand, played as much a part in the breakdown of my marriage as my first wife's thoughts and actions.

At my point of greatest need, Vanessa became my primary supporter in my network of support. She did so without reservation and made it abundantly clear that she was there as a friend only, not as an emotional substitute.

I know one of the reasons God placed Vanessa in my life was to minister to me in this critical moment of need. She helped me carry on when I did not feel as if I could do so. She showed me there was more living to do outside of my workaholic existence. On one occasion after work, when I did not want to return to an empty house, she suggested that we get something to eat at a dinner club that had live music. I said to her, "Oh yeah, I guess people do go out and do stuff after work."

Our roles reversed when I began to ask Vanessa questions about why my estranged wife was doing what she was doing. Initially, she offered her opinion and tried not only to explain but to rationalize the behavior. Eventually, she stopped trying to explain when it just seemed to be bad behavior. That helped me because Vanessa was not only someone I could confide in, but she was also one of my support team members that I could count on when I needed a sanity check. That is critical when one is going through a life crisis.

Once it became clear that reconciliation and restoration of my marriage were not to be, Vanessa helped me to establish the new normal. I learned how to be a single parent raising my children on a part-time basis. Vanessa would come along on some family activities and established relationships with Bart and Talia. Also, she introduced me to her circle of friends, primarily coworkers and church members. That was not how I envisioned my life to be, but I was learning to be content in my circumstances and envision a new future as a healthy and whole individual looking forward to what God had in store for me.

My divorce became final after 26 months of hearings, negotiations, and ultimately a settlement agreement. Afterward, Vanessa and I remained as friends for the next two and a half years. We would do things together, but I spent much of my time being a single parent and reconnecting with friends I had lost touch with while I was married. Valenda and I would get together regularly on play dates for our children and to celebrate their birthdays. I also became active in my church, where I found a community of believers that welcomed my children and me as part of the church family. Vanessa was involved in one or two relationships during this time, but nothing really serious.

AND THEY HEEDED THE CALL
Cancer Treatment Centers of America, Zion, IL
July 2015

Over the course of the journey, more than 200 people from different states, countries, and continents either became members of the Secret Facebook Group or received emails on my status because they did not have Facebook accounts. They heeded the call when they heard of the situation we were facing. This group of people came to be known simply as "The Prayer Team."

Those who responded to a call to arms made a personal commitment and sacrifice to become part of something bigger than themselves. In this case, The Prayer Team consisted of people willing to pray for Vanessa and me and decided to join us on this journey. They decided to come alongside us during this time in our lives to journey with us, to walk their life's path in parallel with ours.

I believe The Prayer Team members were called not just by Vanessa but by God. I believe that it was something in their spirits that caused them to heed the call. I believe they heard the Shepherd's voice, and they drew near unto Him.

Therefore, The Prayer Team became a significant part of the story, not just because of their prayers, which in themselves would be a powerful source of healing, but because the impact of the journey on them also would be as significant to them as it would be to Vanessa and me.

So the stage was set. Vanessa and I and The Prayer Team were about to embark on a journey together. In Zion, where God dwells, is where everyone got on board to provide the prayers so desperately needed to help bring about the miraculous healing that God performs when his people cry out to Him. In Zion, where God's people came for refuge in times of old, is where we found ourselves drawn together for a time such as this. Zion is where we looked for God to show up and show out.

Even in the midst of trouble and uncertainty, there is a certain expectation present, a certain excitement to see what God will do. There is an expectation for good for those who love the Lord and are called according to His purposes. I felt that excitement and had that expectation. There was no fear, just anticipation. What a mighty God we serve!

Chief Among Them

Everyone on The Prayer Team was special in their own way. Aside from their prayers, they commented on Vanessa's posts, providing insight into how the journey affected them personally. Their comments were testimonies in themselves on what God was doing in their lives.

It would be impractical to include all of the comments we received from The Prayer Team. In the telling of this story, however, their experiences are an essential part of the journey. Their collective perspective is as unique as Vanessa's and mine. Without their point of view, it would be impossible for you, the reader, to get a broad sense of what God did in the lives of all that were part of the journey. The telling of this story, in some ways, would be incomplete. It is therefore vitally important to share their thoughts and words in a meaningful way.

To that end, I have included some comments Prayer Team members made in response to some of Vanessa's postings. It is my intent to provide you, the reader, with some insight into their point of view along the journey.

Also, chief among them were the key individuals mentioned in the Preface. They were as faithful as Dr. Suess' Horton the elephant in his commitment to hatching the egg.

So, it was time for us to begin the journey God set before us all. Together, we would see the miracles God had in store for us along the way.

Fighting the Good Fight

"Finally, be strong in the Lord and in His mighty power. Put on the full armor of God, so that you can make your stand against the devil's schemes. For our struggle is not against flesh and blood, but against the rulers, against the authorities, against the powers of this world's darkness, and against the spiritual forces of evil in the heavenly realms." — Ephesians 6:10-12, Berean Study Bible

Cancer Treatment Centers of America, Zion, IL
July 23, 2015

A COUPLE OF DAYS AFTER THE GOOD NEWS ABOUT MY KIDNEYS, I STARTED TO FEEL SOMEWHAT BETTER. Part of my weakness was from the toxins accumulated in my body when my kidneys were not functioning. Now, I had a little more strength and felt as if I could do a little more to help with my recovery.

I also had a change of scenery. I was not in the room I was brought to when I first checked in to the hospital five days earlier. My original room had a window, but all I could see was part of the roof of my building and the side of another building on the hospital grounds. Not much to look at. My new room had a view of Shiloh Park with its well-kept grounds and lake. I could see people walking around the park and hospital employees who had gone outside to eat lunch. It was a much better view. I also wanted to be outside walking. I have always enjoyed walking, and I made a goal to one day go out and walk around the park.

My physical therapist had encouraged me to get out of bed whenever possible to minimize the loss of muscle tone. The Physical Therapist gave me out-of-bed exercises to do in the room and told me to walk around the nurses' station outside on the wing of the floor. In my mind, my first few attempts at exercise and walking were impressive only because I tried. I was amazed at how weak I was after only five days in the hospital. I was not deterred, however, even though my performance was underwhelming. You have to start where you are at and build from there.

I set a goal to walk a mile in the hospital to have the stamina to walk around the park. I found out from the nurses that I would have to walk around the nurses' station 35 times to complete 1 mile. So, I set my sights on 35 laps and tried to increase the number of laps I did each day.

I pushed myself every single day. As I made my way around each lap, I repeatedly told myself, "Do what you can with what you've got," and "I can do all things through

Christ who strengthens me." But I may have pushed a little too hard.

 Vanessa Foster-Dotson
July 23, 2015

Update for Thursday, 07/23/15:

Well, this is the second full day of the intense portion of Henry's treatment plan. Henry's kidney numbers are continuing to improve, and he is in slightly less pain. He started at a count of 8 and is now at 2. The goal is .1 to 1. On the other hand, Henry's blood pressure is high, and he is weaker. He was not as upbeat as he had been on Wednesday, and his voice was gruff again. He was even cold, and Henry is seldom cold.

As part of his physical therapy, Henry has a self-imposed goal to walk a mile around the nurses' station. A mile is 35 times around. On Monday, he and his PT walked two times. On Tuesday, he walked seven times. Today he walked 15 times. Henry may have overdone it a bit. Although the additional distance is great progress, between the exercise, the chemo, and a breathing treatment that protects him from getting pneumonia, Henry was very tired. He ended up going to bed at around 4:30 p.m. I was concerned, but the doctor and the nurses said that being weak like this is "normal".

I am about to check on him again.

Thank you for continuing to pray! The marathon continues.

👍 23   Seen by 172

 Our thoughts and prayers are with you, Henry! Prayer warriors in the Holy Name of Jesus Christ are praying for strength, determination, and healing!

 The Greater One LIVES on the inside of Henry, and His Light dispels ALL darkness; therefore, sickness and disease CANNOT rule nor reign in Henry's body! - it MUST bow down to THE Greater One... Keep walking by faith (not by sight), my friend... Hugs.

 Thanks for the update. I'm just lost for words this morning. The update really helped.

 That's Henry for you; driven and determined! God is good!

July 24, 2015

I was wiped out when I woke up this morning. It was no longer a maybe...I definitely pushed too hard yesterday. I learned a valuable lesson. When fighting a serious disease, you must save your strength so your body can use that energy to put up a good fight. While I did have the energy to walk, I needed to make sure I saved enough to remain engaged in the battle. I probably should have stopped my walk somewhere between lap 7 and 10 instead of pushing it to lap 15.

Also, additional side-effects of Hyper CVAD were beginning to kick in. The chemo started sapping my strength and appetite. Sitting up had become a chore. My feet were also beginning to swell. I had absolutely no desire to eat. Neither the sight nor the smell of food would stimulate my body's natural response to prepare to eat. I did not salivate; I did not have hunger pangs, no anticipation for a meal, nothing. Eating was just the mechanical exercise of chewing up the food in my mouth and drinking

> **Neuropathy Caused by Chemotherapy**
>
> Some chemotherapy drugs can cause peripheral neuropathy, a set of symptoms caused by damage to nerves that are away from the brain and spinal cord. These distant nerves are called peripheral nerves. They carry sensations (feeling) to the brain and control the movement of our arms and legs. They also control the bladder and bowel.
>
> Chemo drugs spread through the whole body, and certain types of chemo can damage different nerves. Symptoms tend to start farthest away from the head but move closer over time. In most cases, people will notice chemo-induced peripheral neuropathy (CIPN) symptoms in the feet, then later on in the hands. Symptoms may start in the toes but move on to the ankles and legs. Likewise, symptoms can move up from the fingers to the hands and arms.
>
> CIPN most often affects both sides of the body in the same way. When it affects both hands and both feet, doctors may call it a stocking-glove distribution.
>
> CIPN can begin any time after treatment starts. It often gets worse as treatments go on.
>
> Many treatments have been used to try to prevent chemo-induced peripheral neuropathy (CIPN). Certain vitamins, dietary supplements, and other drugs are being looked at to see if they can help protect nerve cells from damage. Many of these are being studied as supplements given before and after chemo.
>
> So far, there's no sure way to prevent CIPN. But this is a major problem for some people, and doctors are looking for medicines that work. A lot of research is being done in this area. Clinical trials are needed so that volunteers can help researchers find out more about what helps.

water to wash it down. It was not that the food had no taste or flavor; it was just not enough to compel me to want to eat.

Secondly, neuropathy started to occur. I did not know the medical term for what was happening; I just began to feel tingling in my feet and hands. It was very uncomfortable and just felt strange. Dr. Abutalib came in to check on me and just so happened to say neuropathy is a possible side-effect of chemotherapy. Vanessa asked him what that was, and he began to describe what I was feeling.

"While neuropathy occurs in almost all patients receiving chemotherapy, the severity and degree of discomfort vary greatly from patient to patient," he said in response to Vanessa's question.

I raised my hand while he was talking.

"You have a question?" he asked.

"I can feel what you are talking about happening now," I said.

"So, you are just confirming what I described," he said.

"I guess so," I replied. But I wanted to know more. "Will it go away?" I asked.

"It can get better over time, but it typically gets worse before it gets better," he said. "Everyone is different, so we cannot say how bad it will get, how soon it will start to get better, or how much will be permanent," he continued.

Another hill to climb, I said to myself. Amid my increasing suffering, I asked God to give me the strength to get through it.

Vanessa Foster-Dotson
July 24, 2015

Update for Friday, 07/24/15:

Today was pretty rough. Henry was weak, spoke very few words, and seldom opened his eyes. His vital signs were slightly worse, so adjustments were made as needed. He doesn't have an appetite, but he did force down two containers of an Ensure-like drink. He is also in a bit more pain. I could go on with additional challenges that he is facing, but the bottom line is that it was a difficult day. Thankfully, Henry is on his last dose of chemo for this cycle. At the end of the day tomorrow, his first cycle of chemo will be over!

There are so many cancer patients here. It is really amazing and sad. They each have unique "cocktails" that their bodies are having to endure. All of these "cocktails" consist of strong drugs with serious side effects. So additional drugs are given to combat the side effects. Absolutely crazy! I have a renewed respect for cancer patients. There needs to be a better way.

continued

> But for now, this is what is available from the medical profession to save my husband's life. Thankfully we know that God will give Henry the strength to fight and is holding Henry in his arms. Also, Henry has each of you supporting him. He/we are so blessed. We say thank you. We feel and appreciate your love.
>
> 👍 42 Seen by 172

FD We love you both and continue to pray for you both. God has truly blessed us with the gift of You as you give your love and support to our nephew. God IS good, and Bernard is in the best hands in the universe, namely, JESUS! May He continue to give you strength as He strengthens Henry in His healing process!

AM We are calling on all our friends and family to a special two days fasting prayer for our beloved brother Henry. On Sunday and Monday, please skip at least one meal and spend that time in prayer, focusing on praying for his healing and pray for sister Vanessa and the family to stay strong. God bless you.

VP Hang in there, Big Sis!

PM Be comforted in the knowledge that through it all, you and Henry are not alone. Having walked in your shoes with both twins, I've learned that God is faithful and will never put more on the patient or caregiver than they can bear.

July 25, 2015

My condition seemed to improve some overnight. The PCA had raised the foot of the bed before I went to sleep, which elevated my feet. That helped to get the swelling down. The neuropathy had persisted and indeed was spreading. But at this point, I was thankful for the things we often take for granted, like waking up to see another day.

My vital signs continued to fluctuate. My blood pressure was a little high, my oxygen saturation in my blood was a little low. My temperature was slightly elevated, and my pulse was somewhat high, but still in the normal range. My vital signs were checked several times during the day.

Towards the end of the day, I felt a fever coming on. I also started having trouble breathing. I was put on a respirator as a precautionary measure.

Despite all this, I thought about God's goodness. It helped me to carry on and do what I could. I found the strength to get out of bed and to do a little physical therapy. I was not able to do any laps around the nurses' station, but I knew that would come in time.

 Vanessa Foster-Dotson
July 25, 2015

Quick Update for Saturday, 07/25/15:

Henry is doing better today. He is more alert and talking a bit more. The swelling is down in his feet and legs. They are still working on stabilizing his vital signs, though. But all and all, today is starting out to be much better than yesterday. Praise God!

 44   Seen by 172

CL   Keeping Henry and you lifted up before God. Calling your names out, just like Pastor Ed taught us to do. Be encouraged, Vanessa. Tell him that he has hundreds of people praying for him. Tell him that the Langleys love him. Tell him that we have asked God to send legions of angels to minister to him. Your family in Christ is standing in the gap for him, interceding!

VH   God can and does perform miracles, and you have many, many people uplifting you in prayer. Thank you for the update.

 Vanessa Foster-Dotson
July 25, 2015

*** Continued Update for Saturday, 07/25/15:

Although he was still weak, Henry remained alert and showed improvement externally. He even watched a movie and did a little PT. Henry has gotten out of bed every day and sits in his chair for long periods of time. This a good thing!

Unfortunately, Henry's vital signs still were not stabilized. He had a fever, continued to receive oxygen as his respiration went below normal at times, his blood pressure was a little high, etc. The nurses are watching him carefully and are consulting with the doctor as needed. Also, Henry is still not eating. (I did get him to drink one Naked Juice.) At 3:00 pm, Henry went back to bed as he wanted to sleep off the rest of the last chemo dose for this 1st cycle.

continued

My baby is strong! God has given Henry the strength to complete his first round of chemo! We do not know what the future holds, so I must continue to focus on the present. As you may know, I am the ultimate planner, so not knowing is very difficult. However, I've drawn strength 1) from God, 2) from watching Henry fight, and 3) by feeling your love and your prayers. I am not sure why God told Henry to come all the way out to Chicago or why we were led to start an online prayer team. But no matter what the distance is, we do not feel like we are alone. Henry and I continue to say thank you for your prayers and support. We are truly humbled, and we are walking by FAITH!!!

 38   Seen by 185

MS One step at a time, patience is all that we need to consider, for it is one of the gifts of the spirit. So, we give God the glory and are grateful for God's favor in each and every step that Henry is passing, and keep pouring your heart as you update us, Vanessa. God surely is at work in our lives. Let's keep the faith. He cares.

RN Continue to walk by FAITH! Stay strong, Vanessa and Henry. Be encouraged. You shall believe the report of the Lord!! I love you guys! Henry is strong. Please tell him to hang tough, and this too SHALL PASS!!

VH Vanessa, as one who has been through and survived Stage III breast cancer twice, I really have an idea of what you and Henry are going through, and my heart goes out to you. Chemotherapy is extremely difficult on the body, and sometimes it is very hard to eat, and all you want to do is sleep. I've been there. I had 13 rounds each time, and my breast cancer was very aggressive. But I made it, and I believe that Henry will too...one day at a time, one step at a time. It takes a long time for the body to heal, but it is very encouraging to hear that Henry seems to be getting stronger. I was on a respirator, too, when I was sick, and my vitals were all over the place. Try not to despair; it takes a while for them to stabilize. God will never leave you nor forsake you. Continue to put your trust in Him that He will lead you and Henry B. Dotson III out of the valley and that his health will be restored. I pray that God will continue to keep you in His care. Love you both.

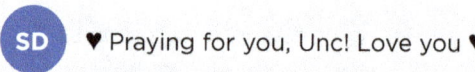 ♥ Praying for you, Unc! Love you ♥

July 26, 2015

Standing your ground is an ongoing activity. It is a daily challenge to stay vigilant through the highs and the lows we encounter. My father called them "The vicissitudes of life." I thought about his words and their meaning as the days wore on. When he first uttered these words, I immediately went to the dictionary because I did not know vicissitude's meaning. My father also taught us to look a word up in the dictionary instead of simply asking someone what it means. He wanted us to get into the habit of using the resources around us to learn things instead of passively being fed information.

I discovered the fundamental definition of the word "vicissitude" is the alternation between opposite or contrasting things. When used to speak of life events, it has a narrower definition of 'a change of circumstances or fortune, typically one that is unwelcome or unpleasant.' Surprisingly, I also found an example of the use of the word that expressed what my father was trying to tell me,

> "It's futile to happify your way through life's vicissitudes, which are an inescapable part of the human experience."

With these thoughts rummaging around in my head, I was able to concentrate on making it through yet another day.

 Vanessa Foster-Dotson
July 25, 2015

Oh, and for those of you that are fasting today and tomorrow, as per Abraham Manase's previous comment on Friday, 07/24...thank you so much! I will be joining you. Please include prayer for Henry B. Dotson III's complete healing...body, mind, and spirit...continued strength, improved vital signs, and renewed appetite. Thank you again!

 God, please heal and bring Henry out of the woods. God, you are able!! Touch and heal in Jesus' mighty name! Heal Henry Lord. We love him!!

(Isaiah 40) He gives strength to the weary and increases the power of the weak. Even youths grow tired and weary, and young men stumble and fall; but those that hope in the Lord shall renew their strength, they shall mount up on wings as an eagle that soars they shall run and not grow weary they shall walk and not be faint. (John 14) Very truly, I tell you, whoever believes in me will do the works I have been doing, and they will do even greater things than these because I am going to the Father. And I will do whatever you ask in my name, so that the Father may be glorified in the Son. You may ask me for anything in my name, and I will do it. (Romans 8) And if the Spirit of him who raised Jesus from the dead is living in you, he who raised Christ from the dead will also give life to your mortal bodies because of his Spirit who lives in you. (Psalm 46) He says, "Be still, and know that I am God; I will be exalted among the nations, I will be exalted in the earth" The Lord Almighty is with us: The God of Jacob is our fortress.

Vanessa told me about the upcoming fast and that she was going to participate in it. I was encouraged by the sacrifice others were willing to make on my behalf. Not only because they were willing to give more of themselves than their prayers, but because I know when fasting is combined with prayer, God will do more extraordinary things.

> *"Jesus rebuked the demon, and it came out of the boy, and he was healed at that moment. Then the disciples came to Jesus in private and asked, "Why couldn't we drive it out?" He replied, "Because you have so little faith. Truly I tell you, if you have faith as small as a mustard seed, you can say to this mountain, 'Move from here to there,' and it will move. Nothing will be impossible for you." "But this kind does not go out except by prayer and fasting."*
> — Matthew 17:18 – 21 New International Version

Vanessa's willingness to participate in the fast meant even more to me. She was my primary caregiver which was often very demanding. She was in charge of my well-being and made all decisions about what would and would not be done on my behalf. Yet, with all of this, she was still willing to fast so that she could call on more of God's goodness for me.

She has always been willing to do what it takes to be a helpmate in my times of trouble, as I've gone through "The vicissitudes of life."

Monrovia, CA
January 1997

MY LIFE BEGAN TO CHANGE IN 1997. First, I began to feel as if I was ready to start thinking about dating. One of the positive things that happened due to my divorce was that I received counseling and learned about healthy relationships. I read many books on divorce, single parenting, blended families, and God-honoring marriage. I knew that I wanted the type of marriage described in the Bible. One that put God first and had Christ at the center of the relationship. I wanted to apply the principles I had learned about being a good husband. I believe God put the desire in my heart to have a life partner.

I was motivated, but I did not know precisely how to go about dating after seven and a half years of marriage and four and a half years focusing on my children and healing from the most crushing blow of my life.

The first opportunity I had to "date" came when the single adults' ministry leaders approached me at my church. They had come up with the idea to have a date auction as a fundraiser around Valentine's Day. They were seeking eligible men to auction off for the event. I was hesitant, even apprehensive, but I felt it might be interesting. After some thought, I agreed to participate. Vanessa did not think it was a good thing to do. She knew she would never do something like that. She thought it was akin to a meat market but to each his own.

As the time approached for the event, I began to get cold feet. I decided to put a safety valve in place. I asked my trusted friend Lisa from college to attend the event and bid on me if she thought things were getting dicey. Things did not go well. A determined bidder outbid Lisa, and the date was memorable for all the wrong reasons. Vanessa thought God intended to teach me a lesson - never do that again! After that fiasco, I decided to listen for God to direct my path.

I thought I heard from Him one Saturday afternoon at another single adults' ministry activity. I do not recall what the occasion was, but before it began, the leader asked one of the attendees to give an opening prayer. I did not see who that was; I just bowed my head and closed my eyes. What I heard was a captivating female voice uttering a heartfelt, fervent prayer! I kept my eyes closed, but I thought to myself, *Man, she sure can pray! I need to find out who that is!* I was instantly attracted to her sight unseen because of how she prayed.

I looked for her as soon as she finished praying, but I did not see her. There were a lot of people at the affair, so I was looking through the crowd. It turned out that she was petite, so I had to make my way towards the voice before seeing her. I did not come up to her right away and introduce myself. I decided I would wait to find someone at church I knew who also knew her and asked them to introduce me. I also thought I might find out more about her than just her ability to pray.

We eventually met, and I was enamored. We had a few conversations at church over the next few Sundays. Then, we met once away from the church. I discovered she had been in a relationship that ended in uncertainty a little while ago. Undaunted, I invited my father and Vanessa to church one Sunday, where they met her.

My father did not say a word, but he gave me one of his looks that let me know he was not impressed. It was subtle, but I understood its meaning full well. My father was not one to discuss matters of the heart with me. He almost always kept his thoughts and opinions on the subject to himself. But his facial expression, though subtle, spoke volumes.

Vanessa shared my father's opinion, but she was far more vocal. Vanessa said she certainly did not see what I was seeing. Vanessa did not dislike her; Vanessa just thought she was not my type. I think Vanessa had in mind the kind of person she thought I needed and would be suitable for me. That did not look like a good fit to her. My father's nod of approval of Vanessa's comments punctuated their mutual sentiment. Case closed.

It became clear to me at this point that I needed to be a little more patient with God and perhaps to adjust my expectations of the single adults' ministry at church.

Monrovia, CA
Summer 1997

In the Summer of 1997, I became reacquainted with someone I knew from college. She called me on the recommendation of a mutual college friend who thought I might be good to talk to. She was going through a difficult divorce, and our mutual friend was impressed with how well I seemed to have navigated those turbulent times in my life.

Our initial phone conversation led to a face-to-face meeting that led to more and more, and ultimately it led to a fledgling relationship. Unexpected but welcomed. We shared the Christian faith, and that was an absolute necessity for me. We were not raised in the same denomination, but this is not uncommon, and initially, I thought it was nothing to worry about.

As time went on and we got to know each other better, a singular but significant difference in our faiths began to surface that I knew would be a stumbling block if our relationship was to move forward. We had several long and deep discussions on this sticking point but could not find our way around it.

This was very troubling. I wanted the relationship to work, but I did not know how to get past such a significant stumbling block. I needed some help. I needed to hear from someone whose opinion and insight I trusted. I needed to hear a woman's point of view. I needed Vanessa.

Vanessa knew me well. I trusted her and respected her opinion. I never had to guess what she was thinking because she always spoke her mind about things she cared about. And I knew she cared about me. I knew she had my best interest at heart. So if anyone would have something constructive to say, I knew it would be Vanessa.

Pasadena, CA
September 1997

I went to see Vanessa one evening and unloaded my troubles. We sat on the sofa, and I began to share with her my dilemma. I told her how I wanted the relationship to work but did not see how it could. I let her know I was at a loss as to what to do. I asked her what she thought I should do. I anticipated what she had to say. I was leaning on her again for the support I desperately needed. I was confident that she would utter the words I needed to hear.

I was so, so wrong.

After hearing my plight, Vanessa stood up, walked over to the stairs, and announced, "I think it is best if I keep out of the situation and leave you and her to work this out on your own. As a matter of fact, I think I should just stop spending time with you altogether so you can focus on making it work."

I was stunned, confused, and did not understand. Why would Vanessa leave me hanging in my desperate time of need? I had never done anything like that to her. Whenever she came to me with man troubles, I did my best to help her out. I asked her why she wouldn't help me figure this out.

"I've been thinking about what I want to do with my life," she began. "I came out to Southern California because of a job opportunity, but I have no family here. I met Rosalind, and we became best friends, so that was cool. But now Rosalind is married and has moved away to Northern California, and nothing is keeping me here now."

Vanessa then got up from the sofa, crossed the living room, walked up the first three or four steps of the stairway leading to the second floor, and sat down on the stairs. At that moment, I stopped thinking about my situation and began to listen to what Vanessa was going through.

"So, what are you thinking about doing?" I asked.

"I'm seriously thinking about moving back east to be close to my family," she replied.

It appeared that her situation was not the same type I was dealing with, and I quickly returned to being self-centered. I understood her problem and appreciated the implications of her solution, but what did that have to do with helping me when

I **really** needed her to help me work through my problem? She could move back east and still help me. I had no problem talking this out with her from long-distance. This was not adding up. Something was missing from her logic.

I walked over to the stairs. "I still don't see why you can't help me with this," I insisted.

"Well, there's something else," she said slowly, looking down.

"What is it?" I blurted out as I got close to her, face to face.

My sense of urgency was half due to wanting to get her to help me and half because I wanted to know if there was anything I could do to help her.

"I've come to realize that my feelings for you are stronger than I thought," she said softly, still looking down. When she looked up, she had tears in her eyes.

I was shocked, but I reacted quickly. In my head, I did the calculus to figure out how to solve both of our problems simultaneously.

"Oh, this is easy," I said. "My relationship with you is much more precious to me than the relationship I am struggling to make work. After all we have been through together, I am not willing to give that up. You should just stay here with me."

As I spoke these words, the truth of the matter went from my head to my heart. In my heart, I started to feel something powerful that had been growing over the years. It had finally overflowed and burst through to connect with the logic in my head. I loved Vanessa, and I loved her deeply! I knew it in my heart and my head!

I immediately embraced her and kissed her on the forehead while she sat on the stairs. I lifted her head and softly kissed the tears on her cheeks. Then I kissed her softly on the mouth for the first time. Then I just held her as she sobbed quietly.

"I'm not sure what to do," she said after a few minutes.

"It will be okay," I said. "Just stay here with me."

Vanessa did not answer but leaned into me as I held her.

When I left shortly after that, I wasn't sure what the future held for us, but I knew she would stay in Pasadena long enough to figure that out.

In retrospect, it is clear I was clueless. I was looking for love in all the wrong places. The one for me was there all along. Our song became "You Went And Saved The Best For Last" by Vanessa Williams.

Cancer Treatment Centers of America, Zion, IL
July 26, 2015

Change can come quickly, or change can come gradually. It can be for the better, or it can be for the worse. Today, it was for the better, and it was gradual. I was taken off of the respirator, and I regained a bit of strength. I am still tired and have a slight fever, but I can still praise the Lord for what He has done!

Vanessa Foster-Dotson
July 27, 2015

*** Update for Sunday, 07/26/15:

Sunday turned out to be a little different from what I expected. The good news was that Henry was removed from the respirator, ate a small amount of applesauce, and was able to do a bit of walking during his PT session. He also talked more. Unfortunately, Henry was still very tired, pretty weak, and still had a slight fever. I am learning that being tired and sleeping is not all bad. Henry's body heals while he is sleeping. So, I guess his body is healing A LOT.

In any event, I was naively hoping that my best friend would show more signs of improvement since the first cycle of chemo was over.

I have to remember that this is a journey, one day at a time. And everyone responds differently. Yesterday provided some tough lessons.

Please know that it may be a little while before Henry can receive visitors, either in Chicago or in Pasadena. Henry's immune system is compromised, and the chemo is making him weak. I know that you all love him dearly and want to see him, but I must ask for your patience. He/we love you as well and appreciate your prayers, concern, and support. I promise that I will let you know when he can receive visitors or respond to phone calls. I am learning daily about my role as his primary caregiver. First and foremost, I must do all that I can to help Henry fight and WIN!!! That includes saying "no" sometimes when I really don't want to. I ask in advance for your understanding and cooperation. Praise God for continually providing insight, wisdom, and direction!

I also praise God for those of you that fasted yesterday and will fast today. We feel your prayers.

Prayer requests:

1. Complete healing: body, mind, soul, and spirit. (no cancer, no fever, no anemia, healthy kidneys, etc.)
2. Renewed appetite
3. Renewed energy and strength

👍 44   Seen by 48

MH Vanessa Foster-Dotson, this journey is so hard on the primary caregivers as well. I pray for your strength, stamina, peace of mind, and spirit in this walk. Please let us know how we can help with the day-to-day things you can't do. God bless.

HR Prayers and best wishes for miraculous healing from the Rizvi family and all his classmates at AAA Institute.

CD Praying and standing in faith with you, sis. Be encouraged with Luke 1:37, "For nothing will be impossible for God," and 2 Corinthians 12:9, "And He said unto me, 'My grace is sufficient for thee: for My strength is made perfect in weakness. Most gladly, therefore, will I rather glory in my in firmities, that the power of Christ may rest upon me'. Love you both!

July 27, 2015

Today I was able to do more! Recovery is slow, but today is better than yesterday. I continue to push myself because I know that is what it takes to get better. I just need to be careful not to overextend myself. I still remember what happened a few days ago, and I do not want to repeat that experience!

Vanessa Foster-Dotson
July 28, 2015

*** Update for Monday, 07/27/15:

Monday was awesome! Henry's fever broke. His kidneys improved a bit, and he even ate some dinner! As I was trying to say yesterday, he no longer needs additional oxygen as his normal breathing is providing adequate oxygen levels. (I mistakenly said respirator.) The physical therapist came around 9:30 a.m., and Henry got out of bed and began physical therapy. He even did some walking exercises in the room. (He is building back up to doing the laps around the nurses' stations.) The therapist came back later in the day, and Henry more than doubled the distance that he had walked in the morning. He told the therapist, "I want to walk some more." (Fighter!!!) On top of all of that, Henry stayed out of bed all day until about 9 p.m. and was awake, alert, and talking.

Now, Henry's voice is still gruff and labored, he is still weak, but progress was definitely made! It is expected that his blood counts will go down more over the next few days and then improve. But for now,

continued

I am thankful for his success.

And for those that want to know how I am, I am good. Sunday, I received a needed lesson..." one day at a time"...but I am OK. Taking care of myself is a part of taking care of Henry. I am not a superwoman, and there may be low moments. But I have to pick myself up, learn, move forward, and stay strong. I may need help at times, and I have to learn how to ask, but I am well for now. Thank you, Jesus!

Thank you all for your concern. Thank you again for your prayers! Thank you for fasting! Thank you, Zoe, for your Late-Night Prayer on Friday. Thank you to a special pastor and his wife who prayed with us on Sunday. Thank you, God, for your continued grace, mercy, and healing. Monday was a good day!!!

Prayer Requests:

1. Complete healing: body, mind, soul, and spirit. (no cancer, no pain, no long-term anemia, no permanent back damage, healthy eyes, healthy kidneys, etc.)
2. Continued appetite
3. Renewed strength and movement
4. Complete clarity of thoughts and words

👍 45   Seen by 56

JM Yes!!! We are thanking God for the manifestation of Henry's healing!! Jesus took stripes for Henry over 2000 years ago! Jehovah Raha, the God who heals!! I'm excited in my spirit as I offer prayers of thanksgiving this morning!! It's done in Jesus' Name!!

FD Praise God from whom ALL blessings flow! Thank you for your concise updates, Vanessa, as well as your continued love and devotion. You two give the term 'marriage' a definite shot in the arm, and I know God is well pleased. Continued prayers are going up while blessings continue to come down.

LD Amen, amen, amen! Constantly praying for all your requests above. Keep Jesus foremost on your mind and lips!!! All is well, EVEN IN THE FIRE!! We who are praying are y'all's "arms-holder-uppers," and Jesus is the lifter of your head! Be strong in the Lord and in the power of His strength! YEAH!!

July 28, 2015

I was not in the mood to speak much today. Instead, I was focusing on accomplishing my goal of two laps around the nurses' station. Still, I have to keep in mind to pace myself as I continue to regain strength. I am still a little tired, and I am unsure if I have entirely recovered from "Chemo Brain."

I am surprised at how strong my desire is to make my father proud of me by following his instruction to "do what you can with what you've got." I have to ask God for the spirit of discernment so as not to overdo it. Today I went to bed early to give my body longer rest and recovery time.

 Vanessa Foster-Dotson
July 29, 2015

*** Update for Tuesday, 07/28/15:

One day at a time! Monday was awesome, and Tuesday was good as well. As expected, after having the type of chemo that he received, Henry's blood counts went down. As a result, he was tired, weak, and spoke few words. He also would not eat much, just a couple of shakes. However, Henry's kidneys continued to improve. He was alert, and. he is back at it; my man is doing laps again! He walked around the nurses' station twice! And the only reason that he stopped was that nature called. He may have overdone it a bit because he went to bed at 6:00 p.m. But Henry is still fighting! The doctors are saying that Henry is progressing well (thanks to all of your prayers!). Henry even has favor with the nurses as they moved him to the biggest and nicest room last week; more natural light and a better view; better for his recovery.

Henry is a special guy. God's got this!

Thank you all for your continued prayers!

Special thanks to Margaret and her husband, Jerry. Margaret is Henry's friend that strongly encouraged Henry to come to CTCA in Zion, IL, near Chicago ASAP. After hearing from God, Henry agreed to go. Henry was admitted immediately due to kidney failure and anemia and quickly diagnosed with Multiple Myeloma. We did not know that Henry had these conditions, but God did. Margaret is a believer, and she has an amazing testimony. Her husband, Jeff, is Margaret's primary caregiver and I am looking forward to learning from him. Thank you so much, Margaret and Jeff!

continued

Prayer Requests:

1. Complete healing: body, mind, soul, and spirit. (no cancer, no pain, no long-term anemia, improved blood counts, no permanent back damage, healthy eyes, healthy kidneys, etc.)
2. Improved appetite
3. Renewed strength and movement
4. Complete clarity of thoughts and words

 33   Seen by 39

MS   Thank you, Vanessa. Thanksgiving prayer to the Lord is offered. Praising, worshipping, and glorifying the Lord for what He has done… Just keep your faith and stay blessed as we thank God continuously for restoration. One day at a time, one step to another, may God be glorified in Jesus' name. Amen.

VW   Praise God! We are continuing to pray and believe for total healing. We serve a God that is able to do exceedingly abundantly above all that we ask or think! That's why the process you report is not surprising to me. Just an indication that our God remains on the Throne and that His Word is true now and forever. Halleluiah!

AR   Thank you for the update, Vanessa. Tell Henry that, inspired by his strength and fight, I almost exclusively took the stairs yesterday, but it looks like I still owe two laps around the building!! Today, I am specifically praying for improved blood counts. Love to you both.

PM   I smiled when I read, "Henry is a special guy." How could he not be? He has you…the epitome of specialness! Thank you, Vanessa, for being who and what you are. You are God's co-pilot in this journey, and the battle has already been won! Glory to God!

July 29 2015

Today was another good day. I realize going to bed early paid off. I increased my number of laps around the nurse's station without feeling any more tired than yesterday. Yet and still, I am a little weak because one of the side effects of chemotherapy is a loss of appetite, so I am not taking in as many calories as I should.

But I think God was looking out for me today in a unique way! Like manna from heaven, I received a cheesecake from my best friend, Norman! It was not only a delicious form of calories; it was food for the soul. You see, cheesecake is my favorite cake. Back in the day, I loved it to a fault.

When we were in college, most of my friends knew about my voracious appetite. So, for my birthday one year, I bought myself a cheesecake from Marie Callender's. I took it back to the dorm room Norman and I shared and started to dig in. When Norman returned, he asked if he could have some. Much to his surprise, I not only did not share, I just ate the entire cake right there in front of him! Norman could not believe what he was seeing. I don't know if it was gluttony, but if it wasn't, I was a spoonful away from sin.

In retrospect, it is certainly something I am not proud of. At this moment, it reminds me that I have a lifelong friend that is willing to do what he can to lift my spirits and support me in my time of need, despite my inconsiderate behavior in the past. He cares for me and has shown it in a way that only he could.

After eating a slice of cheesecake, I tried to complete all of my physical therapy exercises. I was motivated by Norman's thoughtful act of kindness.

Vanessa Foster-Dotson
July 30, 2015

*** Update for Wednesday, 07/29/15:

Wednesday was a good day! Although his blood counts are still low and Henry is still weak, he is pushing forward. In the morning, he did four laps around the nurses' station, and in the afternoon, he did three more! (Annie...smile!) He is also doing leg exercises in the bed on his own, and he has started doing a breathing exercise that will help to ensure that he does not get pneumonia. Henry is determined to do all that he can do to get well.

Although he ate better yesterday, he did not eat much solid food, so the dietitian is still encouraging him to eat more. And because he is tired, Henry's voice is still weak and labored.

But yes, Wednesday was a good day, and I am extremely thankful for

continued

the steady progress that Henry is making. We are also thankful for the cheesecake that arrived from a dear friend. Henry LOVES cheesecake. So, once the cheesecake arrived (and he was cleared to eat it), Henry would not do PT or anything else until he had a slice. There is a lot of cheesecake left, so I am sure that he will be enjoying it for a few days to come.

And I need to make a quick correction to my note yesterday. I said thank you to Margaret and "Jeff." I should have said "Jerry" instead of "Jeff." I sincerely apologize.

Prayer Requests:

I keep trying to keep these updates short, but at the same time, I must follow God's prompting. In addition to praying for Henry today and the prayer request items that I mentioned yesterday, please say special prayers for your other family members and friends that have been recently diagnosed or are suffering from cancer or some other life-threatening health challenge. Like when you buy a new car and all of a sudden you start becoming more aware of that same car on the freeway, it is amazing to me how many people in our circle have cancer or some life-threatening disease. Their fight is difficult. But God is all-knowing, and He is able to heal them all!

Thank you once again for your prayers for my beloved Henry!

Q: What were your intentions in sending the cheesecake to me in Chicago?

NORMAN: Appetite stimulation because I knew that you LOVED cheesecake. And, it was a chance to revisit a funny moment in our past. It provided ammo for me to egg you on to eat. Really, the primary thought was, what does Henry love to eat? Cheesecake was something I saw you consume with gusto and some greed ;)

RUTH: As a bystander, I thought Norman's sending you cheesecake in Chicago was Norman's way of honoring your 40+ years of friendship and bringing you a smile as well as needed calories in a joyful way.

 So wonderful to hear Henry is doing a little better and fighting hard. Enjoy that cheesecake, Henry!! I am continuing to pray for you guys every day.

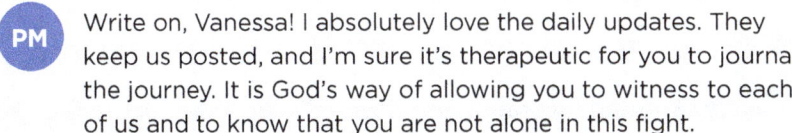

Write on, Vanessa! I absolutely love the daily updates. They keep us posted, and I'm sure it's therapeutic for you to journal the journey. It is God's way of allowing you to witness to each of us and to know that you are not alone in this fight.

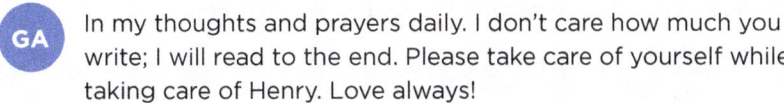

In my thoughts and prayers daily. I don't care how much you write; I will read to the end. Please take care of yourself while taking care of Henry. Love always!

July 30, 2015

God continues to move in this place! We received news today that my kidneys are back to normal!

In the first five days, the doctors were trying to save me from death due to kidney failure. That miracle happened today by God's grace. Even so, the doctors did not know if there had been any permanent kidney damage. Only time would tell.

Today we saw what was done in heaven made manifest here on earth!

My appetite is slowly coming back, and I stress the word "slowly." I am still setting goals for myself to keep me on track with my physical therapy. It is a little tricky due to my back pain, so I still try not to overdo it.

 Vanessa Foster-Dotson
July 31, 2015

*** Updated for Thursday, 07/30/15:

Another day of progress! Yes! I had to fill out some papers for Henry, so I arrived at his room about one hour later than normal. Henry's oncologist was in the room for his daily visit. His kidney doctor arrived a bit later. Both said that Henry's kidneys are back to functioning normally. No renal failure! No permanent dialysis! Yes! Yes! and Yes!

He was able to do five laps around the nurses' station in the morning and 5 in the afternoon. (Annie...I told him that you are keeping up with him, and he smiled. He enjoys challenges.) Henry even ate a hardy breakfast. I was also excited that his voice was much clearer and that he was back to making witty remarks. Everyone noticed that his eyes were clearer as well. He is not talking as much as normal, but that will come. One day at a time!

Now Henry is still working on lunch and dinner, as it seems as the day progresses, his appetite diminishes. But Henry usually will at least

continued

drink an Ensure or an Ensure-like shake for those meals.

The biggest thing now is that Henry's blood counts are still very low. Although expected as a result of the type of chemo he received, the counts have to start coming back up to strengthen his immune system. He is pretty isolated now and has a special diet...no raw anything...except bananas and oranges.

Henry is also still experiencing pain in his back whenever he gets out of perfect alignment...especially when sitting up or down.

Multiple Myeloma is statistically most common in African American men around the age of 65. Of course, there are other factors as well. Henry is not 65, and we had no idea that he had any issues other than back pain "as a result of helping someone move." However, when we arrived at CTCA, 90% of Henry's blood was affected by Myeloma. (Thank God for the move!) Please make sure to get your check-ups, both men and women. And ask for extra checks, blood analysis, x-rays, etc., at times.

And please keep those prayers a-comin'! God Bless!

Prayer Requests:

1. Complete healing for Henry's body, mind, soul, and spirit. (no cancer, no pain, no long-term anemia, improved blood counts, no permanent back damage, etc.)
2. Improved appetite
3. Improved strength and movement
4. Continued clarity of thoughts and words
5. General prayer for all of the family members and friends of anyone that is reading this update and has been recently diagnosed, or is suffering from cancer or some other life-threatening health challenge.

Prayers Answered:

1. Healthy kidneys
2. Healthy eyes

 Tell my nephew that we are locked hip to hip and shoulder to shoulder fighting the good fight. I pray continually for his complete healing and our victory testimony. I also pray for you as you minister to his spirit and his mind. Be Blessed.

Amen, we give God the praise for all the progress and updates you are giving us, Vanessa. God's still in control and at work with you guys; your journey awaits you in your calling, teachings, and leading and praying for others. I hope you were branching out to carry with you a great testimony, to testify ahead of those that will be under similar attacks. Restoration, for now, is a process. God is at work, working us and working in us. Amen

 Uncle Alfred Dotson, these prayers are for you as well since you are fighting your way to victory over Multiple Myeloma. We already know that the battle is won for both you and Henry! There is no way that Satan can win with all of these prayers going up! God's got this!

Visits From Home

"I am treating you as my friend by asking you to share my present minuses in the hope that I can ask you to share my future pluses."
— Katherine Mansfield

July 31, 2015

It is no secret how encouraging it is to be visited by family and friends when one is in the hospital. It does not matter where you are or how ill you are. Any time taken to visit the sick is much appreciated. It is an even greater blessing when those who care about you travel a great distance to be at your bedside.

I was blessed with five such visitors. Margaret came to visit a couple of times during her routine cancer treatment appointments. Our son, Bart, our daughter Talia, and our assistant pastor and his wife came to see me while in Zion!

Vanessa told me our children were coming because they wanted to be there with me. That was only part of the truth. Much later (after we had returned home), Vanessa told me much later that the doctors had advised her to call the children and tell them to come to see me because it may be their last time to see me alive. Our assistant pastor and his wife were already in Chicago to attend his father-in-law's funeral.

In addition to the visits, I began receiving scores of messages from all over the world with expressions of love, prayer, blessings, and encouragement. I was moved by the number of people investing their time to let me know they cared. I am sure that this was part of my healing.

Here are the thoughts and feelings my visitors expressed in their own words.

Q: When did you understand how serious my condition was?

MARGARET: I realized it when you arrived at the hospital and could not go to dinner with us because you had to have blood transfusions and kidney treatments. I knew you were in trouble, but it was not until then that I realized you, like me, had arrived just in the nick of time, and that it would take a team that would pull out all the stops to get you well. That Thursday night, I realized you might not make it, and I stayed in prayer most of the night. The next morning, I felt you had a chance, but I didn't really have any real reason to think so – I just felt that God was not finished with you yet.

Q: Did you ever seriously question my survival?

MARGARET: When we came to visit you in the Stem Cell "lock-up," I was very concerned that you might not make it, and I knew we had to redouble our prayers and keep praying until you were out of danger. You really looked like you were in trouble, and we were very concerned. I sent out emails and text messages to all my prayer chains and asked them to add you to them, and I continued my prayers as well. I didn't feel helpless, but I knew that only the Lord could save you. I don't think you knew this, but I have over 30 prayer chains praying for me, and I asked them to include you. You had people praying for you around the world – even in Africa.

Q: What did you think when you first saw me after my diagnosis?

MARGARET: I thought you were sick, but I also knew that you were in the best place you could possibly be – I knew the team of doctors would do everything in their power. And that, coupled with our prayer, gave me encouragement that you would survive and get healthy again.

Q: What did you feel when you first saw me after my diagnosis?

MARGARET: I felt scared for you, but I also felt that you would make it if you could handle the treatment. I also knew that Vanessa was not going to just let you go – she was going to pull you through. She would make sure you were doing everything the doctors said and make sure everything that could possibly be done was done. She was "on a mission" to save you, and I don't think she would have allowed you to die!

Q: Was it difficult for you to see me in my physical condition?

MARGARET: Yes, it was difficult, but only because I had just been through some of what you were going through, and I knew how bad it was. However, I also knew that you would not "feel" most of it – those doctors are good at masking the pain and side effects.

Q: What were you thinking and feeling when Vanessa said you needed to come to see me in Chicago?

BART: If I remember correctly, I communicated that I wanted to come to Chicago before Vanessa asked me. I knew that I needed to be there for you.

TALIA: When Vanessa said I needed to come to Chicago to see you, I knew that I needed to be there, and nothing would stop me.

Q: What did you think when you first saw me after my diagnosis?

BART: I didn't know what to expect when I walked down the hall to see you. You looked both better than I expected and worse than I expected. Your body was frail, but your spirit seemed strong. You did not appear close to death as it had seemed on the phone.

TALIA: When I first saw you, I thought that you looked ill. You had lost a lot of weight, but mostly I was thinking that I did not want you to be in pain.

Q: How did you feel when you first saw me after my diagnosis?

BART: I remember feeling overwhelmed. I felt great sadness at your condition, hope that you could recover, pain with seeing you suffering, and comfort seeing Vanessa there to care for you.

TALIA: It was emotional. I felt concerned, helpless, worried, and remorseful. At the same time, I did not feel hopeless, and I was not fearful.

Q: Was it difficult for you to see me in my physical condition?

BART: It was quite difficult to see you in such poor condition. I remember attempting to make a few jokes to lighten the mood and make myself feel more comfortable, but they didn't go over well.

TALIA: It was difficult because things that were so simple before were huge challenges. Even talking, your favorite pastime, was exhausting and sometimes impossible for you. It was also difficult to see because I knew that you were doing the best you could, and it was scary to think that what I was seeing was your best.

Q: Did you ever seriously question my survival?

BART: While your situation was dire, I wasn't aware of how close you were to death until quite a time after you recovered. Because of this, I didn't seriously question your survival.

TALIA: Never. Like I mentioned before, I was numb at first, yet as the realization of what you were going through sunk in, there was no underlying feeling of despair. Through everything, I had an overwhelming sense that everything would be alright. Not to minimize the seriousness of your illness, but I always felt that God would not allow that to happen at this time. It looks like I was right!

Q: What were your thoughts and feelings as you saw me go through the critical days of my treatment?

BART: I remember one specific instance during the time of your critical care. It was midday, and your physical therapist came into the room—his goal for you: complete at least one lap around the hospital wing. I walked with you as you slowly, painfully did that lap around the wing. As you rounded the final corner, my eyes were filled with tears. To see my father, who was once so strong and healthy, struggling to walk even an eighth of a mile, was difficult. At the same time, seeing my father, who was once so strong, still pushing forward and not giving up, was incredibly moving.

TALIA: Seeing you go through the critical days of your treatment was difficult. My preoccupation was that you were going through all of this with still no treatment to your back. I did not want you to be in pain and did not like to see you in any discomfort. I was very proud of the efforts you made and the immense patience you demonstrated, keeping a practical attitude and moving forwards. Probably the most difficult part was witnessing you go through "chemo brain." It was devastating to see you without full control of your thoughts. I would fight tears any time you would forget what you were just speaking about or lose your train of thought.

Jeff and Charale

Pastor Jeff and his wife Charale clicked with Vanessa right away. All three of them are from back East, and Jeff is also from Pennsylvania. Vanessa and I worked very closely with Jeff on several mission trips to South Africa and Ghana. Over the years, we have continued to nurture our relationship.

Q: How did you hear about my diagnosis?
JEFF AND CHARALE: Our recollection of being informed of your diagnosis was we heard it directly from you and Vanessa.

Q: Had you heard of multiple myeloma before hearing of my diagnosis?
JEFF AND CHARALE: We had never heard of Multiple Myeloma before.

Q: How did you feel when you learned of my diagnosis?
JEFF AND CHARALE: We remember processing through a number of feelings ranging from sympathy, compassion, and a sense of anger at the devil for his attempt to take you out with such a diabolical scheme. Our

immediate charge was to respond in continuing prayer and intercession on your behalf. We also wanted you to know that your extended family was going to be there to support you by going to the throne of grace to be in agreement with you in appropriating the healing that belongs to you by virtue of the sin debt already being paid on your behalf.

Q: When did you understand how serious my condition was?
JEFF AND CHARALE: The seriousness of your condition was not immediately known to us, but as we continued to receive updates, we realized that it was a life and death battle. We received updates from Vanessa primarily after our initial conversation, one or two telephonically and then through the Facebook support page that she created.

Around the same time that you were led to seek help at the Cancer Treatment Centers of America in the greater Chicago area, Charale received news that her dad had passed. As we made preparations to travel back to Chicago for his Homegoing, we resolved to visit you while we were back there.

We found out that it was some distance (approx. 2 hours) outside of Chicago itself, but we said we couldn't come all this way with you being this close and not check in on our brother. What's a couple of hours anyway when we spend nearly that amount of time in L.A. traffic to go somewhere that is not nearly as far distance-wise?

We phoned Vanessa a couple of days prior to visiting you to let her know that we were out there for the funeral and wanted to come by to pray with you guys and encourage you. Vanessa shared that she would need to get back with us to confirm a time/day that would work based upon the treatment plan for the week.

She also shared that your immune system had been compromised. We got a sense that she was struggling with being protective of your physical condition and trying to accommodate our being out there and the benefit of the visit and support. In any event, we worked out a time that she felt comfortable with that would properly balance the tensions and priorities.

Q: What did you think when you first saw me at the Cancer Treatment Centers of America, Chicago?
JEFF AND CHARALE: We arrived at the facility and were blessed by the peaceful serenity of the environment. We remember being particularly blessed when we found out that it was in "ZION," Illinois. As we walked

into the room, we were greeted by our dear sister's warm smile and strong embrace. We were so blessed that we were able to make it out there to see you.

When we first saw you, it was apparent that you had been "going through it." You appeared very weak, lost a lot of weight, maybe even looking a bit jaundiced, but your spirits were still very high. That is what we have come to know, expect and love about you, that you are a man of great strength, strength of conviction, strong in faith.

The real deal.

Q: Did you ever seriously question my survival?

JEFF AND CHARALE: Based on the details of what was shared, how you looked, the aggressive nature of the disease, although never spoken, we both had thoughts that came into our minds of possibly losing our brother. We never gave voice to them, though in a desire to guard our faith, our prayers, and the environment needed for healing to manifest.

Q: What were your thoughts and feelings as you returned home from Chicago?

JEFF AND CHARALE: We were so relieved that we took the time to come out your way. It was a sacrifice to leave Charale's family during their time of bereavement, but one that we would gladly make again as you are our family as well. We were called to go back to Chicago to minister to family during a time of need, and after our visit, we felt that we had been truly obedient to what we were called to do. We felt a sense of joy from both of you in having a familiar face from home so far away that was right there with you. We experienced unspeakable joy in being able to share that time with you guys.

Q: What did you share with the ZCF staff about my situation after visiting me?

JEFF AND CHARALE: Upon returning to California, we only shared our visit with a few folks, Bishop, Dorri, Minister Carter, and some of our South Africa team members. We told them of the strength and resolve we saw in you and of the tremendous love, dedication, and sacrifice we saw from Vanessa. We shared that there was a long journey ahead, but if anyone seemed to be poised for the battle, it was you guys. We thought it vital to spread words of faith and hope to continue to guard the environment of faith.

Vanessa Foster-Dotson
August 1, 2015

*** Updated for Friday, 07/31/15:

Friday was AWESOME! We figured out how to get Henry to eat. Bart, and Talia need to be by his side. Yes, both of them are in town, and Henry is extremely happy. He ate three full meals! He also completed his first balancing exercises and his first laps around the nurses' station with a cane instead of a walker. Because his blood counts are still VERY low, Henry was pretty tired after all of the exercises...but he pushed himself both in the morning and in the afternoon and got it done!

After speaking to a nurse, Henry was excited to learn the reason that his back was still hurting. He was told that the back pain would persist as long as his spine is healing. And his spine is healing because the Myeloma caused small fractures. Now that it makes sense to him, I believe that Henry feels that he will be able to deal with the pain better (Although he was already dealing with it pretty well, in my opinion.).

Now back to Bart and Talia. Having them here is great. They each provide Henry with different strengths and motivations. It is also good for them to see first-hand how their dad is doing, the fight that is in their DNA, and to be able to help him recover, each in their own way. Bart initiated a family prayer and comforted his dad in several ways. Talia provided additional nurturing and food advice.

But most of all, they demonstrated their deep love for their father, and he felt it. The best medicine in the world – the love of your family! No matter what the circumstance, never take your family for granted. God Bless, and thank you once again for your prayers and support! (BTW, Henry is thoroughly enjoying your cards, notes, gifts, and prayers. Thank you for those as well!)

 Perfectly wonderful news. We Dotson's have struggle and survival in our lineage, but at the core of it all is our unwavering faith in God! We thank everyone who has joined in undergirding us with your prayers and words of encouragement. As a family, we are facing many medical challenges at this time, but our confidence is in our Heavenly Father! He's handling His business!!!!

Praise God for Family! I thank them, especially Vanessa, Bart, and Talia and pray for your strength in Him.

Vanessa, thank you for this update. And, thank you so much for posting the photo, which is a 1000-word praise report in and of itself! We can see just what God is doing. Your smiles did my heart good and reminded me (and my knees) that the flights of stairs (7+ on Thursday, 10+ on Friday), that I am in agreement with all of you. I have been exclusively taking the stairs up, though not always down since I took on the challenge of keeping up with Henry's laps. But I don't know. Henry might have to send me the walker he's no longer using! Just kidding.

I'm learning from you both that strength is gained from the push. For a long time, I have been exercising my faith. It's amazing that from Chicago, you and Henry are getting me to do something that you couldn't get me to do in Pasadena; Exercise my body! God is indeed good!!

Today, I am praying specifically for Henry's blood counts to improve.

God is our refuge and strength, an ever-present help in times of trouble. Glad to know you have your help around you as God continues to manifest the healing miracle. I continue in prayer.

> "When everything goes to hell, the people who stand by you without flinching – they are your family."
> — Jim Butcher

GoFundMe
August 1, 2015

I think yesterday's excitement got the better of me. I am drained, so I am going to listen to my body and take it easy. I am not hungry, but I know I need to give my body energy to fight the disease. So, I will do the best I can to take in some calories today. All I really want to do today is rest.

Vanessa Foster-Dotson
August 2, 2015

*** Updated for Saturday, 08/01/15:

One day at a time indeed! After several days of progress, Henry did not have his best day on Saturday. He was able to do a small amount of PT in the room. No laps. Henry's low blood counts are still causing him to be extremely tired and weak. Bart and Talia have suggested a couple of goals that are motivating Henry to eat. As a result, Henry did eat two full meals. Yes! However, he went to bed around 1:30 p.m., just too tired to push it any further for the day.

Soon after being in bed, Henry developed a fever. Cultures were taken to ensure that he did not have an infection. His nurse said that fevers are common when blood counts are as low as Henry's. They restated that his immune system is extremely weak and that they strongly suggest that he not have any visitors. As the day/night progressed, they were able to stabilize Henry's temperature. Praise God!

Yesterday brought me back to the reality that we are truly on a "one day at a time" marathon. I am basically okay with this reality as our future is completely in God's hands...a faith walk. However, I still keep trying to get some insights regarding what I will need to prepare for at home. I want to make sure that Henry has what he needs... especially as I return to work. The doctors and nurses are still saying that "every person responds differently."

As I further accept the reality of unknowing, I have also been encouraged by several people to set up a donation fund. Although I know that Multiple Myeloma is one of the most expensive cancers to fight, initially, I was not in favor of the donation fund idea at all! But this is not about me or my comfort...it is about Henry and his life! And for some reason, I believe that God placed people in our life at this time to encourage me to agree to have the fund set up.

So, if you are so inclined, I will be providing a link to Henry's donation fund via a separate post. Once at the link, the description provides more details.

Thank you once again! Both your continued prayers and financial support are greatly appreciated. God Bless!

Prayer Request: Please pray for Henry's blood and platelet counts to increase along with his pain to decrease.

Yes, we would like to have the link for the donation!

 Whatever I can do to help!

August 2, 2015

 I felt better today. I had a slight fever last night, but my healthcare team did an excellent job of getting it under control. I am glad I listened to my body and went to bed early yesterday.

 Vanessa and I spoke about creating a GoFundMe account. She wanted to know how I felt about it. To be honest, I did not like the idea when she brought it up. I did not want the Prayer Team to think that this was our plan all along, to set them up so they would give money for my care. It just felt like my integrity would be in question. Vanessa admitted it was also out of her comfort zone.

> Vanessa Foster-Dotson
> August 2, 2015
>
> Hello Family and Friends!
>
> As per the update for Saturday, 08/01, I have been encouraged to set up a GoFundMe account for Henry. Definitely out of my comfort zone, but it is not about me; it's about Henry's life. So, the link for the account is below. Once at the link, please review the description for more details.
>
> http://www.gofundme.com/.....
>
> Thank you in advance for your support!
>
>

 Henry Dotson. You are looking so strong!!! God is Great!!! Praying for God, please heal his body. Soul!!

 Count me in.

 I am not sure I ever got comfortable with the GoFundMe account. What helped to mitigate some of my discomfort was reminding myself that some people very much wanted to be a financial blessing to us, and it was not up to me to decide how I was to be blessed.

I did not think about not being able to earn a living. Since I was self-employed, I was not concerned about being fired. Living on one income also did not become a major concern to me. Most certainly, losing my income and facing unknown medical expenses was a real issue.

However, as I stated before, when you are diagnosed with cancer, everything else really doesn't matter. Therefore, all of my attention was focused on what needed to be done to deal with cancer. When I did think about the unknown cost of my health care, I also placed that in God's hands. I trusted that He would provide a way somehow.

Sometimes having your financial needs met by God is more about allowing someone else to be blessed to be a blessing than it is about the money you are receiving from the person. It is a little counterintuitive, but in God's economy, the books balance.

The Empire Strikes Back

"For we do not wrestle against flesh and blood, but against the rulers, against the authorities, against the cosmic powers over this present darkness, against the spiritual forces of evil in the heavenly places."
— Ephesians 6:12, English Standard Version

Cancer Treatment Centers of America, Zion, IL
August 2, 2015

I started feeling sluggish today. My energy was low, but I was determined to do what I could, even if it was not much. I was able to do some physical therapy, but I did not have the strength to do laps around the nurses' station. I am getting much better at knowing when it is best not to push.

When my body tells me it is time to rest, I pay attention. So, I climbed back into the bed shortly after lunch.

Vanessa Foster-Dotson
August 2, 2015

I am so blessed! The doctor just made a special visit on his day off to assure us that "Henry is on cruise control now"…just waiting for his counts to go up. His kidneys are still good, and his white blood count increased from 0.00 to 0.10 (should be from 4.0 to 10.50). Still have a ways to go but progress! On top of that, Henry said that he wanted to take a lap around the nurses' station, and once he went around once, he said, "1 more". Absolutely AWESOME!!!

 Keep up the good work Henry, one step at a time, one day at a time. You can DO IT. We are praying for you every morning.

 Yes, Lord!!! Go, Henry!!!

 Praise God!! He is awesome!

Now please know that the doctor is saying cruise control for this week for getting blood counts up. We are just waiting for the counts to go up. Henry will still have at least four more cycles of chemo over the next 16 weeks. Sorry for any confusion. We are still on the marathon.

August 2, 2015

I spent some time in prayer last night, and I asked the Lord if there was anything more He wanted me to do. When I woke up this morning, I had my answer. He said, "Be faithful."

I knew it was from God because it resonated in my spirit. Still, I had to figure out what it meant in terms of how I was to put it into practice. I meditated on it for a short while, and the scripture in James came to me that says, "Faith without works is dead."

Again, this word from God resonated in my spirit. It was telling me that as long as I have breath in my body, I need to be working for the Lord. It said to me if God were to decide my time on earth had come to an end, that the last words coming out of my mouth should be about His goodness and mercy. It exhorted me to be faithful until the end, whenever the end comes.

This message lifted my spirits. I felt as though I had a new wind beneath my wings. From that moment forward, I made it a point to reach out to whoever came into my hospital room and speak a word of encouragement to them. To tell them that God loves them and that He has a purpose for their lives. In doing so, I was constantly reminded that He still had a purpose for my life despite my circumstances, for as long as He decides I will be on this side of eternity.

So, whenever someone came into my room, I would engage them in conversation. I had learned from some training on how to look for business prospects that open-ended questions about work and family lead to more meaningful conversation.

I would start with the question, "How long have you worked here?" followed by, "What do you like about working here?" I would then ask, "Do you have to travel far to come here to work?" That would lead to, "Where do you live?" and "Do you have family living with you?"

Once people started talking about their families, something would inevitably come up in the conversation about some issue they were dealing with. That is when the spirit moved me to speak a good word of hope into their lives. I did not have anything prepared to say, but whatever I said seemed to be just what they needed to hear at that moment.

I knew that when I made myself available to God to be used to minister into the lives of people that He would put the right words into my mouth through the power of the Holy Spirit. People would respond by sharing even more details about what mattered to them because I was a non-judgmental listening ear, something most people do not have in their lives.

Our conversations were usually brief, but I made sure that they always ended in prayer. I would say to the person, "I would like to pray for you now. Would you let me pray for you?" No one ever said no. After I prayed for them, I would ask them, "Would you do me a favor?" Again, no one ever said no. I then asked, "Would you pray for me now?" Again, no one ever said no.

I called these brief interactions "divine appointments."

After each one, I knew that I was faithful to the best of my abilities. What a mighty God we serve!

Vanessa Foster-Dotson
August 3, 2015

*** Update for Sunday, 08/02/15:

Sunday was such a special day! Henry was still very weak and tired. As we began our 3rd full week in Illinois, we are still waiting for his counts to go up and for his immune system to strengthen. As previously mentioned, his white blood count did increase slightly, so that was great news. Henry ended up having to get a platelet transfusion last night to help with boosting his platelet count.

Also, as previously stated, the doctor stopped by and said that we are on "cruise control" now regarding waiting for Henry's counts to improve. Once the counts have improved sufficiently and his immune system is functioning properly, Henry will be released as an outpatient and will commute to CTCA from a local hotel here in Zion. When the doctors and nurses feel that Henry is functioning okay, Henry will be released to go home. The current thinking is that Henry will only be an outpatient in Zion for a few days. Once at home, he will continue to receive chemo treatments for at least 16 weeks. During that time, he will return to CTCA once a month for status checks. The journey after that depends on how Henry's body reacts to the treatments.

Yesterday, Henry proved numerous times again that he is such a special person. Although very weak, Henry pushed himself as much as possible. He pushed himself to get out of bed. He pushed himself to walk two laps. He pushed himself to meet his eating goals.

continued

He pushed himself to stay out of bed. He pushed himself to minister to a single young black father of four who works as a janitor at CTCA. He also pushed himself to minister to Bart, Talia, and me. Although his voice was very winded and labored, he had something to say, and he was determined to get it out. It was amazing! All that I can say is watch out when he returns. God will be using him in miraculous ways! Henry will definitely have a testimony. I am so proud of him! Thank you, God!

I also want to say thank you to my manager and employer for allowing me to stay by Henry's side. I believe that it has made a difference in Henry's recovery.

And I want to apologize to anyone that I owe a phone call, email, text, or thank-you to. I have not forgotten and will respond as soon as possible. Hopefully, you understand that I have to devote this time to Henry, and EVERY DAY has been full of activity and surprises.

God Bless!

MS — Amen, to God be the glory. Testimony is evidence of victory. Like I said before, you are carrying out testimony indeed ahead of you. Restoration in its process of his recovery continues, and it shall be fulfilled and reach its end in Jesus' name, stay blessed, and thanks for the update, Vanessa.

RH — Amen. Thank you for sharing, Vanessa. Henry has always walked in greatness; he's just doing it for himself now. He is lucky to have you by his side, even if you are the most anal person I love! Henry knows more than most that you are a person who will get things done and done right! I have always admired your strength and determination. Sending love and prayers to you and Henry!!

CC — You are blessed to be a blessing. The courage that you and Henry are exhibiting is an inspiration to all. Love and continued blessings!

PM — God has given Henry a healing victory, and you are a major part of that victory. Don't worry about us; just continue to be strong for your husband. You're doing a fantastic job, Nessa.

Vanessa, you are amazing, and I am proud of you. Henry has a special and loving wife at his side, along with family and blessed friends praying around the clock. Vanessa, it is a lot, and I understand how you feel. Just know everyone knows you are fulfilling your wedding vows. So they have your back, and everything else can wait. We need both of you strong as God continues to show himself strong. God will restore Henry's health. We love you, the Picott's!

August 3, 2015

Despite the work I was doing that was motivated by my faith, my body was still under attack. But this did not bother me. As long as I knew my will was aligned with God's Will, I was taking care of what I needed to, and He was taking care of the rest.

I had contracted a Staph infection. The doctor said it was a common occurrence in hospitals and that it must be dealt with right away. It could become deadly if not treated. I was not worried because I was in the best place to combat the infection. I believe I was diagnosed as soon as possible, so I had the best chance of obtaining the best possible outcome. I remained focused on what I could do and left the rest to others who did what I could not. Mainly, I left it to God to do what only He can do.

Vanessa Foster-Dotson
August 4, 2015

*** Update for Monday, 08/03/15: Another day at CTCA. Henry is so ready to leave the hospital! His kidneys are still doing great, and his blood counts have started going up a bit more. He continues to do laps around the nurses' station and even added steps to his routine as he prepares for the eight steps at our house that he would have to ascend to reach our bedroom. (We may have to put a bed downstairs...we'll see.) Henry did not eat much, and he went to bed pretty early. When asked how he is feeling, he simply repeats, "I'm tired."

I neglected to mention in yesterday's update for Sunday that we had a family prayer and laid hands on Henry after he ministered to us. It is a wonderful thing to see your children's ability to minister to their parents. As our Pastor Ed Smith would say, "It was powerful!"

continued

I was told that once Henry's counts start going up, it is not uncommon for the counts to start increasing very quickly. So, during your prayers today, please pray that Henry's counts rise exponentially! Please also extend your hands and pray for Henry's complete healing and that his body is properly prepared to leave the hospital and enter outpatient status in Illinois within the next day.

God Bless, and thank you once again!

(Oh, BTW, I met with Henry's care managers yesterday to go over one of the meds that Henry will have to take once he is home. I vaguely remember reading that that particular med is $500 per PILL. I asked the care managers for confirmation. They said that indeed the med is $8,000 for a 21-day cycle. Amazing! The care managers are working on getting the price down for us, but still. Why make medicine that very few can afford? Absolutely ridiculous! The faith walk continues!)

CW — Vanessa, I know Henry thanks the Lord for you and your children! I have not seen a better example of a wife praying for her husband. It is an honor to join you and your family and church family in prayer for our brother.

Sondria and I will continue to pray for Henry's complete healing and speedy recovery and for you and your children to be strengthened. God bless you!

RH — We are praying for you both, and agreeing and declaring total healing and restoration. Due to unforeseen circumstances, we have not been able to make the 2.5-hour journey across Illinois, but our prayers are not bound by distance. We stretch our hands in faith, knowing that our God is a healer and healing is yours! We are Standing with you! Blessings!

CS — The cost of medication is shameful.

RZ — Praise God! Stay faithful and focused. All of this sounds so familiar to me. I completely understand how "little" things such as taking a walk become so priceless.

VP — Yea. It's the treatment!! Hang in there. Henry Dotson. And Vanessa. You take care of yourself as well.

August 4, 2015

I seemed to be a little stronger than yesterday. I realized if I paced myself and did not overextend myself, I could make good steady progress. I created a personal challenge in my mind to work hard with my physical therapist. I wanted to increase the number of laps I did around the nurses' station each time I went for a walk.

Negotiating the stairs was added to my physical therapy routine. That reminded me that I needed to prepare myself for my eventual departure from CTCA. Until this point in time, I was only thinking about the very next day and nothing beyond that. Just one day at a time was all I could concentrate on. I began to give quiet thanks to God for bringing me this far.

 Vanessa Foster-Dotson
August 5, 2015

*** Update for Tuesday, 08/04/15:

Still waiting! Although Henry's blood counts did improve slightly, we are still waiting for them to increase to a level that allows him to be released. He continues to look forward to PT. He was able to walk two laps in the morning and afternoon along with eight steps both times as well. His general attitude is very positive and thankful. He just wants to leave the hospital...which the doctor is saying is a good sign regarding his level of recovery.

Thanks once again for your prayers. We believe that Henry's counts will be much better on Wednesday.

God Bless!

JR We are in agreement with our Lord and our Henry.

BC Praise God for Henry's perseverance and strength! Tell brother Henry that the finish line is within sight... Continuing to pray for your entire family through these challenges.

CL Vanessa, greet Henry for us. Let him know that we love him and you and the family. Greet Talia and Bart for us. Tell them that the Langleys are lifting their Dad up in prayer every day. Be encouraged. Is anything too hard for the Lord? Gen. 18:14 I read these scriptures and thought of Henry; Matt. 19:26, Luke 18:27, Ps 34:1, Acts 12:5.

LD Praying, praying, all the time, and believing God's word for Henry's healing. Keep up the excellent work!!

VH A positive attitude is more than half the battle! Praise God for improvement.

August 5, 2015

Today Bart and Talia had flights to return to Phoenix and Los Angeles, respectively. It was wonderful having them here, but it was time for them to return to their daily routine. Before they left, we gathered together as a family and prayed for one another.

In my prayer, I gave a father's blessing over his children. I wanted to confer my blessing over their lives for the rest of their lives in case I would not have the opportunity to do so in the future. I think it is critical for children to receive their father's blessing to help carry them through in times of trouble.

As Bart, Talia, and Vanessa prayed, I felt the presence of the Holy Spirit in our circle. It soothed my soul and gave me such peace! I felt God's love as He ministered it to me through my family. I was more than encouraged; I felt restored.

After the children left, I began to wonder what thoughts they carried with them on the way home and how this experience had affected them. Later on, they shared their thoughts with me.

Q: Did your perception of me change as a result of your visit with me in Chicago?

BART: While in Chicago, I had never seen you so physically weak and yet so spiritually engaged and hopeful. My perception changed as I saw your great faith and reliance upon God through difficulty. I've always seen you as a strong man – physically and mentally.

This experience showed me that you are a strong man spiritually, as well.

TALIA: I guess after I left Chicago, I realized more and more how diligent you are. I was really proud of you, and I think I gained more respect for the experiences you've had leading up to this point in your life and how you've handled them.

Q: What were your thoughts and feelings as you returned home from Chicago?

BART: Honestly, it was hard to process through everything that I experienced while in transit back to Phoenix. I spent more time in prayer and quiet, a non-focused reflection more than anything else.

TALIA: When I returned from Chicago, I felt more determined to get my own life in order. To follow the example that you were setting and do the best I can do in all things, mainly because there was nothing I could do to help your condition, but I could make sure that I was optimal so I could be there if you needed me.

Q: How did your experience in Chicago affect your relationship with Charity?

BART: The visit to Chicago affected my relationship with Charity in many ways. Initially, it served as a bonding experience since Charity had experienced the near-fatal physical illness and subsequent prolonged hospitalization of her sister.

Charity helped me to identify a flight out to Chicago. After I returned, we had many conversations about health, relationships, and God. I know that Charity felt that my opening up to her really showed how much I trusted and cared about her.

Charity

Charity is Bart's wife. At the time, they were just friends, not even dating. It was later during the journey that they were married. She has been a blessing to Bart throughout this journey and a wonderful daughter-in-law. I also asked her to provide answers to some specific questions.

Q: Had you heard of multiple myeloma before hearing of my diagnosis?
CHARITY: No, I had not.

Q: How did you feel when you learned of my diagnosis?
CHARITY: I'll never forget- it was July 2015, and Bart and I had only been friends for barely a couple of months. But I could tell something was off with him when he came to our small church group. I didn't feel it was my place as a more casual friend to press him about what was wrong, but I wanted him to know that I was there for him.

I texted him, later on to let him know I was here to help however he needed it. He called me and confided in me that you were just diagnosed with cancer. I was shocked and devastated. This was heartbreaking to hear, but I was honored that he would share such personal news with me. As I sat and listened and offered emotional support to him over the phone, little did I know God would use this awful news to deepen our friendship. What the enemy intends for bad, God uses for good!

Q: When did you understand how serious my condition was?

CHARITY: I think it was when he got back from visiting you in Chicago and told me about his experience with you in the hospital.

Q: Did you ever seriously question my survival?

CHARITY: Because I didn't know you when you were going through the thick of it, I didn't necessarily question your survival but was always relieved to hear updates from Bart on your progress.

Vanessa Foster-Dotson
August 6, 2015

*** Update for Wednesday, 08/05/15:

And we are still waiting! Henry's blood counts are improving but are not where they need to be. One of the main counts, the Absolute Neutrophil Count (ANC), is now at 1.17. This count was at 0.0 most of last week and did not get up to 0.17 until this Tuesday. So, a jump to 1.17 in one day is great. Our prayers are being answered! The doctor wants Henry's ANC to be at 3.00. So, we still have a bit to go.

He continues to do PT in the morning and afternoon. He has added additional balancing and bed entry/exit activities to the two laps and eight steps that he is doing per session. Henry is consistently eating a good breakfast. However, lunch and dinner are hit and miss. His pain level is pretty consistent as well, around a level 2 or 3, where ten would be considered extremely painful.

He mainly has pain when his back gets out of alignment. (In the days to come, it may take a while for his back pain to subside because of the compression fractures that he has in his spine.) Henry was very alert most of the day and stayed out of bed relatively late. Great improvement! More improvement should come as his counts continue to go up.

There was a slight setback yesterday as he contracted another mild infection. Because Henry's immune system is extremely low, infections are common. This is the main reason that we have to limit who/what he comes in contact with for a while. But one great thing about being at CTCA is that infections are detected, addressed, and

continued

remedied VERY quickly. I am believing that the infection will be gone on Thursday.

Sad to say, Bart and Talia have returned to their homes. I am so thankful that they were able to come. Their visit made a huge difference! Although Henry was already positive, I believe that he now has more drive and determination. He has recently stated, "This is in God's hands. So, all that I can do is my part." I believe that Talia and Bart's visits confirmed that Henry's part is huge. I believe that Henry not only wants to do what he needs to do to address his cancer, but he also has so much more to contribute to Bart and Talia's lives as well as the lives of all of you and others. I walked in, and he was ministering to a young nursing assistant. All that I can say is that I can already see that God is going to be using Henry in a great way. Are you ready?

Lastly, thank you to all of you that have given or plan to give to Henry's GoFundMe account. I have faith that God and the care managers will lower the cost of Henry's prescriptions as much as possible. However, there still will be some prescription costs as well as other costs. One example is our hotel costs while at CTCA. We had only planned on being here for six days at most. We are now on day 23. Some may ask why didn't we stay in CA. As he heard from God, this was definitely the right place for Henry. So, back to our faith walk!

Thank you for your continued prayers!

Prayer Requests:

1. Complete healing for Henry...body, mind, soul, and spirit. (no cancer, no pain, no long-term anemia, no permanent back damage, no infections.)
2. Exponential blood count level increase
3. Immediate release from the hospital
4. Improved appetite
5. Improved strength and movement
6. General prayer for all of the family members and friends of anyone that is reading this update and has been recently diagnosed or is suffering from cancer or some other life-threatening health challenge.

continued

> Prayers Answered:
> 1. Healthy kidneys
> 2. Healthy eyes
> 3. Increased platelet count
> 4. Clarity of thoughts and words

JD — Continued prayers and God's Blessings.

RH — We stand with you, Henry and Vanessa. Our God is awesome! We thank God right now for providing all that is needed physically and financially.

RH — Thank you for the update, Vanessa. Glad to hear of the improvement. Mike and I will continue to pray for Henry and you. Love you.

VP — Henry Dotson, keep your faith. God will see you through this storm!!!!

VH — Prayers are being answered. Henry is improving daily! God is watching over you both, Vanessa. Keep the faith!

GT — Amen, thank you for answering the prayers of your children.

Toward the end of the day, I was beginning to feel a little weaker. Something was going on in my body that I could not put my finger on. After my lab results came back, I was told I had contracted another infection – called C-Diff. Another infection commonly seen in people with long hospital stays must be addressed immediately or lead to death.

I once again focused on what I could do and left the rest to God and the medical staff. I did not put any energy into worrying or being fearful. That was energy better used to speak with others about God's goodness.

Although Pat and Kathy, and Cecily did not come to visit, they saw the photos of Bart and Talia's visit on the Facebook page. That was the first time they had seen me since the diagnosis. Here is what they shared about that moment.

ZION

Q: What did you think when you first saw me after my diagnosis?

PAT: Every day I began searching for news about you. And then, without warning, the picture came. I saw this scrawny little shell of a man.

KATHY: I thought I was looking at another person. It was only a picture, but the toll the disease had taken was evident.

CECILY: You look very ill. You had lost a lot of weight. You looked aged and like death warmed over.

Q: How did you feel when you first saw me after my diagnosis?

PAT: With you and Vanessa being gone to Chicago, it seems that my life became one big knot! When I saw the picture, I was hit again by another brick! I was broken.

KATHY: I was completely taken aback. The first thought that came to mind was one of the "lost boys" from Africa. You were so drawn and thin. Your skin looked ashen. I just kept staring in disbelief.

CECILY: I was sad and heartbroken. I was very emotional.

Q: Was it difficult for you to see me in my physical condition?

PAT: As children, everyone always thought we were twins. Especially when we told them for 17 days, we were the same age (That's because the three of us, Ira, Bernard, and myself are all born in October, and all are less than a year apart. So, with Bernard and I, there are 17 days each year that we are the same age). There is a picture floating around somewhere with both of us with bald heads, and the resemblance is striking!

So, to see you so small and dark, and to not see the light that was always in your eyes, was hard.

My faith again was on the rocks!

KATHY: Yes. You just looked so weak and unlike the robust man I had just visited the year before. I was astonished at seeing the human body in the throes of the disease. I had never had that experience.

CECILY: You had always been robust, muscular, and energetic. I saw you on Facebook, and at first, thought you were not going to make it through the treatments you were getting in Illinois.

Q: Did you ever seriously question my survival?

PAT: Is he going to make it? Will he pull through?!" I said it over and over in my mind. The words I would never accept or say were, "He's NOT going to make it."

KATHY: Yes. Again, everything that I'd read talked about short-term survival, if at all. It was not a very optimistic picture, and after knowing how close to the edge you were was a very shaky feeling.

CECILY: There were a number of times in Illinois I thought I would never see you again. When Vanessa would call and discuss your case, there were times when it was grim. But one thing she would always say is, "Henry has the strongest faith, and he believes he will be saved/healed."

August 6, 2015

We spoke with the doctor and the nutritionist today. The doctor said my ANC was back in the healthy range. The nutritionist told me I am still not getting enough calories. I was simultaneously grateful for the good news and trying to come up with a way to get a better report from the nutritionist the next time.

> **ANC**
> Absolute Neutrophil (NEW-truh-fil) Count. The most important infection-fighting white blood cell (WBC) is the neutrophil. The number doctors look at is called your **absolute neutrophil count** (ANC). A healthy person has an ANC between 2,500 and 6,000. The ANC is found by multiplying the WBC count by the percent of neutrophils in the blood. Sometimes the ANC is divided by 1,000 and reported in parts per 1000, which makes the healthy range between 2.5 and 6.0.

I am trying, but I don't have much of an appetite. What little I do eat makes me feel full. I shared this with the nutritionist, and she suggested I try eating frequent smaller meals. Knowing that I will not be discharged until I am regularly eating food has motivated me to set new goals. I achieve more when I set goals, so I told Vanessa I am going to set some daily eating goals. I also asked her to hold me accountable for reaching my goals. She said she would. I am blessed to have her as my caregiver. I believe I will be equally blessed by her being an empathetic accountability partner.

Vanessa Foster-Dotson
August 7, 2015

*** Update for Thursday, 08/06/15:

Well, first with the good news. Henry's ANC has gone up to 4.13. It has exceeded the level that the doctor wanted. Yes! However, Henry is not being released into outpatient status because the doctor feels that he is too weak. Although Henry is trying to eat, he is feeling full too fast. So, he is now willing to try frequent smaller meals...7 a.m, 10, 12, 3, 6, and 9. Getting stronger is something that he can apply effort towards, so that is Henry's new goal.

Thank you once again for your continued prayers! They are truly making a difference.

SM Amen and Hallelujah, too, for the progress Henry is making. God is not through with him yet. Someone else may need to see the miracle that God is doing through Henry for them to turn their lives around. WE will continue to give God all the glory for what He is doing in the body of Christ.

AR Praise God for the improved blood counts! Today, I am praying specifically for renewed and increased strength for both of you. God is answering our prayers and renewing and increasing my faith through your testimony. Love you both.

VP Mommy said she's going to give you a call today:-)! So, tell Henry he has someone else in his corner :-)!

PM Thank God for each health challenge that Henry is conquering. Prayerfully his appetite will eventually return. The 2-hour feedings and small portions are a good idea to induce the desire for food. Since he is goal-oriented, he knows he has to eat to regain his strength. Stay strong, Nessa, because his strength comes from you too!!!!

VP Yea. When they see a lot of food before them, they tend to get full faster. Smaller portions are better. It works for my mom.

BC Hang in there, Henry. God is testing your patience. Have a blessed day, my friend!

August 7, 2015

"Eat, eat, eat" has become my mantra. I am determined to get in shape as soon as possible. My higher goal is to become an outpatient. Becoming an outpatient is one step closer to going home.

I just remembered it's my mother's birthday. She would have been 84 today. I am glad she did not live to see me this way. She would have been very anxious and worried. At the same time, I am very thankful that she and my father provided us with a Christian home that helped lead me to Christ. I can't imagine what shape I would be in if I did not put my faith in God.

I honestly don't know how people get through life-threatening circumstances without Him.

Vanessa Foster-Dotson
August 8, 2015

*** Update for Friday, 08/07/15:

Henry is doing well. The smaller meals worked better. And he was able to do two laps with only a cane twice yesterday...4 laps total! This was great progress.

Henry's kidney numbers were slightly elevated, and other counts were slightly out of balance as well. Therefore, the doctor decided to start Henry's next cycle of chemo last night instead of waiting until next week, when it was originally scheduled for. The doctor wants to make sure that the Myeloma is kept under control. It seems like as one count gets a favorable reading, another count shifts negatively. I am not claiming this, but I do ask for prayer that Henry's counts stabilize and are all positive.

Henry's focus is now on doing what he can do to get stronger and get out of the hospital. As he says, "eat, eat, eat, eat, eat, eat, eat!" I have started placing more focus on preparing for our return. We are still not sure when we will return to CA, but I have to believe that it will be sooner versus later. I am finding that there is a lot to consider regarding our return.

However, I may have to ask for more help than I am comfortable with. I have to remember that this is all in God's hands and that I have to listen for His guidance from the various voices that He places in my path.

Thank you, God, and thank you all!

VW — Vanessa and Henry, I continue to pray and believe for Henry's total healing to manifest! To God be the glory!!!!! Please know that I am here for you both, and whatever I can do to help, I will.

RH — I am continuing to PRAY. I will be back in Carson in a few days, but willing to help in whatever way I can. (Errands, prayer support...)

VH — One day at a time. God WILL work it out! A cancer diagnosis changes your life forever, but hopefully, you will both emerge from it stronger. Remember that God will not put any more on you than you can bear.

DM — Surely the Lord will make a way. Be encouraged, stand still and hear and feel the Lord's Guidance. So often, he will show us things that we are not in line to receive, for whatever reason. I have learned and am still learning how to totally lean and depend on God's unchanging hands. When I'm off balance out of my lane, God's got me covered.

All this to say, direct caregivers take on many roles and responsibilities. Pray for discernment as you will need it.

Love you both; however, God loves you more.

I pray for strength for you both as you continue to go through.

DK — Sis, please set up the fund. All we want is the will of God for Henry and his family. In Jesus' name, amen.

CS — It takes courage to ask for help. Good for you!

LD — Vanessa and Henry, we are praying and believing with you!! Let us know what we can do to help when you get back home—loving you both and praying! God will supernaturally provide all the help you need with Henry, but you will have to let us know what is needed!

RN — Let me know if I can assist you when you and Henry are back home in Cali.

GA — Constantly in my thoughts and prayers.

"Be of sober spirit, be on the alert. Your adversary, the devil, prowls around like a roaring lion, seeking someone to devour."
— 1 Peter 5:8, New American Standard

The Force Is With Us

"But the Lord stood at my side and gave me strength, so that through me the message might be fully proclaimed and all the Gentiles might hear it. And I was delivered from the lion's mouth."
— 2 Timothy 4:17, New International Version Bible

Cancer Treatment Centers of America, Zion, IL
August 8, 2015

At most hospitals, the nursing staff and the Patient Care Assistants (PCAs) have 12-hour shifts from 7 a.m. to 7 p.m. CTCA was no different. After three weeks in the hospital, I thought I had met everyone who was providing me care. Yesterday, however, I met a nurse who would be my night nurse for the first time.

Yesterday, around 6 p.m., my day shift nurse came in to introduce me to my night shift nurse. Vanessa was just getting ready to leave for the hotel. This particular evening Vanessa had decided not to spend the night in the room with me. I do not remember the night nurse's name, but she caught my attention because I had never seen her before, and she was the first (and only) African American nurse I had while at CTCA.

"Hi, Mr. Dotson," the nurse said. "My name is __, and I will be your nurse for the evening."

"Hi," I said with a half-smile.

"Hi," Vanessa said. "I am his wife. I am just getting ready to go to the hotel for the evening."

"Don't you worry, Mrs. Dotson. I am here to make sure your husband is taken care of tonight. Everything will be alright."

"Alright," Vanessa said to the nurse.

Vanessa gathered up her things and headed for the door. Before she left, she turned to me and said, "I'll see you in the morning Dot. I love you!" and out the door, she went.

"Do you need anything, Mr. Dotson?" the nurse asked.

"No, I'm fine. Just a little more tired than usual," I said.

In truth, I was beginning to feel a little worse than just tired, but this was not unusual. My body would go through its ups and downs two to three times a day with no explanation other than reacting to the chemotherapy I was given.

"Well, you just let me know if you need anything," she replied. "I will be outside if you need me."

With that, she left the room. I watched television for a little while, but I really felt I needed to get some rest. So, I turned out the lights well before 9 p.m. and called it a day.

I awoke in the middle of the night in distress. I was sweating, I could feel that my pressure and heart rate were up, and my body was in pain all over. While this by itself was concerning, there was something more going on that I was even more concerned about. I was under spiritual attack!

I knew that I was under spiritual attack because I had been under severe spiritual attack before...

Tzaneen Country Lodge, Tzaneen, South Africa
August 2010

Vanessa and I were leading a mission trip in Tzaneen, South Africa. That was our second mission trip as team leaders and our fifth mission trip to Africa. Nothing was going well. There were many problems, but the main one was we had very limited access to our funds. We had deposited most of our money in a South African bank and had significant difficulty using our ATM cards.

After each day of mission work, I spent evenings making phone calls to the US to resolve our banking problems.

I was burning my candle at both ends, and I was physically exhausted. Consequently, I got sick and was starting to have trouble breathing. What I did not know at the time was that I had bronchitis. Up until this point in my life, I had never been very sick. What had me most concerned was we were not close to a good hospital.

On our last mission trip to the same area, we had to take one of our missionaries to the local hospital. The hospital was not up to standards that I was comfortable with.

One day I could tell I was getting progressively worse by the hour. On this particular day, the team was going out on their one sightseeing day of the trip. We were going to the local mountains to a scenic location called "God's Window." I was determined to go out sightseeing with the team. One of the missionaries, who happened to be an elder of the church, looked at me and said he thought it would be best if I stayed at the hotel and tried to get some rest.

"I really want to go out with the team and see 'God's Window,'" I pushed back.

"Brother Henry," the elder said, "You may want to see 'God's Window,' but we want to make sure you don't go through 'God's Window' today."

"Do I really look that bad?" I asked.

"Yes, brother, you do," he said.

"Okay, I'll stay and get some rest," I conceded.

"Don't worry, brother, Vanessa and I have your back," he assured me.

Vanessa was relieved that the elder spoke to me about staying. She was not sure that she would convince me to take care of myself without some reinforcements.

The team was going out in the evening after sightseeing to continue with mission work, so they would not be back until late at night.

I tried to get some sleep once the team left to go sightseeing, but it was a struggle because it was hard to breathe. I finally was able to fall asleep after a few hours. Once asleep, I began to have a strange dream. I dreamt that there were hundreds of small bug-like creatures inside my skull attacking my brain. They were crawling all over the surface of my brain in the space between my brain and my skull.

I am not certain what was fighting on my behalf, but I believe whatever it was, it was coming from my natural defense system. As the battle raged, it seemed as though neither side was winning. I awoke because my body was in distress; I was having difficulty breathing. I immediately discovered that even though I was awake and my eyes were open, the dream continued. That was a very strange and somewhat surreal experience. I was trying to figure out what was going on when I got a word in my spirit that said, "This is a spiritual battle."

Once I realized what was happening, I said to myself, *"Oh, now I know what to do. If this is a spiritual battle, then this is not my battle to fight. I just need to pray."*

I started to pray in tongues. The New Testament describes "tongues" largely as speech addressed to God and as something that can potentially be interpreted into human language. *It is the utterance of your spirit to the Holy Spirit that is edifying to the hearers* (1 Corinthians 14:5, 13).

Once I started to pray in tongues, I could see the small bug-like creatures literally lifting off my brain and disappearing. My breathing became much more relaxed and natural. I could feel my body and my spirit being uplifted to a better place.

When Vanessa returned from the mission work, she was surprised to find me in such good spirits and much better physical condition. In the next few days, my health continued to improve. That was the first time I had ever experienced a spiritual battle.

But I knew that I was just in one.

> *"So you shall serve the LORD your God, and He will bless your bread and your water. And I will take away sickness from among you."*
> — Exodus 23:25, Berean Study Bible

Night Angel

"Last night, an angel of the God to whom I belong and whom I serve stood beside me." — Acts 27:23, New International Version Bible

---

Cancer Treatment Centers of America, Zion, IL
August 7, 2015, Late Night

Again, once I realized what was going on, I knew what to do. I began praying in tongues. I expected to get the same results that I had in Tzaneen, South Africa. After praying for some time, nothing seemed to be happening. I did not panic, but I knew that I needed some help.

I pressed the button on my controller to page the nurse. The night nurse's voice came through on the small speaker in the controller.

"What do you need, Mr. Dotson?" she asked.

"I'm having some trouble, and I need some help," I replied. My tone was not alarming, but I did want to communicate a sense of urgency.

"I'll be right there," she replied.

In less than a minute, she opened the door and came to my bedside. She left the lights off and asked, "What do you need?"

"This might seem a little strange." I said, "But I am in a spiritual battle, and I need some help. Can you just pray with me?"

What happened next was simply a miracle.

She calmly but emphatically said to me, "Mr. Dotson, I told your wife that I would make sure nothing happens to you. That is why I am here."

She began to pray in tongues with both passion and conviction. She then laid her hands on my abdomen and chest. When she touched me, my body began to tremble. As she continued to pray in tongues, my body started to shake. I could see in my mind's eye darkness being drawn out of my body. As the darkness was being drawn out of my body, I began to feel lighter and stronger.

That continued for about a minute until I could see no more darkness coming out of my body. My body then stopped shaking and began trembling again. The trembling continued for 10 to 20 seconds and then came to rest. At that moment, the nurse stopped praying in tongues and removed her hands from my abdomen and chest.

She again calmly but firmly said to me, "Mr. Dotson, you will be alright." With that, she walked out of the room and closed the door.

It took me a few moments to gather myself and internalize what just happened. My body was no longer in distress, and my mind was racing. I knew that I was undeniably the beneficiary of a miracle. My body had been touched by the hand of the Master Physician who takes away all sickness and disease.

I never saw that nurse again.

> *"May the LORD answer you in the day of trouble; may the name of the God of Jacob protect you. May He send you help from the sanctuary and sustain you from Zion."*
>
> — Psalm 20:1-2, Berean Study Bible

Vanessa Foster-Dotson
August 9, 2015

*** Update for Saturday, 08/08/15:

As I entered Henry's room on Saturday, he looked different. He looked vibrant and sounded more like the old Henry. His voice was the strongest that I had heard in weeks, and he was way more talkative, witty, and engaged. He told me that he had prayed with one of the nurses at some point during the night. It appeared that his spirit had truly been renewed. I was somewhat awe-struck as I witnessed this transformation during the remainder of the day. A few of his comments were as if Henry had just awakened from a long slumber. I can't really explain it, but it was definitely real. All I can say is to God be the glory! During the day, he was more determined than ever. We walked three times around the nurses' station in the morning (without the PT), and he worked on strength exercises and steps (10) in the afternoon. He was able to eat his targeted six small meals and even stayed up past 9:00 p.m. to make sure that he completed the last meal. (He was fully awake the entire day!) The dietitian said that it would be great if Henry ate 2,380 calories a day with a focus on proteins and carbs, for now, to get his weight, strength, and energy back. We have been using an iPhone app to track what he eats. Henry's goal is to exceed the dietitian's suggestion, and he was successful yesterday. Henry is truly doing what he can do to get better, but he knows that the rest is in God's hands.

As previously mentioned, Henry had another round of chemo on Friday. As his treatment plan stands now, this was the first of 16 weeks of chemo. During these weeks, Henry will receive chemo injections one day per week. He seemed to tolerate this first injection very well. His blood counts have not stabilized completely, but I

continued

As previously mentioned, Henry had another round of chemo on Friday. As his treatment plan stands now, this was the first of 16 weeks of chemo. During these weeks, Henry will receive chemo injections one day per week. He seemed to tolerate this first injection very well. His blood counts have not stabilized completely, but I have been told that the current fluctuation is not uncommon. More questions to ask the doc on Monday.

So, all that I can say is thank you once again for your prayers and support. Our prayers are being answered. Thank you on behalf of our entire family.

Continued "blessings" to each of you, as our daughter would say!

Prayer Requests:

1. Complete healing for Henry: body, mind, soul, and spirit. (no cancer, no pain, no long-term anemia, no permanent back damage, no infections.)
2. Stabilized blood counts; all counts being positive
3. Stabilized kidney counts
4. Immediate release from the hospital
5. Improved strength and movement
6. General prayer for all of the family members and friends of anyone that is reading this update and have recently been diagnosed or is suffering from cancer or some other life-threatening health challenge.

Prayers Answered:

1. Healthy kidneys
2. Healthy eyes
3. Increased platelet count
4. Clarity of thoughts and words
5. Exponential blood count level increase
6. Improved appetite
7. Renewed spirit

 43   Seen by 172

RN Hallelujah. Great praise report. Let's keep praying and praising. Thank you, Lord!! Jesus!! Nobody but You!! Nobody Greater!!

MS To God be the glory indeed Vanessa, it is beautiful to find courage from knowing that the flesh is interconnected with the earth, and therefore it is a good thing that Henry has to eat as determined by the dieticians, and so his spirit is connected to the Source of life according to God's Word. In the name of Jesus, all prayer items observed and restoration in progress, and thanksgiving from the answered prayers recovered. Thanks for the updates. It finished. Amen.

CP The joy of the Lord is your strength. What a mighty God we serve. God is working it out for Henry's good. We continue to stand on the word of God and see the prayers of the righteous avail much. Decree and declare the word over both of your lives daily as we stand with you as one body and mind in Christ Jesus. We love ya'll.

BC Gamba Henry! Kick Cancer in the a$$! Praise God for his strength and protection!

VH Excellent praise report! Keep fighting, Henry!

August 9, 2015

I may have overdone it today doing my exercise. As much as I want to be discharged, I have to pace myself. Today is Sunday, so maybe it should have been a day of rest. Vanessa and I did hold our own church service. We haven't done that in a long time. I do miss going to church. I wonder when I will be able to do that again.

Vanessa Foster-Dotson
August 10, 2015

*** Update for Sunday, 08/09/15:

Sunday was a good day. Henry was a bit more tired than he had been on Saturday...still very alert and engaged...just tired and a little weak. He pushed to meet (actually exceed) his eating and exercise goals. We conducted our own "church service" as we prayed, read Our Daily Bread, read healing scriptures, and listened to gospel music. Henry's blood counts continued to fluctuate some, but they seem to be going in a more positive direction overall.

So, the fight continues. One day at a time!

Thank you for your prayers and support.

God Bless!

WL — Our God reigns, One day at a time, step by step. May God overshadow you with his comfort and healing.

CS — So he starts chemo tomorrow? Is it a combined or separate drug? If separate, ask why they are not giving him combined? Please. I'm learning more about this disease. I had a patient yesterday who has had it for eight years. She is head of the local chapter in Redding. She talked to me a lot and gave me the name of the doctor you need in your circle at Cedar Sinai. She is going to drop me off some literature. If you have the energy, support the Google group in your area. Let me know how you and Henry are doing. I love your posts; thank you.

FD — Bless the Lord, and thanks for the praise report/update. Love you guys.

LD — Keep up the good work! And after having done all, STAND!

An Outpatient in Zion

"Getting out of the hospital is a lot like resigning from a book club. You're not out of it until the computer says you're out of it."

— Unknown

Zion, IL
August 10, 2015

WE WERE TOLD THAT I WOULD BE RELEASED FROM THE HOSPITAL THAT DAY FOR THE PAST FEW DAYS. It was good news to my ears, and my hopes were high. But each day, sometime in the afternoon, someone told us that it would not happen that day because of red tape.

I soon discovered there is a certain amount of bureaucracy one will experience during the discharge process. Sometimes someone needed to come to see me before I left. Other times, someone (including me) needed to sign off on some document. Other times, my medical records required updating in "the system."

After the second day of delay, I decided to adjust my expectations. My new expectation has been, "I will believe it when I am outside the hospital." Adjusting my expectations has served me well. The delays did not surprise me, nor did they disappoint me.

Well, today, I was finally discharged from the hospital! That is a big step in my recovery. I purposely had not thought about what happens next because I did not know if I would walk out or be carried out of the hospital.

Now that we knew I would remain in the land of the living, Vanessa and I discussed with the doctors what my treatment plan would be moving forward. I would stay an outpatient at CTCA until medically cleared to return to CA to receive ongoing treatment at City of Hope under the supervision of CTCA. Now I have something new to think about.

Once my discharge was sure, I began to get dressed in street clothes for the first time in 26 days. I had been in bed so much of the time that I lost 40 pounds and a lot of muscle mass. And when I took off my hospital gown and looked at my legs, I thought to myself; *I look like I spent time in the German World War II concentration camp at Auschwitz.*

It felt bizarre when I put on my pants. It had been a long time since I had clothes rubbing against my legs. The pants felt coarse and very loose. Putting on the rest of my clothes was not unfamiliar; it just took longer than I expected. I was a little unsteady standing up, but a wheelchair soon arrived, so I did not have to stand for very long. Despite all of the physical therapy that I did, I was very weak.

When we got outside of the hospital, we waited for the shuttle bus that would take us to CTCA's Guest Quarters North, a local hotel where outpatients stay. As we waited, I just enjoyed being outside. Breathing the warm summer fresh air lifted my spirits. Feeling the sun warmed me up. It felt great to be outdoors!

When the bus arrived, the driver opened the front passenger door to let the passengers on the bus who were able to take the stairs. He then got out on the driver's side and said to the rest of us that he could assist us in getting on the bus. I was lifted into the bus using a wheelchair lift at the rear passenger door. That was a first for me.

The driver lowered the ramp and assisted me with getting on the ramp. Then he secured me to the ramp to make sure I did not fall off while being lifted. The driver then unstrapped me from the ramp and brought me inside the bus. Once inside the bus, I stayed in the wheelchair, and the driver secured it to the bus with a special wheelchair harness.

It felt strange needing so much assistance. I began to appreciate what disabled people go through just to get from one place to another. *Now I are one* I thought to myself. Other passengers needed wheelchair assistance, so it took some time for the driver to get us all aboard. Vanessa found a seat close by, and once all the passengers were aboard, we took off.

The ride to the hotel was surprisingly uncomfortable. The shuttle bus was like any other bus; any bumps in the road resulted in jolts in the passenger compartment. Those jolts were exceptionally painful for me because of my bad back. I tried to lift myself off of the seat of the wheelchair when I could tell we were about to hit a bump, but I was not able to anticipate most of them. I was beyond relieved when the ride was over. I did not say anything to Vanessa about my discomfort. I tried to concentrate on the blessing of just being outside and out of the hospital.

We did not go directly to the hotel. We made one stop west of CTCA to drop off some people before turning back east to get to the hotel. That made the ride twice as long as it would have been if we traveled directly from the hospital to the hotel. Twice the number of bumps and zings to my back. I just looked forward to getting off the bus.

Vanessa Foster-Dotson
August 11, 2015

*** Update for Monday, 08/10/15:

At last, one step closer to California. On Monday, Henry was released from the hospital! After being in the CTCA hospital for 26 days, Henry was finally well enough to get dressed in regular clothes (no hospital gown!), leave the 4th floor isolated Stem Cell Unit, get wheeled outside to the fresh air, and then driven to a local hotel. Absolutely AWESOME!!!

We will remain at the local hotel for at least a few days. During this time, Henry will have his blood tested daily on an outpatient basis, and we will begin adjusting to our "new norm." We will also prepare for Henry's ongoing remote care, which will take place in California and be supervised by CTCA. Once the doctors and PT feel that he is ready and everything is in place in California, he will be released to return home.

During the day, Henry was cautiously excited about leaving the hospital. Due to prior false alarms, he did not want to get too excited until he was actually at the hotel. Once at the hotel, his first thought was to get some sleep. While staying at the hospital, he was often awakened several times during the night to take meds, go to the bathroom, or get vital readings. So most of the remainder of the day on Monday, Henry slept and worked to adjust to his new norm.

One more step towards the goal; full caregiving responsibilities have begun.

God Bless!

👍 23   Seen by 172

 Just what we have been believing. Healed and totally recovered. Nothing is too hard for God!!

 Praise God! Henry's journey is a testimony of God's faithfulness and healing power!

 Take good care of the patient but as the caregiver, get support and take care of yourself. The county where you live should be able to provide an aide as needed to free you up if contacted. We did this for my dad and had wonderful support - also checkout an org called visiting Angels.

And as someone who was hospitalized for two months at the end of 2013, I know how Henry felt when he was out in the FRESH AIR for the first time in a few weeks! It's an amazing feeling. Keep getting better, Henry, and please take care of yourself, Vanessa. God is amazing!

Zion, IL
August 11, 2015

I didn't quite know what to do when I woke up this morning in the hotel. I was so focused on just getting discharged that I did not think ahead to what would come next. All I could think of was my physical therapy exercises. They were not fun, just familiar. Our room is not very big, but I tried my best to do laps with my walker. I also had my apparatus to do breathing exercises, so I did that too.

My appointment at CTCA today was not until the afternoon, so I had some time just to get acclimated to my surroundings. Vanessa got us something to eat, even though I was not that hungry. It felt so unfamiliar not eating hospital food off of a tray.

Eventually, the time came to get ready to go to the hospital. I was still a little weak as I made my way to the bathroom with my walker. Once I stood before the sink and mirror, I realized this was the first time I had to clean up and get dressed by myself in almost a month! Everything was so challenging, even using a regular height toilet. I did not realize how low the seat is! It was a struggle for me to take care of myself. Vanessa helped some, but she knew it was best to step in only when I asked for help, or when it was evident that it wasn't safe for me to try something by myself.

I was not looking forward to the ride between the hotel to the hospital. The road is very bumpy, and because I ride on the bus in my wheelchair, I am always sitting right next to the rear wheels. Every time we hit a bump, I'd get a jolt up my spine. It was very uncomfortable, and even the slightest bump caused pain. But if I just concentrated on the fact that through the grace of God, I was alive, it didn't hurt as much.

I did get a favorable report from the doctors today, so I am very grateful. They said it would take some time, but I should have an excellent recovery. They also drove home the point that I need to drink more water. It is vital since I have an active case of cancer. Water is required to help flush out the toxins introduced when I receive chemotherapy medication. Drinking water will help keep my kidneys and liver from being damaged. It's a good thing I like drinking water. I just have to be sure I remember to keep it up throughout the day.

Vanessa Foster-Dotson
August 12, 2015

*** Update for Tuesday, 08/11/15:

Henry's first day as an outpatient was quite different than being in the hospital. Henry started his day by taking laps back and forth in the room using his walker. He also did a few breathing exercises. However, as the day progressed, differences in his routine became more apparent. Gone are the comforts of having everything come to him. Although I assisted, Henry now had to take more responsibility with tasks like getting washed up and dressed. He was successful with accomplishing "little things," such as getting down to sit on a regular toilet seat. There are many things that we take for granted that Henry has to relearn.

As we were driven to the CTCA hospital, Henry had to endure numerous bumps in the road. These bumps seemed insignificant to me, but the compression fractures in Henry's back made him fully aware of each little hill or pothole. Once at the hospital, the outpatient clinic was very congested and totally overwhelming for Henry. As I figured out how to maneuver his wheelchair and walker in the tight area, he was eventually able to get his daily vital signs read and his blood drawn.

In a couple of hours, we met with the doctor to discuss the results of Henry's blood work. I also received answers to several questions. In general, the doctor was pleased with Henry's progress. The doctor reiterated that Henry was VERY, VERY, VERY sick when he arrived. That is why they had to start him off with the 5-day, aggressive chemo treatment to literally save his life. Although the treatment also caused Henry to be extremely weak, tired, etc., he is here and will recover over time. The doctor said that Henry might not recover to 100% of where he was before, but he should come close. The main concern that the doctor expressed was for Henry to drink more fluids. Henry ended up having to receive fluids intravenously before taking the bumpy ride back to the hotel and going to sleep.

So, in addition to praying for Henry's complete healing, please pray for increased fluid and food intact. Also, please pray that we can continue to get all of the required support systems and medical equipment in place that is needed in California.

Thank you once again, and God Bless!

👍 29   Seen by 48

RH We are agreeing with 100% recovery and that Henry will soak up fluids like a sponge! Our God HAS provided all things needed and will continue to guide and direct you in ALL matters. We will stay on the prayer watch as God manifests all things needed.

RH Good job, Henry! Now you have to drink more. Drink as much as you can for yourself, then drink a little more for Vanessa, then a little more for Bart, and finally, a tiny bit more for Talia.

I am praying for 100% recovery. If the doctor can get you to 95%, God has the rest. Amen.

PH I am agreeing in faith! Speaking the Word over this situation! Henry is fully recovered and healed in every area of his body and mind! Every need is met thru Christ Jesus! You and Henry have everything you need for care and speedy recovery! In Jesus' Name!

GT I am praying right now for all requests. I still attend Cedar Sinai cancer center for monitoring. It's part of the routine. Let me know if you need any information.

CS Go buy him a sports bottle with a hook-on in. He is to drink a minimum of half his weight. If he weighs 170 pounds, then he should drink 85 fluid ounces minimum.

RZ You probably know this, but remember grapes, oranges, and melons, are also great ways to get fluids and a few calories too. You might try to keep a bowl of such near Henry in addition to water.

SB Awesome! It sounds like a good follow-through diet to get your strength back. I am praying for a blessed recovery!

My God shall supply all your needs according to His riches in glory!!

JR In the prayer request box, all the above-mentioned requests were listed; I made sure of that. All your prayers are being addressed and covered! XXX!

August 12, 2015

I had a better attitude today. I started out by drinking all the water I was supposed to drink before my appointment at the hospital. My attitude was tested when I found out my counts for my kidneys were still not where I wanted them to be. I had to get fluids, and that stretched my visit another three hours.

My first response was disappointment. Since I am goal-oriented, it was disappointing not accomplishing the goal I set for myself. It was also frustrating because it meant I would have to stay at the hospital much longer than I had anticipated. But it is in my nature to always look for the silver lining around the gray clouds. So, I told myself, *It's not like you have anything special to do once you go back to the hotel, so you are not going to miss anything.* A small concession, granted, but it was something.

I felt better when the nurse explained that it was not totally up to what I was doing. It was also dependent on what my myeloma cells were doing.

Once I realized I was still battling the enemy, I got in the right frame of mind. It just took a little enlightenment.

Vanessa Foster-Dotson
August 13, 2015

*** Update for Wednesday, 08/12/15:

One more day, one more blessing. Henry woke up determined to drink all of the water that he had been told that he needed. He drank 64oz before we departed in the morning to go to the hospital. (Thank you for your prayers!) However, later, when the results of his blood work came back, his kidney counts were up, and he still had to sit and get fluids intravenously for three hours. Henry was frustrated. He did as he was told but did not get the outcome that he had expected. I asked the nurse to talk to him. She explained that, although the myeloma had been "shut down," it is still active in his body. Hence the reason that he will need to get chemo every week for the next 16 weeks at least. Henry was satisfied with the explanation. Meanwhile, I became a bit discouraged when the nurse was speaking but shook it off as I know that 1) we have been truly blessed to have Henry still here, 2) we have been truly blessed that he is progressing positively overall, and 3) we are truly blessed to have the prayers and support of each of you. Like Henry's rides to the hospital, there may be hills and potholes along the way to our destination, but we will arrive! God's got this, and we just have to keep our eye on the prize.

continued

We love you all, and God Bless!

Prayer Request:

1. In addition to praying about Henry's complete healing, please include a prayer today for additional discounts on Henry's medicine as well as final coordination of the immediate resources that are needed in California.

 29   Seen by 48

CP Vanessa Foster-Dotson, there is nothing too hard for our awesome God, who is the author and finisher of our faith. May the joy of the Lord continue to be your strength. Psalm 121 all of your help comes from the Lord? Yes, keep your eyes on the Prize Christ Jesus! Victory is ours! The battle is the Lord's.

RH It's okay, Henry. I pray the kidney count improves and the discounts flow. I love you guys, and you are in my thoughts every day.

PM The Lord is executing Henry's recovery. Each day is a challenge, but ultimately the victory is realized. When either of you feels discouraged, look back to how far you've come. The Lord has always been and will always be faithful.

WL You have come this far by faith. God will continue to lead and guide you with the CLOUD by day and the FIRE by night. God is in the midst of this challenge because he said, "where two or three are gathered in MY NAME, I AM, THAT I AM, THAT I AM." BE BLESSED.

RN Still praying. Thankful for the positive feedback on Henry's condition. Stay strong, Henry. God is fighting your battle. Stay encouraged. The road may be bumpy, but you are still riding in the car!! #trueblessing

VH It is amazing how far you have come in a short time. God will continue to be there for you and Henry; the battle is His! Love you both!

JD God has been and still smiling on you and Bernard. I am sending both of you continued blessings and thanking GOD for all he is doing. Much love!

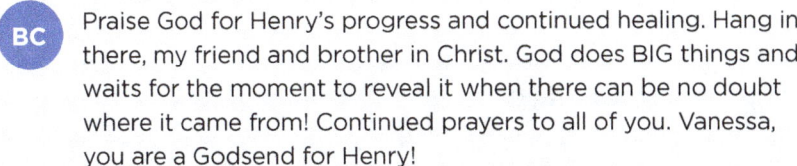

BC Praise God for Henry's progress and continued healing. Hang in there, my friend and brother in Christ. God does BIG things and waits for the moment to reveal it when there can be no doubt where it came from! Continued prayers to all of you. Vanessa, you are a Godsend for Henry!

SM God is still in control, and He knows the beginning from the end. I am standing in the gap for Henry as well as you. Love you both!

August 13, 2015

TODAY I WENT UP AND DOWN ONE FLIGHT OF STAIRS DURING PHYSICAL THERAPY! I will admit that at first, it looked a little daunting. It has been a long time since I've even seen a flight of stairs, let alone attempted to go up and down a flight of stairs. The stairs looked foreign because we were in a stairwell. I was trying to use visualization techniques to see in my mind's eye a successful outcome, but I did not envision stairs in a stairwell. I saw myself going up and down the stairs in my house. I calmed myself by imagining all of the physical therapy sessions where I stepped up and down on the stepping blocks. That helped. I knew if I took my time and made sure I used the stair rail, I could do it.

The physical therapist asked me to go up and down a couple of times. I went up and down four times. I wanted to make sure she saw that I was able. That was important because I cannot return to California until I can demonstrate that I can go up and down stairs.

I did not want to leave any room for doubt. I stopped after four trips because I was beginning to get tired.

Today was a good day!

Vanessa Foster-Dotson
August 14, 2015

*** Update for Thursday, 08/13/15:

When Henry got up on Thursday, the first thing he wanted to do is eat. (Yes! He has an appetite!) I had ordered take-out the night before, but Henry had gone straight to bed and did not eat his. So he started the morning by nibbling at the take-out and drinking 48oz of fluid. Breakfast continues to be Henry's best meal of the day.

The remainder of Thursday was basically a repeat of Wednesday. We got up, got dressed, rode the van to the CTCA hospital. Henry had his vitals and lab work done. Henry picked at his lunch, he went to PT, sat two hours while receiving intravenous fluids, rode back to the hotel, drank a couple of protein shakes for dinner, and went to bed for the evening...waking up frequently until the wee hours of the next morning when it is now time to start all over again. That has become Henry's outpatient routine. Somewhat simple but very tiring...for both of us.

One key thing that happened yesterday during PT is that Henry was able to go up and down 12 REAL stairs for the first time! His legs were quite fatigued afterward, but he did it! This means that at some point, Henry should be able to go upstairs once at home. Henry is really pushing to do all that he can to get well. I am so proud of him!

And thank you once again for your prayers. Unfortunately, Henry was not able to get any other prescription discounts. Initially, our insurance company agreed to cover part of the cost of the $8,000/month prescription so that the new price would be $450/month. (Praise Him!) However, after your prayers yesterday, it appears that the price will go down further to $295/month. (Thank you all again!) When added to the $120/month for the rest of his prescriptions, this is still a very high bill. However, it is better than $8,120, and Henry should continue to progress positively.

In addition to covering our high insurance deductible, we are hoping to use the monies from the GoFundMe account to cover these monthly prescription costs. So again, thank you so much for supporting us via GoFundMe. Please feel free to share the link for the GoFundMe account with others if you are led to do so. This is truly a humbling experience.

Lastly, please continue to pray for Henry's complete healing as well as the final coordination of resources that are needed in California...

continued

medical equipment, at-home PT, doctors, etc. We are ready to return home!

So, thank you! Thank you! Thank you! Not sure what else to say. We are so appreciative of you all! Thank you again! And thank you, God!

VH Breakfast is Henry's best meal, which is great because it's the most important meal of the day. I'm glad to hear that his appetite is returning. Healing comes in small increments...truly one day and one small step at a time, Vanessa. Prayers will continue to go up so that blessings come down. Love to you both.

PM I begin each morning anxiously looking forward to your daily update on Henry. I know you must be worn out at the end of the day, so allow me to thank you, Vanessa, for taking the time to keep us abreast of Henry's progress. Praise God for the good news!!

Thank you, Lord, for hearing our prayers and supplications. Thank you for Vanessa's love, support, and devotion for her husband as they travel this challenging journey. Please keep her strong and healthy for the warrior she is as she fights the good fight of faith for Henry. In the name of Jesus. Amen.

FD Thank you, Lord, for all that you've done and are doing for our family. Thank you, Ms. V, for loving my nephew and keeping us informed. As a fellow caregiver I fully understand the challenges you face on a daily basis. Know that you both are in my prayers for your complete recovery and renewing of your strength.

RN Thank you, God. He is coming home. I pray for his continued healing and strength in Jesus' name. It is so!!

August 14, 2015

THE BEST THING THAT HAPPENED TODAY WAS FINALLY MAKING THE PLANE RESERVATIONS TO GO BACK HOME! The last box checked in terms of my physical condition was that I could go up and down stairs during physical therapy. I showed I could do that yesterday, so I had done all that I could do. The rest was up to how well my body responded to the treatments.

My outpatient days have become routine to me. It is not easy, but it is routine. Each day I wake up, I thank God that I have lived to see another day. Getting ready to go to the hospital in the morning takes some time, but I am doing it on my own. I wash up in the sink and put on my clothes. Breakfast is available daily downstairs, so Vanessa will get some fruit, some oatmeal for me, and maybe a small croissant and bring it back to the room. We eat, and then I brush my teeth.

We then go downstairs and wait for the bus with the other outpatients in the lobby. There may or not be small talk until the bus arrives, depending on who feels chatty. When the bus comes, we all load up. I get on the bus through the rear door lift in my wheelchair. The driver secures my wheelchair to the frame of the bus with straps. Then I make the uncomfortable bus ride to the hospital.

Once I check in for the day, I get my blood drawn and go to my scheduled appointments. That usually includes physical therapy and some other treatments based on my lab results. I consciously try to maintain a positive attitude as I go through each appointment. My attitude is the one thing that I have total control over, and a good attitude is the best thing to have.

While at the hospital, Vanessa and I have lunch and discuss what my doctors and other healthcare providers have explained about my condition. There are usually more appointments in the afternoon. When finished, we get back on the bus for another bumpy return ride to the hotel. Vanessa will order something ahead of time for dinner and pick it up after settling in the room. After dinner, we may watch some TV and then go to bed.

I thank God for the day after the lights are off, and I ask myself if I did all that I could do that day. Most of the time, I think I have. That helps me to get a good night's sleep.

I think it is good to have a routine. It helps bring some consistency each day, which is easily lost when you are unfamiliar with your surroundings.

Vanessa Foster-Dotson
August 15, 2015

*** Update for Friday, 08/14/15:

The fight continues! There were a few small challenges yesterday, but God prevailed. The routine was the same as on Thursday... up, dressed, ride, hospital, lab work, lunch, PT, lab results. One big difference is that Henry's hemoglobin count was low, so he had to get a blood transfusion that took FOREVER. He then had to get a chemo treatment.

We arrived at the hospital at about 9 a.m. and did not get back to the hotel until about 9:00 p.m. While waiting, I worked with the care managers and various resources in California to try to get things in order for us to come home. This is where we ran into a few additional challenges, but God is good, and we have great friends! We have faith that everything will work out.

As the time to come home draws closer, the thought of being totally on our own, without any help from the fantastic CTCA staff, can be a little overwhelming. I believe that I have had my time of concern and am now ready to do whatever needs to be done to adjust to the new norm. However, Henry may be just starting to accept that we will be leaving at some point...hopefully soon.

We have been told so many times that we can leave in a few days that we now have a "we will believe it when we are in CA" attitude. I am glad that they will not release Henry until they are confident that he is ready. His health is top priority! However, as the time to leave draws closer, the thought of how different life is going to be once we return can be a lot to deal with...especially for a patient. Imagine having to relearn most of the physical things that you do and feeling weak and tired while relearning. Henry will have to take it slowly...one day at a time. Please pray for an "easy" adjustment.

God Bless!

Additional Prayer Requests:

1. Complete healing for Henry: body, mind, soul, and spirit. (no cancer, no pain, no long-term anemia, no permanent back damage, and no infections.)
2. Stabilized blood counts; all counts being positive
3. Stabilized kidney counts
4. Immediate release from the hospital

continued

5. Improved strength and movement
6. General prayer for all of the family members and friends of anyone that is reading this update and has recently been diagnosed or is suffering from cancer or some other life-threatening health challenge

Prayers Answered:

1. Healthy kidneys
2. Healthy eyes
3. Increased platelet count
4. Clarity of thoughts and words
5. Exponential blood count level increase
6. Improved appetite
7. Renewed spirit

VW — Amen! The best thing about someone close to you being your caregiver when you're sick is you learn each other a WHOLE lot better. You learn an other side of them, you get a better relationship with them, and you get to depend on God together. We love you guys and are praying!

RN — I am praying for you both. I know it may be challenging, but the transition will take care of itself. Continue to believe God has it under his control. You are just the vessel...

SB — What our Lord and Savior has done thus far calls for our "Thanks" to begin. He is our Awesome God who can do over and beyond what we think or ask, done wonderful miracles, and will continue to do the same. We declare that his faith has healed him and is not coming back, so we Thank you, our God and Savior Jesus Christ, for this, your wonderful miracle on Henry "Bernard" Dotson.

WL — You have seen what GOD can and will do for those that LOVE him. You and Henry LOVE the LORD, so he will do MIGHTY THINGS on your behalf. Fight on soldiers and see the HANDS of GOD.

DK Lord Jesus, I'm in agreement with everything my sister Vanessa has prayed! Let everything run smoothly as she prepares to come home. Continue to strengthen Henry's body, mind, and soul, surround her with your presence, let her walk by faith and not by sight, trusting your every step of the way. Meet all their needs, traveling blessings in Jesus' name, amen! Love you guys!

 PM Just like the ride to the hospital each time you and Henry go, there're going to be bumps in the road to recovery. Don't worry though; you won't be alone. God said, "The battle is mine." He's been with you in Chicago, and he'll be with you every step of the way when you return to Cali.

Q: How did you feel when you learned I would be returning to California?

BART: I was overjoyed to hear that you were returning to California. In my mind, it signified a significant milestone on your road to recovery.

TALIA: Relieved and grateful.

August 15, 2015

TODAY WAS A GOOD DAY! I walked from the hotel to the hospital for my appointments and back again!! It was only 0.3 miles from the hotel to the hospital, so it was definitely within my abilities (*see photo next page*). I had walked farther than that when I was doing laps around the nursing station.

I did not want to push too hard, so I took my time. I was using my walker to assist me and help keep my balance. We walked south on Sheridan Road for a block. We stopped at the Dollar General store on the corner to buy some sundries. It was wonderful.

It was the first normal thing I had done in many weeks.

We then continued to walk south down Sheridan Road to the end of the block to Shiloh Boulevard. We walked down the east side of the block-long Veterans Memorial Park and turned right onto Shiloh Boulevard to walk along the park's south side. It took us about an hour to travel the 0.3 of a mile, but there were no bumps to hurt my back! I took the stairs to get inside the hospital instead of wheeling up the ramp in a wheelchair.

I don't remember much about the appointment because I was so excited about walking to the hospital. The appointment was over in mid-afternoon. What was memorable was taking the time to thank the doctors and nurses who provided my care. They wished me well, and Vanessa and I planned on seeing them again when I was ready for a stem-cell transplant.

Again, I walked down the stairs outside the hospital and walked back to the hotel. Vanessa and I stopped along the way on the return trip to pick up some dinner from a little restaurant to take back with us to the hotel.

I was tired when we returned to the hotel, but it was the good tired that you feel when you've worked out just the right amount. Vanessa and I ate dinner, and I got a good night's sleep.

What more could I ask for?

Vanessa Foster-Dotson
August 16, 2015

*** Update for Saturday, 08/15/15:

Oh My Goodness!!! What a day! A nurse had told me that after receiving a blood transfusion and chemo treatment Friday, Henry might be more energetic. And many of you had said to expect the unexpected. Never would I have imagined what took place on Saturday. Henry woke up and started walking around...without his walker. I watched out of the corner of my eye to make sure that he was safe. He moved slowly and deliberately, but he was walking unassisted! Absolutely Amazing!

The van was running late, so I asked Henry if he wanted me to just push him in the wheelchair to our appointment at the hospital. He said, sure, let's try that. Once outside, Henry told me, "Last night's van ride from the hospital to the hotel was the worse that I had experienced. (extremely bumpy)

I promised myself that I would do all that I could do to not have to get back on another van." So instead of me pushing Henry, he decided to use his walker to walk to his outpatient appointment at the hospital! And along the way, he asked to stop at a store. It took us about an hour to go a little less than one mile, but he made it. Henry used his walker, and I followed with the wheelchair. And once at the hospital entry, Henry really wanted to use the stairs instead of the ramp. I was very hesitant, so I made myself available to assist if needed.

He did great on his own.

During the appointment, he had to get more fluids, so we were at the outpatient clinic for approximately five hours. Henry talked almost the entire time. Fantastic! And afterward, he again wanted to use his walker instead of the wheelchair and van to walk back to the hotel. This time he walked down the stairs in the hospital entry. We also stopped along the way to get some fish that we discovered he likes.

An AWESOME day! I know that there will be hills and valleys, but I am going to cherish being on top of this hill for now. Thank you, God!

 Praise God! Good job, Henry! We can't wait to see you come home. Keep fighting the good fight! Continued prayers for all of you.

MS — This is a great heart of faith in action. Thanks for the update, God is really at work, and courage is seen in the doing. To God be the glory in Jesus' name. Healing and more healing of total strengths amen.

CP — How Great is our God? Exceedingly and abundantly above all, we can think. Powerful Vanessa Foster-Dotson. Our prayers are with you, Sis. God has you both. Be encouraged that Henry is healed and delivered. Love and miss you both.

JH — Vanessa Foster-Dotson, now that you can see the path to coming home, please let me know what I can do to help when you get here.

WL — AMEN, Ps.23:4, "When you walk through the valley, YOU fear NO evil BECAUSE God is with you, God's ROD AND STAFF will PROTECT and GUIDE YOU." LIFT up YOUR eyes and HEART and GIVE GOD PRAISE. May GOD continue to order your STEPS.

RM — Bless The Lord! Vanessa - almost every sentence in this post caused my head to "jerk back" in awe! I am so happy and encouraged to hear of Henry's perseverance in The Lord! And you as his "Help Meet" - I can't begin to express the respect I have for your tenacity and your steadfastness to write these daily updates. Continuing to intercede for you both!... Hugs.

DM — Praise God for healing, clear mind to press on anyway. Thank God for the will to do more every day and even more for the love and support that you provide for him. I love you both.

CD — Amen and amen! God is truly good. And Vanessa, I pray that God will continue to strengthen you and give you the grace that is needed as you minister (serve, help, give aid) to your husband and best friend. I am thanking God for more of the miraculous testimonies yet to come! Love you both.

"Because he has loved Me, therefore I will deliver him; I will set him securely on high, because he has known My name. He will call upon Me, and I will answer him; I will be with him in trouble; I will rescue him and honor him." — Psalm 91:14-15, Berean Study Bible

You're Free to Go

"Being away is fine, being home is best." — Swedish Proverb

Zion, IL
August 16, 2015

ONE DAY AND COUNTING. Today I wanted to do three things: mentally and physically prepare for tomorrow, and spend some quality time with Vanessa. I was able to do just that.

I decided to think of my physical preparation today the same way I did when I had a gymnastics meet the following day—just a light workout to help my muscle memory. I went through some of my physical therapy exercises, including taking the stairs to go down to the lobby and back. I spent some time in the room walking back and forth with and without my walker. I did not want to put in a lot of work, just enough to warm up my body without breaking a sweat.

Vanessa and I relaxed and watched television. We talked about going home and what that would be like. We discussed how we wanted the day to go tomorrow. Most of the time, we just enjoyed each other's company in silence, broken only by my comments about what was happening on television and Vanessa telling me to be quiet.

A slight return to normalcy.

After Vanessa went to sleep, I started to reflect on my time in Zion. I thought about my physical condition when I arrived and my current condition. I arrived not feeling good only to discover I was near death with my survival odds against me in the natural. Today my odds of survival have greatly improved, but at a cost to my body. Multiple Myeloma and chemotherapy have taken their toll. Multiple Myeloma has left me with bone lesions (small fractures) throughout my body. My crushed T7 vertebra has resulted in me being three inches shorter than I was before.

My bones are not as strong as they used to be. My right tibia (shinbone) now has a slight twist to the right, which causes my right foot to point outward and affects my gait. The side-effects of chemotherapy have left me weak, underweight, and with a compromised immune system. I also have neuropathy, which affects my peripheral nervous system. I have numbness and tingling sensations in my extremities. I don't have much of an appetite, and my sense of taste is mostly gone. I was not lamenting my health condition, just making an objective assessment of my physical state of being.

I then turned my attention to my state of mind. I seemed to have all of my faculties, and I continued to have a positive attitude. That was the best I could hope for at the moment.

Lastly, I thought about what God has done during my time in Zion. First and foremost, he literally saved my life. He brought me from the brink of death back to safer ground. That thought alone brought tears to my eyes.

I wept silent tears of joy at that moment. I continue to do so now. I next thought about my time in the hospital bed when no one else was in the room. I never felt alone... more tears of joy. I then thought about every other waking moment I spent as an inpatient at CTCA Chicago. Through all that went on, again, I never felt alone, more tears of joy.

I finally cried myself to sleep. Sometimes I simply have no words to express what He's done for me.

I do not express it audibly, just with tears, tears of joy.

 Vanessa Foster-Dotson
August 17, 2015

*** Update for Sunday, 08/16/15:

Sunday was pretty low-key. No medical appointments. No trips to the hospital. We stayed in the hotel room, watched television/movies, and just enjoyed being together. Henry continued to walk around the room without his walker or wheelchair. The one time that he did leave the room to go downstairs, he only used his walker. He did not talk as much as he had on Saturday, but all was well. It was a good day.

It was a day of progress and peace.

AC — "But let all who take refuge in YOU be glad; let them ever sing for joy, And may You shelter them, that those who love Your name may exult in You." Psalms 5:11 (exult means - show or feel elation or jubilation, especially as the result of a success)

PM — Good! You both needed a day like that. Saturday was such an awesome day. You could bask in the glory of God and behold the wonders and Grace he has performed.

RN — Enjoy your good days and all the great ones that are around the corner!! Keep the faith!! God is able to see you through!

Return to Cali

"Go home to your own people and tell them how much the Lord has done for you, and how He has had mercy on you."
— Mark 5:19, New International Version Bible

Zion, IL
August 17, 2015

THE DAY TO GO HOME HAD FINALLY ARRIVED. I woke up early to get ready for the trip. Although it had been 33 days since my last plane trip, I vividly remembered how difficult it had been. I wanted to do all I could to not repeat that experience. I did a few laps in the room to wake up my atrophied legs. My adrenaline was flowing as I washed up and got dressed.

Vanessa had done most of the packing the night before, so all we had to do was wait for our ride to the hospital. I thought about walking from the hotel to the hospital to avoid another bumpy ride, but I wanted to save my strength for the return trip home. Also, when I looked at all of the luggage we had to carry, I knew it was not a good idea to walk.

It was a beautiful day in Zion. The sun was out, and there was not a cloud in the sky. The ride to the hospital did not disappoint. It was just as bumpy and uncomfortable as usual, but today, I did not care. I was going home.

I got into a limo to go to Chicago O'Hare airport. I remembered how difficult it was to get into a limo the last time. *So far, so good,* I thought.

We arrived at O'Hare airport in the evening on the trip from California. Today, we would arrive at O'Hare in the morning for the journey home. It is about a 40-minute ride from Zion to the airport, so I had a chance to take in the scenery. It had been many years since I was last in Chicago, so I was trying to see if I could tell what had changed. Just something to do to pass the time. I did not want to think about what it would be like once we got home. I did not recognize many landmarks, so I gave up after being on the freeway for about 15 minutes.

Getting through check-in, security, and boarding was very easy because I was a wheelchair-assisted passenger. We avoided all lines after our bags were checked. Vanessa and I settled into our seats and waited for the other passengers to board. Throughout the flight, Vanessa and I were not very talkative. We each were alone with our own thoughts. Vanessa stayed away from boredom by playing solitaire.

I stared out the window with not much on my mind, occasionally drifting in and out of sleep.

All was well until the flight attendant announced that we were about fifteen minutes away from landing at LAX. Right after that, I had a sudden urge to pee. I had used the restroom once before during the flight, but the urge was back again. I was sitting by the window, and I didn't think it was worth the trouble to try to get up and make my way to the line already forming at each restroom. Besides, I thought I could hold it until we landed and disembarked. I was sadly mistaken.

I found myself straining when the plane was at the gate, and the passengers were getting off. While we were the first ones on the plane due to my wheelchair status, we would be the last ones off for the same reason. It was then that I told Vanessa that I had to use the restroom.

"Well, can you hold it until we get off the plane?" she asked.

"I don't think so," I replied.

Vanessa started looking around to see what it would take for me to get to a restroom. The passenger who shared our row had already left, but there was a stream of people blocking the aisle. There did not appear to be a break in the line of disembarking passengers

As Vanessa continued to look, I realized I was not going to make it. I unbuttoned the top button of my pants to try to relieve some of the pressure it was putting on my bladder. That helped, but not enough. I thought to myself, *After all I've been through, damp pants will certainly be the least of my problems.* I decided not to resist the urge and deal with the consequences. Just at that moment, Vanessa turned around to see a stream coming up from my pants. Her jaw dropped in disbelief. My muscles relaxed with a sense of relief.

Fortunately, no one was paying attention to what was going on in row 12. They had places to go and things to do. After the waterworks were over, Vanessa got my windbreaker jacket, and I put it on in an effort to look more presentable. It was not a big deal because I was in a wheelchair when I got off the plane until we picked our luggage at Baggage Claim. I was not embarrassed or even concerned. When we would run into obstacles on mission trips, we learned to "go with the flow" (no pun intended).

The most important thing was that I was back in California!

My brother Ira was at the airport waiting to take me home. Our friend Cedric brought my car to the airport for Vanessa to drive back to the house. We had left my car with Cedric while we were out of town. He lives close to LAX and had space for my car at his apartment. I was glad to see familiar faces. It had been a long time since our visitors from home when we were in Zion. I took a little moment to say a silent prayer of gratitude for a safe trip back to Los Angeles.

We all stopped to get something to eat near LAX before we headed home. Ira was talkative as usual, but not as much as I've come to expect. He asked some questions about my time at CTCA, but he spent more than an equal amount of time trying to catch me up on what had happened while I was away.

When we entered our house, I was greeted by our neighbors from down the street, Larry and Pam, our friend Butch, and our friend Maude. They had set up a hospital bed in the family room where I would stay at first. That was to avoid having to go up and downstairs too often. I went up and down the stairs a couple of times just to see what it was like, then I sat on the edge of the bed and chatted for a little while. It was great to see everyone, but soon it was time for Vanessa and me to be alone.

"We're finally back home!" Vanessa said. "What do you feel like doing? Are you tired? Do you just want to rest?" she asked.

"Well, the first thing I want to do," I said, "is to get out of these wet clothes. The next thing is just to lay down and relax. It has been a busy day so far."

Once I settled in bed, I thought about how much my life had changed in less than a couple of months.

I also thought about what God had done for me. More tears...

Vanessa Foster-Dotson
August 18, 2015

*** Update for Monday, 08/17/15:

From ordinary to extraordinary! Sunday had been a low-key day, relatively ordinary. Meanwhile, Monday was extraordinary. So, on day 33, Henry woke up very early, again walked around unassisted, and got dressed. He ended up having to take another ride in the van. However, this time, we transferred to a limo once we arrived at the hospital entry. The limo then took us to the airport. YES, AT LAST, WE ARE BACK HOME!!! Thank you! Thank you, family!

Thank you, friends! Thank you, Jesus!

The flight was uneventful, and we were picked up at the airport by Henry's brother, Ira, and friend, Cedric. Once in Pasadena, we were met at our home by my dear friend Maude who had assisted with house sitting and preparing the house for our return (although I forgot to tell her the exact day that we were returning...oops! I probably forgot because I did not know our exact return date until fairly late. You see, one of the doctor's requirements for coming home was that Henry had to have a hospital bed, wheelchair, walker, etc., in place before we arrived. The doctor did not want Henry to have to go up/down any stairs. So once the doctor finally said that Henry was physically ready to go home, I then had to scramble to make

continued

arrangements to move furniture out of the family room and to then have the hospital equipment delivered and set up.)

During Monday afternoon/evening, Henry seemed full of thoughts and held a moderate amount of conversation. I guess he was reflecting on all that had taken place and possibly thinking about what was to come. Time will tell.

It appeared that Henry's appetite was back to some degree, as he was anxious about getting our Thai food order picked up quickly so that he could eat. We knew that Henry would have to go upstairs at some point, at least to take a shower, so while Ira and Cedric were available to assist, Henry demonstrated that he was able to go up and down the stairs in our home. However, he was not completely stable yet, so he was not going to be going up the stairs too much. A physical therapist would be coming to assist him with regaining comfort with the stairs and other things.

So now that we are back home, I have to get back to my J.O.B., which is a good thing. I am still not sure how all of this is going to mesh together, or what assistance we will need.

But I will definitely reach out as appropriate. Please be patient with us as we get used to the new norm and determine what Henry can and cannot do. We may not be able to take visitors for a while. Also, I may not be able to send as many updates. We'll see how things go.

The main thing that I do know is that Henry is alive, he is fighting to stay alive, you all are fighting with us, and that God has got our back and is also directing! One day at a time. Thank you for continuing to pray as Henry forges ahead on this marathon.

Thank you, Ira, Cedric, Maude, Butch, Larry, and Pam for assisting us with getting home and beginning the transition back to being in CA.

May God continue to Bless You All!

 To God be the Glory, and thank you, Vanessa, for this notice at this stage of being back at home, back at your known territory. Your ground rules are in order and relevant. May your returning to your J.O.B be in order, and may God keep Henry in control as well. Thirty-three days away carries reasonable testimonies and break thru for coming back home. All the best in all your recovery and catching up in Jesus' name. Stay blessed and enjoy.

WL: May GOD'S Abundant LIFE continue to overshadow you as you take steps through this JOURNEY of TRUST and FAITH. WELCOME BACK HOME.

HL: Welcome back... tell Henry I'm praying so hard that I have to use the dictionary to find new words to ask God to fix him.

RZ: Congrats on the milestone of making it back home in good condition. I agree for continued improvement. I won't visit, but if you give me a few days' notice, I'll be happy to drop off a healthy casserole.

RH: Amen. Amen. Amen. So happy to hear Henry is home. I pray the transition goes especially well. I pray those around Henry are able to help him where they can. I pray my incredible life-long friend, Vanessa, continues to be Henry's soul mate and caregiver. I pray traveling this journey with Henry and Vanessa teaches us all how precious life is, and we all need one another. I pray for healing, love, and peace. Amen.

CL: We are joyful and continuing in prayer for Henry. Tell him we love him! Give him two hugs, one from William, one from me.

Q: What did you think when you first saw me after my diagnosis?

IRA: Vanessa called ahead and asked me to pick you up from the airport. She told me by phone that whatever I saw, do not act surprised or alarmed. When I pulled up to the arrival area, I saw you sitting in a wheelchair. Even though it was the summer, you were wearing a heavy cotton tracksuit.

You needed to stand up to get into my car. It was when you stood that I saw the severity of the disease. From the front, you looked normal. Since you needed assistance walking and getting into my car, I helped you from the chair and supported your weight and your body as you made your way to your seat.

When I got next to your side, I was able to look behind you. There was nothing behind you. The tracksuit was just resting on your bones. You had no depth to your body. It was as if your face, arms, and legs appeared normal. But the reality was they were just a façade hiding the degree of stress your body had been suffering from. I made eye contact with Vanessa, and I immediately understood what she meant from our earlier phone call.

She was helping you on the other side of your body. I could see the concern in her eyes, but I could tell she had determined to be upbeat and positive regarding the welfare of her husband. Her courage inspired me. I knew that she had seen the worst for over a month. Yet, her resolve was resilient. She had taken the first blow of your illness. After the shock wore off, it was apparent that she had made up her mind to fight back. She was not going to be intimidated by what she saw. She was determined to walk by faith and not by sight.

I always knew that Vanessa loved you. It was not the frivolous love of young people who are propelled by emotion, but it was a love that began with her heart, yet it was rooted in the decision to love him no matter what happened. I saw her love for you at the wedding, but I could tell that her love for you had grown deeper. I knew that you were in good stead with her at your side.

Q: How did you feel when you first saw me after my diagnosis?
IRA: My first feeling when I saw you was a feeling of compassion. You had several physical problems in your youth. You were born with asthma. There were several times when we had a steamer in our bedroom for you to be able to breathe throughout the night. Whenever you had a cold, you needed to be rubbed with Vapor Rub and wrapped in your robe to keep the warmth around your torso.

Later you contracted a serious infection in the back of your head. In the '60s, the scalp disease called ringworm was passing around our community. When mom saw two large patches on your head, she placed a cap on your head so the disease would not spread to others. (Not a normal cap. It was a cap made from some type of cotton that had two straps attached to either side. Once the cap was on the head, you tied the straps underneath the chin to secure it.)

Unfortunately, Mom treated your head with some ointment and put a stocking cap on your head to wear overnight. Because you perspired overnight, the dye transferred to your scalp. As a result, the ringworm became infected. The two patches in your head began to have open sores that were filled with pus and fluid that would cause the cap to stick to your head. Whenever it had to be removed, you would let out a small cry. It took some time for those wounds to heal. When it was over, you had two bald spots on the back of your head. The hair follicles were gone, and all that remained were these glaring spots.

In high school, you decided to become a gymnast. You were an all-around competitor. This meant an all-around athlete competed on every piece of equipment. You were working on a double rotation dismount on the rings. Unfortunately, you did not complete the final rotation. Instead, your pointed toes slammed into the mat instead of the soles of your feet. Initially, you felt pain, but you walked it off. However, when we went home, your pain increased. When we arrived, our parents felt you needed a doctor to examine you.

When they took x-rays of your feet, you had fractured both feet. The force of you striking the mat was enough to create these injuries. You had to live with this injury during the competitive season for the gymnastic team. It was tough for you to just watch and not participate. You had experienced many physical setbacks early in your life.

But now, you were in for the fight of your life. I knew what kind of heart you possessed. I knew that you would give 100% to fighting this disease. I was sorry that you had another mountain to climb. I wanted you to know that this is what brotherhood is about. When you were down, I was available to pick you up.

Q: Was it difficult for you to see me in my physical condition?

IRA: It was difficult seeing you for the first time after your stay at the Cancer Treatment Centers of American in Chicago, Illinois. I had to remember what the Holy Spirit had witnessed to me two months previous. As bad as you looked, I was confident you would survive.

> *"Heal me, LORD, and I will be healed; save me and I will be saved, for you are the one I praise."*
> — Jeremiah 17:14, New International Version Bible

PART THREE:
MIDDLE PASSAGE
August 20, 2015 – November 15, 2015

"I keep sailing on in this middle passage. I am sailing into the wind and the dark. But I am doing my best to keep my boat steady and my sails full."

— Arthur Ashe

The Middle Passage

THE MIDDLE PASSAGE is known as the 300-year period in world history when more than 12 million Africans were taken by force from their homelands and enslaved in the "New World." It was called the Middle Passage because it was the second leg of a three-leg triangular sailing trade route.

The route started in Europe and went to Africa, where trading ships were filled to capacity with captured Africans (leg one). The vessel then traveled to the "New World," where the Africans were dropped off and sold into slavery, and the ships were filled with New World goods (leg two). Then the ships heavy-laden with cargo would sail back to Europe where the goods would be sold for tremendous gain (leg three).

Africans captured by other African tribes were traded to Europeans who had established trading posts on the West Coast of Africa. They were taken from what was familiar to miserable slave castles where they were placed in deplorable living conditions for about six months.

Anyone trying to escape was killed as an example to the others. Some of the women were raped by the commanding officer of the castle.

The slave castles served two purposes. First, they were used to hold the captives until the trading ships arrived from Europe. This was because it took about six months for the trading ships to complete the roundtrip journey back to Africa along the trade route.

Second, the deplorable living conditions and inhumane treatment were intended to physically weaken the captives and break their fighting spirit so they would be easier to manage as they were taken aboard the ships.

As horrible as the time spent in the slave castles was for the captured Africans, it was during the Middle Passage when Africans suffered the most traumatic part of their journey. They went from horrendous living conditions and cruel treatment into the unknown by way of a horrific and inhumane transatlantic crossing.

Many died at sea due to sickness or by jumping overboard if they had the chance. Only the strongest survived to be enslaved in a foreign land. It was truly by the grace of God that any survived the journey at all.

From Zion to a City of Hope: A Journey of Faith

Arthur Ashe, the first black tennis player to win the U.S. Open tournament and Wimbledon, referred to his life's journey as a black professional tennis player in the 1960's as a type of Middle Passage. In August 1969, he told *Sports Illustrated* he lived in an abnormal world where he felt like he was floating down the middle and was never quite sure where he was.

I view the time from late August 2015, until the end of November 2015, as the Middle Passage of my cancer journey. My Middle Passage is similar to the historical Middle Passage in that: 1) I had to leave the place that had become safe and familiar (Zion); 2) travel to an unknown place (City of Hope), and 3) do so with much uncertainty about the condition I would find myself in after the Middle Passage was over.

My Middle Passage is similar to Arthur Ashe's Middle Passage in that I did my best to keep my boat steady and my sails full throughout this transitional period.

It is not about the actual physical journey from Zion to City of Hope that I speak. Nor is it about leaving the known care of an excellent healthcare provider that saved my life and transitioning to receiving care from an unknown healthcare provider that I speak.

It is of my emotional and spiritual Middle Passage from Zion to City of Hope.

I speak of the emotional Middle Passage from a place of comfort to an unknown emotional place. A passage through anxiousness, feeling overwhelmed, and cautiousness challenged my need to make a timely critical decision.

I speak of the spiritual Middle Passage from a place of peace to an unknown spiritual place, a passage through times when my spirit was not at peace.

I do not know who the Africans prayed to during their Middle Passage. Likewise, I do not know if Arthur Ashe put his total trust in the supernatural to keep his boat steady and his sails full.

What I do know is that I put my trust in the One that, when a violent storm came upon the sea, rebuked the winds and the waves, and it became completely calm on the sea (Matthew 8:24-26). I did not know where I was going, but I trusted the Lord to guide my path and get me there.

> *"Then they cried out to the Lord in their trouble, and He delivered them from their distress. He led them on a straight path to reach a city where they could live."*
>
> — Psalm 107:6-7, Berean Study Bible

Middle Passage

Check-In at COH

City of Hope, Duarte, CA
August 20, 2015

TODAY I BECAME A NEW PATIENT AT CITY OF HOPE. It is located 8.5 miles driving distance from our house in Duarte, CA. Its proximity to our home is a true blessing. We can get there either by the freeway or on the surface streets in 15 minutes.

That was only the second time I had ever visited the cancer center's campus. I came here before to visit my aunt, who had received a Stem Cell Transplant. She too had been diagnosed with Multiple Myeloma. What a coincidence. She is my aunt by marriage, but I have a cousin and another biological uncle who both have been diagnosed with Multiple Myeloma.

We followed our driving directions to City of Hope and turned right onto Hope Drive, the main entrance to the campus. As we drove past the empty guard shack on the left, I read City of Hope's credo on a large metal sign on the right:

> *"There is no profit curing the body if in the process we destroy the soul."*

Wow, I thought to myself. *I think we've come to the right place.*

We arrived at the patient drop-off/pickup location at the end of Hope Drive, in front of a large artistic fountain. In the middle of the fountain was a large statue of a man, woman, and child entitled "Hope Rises." The man and woman are holding the child above their heads.

We used valet parking, and I got in a wheelchair. Vanessa pushed me from there into the entrance of the main medical hospital on campus (there are two hospitals on campus).

We were greeted at the main entrance desk by a member of the administrative staff and directed to a waiting room where new patient registration takes place. I was now somewhat familiar with the new patient registration process based on my experience at CTCA, so I did not question what would happen next – a lot of paperwork. So, I began to take in my surroundings while we were waiting for my name to be called.

For some reason, it seemed as though City of Hope was busier than CTCA. Many people – patients, caregivers, healthcare providers, and staff – were moving at what I perceived was a quickened pace. I knew this was not a fair comparison because I was moved into a hospital room so fast at CTCA that I didn't have time to notice much of anything.

But what did stand out was City of Hope appeared more business-like, more academic than CTCA. CTCA looked and felt more casual, more personable. I knew all of this had very little to do with the level of care I anticipated I would receive. It was just an observation.

At hand, the main business was registration and seeing how my treatment plan prepared at CTCA would be carried out at City of Hope. CTCA was still my primary care provider and would supervise City of Hope as they follow CTCA's plan. While at CTCA, I had expressed concerns about who would be my oncologist at City of Hope and how well the doctor would understand the treatment I had received at CTCA.

CTCA, Zion IL
August 10, 2015

As part of the discharge and planning conversations, Vanessa and I met with my doctors to discuss my remote care in California. It was vital for me to understand how this was going to work. We met with both Dr. Abutalib and Dr. Redei during my outpatient treatment. It was during this conversation that I expressed my concerns.

"We need to discuss what will happen when you return to California," Dr. Redei began.

"Yes, I want to know where I will receive treatment and who my oncologist will be," I replied.

"Well, we spoke to your family doctor, and she said City of Hope in Duarte is where she referred you to first, and she thinks you should receive treatments there," he replied. "We have contacted City of Hope to discuss your case. They are prepared to provide your continuing care."

"That's good," Vanessa said. "We wanted to go there first, but none of the oncology doctors were available."

"Well, things have changed," Dr. Redei replied. "A doctor is now available and is prepared to take you on as a patient."

"Do you know much about him?" I asked.

"Yes, as a matter of fact, I do," said Dr. Abutalib. "I am working on a book about bone marrow transplantation as one of the authors, and he is one of the contributors to the book."

"So, you know him personally?" I asked.

"Yes, I do. He is an excellent doctor," Dr. Abutalib replied. "I called him, and we have discussed your case."

I felt much better learning Dr. Abutalib knew the doctor at City of Hope personally. I felt in my spirit that God was navigating the circumstances in my life and my healing.

"So, how will this work?" Vanessa asked.

"Well, you will still be a patient here at CTCA," Dr. Redei replied. "We will come up with your treatment plan and supervise its implementation at City of Hope. You will return here when the time comes for your Stem Cell Transplant."

"When do you think that will be?" I asked.

"It depends on how you respond to the treatments," Dr. Abutalib answered. "We have planned for chemotherapy treatments until the end of the year. We will do an evaluation at that time."

"I see," I replied. I was beginning to process the fact that I would be receiving chemotherapy treatments through the end of the year.

"We will not discharge you until everything in California is ready and your physical therapist says you are ready to leave," Dr. Redei said.

"Okay, well, thank you," I said. "Do you have any other questions, Vanessa?" I asked.

"Not now," she replied. "But I'm sure I will have some later after I think about it."

"Okay, we will talk again soon," said Dr. Redei.

City of Hope, Duarte, CA
August 20, 2015

At the end of our discussions at CTCA, everyone understood that CTCA was still in charge of my case. I would see City of Hope as my local case manager following instructions from CTCA. I felt at ease knowing CTCA was still in charge. After all, they were the ones who, through God's grace, had saved my life.

We set this arrangement up primarily because the logistics of continuing to receive treatment at CTCA was impractical. Taking all of this into consideration, I was very comfortable with the arrangement.

After I registered as a patient, we went on a tour of City of Hope. We saw the two hospitals on campus, the outpatient treatment areas, the pharmacy, the main lab, and the places on campus where we could get something to eat. We finished the day with a trip back to the main lab to have my blood drawn.

Not bad for the first day, I thought.

Vanessa Foster-Dotson
August 21, 2015

*** Update for Thursday, 08/20/15:

Success! One goal for Thursday was to take another step towards adjusting to being back home. We awoke very early. Henry completed his morning activities, and then we were off to his first oncology appointment in California. This was a new patient appointment at City of Hope. It took a lot of persistence to get this appointment.

But at last, it became a reality. And at 5:30 p.m., we finally received a call for Henry's next chemo treatment. It will be on the exact day that we needed it to be. For various reasons, we had been pushing for these appointments for weeks. So, Thursday was a good day.

Henry again was pretty quiet. His appetite was still good, but he went to sleep very soon after we returned from his appointment. Please pray that Henry's strength and energy level increase. God Bless!

👍 43 Seen by 45   13 Comments

CP Praying for Henry can do all things through Christ who strengthens him in Jesus' Name!

VP Henry. Keep your faith. God sits high and looks low!!! We r family!! Love you guys.

BC Hang in there Brother Henry! God is testing your patience every day... remember that the race is a marathon and not a sprint. Continuing to send love and prayers to all of you!

RH One day at a time. Keep up the effort, Henry. You are amazing! Love you guys!

VH Yay for Henry! He truly is an amazing, extraordinary person. His strength will return, but chemo does tire a person out very quickly, and getting enough rest is imperative. Sleep is healing and restorative. One day at a time, Vanessa, truly one day at a time. I'm speaking from experience, as you know. Stay prayerful.

August 22, 2015

I RECEIVED MY FIRST CHEMOTHERAPY TREATMENT AT CITY OF HOPE ON FRIDAY. It was very similar to the chemotherapy treatments I received as an outpatient at CTCA. The main difference was the treatment area at City of Hope, and the waiting room was larger than the respective areas at CTCA.

It looked more like a hospital, whereas CTCA looked and felt more... comfy. I think I will be making these mental comparisons for a while until I get comfortable with my new setting.

I was a little sluggish on Friday. I attributed it to the wear and tear of travel and getting settled back at home. But when we arrived at City of Hope, we were told I had a persistent fever. So, I received a broad-spectrum antibiotic in addition to the chemotherapy medication. The nurse merely added another bag to what was given to me intravenously.

I felt better by Saturday. I am beginning to realize the new normal may include getting some help for my immune system when fighting off some kind of bug. Thank God something can be done when I need help.

 Vanessa Foster-Dotson
August 23, 2015

*** Update for Fri, 08/21 - Sat, 08/22/15:

Things change so quickly. When we were at the doctor's office on Thursday, they detected that Henry had a slight fever. As a result, a blood culture was performed as a routine precaution. We woke up and got dressed very early on Friday as we prepared for Henry's first chemo treatment in California. Yes!!!

Henry had a 7 a.m. appointment, first lab work, and then treatment; the new routine. When I took his temperature at home that morning, Henry still had a fever, so I was relieved that he was going in for treatment.

Once at his appointment, the lab work also confirmed that Henry still had a fever. I had been told in the past that fevers are relatively common since Henry's immune system was compromised. But the fevers do have to be addressed. So, in addition to receiving his chemo treatment on Friday, Henry also received antibiotics to fight his fever.

By Saturday, Henry's fever had disappeared, and he was feeling much better. His appetite had improved, and he was very alert. His

continued

appetite had improved, and he was very alert. His breathing is still a bit labored, but all of his breathing-related readings are in order. We will have a discussion regarding Henry's breathing the next time that we see the doc.

While Henry was getting his treatment, I was able to attend my first work-related conference call. It appears that a lot has changed since I was gone, so I have some catching up to do. I work with a great team. They are extremely supportive. I am very thankful!

Henry and I are truly blessed in so many ways! We knew that we were blessed before, but our blessings have become even more apparent since we have returned to CA. The love and caring that have been demonstrated by so many of you have been tremendous. One example was provided by Lois who was kind enough to perform some errands for us. How awesome is that?! Thank you so much, Lois!

I realize that being back home is more difficult than being in Illinois. When we were in Illinois, I did not need to focus on the normal at-home tasks. My main goal was to do all that I could to support Henry's fight and then get back here.

But now that we are back, it is amazing how much has to be done in addition to helping Henry with fighting his battle. Sure, before we returned, I knew that life would be more demanding, but WOW! Now, please know that I am not overwhelmed, so there is no need to worry about me. I do know that taking care of me is part of taking care of Henry.

As a result, I am becoming more comfortable with asking for and accepting help. We are just so blessed that so many of you are willing to help. "Thank you" does not begin to express how much we appreciate your demonstrations of love.

Thank you so very much!

Prayer Requests:

1. Complete healing for Henry: body, mind, soul, and spirit. (no cancer, no pain, no long-term anemia, no permanent back damage, no fevers, no infections, etc.)
2. Easy transition to being in California
3. Stabilized blood counts...all counts being positive
4. Stabilized kidney counts
5. Improved strength and movement

continued

General prayer for all of the family members and friends of anyone that is reading this update and has recently been diagnosed or is suffering from cancer or some other life-threatening health challenge.

Prayers Answered:

1. Healthy kidneys
2. Healthy eyes
3. Increased platelet count
4. Clarity of thoughts and words
5. Exponential blood count level increase
6. Improved appetite
7. Renewed spirit
8. Release from CTCA and return home

👍 39 Seen by 57   11 Comments

ML Great news! Still praying for you both.

DK Welcome back! Thank you, Lord Jesus, for healing Henry's body, mind, and soul, strengthen Vanessa and meet all their needs in Jesus' name, amen!

RH Amen. It's a lot to deal with, Vanessa. Glad you're letting others help. Very proud of your breakthrough! Love you guys! Praying for Henry.

SB I can just hear the praise team singing: "God is" He does not change, but we do. Wait on the Lord! Be Still...

RH Thank you for sharing. I'm praying for Henry and the other people in my life who have received a cancer diagnosis this summer. I pray for God's healing mercy. Love you guys!

Q: What did you think when you first saw me after my diagnosis?

LOIS: It wasn't immediately that I saw you after your diagnosis. I saw you before you went to the Cancer Treatment Centers of America in Chicago, and while I knew you were in pain, you basically looked the same. However, when I did see you on your return, I was shocked, though I didn't want to show it. You looked very bad, very ill, very dark. I didn't know what to say or think. You looked like death warmed over, and I knew you didn't feel well.

Q: How did you feel when you first saw me after my diagnosis?

LOIS: I felt terrible seeing you in that condition. I honestly didn't know about your healing at that point.

Q: Was it difficult for you to see me in my physical condition?

LOIS: Yes, of course it was difficult! I didn't know if I should go on believing God for your healing or just give assent to praying along with you. It was very hard, but I decided I wanted to stand in the gap for you and not allow myself the option of giving up on my prayers and standing with you!

August 24, 2015

I STARTED MAKING A FEW CALLS TO FAMILY AND FRIENDS TO THANK THEM AND TO RECONNECT. I did not want to be overwhelmed with calls, so this was a "Don't call us, we'll call you" arrangement. It was great to hear familiar voices, but it was more tiring than I had anticipated. I think it was because I was doing most of the talking on each call.

People seemed more concerned about my condition than they were about sharing with me what was going on with them. I guess I should have expected it, but I hadn't thought about it before making the calls.

We did receive one special and memorable call. It was from our pastor, Ed Smith, and his wife, Vanessa. Vanessa and I got on the call at the same time to speak with them. The most important thing that happened on that call was they prayed over us and gave us words of encouragement. Exactly what we needed to hear. After the call, my burden did not seem as heavy. Oh, the power of prayer!

Vanessa Foster-Dotson
August 25, 2015

*** Update for Sun, 08/23 - Mon, 08/24/15:

Henry remained pretty alert on Sunday and Monday. He was even able to talk a bit more to a few family members and friends. However, he is still very weak and continues to get tired quickly. Most that have spoken to Henry have stated that he seems good for all that he has been through.

But they do notice that he has not yet returned to being the talkative, fun-loving, and full-of-life guy that they are accustomed to. So, although Henry has made significant progress over the last month-plus, the road that he is traveling is definitely a marathon and not a sprint. Thank you for your continued prayers!

On Monday, Henry was blessed to receive prayer from the pastor and first lady of our church...Pastor Ed and First Lady Vanessa Smith. Outstanding! I am confident that their words of encouragement and support will aid in Henry's path to full recovery. Thank you, Pastor Ed and First Lady, for who you are and everything that you have done to support us!

Now, I know that these updates are about Henry, and I do not want to take the focus away from him. However, I have been led for several weeks to mention some of the people around us that are facing health challenges. Absolutely unbelievable! I will list some of the challenges below just to illustrate my point.

Henry asks me for a status update on at least one of them most mornings. Please do not be discouraged if you read the list. Most of the people that are mentioned are believers, and they will have victory one way or another. I am sure that you know others that you can add to the list as well. Totally unbelievable! The storm.

I am not sure why all of these challenges are occurring at approximately the same time, but God knows. One thing that comes to my mind is that each of us should not take ANYONE for granted. Tomorrow is not promised. Let your family and friends know that you love AND appreciate them. Search deep within and take the focus off of yourself. Do all that you can to nurture and cherish the precious relationships that you have been given. Also, appreciate your numerous blessings...no matter how small.

These are just my thoughts. Next time, back to Henry.

continued

WE ARE ALL SO TRULY BLESSED!

*** Challenges in July and August ***

1. Henry's Aunt is fighting colon cancer and had surgery in July.
2. Henry's Uncle is fighting Multiple Myeloma and his chemo treatment increased in July.
3. Henry's other Aunt recently received a Stem Cell Transplant to fight her Multiple Myeloma.
4. In July, yet another Aunt of Henry's had an aneurism.
5. One of my Aunts became unresponsive in July.
6. In July, the father of my "play little brother" was diagnosed with Stage 3 kidney failure as well as lung damage.
7. Our matron-of-honor, and my very, very close friend, was diagnosed with ovarian cancer in July and started chemo treatment on Monday. While undergoing her treatment, she texted me to see how Henry was doing.
8. Another close friend was diagnosed with breast cancer in July, and her husband received the news that his mother passed just a few hours before his wife's lumpectomy surgery last Wednesday.
9. The husband of a dear co-worker is fighting an advanced stage of pancreatic cancer.
10. A close family member is battling an advanced stage of brain cancer.
11. A close friend passed away in her sleep at age 51 last week—no major prior illness. On August 5th, she had just sent me a picture of the two of us and one other person on the mission field in South Africa. She said, "This is my favorite picture." In July, she had helped me by organizing a gift basket for the medical staff at CTCA.
12. The middle son of two very close friends (the wife has been my prayer partner since 2001) was released from the hospital on Monday after fighting a blood-related disorder for 38 days.
13. Last week, the dear friend that told Henry about CTCA received what is hopefully her last chemo treatment before going into remission. She was told by her local doctor in November of 2014 that she had a 20% survival rate from her ovarian cancer. Look at God!

29   Seen by 42   13 Comments

TM: We thank God and continue to pray for him.

GT: Praise God for his healing power, no matter what it looks like. Glad for Henry's progress one day at a time.

VH: This is loss and a lot of adversity, Vanessa; and I am sorry for your loss, but happy to hear of the victories! But God! One thing that I've learned is that everything happens in God's time, not ours. We just have to keep trusting and believing, no matter what the outcome.

LW: We are praying for peace, comfort, and healing for you, Henry, and all who are touched by cancer.

RH: Thank you for sharing. I'm praying for Henry and the other people in my life who have received a cancer diagnosis this summer. I pray for God's healing mercy. Love you guys!

Sandra

One other person I reached out to was Sandra, our longtime friend and housekeeper. She and her crew come in every two weeks to take care of the routine house cleaning. As a result, she was one of the few people that would see me regularly after my return from CTCA. I asked her to answer a questionnaire to give her perspective on this journey.

Q: How did you hear about my diagnosis?
SANDRA: You told me about your diagnosis in August 2015.

Q: Had you heard of multiple myeloma before hearing of my diagnosis?
SANDRA: I had heard of Multiple Myeloma before your diagnosis from a dear friend of mine who lost his life to Multiple Myeloma.

Q: How did you feel when you learned of my diagnosis?
SANDRA: I felt petrified upon hearing of your diagnosis, especially since I had lost that dear friend to the same disease.

Q: When did you understand how serious my condition was?
SANDRA: I understood how serious your condition because of my dear friend.

Q: What did you think when you first saw me after my diagnosis?
SANDRA: I thought I might lose you when I saw you after your diagnosis.

Q: How did you feel when you first saw me after my diagnosis?
SANDRA: I felt sympathy, pity, and hopelessness after I saw you.

Q: Was it difficult for you to see me in my physical condition?
SANDRA: It was extremely difficult for me to see you in such an atrophied state. I couldn't believe that this happened to you so fast, and just to watch the disease rapidly eat you up was painful to watch.

Q: Did you ever seriously question my survival?
SANDRA: Yes. I did question that you would survive through such a terrible disease.

One Last Assault

"We do not lose heart. Though outwardly we are wasting away, yet inwardly we are being renewed day by day. For our light and momentary troubles are achieving for us an eternal glory that far outweighs them all."
— 2 Corinthians 4:16-17, New International Version Bible

City of Hope, Duarte, CA
August 25, 2015

TODAY WE FOUND OUT THAT MY FEVER IS DUE TO RESIDUAL INFECTION. More test results came in from the blood culture taken on Thursday. I have a residual infection from either the C-Diff or Staph bacteria I picked up at CTCA. It could be life-threatening! I was admitted to City of Hope for further treatment.

I am very disappointed. I was looking forward to getting home and settling down, getting adjusted to the "new normal." Instead, I am back in the hospital again. But I am determined not to let my disappointment have a negative effect on my attitude.

I keep reminding myself of three things: 1) my attitude is the only thing I can control; 2) people with a positive attitude have better outcomes than people who don't, and 3) God will not give me more than I can bear. Despite this unexpected turn of events, it is no surprise to God.

I will be in the hospital until the infection has cleared up. My doctor wants to know if any damage has occurred due to the infections since they have persisted for so long. Since both infections are in my bloodstream, my doctor wants to make sure there has been no damage to my lungs or heart.

He has ordered chest x-rays, an MRI, and a Trans Esophageal Echocardiogram ("T-E-E" for short). I know what the first two procedures are, but I have never heard of a T-E-E. I will cross that bridge when I get to it. The T-E-E procedure was scheduled for tomorrow, but later this evening, it was moved to Friday…and so it begins.

Vanessa Foster-Dotson
August 26, 2015

*** Update for Tues, 08/25:

And the beat goes on! Life has not been quite what we hoped. We were really looking forward to getting back to California and getting adjusted to our "new norm." Instead, we have seen various doctors every day since Henry's fever was detected. And yes, after taking antibiotics, Henry's fever did break. However, with additional testing, it has been determined that the fever resulted from yet another infection. My heart aches for Henry. He just wants to reestablish his life.

Henry is doing all that he can to "get back to normal." He is eating. He is exercising. He is engaging in conversations about his health when asked by various doctors. But his body is giving him challenges. I know that these challenges can be common with Multiple Myeloma but still, I ask why. Why does Multiple Myeloma even have to exist? Why did Henry have to get Multiple Myeloma? Sure, Henry says, "Why not me?" But I still ask why. And why was Henry led to take the road from California to Illinois to California for treatment? We are trying not to compare, but the medical staff and procedures at City of Hope are quite different from those at CTCA. It is really taking a lot of effort and restraint to get used to the staff at City of Hope.

The good news is that Henry's new doctor wrote a chapter in the medical textbook that is being written by Henry's doctor at CTCA. So, they at least know each other, and we have asked that they discuss Henry's treatment. What a great "coincidence." Favor!

Each day I wonder what does God have in store for Henry's life after he overcomes all of this? Only time will tell.

We found out late on Tuesday that Henry will be receiving a procedure on Wednesday to try to determine the source of his infection. Please pray that the procedure is successful and that all infections are removed from his body permanently.

God Bless!

👍 29   Seen by 47   27 Comments

   Praying every day, Cousins! Love you!

   God is Able! I shall continually be praying with you.

I trust that God will continue to strengthen you as you go through this fight of faith. We know that these fiery darts are from the enemy, BUT GOD raises us up in the STORM. One saint PRAYING will put 1000 of the enemies to flight, but you have a mighty ARMY of PRAYER WARRIORS who are making MILLIONS of the enemies to FLEE from HENRY. May the GOD OF PEACE REST UPON YOU. XOXOXO for You and Henry.

I love you both and praying for you both for strength, courage, endurance, and patience with each other and the medical staff in California. As we pray, keep holding on to God's Unchanging Hands. Draw your strength from God, and he will bring you through and even reveal his will for you both.

Cry. Cleanse your soul and come back renewed. For Joy does come in the morning. Find comfort in the small things. Love and prayers.

I need to share this. It was shared with me this morning—it is sufficient food from the Lord. God says Trust Me in the midst of a messy day. Your inner calm/ your Peace in My Presence need not be shaken by what is going on around you. Though you live in this temporal world, your innermost being is rooted and grounded in eternity. When you start to feel stressed, detach yourself from the disturbances around you. Instead of desperately striving to maintain order and control in your little world, RELAX and remember that circumstances cannot touch My Peace.

Seek My Face, and I will share my mind with you, opening your eyes to see things from My perspective. Do not let your heart be troubled, and do not be afraid. The peace I give is sufficient for you.

John 16:33 — "I have told you these things, so that in me you may have peace. In this world you will have trouble. But take heart! I have overcome the world."

Psalm 105:4 — "Look to the Lord and His strength; seek his face always."

John: 14:27 — "Peace I leave with you; my peace I give you. I do not give to you as the world gives. Do not let your hearts be troubled, and do not be afraid."

CP The blood of Jesus has never lost its power. Vanessa Foster-Dotson, your husband and you are covered by the blood. Henry is an heir of the King, and he is healed of all infection. Begin to command all infection gone and delete all doubt.

Vanessa, words may never express the depth of what you are feeling, but God knows. Walk in your authority this very moment for Henry. This too will pass, Sis. Saturate yourself in only the word of God with prayer.

AM We continue to pray and trust God for his complete healing. You are not alone; you will always have our support; stay strong.

CC You are completely healed in the name of JESUS. You and Henry will be great advocates for others with similar health issues.

VS Yes! I am praying for you. And may our God manifest himself to you in such a BIG way that you have no question that it is him!

PM Vanessa, I've walked in your shoes, so believe me, I feel your frustration. It's impossible to pass through life without experiencing times when you cannot see your way through a deep valley.

When you are caught in the grip of affliction, you may be going through some of the hardest days of your life. You may be wondering, Why? Why me? Why this trial?

When you persevere through a trial, the reward is that God gives you a special measure of insight. You become the recipient of the favor of God as He gives to you something that would not be learned otherwise.

You and Henry stay strong like the warriors that you are. God will bring you through this storm.

CB It's already done; he is healed and has been healed. The healing continues to manifest day by day throughout his body, from his head to his toes. Jesus didn't die on the cross for nothing!!!

KI Henry is a strong man. I pray for him every day. He is the big brother I never had. We love you all.

You are experiencing all normal emotions, thoughts, and doubts. I'm sorry, no one has the answers yet. It's a journey. Take one day at a time. I know it's overwhelming looking long-term and or at the unknown.

I, too, say why Henry. He is a special, kind, lovable, faithful man. We don't have the answer yet. We will in time. I know there's no wisdom or words that will comfort you. You both are in God's hands, and I know you are excellent emotional and knowledgeable support for your husband. Hugs to you both.

Q: How did you feel when you learned I needed to be admitted to the hospital after returning to California?

BART: Honestly, I was dismayed but not afraid. You had made it through the worst, and I was confident that you would continue to recover.

TALIA: I was concerned. I thought maybe we were doing something wrong or had been careless. I was reminded again of how delicate your body was at one point.

Q: How did you feel when you learned I had residual lethal infections after returning to California?

BART: I remember learning about the lethal infections after knowing that they were lethal. At the time, I realized that there were further complications, but I didn't realize that there was a significant possibility of your passing.

TALIA: I was worried but honestly felt as though the largest obstacle had been crossed. As I mentioned before, through this whole process, there was an overwhelming sense of peace and comfort, as though things would be alright, so when I heard about the infection, I was worried about you potentially becoming more physically debilitated, but I was not afraid.

Vanessa Foster-Dotson
August 26, 2015

*** Update for Tues, 08/25, Continued:

Henry's procedure was moved to Friday. Not sure about the exact time as yet. Thanks!

 8   Seen by 14   1 Comment

   We will continue to pray Ephesians 6:10 — *"Strong in the Lord and the power of His Might."*

Vanessa, your husband is more than a conqueror (Romans 8:37).

City of Hope, Duarte, CA
August 27, 2015

TODAY WE FOUND OUT THAT I WILL NEED RADIATION TREATMENTS FOR MY SPINE. I will also need a back brace to support my spine. The radiation treatments are intended to eliminate the Multiple Myeloma cells in my spine.

We spoke to the radiation doctor, and he said I would need to undergo radiation treatments for 12 consecutive days. I thought back to when I would take my sister to her radiation treatments for breast cancer. Each treatment itself was not bad, but the side effects were very difficult for her.

She had radiation burns that were cumulative very painful. She also felt sicker after each treatment. I know each person is different in terms of how effective treatments are and the side effects they experience. Still, my sister's experience made me think my experience could be a significant hurdle to overcome.

Again, I focused on my attitude. I reminded myself that I was not in control, but God is. That reminder lifted my spirit.

We were also visited for the first time by Dr. Chen, the neurosurgeon assigned to my case. I liked Dr. Chen from the beginning. He was, in some ways, matter-of-fact, but he gave us all the facts and answered all of our questions.

I asked Dr. Chen, "Can you explain a little more what is going on and how the brace will protect my spine?"

"Well," said Dr. Chen, "Think of your spine as a sapling tree. It is very long compared to its thickness, and it has a good part of its weight at the top. Now picture a dent in the tree. The tree will begin to bend over at the point where the dent is because it is unable to support the weight above the dent.

Left unchecked, the tree would eventually bend until it breaks. To correct the problem, a gardener will put a splint on the tree to give it more support and allow it to heal as it grows.

In your case, the weight is at the top is your head. It weighs about 10 pounds. The back brace will act in the same way as the splint would on a damaged tree. It will help keep you upright and not continue to bend over."

I understood completely. It was just physics and a little mechanical engineering statics; both I had studied in engineering school. God knows how to speak to his people in ways they understand. All in all, I am up for the challenge, and I want to see what God will do.

Vanessa Foster-Dotson
August 28, 2015

*** Update for Wed, 08/26-Thurs, 08/27:

> "But Christ, as the Son, is in charge of God's entire house. And we are God's house, if we keep our courage and remain confident in our hope in Christ." — Hebrews 3:6

> "And we know that in all things God works for the good of those who love Him, who have been called according to His purpose." — Romans 8:28

> "The sufferings of this present time are not worth comparing to the glory that is to come." — Romans 8:18

As I read these scriptures/words, I find encouragement. This week has been trying. But they dictate, and Henry's attitude is that "God's got this!" Henry has total faith that God is directing the path of the doctors and his healing. I have faith as well, but I still struggle at times with the realities of all that is happening.

On Wednesday, Henry did not get the procedure for the infection that he had been fasting for. Instead, he received an MRI of his back/spine. Also, on Wednesday, Talia stopped by. We were both truly blessed!

On Thursday, results from the MRI came back, and it was determined that, in an effort to avoid pain, Henry has been leaning forward more than he had in the previous MRI, which was taken at CTCA. Continued leaning would start having a negative effect on his spine.

Instead, the surgeon ordered a hard-case back brace to replace Henry's existing brace. The goal is that the brace will allow the compression fractures in Henry's back to heal properly. Once the diseased cells that are near his spine are removed, the leaning should go away.

continued

The radiation doctor stated Henry needed to undergo 12 days of radiation to remove the diseased cells that are near his spine. The radiation will be more focused than the chemo.

However, since Myeloma is a blood-related disease and blood goes throughout your body, Henry still needs to maintain his chemotherapy. So, on Friday, Henry will have three procedures:1) infection-related procedure, 2) radiation, and 3) chemotherapy.

One good thing on Thursday is that the PRELIMINARY results of Henry's latest blood culture indicated that his infection might be gone. Yes!!! Hopefully, we will know more on Friday.

Meanwhile, I am placing an increased amount of focus on work. I enjoy my work, so it's pretty nice to be back. Fortunately, I can do quite a bit of my work from home.

Thank you again for your prayers and support! "God's got this!" One day at a time.

RIP Millie, Jeff, Rickey, and Mrs. "Carr"

👍 33   Seen by 43   14 Comments

RH Thanking God for answering all prayers. Thank you for the update. Go, Henry! Love you guys!

DK Henry, the battle is not yours; it's the Lord's! Keep walking by faith and not by sight, trusting the Lord all the way, to meet all your needs in Jesus' name, amen! Love you guys xoxo.

PM You are such a blessing to Henry and his prayer team. Thank you for so diligently keeping us informed. I look forward to your updates, even though I know that you are extremely busy.

God is blessing you in so many ways. Especially with your job and that you have the flexibility to work and care for Henry. I wish I were there so I could offer you a respite and some "me" time for yourself.

KI God is good all the time, and all the time, God is good!

CC You may have tried this already but, attach a cushioned pad to his back brace, especially around the edges. It should help reduce it being uncomfortable. I love you both!

City of Hope, Duarte, CA
August 28, 2015

TransEsophageal Echocardiogram

My oncologist is concerned about the extent of the damage caused by the infections I have in my blood. He is most concerned about any damage to my heart. He wants me to undergo a procedure called a "transesophageal echocardiogram" to rule out endocarditis – a life-threatening inflammation of the inner lining of the heart's chambers and valves.

Dr. Tran from Cardiology came to visit me in my hospital room to discuss the procedure. He had a calm demeanor and explained the entire procedure with a very scholarly tone.

"The Transesophageal Echocardiogram, also known as T-E-E, is a procedure used to determine if there is any infection in your heart. This is done by looking at an echocardiogram, which is an ultrasound of the heart. We can detect infection by seeing the way blood flows through your heart.

The difference between how blood flows in an infected heart and a non-infected heart is very small, so we need to get the probe as close as possible to your heart. That is why a probe is inserted in your esophagus."

"So, what exactly does the procedure entail?" I asked.

"Well, the probe is attached to the end of a cable about the size of a garden hose. The probe is inserted…"

"Surely, I will be sedated when this procedure is done," I interrupted. I could not imagine myself being awake when a garden hose is pushed down my throat.

"Oh no, Mr. Dotson," Dr. Tran replied. "You must be awake. We have to make sure your airway is not blocked, so we need to see that you are breathing on your own. We will give you a general anesthesia to calm you down, but you will be awake."

I could tell this was not going to be pleasant. Dr. Tran continued with his explanation, but I was not paying any attention to what he was saying. My mind was fixated on the thought of a garden hose being pushed down my throat.

My attention returned to what Dr. Tran was saying when he told me, "We have scheduled the procedure for later this afternoon."

"Hmmm," I said. "I'd like to think about it." That was the only time I ever considered not having a procedure done.

"Okay," said Dr. Tran. "We will check with you later to see what you want to do."

Vanessa came by later to visit, and we discussed the procedure. We agreed that

I needed to do it, so I would just have to get through it the best I could. I prayed silently for strength.

The T-E-E procedure was scheduled to take place shortly after my radiation treatment. Getting up and down from the radiation table left my back aching. An orderly returned me to my room with just enough time to speak with Vanessa before another orderly came to take me to my T-E-E procedure.

I was placed on a gurney and wheeled into the procedure room. I saw Dr. Tran, along with two others who would be assisting him. They were engaged in small talk as if this was a simple non-surgical procedure – a piece of cake. I was given a small dose of Ativan as general anesthesia. Shortly after that, Dr. Tran said he was ready to begin.

When I saw the actual probe, it looked like it was much bigger than a garden hose. I thought to myself; *He will never get that down my throat!*

But, I was surprised at how much my throat expanded. It was the same sensation I've felt when I've swallowed a large portion of food in one gulp. Only this time, the feeling did not go away. I was also surprised that I was not gagging. I was just trying to breathe.

Dr. Tran and the others continued to make small talk as the probe made its way down my throat. The probe came to a halt about halfway down my esophagus.

As Dr. Tran asked the team what they planned to do that weekend, I felt the probe make a turn to the left. I could feel the probe under my heart! It was a very eerie and uncomfortable feeling. It felt like something was pressing up against my heart from the inside.

As I heard about plans to go to the beach and other weekend activities, a tear rolled down my left cheek. I said to myself, *This is what I imagine it would have felt like just before the creature popped out of the astronaut's chest in the movie, Alien.*

I don't know how long the probe rested against my heart. I could feel Dr. Tran rotating it from one position to another. I just concentrated on breathing and not on what I was feeling.

Finally, I heard Dr. Tran say, "We're done."

Removing the probe was almost as uncomfortable as its insertion.

"Good job, everyone!" he added, "Enjoy your weekend." He looked at me and said, "You did just fine, Mr. Dotson."

An orderly came shortly after that and wheeled me back to my room. Vanessa was there waiting for me. After I was situated back in bed, Vanessa asked me, "So how was it?"

I thought about my mother's colonoscopy and said, "They hadn't ought treat people that way."

The T-E-E has been the most difficult procedure I have gone through to date.

The good news is the results came back quickly. By the grace of God, there was no infection in my heart! I praised Him for the victory and for seeing me through the procedure.

Vanessa Foster-Dotson
August 29, 2015

*** Update for Friday, 08/28:

Friday was busy but relatively successful. Henry's infection-related procedure revealed that Henry does not have any infection near his heart. Thank you, Jesus! In addition, his last two blood cultures are still providing PRELIMINARY indications that his infection has cleared up. Unfortunately, he now has another infection.

Henry's radiation treatment was a bit rough. To situate Henry appropriately, he was moved around quite a bit. His brace had to be taken off and put back on. His back was very irritated when he finished the treatment.

Meanwhile, Henry's chemo treatment was becoming routine, a shot in the belly and a few pills. The main side effects from the chemo thus far seem to be hair loss along with dry and darkened skin and some fatigue.

The day ended with a long overdue, heart-to-heart conversation with Henry's oncologist. Let's just say that we are still adjusting to being in California.

With the huge exception of the pain that Henry suffered in his back, Friday was a productive day. One day closer to complete healing! God continues to hear our prayers. Thank you!

 32   Seen by 37   13 Comments

 Stay strong! Healing and breakthrough are coming! Jesus did it through His stripes!

 Know about the fatigue, rest when you can, and don't try to go too fast. God has all the time in the world to complete this healing miracle. During the downtime, try to discover just what it is that God is saying, trying to teach or affirming in your spirit. There is something special that God is doing. Discover what it is and be Blessed.

 Blessings and tests each and every day... and we rarely notice one without the other. Continued prayers for all of you!

Vanessa, that radiation is rough. And Henry's body is going through serious changes. But remember. God has the light shining at the end of the tunnel!!!! Keep your faith. Give God the glory. He is an awesome God. Thank you, God!!!!!

 Vanessa, expect Henry to be very tired from the radiation. Also, get some Eucurin lotion to smooth on his skin in between treatments from the chemo and radiation. However, don't do it too close before the radiation, or he will suffer from serious burns. Love you both.

August 30, 2015

I RECEIVED MY SECOND AND THIRD RADIATION TREATMENTS THIS WEEKEND. My first treatment was on Friday, but I really did not pay much attention to it because of my traumatic experience with the T-E-E procedure.

The radiation treatment itself only lasts five minutes, tops. It is also painless. On the other hand, it takes 15 minutes to get from my hospital room onto the radiation table, and another 10 minutes to get back to my hospital room.

Getting on and off of the radiation table is a bit complicated and painful. Before I can get on the table, I have to remove my back brace. It has several straps and snaps that take time to remove. Once the brace is removed, my spine is no longer supported, and I have to climb up on the table.

It is the getting on and getting off the table that is most difficult. Trying to maneuver without causing my back to hurt is nearly impossible. I don't mind the pain so much as I don't want to damage my spinal cord. I am most vulnerable without my brace, and I can tell that I have lost the support that it gives me.

I am just thankful I only have 12 treatments planned. Three down and nine to go. I can do all things through Christ who strengthens me.

 Vanessa Foster-Dotson
August 31, 2015

*** Update for Saturday, 08/29 - Sunday 08/30/15:

A time for recharge and renewed faith. The weekend was basically uneventful. Henry continued to recover from his infections. He was alert, talkative, and God-focused. On Saturday, Henry started the morning by listening to sermons. He has total faith that God is leading every step of his recovery.

continued

Henry's face is a bit smaller than it had been in May, but it is still full and vibrant. His beautiful smile is still brightening my world! Now that his back is secured with the brace, He's doing a bit more walking. We spent time on Saturday watching movies, and on Sunday we watched TV. It was nice to just enjoy being with each other.

A peaceful weekend! Much needed.

Prayer Requests:

1. Complete healing for Henry: body, mind, soul, and spirit. (no cancer, no pain, no long-term anemia, no permanent back damage, no fevers, no infections.)
2. Easy transition to being in California
3. Stabilized blood counts…all counts being positive
4. Stabilized kidney counts
5. Improved strength and movement
6. General prayer for all of the family members and friends of anyone that is reading this update and has recently been diagnosed or is suffering from cancer or some other life-threatening health challenge.

Prayers Answered:

1. Healthy kidneys
2. Healthy eyes
3. Increased platelet count
4. Clarity of thoughts and words
5. Exponential blood count level increase
6. Improved appetite
7. Renewed spirit
8. Release from CTCA and return home

Praise God! Let me know when he is feeling up to some company. Tell him my mom and I love him.

I am always touched and inspired by your updates. My prayers continue to be with you all.

PM Thank God who is not only hearing our prayers but also is answering them. We can look forward to the latter list being longer than the former. Amen!

CP Vanessa, it is powerful and key that both you and Henry's faith are based on the foundation of prayer and the Holy scriptures. God truly heard the prayers of your heart and those standing in the gap. The word of God speaks and will not return void.

So be encouraged, Sis, for God is unfolding this plan, and it has already begun to transform for the better. For thou, oh Lord are a shield for me the glory and the lifter of my head. We love you guys!

AC Thank you, Lord, for what you have already done and what you are continuing to do. You said that you would never leave us or forsake us, and we believe your word!

"I will call upon the LORD, who is worthy to be praised; so shall I be saved from my enemies." — Psalm 18:3, Berean Study Bible

Turning Back the Tide

"When you get into a tight place and everything goes against you, 'til it seems as though you could not hang on a minute longer, never give up then, for that is just the place and time that the tide will turn."
— Harriet Beecher Stowe

City of Hope, Duarte, CA
September 1, 2015

MY ONCOLOGIST ADJUSTED MY MEDICATION TO DEAL WITH THE INFECTION. He added antibiotics to the medications I take intravenously to combat the infection. My early morning visit by the phlebotomist includes collecting one more blood sample to check for blood cultures. That is an easy adjustment to make since my blood is drawn through my PICC line.

Each day my oncologist comes by and tells me the results of the blood culture test. Each day for the past five days, the results were the same – positive on the blood culture. That means the infection was still present. The daily results do not deter me. I know if I just stay on the battlefield, victory will be mine in the name of Jesus.

Today, the sixth day, my oncologist came in on his daily rounds and said, "The blood culture results were negative today. We need to get several consecutive days of negative results before we can conclude the infection is gone."

"That's good news," I said in an upbeat tone. *Thanks be to God,* I thought. I made a silent petition to God for nothing but good results from the blood culture tests over the coming days so I could give Him the victory.

After a few more days of testing, my oncologist said, "We have had several days of negative blood culture results, so we can conclude the infection is gone."

Hallelujah, thank you, Jesus, I thought. I felt a change in the momentum of the battle at that point. I felt as though we had finally defeated the enemy's lethal infections sent my way to destroy me. I felt as though whatever strength I had in my body could now be focused on fighting cancer, and not be divided between contending with infection.

I thought to myself; *Soon, I will be able to leave the hospital and go home for good, at least until my next planned in-patient stay.* I tempered my rejoicing because I was still not out of the woods. I would celebrate once I was back home.

"We still need to continue the antibiotics for four weeks to make sure the infection is eradicated," he continued.

"How long will I have to remain in the hospital?" I asked. I wanted to set realistic expectations about when I would be discharged and not be disappointed due to unrealistic expectations.

"Oh, just a couple more days, I think," he replied.

"How will I receive the antibiotics?" I asked. "Will I have to come in every day for infusions?"

"No, that won't be necessary," he said. "We can set you up with a portable pump that you wear that will administer the antibiotics."

"How does that work?" I asked. *This is going to be different,* I thought.

"The nurse will come and explain everything when the time comes," he said. "You can ask questions at that time."

"Okay," I said. I let it go for the time being. My doctor had other patients to see on his rounds. I decided to wait and ask the nurse once Vanessa and I had had a chance to talk about it and formulated our questions.

On the cancer treatment front, I am still receiving chemotherapy medication every day and undergoing radiation treatments. I am thankful for the continued minimal side effects from the chemo (mainly weakness, neuropathy, and slight nausea). I am taking pain medication before my radiation treatments as a precautionary measure to minimize the back pain I experience each time I climb up and climb down from the radiation table.

The next time I spoke with Vanessa, I gave her the good news.

"Really!" she said, smiling.

"That's what he told me," I replied.

"Did he say where it came from?" she asked.

"No, and I didn't ask. I assume there was some residual amount still there from CTCA. I'm just thankful it's gone," I said.

"Hmmm," she said. "I would like to know where it came from. I don't want it to come back. I want to make sure it's gone for good. I will ask the doctor when we see him tomorrow."

"Okay," I said. I knew Vanessa was still a bit anxious. I remember how shaken she was when the doctors at CTCA told her the infections were lethal and had to be dealt with right away. She wanted to be sure it was gone once and for all. As for me, I left it at the feet of the Master and continued to claim the victory.

"He said I would still need to take antibiotics for the next four weeks to make sure it is completely removed," I told her. I hoped this would ease her mind some.

"How will you get the antibiotics?" she asked.

"They have some type of portable pump that I will take home," I said. "I don't exactly know how it works, but the doctor said the nurse would explain it."

"Well, we need to be sure to ask about that too," she said. She was making her list of questions for the doctor again.

"Okay," I said. "Let's see what tomorrow brings."

 Vanessa Foster-Dotson
September 2, 2015

*** Update for Monday, 08/31 - Tuesday 09/01/15:

Henry has been receiving antibiotics since Friday, 08/21, for his infection. He has been seeing the doctor daily and has also been receiving daily blood culture results. The last positive blood culture reading was on Tuesday, 08/25. So, his doctor is now saying that the infection is gone! Yes! This is huge progress.

However, after undergoing several tests, there is concern that the source of the infection is still unknown. It may be residual from the infection that he had while at CTCA. As a result, the current plan is that Henry will continue receiving antibiotics for an additional four weeks to ensure that the infection is completely removed.

He now has a new PICC line, and he will no longer need to see the doctor every day. So, although the antibiotics may be necessary, please pray that they don't affect Henry's body negatively.

Meanwhile, he has completed day four of his 12 days of radiation for his back. He has started taking pain medication before going to radiation. Henry now has less pain after his treatment. However, he is feeling a bit nauseous.

Henry has completed his first full month of chemo treatments with seemingly minimum side effects...3+ months to go. The doctor has stated that Henry's protein levels are better and that his body is responding positively to the chemo.

He continues to improve daily...more alert, more animated, more active, more talkative. His voice is stronger, almost back to normal. He has some challenges with concentration and short-term memory. So, I am trying to think of activities that will exercise and renew the cells in his brain.

But thankfully, from what I can see now, he is still the intelligent and thoughtful man that I fell in love with and married 17 years ago.

Praise God that Henry will continue to improve daily! We are doing all that we can to ensure that he does not get any more infections. Thank you once again for your prayers.

👍 38   Seen by 54   20 Comments

CP Powerful report. We shall continue to believe the report of the Lord. He is the ultimate healer. Vanessa, it is a joy seeing God's hands all over both you and Henry.

DM I had no doubt that God would bring Henry and you through this test. For his plan for you both has not been completed. Truly, the half has not been seen or told. No question God is in this for us to learn. You visit unconditional love, measures of discomfort, some doubt. Your mind questions, "When?" The answer: Draw nearer to the Lord. Be open to his complete anointing. In this place, things become very clear.

Vanessa and Henry, I love you both; however, God loves you best. I furthermore pray for your spirits to be empowered in unity. Peace for you, Vanessa as an advocate on Henry's behalf. In closing, be steadfast. The blessing of our Lord and Savior rest, rule, and abide with you both now and forever.

JD Praise God !!!! Food for thought: you may want to get Bernard a crossword puzzle book. I do the crossword daily. God Bless your union of 17 years and continue 17x17x17 more as you set an example of what's it like to be equally yoked. Much love!

RH Glad to hear progress is happening and Henry is mending. I am praying for Henry and sending my love and prayers. Praying. My heart is extended to you and Henry and his children. I wish I could do more. God can!!

SM Powerful praise report. God is not through with him yet. He has an awesome testimony to tell. I would love to be there for that one!

PM I suggest Word With Friends. Once downloaded, he can connect with other FB friends who also play. It's a good brain teaser for those who love words.

Q: How did you feel when you learned my lethal infections had been eliminated?

BART: I found out that the lethal infections were eliminated, and at the same time, I learned that they were, in fact, lethal. I was greatly relieved to hear that you were better.

TALIA: Relieved, grateful, and proud.

City of Hope, Duarte, CA
September 2, 2015

The next day, Vanessa came to City Of Hope in time to meet with my oncologist when he made his rounds. After he provided an update on the day's lab results, we started to discuss our next steps.

"The lab results continue to look good," he began. "The infection is gone, and we are preparing for your discharge."

"Did you ever find out where the infection came from?" Vanessa asked.

"Not for certain," he replied. "We know that Henry had the infection when he first arrived here, and it is the same type of infection he had while in Chicago. It is reasonable to assume there was some residual infection present when he returned to California."

"As a precaution, we will continue giving him antibiotics for four weeks to make sure the infection is completely gone."

"How will Henry receive the antibiotics?" Vanessa asked while reviewing her list of questions.

"There is a portable pump that he will wear, and it will administer the antibiotics automatically every four hours through his PICC line."

Vanessa followed up her question with, "Where are the antibiotics?"

"The antibiotics come in a bag that fits inside the case that holds the pump. You will receive a supply of antibiotics by courier every week. The antibiotics need to be kept in a cool place until you are ready to use the bag," he said.

At this point, I thought to myself; *This is going to be interesting. I will have to have a bag somehow strapped to me to receive medication when I am away from the hospital.*

I have seen others at City Of Hope with bags at their hip and a strap slung over their shoulders to carry it. Now I know what that was all about ⊠ just another hill to climb.

Thank you, Lord, for the miracles of medicine and science that will allow me to leave this hospital and go home.

"Who will change the bags?" Vanessa continued.

"A nurse will come out at the beginning to change the bags. But eventually, you or Henry will have to learn how to change the bags."

"Also, his PICC line needs to be flushed every day and changed once a week. It is not that hard to do. I am sure you will be able to do it," he said assuredly.

Now, Vanessa is gifted and blessed with many talents. However, working with needles, medical devices attached to the human body, and blood is not among those gifts and talents. I knew this was going to be a problem for her.

"I may be able to learn how to change a bag, but I won't be changing his PICC line," Vanessa said emphatically.

My doctor looked a little surprised and perplexed at Vanessa's firm reply. "Other caregivers have been able to do this without much trouble at all," he said. "I truly believe you can do it." I think he was trying to get her to warm up to the idea.

"I'm not doing it," Vanessa announced.

I knew Vanessa's mind was made up about this issue. I began to think, *What can we do to get past this stumbling block?*

At that very moment, an idea came to me, and I said, "We have to come to City of Hope once a week for lab work, so would it be possible for the lab technicians to change the PICC line during that appointment?"

"That will work out fine," my doctor said. "I can order a PICC line change once a week when you come in for your lab work."

Crisis averted, I thought. *Thank you, Jesus!*

Later on, Vanessa told me not only did she feel uncomfortable working with that type of medical equipment, but she was more concerned about doing something that could hurt me. And that she could not live with.

> *"Hear the shouts, hear the triumph song, 'The hand of God has turned the tide! The hand of God is raised in victory! The hand of God has turned the tide!'"* — Psalm 118:16, Message Bible

Ironman

"If you would seek health, look first to the spine...." — Socrates

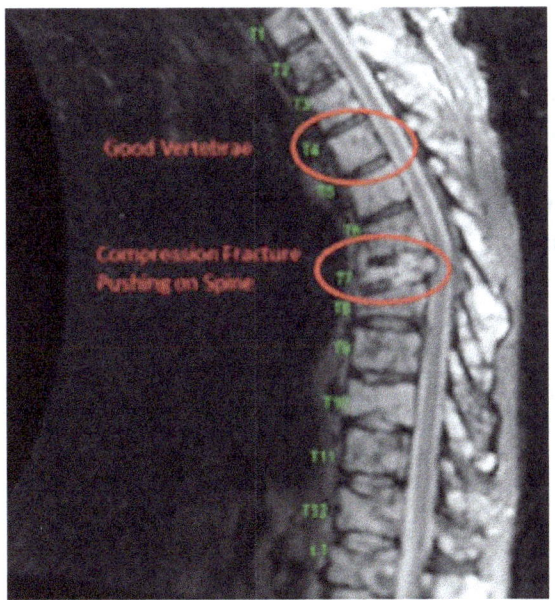

Annotated MRI image from 08/26/15

City of Hope, Duarte, CA
September 3, 2015

THE NEXT DAY, IN THE LATE AFTERNOON, I WAS VISITED BY DR. CHEN. He was there to discuss the results of my latest MRI.

"It looks like you have a severe compression of your T7 vertebra," he began. "From the MRI, we can see that the damaged vertebra is very close to impinging on your spinal cord. If that happens, you could be paralyzed or worse." His tone was somber. "The only permanent solution is to replace your T7 vertebra through surgery."

"What we need to do between now and the surgery is to make sure the situation doesn't get any worse. I am going to prescribe a more rigid back brace to prevent spinal cord injury. It won't make things better; it will just protect your spinal cord."

Dr. Chen's tone told me the situation was serious. If we were not careful, my life would be very different when all was said and done. I immediately said to myself, *Lord, this is another situation that is totally in your hands. You already knew about the damage to my spine due to Multiple Myeloma, so this is no surprise to You. I trust that Your Will will be done.*

"I understand," I replied. "Do I have to wear it all the time?"

"You should wear it all the time except when you bathe," he said. "Wait here. An occupational therapist will come to see you with the brace and show you how to put it on."

We thanked him, and he left the room.

"Wow!" Vanessa said. "You will have to wear the brace until they decide when to do surgery on your back. That could be a long time."

"Well, it's just the next thing," I said. My thoughts were more focused on being discharged. I wanted to go home, and getting this brace was the last thing I needed to do before we could leave.

Time dragged on. I decided to order a sandwich from the cafeteria because it was getting close to 5 p.m. It took over an hour after that before the occupational therapist showed up. I was not agitated or stressed. I had learned to be patient on discharge day based on my time at CTCA. There is always something else left to do.

When the occupational therapist did arrive, she was very apologetic.

"I am so sorry it has taken so long," she began. "We were very busy when we got the prescription from the doctor, and no one was available to handle the order. I took the order because City of Hope is on my way home."

Before I answered, I noticed the brace she was carrying. It was quite a work of engineering. It had sections of white rigid plastic and gray padding held together with several straps and snaps. There was the main back piece that provided most of the back support. The other components held the whole thing together and gave my arms a full range of motion. I did not expect to see something as elaborate as this.

"No worries," I said. "That is quite a brace."

"Well, it looks a little overwhelming at first, but once I show you how to put it on, you will see that it is not so bad."

It took about 10 minutes for her to get everything adjusted. When she was done, my entire upper body felt encased in semi-rigid armor. I wondered how long it would take Vanessa and me to figure this out.

On the one hand, the brace felt a little awkward and confining. On the other hand, I could tell I was more upright than I had been in a long time, and I felt protected with the brace covering the upper part of my 140-pound frame.

I felt like what I imagined Ironman from the Marvel comics felt like. A weakened body surrounded by a tough outer shell. I was reminded in my spirit about what the Word of God says.

"Finally, be strong in the Lord and in His mighty power. Put on the full armor of God, so that you can make your stand against the devil's schemes. For our struggle is not against flesh and blood, but against the rulers, against the authorities, against the powers of this world's darkness, and against the spiritual forces of evil in the heavenly realms." — Ephesians 6:10 - 12, Berean Study Bible

Before I left the hospital, I was outfitted with a portable pump for my antibiotics. A belt holds the device around my waist. There is a compartment for the electrical pump and a compartment for the medication. Vanessa will have to change the medication in the pump daily.

When I left my hospital room for the last time, I felt like Ironman. With my rigid back brace and portable pump, I was ready to battle with the evil one.

I was finally discharged from the hospital around 7 p.m. About 20 minutes later, Vanessa and I were back home for good.

"Be it ever so humble there's no place like home."
— John Howard Payne

Battle on the Homefront

"If it is disagreeable in your sight to serve the Lord, choose for yourselves today whom you will serve...but as for me and my house, we will serve the Lord." — Joshua 24:15, New American Standard

---

Pasadena, CA
September 5, 2015

I HAVE BEEN STAYING DOWNSTAIRS IN THE FAMILY ROOM SINCE I RETURNED FROM THE HOSPITAL. My doctors at CTCA did not want me to go up and down stairs unless absolutely necessary. There is a half bathroom next to the family room, so I don't have far to go when I have to go. With the kitchen just six steps up from the family room (we live in a split-level home), it is easy for Vanessa to bring me my meals. The wall-mounted television makes the arrangement complete. It is the most convenient arrangement we could come up with.

Yet, it feels somewhat strange sleeping in the family room overnight. I am home but not really home. I am in the house, but I am not in my bed with my first wife at night. It is as if I am still in transit from hospital to home.

At bedtime, and when I wake up early in the morning, I am in the dark, alone with my thoughts and with God. I trust in the Lord and have no fear, but I wonder where I am going.

When will I reach the "new normal" Vanessa and I keep talking about? Is there really such a thing as "normal," or will it always be a changing landscape driven by the effects of Multiple Myeloma and the side effects of chemotherapy? I know no matter what comes, I will continue this journey with a positive attitude because I know God is in control.

As I continue to wrestle with these thoughts, I begin to think about how good God has been to me. I think about how He saved me from the numerous bumps and scrapes throughout my childhood and adolescence that could have left me disabled or even dead. I think about how He brought me through the devastation of divorce to my lifetime partnership with Vanessa. I think about how He brought me through the painful loss of my "sister from another mister," Valenda and used it to make me aware that I had Multiple Myeloma eight and a half years later.

These new thoughts about the goodness of God replace my thoughts about what the future holds and brings me to a place of gratitude.

The physical manifestation of my healing has not come yet, but I know in God's infallible timing, it will come to pass. That is the reason for the hope and the joy that lives within me. I have gone through this mental exercise every early morning in the family room and arrive at the same place of gratitude.

And each day, at about that time, the sun's light begins to creep into the family room. I've seen joy come in the morning time, and it gives me peace.

We met with the director of the company that will be providing home physical therapy on Friday. We had first met earlier in the week when Vanessa and I were deciding which company to go with as the service provider. We had spoken to a couple of other companies and settled on this one. We set up my physical therapy schedule and will begin next week.

The director was impressed with my progress since our last meeting. I asked if it were okay for me to go up and down the stairs. She said I should not use the stairs without the help of two people—one in front of me and one behind me. I seized the opportunity and asked if she, along with Vanessa, would help me go upstairs to the master bedroom.

With the help of the physical therapist and Vanessa, I made my way upstairs for the first time since returning from CTCA. For the first time, I felt like I was home.

Being in my own bed set the wheels in motion in my mind about how I could make this move back upstairs permanent. I would need someone who would come by and help Vanessa get me up and down the stairs. There would only be two times that I would have to go downstairs; when I need to do physical therapy and when I need to leave for my radiation treatments.

I figured the physical therapist could help Vanessa get me up and down the stairs when I was doing physical therapy. I still need to figure out who would come by to help get me to and from my radiation treatments at City of Hope. I would have to think about that some more.

In the meantime, Vanessa and I were able to celebrate our wedding anniversary in the comfort of our bedroom. I had enlisted the help of our friend Lois to go out and find an anniversary card that I could give to Vanessa. It was a great time to celebrate our anniversary and a time for me to give honor to Vanessa for seeing me through the difficult days in Zion.

Maybe this is the start of the "new normal."

Vanessa Foster-Dotson
September 6, 2015

*** Update for Wednesday 09/02/15 - Saturday 09/05/15:

Adjusting. It's been a while since the last update, and quite a bit has happened. First, Henry is doing well. He continues to improve daily. On Tuesday, 08/18, Henry was assessed by his at-home physical therapist (PT) for the first time.

Now that Henry is no longer seeing the doctor daily, the physical therapist could come out again on Friday, 09/04. She was extremely excited to see Henry's progress. In addition to being more engaged, she stated that Henry is physically stronger. He is still in a wheelchair and needs more recovery. However, he is very positive, determined, and God-focused. He has even started using his laptop.

We know that his forward progress is a direct result of your prayers. Thank you!

As we work to establish our new norm, much has changed. Thursday, 09/03, was the first day Henry started receiving antibiotics for his infection intravenously at home. He has a small pump that administers his antibiotics every four hours automatically. The pump and the medicine are carried in a small bag that Henry can place over his shoulder. Right now, a nurse comes out every day to change the medicine.

Currently, our insurance only covers five visits from the nurse, so I will have to learn how to change the medicine. Definitely not in my comfort zone!

Another big change on Thursday was that I took our beloved dog, Niko, to the dog sitter for an undefined length of time. This was really hard. However, I prayed about it, and God provided clarity that this was the right thing to do...for Henry and Niko. I miss Niko.

Part of the reason that I took Niko to the sitter was that I wanted Henry to be able to spend time upstairs. He had only been upstairs once since we have been back. The PT had previously told me that there should always be two people available to assist Henry with going up and down the stairs.

Although Henry can really navigate the steps on his own, having someone in front and back of him provides extra safety. So, the PT assisted me with getting Henry upstairs on Friday.

Although I was very tired on Thursday and Friday, it was nice having Henry upstairs. For one thing, we were able to sleep in the same

continued

bed! Yes! Luckily, Henry had bought a Sleep Number bed for me a year or so ago to help my back. Now he is able to use it to raise and lower his head and feet as needed, just like his hospital bed. So, he is comfortable.

Being in the same bed was extra nice because Friday, 09/04/15, was the 17th anniversary of our wedding. Henry gave me a beautiful card which I will always cherish. (Thank you, Lois!) I am still trying to figure out the best way to celebrate this special anniversary.

First, I am so blessed to have Henry here to celebrate with. We came extremely close to that not being the case. But second, the whole concept of our marriage vows, and especially "in sickness and in health," have taken on an entirely new meaning. It's beyond gifts. It's beyond words. It's a heart thing.

I truly love Mr. Henry Bernard Dotson, III. He is my treasure from God. Happy Anniversary, Babe!

👍 40   Seen by 60   19 Comments

WL It is great to learn more about Henry and your JOURNEY. Happy ANNIVERSARY and may GOD bless you with many more years. The Value of LOVE is not measured BY a movie, a trip to Aruba, or WINNING a MILLION DOLLARS. IT is MEAS URED by the ABILITY to be ABLE to LAY DOWN ONE MORE Minute, Hour, Day, Week, Month, Year, and all the DECADES together. HIP, HIP, HOORAY!!!

RH How lovely, Vanessa! Glad to hear the update. Tell Henry he remains in my prayers every day. Happy Anniversary! I remember your beautiful wedding day and remain honored to have been a part of it. I remember Henry really cutting a rug on the dance floor. Tell Henry, Mike and I are coming out for a visit, and he and I will dance! Love you guys!

LD Happy anniversary!!!! It is so good to see God's blessings in this journey of your lives. We will continue to pray for you and Henry.

SR Vanessa - so glad to hear that Henry is doing well. You will learn how to change the medicine, NO PROBLEM, I am sure of it! Happy Anniversary and you both are in my prayers...

Pasadena, CA
September 8, 2015

I STILL NEEDED TO FIGURE OUT HOW I WAS GOING TO GET TO AND FROM MY RADIATION TREATMENTS. Vanessa was starting back to work and could have schedule conflicts that we would have to work through. As I continued to think about it, I received a call from my friend Jim. He was checking up on me to see how I was doing.

Jim

I met Jim at work when I was working at Southern California Edison. He was a manager in another IT organization that I would occasionally meet to discuss his people's work on my projects. After a reorganization, Jim became my manager.

Jim volunteered me to get involved in a project where I ultimately developed subject matter expertise that enabled me to start my own consulting business after leaving Southern California Edison. Jim also became a consultant in the same area after leaving Southern California Edison, so we found ourselves working as colleagues in a niche market.

When I returned to California from Chicago, Jim called to see how I was doing and asked if there was anything he could do to help. Vanessa took him up on his offer, and asked him to take me to my daily radiation appointments to allow her to catch up on her work.

Jim stepped up and helped out on several occasions during my battle on the home front. Vanessa and I will be forever grateful for him taking the time to provide support when we desperately needed it. He shared some of his thoughts about this journey.

Q: Had you heard of multiple myeloma before hearing of my diagnosis?
JIM: I had heard of Multiple Myeloma prior to hearing of your diagnosis but did not know anything about it.

Q: How did you feel when you learned of my diagnosis?
JIM: I guess shocked would be a good word. I knew you had been having back pain, but the fact that it could be related to something so serious was a shock. That you were so close to the edge made it even more of a shock. I am so grateful that you had an angel named Margaret to point you in the right direction.

Q: When did you understand how serious my condition was?

JIM: I understood how serious your condition was when I heard the state of your vital signs. The fact that you went all the way to Chicago underscored the serious nature of your condition. I could relate to it, having been there myself many years ago when I needed an infusion of seven pints of blood and even my more recent hospital stay a couple of years ago.

Q: Did you ever seriously question my survival?

JIM: I did some research on Multiple Myeloma, and I became aware that your survival was at stake, and the odds were not in your favor. That shook me up even more than initially finding out about your condition.

Q: What did you think when you first saw me after my diagnosis?

JIM: I can't recall any specific thoughts about first seeing you, other than being glad that you were still there to be seen.

Q: How did you feel when you first saw me after my diagnosis?

JIM: I was scared for you and Vanessa. I knew that you had a battle ahead of you and that it was going to be a rough one.

Q: Was it difficult for you to see me in my physical condition?

JIM: Your physical appearance was pretty much what I expected, given your condition, although I am still adjusting to your slightly shortened stature. If anything, you probably looked better than I might have expected.

Q: How did your accompanying me to hospital appointments affect you?

JIM: Accompanying you to your appointments was a pleasure (if that is the right word) for me, as it allowed me to be part of your journey. If anything, your spirit and attitude lifted me up and helped me in my faith that you would survive.

Vanessa Foster-Dotson
September 9, 2015

*** Update for Sunday 09/06/15 - Tuesday, 09/08/15:

Steady as he goes! We had a quiet anniversary and holiday. We spent most of the time talking to family and friends as well as watching television. One of our favorite sports to watch together is tennis. Watching portions of the US Open is a tradition for our anniversary.

However, we are usually not at home as we try to go somewhere different each year. In even years, Henry picks the location, and in odd years, I pick the location. (One year, I want to attend the US Open!) But this year, we thoroughly enjoyed just lying together quietly in the comfort of our own home.

We were blessed by a visit from Talia as well as a call from Bart. They each provide a unique way of supporting their dad...medicine for the soul that only your children can administer.

Henry was generally stable. His energy level cycled, and he is again struggling with eating. (So no anniversary dinner.) But he has gained a bit of weight and is pushing himself on several fronts.

On Sunday, he was at the computer for a few hours as he created a framework for his daily Bible study. And then, on Tuesday, after returning from his eighth radiation session, and while still feeling weak, Henry pushed himself to work out a little with his physical therapist.

Also, on Tuesday, he was back on the computer as he assisted with submitting paperwork. Henry's efforts are very inspiring to me, especially on the computer. Although chemo can challenge your concentration, Henry's work on the computer is providing him with mental exercise and is demonstrating his determination.

Now when it comes to determination, I also exhibit this characteristic at times. When the nurse came on Tuesday, in addition to changing Henry's medication, she also taught me how to clean and replace the dressing for his PICC line. This has to be done weekly.

While I have become comfortable with changing his medication, I am determined to find someone other than myself to change the dressing for his PICC line. Too many things can go wrong with dire consequences. I will figure out another option besides myself.

continued

As we continue to define the rhythm of our "new normal," we find peace in knowing that the best is yet to come. This is all in God's hands!

Thank you, Verbon and Annie, for your support this weekend!

👍 40   Seen by 51   18 Comments

SM Thank you, Jesus, for your continued healing and promises of your Word concerning your faithful servants Henry and Vanessa. YOU are not a man that you would lie, so I thank you for doing what you said you would do. In Jesus' name, Amen!

GT Thank you for your updates. I understand this journey as I read your updates. It helps to renew my strength by praising God for all the victories day to day. I still have a PICC line in, and my last chemo was in 2012. God is in total control. Blessings and favor for you both.

DM So long as God is first and the head of your household, goodness and mercy will follow. I thank and praise God for blessing and keeping you both connected and strengthening on all levels daily. Truly an example of unwavering love and compassion one for another as Christ has taught us all.

RN All in Gods hands. . . It is a God thang! So proud of Henry and how determined he is during his fight. I love it!! What strong character he is as a person. Faith. . .Keep the Faith in God, and He shall bring it to pass!! Go, Henry!!!!

RH Yes, my dear friend, God is taking care of Henry and you. Henry's progress is amazing. He (and you) have been through so much. I continue to pray every day for Henry's healing. Love you guys!

VH Vanessa, my mother was saying how much we look forward to your updates and how you write so beautifully. May God continue to bless your journey; it is truly in His hands. Praise God for the healing that is to come. Love you both.

Don't Sweat the Small Stuff

"And which of you by being anxious can add a single hour to his span of life? And why are you anxious about clothing? Consider the lilies of the field, how they grow: they neither toil nor spin... but if God so clothes the grass of the field, which today is alive and tomorrow is thrown into the oven, will he not much more clothe you, O you of little faith?"

— Matthew 6:27-28, 30, English Standard Version Bible

Pasadena, CA
September 12, 2015

I STILL FEEL AS THOUGH I AM IN TRANSITION, BUT THINGS SEEM TO BE LEANING TOWARDS A ROUTINE OF SORTS. Radiation treatments have become routine (still uncomfortable getting on and off the radiation table), and working with the portable pump is not so bad either. There have been some challenges along the way, but they are minor compared to what Vanessa and I have been through thus far.

All past struggles make these challenges seem like bumps in the road, not amounting to a molehill, let alone a mountain.

But I know this stage of the journey will come to an end soon. Soon I will complete my radiation treatments. Soon I will complete my at-home antibiotics infusions, and the pump will be a thing of the past. At that point, we will again redefine "normal."

God is taking care of all the "big" things. By His grace, I am getting stronger and stronger each day. He has made it, so there is no copay for my chemotherapy medication. I am sure He is also doing great things that I am not even aware of, not yet, at least.

I am testing out my mental faculties by getting on the computer and trying to stay focused enough to get something done. I am also getting back to my daily Bible study. It's amazing how much time you have on your hands when you are only focused on what is important. You become acutely aware of all the other things you do that are just busy work or distractions.

With this clarity, it is easy not to sweat the small stuff.

Vanessa Foster-Dotson
September 13, 2015

*** Update for Wednesday 09/09/15 - Saturday, 09/12/15:

Don't sweat the small stuff! As I thought about what to write, I thought about a few challenges that "we overcame" over the past few days. So, the initial "title" that came to mind was "We shall overcome!" However, as I read my daily devotion today, I was reminded that the challenges were small in the grand scheme of things, that God is the one that really handled them, and that we, really, I, need to allow and trust God to handle the small things in the same way that He is handling the big things.

> *"Are not two sparrows sold for a penny? Yet not one of them will fall to the ground apart from the will of your Father. And even the very hairs of your head are all numbered."* — Matthew 10: 29-30

First, there weren't any new challenges with Henry's health. His physical therapist was even more excited than before about his progress. "He is stronger! It will be safe for you (Vanessa) to take him up and down the stairs by yourself very soon."

Henry's oncologist was excited as well. He had not seen Henry in a week, and he said that Henry looked great! Almost all of Henry's blood counts were as they should be. The only real challenge is that Henry is not eating enough. He has lost a bit more weight.

God is continuing to take care of our biggest challenge. We are so thankful for Henry's progress!

But there were a few "small" challenges that God handled as well.

1. On Wednesday, the nurse was supposed to come at 6 p.m. to change Henry's intravenous antibiotic medicine. She called at 6:15 p.m. to say that she would not be coming because her company had not received authorization from our insurance as yet. So, at that point, I had 10 minutes to change Henry's medicine myself. Success! God showed up!

2. Also, on Wednesday, we had Henry fitted for a new wheelchair because the seat in his current one was too short. The new chair was supposed to be delivered Wednesday afternoon but was not. Henry was extremely disappointed. I was frustrated. After numerous calls and hurdles, we were finally able to pick up the new one on Friday! (Thank you again, Lois!) God showed up!

continued

3. As previously stated, I am comfortable with changing Henry's medicine, but I am not comfortable with changing his PICC line dressing. Early in the week, I started asking for help. On Thursday, we were told that the nurses at City of Hope would change Henry's PICC line dressing on Fridays when he goes in for chemo. Yes! God showed up!

4. Remember the $500 per pill medicine ($10,500 for 21 pills) that we were blessed to get for $300 for 21 pills last month? Well, this time, we were told the cost would be $0! Not sure what changed, but God showed up!

5. On Friday, when we went in for Henry's 11th radiation treatment, we were told that the radiation doctor would meet with us on Monday since that will be Henry's last treatment. I have a previous appointment that I had scheduled months ago, so Jim was kind enough to agree to take Henry to his radiation treatment on Monday. (Thank you, Jim!)

When I was making arrangements with Jim, we did not know about the meeting with the radiation doctor. So, we asked if we could meet with the radiation doctor on Friday, 09/11, after Henry's treatment. They agreed and even showed us the attached image of Henry's spine.

The image highlights the good vertebrae in his spine, which look almost like a square, as well as the bad vertebrae that have been affected by the Multiple Myeloma cells.

Although Henry's damaged L2 vertebra did not appear on the image, the compression fracture on T7 was very apparent. It was clear that the compressed T7 vertebra was starting to push on Henry's spinal cord. This is serious!!! Even though I initially questioned whether Henry should have the radiation treatment, Henry was right.

Henry said that he had full faith that God was directing the doctors. The image is extremely helpful with understanding the effects of Multiple Myeloma. Again, God showed up!

Lesson learned...don't sweat the small stuff. "God's got this" means everything...both big and small. Go to Him in prayer for EVERYTHING!

Please pray for full repair of Henry's back, no damage to his spinal cord, and complete renewing of his appetite.

God Bless!

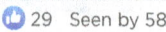 29   Seen by 58   14 Comments

VH: God will continue to show up and show out again and again! Wonderful Praise report, Vanessa. Keep fighting, Henry!

PM: Just keep on praising God for always showing up! He is always faithful great or small. If you find yourself in the position of having to change the PICC line dressing, don't be intimidated. I had to do it for Ness, and I said I couldn't do it because of the risk of infection. God guided me as I followed the instructions, and before I knew it, it became a breeze as I did it. Just trust God!

WL: Every morning when we pray, we lift up you and Henry. GOD will continue to give you the strength to overcome. The victory is in your hands. Have a great day.

JD: Thank you, Lord! Just continue to trust him because he is an on-time God. I know because I have never stopped. When prayers go up, blessings come down. So I am thankful for everyone praying and agreeing for you and Bernard. Much love, my dear niece and nephew. God is so good!

JD: We are continuing to pray for both of you, my sweets. Thank you, Vanessa Foster-Dotson for the photos of his back. It allowed me to spiritually lay hands on his back and pray for him by laying hands on the picture, although I am not physically there to do it. Love you, my friend

Q: How did your visits to the hospital to see me affect you?

LOIS: In the beginning, it was difficult seeing you because you were so very sick, so mostly I was there to sit with you as a companion and to hear anything the doctor might say if he came into the room. I offered to help Vanessa just be present with you whenever she couldn't be there, also to allow her to do errands. You weren't very responsive at first because you were still in the throes of the illness. As you got better, it was easier to be with you because you were more communicative and were feeling somewhat better.

Taking Care of Business

"All growth depends upon activity. There is no development physically or intellectually without effort, and effort means work."

— Calvin Coolidge

Pasadena, CA
September 17, 2015

I RECEIVED MY LAST RADIATION TREATMENT ON MONDAY. It was anticlimactic because it was just business as usual. I went through the same motions that I have done 11 times before, except this was the last time. I was thankful it was over, but in my mind, it was just another box to be checked on the road to recovery.

It reminded me of when I completed my last final as an undergrad and went to the administration building to get my grad check signed off. The clerk went through my records and said, "Everything is in order; you're done." As I left the building, I thought, *Is that it? Finally, after years of hard work, it comes down to a clerk saying, You're done?*

I learned from that experience to temper my expectations when it comes to recognition for taking care of business.

As I was getting dressed and preparing to leave, I was surprised by the radiation technicians. Throughout the treatments, they had become adept at helping me remove and put on my rigid brace. They knew how cumbersome it was, and they appreciated how difficult and painful it had been for me to get on and off the radiation table. During each treatment, we worked as a team to get it done.

Before I left, the technicians presented me with a certificate of completion they had printed on stationery with a gold border. It read:

CITY OF HOPE RADIATION ONCOLOGY
THIS CERTIFIES THAT
Henry B. Dotson, III
has successfully completed his radiation treatment and is therefore awarded this
CERTIFICATE OF COMPLETION

It was signed by two of the radiation therapists. One of the radiation therapists handed it to me and said, "We know how difficult radiation treatment can be on our patients. We want each patient to know that completing these treatments is a true accomplishment that should not go unnoticed or unrecognized."

The gesture genuinely touched me. It felt good to know City of Hope service providers were pulling for me to get better. And they did it tangibly. I left the radiation treatment lab that day with my head held high.

I am also taking care of business at home. I do not like physical therapy, but I know that it is the only way to recover my physical strength. I push myself to do one more repetition when I feel it getting harder. As a result, I need only one person to help me use the stairs.

It seems like a small thing, but I am one step closer to recovery. It is the many small victories that come before accomplishing a major goal. And they, in themselves, should be recognized and celebrated as part of the journey to get to the final destination. I count it all joy.

 Vanessa Foster-Dotson
September 18, 2015

*** Update for Sunday 09/13/15 - Thursday, 09/17/15:

Day by Day! The last few days have been up and down. Henry was pretty energetic on Sunday and Monday. Monday, he had his last radiation treatment! This is a huge accomplishment. Now we will wait a couple of weeks to determine whether his spine is any better. Henry will continue to wear his brace during this time and is still receiving antibiotics intravenously.

On Monday, Henry also did very well during physical therapy. He has been officially cleared to go up and down our stairs with only my assistance. We no longer have to ask others to come over and help. Awesome!

By the afternoon on Monday, he was tired and didn't have much of an appetite. He was the same way most of the day Tuesday and Wednesday. Occasionally, he would get up from his wheelchair and walk down the hall with his walker to achieve a little exercise. But for the most part, he simply watched television.

He did have some PT again on Wednesday. But his body is frail, and his strength is limited. I have been working on putting together a nutrition plan for him as I try to capitalize on breakfast which is the main time that he has an appetite. I will share the plan with you once it is completed.

continued

But on Thursday, he rose! No more television. He said enough. He was still weak, but he got on the computer and got some things done. He even ate 2,000 of his 2,300 daily calories target. (Thank you to our niece Stefanie!). Henry's weight is still down, but he is making progress.

So, we are moving forward as we establish our new norm, and I am working more and more every day. I am not traveling right now, but I am doing as much as I can from home. I have been blessed with a great employer, and I feel I have to "earn my keep."

When Henry is tired, he calls on me frequently throughout the day, which is fine; however, I am often doing a balancing act, and some home tasks are taking much longer than normal to complete (like sending this update…smile!).

But such is LIFE. And although I get frustrated and overwhelmed at times, I am thankful for LIFE. I am thankful for Henry's LIFE. I am thankful for my LIFE. I am thankful for your LIFE. As per my devotion on Wednesday…"God is faithful to help me day by day." He is helping Henry and me during this journey, and so are you!

Thank you!

 26   Seen by 29   12 Comments

 I look forward to each of your updates, Vanessa. I must admit that I weep as I read them because I am filled with so much compassion and empathy for you and Henry.

My tears are those of joy for God's goodness and faithfulness. For Henry's determination, mental and physical fortitude, and for never giving up.

Finally, for YOU, my beloved woman of God. I thank him for putting you and Henry together for 17 years because you know the meaning of cleaving unto your husband.

The two of you are ONE indeed. Your posts are a tribute to your love for each other.

CP: I get teary eyes sometimes because I know what you are feeling. But this is where you have an awesome support team to help lighten the load. The songwriter says, "I've had some weary days, I've had some hills to climb, God knows what's best for me although my weary eyes can't see, I just say thank you Lord I won't complain!"

LW: Be encouraged. God is working it all out for your good. Hallelujah!

Vanessa, when you're frustrated and overwhelmed (which is normal), I hope you feel the love and hugs from us, who are cheering for you both on this new journey.

"See how blessed we consider those who have persevered. You have heard of Job's perseverance and have seen the outcome from the Lord. The Lord is full of compassion and mercy."
— James 5:11, Berean Study Bible

Pasadena, CA
September 22, 2015

MY STRENGTH IS GRADUALLY RETURNING. I can tell by my accomplishments and the small things I am able to do once again. My mobility has improved; I have gone from wheelchair to walker to cane. I typically have a little more energy each day. I am able to go up and down the stairs on my own. These baby steps inspire me to try toddler steps – a little wobbly at first, but within reason. I do not want to overextend myself.

Saturday, Vanessa and I went to a Multiple Myeloma support group meeting near LAX. Our friend Zephran invited us to attend this meeting. He also has Multiple Myeloma and lives close to LAX. The speakers presented a lot of good information, and we had some time to chat with Zephran afterward. Then we headed home because Los Angeles traffic could prolong the 36-mile trip.

Saturday was hot. On the way back home, I started to get very uncomfortable. The rigid back brace was causing me to retain heat. I felt like a turtle slow-cooking in his shell. And the heat was sapping my strength. By the time we got home, the only thing I wanted to do was to get out of that brace and lie down!

As soon as Vanessa turned the engine off, I got out of the car, made a beeline upstairs, took off my brace, and flopped onto the bed. It was the first time I had gone up the stairs unassisted. You don't know what you can do until you are in a situation that requires more of you than usual. I have been going up and down the stairs unassisted since then.

One of the highlights of my week was that Vanessa and I attended our local couples' Bible study meeting for a brief while. The members have been so faithful in their prayers, and I wanted to thank them in person.

Vanessa was reluctant about going out on a cool night in my condition, but I was insistent. I wanted to thank them and encourage them with my testimony of what God had done so far. Fatigue did not allow us to stay for the entire meeting, but I had a wonderful time amongst the saints.

Q: How did you feel when I was able to make my first appearance at Life Group after my diagnosis?

LOIS: It was quite a while before you were able to return for a visit to Life Group. But when you came, it was soooo exciting and everyone was so happy for you and Vanessa. You were thin and had on a back brace and could only stay for a short time, but you looked wonderful to me. God had come through for you, and what a testimony!

Vanessa Foster-Dotson
September 23, 2015

*** Update for Friday 09/18/15 - Tuesday, 09/22/15:

All is well! Henry has been doing pretty well since the last update.

On Friday, he had his weekly chemo treatment and had a great nurse, Wendy, who he chatted with quite a bit. (She even got scolded a little for spending so much time with Henry...smile!).

On Saturday, he was very energetic. We went to a Multiple Myeloma (MM) support group meeting, which was quite insightful. (Thank you, Zephran!) It was great to observe the positive quality of life that others are experiencing after getting their MM under control. It was good to obtain new information.

Henry may have to take medicine for the rest of his life, but he will be able to live a somewhat normal life. Praise God!

When we returned home from the meeting, Henry was so energetic that he did not wait for me to go upstairs. He was hot and wanted to get comfortable. I was concerned from a safety perspective, but he explained that he had to do whatever he was able to do, and he felt that he could go up the stairs safely by himself.

continued

He is determined! I understand, but I am still concerned. I saw how sick he was and never want him to go back there, not even close.

On Sunday, Henry woke up pretty tired and weak. His energy level was low, and his eating was pretty poor. He returned to bed relatively early.

On Monday, he had more energy. He met with his physical therapist, and they practiced using a cane. Henry really likes using the cane because he feels that he has a bit more stability and freedom, especially on the stairs.

On Tuesday, Henry continued using the cane. His energy was good, and even asked to make a very quick visit to our bi-weekly couples' life group meeting, which is hosted by Mike and Lois. I was concerned, but Henry was insistent. He wanted the group to see that he is doing well. He wanted everyone to know that their prayers are being answered. He wanted to say thank you in person.

The group was surprised, and they blessed us. They laid hands and provided powerful prayers. It was awesome! So once again, he was right. But, of course, I still want to proceed cautiously.

So yes, Henry continues to make good progress. His sister Pat visited on Monday. She had not seen Henry in a few weeks, and she was very pleased to see the difference in his appearance. God is good. NO, God is great!

Many of you have asked when you can visit Henry. The time is coming soon. I just want him to be a bit stronger on a consistent basis. He is truly getting there. This week has been good so far because although he was weak/tired on Sunday, he bounced back on Monday.

He has lost 40 pounds since July, and he still does not have much of an appetite. So, he needs to consume more calories and protein. But all things considered, he/we are doing well.

Thank you once again for your prayers.

Prayer Requests:
1. Complete healing for Henry: body, mind, soul, and spirit. (no cancer, no pain, no long-term anemia, no permanent back damage, no fevers, no infections.)
2. Increased appetite and weight
3. Improved strength and movement

continued

4. General prayer for all of the family members and friends of anyone that is reading this update and has recently been diagnosed or is suffering from cancer or some other life-threatening health challenge.

Prayers Answered:
1. Healthy kidneys / no dialysis
2. Healthy eyes
3. Increased platelet count
4. Clarity of thoughts and words
5. Exponential blood count level increase
6. Renewed spirit
7. Release from CTCA and return home
8. Easy transition to being in California
9. Stabilized blood counts, all counts being positive
10. Stabilized kidney counts

👍 28 Seen by 58   16 Comments

RH Great to hear Henry is fighting and prayers are being answered. You guys are in my thoughts and prayers every day. Love you and wishing and praying for Henry's recovery.

CP What a mighty God we serve! It is always a blessing to see how God is doing a great work in our brother. It is awesome to hear you are both doing well because of your walk with the Lord. As we continue to lift you both in prayer, the Lord will show himself strong. Psalms 121 all of your help comes from the Lord.

FD Thanks for the praise report. God Is, and we continue to trust Him for Nard's complete recovery as well as YOUR continued strength. Love you both.

MIDDLE PASSAGE

A Little Help Around the House

"Needing help doesn't have a look, but asking for it always looks beautiful."
— Brittany Burgunder

"When we give cheerfully and accept gratefully everyone is blessed."
— Maya Angelou

Pasadena, CA
September 30, 2015

THIS WEEK A CAREGIVER STARTED WORKING WITH ME TO GIVE VANESSA SOME NEEDED RELIEF. Work has picked up for Vanessa, and it is clear that she needs help. We were able to get help through our long-term care insurance policy.

I highly recommend getting long-term care insurance. Most of us, at some point in our lives, will need long-term care. Without insurance coverage, the out-of-pocket expense may be too much of a financial burden to bear. I suggest speaking with an insurance broker to find out more.

I liked Mylene from the start. She has a very interesting life story and is talkative – something I appreciate. She helps with my meals and reminds me when to take my medication. She also puts my shoes and socks on my feet because I cannot reach down to do so with the rigid back brace on. The main thing is there is less work for Vanessa to do.

Vanessa Foster-Dotson
September 30, 2015

*** Update for Wednesday 09/23/15 - Wednesday, 09/30/15:

"I got my baby back, baby back, baby back!" Yes, Henry has truly made great progress over the last week. With the exception of his appetite, weight, and strength, he seems very close to being the old Henry. His mind is sharp. Henry is talkative and energetic. He is going up and down stairs on his own at will. He is extremely thankful for all that God has done to bring him this far so quickly and continues to share his faith and testimony with others.

One thing that I have been learning is that it is important to monitor Henry's lab results. Following are some of the key results that indicate

continued

Henry's progress to date. God has definitely brought Henry a long way, and the trip to CTCA (07/15 - 08/17) was totally worth it!

Multiple Myeloma Status Measure: IgG Goal: 700 – 1600	Kidney Status Measure: Creatinine Goal: 0.40 – 1.20	Body Mass Status Measure: Weight Goal: 175 – 180
07/16 (CTCA): **13,000**	07/16 (CTCA): **8.84**	06/01 (Home): **190.02**
08/20 (COH): **7,240**	08/20 (COH): **1.22**	07/16 (CTCA): **181.44**
09/25 (COH): **1,340**	09/25 (COH): **0.77**	08/20 (COH): **158.73**
		09/29 (Home): **150.07**

Praise God!

As for me, I am tired. We have made significant progress in regards to establishing our new routine. I am very thankful that several people have provided assistance since we have been back in California. However, at times my daily home/Henry activities along with work are exhausting and overwhelming.

We set some goals for October 1st, and we have achieved many of them. One goal was to have a caregiver come twice a week for a few hours to help out with Henry's morning activities and assist me with some minor housekeeping.

The caregiver's first day was on Tuesday, 09/29. She did pretty good with Henry, but other than that; I was really disappointed. Maybe I was expecting too much. Maybe we need a different type of service. I guess I am going to have to figure out other options to obtain the minor routine assistance I need.

Meanwhile, I have to pick myself up, dust myself off and keep it moving. But right now, I am a little down. This, too, shall pass. The important thing is that Henry is doing better every day.

Thank you for your continued prayers.

👍 46   Seen by 70   24 Comments

RN — A caregiver's role is a tough but noble one. Try to steal away a couple of hours when your hired help is around to go and relax with a manicure. It will be hard to do because you will worry about how he is doing the entire time you are away. But keep your phone with you and try to steal a moment for your mind to have some diverse time. Reenergize a little so you can be there for him even more. I am speaking from my experience.

BC — Praise God for Henry's progress and the example he is for all of us! Keep fighting the good fight, brother! Vanessa, you are Heaven sent specifically for these challenges. You are doing a great job standing watch over Henry and taking care of your family.

KI — Hello Dotson family. I'm sure you are swamped with calls from 100's or thousands of friends. We would call also, but we know Henry needs to rest and recover. So, know this. He and you are in our daily prayers. God is good. All the time. All the time. God is good.

DM — I am praying for you both; I am praying that at this crossroad, you hear the Lord's voice and lean on him for Guidance. I promise you joy will come in season. Find comfort in the fact that you are doing a remarkable job given all things. Even greater is your love and respect for Henry. This all shows in the results.

Yes, you may have to go through a few people until you find the right one. I pray that God will provide you the strength you need during this time. I further pray you find some comfort in these words.

I Love you both.

SM — Continual prayer is going up on both of your behalfs. Caring for a loved one is a job in itself. I've done it for 35 yrs and counting. God will provide everything you need in His own time. Be encouraged, my sister, and know that great is your reward. Love you both!

LW — Wow. What a journey! I would suggest you keep trying out service providers until you find "the one." You and Bernard are a remarkable couple. And you're continuously in my thoughts and prayers.

WL — You have come this far by FAITH. YOU and HENRY are getting better day by day. GOD will continue to give you PEACE and STRENGTH. You can only do what you do, BUT GOD CAN DO WHAT WE CAN'T. BE ENCOURAGED because GOD HAS YOUR BACK. TREAT YOURSELF to a NICE FUDGE SUNDAE.

JD — Continue to hold on to God's hand, YOU are human, and there will be some low moments. Just know this too shall pass. God has brought Bernard a mighty long way, and I believe as we continue to send prayers and give God the praises for what he has done thus far, we will continue to see his mercy and healing in Bernard.

I was told that for a caretaker, you have to write down step by step what you want to be done. For example, dust a countertop..(you want items to be moved first, then wipe, then spray furniture polish and wipe again.) Something we never think about is their understanding of dusting may be different than ours.

This is something just for thought because I never thought about it until it was brought to our attention. Love you both, and I Thank God for you.

RH — Very good news about Henry. He is progressing nicely. Prayers have been answered. Amen. Vanessa, just take one day at a time. Give yourself a pass on the "perfect" for a while. I know it is difficult for you but do it anyway...at least during Henry's recovery. I am praying every day for you and Henry to have the strength to persevere. Love you guys!

BC — Praise God for Henry's progress and the example he is for all of us! Keep fighting the good fight, brother! Vanessa, you are Heaven sent specifically for these challenges. You are doing a great job standing watch over Henry and taking care of your family.

Pasadena, CA
October 4, 2015

Vanessa and I are still making adjustments as we try to establish our "new normal." I am beginning to realize it may take a while to get to the "new normal." My chemotherapy regime is set, but everything else seems to be in a state of flux.

She is getting back into her work routine. I am gaining strength, and I am able to do more, so what is "normal" keeps changing. I am convinced we are still transitioning, and "normal" has not yet come into view.

We are adjusting to having Mylene provide care. Vanessa's expectations are not the same as my expectations. We had a long discussion about expectations and worked through our differences. Once we were in agreement, we spoke with the home care service provider.

Things are working better now. I think when all is said and done, we just need to extend a little grace and time to one another to help smooth out the rough edges.

I had an experience that is a significant event in my eyes regarding moving towards the "new normal." I received my disabled person's blue placard from the DMV in the mail. It was a tangible indication that my life had changed; I am not the person I used to be. I think there is a good chance that the placard will be a part of my "new normal" from here on out.

Not that I no longer believe I will receive my ultimate healing, but rather, it may become a reminder of some type of "thorn in my side" that reminds me that God's grace is sufficient.

But more importantly, I felt instant empathy for all of the people I had seen before who had these placards hanging from their rearview mirrors or as a sticker on their license plates. I know some people who are not really disabled have placards, but I think the majority of placard owners are disabled.

Now that I have one, I am much more aware of other vehicles with these tags. I know what I have gone through to be eligible for the placard, so now I wonder what life-changing event occurred in another person's life when I see a placard.

They, too, have a story to tell. They, too, are on a journey similar to mine.

Vanessa Foster-Dotson
October 5, 2015

*** Update for Thursday 10/01/15 - Sunday 10/04/15:

Rounding the corner! I wanted to start off with a quick update on me. I indeed dusted myself off and am doing much better...thanks in large part to my fantastic husband. As usual, Henry calmed me down. He constructed an assessment of the caregiver's visit.

We then shared the assessment with the management of the caregiving organization. The assessment was well received. So, when the caregiver came on Thursday, she took great care of Henry and also completed the minor household activities that I had requested. Henry and I were both pleased. A corner has been turned.

One of the tasks that we want the caregiver to assist Henry with is physical therapy. So, Henry had a major milestone on Thursday. He was able to walk around the block, approximately 0.35 miles, with only the aid of a cane. Our block has an incline, so this was huge! Henry took about 30 minutes and was tired when he returned, but he did it!

He was able to walk around the block again on Saturday with me. This time he only took 15 minutes. Absolutely FANTASTIC!!! Another corner was turned, literally.

Friday was Henry's weekly chemo day, and Saturday, a friend hung out with Henry while I went to a meeting and ran errands. But then, on Sunday, we celebrated. As Henry put it, "we celebrated 205 months of marriage" (17 years and one month). It was all a surprise to Henry. He is now well enough to go out occasionally as long as he is wearing a mask and we avoid crowds.

So, we started out early on Sunday. We got much-needed manicures, saw the movie "War Room," had a great meal, and then he had a facial while I had a massage. We both enjoyed ourselves. Just a month earlier, we were not able to really celebrate because Henry was too sick. It is absolutely amazing how much Henry has progressed in such a short time. Even his appetite has finally improved!!! His Uncle Fred suggested that he just get the food down, and that is what Henry is doing. Another corner! When we were at CTCA, I told Henry's Mind-Body therapist about our Facebook group, and she told me about a book by Larry Dossey which is called "Healing Words." The book discusses the healing power of prayer as a complement to medicine. As I am witnessing Henry's daily improvements and as we

continued

attended the must-see movie "War Room," my conversations with the therapist came to mind. I have a renewed awe regarding the power of prayer. God is AWESOME, and we are so blessed to have EACH of you joining us in prayer.

You are literally providing medicine for Henry's mind, body, and soul. As I observe different people at both the hospital and support groups, I do not know how others can go through something like this without prayer. Thank you once again for partnering with us!

We believe that Henry is well enough to start having visitors on a limited basis. (Another corner turned.) Of course, he will not be able to see everyone at once, and there may be times when he is not able to see anyone. Henry's immune system is still fragile, so please understand that we will have to turn you away if you are sick. Feel free to inbox me if you are interested in visiting.

God Bless!!!

👍 36   Seen by 70   26 Comments

ES   God is good! Glad to see your Progress, Henry! Praise God!!

CP   Vanessa Foster-Dotson, it is powerful and a blessing to hear and see the abundance of prayer nationwide for Henry and yourself. I am so glad you wiped the dust off with the help of Henry. Thank you for your continued strength and trust in the word of God that keeps you stable and strong in your faith.

The favor of God is truly amazing and upon you both. We will set up a time to call before visiting. Love and miss you guys.

JR   GOD IS FAITHFUL, HE IS THE LIVING WORD!! HE WILL NEVER LEAVE YOU OR FORSAKE YOU: AND NO WEAPON IS FORMED AGAINST YOU THAT WILL PROSPER: WORD! AMEN? AMEN!!!

RN   Thankful that you both are turning the corners by the grace of God Almighty! Keep trusting God. Keep believing. Keep the Faith. He shall bring this to pass!!

SZ   I am praying for you and Henry! Hang in there.

WL   To GOD be the GLORY. It is not how fast we get around the block, but that we get AROUND the BLOCK. May GOD continue to BLESS you GUYS as you ENJOY your time together and reflect ON WHO GOD IS. HE IS ALIVE. HE IS ALIVE IN HENRY'S BODY.

RN   Thankful that you both are turning the corners by the grace of God Almighty! Keep trusting God. Keep believing. Keep the Faith. He shall bring this to pass!!

GT   Praise God for all of his blessings! Vanessa, I am so thankful and encouraged by all of your updates. I am looking forward to abundant life and continual blessings for you both as well as myself.

BC   This is great news, Vanessa! Praise God for how He is using both of you as faith warriors… despite the test that you are experiencing. Thank you for letting us pray for you and Henry. I am sure that when Henry is strong enough, DG and I will look forward to coming over to harass Henry. May God continue to watch over and bless each and every one of your days!

CB   Soooo! Happy and excited for my brother and sister in Christ. God is truly amazing with the supernatural healing powers that He bestowed upon Henry. We love you two, to the moon and back. Continue to receive your blessings.

Pasadena, CA
October 12, 2015

Vanessa and I were able to meet with our goddaughter for dinner tonight. We had to drive about 25 miles to see her. She is touring one of the colleges she might attend, and it happens to be close enough for us to connect. Joslyn is the daughter of Vanessa's best friend, Rosalind. The family lives in Delaware, so it was a treat to be able to see her. The visit was great.

I decided to wear short pants for the occasion. I did not pay attention to my appearance other than my shirt and pants matched. We had someone take a picture of the three of us, and I noticed how skinny my legs were. It reminded me of one of the rare times my father wore short pants, exposing his thin legs and knobby knees. We were heading to the beach on a family outing. My mother looked at my father's legs and said:

> *"Henry, your legs are so skinny your body is going to sue for non-support!"*

We three children in the back seat of the car howled.

That memory reminded me of how much I missed my parents and how grateful I am for having them as parents.

Let's Get Physical

"Without health life is not life; it is only a state of languor and suffering - an image of death." — Buddha

---

Pasadena, CA
October 13, 2015

I AM FOCUSED ON GETTING INTO GOOD SHAPE. According to my treatment plan, I should be ready for a Stem Cell Transplant around December. I need to put on some more weight, build muscle tone, and do more aerobic activities. It will help me get through the transplant. I also want to be in better shape for the trip back to CTCA.

To that end, I have been walking a lot more. Mylene and I go out at least once a day when she is here. I have also been working hard with my in-home physical therapist. He says I am ready to start outpatient physical therapy. It is hard work, but I can see the improvement, which motivates me to carry on.

I also drove my car for the first time since my return from CTCA. I did not go very far, just around the block to see how I felt. I felt fine, but I noticed that I was moving slower than I did before. I don't know if I am ready for doing anything more than drive around the neighborhood. Driving will take some getting used to.

I met with Dr. Chen on Friday to see how my spine is doing. He reiterated that I would need vertebra replacement surgery as the permanent solution to the problem. He explained in a little more detail what the surgery would entail.

"We will need to make a long incision down your spine to expose the damaged T7 vertebra and the three vertebrae above and below T7. We will attach the replacement vertebra harness with screws to the upper and lower vertebrae."

"That sounds complicated," I said. My engineering mind started to think about how to choose the hardware. "Do you have options for the replacement vertebra? If so, how do you decide which one to use?"

"There are different ways to replace your vertebra, but you let me worry about all of that," Dr. Chen said. "I am in surgery every week doing procedures like this."

His remarks put me at ease and reminded me that I didn't need to know how they make the sausage; I just wanted the sausage.

"When do you think you will schedule the surgery?" I asked.

"Let's make sure you're going to survive your cancer first before we start planning back surgery," Dr. Chen said. "It would not be worth all the pain you will have to go through in recovery if the prognosis for your cancer is not good. Let's see where you stand after your Stem Cell Transplant."

I appreciated Dr. Chen's honesty. I much prefer being told the unvarnished truth instead of fluffy ambiguities intended to soften the blow of reality. Dr. Chen was right. The results of the Stem Cell Transplant would be the determining factor in what to do next.

In the meantime, I will continue to put my trust in God.

Vanessa Foster-Dotson
October 14, 2015

*** Update for Monday 10/05/15 - Tuesday 10/13/15:

No news is good news. Well mostly. Henry is continuing to progress positively. He is still eating even when he is not hungry. Five or six mini-meals a day is still the goal. This goal supports his overall physical target.

He wants to make sure that he is as fit as possible by December. Henry set this target because, in the December/January timeframe, he will be evaluated to determine whether he can receive a Stem Cell Transplant which is the next phase of his MM treatment. In short, during a Stem Cell Transplant, his diseased bone marrow will be replaced by healthy bone marrow.

As a result of his increased food intake, Henry has gained four pounds. This is a huge step in the right direction. Henry has also been told by his in-home physical therapist that "he has graduated" and should now start doing outpatient therapy so that he will have access to machines and weights. Great progress!

Another big improvement in Henry's physical condition is that he is now walking totally unassisted; no cane, no walker, no wheelchair. And he walks pretty quickly unless he is tired. On Sunday, our daughter Talia visited, and she walked approximately a half-mile with her dad. This was .2 miles farther than Henry had walked the previous week. It was great to spend time with Talia.

Henry's spiritual focus has improved as well. He has a Leadership Bible that he has had for quite some time and has used to conduct several studies. His current study is focused on servant leadership and leadership development. The study is validating and sharpening what he had already started doing when he was in Chicago, sharing wisdom, knowledge, and his faith with others, as he allows Christ's light to shine through him. Pretty awesome to watch and hear about.

continued

Lois hung out with Henry on Tuesday, 10/13/15, while I went to my first out-of-the-office work meeting. She has seen Henry a few times since we returned from Chicago and commented on how amazed she is about his progress. I am amazed as well. But God!

Now with all of this progress, Henry is ready to "spread his wings" a bit further. Last Wednesday, 10/7/15, he suggested that he drive his SUV around the block. His SUV has a manual transmission.

I was not ready for this! I asked if it would be okay if we consulted with the doctor on Friday during our already scheduled appointment with the surgeon that had prescribed the back brace for Henry. I wanted to make sure that maneuvering the manual transmission would not agitate his back. The surgeon said that it would be okay for him to drive around the block. The surgeon also had some additional news.

On Friday, as the surgeon reviewed an x-ray of Henry's back which was taken early that day, he stated that Henry is leaning forward a bit more. If you recall from the MRI image that I sent a couple of weeks ago, the more Henry leans forward, the closer the compressed vertebra, T7, will come to pressing his spinal cord.

As a result, the surgeon is saying that Henry will need to get back surgery in the future. The surgeon wants to conduct the surgery after the Stem Cell Transplant. My prayer is that God repairs Henry's back FULLY and that surgery will not be needed.

So, I ask that you please join me in praying for Henry's complete healing, especially his back.

We are blessed!

Thank you for your continued partnership and friendship!

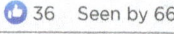

👍 36   Seen by 66   22 Comments

DK We know we serve an awesome God! So happy for Henry and Roman 8:28. Stay blessed, my sister, and when we get back in town, we plan to visit—sending our love and prayers.

JR Glory to God. Remember that no weapon formed against you shall prosper! And this is the confidence that we have in Him, that if we ask anything according to His Will, we know that He heareth us, and if we know that He hears us that we have the petitions that we desire of Him!!!!!

CP Wow! But God, he is truly amazing! Vanessa Foster-Dotson, oh what joy floods my soul hearing and watching God working things out for both of your good. There's nothing too hard or impossible for our God. We will continue to stand in agreement with you both for total healing of Henry's back as well as getting a Stem Cell Transplant. We thank God for you both.

TM Vanessa Foster-Dotson, you are a strong woman of God. God continues to bless you. Tell Henry "absheni." We love him.

SM Awesome praise report. God IS still in the healing business. I stand in agreement with you, as well as the other prayer warriors, that miraculous healing will be done regarding Henry, and God will be glorified for it. In Jesus' name!

PM God is the potter; Henry is the clay. I am in total agreement that Henry is already healed. We're just getting the opportunity to see the progression of that remarkable healing. Praise God for his faithfulness.

Q: How did your being my caregiver affect you when Vanessa needed you to do so?

LOIS: It made me feel like I was putting my prayers into action, not just praying for you to get better; I was participating. I felt that I was there for Vanessa, too, even though she seemed to be doing very well. I admired her greatly!

Q: How did you feel when you learned I was going to undergo a stem cell transplant?

IRA: The stem cell surgery was instructive. Since you had bone cancer, I did not know what the solution to that illness was. Unlike cancer in an organ that can be removed, your form of cancer created a unique solution. (I did not make the connection to your stem cell replacement therapy until I remembered my friend that had the same cancer you did.)

As you explained the process to me, it seemed like the only solution. The chemotherapy you were experiencing was necessary for this treatment to be successful.

My concern was for your ability to endure the process. I knew your immune system was compromised. I knew this phase of your treatment was critical, but it was another challenging stage of your recovery.

CRIS: I felt good about it being done because I believed it was going to help you for the better.

PAT: When I heard about the Stem Cell Transplant I was very hopeful. I was concerned, however, about the pain that you would have to go through. You had already been through so much! But I knew that if God had brought you this far, he would take you all the way.

BART: When I heard that you would be undergoing a Stem Cell Transplant to replenish your cells, I was initially surprised. I wasn't aware that this was the next step in treatment. While there were inherent risks, I was excited by the possibility of you quickly getting well.

TALIA: I didn't anticipate any problems.

BERYL: When you survived CTCA and permitted to go home, I rejoiced and gave thanks to God for bringing you through what I thought was the most difficult part of the journey. When you first told me about the Stem Cell Transplant, I thought, Hasn't he been through enough?

What helped me was knowing that you were physically closer to your support network. I could hear it in your voice (how beautiful it was to hear your voice) as you went into detail about what would happen during the Stem Cell Transplant and experiencing the power of being a part of a group of online family and friends praying individually and collectively for you.

KATHY: By that time, I was hopeful. Also, I thought of journalist Tom Brokaw who has MM and underwent a Stem Cell Transplant, if I remember correctly. And he is doing quite well. So, I felt confident that it could work for you too.

SANDRA: I felt a burst of hope and relief when I heard that you were getting a stem cell transplant.

NORMAN: Good. Very good. It seems like it is the standard for blood-related cancers. Kill all the blood-producing cells and then rebuild. It was an indicator to me that you had exited one danger zone and moved to another.

It seemed less dangerous, though. SCT is pretty common these days, not without danger, but I think it is much better understood than, say, ten years ago.

On the other hand, the slow harvest rate was disconcerting for me; you too, I suspect. That was the most worrisome thing for me after the first extraction Ð after three, would there be enough. And, if not, what next?

RUTH: I was scared. I thought at best it might give you a few extra months, and I did not want to see those few extra months be ones of extraordinary pain or helplessness/hopelessness for Vanessa.

JEFF AND CHARALE: We remember feeling that it was such a great thing that you were in tune with the voice of the Lord to go get the best treatment from the best facilities available that specialized in all forms of cancer, as well as combined faith, as part of their healing regiment.

LOIS: My feeling was that whatever even MIGHT work, I was all for it!!

CECILY: Confident with Stem Cell Transplant. Just concerned if you would be able to harvest enough stem cells. I read Tom Brokaw's autobiography; he also has Multiple Myeloma.

JIM: I knew the Stem Cell Transplant would not be an easy procedure for you, but given the spirit you had shown up to that point, I knew you perceived it as just another step in the journey you were on and one that you would get through.

MARGARET: I was relieved. I had talked to some of the folks at CTCA about your type of cancer, and they told me that the key to full recovery was to get the Stem Cell Transplant.

They also told me that you would have to be strong to be able to get through it. So, when I heard you were getting it, I felt that it meant that you would come out of this mostly whole (as much as any of us that have been that close to death can get).

Q: Did you donate blood on my behalf when you learned of the stem cell transplant?

NORMAN: I think I would have offered to donate platelets. I have in the past for someone at Sari's middle school. I probably offered when I first heard they were going to do a Stem Cell Transplant because I know that no platelets are a by-product.

I do not know the time span between when I probably offered and when they might have been needed. In fact, did you get any platelets or just whole blood? It is also possible that the time of need was within the 56-day window after I donated on my regular rotation. 12.375 gallons to date.

Welcome To The Community

"A community is the mental and spiritual condition of knowing that the place is shared, and that the people who share the place define and limit the possibilities of each other's lives. It is the knowledge that people have of each other, their concern for each other, their trust in each other, the freedom with which they come and go among themselves."
— Wendell Berry

Pasadena, CA
October 22, 2015

DURING ONE OF MY APPOINTMENTS AT CITY OF HOPE, VANESSA AND I MET WITH A FAMILY COUNSELOR. She recommended that we get involved in one or more cancer support groups, and several were there at City of Hope. She then asked where we lived and suggested that we check out Cancer Support Community Pasadena.

I am not opposed to counseling. In fact, I advocate counseling. I first went to see a counselor during the turbulent days of my divorce. She was a godsend. I know counseling helped me get through and recover from the trauma of divorce much faster than I ever could have done without it.

Vanessa and I went to see the same counselor early in our marriage as we sought ways to work through challenges newlyweds often face that we could not work out on our own. Years later, we returned to counseling with a different counselor for help with a new set of marital challenges. In both instances, counseling proved to be effective.

I highly recommend counseling when you find yourself stuck and cannot see how to get unstuck and move forward.

I knew counseling had worked well for me in the past, but that was one-on-one and marriage counseling. I had never been involved in a counseling support group before. But based on my past experience, I was willing to check it out with cautious optimism.

When Vanessa and I committed to attending cancer support group meetings, we went in all the way. We joined one on-campus group at City of Hope and two at Cancer Support Community Pasadena, and we had already attended a meeting of a group near LAX.

Each of the first three had a different focus and therefore sought to provide different types of support. The LAX group was similar to one of the first three. We settled on attending the two support groups at Cancer Support Community Pasadena facilities.

We chose Cancer Support Community Pasadena because the logistics of travel were more convenient and partly because it provided two different types of support – both of which we needed.

Vanessa and I made the trip from our house in northeast Pasadena to CSCP in southwest Pasadena last night for the first time. During the 20-minute drive, I wondered to myself how this evening would turn out. I was curious and hopeful but not sure exactly what to expect.

We pulled into the underground lot, parked in a handicapped space, and searched for the elevator. We took the elevator to the first floor and stepped out into an open courtyard surrounded by four two-story buildings.

Our Indian Summer ended early, and it was a little chilly for me because I don't have much meat on my bones. The jacket I was wearing provided some protection from the cold, but I was really looking forward to getting inside the building.

When we entered the front lobby of CSCP's office suite, the warmth of central heating greeted us. I don't know why that was so important to me, but it did help make me feel comfortable.

The front lobby looked like a living room instead of a place of business. There were two sofas facing each other with a coffee table in between. There were also a couple of other comfortable chairs. A baby grand piano was next to the front desk. A horn of plenty and other items signaling the harvest season decorated the carpeted room.

There were informational brochures covering many different cancer-related topics available to take. The director's office was to the left of the front lobby. All of the other rooms were down a hall to the right of the front lobby.

We signed in at the front desk as first-time visitors, and I picked up our free parking sticker. We arrived a little early for our appointment, so we were asked to keep our voices lowered because sessions were going on that would be ending in a few minutes. While waiting, Vanessa and I met Laura Wending.

"Welcome to Cancer Support Center Pasadena," she said with a broad smile. "I am Laura Wending, the Program Director here at the center. Are you here for the first time?"

"Yes," Vanessa said. "I called and made an appointment. And this is my husband, Henry."

"Hi," I said as I shook her hand.

"How did you hear about us?"

"Henry goes to City of Hope and a counselor there recommended that we come by. He was diagnosed in July with Multiple Myeloma."

"Well, we have several weekly support groups and other educational workshops," she began. "One of our staff will explain how you go about picking a support group."

"You are in luck," she continued. "We also let the San Gabriel Valley Multiple Myeloma Support Group use one of our rooms to hold their monthly meetings the first Monday of the month. I encourage you to take a look at them too. That group has Multiple Myeloma patients and their caregivers as members. Nice to meet you both."

We thanked Laura, and she introduced us to one of the staff workers. She explained the support groups at CSCP. They had groups for newly diagnosed patients, patients in treatment, and patients living with cancer.

The CSCP groups meet weekly, and the caregivers meet separately from the cancer patients. Caregivers and patients have different needs. Caregivers need to be in a place to share their concerns away from the patient they care for. They need to be free to express things they cannot / should not say within earshot of cancer patients.

The same goes for cancer patients. Joining a support group is similar to finding a counselor that you can work with. You need to spend a session or two feeling each other out. There is no one size fits all.

Selecting a specific support group is an important decision to be made. You must agree to keep all session conversations confidential. CSCP tracks attendance to make sure group members are regularly attending.

Most of the support comes from interactions between group members. Members develop trust in the group by meeting weekly. They feel safe sharing what they are thinking and feeling as they travel on their cancer journey.

The staff worker advised us to attend a couple of different groups whose focus is to support those recently diagnosed with cancer or who had never been a part of a cancer support group. Vanessa and I chose separate respective subgroup meetings of one of the support groups.

I was struck by how welcoming the group members were to me. When I introduced myself, I shared my cancer journey up to this point (the short, short version). Just being able to tell my story with others who had similar stories made me feel better.

Looking into their eyes, I could tell they understood me. It struck the same emotional chord within me that was struck when I saw the movie *Avatar,* and the character Neytiri (Zoe Saldana) said to the character Jake Sully (Sam Worthington), "I see you." I bought into the idea of participating in cancer support groups at that moment.

When the subgroup sessions were over, Vanessa and I got back together.

"How did it go?" Vanessa asked.

"I really enjoyed it," I replied. "How about you?"

"I'm not sure yet. I think I need to sit in a couple more times before I can decide."

I was not surprised. Whenever Vanessa is in a new situation with people she does not know, she mostly stays quiet and observes what is happening. She tends not to make hasty decisions.

"Well, I guess we will have to come back again next week and check out another group."

"Okay."

Before we left to go home, we were fortunate to meet a San Gabriel Valley (SGV) Multiple Myeloma Support Group member. The member invited us to attend their November meeting in a little over two weeks. We accepted the invitation and plan to attend next month.

Outpatient Physical Therapy

I settled on an outpatient physical therapy service provider based on a recommendation from Jim. It was the same one he used when he needed to do some rehabilitation work. I liked the setup and Edgar, the manager of the facility. The facility is located in the heart of Pasadena.

The goal of physical therapy is rehabilitation to get patients back in shape to resume regular exercise. I went through an assessment with Edgar, which included a light workout. The last time I worked out was before I pulled the muscles in my back. It felt good to work out, even though I had to wear the rigid back brace. After the workout, I set up a schedule with Edgar. He will be my physical therapist.

I look forward to working with him.

Vanessa Foster-Dotson
October 23, 2015

*** Update for Wednesday 10/14/15 - Thursday 10/22/15:

Closer to the new normal. Henry is doing well! His numbers are good, his pain is minimum, and he seems to be feeling better every day. Now, there are still days when his energy level is low, typically on Sundays, two days after his Friday chemo. And although Henry has been forcing himself to eat more, there have been times when his stomach has been upset, and he just could not make himself eat. But other than that, he is doing really well. Walking FAST!!!

I am so proud of Henry. As we have been attending support-group meetings and observing patients at City of Hope, I am constantly reminded how important a positive attitude is. As it has always been, Henry's attitude is super positive and full of faith. I am so thankful!

continued

1. Last Monday, 10/12, we were with one of our Godchildren, Joslyn. She is one of three triplets and is hoping to attend Pomona College in Claremont. It was awesome to spend time with her! It was so wonderful to see her, spend time with her, and observe how she is growing up. Thank you for blessing us with a visit, Joslyn!

Josyln's mother, Rosalind, is my sister-friend. She was the first person to say hello to me when I came to California. We worked together, we bought our first house together, we were roommates, and she was the matron of honor at our wedding. About two weeks after Henry was diagnosed, she was also diagnosed with Ovarian cancer. She is doing well. Life is interesting.

2. Henry and I were able to attend our couples Life Group meeting this week. It was refreshing to learn, share and fellowship with other believers.

3. Henry has a new physical therapist. (Thank you for the recommendation, Jim!) He went to his first outpatient session on Wednesday, 10/21. During the session, the PT assessed Henry's capabilities so that he could design a custom workout for him. The assessment lasted about 1 hour and 30 minutes and included 10 mins of cycling. Henry was able to work out the entire time!

4. We have started going to a weekly cancer-support group meeting. (These meetings are not specific to Multiple Myeloma. The MM meetings are held monthly.) During the weekly meetings, patients and caregivers meet at the same time, but separately. Henry seemed to really get a lot out of his session. The jury is still out on mine.

5. I am getting out a bit more, thanks to the support of friends and my husband, who promises me that he will not go down the stairs while I am gone. If he is by himself, I do not stay away long. However, I have been able to return to the gym, walk around the Rose Bowl, attend a couple of work and non-work-related meetings, grab a quick bite, and also go grocery shopping. Getting away by myself at times is a good thing.

6. Last but not least, Henry drove around the block! After going walking around the block one day, we then decided to see how he did behind the wheel. Henry did fine.

So, as you can see, as Henry's condition improves, we are starting to pick up the pace a bit regarding establishing our new norm. Henry is

continued

still working hard to prepare himself for a Stem Cell Transplant. He wants to gain weight and build lean muscle. Probably our biggest challenge right now is food and food preparation, especially since Henry is trying to gain weight and I am trying to lose weight. Some of you have offered to provide meals in the past, so I have finally finished documenting Henry's diet guidelines and will be posting them separately.

I am trying to make sure that we enjoy ourselves. I tend to be very task-oriented, which has been helpful during the last few months. However, one thing that I continue to learn is that life is precious. God blesses us every day that He allows us to wake up, and we should do all that we can to experience joy, peace, and happiness during the hours that we are awake. Nothing should be allowed to steal the joy that God has given us!

May God Bless You All!

As you continue to pray for Henry and everyone who is reading this update, please say a special prayer for Brad Chang and his family as they celebrate the home-going of his young son Derek. Please also say a special prayer for my brother-in-law Jarvis, his sisters Val and Vanessa, along with their families as they support their mother, Mealy Parker, who is in hospice and is suffering from brain cancer.

Remember, we are ALL truly blessed!

👍 61   Seen by 172   20 Comments

LW Again, thank you for the update. It's always inspirational. Glad you're taking care of yourself as you're taking care of Bernard. Our prayers continue to be with you and all around you.

RH Thank you for the update, Vanessa! Thank you, God, for helping Henry to heal and persevere and for helping my friend hold everything down. I am sending love and prayer to Jarvis and his family. I am still praying every day for you and Henry. Love you guys.

LD I'm not sure I knew you lived in Pasadena. You said you walk the Rose Bowl. I was in town last week. My mom lives on Harriet. I need to try and see you guys on my next visit.

PM — My dearest Vanessa, you are surely the definition and epitome of a true earth angel. What would Henry do without your love and dedication? Thank you for ALL that you do!!

With you doing due diligence in every aspect of his care, you are so much responsible for his recovery. God is happy to share his glory with you. As his servants, you are all that God asks us to be and His perfect example.

God bless you for remembering that your friends are in need of prayer as well in their time of tribulation. I am praying that the Holy Spirit offers them the comfort that will sustain them.

RN — Hey Dotson family. Hey Henry. You look great. I'm sooo happy to see you up and about. Praise Jesus!! Hallelujah!!! Thankful.

EC — Praise God! It is said that a picture is worth a thousand words. This picture says so much. So good to see Henry up and about and with a big smile. God is faithful.

DK — You are looking great! God is awesome. May He continue to bless and heal and restore everything to everyone in Jesus' name, amen. Xoxo

SM — Praise God! Sooooo good to see you guys. Yes, I agree that a picture is worth a thousand words. Looking good, brother!

RG — Great picture, so pleased and joyful to see you all are looking fabulous! Henry B. Dotson III, you look wonderful, to God be the Glory. I love you, and many blessings!

DR — Hey, glad to hear that. I just want to say Henry and you look good. Our God is truly awesome!! Love and Hugs to you both!

Pasadena, CA
November 3, 2015

San Gabriel Valley Multiple Myeloma Support Group

The San Gabriel Valley Multiple Myeloma Support Group (aka SGV Myeloma Group) was founded in April 2013. Their mission is to help Multiple Myeloma patients, their family, friends, and caregivers find answers to questions about Multiple Myeloma. The organization is closely affiliated with the International Myeloma Foundation (IMF), based in North Hollywood, California.

Vanessa and I attended our first SGV Myeloma Group meeting last night. The caregivers and the patients all met together. Only occasionally do they split into subgroups.

This support group also has speakers from time to time to share information of interest to Multiple Myeloma patients and their caregivers. Confidentiality is also required, but the commitment for regular attendance is not.

There is no professionally trained facilitator conducting the meeting. Instead, the leader is either a patient or a caregiver. However, the leader does attend some annual training sessions held by the IMF. Everyone takes a turn sharing what has happened since the last meeting, and newcomers introduce themselves when it is their turn to share.

Food is available at the meeting (sometimes provided by the speaker if they represent a pharmaceutical company). The people are very friendly and welcoming, but it seems as if sharing information is more the type of support one receives. I could tell the group's regular members had developed a rapport with one another based on how they interacted.

I found this type of support group very helpful too. I heard the same medical terms my oncologist was using, and the group members could help explain what they meant. That satisfied my analytical side that wants to understand the facts.

I also found it very helpful hearing how others dealt with the challenges they were facing as Multiple Myeloma patients. They talked about things that I have yet to experience in my treatment plan. It was good to hear such frank and candid conversation. I was encouraged by what I heard. I definitely plan to become a regular with this group.

> *"I am struck by how sharing our weakness and difficulties is more nourishing to others than sharing our qualities and successes."*
> — Jean Vanier

Since the specifics of what takes place during a CSCP support session are confidential, I can only share with you the key takeaways I got from my experience with the support group in general terms and comments made by group members in anonymity.

- First and foremost, there truly does exist a cancer community in the highest sense of the word. A community where its members obviously care for one another, are empathetic, and honest about what they are going through. One of my group members said,

  "We are all involuntary members of this community. We are not here by choice. But despite that, being part of this community is one of the best things I have ever been a part of in my entire life."

  Another one said,
  "I can honestly say I am thankful that I got cancer. It has helped me to realize my purpose in life."

- When cancer patients get together in a support-group setting, they share feelings that they will not share with anyone else. Not their caregiver, their doctor, loved ones, or even their spouse / significant other. What makes it more impressive is that some readily share these things during their first session with total strangers. There is a strong need to connect with someone you know understands what you are going through because they are going through it too, or have already been where you are going. And cancer patients know they do not have to be pretentious around other cancer patients.

- Members of a cancer support group are incredibly giving of themselves to help others in the group. I believe that cancer-support groups are one way God ministers comfort and compassion to people. Sincere words of encouragement are shared, along with words of reassurance that we are not alone on our cancer journey.

One group member said something very poignant that has remained with me, and I think I will never forget it.

He was very, very ill, and his prospects for survival were very, very low. Each time we met, the group was not sure if he would show up. He was relatively young (in his mid 30s?) and had had other significant health and financial struggles in his life. During one of his last meetings, he said,

> "When I look back at my life, I am very grateful. I have had struggles in the past, but I have always had people around me that cared about me and cared for me. I don't have much, but whatever I have, I am always willing to share."

Another group member said,

> "I heard someone give a talk about what it means to enjoy life. As part of his talk, he looked at where the word 'enjoy' came from, what its origin was, and what does it mean.
>
> He said it came from the notion of one entering 'into joy.' He went on to say, the only way we can enter into joy is to first have a sense of gratitude. We must first be grateful for the life we have before we can enjoy the life we have."

> "Healing is impossible in loneliness; it is the opposite of loneliness. Conviviality is healing. To be healed we must come with all the other creatures to the feast of Creation." — Wendell Berry

Another Trip Around the Sun

"Each new year of life added to your past, changing the way you viewed every new day, influencing how you reacted to everything from the simplest daily routines to complex events touching you, your family, and the world you lived in." — Paul Snyder

---

Pasadena, CA
October 27, 2015

WE CELEBRATED MY BIRTHDAY EARLY THIS YEAR. We celebrated the Sunday before because my birthday will be this Wednesday. Vanessa made another valiant attempt to surprise me, but I was not caught unaware. I knew she would want to have some type of celebration for a birthday that we were not sure I would see a few months ago.

What made it exceptional was that I celebrated it with my siblings; only the second time in our lives that we have had a joint birthday party. Our first joint birthday party was the only birthday party we had while we were growing up. It was an overwhelming experience for my mother.

You see, all three of us were born in October, a little less than one year apart. My mother decided to host a joint birthday to celebrate us turning two, three, and four. Up until then, she was too busy trying to take care of three children under three years old to even think about having a party for an individual child.

The joint party idea was intended to kill three birds with one stone, so to speak. A joint party would eliminate the stress of having three separate parties, all in October. If all went well, this could become a family tradition.

My mother was prim and proper, and she wanted everything to go exactly according to her plan. That was the way she ran her classroom as an elementary school teacher. Unfortunately, when working with a group of toddlers, nothing goes according to plan. My mother told me things became too chaotic for her when the time came for the children to eat the cake and ice cream.

> *"The children would not sit still at the table. We parents were chasing after them. I looked up and saw you eating ice cream with your fingers. Everything was a mess. I told myself, 'I'll never do this again.'"*

Here endeth the Dotson family tradition of children's birthday parties. Instead, we would each be recognized on our respective birthdays and made to feel special. We would get to do something we liked, and everyone would participate.

This year's birthday celebration was extra special because it was more than 50 years in the making. Praise God from whom all blessings flow!

 Vanessa Foster-Dotson
October 27, 2015

*** Update for Friday 10/23/15 – Monday 10/26/15:

Time to celebrate! Henry is still doing very well. Yes, he is walking, standing, and looking a bit differently. And yes, he weighs much less. And yes, he is having some digestion issues right now. But each day, he is talking and acting more and more like the "old" Henry that we all love. We are thankful!

These past few days have been eventful. Friday was Henry's normal chemo day. The appointments were relatively quick, so afterward, I was able to return to work. But the big event on Friday was that Henry drove us to and from City of Hope for the first time! This is about a 20-minute drive on the freeway one way.

Henry did well! The manual transmission did not seem to negatively affect him physically. I think that he really enjoyed being in control. I know that my knees were happy that I did not have to maneuver the transmission pedal. (smile!)

Saturday, Henry ended up hanging out at home by himself for a while as I got my hair done by a new hairdresser in Pasadena. My hair even felt the heat of a hot comb for the first time in years. (I will be returning my hair to its natural state ASAP.) I wasn't far away, and Henry again promised he would not navigate the steps while I was gone. Henry was fine when I returned.

On Sunday we partied!!! We had a surprise party for Henry. His birthday is on Wednesday, Oct. 28th. Only Henry's siblings and their children were invited in order to minimize his exposure to illness. So, there were about 12 people in total. Bart and Lashae (Pat's daughter) both live out of state and were not able to make it. (They were missed!) Talia came early and stayed late to assist me.

As you can see from the picture in our kitchen that our niece Stefany posted yesterday, Henry had a great time. He even played the piano for a while. I learned a long time ago that the best gift/medicine for Henry is being around people, especially family. So, this immune

continued

system challenge has been difficult. You all know how social he is. Thankfully his immune system is stronger right now.

During the party, we also celebrated Henry's brother's and sister's birthdays. Ira E Dotson's birthday is October 31. Patricia Jones's birthday is October 11th. Unknowingly, this was the first time the three of them had celebrated their birthday together in 50 years. Truly special!

We are so blessed that Henry will be here to celebrate his birthday on Wednesday (God willing). When he arrived in Chicago in July, Henry was EXTREMELY close to not being alive. But God had a different plan!

I don't understand why some people live and others die. I don't understand why some people get cancer and others don't. But I do understand that God orders our footsteps. And I am thankful that He has orders for Henry to do more on this earth with all of us, especially with me (smile!).

If you care to celebrate Henry's Birthday with us, please call him, text him or arrange a visit. Please flood him with an outpouring of your love. Inbox or email me, and I will provide his contact info.

If you really would like to give a gift, you can also donate via our PayPal account or Henry's Go-Fund-Me account. In addition to his medical and home care, there are a few things that I need to buy him.

So Happy Birthday, Baby! Thank you for blessing us all with another year of the joy, happiness, and love that you bring!

33   Seen by 37   9 Comments

 Happy Birthday my carpool buddy! Praising and thanking our God with you and for the gift of another birthday!

 Wow! Happy Birthday, Bernard! So glad the Dotson sibs celebrated together. So glad that you are in his life, Vanessa! Peace and healing be with you!

 Happy, happy birthday, Henry. I know you will be around to celebrate many, many more! Hugz. I am vanpooling right now since I live so far away, but when I drive, I will see if it is a good time to visit. Take care, my friend—prayers to you and the fam bam.

I am OVERJOYED to see my uncle snap back from being on his deathbed to his old goofy self!!!! He's not 100%, but he has come a looooooong way!!! I love you, Uncle Bernard!!!!!

Q: HOW DID YOU FEEL ABOUT PARTICIPATING IN THE BIRTHDAY CELEBRATION FOR YOU, ME, AND PAT?

IRA: I do not remember that birthday celebration. Nevertheless, the most important aspect of that event was that it was the first time in over forty years that the three of us were together.

Q: How did you feel about participating in the birthday celebration for you, me, and Ira?

PAT: The birthday party was bitter-sweet for me. I loved being able to celebrate your birthday, but with a seemingly uncertain diagnosis, my heart was heavy. Seeing you in that bed downstairs was tough.

I had to put on my "happy smile" to hide my tears. Was this the last birthday? Was this as good as it gets? Your frail body and tired look reminded me of so many others I saw when I was dealing with my cancer.

I felt privileged to be able to spend that time with you, even though it hurt to see you so small and sickly.

Q: What did you think when you first saw me after my diagnosis?

CRIS: I was a little numb to think anything.

Q: How did you feel when you first saw me after my diagnosis?

CRIS: I was somewhat sad, and I was in disbelief that you had cancer.

Q: Was it difficult for you to see me in my physical condition?

CRIS: Yes, it was a little difficult. You didn't look like you.

Q: What were you feeling when you saw Ira, Pat, and me celebrating our birthdays together in Oct-2015?

CRIS: I thought it was cool for us to celebrate all of your birthdays together. I think it was a first.

Pasadena, CA
October 28, 2015

A Birthday to Remember

"God gave us the gift of life; it is up to us to give ourselves the gift of living well."
— Voltaire

"Count not the candles...see the lights they give. Count your age by friends, not years. Count not the years, but the life you live."
— Birthday.Kim

Henry B. Dotson III
October 28, 2015

Happy Birthday to Me!

Today's status update is written by me – Henry because it is my birthday. Vanessa has done such an excellent job keeping you informed of my progress, so I am honored that she allowed me to make this special entry.

Some of you know that birthdays are special to me. I try to call many of you on your special day to wish you well and let you know you are special to me. On my birthday, I take time to reflect, give thanks, and look forward to what the future will hold.

With that in mind, I want to give a first-person account of my status and share my thoughts for the day.

Reflections

This past year has definitely been a year of change. This time last year, I was 11 days into my involuntary "retirement" from my employer, deciding what to do next. In January, I started my consulting business. In March and April, I was awarded my first two contracts. In July, I started this amazing journey that has challenged my health, my faith, and my perception of the significance of my life in the lives of others.

In retrospect, God was preparing me for a new season in my life. I continued to learn to trust in Him and Him alone, and to listen for His small, still voice when I needed to make a major decision. The time was right for me to start a new business. It was the right decision to go to Chicago for my care. My faith was tested when there was

continued

nowhere else to turn. In each instance, God was faithful.

In the midst of it all, I learned that I had made a difference in the lives of others. The outpouring of support came from so many that I could not keep up with everyone. Thank God for Vanessa setting up this Facebook group as a means to communicate with you all.

As a result, I was inspired to continue to be used to speak into others' lives even as I was going through my own trials. I shared with anyone who came into my hospital room, and God had a word for those who were ready to hear. I learned that the purpose for my life did not take a break just because I was facing my own challenges.

Finally, I learned that everyone that supports me pays a price of their own. You give of yourselves in my moment of need. For those who saw me firsthand, my physical condition affected their emotions and state of mind. It has made me sensitive and empathetic to what you put yourselves through when you step out of your comfort zones and make such a personal sacrifice on my behalf.

I am overwhelmed with gratitude and humility.

Giving Thanks

Every day I give thanks to God for allowing me to see another sunrise. He has carried me through the valley of the shadow of death, and I feared no evil. I had no idea that I was a sick as I was. With a faith as innocent as that of a child in his parent's love and protection, I have been blessed to see Him work true miracles in my life.

Many of my health care providers have said my survival is nothing short of a miracle. My kidneys have been restored (no dialysis required), and the markers for my cancer are within the normal range. While my full restoration has not manifested itself in the natural, it has been ordained in the supernatural.

I give thanks every day for God putting Vanessa in my life. I literally would not be alive today had she not been there for me. She is my Proverbs 31 woman and has lived up to the vows she made on our wedding day to love, honor, and cherish me in sickness and in health. With God's help, I strive to keep my commitments to her in the midst of my journey.

I also give thanks for all of you who have supported me with your prayers, words of encouragement, and finances. God works through the hands, feet, and voices of others that He puts in our lives. I have seen Him work through all of you. I am truly blessed.

continued

The Future

I look forward to what the future will hold. My health continues to improve. I actually drove to the hospital with Vanessa last Friday for my weekly appointments. I am in outpatient physical therapy and building my strength. I have Stem Cell Transplant procedures to go through in 2016 and possible back surgery afterward.

God is able, and I will trust in Him as He has shown Himself trustworthy. Please continue to pray for me and be the blessing in my life that helps sustain me as I run the race before me.

I thank Vanessa again for allowing me to make this entry on my status. I hope you have found it informative and encouraging. God has a plan for each one of us. Your decision to be a part of my journey is part of His plan for us all. Thank you for getting on board and seeing what He will do.

May God continue to bless you and keep you. I look forward to hearing from you on this special day in my life.

-- Be Well!!

Please call, text, or arrange a visit if you have a chance.

👍 52   Seen by 62   31 Comments

GT Happy Birthday!!! Henry, again I truly thank God for your healing. It is wonderful hearing from you today. These updates continue to bless me, and I am learning to be more patient each day as God shows up in my journey daily. Love you guys, Henry and Vanessa ☺ P.S. Brianna sends her Love and Prayers!

LW First, I want to say, "Happy Birthday, Bernard!"

Second, I believe you and Vanessa are role models of Christian love and marriage. And to that end, I hope you publish your inspirational thoughts.

Every morning, I look forward to seeing Vanessa's updates on your progress. It makes my day!

You both are thoughtful writers who have an audience ready and needing your messages.

May you continue to allow God to be the light in your life.

Love you, my SBC brother!

DM — I first for most give honor, glory, and praise to God for this day.

A day that He has seen fit to bless and mark it as special, to acknowledge you and all that you are to so many. That being said, Henry, Happy Birthday. Surely, in addition, I acknowledge Vanessa, your wife, helpmate, and bridge over troubled waters, for her unwavering faith and trust in your well-being. I thank God for you both. A testimony of love in this day. I pray for God's continued blessing in your life this day and always.

RN — Happy Birthday my friend Henry Dotson. I wish you all of God's Blessings. God is in the healing business. Amen. So happy to see you doing better. I love you and Vanessa!

LD — So beautifully written and testifies of your journey with God!! Oh man of God, you are a blessing Hallelujah Henry! May you have beautiful sunrises every day!

Happy birthday, brother Henry. What a journey! I pray that God will keep you and Vanessa strong and encouraged. I hope you had a good day. Peace.

WL — Dear Henry, you and Vanessa have, and continue to be, a blessing to us, the Langley's, as we see the strength and power of God's LOVE BEING POURED OUT ON YOU. In this JOURNEY of LIFE, GOD'S GRACE and MERCY IS SUFFICIENT. HE PREPARES A WAY OF ESCAPE. HE DOESN'T BRING THE STORM, BUT HE TELLS THE STORM, PEACE, BE QUIET, BACK AWAY, LEAVE, ABANDONED, BE STILL, AND LEAVE MY CHILD.

VH — Dear Henry, oh, you most certainly are a significant presence in all of our lives, and as you can see, you are deeply loved and cherished by many. You and Vanessa are truly blessed to have each other. Your status is one of the most beautiful I have ever read on this forum. May God continue to keep you in His care, and I hope that this very special birthday is everything that you want it to be. Love you, my friend.

CP — Happy birthday, Henry. This is the day the Lord made. Let us rejoice and be glad in it. God had a plan for you, Henry. Many are called, but few are chosen. He chose you to be his emissary and living testimony to minister to all those who will listen to the goodness and glory of God.

CP Happy birthday to an awesome man of God and valor. Henry, words cannot begin to describe how blessed I am with Earnest to send a shout out to you on this special day. God created you for such a time as this. We truly appreciate and thank God for you being a part of our life. You are a vessel full of Power guided by the Holy Spirit. We love you.

AV I wish you continued blessings, Henry. May your Birthday be filled with love and laughter.

Vanessa Foster-Dotson
October 28, 2015

*** 10/28/15 ***

Happy Birthday to my best friend, Henry B. Dotson III! He just happens to be my husband as well. God blessed me with this friendship in 1988, and 10 years later, we were married. It has been a fantastic journey! Henry is definitely the soul mate and lover that I was meant to spend the rest of my life with. He is fun, intelligent, loving, and God-fearing. He is also a great father, brother, uncle, and friend, a social butterfly that knows no stranger.

As you may know, our journey recently encountered a major twist in the form of Henry being diagnosed with Multiple Myeloma. It has been awesome to watch how Henry has navigated this twist with faith, humility, and unexpected gratitude.

Henry is truly a fantastic person. I am so blessed to have him as a husband and thankful to be given another birthday to share with him.

Happy Birthday, My Dear Henry!

BD Happy Birthday, Henry. Wishing you a year of joy, prosperity, love, improved health, and peace. Warrior on!

VH Happy Birthday earth angel, Henry! Vanessa, what a blessing! Beautiful tribute ♥

PM Vanessa, God bless you for being there to do all that you have done to ensure Henry is enjoying another birthday.

This birthday is definitely a significant one I will never forget.

There was another birthday I celebrated with Vanessa. However, that is just as memorable as this one and arguably even more significant.

Pomona, CA
Friday, October 30, 1997

VANESSA WANTED IT TO BE BIG, AND SHE WANTED IT TO BE A SURPRISE. Since my 40th birthday was on a Wednesday that year, she decided to have a party on the weekend. She decided to have a surprise party Friday night because it was the day before Halloween. Vanessa didn't want to have it on Halloween night because she knew people would already have plans to be out celebrating that occasion, and turnout for my party would be less.

To make it interesting, she decided that the party would be in keeping with the season by having a Halloween theme, which would call for guests to wear costumes; and that it would include a time to "roast" me, so the guests would need to come prepared to speak. Planning is Vanessa's wheelhouse. She is logical and analytical.

Vanessa diligently and discretely searched to locate as many friends of mine as she could find. She discretely used my address book to get my friends' contact information. She contacted friends of mine to help her find other friends of mine. She found old address books of mine and went through them to find even more friends of mine. When Vanessa sets a goal, she is determined and persistent to achieve it.

She needed to make arrangements. Vanessa contacted a close college friend of mine who taught at a Christian school run by a church. My friend got permission from the church to use the school's auditorium for the party. Vanessa hired a caterer and a DJ. In the weeks leading up to the event, she collected the necessary party supplies. She got volunteers to be part of setup, decoration, and cleanup crews. Not only is Vanessa determined and persistent, but she is also very organized and very thorough.

The children were with me that weekend, so it worked out that they would attend without disrupting the schedule I had established with their mom. Vanessa waited as long as she could before she told them about the party and that it was a surprise, so they did an excellent job of not letting on.

Try as she might, the event itself was destined not to be a total surprise to me. Vanessa knew I considered my 40th birthday one of those milestone events in my life. She knew it, and she knew I knew she knew it. So, it did not take much for me to deduce that she was going to do something.

The unknowns for me were the actual date, time, and location. The "surprise" for me would be what was what she had planned to happen during the event. I did not know what exactly she was scheming, but I knew it would not be small. I also knew she knew I loved getting together with friends to celebrate the significant events in my life. So, whatever it was going to be, I knew it would involve many of my friends.

That is the challenge we face when it comes to really surprising each other on special occasions. We know each other well, and we are both analytical. Therefore, most, if not all, of the usual elements of surprise are not in play simply because of the way we think. Subtleties buried in the details are our most effective elements of surprise.

On my birthday, Vanessa called and wished me a happy birthday. I took the day off, so I would not see her at work that day. She said she would meet me later and we could do something to celebrate.

I received some phone calls from others, the most important being the one from my mother. Vanessa and I went out as planned to celebrate. While it was not the "big" event, it was a wonderful evening. I shared with her some of the reflections and observations I had made during the day.

"I hope you remembered to keep Friday night open," Vanessa said nonchalantly. "The kids and I want to do something special to celebrate your birthday."

"I remembered," I replied equally as nonchalant. I played along, not to give away the mental gymnastics I had already gone through in my head about the event. Her comment had just eliminated one of the unknowns – the date – and narrowed the time down to the evening. I did not want to show any signs of how this information had helped me fit a few more pieces into the puzzle.

While I knew I would not be surprised, I wanted to give as much of the appearance of a surprise to Vanessa as possible when the time came to do so. In addition to being very analytical, Vanessa is very good at picking up my nonverbal communication and using her intuition to figure out where my head is. I did not want her to figure out how much I already knew.

On Friday morning, Vanessa called and told me that the children and I should dress up for the evening. She said she planned for it to be a "special" celebration. I said I would do as she asked. I picked up the kids after school, and while driving home, I asked them if they knew what we were going to do that night. They just giggled and said, "We can't tell you!"

Vanessa called as evening approached and said she would come by to pick us up around 6 p.m. to take us out.

She showed up at the appointed time. She honked her horn for us to come out to the car. Vanessa was wearing a beautiful black and gold sequined dress. She was also wearing makeup, something she normally did not do.

"Wow!" I said. You look nice."

"Thank you very much," she said in a way similar to Elvis Presley.

We got into the car and headed east on the 210 freeway. I was trying to figure out where we were going in silence. Vanessa was paying close attention to the freeway because we were in rush hour traffic. Bart and Talia were sitting in the back, just smiling.

I would occasionally reach back and squeeze one of their thighs to make them laugh. They would jump and squeal, "Stop, daddy!" When things got too busy, Vanessa would say, "Henry, leave them alone!" I would stop for a while and start up again after a few minutes.

We took the 210 freeway east to the 57 freeway south and then on to the 10 freeway east. After a 45-minute ride, we exited the 10 freeway at the Indian Hill offramp. We headed south on Indian Hill into the city of Pomona.

I was still trying to figure out where we were going until we turned right onto Lincoln Avenue, and I saw the Christian school where my friend worked. I knew we had arrived.

The party was a success. I was surprised to see the number of people in attendance. Vanessa did a great job contacting people that I had not seen in a long time. The decorations, music, and food were perfect.

The roast, however, did not go as planned. When the guests that decided to speak took the "mike," they each said they could not think of anything to say that would "roast" me. Instead, they each got up and said what a wonderful friend I had been over the years. What was to be a roast turned into a sentimental expression of appreciation.

The last person to speak was Valenda. She didn't get very far into her remarks before she became emotional. We had supported one another as we each went through very trying divorce proceedings. We had become like family, supporting one another as single parents. We had shared things with each other that we had not told anyone else.

Valenda was not making eye contact with anyone as she gave her remarks. She mostly looked around and occasionally at the floor. As her eyes filled with tears, we made eye contact. Her tears began flowing almost as much as mine. After her remarks, we hugged each other for a long time.

After the event came to a close and most of the guests had left, the volunteer cleanup crew began to take down all of the decorations. The caterer and the DJ were already packing up their equipment. Vanessa was overseeing everything to make sure the auditorium would be ready for Sunday school in a couple of days.

I was helping a little with the cleanup, but I was mostly taking in how wonderful the event had been. So many people were there, and I could not have been more humbled by their kind words. I thought about the great job Vanessa had done putting it all together. I looked to see where she was. My eyes found her in the middle of the room, sweeping.

As I looked at Vanessa, it seemed like the lights in the room dimmed, and a spotlight shined on her. The gold sequins on her dress seemed to shimmer as she went through her sweeping motions. Then I heard a voice as if someone was standing directly behind me, although no one was there. The voice said:

> "Henry, I know the desires of your heart. I know you want to have the kind of marriage the Bible talks about. You asked Me to bring you a helpmate as I did for Adam. I have brought Vanessa to you."

There was a slight pause, and then the voice continued:

> "Now you have a choice. You do not have to choose Vanessa to be your helpmate. You asked Me to make it clear to you who that one is because you can be a little dense. So, to make it clear, Vanessa is the one I have brought to you."

A couple of seconds later, there was no spotlight on Vanessa, and the lights in the room returned to their previous brightness.

I could hardly believe what just happened. It felt so surreal. But I did recognize His voice. I knew it was God because I had never thought about Vanessa being "the one." I also knew it was Him because He honored my request by making it undeniably clear that it was Him when He spoke of me being dense.

I then said to myself, *Henry, you would be a fool if you don't marry that woman.*
It was at that moment I decided I was going to marry Vanessa.

Pasadena, CA
November 5, 2015

I CONTINUE TO WORK HARD IN PREPARATION FOR MY STEM CELL TRANSPLANT I am scheduled to complete my sixth round of chemotherapy in December and then return to CTCA for the procedure. I am determined to be in the best shape possible when it is time to go.

I work out twice a week in outpatient physical therapy. I make sure I do one more repetition of every exercise to push myself just a little bit further. Vanessa and I now go walking twice a week. I now drive to Victory Park with Mylene, and we walk around the park. I think Mylene gets more tired than I do when we walk the park.

Some days, I slow down because of the chemotherapy treatments. But, I am determined not to let that be an excuse for me not to do my best. I am more than a conqueror!

Vanessa Foster-Dotson
November 7, 2015

*** Update for Thursday 10/29/15 – Thursday 11/05/15:

Less is More. Time has been moving quickly. All things considered, Henry is doing really well. If you did not get a chance to read his birthday update on 10/28, I strongly encourage you to do so. Henry is having fewer and fewer challenges with his Multiple Myeloma.

He has gained about 11 lbs. and now weighs about 161! The numbers from his lab work continue to improve. His kidneys are stable. His immune system has improved. He is driving more with others in the car. He is getting more things done on his computer. Henry's hair is even growing back! (He has soft, straight, fine hair. I affectionately call him "Fuzzy.")

Henry is again experiencing low energy on Sundays after receiving his weekly chemo regimen on Fridays. Lately, he has not wanted to get out of bed much on Sundays. After the last two chemo treatments, he has also been tired on Mondays. We have been reminded that his low energy is expected as a result of the steroids that he receives as part of his regimen.

However, although expected, he gets a bit frustrated as he wants to be productive, but his body just won't let him. His frustration is totally understandable. We are learning that it is important that we keep the lines of communication open during these times so that I understand how he is feeling.

I know he is sick and that he is dealing with more than I can even imagine. However, when he is frustrated, he gets a bit snappy at times which can be difficult for me to deal with. Time to pray!

Henry continues to focus on doing all that he can to be accepted as a Stem Cell Transplant recipient, and I am trying to help him. He is still going to PT twice a week. They have increased the intensity of his workout to build his strength.

continued

In addition, we are walking on our own sometimes twice a week. He also walks two times a week with his caregiver. (The caregiver is now coming 4 hours a day twice a week...thanks to your financial support!)

Food continues to be a challenge. Henry is eating, but he is pretty picky, and sometimes he still does not have an appetite. But at the same time, he is trying to gain weight (and I am trying to lose weight). So, I have been spending quite a bit of time refining his/our diet plan as well as planning and preparing meals. Just when I think that we have a plan that we can follow and that I can share with you, his appetite changes. Very frustrating, but I am determined to do what I can to ensure his success!

In addition to helping him, I am trying to do all that I can at work. Since I am not able to travel, I feel like I have to do extra to make sure that I am not viewed as a layoff candidate. Being the sole financial provider can be a heavy weight at times. I know God has our back, but sometimes I still have concerns. Faith!

Yes, Henry continues to improve daily. His strength is increasing, and he is having fewer challenges. However, somehow it seems that more time is being required to prepare for the Stem Cell Transplant; more exercise time, more food planning/prep time, more time at work, more time getting our affairs in order. Less is more!

But we are still very blessed. As we attend various support group meetings, I am reminded of how serious Multiple Myeloma really is. Daily, and when you continue to see progress, you can sometimes set aside the magnitude of what is going on in Henry's body.

When Henry shares his story, it reminds me of how close he was to exiting his earthly presence. I am also reminded that there is currently no cure for MM, but new treatments that will keep the disease at bay and extend Henry's life, are constantly being developed.

Henry's current side effects are minimal when compared to others. Sure, he has a major compression fracture in his back, but the brace that he is wearing is limiting his pain. And yes, he has neuropathy in his hands and other parts of his body. But he does not have neuropathy in his feet, so he can walk without pain or concern. He has only had single instances of nausea and diarrhea. We Are Blessed!!!

So, thank you once again for all of your prayers, finances, and other gestures of support. Outside of God, all of YOU are our greatest blessing! You are truly making a difference.

continued

Please keep the Parker and Mack families in prayer as they attend the funerals of both of their matriarchs over the next few days. Interesting times. (RIP)

👍 30   Seen by 53   10 Comments

CP Vanessa Foster-Dotson, no matter what you post, God has His hands in it all the way. It is the effectual fervent prayer of the righteous that avail much. You have so much love and support. Global war rooms are lifting up prayers with and for you guys.

Our God is greater awesome in power Lord you are higher than any other, Lord you are a healer.

So as we continue to send up the praises, the blessings are coming down. Be encouraged as you are for Henry and we decree and declare it so for we still believe the report of the Lord! Hallelujah!

JD May God continue to bless the Parker and Mack families during and as well as after this time of sorrow. In your post, you mentioned what this journey takes, and that's FAITH. God is good, and he has given us a testimony. Continue blessings and much love.

LW I am always amazed and inspired by your love for your husband and your willingness to share the joys and challenges. Know that you have a sis in the Bay Area praying for you, Bernard, and the rest of the family.

WL You guys are traveling a JOURNEY that becomes GOD'S POSSIBILITIES. GOD IS SHOWING YOU THAT HE IS THE GREAT I AM. HE HAS BROUGHT YOU THIS FAR BY FAITH. It is great to see that YOUR FAITH IS SEEING YOU THROUGH. GOD IS MIGHTY, AWESOME, FAITHFUL, and ALWAYS ON TIME. We are LIFTING YOU UP EVERY MORNING.

PH Vanessa Foster-Dotson. I am inspired by your posts to trust God always. We continue to pray and believe God for the full manifestation of healing in every area of concern. Please know that you are stellar examples of acting on and living your faith, and your prayers are answered!

Nessa, I, too, have appetite problems. One day that something tastes good, the next time no. I also lost 75lbs and am trying to gain some of it back.

I drink Ensure to make sure I get the protein I need. I also bought these capsules on Amazon.com called Graviola, and it's supposed to be ten times stronger/better than chemo. I'll send you more info later, but it never hurts to try.

You are always in my prayers, and I know this is an awesome testimony of faith and love. Stay strong, my friends. Hugz

Decisions, Decisions!

"Be willing to make decisions. Don't fall victim to the ready-aim-fire syndrome. You must be willing to fire." — T. Boone Pickens

---

Pasadena, CA
November 6, 2015

I AM ELIGIBLE FOR A STEM CELL TRANSPLANT RIGHT NOW! My oncologist told us last Friday that I had responded very well to my chemotherapy treatments. The amount of myeloma cells in my marrow is down from 90% to 5%.

That is a miracle to me. Some patients do not respond well or at all to the first chemotherapy protocol given to them. I have received the favor of God!

If we decide to move up the Stem Cell Transplant, City of Hope will perform the procedure. My oncologist would also want me to enter into a clinical trial with a different chemotherapy medication. He says I am a good candidate for the trial, and administering the medication would be less invasive because I would take one pill once a week.

If we decide to continue according to plan, CTCA will perform the Stem Cell Transplant, and CTCA will continue to supervise City of Hope as they carry out the treatment plan prepared by CTCA.

With the unexpected good news comes an unexpected choice with significant consequences. Vanessa and I were not prepared to make such an important decision.

To add to the gravity of the decision, City of Hope is advocating a different post-Stem Cell Transplant treatment plan. That means if we choose to go with City of Hope, I will no longer be a patient of CTCA.

Our oncologist asked us to make this decision by next Friday. I believe he wants an answer soon so he can place me in the clinical trial before other patients take all of the openings.

We are feeling pressure to make a decision, but we don't know if we are prepared to decide in a week's time.

"Once a decision is carefully reached, act! Get busy carrying out your decisions – and dismiss all anxiety about the outcome."
— Dale Carnegie

Vanessa Foster-Dotson
November 11, 2015

*** Update for Friday 11/06/15 – Wednesday 11/11/15: Decision Time! We are at a point where we need to make some major decisions, so we are asking once again for your prayers. However, before I continue, let me say that I apologize for not writing this sooner. While contemplating these decisions, time got away from me.

So, what are the decisions? Well, when we went to Henry's chemo appointment at City of Hope (COH) last Friday, 11/06/15, we had an opportunity to see his oncologist. The oncologist said:

Henry would not be receiving chemo that day because:

1. Henry's blood counts had improved to the point that, after four cycles of chemo instead of the six cycles that were originally planned, he is eligible to be evaluated for a Stem Cell Transplant NOW. However, Henry could also wait until later to have the transplant.

2. If Henry decides to do the Stem Cell Transplant (SCT) now, at COH, he could either undergo the SCT on an out-patient basis or an in-patient basis. Henry's original plan was to go back to the Cancer Treatment Centers of America (CTCA) for his SCT.

3. After the SCT, and once in the maintenance phase of his treatment, Henry could participate in a clinical trial that is offered at COH. Participation in the clinical trial could extend Henry's life.

4. The oncologist requested that Henry complete his decision process by this Friday, 11/13/15...although 11/06 was the first time that the oncologist discussed most of these details with us. (We were a bit shocked!)

5. Now the fact that Henry is eligible for his SCT almost two months ahead of the original schedule is a true blessing and is a direct result of all of your prayers. Thank you! Thank you! Thank you! And Thank you, God!

Since last Friday, we have reached out to CTCA and made sure that they have Henry's latest results along with a copy of the clinical trial information. Based on his results, they agree that Henry is eligible to be evaluated for a Stem Cell Transplant. They also feel that the clinical trial is very positive. Unfortunately, they do not offer the trial at CTCA.

Over the last few days, we have also reached out to several Multiple Myeloma patients that we know so that we could better understand their transplant experience. One person, Henry's Aunt Karen, had her

continued

SCT performed at the COH. Her experience at COH was very positive.

To date, our experience at COH has not been completely positive. Probably our biggest concern is the experience level of Henry's oncologist and the level of care that is provided by the medical team, especially some of the nursing staff.

Administering weekly chemo injections is pretty straightforward. However, when it comes to doing a Stem Cell Transplant, that is major.

Henry has already decided that he wants to proceed with the SCT as soon as possible. He has decided that he wants the SCT to be performed on an in-patient basis. He has also decided that he would like to participate in the clinical trial.

So please join us in praying for the following so that we are prepared for our discussion with the oncologist on Friday:

1. Which facility should Henry have the SCT performed at?
2. If Henry decides to have the SCT performed at COH, should he request a new oncologist?
3. If he does receive a new oncologist, please pray that the transition takes place smoothly.
4. If Henry decides to have the SCT performed at COH, please pray that we can maintain our great relationship at CTCA.
5. Please pray that we have peace with whatever decisions are made.

Thank you once again, and God Bless!

👍 28   Seen by 60   23 Comments

BM Prayers that you find the right answers that you need to enter in this part of Henry's journey. I am praying for you both, and I know the Lord will lead you in the right direction.

LD In Jesus' name, we pray for your wisdom and that the eyes and ears of your understanding are open to hearing from God! Amen!!

CS Can he be in the clinical trial only if they administer the SCT?

VFD That is one of the questions that we will be asking on Friday.

CS Well, my suggestion is to research a new oncologist. You want the best. If his oncologist isn't that experienced, look at all the other oncologists you can choose from and read their bios. Nothing wrong with change. If it does not feel right, change to one you have more confidence with.

You just say the patient-doctor relationship was not there. They usually just say okay. What specifics are you looking for? And answer honestly to the new oncologist. Remember always go with your gut; it speaks clearly.

More specifics on clinical trial; What is it? Where's it been tried, and on who or what animal? How many in-trial side effects and risks? Outcomes?

 VFD I can send you a copy of the trial info.

 DM I am praying that our Lord and savior will lead and guide you both in the decision-making that will be most suitable. I furthermore pray that God will use the medical team of your choosing to the fullest potential.

When at the crossroads, lean on the Lord. He is all-knowing and surely able to fill in the gaps. I pray for clarity and peace of mind for you both.

 TM Hey, Henry and Vanessa. We pray for you all the time. I wanted to tell you guys about our knowledge of stem cells. To make a long story short. Our son is a semi-pro baseball player with dreams of playing MLB.

He popped his rotator cuff on his throwing arm. We took him to an orthopedic specialist in Culver City. They told us he would need surgery, and this could possibly be a career-ending injury. So we prayed for him and took him to have prayer from this lady visiting and preaching in Pasadena.

So, she started praying and asking God for new body parts for our son. Fast forwarding, my wife was researching new technology to repair shoulders on the Internet and came across stem cell research.

(We) took him to a specialist in the Valley to have two stem cell injections. The doctor prescribed therapy to get his strength

continued

back in his shoulder for 4-6 months (not exactly sure – memory loss! Lol).

We took him back to the orthopedic specialist for his check-up with the doctor. The doctor took Tony's arm and started to move it around, and asked him, "Does this hurt?"

Our son kept replying no, that it doesn't hurt every time he moved his arm. He tried moving Tony's arm to test the strength.

... The doctor looked at me and said our son's arm is very strong, and we need to do another MRI. The MRI showed no injury and that our son was healed, and his rotator cuff had grown and mended itself back together. The doctor said it's like he's got a new body part!!!

So, the doctor asked us what did we do. We told him we ask God for a miracle and new nody parts!!! God sent us stem cells!!

The doctor is the orthopedic surgeon for the Los Angeles Lakers!! He said he's never seen anything like that before!!

Our son is back playing baseball and has a tryout with an MLB team in January!!! Pray for him!!!

So, Henry, we think stem cells are another one of God's Miracles, and you should DO it. Don't TRY it, but believe you are healed already and that God sent you new body parts.

I hope I didn't sound like a preacher, but it is a true story!!

 So glad to hear the positive report! Praising God! Trust in Him. He will direct you in the right way. God bless you both.

Open to Options

"I know from our talks, you worry about making the right choices in your life. I cannot nor should anyone, tell you what to do. For that, my dear, you must listen to your own heart. And, never fear, it is speaking to you.

"Perhaps I can help a little though, by showing you how I found my own way."
— Ann Warner, Dreams for Stones

Cancer Support Center Pasadena, Pasadena, CA
November 11, 2015

WE NEEDED SOME HELP IN ORDER TO MAKE OUR DECISION. I liked the idea of the clinical trial. It would allow me to get back to work with the least number of challenges to receive my chemotherapy medication.

On the other hand, we have serious reservations about leaving CTCA for City of Hope. We cannot put our finger on exactly what is concerning us, but the feeling is strong.

We got just what we needed from Cancer Support Community Pasadena. The Program Director greeted us when Vanessa and I showed up for our next support group meeting.

"How are you this evening?" Laura asked.

"Well, not so good," I replied.

"Oh, what seems to be the problem?" she asked.

"We need to decide where to have my Stem Cell Transplant procedure done, and we don't know if City of Hope is the right place," I replied.

"Why is that?" she asked.

"We feel we received a different level of care at CTCA.," Vanessa said. She went on to say, "Weekly chemo injections are one thing, but a Stem Cell Transplant is a major procedure."

"Our oncologist asked us to make our decision by Friday," I added.

"Why do you have to make a decision so soon?" Laura asked.

"Our oncologist wants to get me into the clinical trial as soon as possible," I replied.

"I suggest you call and let him know that you may not be ready to decide by Friday," Laura said. "You shouldn't feel rushed."

"Okay, we'll do that," I said.

Laura then went on to explain:

"The Cancer Support Community has created a decision support counseling program called *Open to Options*® that can help you prepare for an appointment in which you will be making a treatment decision."

Laura continued with her explanation of the program. She said the main thing was that we needed to schedule an appointment with our oncologist to discuss our concerns. The program is designed to help patients and their caregivers formulate questions that need answers before deciding what to do.

Vanessa and I decided to go through the program right away. Laura facilitated the program, and we came up with the following results after about an hour:

SITUATION (known facts about my condition): I am a 58-year-old male diagnosed with Stage III Multiple Myeloma in July 2015. I have completed four cycles of chemotherapy.

OPTIONS (possible treatment options):
- Stem Cell Transplant after four chemotherapy cycles
- Stem Cell Transplant after six chemotherapy cycles
- In-patient or out-patient
- City of Hope or Cancer Treatment Centers of America in Chicago
- Clinical trial after Stem Cell Transplant

NETWORK (personal and medical):
- Limited family support in LA and none in Chicago
- Friends in Pasadena
- Two adult children, one in Rancho Cucamonga and one in Phoenix, Arizona

GOALS (my goals and priorities):
- Minimal residual disease.
- Reduce pain from the disease.
- Reduce the risk of infection.
- I want to be able to get back to work, including business travel.
- I would like to gain weight to feel healthier.
- Improve my endurance, reduce fatigue.
- I want to feel confident in my medical team.

EVALUATION (how my options may affect my goals):
- Why do we have to make the decision to go forward with the Stem Cell Transplant today?
- Who will perform the biopsy? How many biopsies have to be performed?

- Would we have better access to you during the process?
- Which physician is actually doing the Stem Cell Transplant?
- How many Stem Cell Transplants have you personally been involved in?
- How many Stem Cell Transplants cases have you been the team leader on?
- Who is on my team, and how many people will be on the team?
- Will the team members coordinate my care?
- How do all the team members assist in reducing the risk of infection?
- How much will additional care will need to be done at home?
- What is the patient-to-nurse ratio in the transplant unit?
- How long does the process take? How is the disease being monitored while not on chemo?
- Are enough stem cells harvested for more than one possible Stem Cell Transplant?
- How long will it take, and how will we know if the clinical trial has been successful?
- How often should the M-spike result be reviewed?
- If I have the Stem Cell Transplant in CTCA, can I do the clinical trial after the transplant at City of Hope?
- Why did you ask us to decide this Friday? Only one week?
- What precautions will be taken to protect Henry's kidneys?

CLINICAL TRIAL:
1. Based on the medications in the clinical trial, what is the expected remission rate of the medications:
    a. Individually
    b. As a combination
2. What drugs are part of the traditional maintenance routine (VRD)?
    a. What is the expected remission rate of these drugs individually?
    b. As a combination?
3. What happens if the clinical trial is not working?
4. The trial indicates a 28-day cycle. You used a 21-day cycle. Which would be used if Henry takes part in the trial?
5. Are there other trials available?
6. Why are you recommending this trial for me?
7. What types of trials are good for me?
8. Why is the trial designated as a safety issue on clinicaltrials.gov?
9. How many have signed up to date?

We decided to use our upcoming Friday appointment to ask the questions we came up with after going through the *Open to Options®* program.

We felt prepared for the appointment. We believed if we got answers to all of the questions we prepared, we would be able to make a decision that we would feel good about.

City of Hope, Duarte, CA
November 13, 2015

THE APPOINTMENT WITH OUR ONCOLOGIST WENT VERY WELL. I was not sure how it would turn out, but I was pleasantly surprised. I thought our doctor would take offense to so many questions, especially the ones that might seem to question his competence.

But on the contrary, every question was well received and sufficiently answered. When we ended the appointment, our oncologist said he actually appreciated all of the questions. He said he felt as though he addressed all of our concerns. He said that was not usually the case with other patients.

We told him about the *Open to Options®* program at Cancer Support Community Pasadena. He thought it was very effective. We could not agree more.

I believe God provided exactly what we needed at exactly the right time.

> *"In the face of all the uncertainties that surround any decision, the wise man acts in the light of his best judgment illumined by the integrity of his profoundest spiritual insights. Then the rest is in the hands of the future and in the mind of God."*
> — Howard Thurman, *Meditations of the Heart*

Should I Stay or Should I Go?

"Sometimes you have to stop thinking so much and just go where your heart takes you." — Unknown

"The LORD replied, "My Presence will go with you and I will give you rest." — Exodus 33:14, New International Version Bible

---

Pasadena, CA
November 14, 2015

WE HAVE ARRIVED AT OUR DECISION. We based our decision on the answers we received to our questions on Friday. The bottom line is we came away from the appointment feeling we would receive the level of care we wanted at City of Hope.

We took a tour of a Stem Cell Transplant wing at Helford Hospital and were duly impressed. The facilities were more modern than those at CTCA, which helped, but, for me, it was observing the staff that convinced me that I would be in good hands. I still think I will not receive the Mother Standard of Care, but I am not as sick as I was in Zion.

Vanessa and I also agreed that the convenience of City of Hope is better for us in case some emergency situation might arise. It would not be very effective for CTCA to oversee a problem from so far away. Lastly, the convenience of the clinical trial medication in terms of me getting back to work was also very compelling.

We informed our oncologist at City of Hope and our doctors at CTCA Chicago on Friday. Our oncologist began scheduling the Stem Cell Transplant and signed me up for the clinical trial. We thanked my doctors and our nurse, Julie, at CTCA for all they had done for me. We promised to keep them informed of my progress.

It was hard to say goodbye, but I knew it was the right thing to do. I will do my best to stay in touch with those special people I met at CTCA. I will continue to put my trust in God.

Vanessa Foster-Dotson
November 15, 2015

*** Update for Thursday 11/12/15 – Sunday 11/14/15:

Decisions have been made! After a lot of prayer, consulting with others, and a tour of the hospital on Thursday, Henry has made the following decisions:

1. Henry will receive his Stem Cell Transplant (SCT) at City of Hope (COH) in California.
2. Henry will not be assigned a new oncologist at this time, but may still speak with the director of oncology at COH about any concerns.

Henry also proceeded with signing up for the clinical trial. However, we are continuing to research the trial. And since the trial would not start for several months after his SCT, Henry can remove his participation at any time if he changes his mind.

Because we live about 15 minutes away from COH, Henry's oncologist really wanted him to receive the transplant on an outpatient basis. This would mean that Henry would drive back and forth to the hospital every day for 2.5 – 3 weeks. It would also mean that I would be responsible for a substantial portion of his daily care...while still working.

We successfully convinced the oncologist that at-home care was not feasible for us. Therefore, Henry will be at COH for at least 2.5 weeks during the latter portion of his transplant process.

Henry will be receiving an autologous transplant which means that his own stem cells will be harvested, frozen, and then used during the infusion phase of the SCT process. Using his cells is much safer than using someone else's. The general phases of the transplant are as follows (more details to come as we learn more):

1. Evaluation and preparation (out-patient, starting on Tuesday, 11/17)

    a. Testing (Lab, EKG, ECHO, stress, bone marrow biopsy, etc.), patient education, scheduling.

2. Validation of transplant eligibility (out-patient)

    a. Test result review, confirmation of insurance coverage, etc.

continued

3. Stem Cell Collection – Harvesting and freezing Henry's stem cells (out-patient, we will have to drive every day).

    a. Approximately 2 – 10 days, 4.5 hours a day.

4. Conditioning (in-patient hospital stay)

    a. Prepare Henry's bone marrow and the body for the infusion phase.

    b. The process starts approximately 1 – 2 weeks after cells are collected. (Probably will be at the beginning of January for Henry.)

    c. Henry will be in the hospital for 2.5 – 3 weeks.

5. Stem Cell Infusion (in-patient hospital stay)

    a. Collected stem cells are placed back in Henry's body.

So, as you can see, this will be a long process, roughly two months. So, we are about to enter a new phase in Henry's Multiple Myeloma journey.

Thankfully, God will be with us the entire time!

The other good news that I should have mentioned earlier is that our dog Nikko has been back for a couple of weeks. Henry's immune system is strong enough now that Nikko is not a threat. It is really nice to have Nikko home, although he will most likely have to leave again for a while during Henry's transplant process.

God Bless, and thank you so much once again!

👍 37   Seen by 55   13 Comments

PM I'm so glad that you did due diligence in arriving at your decisions. It is truly a blessing that you and Henry have been able to involve those who you trust and whose opinions you value. Prayers are still going up, and blessings will continue to come down—all of my love to you both.

CB I will continue to pray and thank God for the team working with Henry at COH. That the surgeon's hands are gifted and being lead by GOD throughout every procedure, and that the staff are accommodating beyond belief.

PH I am continuing to pray for you both! This is wise decision-making. Love y'all!

ES Glad to hear about the progress ... I agree with Henry using his own stem cells

We will continue to pray ...

Let me know (privately) how else we can be of support and help.

The Foundation you helped lay in South Africa continues to be built upon... Today our SA Antioch missions team of 18 people shared highlights of the ministry, including 2,862 people led to Christ.

To God be ALL the Glory...

The missions team training program that Henry developed was key to our ministry accomplishing so much for the kingdom of God and being well prepared.

Thank you !!

We Love you both.

RH Great to hear! Praying all goes well. You and Henry are in my daily prayers. I've been missing your updates. Sis-in-law is in hospital, and Mike has not been well. One day at a time. Sending my love!

The decision to receive my Stem Cell Transplant at City of Hope and participate in the clinical trial marks the end of our formal relationship with CTCA in Zion, IL. The decision was difficult but made easier by the *Open to Options*® program.

It goes without saying that what transpired at CTCA will stay with me for as long as my memory stays with me. I witnessed so many miracles there that there is not space enough in these pages to recount them all.

When I meditate on what the Lord did in Zion, I weep tears of joy.

I also know that our decision to transfer my case from CTCA to City of Hope marks the end of my Middle Passage. It is hard to put into words right now, but it is more than just changing healthcare providers. I may not fully understand it until seeing it clearly in hindsight.

However, I know for sure that we are one giant step closer to the "new normal."

My Middle Passage is behind me now. I can feel it in my bones.

> *"The only requisite to entry into the Middle Passage is to have discovered that one does not know who one is, that there are no rescuers, no Mommy or Daddy, and that one's fellow travelers will do well to survive themselves."* — James Hollis

PART FOUR:
A CITY OF HOPE
November 17, 2015 – August 20, 2016

"At City of Hope, we combine science with soul to create medical miracles."

— City of Hope campaign slogan, October 20, 2015

"There is no profit curing the body if, in the process, we destroy the soul."

— Samuel H. Golter, City of Hope Executive Director

"I wait for the LORD; my soul does wait, and in His word I put my hope." — Psalm 130:5, Berean Study Bible

City of Hope

When I arrived at City of Hope, I knew that it was not Zion in terms of the aura of God's presence. But I knew that God was with me where ever my journey took me. I was reassured of this when I read the words of City of Hope's first executive director as they appeared on the "Golter Gate:"

> "There is No Profit in Curing the Body if in the Process, We Destroy the Soul." — Samuel H. Golter

So, I knew this was where they placed a high value on the soul from this credo. I was further encouraged when I learned of their motto:

> "We treat you as an individual whose life will be made whole again. We combine science with soul to work miracles."

This motto resonated in my spirit. It told me I was in a place where they expect to work miracles. From my Christian worldview, I know that miracles only come from God.

This knowledge removed any lingering concerns I had about being where God wanted me to be.

City of Hope, Duarte, CA
November 17, 2015

THANKSGIVING IS EXTRA SPECIAL THIS YEAR, BUT NOT JUST FOR THE OBVIOUS REASON OF BEING THANKFUL FOR SURVIVING MULTIPLE MYELOMA UP TO THIS POINT. I cannot find the words to express how thankful I am for the Facebook Prayer Team. I am too overwhelmed even to try. I am also thankful for the cancer community I have become a part of.

Time to Give Thanks

> "O give thanks unto the Lord; for he is good: because his mercy endureth for ever." — Psalm 118:1, New International Version

Pasadena, CA
November 25, 2015

Vanessa Foster-Dotson
November 26, 2015

*** Update for Monday 11/15/15 - Wednesday 11/25/15:

Happy Thanksgiving!!! We each have so much to be thankful for. If you are able to read this update, then the first blessing is that you are alive. Some did not make it to see this day. You also have access to a computing device. The device probably experiences the safety of your home. Within that home, you probably have clothes, food, and many comforts of life. Oh, so much to be thankful for!

And please know that this prayer group is something that Henry and I are extremely thankful for. Yes, the last few months have been difficult. Henry's privilege of being on this earth was threatened. But you stood by us, and Henry's life was spared. Praise God, and thank you!

During one of my readings over the past week, I was reminded that Henry and I have become involuntary members of an exclusive club, the Multiple Myeloma club." Only God knows why. Time will tell. Meanwhile, we have been preparing for Henry's Stem Cell Transplant. Last week Henry had several procedures, and we also attended classes as listed below:

1. Gave 21 vials of blood to support extensive testing
2. Bone biopsy in his hip
3. X-Rays
4. Stress Test
5. Heart Test
6. EKG/Echo Test
7. PICC Line removal
8. Social worker consult
9. Training on the overall Stem Cell Transplant process
10. Training on the Stem Cell harvesting process
11. Training on how to care for the Hickman Catheter that Henry will be receiving to support the transplant process.

All of this in one week! Needless to say, we have been busy. And in the middle of everything, I even had a one-day work trip to Phoenix and another one-day trip locally. Amazing!

continued

Henry has not been on chemo and seems to get tired a bit faster. But overall, he is well. His eating is consistent, and his weight is stable... around 160 lbs. So, he still has a way to go to reach his 175 pound. target. His hair is growing, and he has been growing a beard to support a men's health challenge. His attitude remains positive and grateful. He is just anxious to move past this phase in his life.

During the past week, we were also blessed financially. I was paying our bills and realized that our account was overdrawn. I know that funds are tight, so I simply walked away, said a quick prayer, and came back a day or so later. (And yes, I did worry a little...smile.)

When I came back, I looked at our overdraft account, and to my surprise, we had just received some money. A tear literally came to my eyes (which is very uncommon for me). To make a long story short, we had applied for state disability in July but were denied. We had an appeal hearing on 11/10, and we were told that we would receive the ruling from the trial within a week.

We did not hear anything, and then finally, this money showed up, just in time, God's time. The initial ruling was reversed, so Henry is now receiving state disability income! Yes! Of course, the state is not replacing his full income, so funds are still tight, but everything helps. We are extremely thankful!

> *"Put your hope in the Lord. Travel steadily along his path. He will honor you by giving you the land. You will see the wicked destroyed."* — Psalm 37:34

Now, if you are wondering about the funds that many of you have donated, they are in a separate account. To date, we have used half of this money to cover Henry's medical and prescription co-pays. I am trying to save the other half to cover his health insurance deductible next year. So, thank you once again!

There are several more steps to Henry's transplant process, which we will be going through during December. However, we would love to see you during this time before he goes to the hospital, which is tentatively scheduled for the end of December. Please let me know if you are able to stop by.

We pray that each one of you has a fantastic Thanksgiving, full of love, laughter, family, and friends.

God Bless!

Philippians 4:6-7 (Thank you, Jackie.)

👍 36   Seen by 55   Comments

RM: Happy Thanksgiving. May God's manifold blessings revived and renewed health, and abundant provisions abound to you and Henry. Hugs.

CP: Our God is Awesome. Vanessa, your reports about Henry are breathtaking, with amazing results of how God is still making provisions for you both. This has been a tremendous faith walk and prayer time like never before and worth every moment because Thou oh Lord are a shield for me, the glory and the lifter of my head.

Thank you for your love and courage displayed each day as we continue to keep you both lifted up before the Lord. We definitely need to come by before the next procedure. We love you guys and enjoy your day with family and friends. As the song says, "Nobody Greater than You!"

AV: Prayers continue. Blessings for a Happy Thanksgiving!

LW: Again, I say thank you for the status reports. And thank you for being a woman of God, cleaving to her mate. You two are awesome. Happy Thanksgiving!

ES: God is faithful!!

We are glad to hear about Henry's progress. First Lady Vanessa and I, too, will make a visit as well.

Thank you for letting us know it's ok.

God honors His Word and our Faith. You both are great examples. Keep Fighting the Good Fight of Faith!

We are Still praying and standing with you.

With much Love,

Happy Thanksgiving

PM: Such a wonderful update! Praying for you both always! God is able.

BG: Glad to hear how God continues to show us grace and mercy and how he sets up for victories and miracles each and every day of our lives. We have a tremendous loving father. Praise God and continual prayers. Love you both. Happy Thanksgiving.

Pasadena, CA
November 30, 2015

THANKSGIVING IS EXTRA SPECIAL THIS YEAR, BUT NOT JUST FOR THE OBVIOUS REASON OF BEING THANKFUL FOR SURVIVING MULTIPLE MYELOMA UP TO THIS POINT. I cannot find words to express how thankful I am for the Facebook Prayer Team. I am too overwhelmed to even try. I am also thankful for the cancer community I have become a part of.

For these specific things, and all the unspecified things, I give thanks unto the Lord.

We held our annual Dotson Family Thanksgiving celebration on the Saturday after Thanksgiving. The tradition was the brainchild of my niece, Stefany.

Therefore, Thanksgiving Day celebrations are left up to each family household. We do not have anything planned for the extended family that day. Friday is a day of recovery. Saturday, the Dotson extended family gathers at our house. Some bring leftovers from Thanksgiving; others make a dish for Saturday.

Our Dotson Family Thanksgiving gathering this year was limited because my oncologist advised us not to have too many people around me. He was concerned about my weakened immune system. That being said, Bart, Talia, Ira, Cris, Pat, and a couple of close friends did come by.

The gathering was small but impactful. Just being around close family and a few close friends was good medicine. I was glad we did not have to cancel the event.

Q: How did you feel about the Thanksgiving 2015 celebration in terms of my health condition?

TALIA: I was so grateful that the family was able to come together. At that celebration, I had the opportunity to record the stories shared by friends and family members, which is invaluable. I believe that you were our reason to come together to, as you say, show how God is faithful.

IRA: The Thanksgiving celebration was bitter/sweet. I saw your medical bed in the den. It was at this point that I realized you were still in the middle of this fight. You and I would talk about your health and what type of progress you were experiencing.

Your doctors did not discuss their feelings about your progress. Each time you would ask about your progress, they would focus on the current step of treatment you were receiving. Afterward, it was clear to me why they would only discuss your current state. In their minds, they knew the odds of your survival. It was in your best interest to focus on whatever stage you were facing at that time.

CRIS: I felt thankful that you were recovering so quickly and you were able to be there with us.

> *"It is a good thing to give thanks unto the Lord, and to sing praises unto thy name, O most High."*
> — Psalm 92:1, New International Version

Time To Collect

"The most common way to harvest stem cells involves temporarily removing blood from the body, separating out the stem cells, and then returning the blood to the body."

— National Health Service, UK

Pasadena, CA
December 6, 2015

I AM GETTING PREPARED FOR THE STEM CELL TRANSPLANT. My preparation is primarily physical therapy and eating. I don't always feel like working out, and I don't always feel like eating, but I do it anyway. My reward is knowing that I am staying the course and doing all that I can do.

I have a lot of time on my hands. I could do things, but I prefer to be still and meditate on all that has happened to get me to this point. I am not exceptionally tired. I have stopped my chemotherapy treatments in preparation for the Stem Cell Transplant, so I don't get fatigued as much. This time seems to be a period of rest and rejuvenation, a brief respite before taking on what lies ahead. I have three days of stem cell harvesting scheduled for next week.

Vanessa Foster-Dotson
December 6, 2015

*** Update for Thursday 11/26/15 - Saturday 12/05/15:

Relaxed and stable. We pray that each of you had a fantastic Thanksgiving holiday, full of love and laughter. We had a wonderful time with family. Bart and Talia were in town, which was great! And we also received a visit from Junie and Marcia, my play brother from Maryland. We truly had a blessed holiday.

Since Thanksgiving, life has been pretty calm for Henry. He continues to do physical therapy but lies down quite a bit when he is not eating. It seems any exertion that he has in the morning often makes him tired the rest of the day.

He doesn't talk a lot. He simply relaxes as he watches various television shows. Relaxation now is fine because he is about to enter a very busy and possibly stressful portion of his treatment.

continued

He is still wearing his back brace, and his hair is still growing. Now that it is December and the November observance of men's health conditions is over, Henry has even shaved his beard. Yes!

Henry had a positive report from his neurosurgeon on Friday, 12/04. The condition of the compressed T7 vertebra in his back has stabilized. The surgeon said Henry is doing well, and his only request is that Henry continues to gain weight. In order to perform back surgery, the surgeon needs Henry to be healthy and strong after his Stem Cell Transplant.

Regarding the Stem Cell Transplant, the next weeks will be intense. Starting Monday, Henry has doctors/medical appointments every day. Friday, 12/11, is when he will be receiving 11 hours of chemo to "completely" remove all signs of cancer in his bone marrow. After that, Henry will be receiving daily shots until 12/21. The purpose of the shots is to restore his cell count after undergoing 11 hours of chemo. But, chemo can affect both good and bad cells.

On 12/21, his "clean" stem cells will be harvested. The harvesting process will take place for at least four days, four hours each day. So, Henry will possibly be entering the hospital the week after Christmas. This is when his bone marrow will be removed, and his harvested "clean" stem cells will be placed back in his body. He is expected to be in the hospital for a minimum of two and a half weeks.

So, needless to say, it is okay for him to rest now. I just need to make sure that he is eating enough calories. He is eating what is placed before him, so his appetite is still pretty good. However, his weight continues to be around 160. (I would love to be at that weight right now...smile!)

In regards to me, I am preparing myself for an active and emotional period of life. God is with us, and so are you. Here we go! The fight and the journey continue.

 46   Seen by 58   Comments

 RN Thanks for this update. I am praying for you, Henry. I am believing God will provide Henry with a successful transplant and continued long life and good health.

PM This is another challenge for the two of you to meet. Just know that God is with you both and that your prayer warriors are in step as you fight the good fight of faith. Stay encouraged!

EP We continue to be steadfast and interceding for you and Henry. God is at work; continue sharing the gospel through the journey. He is with you.

RB Vanessa, your strength is inspiring. Big hug.

AR Hi, Vanessa and Henry, I haven't been in touch lately, but I continue to regularly and fervently lift both of you up in prayer. I know that God will continue working on us through his work in you. Yours is such a powerful testimony. I am grateful for being blessed by you to witness your steadfast faith in action and the amazing love, grace, and power of God revealed before my very eyes.

DK We stand on God's promises, Amen.

CC Still claiming complete healing in the name of JESUS!!!

Unforeseen Delay

Pasadena, CA
December 11, 2015

WE HAVE BEEN TOLD MY WHITE BLOOD CELL COUNT IS TOO LOW TO BEGIN HARVESTING STEM CELLS. My oncologist plans to delay the start for a week. In addition, my oncologist wants to have another bone marrow biopsy done to see what is going on in my marrow.

I am a little disappointed, but this means I will be off of chemo for another week, and that is great. I am dealing with fewer and fewer side-effects which makes me feel better; more energy.

I've learned to tolerate bone-marrow biopsies. I have them done with local anesthesia only. It feels a little weird and tingly, but I would much rather go through that than be sedated. I have enough medication coursing through my veins and liver as it is. I also do not have to wait after the procedure for the anesthesia to wear off before I can go home.

So, we wait for another week.

Vanessa Foster-Dotson
December 11, 2015

*** Update for Sunday 12/06/15 - Thursday 12/10/15:

Plans change. As previously mentioned, Henry had several doctors/medical appointments planned this week. He only ended up going to three.

On Monday, Henry went to his primary care physician without me. The appointment was routine. The physician mainly wants to keep an eye on Henry's weight.

Meanwhile, in preparation for Henry having a low immune system after his stem cell treatment, we were advised to clean our attic. I had never been in the attic, so to my surprise, we had TONS of items stored there, enough to fill our entire patio, stacked. I had to go through all of the items to determine what would get thrown away, go to Goodwill, or else go back to the attic.

continued

Needless to say, it was a long, dirty, and strenuous job, but it is done! Now, this task is something that I would have welcomed help with; if I had thought about it and had known what I would be dealing with.

On Tuesday, we went to the Center for New Medicine (CNM) in Irvine, based on the recommendation of a dear friend who is also suffering from cancer and the suggestion of our daughter, Talia.

The Center's approach for treating cancer is different from the more traditional approach that Henry is following. They seem to focus more on developing your immune system via nutrition and supplements. They believe that your immune system can fight cancer for the most part.

We are still learning about the Center, but for now, Henry plans on continuing the current traditional plan at City of Hope but will also work with the CNM as a means of keeping the Multiple Myeloma from reoccurring as long as possible.

On Wednesday, we went to Henry's oncology appointment at City of Hope. The oncologist stated that Henry's white blood cell count is low (2.4 out of 3.6 - 10.1), and therefore he wants to postpone the Stem Cell Transplant activities at least one week.

He also mentioned that Henry needs to redo his bone marrow biopsy. Ugh! So, Henry will have another biopsy on Friday, 12/11. Please pray that this biopsy provides all of the data that the doctor needs and that the procedure is not too painful. Please also pray that his white blood cell count increases quickly.

And please continue to keep me in your prayers. I have been fighting a cold for at least two weeks. So, I have to stay away from Henry as much as possible. Thankfully his immune system isn't extremely weak now. I have also developed a sty that is REALLY irritating me. I went to the doctor and rested a lot on Thursday, 12/10. But the beat must go on, and I have to keep things moving.

Thank you for your prayers. We look forward to your visits.

I know that I have not published Henry's diet, but we welcome any meals that you care to send our way. No pork or beef. Moist and easy to swallow. Well-seasoned.

Relatively healthy, yet high in calories for weight gain. Cooking and meals are what we really could use help with. Henry needs to gain weight, and I am tired of cooking (smile)!

Thank you again, and God Bless!

GT — Praise God for all your answered prayers in advance and all the blessings he's already covered you two with. I'm willing to help in any way you need.

LW — I am so glad that you ask for what the two of you need. I wish I lived in So Cal and could help out. My prayers continue for Bernard's healing and your strength.

PM — I'm so glad that you're still able to do all that you do, Ness. God wanted you to slow down and rest at least for a day. I'm praying that the biopsy today yields positive results.

I wish I could be there to help you out with cooking meals. Cooking can be drudgery when you have to do it every day. Have you tried slow cooker meals that you can get more than one meal from? Dried beans, spaghetti, chili, a hearty soup, etc.

So much love can be shown in preparing food. It would give me such a pleasure to cook for Henry and help fatten him up, plus give you a break.

CP — Vanessa, all I can say in all of this is that we stand in agreement with you both for all the requests and petitions to the prayer warriors. We speak Psalm 121 right now, for all of your help comes from the Lord. We definitely will make contact with you. Continue to stay encouraged. We love you guys.

ES — I just prayed again for your total healing and a speedy FULL Recovery... In Jesus Name!

CB — Is chili good for you guys with turkey, or do you prefer just beans? Pastor Jeff and I are thinking and speaking on meals to make and bring you two. I will call you. We continue to keep Henry, and you lifted up in prayer. Have a blessed and joyous day.

FROM ZION TO A CITY OF HOPE: A JOURNEY OF FAITH

Pasadena, CA
December 18, 2015

WHAT A DIFFERENCE A WEEK MAKES. ONE HUNDRED SIXTY-EIGHT LITTLE HOURS! My oncologist says we are "Go" for stem cell harvesting! I am excited and curious at the same time. This could be the start of the knockout punch to my Multiple Myeloma. I am curious to see what my numbers will look like after the Stem Cell Transplant.

But I must not get ahead of myself. First the harvesting, then the transplant. Members of my Multiple Myeloma support group who have gone through a Stem Cell Transplant say it is a painless process. You just have a few days where you are weak and feel terrible. But I am still thinking about the transplant.

They say the stem cell harvesting process is similar to dialysis. Blood flows out of the body into a machine. The machine spins the blood in a centrifuge, and the stem cells are harvested. The blood then flows back into the body. I am interested in experiencing it for myself. It is part of the engineer in me.

Norman and Ruth came up from San Diego to see us this week. That was the first time we had gotten together since Vanessa and I returned from Zion. It was great seeing them. We shared a meal together, even though I was not that hungry.

We also had visits from three other friends who are part of our Prayer Team. It is always good to fellowship with the saints. This was a good week overall.

Vanessa Foster-Dotson
December 18, 2015

*** Update for Friday, 12/11/15 - Friday, 12/18/15:

The time has come. During my last update, I mentioned that Henry's Stem Cell Transplant procedures had been postponed because his white blood cell count (WBC) was too low (2.4). Well, the oncologist called Henry last week and asked that he stop a few of his meds. When Henry's lab work was performed again on 12/15, his WBC count was 5.5 out of 3.6 - 10.1!

So, Henry has now been cleared to move forward with his Stem Cell Transplant. Yes! As a result, on Friday, 12/18, Henry will be going in for 11 hours of chemo/hydration starting at 7 a.m. Then, on Saturday, 12/19, he will start daily injections to increase his blood counts and to stimulate stem cell growth. He won't be staying at the hospital until the first week of January. Please pray that all goes well.

Henry's attitude is positive, and his spirit is strong. He is still trying to gain weight. Meanwhile, he is getting plenty of rest. We have faith

continued

that "God's got this" and that God has more for Henry to do. I witnessed some of Henry's "assignment" yesterday as he fellowshipped and shared his unique and amazing knowledge with our dear friends Janice and DeAndre, who came to visit. (Thank you so much for your visit!) Henry is truly a special and gifted person, and it is my honor to be his wife.

We were also blessed with visits from Norman and Ruth along with Lynda. Norman and Ruth came up from San Diego to bring us a meal. We had not spoken to Lynda in many years, so it was great to catch up with her.

So, the journey continues. Thank you for your prayers that constantly manifest positive results. Please be sure to include everyone that is reading this update in your prayers as well. It seems that many people are encountering challenges. And please know that we continue to welcome your visits, calls, and meals.

God bless!

👍 37   Seen by 48   Comments

PM Hallelujah! God is good! I love how you laud your husband's perfection and knowledge—praying for a successful procedure.

EP I am praying for you and Henry. God's peace, joy, and comfort and His Blessings abundantly!

RG Lifting you up, Henry, in prayer. You are loved by The Lord and us. You are a testimony; keep up the faith walk! We love you!

BM God Bless you, Henry. All the prayers I can muster up are for you and Vanessa. Lord, please take care of this God-fearing couple, and bring them out of this tough time. I know they are leaning on you heavily. I pray we will all come through this with our health and an awesome testimony to share your love. Thank you, Father God. In Your Precious Name. Amen and Amen!

AE Lord, we thank you for Healing Henry. As he goes through this procedure today on his way to complete healing, comfort him, provide peace, and an opportunity to share you with someone else that is in need today. Henry is a minister of reconciliation, use him, Lord, that we can share in the testimony of today. Amen.

Q: What did you think when you first saw me after my diagnosis?

NORMAN: It was a while before we saw you after your return from Chicago, six weeks, maybe eight. You had described the accommodations at home and your condition accurately. So, there were not a lot of surprises except for your weight loss. WHOA! He's smaller. I did not write shorter, just smaller.

RUTH: I thought you were going to die.

Q: How did you feel when you first saw me after my diagnosis?

NORMAN: You know, I am not sure I remember. You looked fragile, tired. As alluded to above, I figure I'd be in a wheelchair or using a walker before you.

RUTH: Shocked. Feeling and seeing your fragility.

Q: Was it difficult for you to see me in my physical condition?

NORMAN: I don't remember it being difficult.

RUTH: Heartbreaking.

Q: In general, did our phone conversations give you any comfort in knowing what was going on?

NORMAN: I was comforted knowing that you survived the vault and walked away from the landing zone; that you were making progress towards health, towards what in Hebrew is called a refuah shlemah – a complete recovery.

RUTH: Yes, in an indirect way: I always heard the updates either from Norman or the occasional email from Vanessa forwarded to me from Norman.

Q: In general, did your visits give you any comfort in knowing what was going on?

NORMAN: Given the geographical separation, there were not many visits. It was good to see you after your return from Chicago. It was good to see the improvement at subsequent visits. Comfort? I guess you could call it that.

RUTH: Very much so! I got to experience your strength of faith, your diligent work on your own health and strength-building, and your being "okay" with whatever would be in God's plan for you.

Pasadena, CA
December 20, 2015

I COMPLETED AN 11-HOUR CHEMOTHERAPY SESSION AS THE FIRST STEP IN PREPARATION FOR MY STEM CELL TRANSPLANT. It was the longest chemotherapy session I've had since my Hyper CVAD treatment at CTCA. During the first and last hours, I received a saline solution. During the middle nine hours, I received the chemotherapy medication in addition to the saline solution.

I received hydration because the chemotherapy medication is very strong. It will wipe out all of the marrow in my bones over the next few days. Without the saline solution, the chemotherapy medication could have damaged my blood vessels.

Before the procedure, I received and signed a disclosure statement that listed all of the known side effects of the chemotherapy medication. The side effects were similar to those listed for other Multiple Myeloma chemotherapy medications I have received in the past, including death.

I have become amused by these disclosure statements. By signing the statement, I give my consent for City of Hope to perform some procedure. Without my consent, I am essentially refusing a prescribed procedure. As a cancer patient, oftentimes, a likely consequence of not having some procedure done is a prognosis of death.

So, I am amused when I think, *"Both my options could lead to death, so what does my choice really mean?"* One option most likely improves my odds of living longer, while the other does not. From my Biblical worldview, all the days of my life are already known to God. So, it humored me more when I thought, *I could sign or not sign the disclosure statement and still get hit by a bus when my allotted days have been completed.*

I chuckled a little when I signed the disclosure statement. Fortunately, the only side effects I've experienced are mild fever and some bone pain. My prognosis continues to be favorable – so far.

 Vanessa Foster-Dotson
December 20, 2015

*** Update for Friday, 12/18/15 – Saturday, 12/19/15:

All is well! Just a quick update to let you know that Henry is doing well, as you can see in his picture. He completed his 11 hours of chemo/hydration along with his first injection to stimulate his stem cell growth (Neupogen).

We were told that he needs to drink a lot of water to protect his bladder from the effects of the type of chemo he received, and his

continued

bones may ache a bit as his stem cells mobilize. Surprisingly, the nurses mentioned that Claritin might help with bone aches.

So far, Henry has only experienced a mild fever and bone aches. He will continue to receive his daily injections on an outpatient basis until Monday, 28th. On the 28th, they will start harvesting his stem cells for approximately four days, or as long as it takes to collect enough for the transplant.

Meanwhile, I will be monitoring him, making sure he does not have a fever and that he is eating and exercising to continue to build up his weight and strength.

This is a new road on our journey so, although the doctors can tell us what others have experienced when traveling down this road, we do not know how his body will react. So, we are extremely blessed that we have your prayers and support and that God is covering Henry specifically. All that we can continue to say is thank you. We are so honored.

Along with Henry, please continue to pray for Henry's Uncle Alfred along with Henry's long-time friend from college. Both are about a week or so behind Henry in regard to traveling down this same road. We were not aware that Henry's friend from college also had Multiple Myeloma until Henry ran into him at City of Hope.

Lastly, please be sure to get yourself checked. We are approaching the beginning of the year. Have you scheduled your annual physical or any other required medical procedures? When you receive your results, question ANYTHING that is not normal. If we had done that, Henry might have started off a bit better.

God Bless!

👍 28   Seen by 42   Comments

CC Our prayers are with you both.

WL God's anointing and power to heal is upon you. You are BLESSED IN YOUR STOREHOUSE, FIELD, AND BODY. BE DELIVERED AND HAVE A MERRY CHRISTMAS.

RG God has your back! Many blessings and much love to you both!

It is such a blessing that you are keeping Henry's prayer team well informed on his treatment and progress. Also, asking us to pray for Henry's uncle and friend speaks to the woman of God that she is. God bless you, Vanessa, for asking us to stay on top of our own health issues as well.

Trying To Get Blood Out Of A Turnip

Pasadena, CA
January 5, 2016

WE HAVE EXPERIENCED ANOTHER UNFORESEEN DELAY. This time it is due to my body not producing enough stem cells for harvesting. Ideally, my oncologist would like to have eight million stem cells available. Only two million were collected on the first day.

That means by the end of the week, probably no more than three or four million stem cells would be harvested because the number of stem cells harvested each day during the week decreases. The plan now is to give my body a rest for a week and resume the Neupogen injections to promote the growth of stem cells.

I am disappointed and a little concerned. I am disappointed because I expected a harvest of at least three million stem cells on the first day. I had heard that harvesting four to five million stem cells on the first day was not unusual. I spoke with a patient today who produced eight million stem cells on her first day. Granted, she is younger (in her 30's), so her metabolism is higher than mine, but I expected to do better.

It seems like harvesting stem cells from me is like trying to get blood out of a turnip.

I am a little concerned about how the delays might impact our plans for what will happen after the transplant. Dr. Chen plans to perform my back surgery after the transplant. He says there is a six-week recovery period after surgery. The clinical trial starts in June, no later than early July. Given the Stem Cell Transplant has a 15-day recovery period, the window of opportunity to perform and recover from both procedures before the clinical trial starts cannot tolerate too many delays.

Focus on the Good

Before I allowed myself to follow a line of thinking that would cause me to worry and drag down my attitude, I began to look for the positives in my situation.

First, I reminded myself of how God had come through for me in the past. I knew He would not leave me nor forsake me. Next, I reminded myself that God was in control, and none of this was a surprise to Him. Lastly, I thought about the many blessings He had already given me on this journey, not the least of which is good health insurance.

Without insurance, the Neupogen injections would cost $8,000 each. I will need four injections when all is said and done, which will come to $32,000. I am

reminded of what my friend said,

> *"All you need to survive cancer is God and good health insurance."*

That reminder lifted my spirits.
Who knows? I thought. *Maybe you **can** get blood out of a turnip!*

 Vanessa Foster-Dotson
January 6, 2016

*** Update for Sunday, 12/20/15 – Tuesday, 01/05/16:

HAPPY NEW YEAR!!! We pray that each of you had a fantastic holiday; full of God, family, friends, love, and laughter. Our holiday was different this year, as we typically travel to the East Coast to spend time with my side of the family. But God had other plans, and we received numerous blessings, more than I can share here. We are SO thankful. To those who blessed us during this holiday season, thank you very, very much!

Henry is doing well. Actually, really well. I believe that he is thoroughly enjoying his vacation from chemo. He is stronger, has more energy, and is spending time with numerous friends. At one point, he had been talking so much that his throat got sore. We continue to work on increasing his weight as he is still around 160 pounds. We have to increase our efforts in this area over the next few weeks.

Henry's Stem Cell Transplant has been postponed because his body did not generate enough stem cells. The goal is to harvest eight million stem cells prior to performing the transplant. Last week, the medical team was able to harvest only two million. So, they are now giving his body some recovery time, and therefore will not do any harvesting this week.

On 01/14, Henry will resume getting shots to increase his stem-cell count. And then, on 01/18, they will resume the harvesting process. If enough stem cells are harvested, Henry is currently scheduled to be admitted to the hospital for his transplant on 01/26. So, man's plans have changed once again, but not a surprise to God. I am comforted by my devotional reading today:

> *"The Lord directs the steps of the godly. He delights in every detail of their lives. Though they stumble, they will never fall, for the Lord holds them by the hand."*
>
> — Psalm 37:23-24, New Living Translation

continued

I believe Henry is a godly man, and God is directing every aspect of his recovery!

Please pray the medical team is able to harvest 8+ million of Henry's stem cells during the week of 01/18.

Please also pray that Henry's Multiple Myeloma does not increase while he is going through this Stem Cell Transplant process because he is not taking any chemo drugs.

God Bless!

👍 37   Seen by 51   Comments

BM You are first on my prayer list! Hope to see you one of these days when I have time to drive to work. I'll let you know. Hugz and lots of prayers!

PH I am in agreement with faith and prayer! 8M+ cells ready and available for harvest and manifestation of healing in every area in Jesus' Name!

LW Our prayers are with you both as always! Happy New Year!

VH Happy New Year, Henry and Vanessa, and Vanessa; thank you for the wonderful praise report. God is guiding both your steps, indeed!

CP Good morning Vanessa. You and Henry are in our prayers continually; I thank God for you being obedient, staying at the feet of Jesus, and allowing the Lord to guide you through this time to draw closer to Him daily in this new season.

Nothing surprises God because he knows all of us and our purpose. Thank you for your faithfulness in keeping us updated on Henry and you. Praise God, for he is still on the throne. We miss and love you both.

CS Thank you so much for the updates.

CW We will be continuing to lift Henry up in prayer.

A City of Hope

Pasadena, CA
January 18, 2016

IT IS TIME TO RESUME STEM CELL HARVESTING. I am certainly looking forward to the restart for all the reasons I have expressed before.

On a related note, when I went to City of Hope to get blood drawn in preparation for the restart, I found myself in the check-in line with an old friend. I was as surprised to see him as he was surprised to see me.

"Hey Steve, is that you?"

"Hey Henry, what are you doing here?"

"I was diagnosed with Multiple Myeloma in July of last year. What are you doing here?"

"I was diagnosed with Multiple Myeloma last year too!"

"What a coincidence! I am scheduled to get a Stem Cell Transplant."

"So am I! They have collected my stem cells so that I will go in for the procedure this week."

"Wow, that's great! Are you going to do it as an in-patient or as an outpatient?"

"We decided I would do it as an in-patient."

"I'm going to do it as an in-patient too. Maybe we'll see each other as in-patients. There should be some overlap in our time in the hospital."

"How many stem cells did they collect from you?" (I had to ask).

"They got about eight million on the first day."

"That's great." (Oh well, so much for needing to be young to have an excellent first-day harvest.) "Okay, let's be sure to keep in touch."

"We sure will."

I believe my running into Steve is what I call a "divine appointment." I believe God navigated the circumstances of our lives such that we would meet at that particular moment, and that we will be going through the Stem Cell Transplant at about the same time and in the same place. What a mighty God we serve!

FROM ZION TO A CITY OF HOPE: A JOURNEY OF FAITH

 Vanessa Foster-Dotson
January 18, 2016

*** Update for Wednesday, 01/06/15 – Sunday, 01/17/16:

The Break Is Over! Well, before providing an update on Henry, let me take a quick moment to say Happy Martin Luther King's Birthday! I pray that you will be enjoying the day and that you will take the time to acknowledge what Dr. King did for us all. It was because of him and other forefathers (and mothers) that Henry is able to receive the same level of care, or better, than others in America are able to receive. I am very thankful for all of the struggles, achievements, and bloodshed.

Thank you, Dr. King!

Henry is continuing to do well. He is active most of the time and still enjoying his vacation from chemo. He hasn't gained any weight, but he is eating well and is still trying to gain. His spirit is positive. He is talkative and is pretty much the same happy guy that he usually is. I am so thankful!!! My buddy is almost back!!!

It is now time for Henry to resume his Stem Cell Transplant process. He will be going to City of Hope (COH) on Monday, 01/18, to restart his stem cell harvesting. The plan is that he will go to COH every day this week for four hours each time until enough stem cells have been harvested.

Please continue to pray that Henry's body is able to produce 8+ million stem cells over the next 1-5 days, and pray that Henry's Multiple Myeloma does not increase while he is going through the Stem Cell Transplant process.

Please also pray for Henry's college/church friend (our friend), who also has Multiple Myeloma and is now about two weeks ahead of Henry. Let's call him Mr. C. I referenced Mr. C in a previous update.

At that time, Mr. C was a week behind Henry. But Mr. C was able to harvest eight million stem cells on his first day of harvesting. So, he entered the hospital last week, has had his transplant, and is now recovering, reportedly the hardest part of the transplant process. We pray God will remove all discomfort in Mr. C's body, and he recovers faster than expected.

Lastly, please say a special prayer for complete healing for Willie Walker, the father of Shelia Walker-Elahee, healing for Tiffany Lyle, and a good report for my mother, Annie Foster. Prayer works!

Thank you in advance, and God Bless!

👍 43   Seen by 50   Comments

RH — Glad to hear Henry's recovery is moving along. Praying Henry achieves 8mil+ stem cells quickly and is able to move to the next step of treatment. Love you!

CB — We have Henry lifted up in prayer for all that is needed for his stem cells and his recovery from the transplant process.

PH — I am praying without ceasing!

SG — I am praying for them all! Happy new year, Henry! My office is no longer on the main campus; otherwise, I would try to catch up with you during your visits. Thanks for the updates, Vanessa. You are truly a strong woman of God!

LD — I am standing in agreement with all you said. Henry looks great!!!! We continue to pray for him. Last Sunday, at our KI meeting, we prayed for him and in our individual prayers too. God bless!!

CP — Good Morning, Vanessa. We stand in agreement, and we petition to the Lord for the eight million stem cells needed to manifest on Henry's behalf. We thank you in advance that all is working for his good. Lord, we thank you for Vanessa being a praying help meet for her husband, and that you strengthen her in this process to trust you and your Holy Scriptures to guide them through. We continue to believe the report of the Lord!

FROM ZION TO A CITY OF HOPE: A JOURNEY OF FAITH

Pasadena, CA
January 20, 2016

ON AGAIN, OFF AGAIN; THERE IS YET ANOTHER DELAY. This time, it is a delay of our own doing. So far, for two harvest-start days in a row, only 3.5 million stem cells have been harvested. The minimum number of stem cells required for a transplant is two million

We want to be able to do two transplants in case I need a second transplant sometime in the future. That means a minimum of four million stem cells need to be harvested. We were told you only go through the stem cell harvesting process once.

If you need another Stem Cell Transplant in the future, you cannot harvest stem cells at that time. You have to collect enough stem cells now for both transplants.

Vanessa and I want to keep as many options open as possible. We pushed to have City of Hope continue to harvest more stem cells, even though 3.5 million is enough for a single transplant. We had to obtain approval from our insurance provider because I will need two more Neupogen injections, which will cost another $16,000.

The injections were approved, and now we have to wait another two weeks for my body to rest and recover before we resume the harvesting.

I am trusting in the Lord that everything will work for my good.

Vanessa Foster-Dotson
January 20, 2016

*** Update for Monday, 01/18/16 - Tuesday, 01/19/16:

Rejoice in the Trial.

> "Consider it pure joy, my brothers, whenever you face trials of many kinds, because you know that the testing of your faith produces perseverance. Perseverance must finish its work so that you may be complete, not lacking anything."
> — James 1:2-4, New International Version Bible

"God's purpose in our lives is not to make us comfortable, but to build our character, and He does that through the trials we face. Don't give up if you fail the test. God will send another and another until you finally pass."

These words are what I read in my devotional today. This is what I needed to hear today.

On Monday, Henry's body only produced about 1.3 million stem cells. So, he now has a total of about 3.5 million harvested. Again, the goal is eight million. However, since he needs two million for a single

continued

transplant, and they typically can only perform the harvesting once, Henry needs to have at least four million stem cells harvested just in case he ever has to have a second transplant.

Now, because 3.5 is close to the minimum four million, the doctors at COH wanted to stop his harvesting short of obtaining the minimum four million. This is because he has to get a special injection the night before the harvest to help to stimulate his stem cells. This special injection costs $8,000 per shot. Insurance typically only covers the first four injections of this type. Henry had his fourth injection on Sunday night, 01/17/16.

So, we had to insist the doctors at COH make a case for the insurance to cover at least one more injection. Now that said, this is a new calendar year, so we will most likely have to cover most of this cost ourselves as part of our deductible. We'll see. But please pray that the insurance company authorizes at least one more injection.

So, man's plans have changed once again. Henry will need to wait another two weeks before they resume the harvesting. His hospital admittance has been postponed again.

Meanwhile, Henry will undergo testing on Friday, 01/22/16, to assess his current Multiple Myeloma level since he has not been on chemo since the end of October.

Also, during the two weeks, we will continue to support our friend, Mr. C, as he proceeds ahead of Henry. We will also support Henry's Uncle Alfred as he joins the Multiple Myeloma Stem Cell Transplant party, as well as another close friend, Mr. H, who was diagnosed with Multiple Myeloma before Henry. Mr. H has not had a Stem Cell Transplant as he is following a different treatment plan.

Now, I do not mention these other gentlemen in an effort to imply that they are competing. Instead, I am just shocked that there are four people in our small circle encountering the same trail around the same time. Yes, they each have different circumstances, but still.

As a dear friend of ours said so eloquently:

"Tis not a race for Mr. D or Mr. C. No one is ahead or behind in a race when the goal is life. God willing, like with HIV, medicine discovers ways to defeat the disease, or to keep it at bay so that both Mr. C and Mr. D (as well Uncle A and Mr. H) get to live full lives. Ideally, a way is found to poison the cancer and not the patient."

Thank you and Amen!!!

continued

So, please, whatever you do, get yourself checked. Make an appointment for your annual physical, and make sure that you go to the appointment. Question ANYTHING that is even slightly abnormal, and then insist on getting additional tests. You have to be your own advocate!

Also, please continue to keep the Walker family in prayer as their patriarch, Willie Walker, has gone home to rest in God's hands.

Lastly, if you know of anything that we can do to promote Henry's stem cell production, please let us know. If you have time to do a little research, that would be very helpful. I am still believing for a harvest of eight million stem cells the next time. If you know me well, I always try to have a plan "B" if it is God's will.

God Bless!

👍 23   Seen by 43   Comments

SB Our prayers of thanks believing that is already done!

WL Dear Lord, we agree that you give Vanessa and Henry GRACE as you shower them with MERCY. YOU are the CREATOR of the STEM CELLS, so we speak LIFE to the multiplication of the stem cells. You stated that YOU would grant us the desires of our HEART. Thank you, FATHER, that the hospital will have empathy and grant your children an exception for the special injection. The race for this healing is not to the swift, but to HENRY and VANESSA, who are enduring to the end.

BC Continuing to pray hard for your family and loved ones!

FD You're both in our prayers. God IS able.

Full Stem Ahead

"Let us therefore come boldly to the throne of grace, that we may obtain mercy and find grace to help in time of need."
— Hebrews 4:16, New King James Version

"Ask, and it will be given to you; seek, and you will find; knock, and it will be opened to you. "For everyone who asks receives, and he who seeks finds, and to him who knocks it will be opened."
— Matthew 7:7-8, New American Standard

Pasadena, CA
February 6, 2016

I AM STILL WAITING TO RESUME STEM CELL HARVESTING, BUT I AM GETTING STRONGER WITH EACH PASSING DAY. The markers for Multiple Myeloma and my kidney function are looking good. During this respite, I have gained weight, started exercising in a regular gym (on top of physical therapy), and have gotten out and about. It is incredible what you can do when you are not taking chemotherapy medication. I have not had any chemotherapy medication since October.

Vanessa and I attended our monthly Multiple Myeloma support group meeting on Monday. I asked some of the members of the group about their experience during their Stem Cell Transplants. Some had done it as in-patients, and others as outpatients. All of them reassured me that it was not bad at all.

Most of them said it was when the stem cells were put back into their bloodstream by infusion; they smelled creamed corn. That is unusual, to say the least. I am going to see if that happens when I go through the procedure. I appreciated them sharing their experiences with me. Oh, the benefits of community. It reminded me that we should not try to walk this journey alone.

I visited my friend Steve during his stay in the hospital while recovering from his Stem Cell Transplant. I asked him if he had been to any cancer support group meetings, and he said he had not. I know the value of being in a community with other cancer patients, so I decided to be his community; we would be a community of two.

When I would visit, we would talk about what it was like being a cancer patient. There was a lot of empathy felt during those visits. It felt good to speak candidly and know you were heard and understood.

Sometimes we would talk about cancer and how we had reconciled it with our faith. Years ago, Steve and I sang together in a quintet while we attended the same church. It is clear to me that we both have put all of our trust in the Lord.

I have kept in touch with Steve primarily by text and sometimes by phone since his discharge from the hospital after completing his recovery from his Stem Cell Transplant. I plan to continue to reach out to him as I go through the procedure and recovery myself. We plan to remain as a support community of two.

Vanessa Foster-Dotson
February 6, 2016

*** Update for Wednesday, 01/20/16 - Saturday, 02/06/16

He is always with you! (Isaiah 43:2). WOW, it's been 2.5 weeks, and God has been good in so many ways. Not only does Henry appear to be doing well externally, but he also is receiving good reports! Since my last update:

1. Henry still has not received chemo since October 30th, 2015, so he is feeling great!
2. As of 01/22/16, Henry's key protein level indicator (M-spike) is down to 0.13. It was as high as 6.0 in August when he first returned from Chicago and even much higher when he arrived in Chicago.
3. We were told the results of Henry's testing in December showed that less than 5% of his blood is currently being affected by Multiple Myeloma (MM). 90% of his blood had been affected when he arrived at the Cancer Treatment Centers of America (CTCA) in July.
4. Henry's key kidney health indicator (creatinine) remains in the normal range (1.16 out of a range of 0.7 – 1.3).
5. Henry is eating much, much better and has gained 6 pounds. He now weighs 166 pounds, closer to his goal of 175. We were blessed with some meal assistance for the month of January which really helped. (Hallelujah!)
6. Henry has been going with me to the gym and is almost able to achieve the same results on the lateral elliptical machine as he was achieving prior to his illness in July 2015!

He still has a compressed T-7 vertebra in his back and is still wearing a brace every day. So, he is not able to do as many exercises as before. However, he is doing very well with the exercises he can do.

7. Henry's immune system is currently strong, and his social activities have increased. In January, we went to a wedding where

Henry proved that he still has his moves on the dance floor.

We also attended two church services. One was for the anniversary of Henry's sister's (Patricia Jones) church, where she is the pastor. The other was for the ordination of the pastor of our church, now Bishop Ed Smith. It was great to be back in God's house and amongst his people.

8. Henry has received numerous visitors and calls, which is excellent therapy. Let us know if you want to connect us.
9. Henry is stating he is in a "medically-induced remission." We are believing that it is a permanent remission!!!

So, what's next? Henry still has to undergo a Stem Cell Transplant to aid with ensuring his MM remains in remission. Now that he has had a two-week break, he needs to resume the stem cell harvesting process.

So next Monday, 02/08/16, Henry will restart the harvesting process in hopes that he can produce at least 500 thousand more stem cells to bring his total to four million. Of course, the original goal of eight million is still desirable. Please again join us in prayer in regards to harvesting eight million stem cells.

After harvesting, Henry will be admitted to begin the in-hospital portion of the Stem Cell Transplant process. Then, in about three months after his Stem Cell Transplant, Henry will need to undergo back surgery.

So the journey continues...

Meanwhile, Mr. C, who I mentioned in previous updates, has completed his Stem Cell Transplant and appears to be doing well. Henry's uncle, Alfred Dotson, has completed his harvesting and will start the in-hospital portion of his transplant next week. Please keep both of these gentlemen in prayer as well.

Please also pray for Larry Huley's complete healing, as well as comfort for the Lopez/Keller, Walker, and Carr families, who have lost loved ones.

I again ask for a special prayer for my mother, Annie Foster.

I am so thankful for all of the blessings in my life. I am overjoyed that Henry is doing well. God has brought him such a long way. I tear up when I think about how he was in Chicago. (Yes, me, the strong one, smile!) But much continues to change in my world.

So, I have to remember and lean on Isaiah 43:2. Thank you for traveling this portion of my journey with me.

God Bless!

35   Seen by 54   27 Comments

JD Love you and in awe and blessed by your strength! I am continuing to pray for you all, Vanessa Foster-Dotson, my sister and partner in Christ.

GT That's awesome news about Henry's stamina and immune system. Keep fighting and leaning on God.

CP Vanessa, such a powerful praise report. God is an amazing God, and he has Henry in his care along with you. You both are faithful, and the word says he has never seen the righteous forsaken nor his seed begging bread.

A long journey to endure, but many prayer warriors in their War rooms are interceding for this miraculous move of complete healing. Yes, you be encouraged and stay strong. With tears of joy, began to shout now! When praises go up, blessings come down.

AO Amen! What an incredible wife!

RB Wonderful news! Vanessa, you walk with and in amazing grace.

WL It was great to see Henry at the ordination of Bishop Ed Smith. I couldn't wait to give Henry a Langley Hug. God is and is the HEALER. He never FAILS because he LISTENS to the VOICE of HIS CHILDREN. STAND STILL and SEE THE HANDS OF THE LORD. YES, HE WILL DO IT. THANK YOU, LORD.

Pasadena, CA
February 9, 2016

    WE HAVE MET THE GOAL OF HARVESTING MORE THAN FOUR MILLION STEM CELLS IN TOTAL! Monday, City of Hope collected 1.27 million stem cells, bring the total to 4.53 million stem cells. Today was another harvesting day, so there will be enough stem cells to do two transplants should the need arise.

    This is such a relief! This means my Stem Cell Transplant will take place in time to have back surgery and recover from it before the clinical trial starts. God always has impeccable timing!

    I look forward to seeing what God will do next!

Vanessa Foster-Dotson
February 9, 2016

*** Update for Sunday, 02/07/16 - Tuesday, 02/09/16

At Last!!! As per my previous update, Henry resumed the stem cell harvesting portion of his transplant yesterday. He is also harvesting today. Yesterday, 1.27 million cells were harvested! Yes! That gives Henry a total of 4.53 million cells from his three harvesting sessions.

We won't know the results of today's harvest until tomorrow, but whatever it is, he has achieved the four million absolute minimum that he needed to move forward with the next phase of the transplant process. I am still praying for the original goal of eight million. However, I am extremely thankful for this progress!

Praising God!!

👍 47   Seen by 47   20 Comments

CP Amen! for an awesome praise report, as we continue to believe God for the eight million coming into view. Our God is awesome; he moves mountains, and this too shall pass. Thank you for continuing to press towards the mark of the high calling in Christ Jesus!

JD Praise God! I'm so very happy. We know God is in charge, and with prayer, everything will be alright. I'm claiming that. Uncle Al will be admitted tomorrow.

JH Let's just call him Stem Cell Henry from now on! Great news!

WL Thank you, Father, for touching and multiplying the STEM CELLS in HENRY'S BODY. YOU are the LORD OF INCREASE. THANK YOU, LORD, FOR HEARING OUR PRAYERS.

Pasadena, CA
February 10, 2016

THE FINAL HARVESTING NUMBERS ARE IN. A total of 4.58 million stem cells were harvested. I am scheduled to be admitted to City of Hope on February 23rd, which means my Stem Cell Transplant will occur on February 25th.

I plan to continue building up my strength and my weight in preparation for the procedure. My oncologist says most patients lose weight during the recovery period, so I want to have more meat on my bones before checking in to Helford Hospital.

I spoke with Steve to let him know what was going on. He wished me well and said the procedure was not difficult to get through. I asked him about the creamed corn. He said he smelled it too.

> *"The whole point of collecting is the thrill of acquisition, which must be maximized, and maintained at all costs."* — John Baxter

Vanessa Foster-Dotson
February 16, 2016

*** Update for Wednesday, 02/10/16 - Monday, 02/15/16

Special Request. All is well with Henry. His last harvest day was on Tuesday, 02/09/16. He ended up harvesting 4.58 million cells which are enough for two transplants if needed. He is currently scheduled to be admitted at City of Hope on Tuesday, 02/23/16, to begin the in-hospital portion of his transplant process. I will keep you posted on his progress.

Meanwhile, please say a special prayer for my mother, Annie Foster. She is having surgery tomorrow, 02/16/16, to have a cancerous growth removed along with a mastectomy. The doctors are not sure what type of cancer she has, but the growth is somewhat aggressive. I will be traveling back east to be with her and the rest of my family and will return in time to be with Henry.

Two of the people that I love most in the world! CRAZY! But I am resting on faith that all will be well with both of them.

Thank you as always for your prayers.

 47   Seen by 64   32 Comments

 Oh my goodness, I didn't know. I've been playing phone tag with Vanna. My prayers will be with Auntie, as well as Henry and the rest of the family. Love Ya!

PJ God's got this, Nessa!! I'll be praying for your mom, and of course, Bernard. You are included too. Stand strong in the Lord, Sis!! I love you!

GA You and the family have been in my thoughts and prayers constantly.

LW Vanessa, I understand first-hand what you're going through. My mother and husband both have the same health condition as the other. It's quite the juggling act when we're in the Bay Area, and she's in So Cal.

I'm praying for your family, knowing we serve a right and perfect God.

PM Oh, Vanessa, so much to endure with your mom and Henry both fighting their respective battles. God has proven that he's in control and will heal them both. I'll be uplifting all of you in prayer. Stay strong as I know you will. Love you so much for the woman of God that you are!

JW I am praying for you and yours. God is good, even in a storm. Love you guys.

AV Prayers go out to you and your mom. As we know, Henry is in good hands. God bless you all.

Dem Bones

"Then He asked me, 'Son of man, can these bones come to life?'
'O Lord GOD,' I replied, 'only You know.'
And He said to me, 'Prophesy concerning these bones and tell them, 'Dry bones, hear the word of the LORD! This is what the Lord GOD says to these bones: I will cause breath to enter you, and you will come to life.'"
— Ezekiel 37:3-5, Berean Study Bible

City of Hope, Duarte, CA
February 25, 2016

TODAY I HAD MY **STEM CELL TRANSPLANT.** It was very anticlimactic. There was more time, energy, and drama in preparing for the transplant than the procedure itself.

The transplant process itself is on a strict schedule from when you check in until you check out.

On the first day (T minus two days), you are admitted to Helford Hospital and placed in a room on one of the special Stem Cell Transplant floors. Patients who provided their own stem cells (Autologous Stem Cell Transplant patients) stay on the fifth floor, while patients who received donor stem cells stay on the sixth floor. My room was on the fifth floor. Each room is pressurized, so air is pushed out of the room whenever the door opens. That prevents germs from entering the room.

On T minus one day, you are given Melphalan, a chemotherapy medication that will remove your bone marrow altogether.

On the day of the transplant (T minus zero days), your stem cells are returned to your bloodstream by infusion. I guess it is more like a transfusion, except you receive your own blood components.

From that point on, you wait for nature to take its course. On average, it takes about 15 days for that to happen. So, your tentative discharge date is T plus 15 days.

When I received the infusion of my stem cells, I could feel them reenter my body. That is because they were still cool from being refrigerated. They keep them refrigerated up until a few hours before the infusion.

Oh yes, I did smell the creamed corn too.

From this point on, my blood will be drawn every day to measure my platelets and white blood cell count. These numbers should go down for three days until they reach zero. That is when I will have no immune system. At that point, I will be susceptible to any and everything. That is why the room has negative pressure.

My numbers should stay low for a few days and then start increasing. The increase indicates the stem cells have migrated back into the bones and are beginning to produce marrow.

After a few days, the numbers will increase to the point where it will be safe for me to leave my room and walk around. By T plus 15 days, my counts should be good enough for me to check out.

We will see how the process goes.

**City of Hope, Duarte, CA
February 26, 2016**

Happy New Birthday To Me!

 Henry B. Dotson III
February 26, 2016

On February 25, 2016, i underwent a stem cell transplant procedure. This is the last major treatment planned for my multiple myeloma. The treatment replaces my original (cancer-producing) bone marrow with new bone marrow that will grow from the transplanted stem cells.

This is a very important day. The healthcare providers say this is your new birthday because you are getting brand new bone marrow and a new immune system.

I have always made it a point in my adulthood to spend time on my birthday to reflect on the year i just completed and to revisit my life's goals. Since this is my year zero birthday (my birth year), i have nothing to reflect upon about the prior year (i still had my 'old' bone marrow).

So, i thought it would be a good idea to see what occurred this day in history and to plan for the year to come.

- In 1862, the U.S. Congress passed the Legal Tender Act, authorizing the use of paper notes to pay the government's bills. This ended the long-standing policy of using only gold or silver in transactions.
- In 1870, Hiram Rhoades Revels, a Republican from Natchez, MS, is sworn into the U.S. Senate, becoming the first African American ever to sit in Congress.

continued

- In 1964 on this day, Cassius Clay knocked out Sonny Liston to win the World Heavyweight boxing title.
- In 1993, a bomb exploded at the World Trade Center in New York. The blast killed six people and injured more than 1,000.
- In 2004, 'The Passion of the Christ,' Mel Gibson's film about the last 44 hours of Jesus of Nazareth's life, opens in theaters across the United States.

These historical events seem to be unrelated to one another and even less related to me. However, they do prompt me to consider my future in terms of what these events represent.

The passing of the Legal Tender Act prompts me to make sure my family's financial plans are in order.

Hiram Rhoades Revels' swearing-in as a member of Congress and Cassius Clay's knockout remind me that great accomplishments can occur against all odds, but trials and tribulations will follow before a long-lasting change is achieved.

Jim Crow laws disenfranchised African Americans from the political process in the South, and Cassius Clay was stripped of his title in 1967 for refusing to be inducted into the Armed Forces during the Vietnam War.

It took 96 years before Edward W. Brooke became the first African American U.S. Senator after Reconstruction, and the Supreme Court of the United States reversed Ali's draft evasion conviction after four years, allowing him to fight professionally once again. In 1974 he regained the heavyweight title.

I am reminded that I must be persistent in the pursuit of my life's purpose.

 Comments

 Happy Birthday! You are an amazing man loved by an incredible woman (Vanessa). I'm so happy for both of you!

 Happy re-birth. Thank you for the well-thought-out post. It is an example to us all. Thank you for keeping it real! Love you, my friend.

 Happy Birthday, Henry! God is using you to inspire others. God bless you!

DM — I thank and praise God for all that he has done for you to bring you to your (new birth). Truly he is a healer, and you are a blessing to many. Happy Birthday and I pray many more.

SB — We celebrate the God that we serve and continue to think about His goodness and His grace, which has set us free from sin!. Happy Birthday, Henry, our fierce leader in missions. Let the Lord lead, He is over all of us, and His Healing is on you!

PM — Happy Born-Again Birthday, Henry! What an awesome God we serve. He has brought you a mighty long way, and your post is beautifully written. The historical events that you intertwined with your own life story are God-inspired.

I'm so glad you added your blessing, Vanessa, in the postscript because the two of you have woven such a beautiful tapestry of your journey. You should do the world a favor and co-write a book of challenges, prayer, inspiration, and victory. It would be a best seller.

Keep fighting the good fight of faith!!!!

WL — To GOD, we give THANKS. I salute your wife and you in this fight of FAITH. The HOPE that we all have is TRUSTING in GOD through the BLOOD OF JESUS TO SET US FREE. The INSPIRATION from you GUYS is that JESUS is ALIVE, and we should NEVER GIVE UP. HIP HIP HOORAY ON YOUR NEW BIRTHDAY. It is not how long it takes to win the RACE, but that we WIN.

RM — What an outstanding reflection and future outlook. May God's manifested grace, restored health, and renewal be yours. Selah.

JB — Happy birthday my friend. Thank you for sharing your reflections. Also, I and many others are further bolstered in our faith by your stand. You are fighting the good fight, and where I am from, the only good fight is the one where we win. Thank you for sharing how to win in Him! I love you, man.

City of Hope, Duarte, CA
March 6, 2016

EVERYTHING IS GOING ACCORDING TO PLAN. My blood-count numbers went down for three days until they reached zero. At that point, I was neutropenic – I had no immune system. I was susceptible to everything, and I could not have any visitors.

Everyone from City of Hope who entered the room had to wear masks. My numbers stayed low for three days and then started to increase. After two more days, my numbers increased to the point where I was able to leave my room and walk around.

I have been taking walks each day since I have been able to leave my room. I have set some goals for myself regarding how many times per day I walk and how far I walk. I find this very helpful because there is nothing else to do except watch television.

My Uncle Alfred came to visit me one day. He was at City of Hope to receive treatment for his Multiple Myeloma and decided to drop by. Visits from home are always welcomed.

City of Hope, Duarte, CA
March 9, 2016

TODAY IS VANESSA'S BIRTHDAY. I spoke to her, but we did not see each other. We are looking forward to my discharge date so we can celebrate her birthday at that time.

I have also asked for and received a keyboard to play in my room. I was looking for something else to do besides watch television.

I am scheduled to be discharged tomorrow. I am so looking forward to going home.

Vanessa Foster-Dotson
March 9, 2016

*** Update for Friday, 02/26/16 - Wednesday, 03/09/16 ***

The best birthday present a girl can have! It's been 2.5 weeks. My baby is coming home tomorrow or Friday after having a successful Stem Cell Transplant!

While in the hospital, Henry walked daily an average of three miles a day and had almost no challenges. They even put a keyboard in his room. I admire Henry's strength, determination, and positive attitude.

I am so happy he is coming home and that he will be HEALTHY! He still has to wear a brace and undergo back surgery in a few months, but we have faith that everything will go great with that procedure as well. The power of prayer!

Meanwhile, my mother is back at the assistant living facility she is comfortable with. She did not like the hospital or acute care facilities at all, and she let everyone know! My sister and I had to take turns spending the night.

Although Mom had a mass removed along with her remaining breast, she has been diagnosed with a rare form of breast cancer, so we still have some challenges ahead of us. The blessing is she will be 83 next week. By faith, Mom is totally healed!

As for me, life has been a bit hectic as I try to cover a lot of fronts. But as long as my family is good, it is all worth it.

God Bless, and thank you so much for your support!

 60   Seen by 63   29 Comments

 Praise God, for he is faithful! So glad to learn my brother Henry is healing. And you, my friend, are amazing! I love you both and wish I could be there.

 Amazing! Look at God! And to God be the glory. My continued prayers for all of you on this journey.

 Vanessa, this is an awesome praise report for your birthday. To God be all the glory. Truly God has shown himself strong on Henry's behalf. We are believing for Mom's healing too. I feel and understand where you are, and God is faithful to his word. We love you guys. An incredible God deserves incredible praise.

CS — I admire your strength. Thank you so much for taking the time to update all of us. You both have role-modeled strength, love, and strong faith. I am so in awe of both of you as you tackle all the challenges, obstacles and continue to journey forward with such grace. Glad you have completed the stem cell process and hope to see you soon. Hugs and kisses.

JB — Praise the Lord! He causes us to be victorious. The devil is no match for our God. Henry, your strong walk of faith, walking in the authority that we, as His children, have been given, to bind and loose, permit and prohibit, is shining through!

DK — Awesome! What's a mighty God we serve. So happy for y'all. Y'all have taken the word of God to the nations, so we knew He would show up and out on your behalf. Forever a God chaser.

JD — May God's continuing healing power move in Bernard's as well your mother's body as they begin to recover. I also ask God to continue to give you the strength of his Grace as you travel this journey with them. Please get the rest you need, and know that we understand and we are standing with you all. I'm here if you need me, my dear niece and nephew—much love and blessings.

DR — God is Good all the time. Stay strong in prayer. You know that Reed Line is strong! Smile hugs and kisses to you and Henry. Love ya cuz.

CL — We keep right on praying, Sis Vanessa and Henry. Faith never quits. Love never fails! Happy Birthday to you!

SM — I am praising God along with you. Such an awesome praise report. Enjoy your birthday too, Sis.

Love you much!!

PM — Always thoughtful and caring, Vanessa, as you keep your prayer warriors updated. God continues to answer our prayers as Henry overcomes every obstacle. We remain in prayer as always!

LD — God is good. Praise going up for your baby! Hahaha! God is good. We will keep Mom in prayer.

Pasadena, CA
March 11, 2016

I WAS DISCHARGED FROM CITY OF HOPE YESTERDAY. My oncologist said my Stem Cell Transplant went precisely according to the timeline for a typical transplant. I think the word he used was "textbook." I was just relieved to get back home.

Today, I am in a more reflective mood. My Stem Cell Transplant is a major milestone in my recovery from Multiple Myeloma and a step closer to the complete restoration of my health. This milestone is also another blessing from God that I can look back on when I face trials and tribulations in the future.

I am looking forward to learning what effect the Stem Cell Transplant has had on the percentage of myeloma cells present in my marrow. I think it will take about a month to find out.

> **Q: How did you feel when you learned i was back home after a successful stem cell transplant?**
>
> **BART:** I was ecstatic to hear that the stem cell treatment was successful. It was at that moment that I was confident that you would go into remission.
>
> **TALIA:** Relieved.
>
> **CRIS:** I was elated!

Pasadena, CA
April 2016

BART AND CHARITY CAME TO VISIT US. It was the first time Vanessa and I met Charity. Bart had told us about her, so we were interested in meeting his "friend."

We have had difficulty in the past figuring out if and when Bart was dating someone. Our dating, boyfriend, girlfriend, and courting concepts do not align or map well with the ideas used by today's young adults. They certainly do not fit Bart and Talia's terminology.

I was interested in meeting Charity because Bart had said she was very supportive when he returned from seeing me at CTCA.

Charity was very nice. She was also friendly and engaging. I was glad to hear that they met at church, and she was into music. She graduated from college with a degree in music and has her own business teaching music to children. She gives private lessons, and she has contacts with the local school districts teaching music to classes during school hours.

We showed her family pictures, including some of Bart's most memorable baby pictures. I'm not so sure he appreciated that so much.

The conversation got around to my cancer journey, and I thanked Charity for supporting Bart when he needed it. It reminded me of the countless times Vanessa has been there for me.

After they left to return to Arizona, Vanessa asked me, "What do you think?"

"I think she was very nice."

"Yes, I do too. She seems to have a good head on her shoulders."

"I agree."

We did not think much more about it. I knew asking Bart what he thought about Charity would only confuse me due to the generation gap. I was content with knowing he had a good friend.

Q: What did you think when you first saw me after my diagnosis?

CHARITY: I thought you were looking pretty good, but it was the first time I had seen or met you, so I didn't have any past experience to make a comparison to. This was in April 2016, so you had been in remission for a little bit, I believe. It wasn't until I saw older pictures of you while visiting that April that I saw how much weight you had lost from the father Henry remembered growing up with.

Q: How did you feel when you first saw me after my diagnosis?

CHARITY: I couldn't make a comparison, but when I saw old pictures, I was thankful you were recovering and starting to feel better and gain strength.

Q: Was it difficult for you to see me in my physical condition?

CHARITY: No, it was the first time I saw you.

Pasadena, CA
April 28, 2016

I RECEIVED MY TEST RESULTS YESTERDAY. Everything is looking good! All but one of my markers is in the normal range. Now, my marrow is only 3% cancerous. It has gone down 2% since before my Stem Cell Transplant; and down 87% from my initial level of 90%. This truly is good news!

I am still expecting even better results when I receive my total healing. I praise God from whom all blessings flow!

Battlefield of the Mind

"If patience is worth anything, it must endure to the end of time. And a living faith will last in the midst of the blackest storm."
— Mahatma Gandhi

ONE OF THE GREATEST BATTLES I FIGHT CONTINUALLY ON THIS CANCER JOURNEY TAKES PLACE ON THE BATTLEFIELD OF MY MIND. It is a crucial battle because it is the primary way the enemy attacks my faith and attitude.

The first assault I had to contend with was the sense of loss.

Part of dealing with cancer is coming to terms with the reality that you value things you have lost. Like any other loss, you must go through the grieving process so you don't get stuck in a rut.

Before I could go through the stages of grief, I had to first identify what was lost in as precise a manner as possible. It would have been impossible to thoroughly go through the grieving process if I didn't know precisely why I was grieving.

For me, what I lost includes 1) the seemingly overnight loss of the person I used to be; 2) the loss of "normal"; 3) the loss of some of my independence; 4) the loss of my ability to work; 5) the time lost to hospitalization and rehab, and 6) the loss of the type of future I had envisioned for myself and Vanessa.

Once I knew exactly why I was grieving and what I lost, I could mourn adequately. I went to the Father in prayer because His word says:

> *Blessed are those who mourn, for they will be comforted.*
> — Matthew 5:4, New American Standard

God answered my prayers. I felt His comfort as I worked my way through all of the stages of grief for each loss until I reached the acceptance stage.

The last stage of the grieving process is acceptance. Once I accepted my loss, I was ready to move on. Moving on meant changing my behavior and attitudes (if necessary) and internalizing them, assimilating them into my everyday life.

For me to reach the point of acceptance, I had to do two things. First, I had to be thankful for the things I did have, those things that remain. Second, I had to look for and appreciate the things I had gained because of what I have gone through.

First, I am thankful I have life itself. I am still here. I am thankful for God, who loves me and sustains me. I am thankful for His promises in the Bible. He is forever faithful, and I have faith enough to believe.

The other things are the things I thought about when Dr. Mahmoud gave me a preliminary diagnosis of Multiple Myeloma: I am blessed with family; I am blessed with friends, and I am blessed with Vanessa. I am blessed with the relationships I have in my life with the people who love me.

As I worked my way through the loss, I remembered what my grandfather said to me in his later years:

> *"Son, whatever you do, do it with all your heart, all your soul, and all your might. Because one day, you will not be able to do it anymore, and you will have regrets. I have friends who are trying to do those things now to make up for the times when they didn't do them, and they are killing themselves trying."* — Henry B. Dotson, Sr.

I took his words to heart, and over the years up until now, I have accumulated no regrets because I chose to follow his advice. There is no excess baggage that I carried into this cancer journey.

What I have gained during this journey up to this point include:
- A greater appreciation for how precious life really is;
- An empathy for disabled people that I would never have acquired without becoming disabled myself;
- A community of cancer patients and their caregivers who welcomed Vanessa and me and continued to help me heal;
- The privilege and blessing to witness Vanessa fulfill her wedding vow to love, honor, and cherish me in sickness;
- An increase in faith because of what God miraculously has done to keep me on this side of eternity.

I will meditate on these things every day to keep the hole filled, the scale balanced as I move forward with no regrets.

The second fiery dart of the enemy that I have battled is the feeling of guilt.

Guilt came during recovery and rehabilitation when I felt better and continued to rest and do nothing. I had been told, "take it easy; don't rush things."

I felt guilty because I thought I should be doing something since I felt better. I felt like I was lazy, that I did not deserve to lie around and do nothing.

Guilt can make you feel unworthy of doing something or drive you to do something you should not do.

Sometimes, I felt like doing something I hadn't done in a long time because of my illness, and I felt guilty because I wanted to do it right then; I wanted to feel somewhat "normal" again.

As I struggled with the guilt, God ministered to me through my friend Steve. He called me to see how I was doing after my Stem Cell Transplant.

"How are you feeling?"

"I feel great! This is the best I've felt in a long time. I want to get up and go, but my doctor told me to continue to rest and do nothing."

"I know how you feel. I felt the same way, too, after my transplant. My doctor told me the same thing, but I didn't listen."

"What do you mean?"

"I hadn't felt that good in a long time, so I decided to do a three-mile hike."

"A three-mile hike!"

"Yes, and it was okay. I felt great when I got home. But a day or so later, I was totally wiped out. It took me several weeks to recover."

I took heed to Steve's cautionary tale. The last thing I wanted was a setback.

My grandfather's words and Steve's experience helped me accept that I am not the same person I was before cancer. That there are some things that I cannot do that I could do before I was diagnosed with Multiple Myeloma. I am okay with this because I have no regrets.

I have also learned that I must give my body time to heal. It may not seem as though anything is going on when I am resting, but my body is fighting the cancer cells on a cellular level, which takes energy. That is energy that I cannot afford to use doing something else in an attempt to feel "normal" again.

I have conquered my guilt by realizing to do nothing at this point is the exact right thing to do.

> *"I have come to believe that caring for myself is not self-indulgent. Caring for myself is an act of survival."*   — Audre Lorde

Through meditation and prayer, I realize that God is speaking to me through my body. When I listen to what my body tells me, I am doing exactly what God wants me to do. My body is His temple, and He will instruct me on what to do to wash away its impurities.

> "Self-care has become a new priority – the revelation that it's perfectly permissible to listen to your body and do what it needs."
> — Frances Ryan

The other attacks are minor skirmishes, but they are more frequent than the first two. These include; 1) side-effects of medications, 2) inconveniences that come about due to my condition, and 3) physical limitations. There are others, but these are the most frequent ones.

I have learned the best way to deal with these everyday frustrations is to maintain a positive attitude and remember that these are minor compared to what I have already overcome in the grand scheme of things. So, when put into context, I have learned not to sweat the small stuff.

I have found it essential to realize I am actively engaged in a battle every day. For me to be victorious, I must do what the Bible says:

> *In addition to all this, take up the shield of faith, with which you can extinguish all the flaming arrows of the evil one.*
> — Ephesians 6:16, Berean Study Bible

and

> *Pray in the Spirit at all times, with every kind of prayer and petition. To this end, stay alert with all perseverance in your prayers for all the saints.* — Ephesians 6:18, Berean Study Bible

Faith and prayer. They are what enable me to continually win on the battlefield of my mind.

Back To The Future

"The greatest discovery of all time is that a person can change his future by merely changing his attitude."   — Oprah Winfrey

---

Pasadena, CA
May 7, 2016

I AM MAKING GOOD PROGRESS AS I PREPARE FOR BACK SURGERY. Once I got rid of the guilty feelings I had for lying in bed, I have had no problems staying put and taking frequent naps. I listen to my body, and when it tells me it is tired, I immediately stop what I am doing and go lay down. I do not try to finish the last little something I am working on at the moment. I go lie down, and after anywhere from 40 to 90 minutes later, I am ready to go again.

It reminds me of when I was in kindergarten. At that age, I looked forward to the afternoon nap period. I now find myself looking forward to naps once again.

I have been off chemotherapy for six months. That is a big part of why I feel so much better. I still have neuropathy, one of the side effects of chemotherapy, but its effects are minimal.

I am looking forward to seeing what God will do when I have my back surgery. I am also looking forward to the future for the first time in a while. I believe there is a future for me here, and God has decided to give me my healing from this disease on this side of eternity.

Vanessa Foster-Dotson
May 7, 2016

*** Update for Thursday, 03/10/16 - Saturday, 05/07/16 ***

Well, you have to have FAITH! It's been quite a while since the last update. (Brace yourself! This one is a bit long...smile). Henry has been progressively stable, so there has not been much to report. He seems to get stronger every day.

He has not been on a chemo regimen since October 2015. His eating is almost back to normal, and he has gained weight. He now weighs 177 pounds! At his last doctor's appointment at City of Hope, which was on April 27th, Henry's blood counts were back in the normal range. His white blood cell count was 5.2.

continued

Henry continues to get tired more than he used to, so he takes frequent naps and still has a bit of neuropathy in a few of his fingertips and feet. Here is a summary of some of Henry's key indicators:

Key Results for Multiple Myeloma (MM) Measure:

- IgG (General indicator of myeloma cells present in the body); Normal Range: 700 -1,600
    - 07/16/15 (CTCA): 13,000
    - 08/20/15 (COH): 7,240
    - 09/25/15 (COH): 1,340
    - 04/27/16 (COH): 499 (Below the norm! Yes!)
- Measure: M-Spike (Key indicator of myeloma cells present in the body). Goal: The closer to 0, the better
    - 08/20/15 (COH): 6.1
    - 09/25/15 (COH): 0.9
    - 04/27/16 (COH): 0.11 (Very good! Yes!)
- Key Results for Kidney Function Measure: Creatinine (Key indicator of kidney function). Normal Range: 0.40 -1.20
    - 07/16/15 (CTCA): 8.84
    - 08/20/15 (COH): 1.22
    - 09/25/15 (COH): 0.77
    - 04/27/16 (COH): 1.4 (Need to keep an eye on this.)
- Key Results for Vitality Measure: Weight (Key indicator of overall vitality). Goal: 175-180
    - 06/01/15 (Home): 190.02
    - 07/16/15 (CTCA): 181.44
    - 08/20/15 (COH): 158.73
    - 09/29/15 (Home): 150.07
    - 04/27/16 (COH): 177 (Reached the goal! Yes!)

The main challenge Henry currently has is with his back. In June of last year, his T7 vertebra, along with other vertebrae, collapsed as a result of the MM. As a result, he started wearing an "ironman" back brace (as we affectionately refer to it) in August and has been wearing it ever since.

continued

His best permanent solution is back surgery. Since his MM counts are good, Henry has been approved to have back surgery on May 18th. He basically will be getting a replacement for his collapsed vertebra. This is a serious surgery (thoracic vertebrectomy), and we are definitely anxious about it.

But we know that we are children of God, so we believe that Henry has been healed in the name of Jesus, and all will be well.

After surgery, Henry will be in the hospital for one week and will then take approximately two to four weeks to recover at home. During this time, he is encouraged to walk as much as possible.

Once Henry recovers, he will start a chemo consolidation phase lasting four months and then go on a low dose chemo maintenance regimen indefinitely.

Henry is now involved in a clinical trial. The trial allows all of his chemo meds to be administered orally. This is significantly less invasive than weekly hospital visits for infusions.

As for me, I still have a lot on my plate. I am extremely thankful that he is close to "normal" and can do much more on his own now. There are a few tasks that Henry cannot yet perform, so I have been picking up the slack in addition to the regular activities that are required to maintain a household.

My work has also become more demanding. I have a new manager and have started traveling again. There have been layoffs already this year, so I continue to do all that I can to ensure that my home life does not impact my work life (and vice versa).

As we are still receiving bills from the Cancer Treatment Centers of America, along with others from City of Hope, I am extremely thankful for my employment and for the insurance coverage that we have, as well as the numerous other benefits that I receive from working. I definitely do not take my employment for granted. I have been led to focus on Galatians 6:4.

I also want to provide a quick update on a few other people:

- My mother, Annie Foster (Rare Breast Cancer): Is doing well. At age 83, my sister and I decided chemo would not provide her the best quality of life, so she has received 30+ days of radiation instead, which she seemed to have handled mostly in stride. (That was a tough decision.) Mom still resides at an assisted living facility and is generally happy.

continued

- Rosalind (Ovarian Cancer): Is doing well. She has some neuropathy but is ready to get back to work.
- Margaret (Ovarian Cancer): Is doing well. As a result of her chemo, she has some minor digestion issues that are controlled by meds.
- Mr. C (Multiple Myeloma): Is doing well and does not seem to have any complications since his transplant.
- Mr. Z (Multiple Myeloma): We need to check in on him.
- Uncle Alfred Dotson (Multiple Myeloma): Has had some severe digestion issues since his transplant.

Prayer Requests:

1. Complete healing for Henry in body, mind, soul, and spirit. (no cancer, no pain, no permanent back damage, no fevers, no infections, etc.);
2. Continued improved strength and movement for Henry;
3. Total favor in regard to all aspects of Henry's back surgery on May 18th, as well as a speedy and full recovery.
4. Please say a special prayer for Uncle Alfred Dotson's quick return to "normal"; no health challenges, full recovery.
5. Please say a special prayer for Lewis's father, who was recently diagnosed with pancreatic cancer.
6. Please say a special prayer for Emily, who has been hospitalized and is very sick, but the doctors do not know why.
7. General prayer for all of the family members and friends of anyone that is reading this update and has recently been diagnosed, or is suffering from cancer or some other life-threatening health challenge.

Prayers Answered for Henry:

1. Healthy kidneys - no dialysis
2. Healthy eyes
3. Increased platelet count
4. Clarity of thoughts and words
5. Exponential blood count level increase
6. Renewed spirit

continued

7. Release from CTCA and return home
8. Easy transition to being in CA
9. Stabilized blood counts...all counts being positive
10. Stabilized kidney counts
11. No long-term anemia
12. Increased appetite and weight

Just think, a year ago this time, we had no idea that anything was wrong with Henry. We have really been on quite a journey these past 11 months! Every day I realize more and more that this has truly been a FAITH WALK. We have been so blessed!

Thank you once again for your prayers. May God continue to bless you all.

Happy Mother's Day to every mother that is reading this update!

👍 40   Seen by 57   27 Comments

CP Amen! Absolutely will pray the prayer of divine healing for by His stripes (Jesus) you are healed!
In the Name of Jesus.

LW God is able and a healer. We stand in agreement with your specific petitions—continued prayers for you and Vanessa.

PO Praying for you, Henry, take care!

RG I am lifting you and Henry up in prayer. You are loved by The Lord and by us. You are a testimony. Keep up the faith walk! We love you!

SB I confess that the power of our Triune God is well aware that your pain and other difficulties are being taken care of in due time. The Triune God that we serve will continue to give you and Vanessa victorious life as we look through a glass dimly.

ES I just prayed again for your total healing and a speedy FULL Recovery... In Jesus' Name!

BG God is good and keeps his promises.

Q: How did you feel when you learned i was going to undergo vertebra replacement surgery?

BART: Of all the major issues throughout the process of recovery (Chicago, the lethal infection, stem cells), the vertebrae surgery was the one operation that I had full knowledge of beforehand.

I felt the most fearful for this operation. I realized that if something went wrong, you could potentially be paralyzed. Or, even if it went well, you could be hindered physically for the rest of your life.

CHARITY: I remember being concerned and lifting you up in prayer.

TALIA: I was concerned about your back and you turning into a bionic man.

IRA: The vertebrae surgery came as a surprise. I wondered during your ordeal if any of your vertebrae had been impacted. Considering all the other procedures you had already endured, this one seemed "normal."

A year ago, the concern was the quality of your life after your recovery. Now you were scheduled to have back surgery. Finally, you were facing something normal.

CRIS: I felt somewhat concerned at first, but I knew it was necessary for the furtherance of your healing.

PAT: Your vertebra replacement surgery, to me, was just par for the course. Everything up until this point had been going so well, well, maybe with a few minor setbacks. I believe my main concern was the mere fact that you were having another surgery. That in itself caused me some concern. Because with any surgery, there are always risks.

BERYL: Knowing that the vertebrae replacement surgery was the last major hurdle, I was bolstered by what had happened up to this point. Although I knew the surgery was serious, I found myself looking past the surgery to the testimony that you would share.

KATHY: Although a little scary, I was very hopeful. So much had happened in your favor that I just figured that this, too, would work out, and it was simply another hurdle that would be conquered.

SANDRA: I felt happy knowing that this could be your breakthrough and that things were getting done.

NORMAN: If I remember correctly, it was more of a "How the hell do they do that?" I did not know that artificial vertebrae existed. It is the engineer in me and the interest in medicine.

RUTH: Frightened, I thought about the "what ifs": What if you weren't strong enough to undergo this surgery? What if you got an infection? What if there was a physician or surgical error?

CECILY: Very concerned about vertebrae surgery as I was not sure you were strong enough and concerned for complications and always the risk of infection and death.

JEFF AND CHARALE: Our hearts went out to you for having to go through the tough road and for Vanessa for having to see her "baby" go through these procedures.

LOIS: Again, I was happy for anything that would help you progress to wholeness!

MARGARET: That one scared me – I had heard horror stories about that surgery, and people never walking again afterward. So, I kept praying and hoped for the best.

JIM: I looked at the vertebrae replacement surgery as a good sign. After all, why put you through that if your journey was not headed to a good destination? I know that may not have been how your doctor viewed it, but that is how I took it.

Pre-Op Prayer Request

Pasadena, CA
May 17, 2016

 Henry B. Dotson III
May 17, 2016

Greetings All,

Once again, Vanessa has given me the opportunity to post an entry to the group. I continue to be blessed by her diligence in providing the means to keep you all informed and making you a part of my journey.

Tomorrow I will have major back surgery followed by an extended recovery period. The surgery is scheduled to last for five (5) hours. My recovery in the hospital is scheduled to last for seven (7) days. My recovery will then continue in an acute-rehabilitation facility for another scheduled two (2) weeks. This will be followed by recovery at home for an estimated two (2) weeks.

I ask that your prayers for me be focused on this phase of my healing. It is through the power of prayer that God enables our stripes to be healed and to be brought into full restoration according to His Word. I have been blessed by your prayers up to this point in my journey, and I depend on your continued support to help carry me through this critical time.

Thank you again for your support through your prayers, words of encouragement, and acts of kindness. I am truly blessed to be part of God's plan to demonstrate His love for us by the way we love one another on this faith walk. We are doing this together, and I can feel His love through what you do. We serve a mighty God who is able!

Stay blessed and be well,

Henry

👍 38   Seen by 39   22 Comments

 Praying for you, Henry, take care!

 God is good and keeps his promises.

LW: God is able and a healer. We stand in agreement with your specific petitions—continued prayers for you and Vanessa.

RG: I am lifting you and Henry up in prayer. You are loved by The Lord and by us. You are a testimony. Keep up the faith walk! We love you!

ES: I just prayed again for your total healing and a speedy FULL Recover. In Jesus Name!

SB: I confess that the power of our Triune God is well aware that your pain and other difficulties are being taken care of in due time. The Triune God that we serve will continue to give you and Vanessa victorious life as we look through a glass dimly.

CP: Amen! Absolutely will pray the prayer of divine healing for by His stripes (Jesus) you are healed! In the Name of Jesus.

City of Hope
May 18, 2016, 6 a.m.

Vanessa and I arrived at City of Hope around 6 a.m. We went to the second floor of Helford Hospital, the same building where I had my Stem Cell Transplant. It felt different coming there as an outpatient when I had spent 17 days upstairs on the 5th floor just two months earlier.

We waited in the open lobby for about 20 minutes. There were a few other people there waiting along with us. Some were other patients scheduled for surgery that day. They were easy to pick out – they were the ones all the other party members were focused on. They spoke in low voices with words of encouragement and occasional reassuring physical touches.

When the patient's name was called, they rose along with their caregiver and went into a small office through a varnished French door with frosted window panes. When they reappeared, the members of their entourage gave them parting hugs, sometimes shed a few tears, and then left. The patient and their caregiver then went into one of the elevators along with an escort.

When my name was called, Vanessa and I repeated what I had seen the others do. We met with an administrative person in the office and went through the pre-op paperwork I had to sign before surgery.

As I read through the documents, it no longer concerned me when I read that one of the possible outcomes could be death. Everything I had signed up to this point had that same disclosure, along with all of the other possible outcomes of the procedure or medication I was about to receive. I had put my trust in the Lord from the beginning, so I signed without hesitation.

We were then escorted upstairs by a staff member to the floor where the surgery would take place. They took me to a pre-op area, where I changed into a gown and climbed onto a gurney. One of the nurses placed a surgical bonnet on my head to cover my hair. Vanessa and I said a little prayer when all was done and waited.

A few moments later, Dr. Chen came by. Our conversation went something like this:

"Good morning Mr. Dotson, Mrs. Dotson. Are you ready?"

"About as ready as I can be."

"About how long will the surgery be?" Vanessa asked,

"About five hours. We have to expose several vertebrae above and below T7 so we can attach the screws that will support the replacement vertebra."

That's a long time, I thought to myself.

"We will take our time," Dr. Chen continued. "With such a long incision and so much of the spine exposed, we must be careful not to do anything in a hurry. This surgery is a complex procedure, and the potential for making a mistake with serious consequences is real."

"I see," Vanessa said. She had a somber look on her face.

I appreciated Dr. Chen's candor. I wanted to know what I was facing without any sugarcoating.

"Do you have any other questions?"

Vanessa and I replied at the same time, almost in unison, "No."

"Thank you, Dr. Chen," Vanessa added.

"Okay. I need to get ready. I will see you in a few minutes in the OR, Mr. Dotson."

"Okay," I said.

After Dr. Chen left, Vanessa had one of the nurses take a picture of us.

Shortly after that, an orderly came and wheeled me into the operating room. I was then lifted and placed onto the operating table. The surgical team got busy hooking me up with monitors and placing disposable coverings over my back.

I don't recall if I had a mask or I received anesthesia through infusion. What I do remember is being asked to start counting backward from one hundred. I can't tell you how far I got into the count. I just remember closing my eyes.

ID We are covering you in our prayers. This will be a successful surgery!

SG Yay!!!! I am praying, believing God for a speedy and complete recovery!

CS Thinking of you.

EP Men of Iron Sharpens Iron prayed, standing, believing, and looking forward to what God has already done—expecting an awesome Testimony. Love you, Bro.

City of Hope
May 18, 2016, approximately 2:30 p.m.

WHEN I WOKE UP FROM SURGERY, I WAS LYING ON MY SIDE IN THE ICU. I was groggy but felt well-rested. The first person I saw was Vanessa.

"Hey," I said. Vanessa looked up and over at me and smiled.

"Hey, how are you feeling?"

"Okay. How long was the surgery?"

"You were in surgery for six hours."

It seemed to me as though I closed my eyes and just opened them again. It was a strange feeling to realize that six hours of my life passed, and I had no recollection of any of it.

"Are you in any pain?"

"No, not really."

"I'm going to let someone know that you are awake."

Vanessa left the room. I started to shift my position in the bed and realized that I had a lot of tubes coming out of me along my backside for the first time. At that point, I decided not to move too much. I didn't want to mess up something. I also noticed my back felt a little numb.

Vanessa returned with a nurse.

"Hello, Mr. Dotson, how are you feeling?"

"Okay. Why am I connected to all these tubes?"

"They are draining tubes. They help to keep the swelling down by draining off excess fluids that your body produces after surgery."

"I see," I said. Since this was the first surgery that I can remember, I had no idea what to expect in post-op.

"We've contacted Dr. Chen to let him know you are awake."

"Okay, thanks."

A little while later, Dr. Chen came by to see me. Our conversation went something like this:

"How are you feeling?"

"I feel okay. Was the surgery successful?"

"Well, Mr. Dotson, with these types of surgeries, we set the bar pretty low for what we consider a success. As I said before the surgery, this was a highly complex procedure. We made an incision in your back that went from T4 to T10. I put 36 staples in your back to close up the incision.

Exposing that much of your spine, replacing the T7 vertebra, and putting all of the necessary support screws into the other six vertebrae increased the risk of something going wrong significantly."

"I see."

"But, to answer your question, I think the surgery went very well. First of all, you woke up. Secondly, you can talk. Thirdly, you can wiggle your toes. Everything beyond that is gravy."

At that moment, I was not sure how to interpret what Dr. Chen said. In all of my previous conversations with him when we discussed the surgery during examinations, he was very frank. But he also showed his very dry sense of humor.

I searched his face and eyes, looking for a nonverbal clue to help my comprehension. I did not find what I was looking for.

There was just a brief pause before he continued talking, so I did not have time to respond to his answer.

"The nurses will monitor your condition. Once your condition is stable, we will move you out of ICU to a regular hospital room to continue your recovery. I will check on you every day when I do my rounds."

"Okay. Thanks, Dr. Chen."

"You're welcome," he replied. With that, Dr. Chen left the room.

"Sounds like things went well," Vanessa said.

"Yes. The process so far is going better than I expected."

I returned to my thoughts about what Dr. Chen had said about the surgery. In my final analysis, I believe that many things could have gone wrong that did not. Since my crushed T7 vertebra was removed, there was a point where my spinal cord was exposed. Vertebrae and discs usually surround it for protection.

The spinal cord is the trunk of the central nervous system. It, along with the brain, controls most functions of the body and mind. If my spinal cord was injured during the surgery or a nerve was nicked or cut, I could have been paralyzed or worse.

Also, Dr. Chen had reminded me of other risks when he came to see me in the pre-op area. Based on this information, I concluded that Dr. Chen's response to my question about how well the surgery went was not dry humor. It was God's honest truth.

For most of my life, I have heard older church members give testimonies that start with, "I woke up this morning in my right mind, with the mobility of my limbs." For the first time in my life, I truly understood what their testimony was all about.

To God be the glory!

After a while, a nurse came in to check on me. She said my vital signs were good, and everything else was looking good. She encouraged me to think about trying to get up out of the bed when I felt I could do so. She instructed me to be sure to call the Nurses' Station and wait for someone to help me before attempting to do so. She said it was an essential part of my recovery.

She said it was also vital that I begin physical therapy as soon as possible. That meant getting up and walking around. I knew exactly what I had to do based on my experience at CTCA and my experience after the Stem Cell Transplant. I decided to rest the remainder of the day and give it a try the next day.

City of Hope
May 19, 2016

THIS MORNING I SET THE GOAL TO START WALKING SOMETIME TODAY IF ABLE. When the nurse came in to check on me, I let her know that I wanted to get up and walk. She said she would let Physical Therapy know, and they would send someone over to assist. I had a light breakfast and waited for the physical therapist.

When the physical therapist arrived, the nurse came in to help me stand. I raised the head of the bed, so my torso was mainly upright. From there, I sat up. I swung my feet over so I was sitting on the bed with my feet dangling over the floor.

She put anti-skid socks on my feet as part of the safety protocol. With the help of the nurse and physical therapist, I slowly slid off the bed and lowered my feet to the floor. I felt fine on my feet. I was not dizzy or wobbly.

The nurse made sure all of my drainage tubes and IV lines were secure and unplugged the connector to the monitoring equipment. She also unplugged the power cord to the IV pumps. I was detached from all restraints that were in place while in bed.

I hung on to the IV/Infusion Pump stand to assist with my balance. I walked slowly out of the room with the physical therapist by my side.

"How do you feel?" the physical therapist asked.

"Pretty good," I replied. That was the truth. I did not feel any pain in my back. I was still receiving pain medication intravenously, so all was well.

"Great. Let's try to walk around the nursing station."

"Okay," I said. It was familiar territory for me. I knew that I had to take my time and walk as far as possible without overdoing it. I knew this was the only way I was going to help minimize my recovery time. My father's words again came to me. "Do the best you can with what you've got."

I am not sure how many laps I did around the nurse's station, but Vanessa arrived while I was walking. She was very excited to see me up and about.

"He's doing great!" the physical therapist told her.

"I see!" Vanessa said.

"I'll be in the room after I finish this lap," I told Vanessa.

She went into my room and waited for my return.

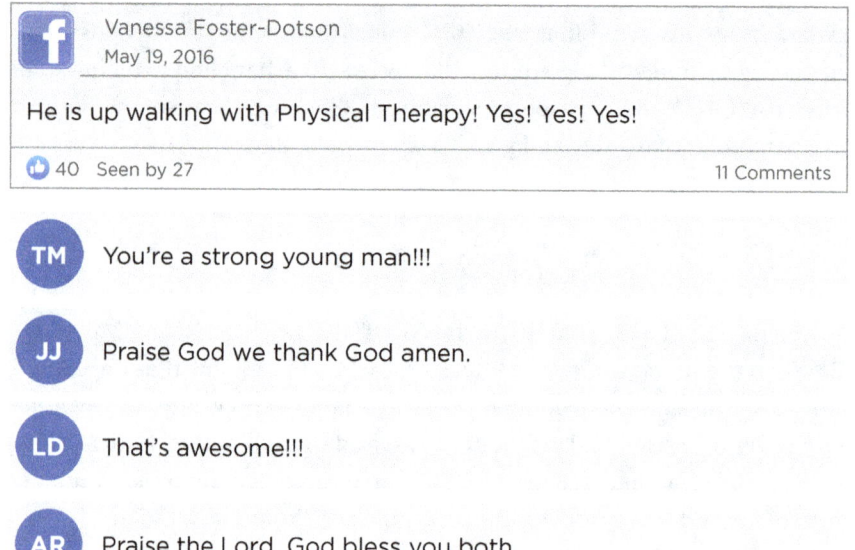

When I finished the lap, I came back into the room and got back into bed with the help of the nurse and the physical therapist. I did not over-extend myself. I could have gone around at least one if not two more times, but I did not want to push it.

"This is an excellent sign," said the nurse. "To get up and walk around the day after back surgery is not the norm."

"I felt I could do it, so I gave it a try."

"You did a good job," the physical therapist said.

"I want to try again later today," I said. "Sometime before I go to sleep for the night."

"Okay, you just let us know at the nursing station so we can get you disconnected," the nurse said.

"Will do," I said.

I did get out later and did a few more laps around the nurses' station unassisted (no help from a physical therapist). It was a good day.

Vanessa Foster-Dotson
May 20, 2016

*** Update for Sunday, 05/08/16 - Thursday, 05/19/16, 84 Days Post Stem Cell Transplant (SCT) ***

The power of prayer! Once again, the power of prayer has proven itself, and God has provided his blessings. Since my last official update, Henry successfully completed his six-hour back surgery on Wednesday, 05/18 and is in the process of recovering. All seems to be going well.

Due to the length of the surgery, he received a very strong dose of anesthesia. After the surgery, he was immediately placed in ICU to ensure that he recovered properly. So, when I first saw him yesterday, he was still a bit groggy and went in and out of sleep. I watched to make sure that he was breathing okay. However, today Henry is coherent and talkative! My baby is recovering well!

Luckily, Henry had been treated to a very good late lunch/dinner on Tuesday by a dear friend because he only drank water after his surgery on Wednesday. But today, his counts are good, even his kidney health indicator, so he has been cleared to have a regular diet.

In addition to getting through a successful surgery, Henry has also been blessed with experiencing very little pain, partially due to the pain meds that he is receiving. He has said several times that the process so far has been better than he imagined.

The ICU nurses said he is ready to be transferred to a regular room because he is currently their most stable patient. So today, we are waiting to see his surgeon, hopefully, get transferred to a regular room and receive physical therapy; yes, already.

Truly the power of prayer! We are so thankful!

👍 31   Seen by 39   22 Comments

 Hallelujah!! I knew God did it!! Our prayers will continue for a speedy recovery. God bless you, Nessa. God will not forget your labor of love.

 I am crying now in gratitude to God for his grace and mercy.

 Oh, what wonderful news!!

JR Glory to God. We serve the living Word that is the same yesterday, today, and forever. "He knows the plans that He has for you, Henry and Vanessa, plans of good, not evil."

JW God surely had His hands in this!!!! Remarkable indeed. So glad Henry is recovering well. Both of you are in my prayers. You already know that—Johnette on Randy's Facebook.

JB The favor of God cannot be bought with any amount of money, but with the fervent effectual prayers of the righteous, in agreement exercising our collective authority, much favor and blessing is what flows from heaven. We serve a mighty God!

KI God is good all the time. All the time, God is good.

Q: How did you feel when you learned I had a highly successful vertebra replacement surgery?

BART: When I learned that the surgery was successful, I was, again, overjoyed.

TALIA: I was very grateful and relieved. I brought you some medicine so that you would not be in pain during the recovery; you were in very good spirits, so it made me feel better about the entire thing.

CRIS: I felt very thankful.

PAT: Being the trooper that you are, you came through with flying colors and were back on your feet so quickly that I knew that it was nothing but God!

The Bionic Man

City of Hope, Duarte, CA
May 20, 2016

I WILL BE DISCHARGED FROM CITY OF HOPE TOMORROW, AND I DO NOT HAVE TO GO TO ANY REHABILITATION FACILITIES. Dr. Chen came to visit me today and said my recovery from surgery has been "remarkable." He said the purpose of rehab is to get the patient up and walking. Since I am already doing that, he said there is no need for it.

The only other criteria for being discharged from the hospital is that a patient can poop and pee. Every day I was asked by the nurses, "Did you have a bowel movement today?" I sometimes felt like a toddler going through potty training.

But it was explained to me that it is crucial to know that my digestive system is functioning before being discharged. The anesthesia not only puts the patient to sleep it also arrests the digestive system. I know of cases where patients were discharged too soon, and the results were catastrophic. So, I didn't mind being treated like a toddler.

I count my rapid recovery as another miracle. I said a silent prayer of thanksgiving for not having to go through two weeks of rehab in another facility.

Although Dr. Chen said I would be discharged tomorrow, I have learned it is better to wait until I am in the parking lot before I believe it. We will see what tomorrow brings.

In the meantime, I did a few more laps before calling it a day.

Here Comes the Bride

"Many congratulations on your wedding. It was a great pleasure to witness this special day of your lives." — Unknown

---

City of Hope, Duarte, CA
May 21, 2016

TO MY SURPRISE, I WAS ACTUALLY DISCHARGED TODAY AT 10:30 A.M. As we headed home, I remembered that my niece Stefany was getting married that afternoon in Santa Barbara, CA. We told her earlier that we would not be attending because I would be in a rehab facility.

Santa Barbara is approximately 100 miles away from Pasadena. I did some quick calculations in my mind and realized we could make the wedding if we left before 1 p.m., so I pitched the idea to Vanessa.

"Hey Vanessa, what do you think about us going to Stefany's wedding?"

"It's a long way to Santa Barbara. Do you feel up to it?"

I was feeling pretty good; no pain, just a little weak.

"Yes, I can make it. I will just recline the seat while you do the driving. We can see if Talia wants to go too."

"Okay, I will call her and see if she can meet us at the house."

Talia said she wanted to go, so when she arrived, we took off.

The trip was uneventful and relaxing. We arrived in Santa Barbara about 30 minutes before the wedding. It was to be held in the chapel at the Superior Court of California County of Santa Barbara. Vanessa parked the car across the street in the parking structure, and the three of us made our way to the chapel.

The three of us sat on the second row on the right, waiting for the ceremony to start. I was so happy to be there. Family celebrations are very special to me. I felt blessed to be among the witnesses to the occasion.

We all turned our focus to the front of the chapel as the music change signaled the start of the ceremony. The officiant came out, followed by the groom. When the groom saw me, he stared for a moment in disbelief. Then he smiled at me and waited for his bride.

When the Bridal Chorus began to play, we all stood up. I peered down the aisle to get a good look at my niece from afar. She was a beautiful bride, smiling and holding on to my brother's arm. As they made their way slowly up the aisle, she was smiling at everyone she made eye contact with.

When she saw me, her expression changed, and her knees buckled. My brother had to hold her up for a moment until she steadied herself.

It never occurred to me that my presence would cause such a reaction. I knew why Stefany appeared to stumble, but I am not sure if anyone did. I felt a twinge of angst because I was the reason for the brief disruption. I just wanted to be there for her. As she passed by the second row, I could see the tears in her eyes.

Vanessa and I were able to catch up with Stefany before the wedding party headed to the reception. I gave her a big hug, and she said,

"I didn't think you would be here!"

I said to her, "I told myself if there was any way possible for me to be at your wedding, I was going to be there."

We hugged again, and she went on to continue greeting other guests.

In preparation for this book, I asked Stefany to share her thoughts and feelings about that day and how she viewed my cancer journey. I am called by my middle name amongst family members, so Stefany refers to me as "Uncle Bernard." The following is what she shared.

Stefany

" I grew up feeling like the luckiest child in the world. I felt very grateful to have an exciting life where I got to be myself and have experiences that were not coming to many black girls I knew. I had a real childhood. The kind of childhood where you ride your bike outside until the sun goes down. Where you get to go camping and fishing and swimming and snorkeling, can you believe that? Snorkeling! I got to walk sand dunes and touch starfish and sea urchins. I even got stung by a sea urchin once. It wasn't the most pleasant experience, but I don't regret it.

Even as a child, I understood on some level that my life was different than most. Unlike most of my peers, I came from a two-parent household with parents who had been together years before I was a thought. I would hear my friends from school and church talk about how their dad or mom wasn't around. Or how their parents had never been married. Or how their parents never intended to have a kid together, and they may have been the result of a one-night stand or a "Situation-ship."

I would hear my friends complain about how their mom would lecture them on how they had to be the man of the house. My middle school girlfriends would be upset because they were the oldest sibling. I witnessed the guilty fits they had because they knew their mother or father expected them to keep house and play a role in helping to raise their brothers and sisters.

Some of my friends lived in group homes or with foster parents because their home life wasn't great. Don't get me wrong; there is no judgment in me mentioning these experiences. I distinctly remember feeling guilty, upset, and hurt for my friends that would have experiences like this.

And then there's me—an only child raised in a household with both of her parents. While I faced my own challenges that shouldn't be frowned upon either, I always remembered that I had friends who did not have some of the advantages that I had. I was grateful for these advantages. I never dismissed them or took them for granted.

When I was about five years old, I realized I had a bonus. I had a secret get out of jail free card. And that bonus was my Uncle Bernard! My dad's brother, my grandmother's son, my cousins' father. He was like an extra dad! He would pick me up and take me on adventures frequently. He would spend time with me and do silly things like color in a coloring book or play Monopoly even though it was the third time we were playing.

As I grew, he would continue to spend time with me and adapt his time spent to my age. He would encourage my curiosity. He would tell me that my opportunities were limitless. He would teach me secret magic tricks or life hacks, like being ambidextrous or the secret formula of **listening** for the purpose of applying what you hear to your life.

Growing up, I remember feeling comforted by the closeness of the relationship between my father and my uncle. We were always there for each other's major life events, including my uncle's marriage to my Aunt Vanessa.

Seeing the way that my Uncle Bernard loved my aunt and demonstrated that love, and everything that he did, changed my views on adults as a whole—watching his willingness to completely intertwine his life with someone else's and his commitment to the love that he proclaimed was astounding. Their love inspired me enough to think that I could also have the same thing for myself.

At 28 years old, I was going through a very rough time in my life. My self-esteem was demolished, my finances were in ruin, and I was very close to losing my s%?# with disciplining my children. I remember thinking, *Who would want me? A baby mama with two baby fathers. What a prize!*

But my Uncle Bernard supported me emotionally, financially, and as a mentor for my career. He really helped me make it through and not give in to the tribulations I was facing. Because my uncle was so supportive, he played a significant role in me improving my self-esteem and my self-worth.

The road wasn't easy, but once I felt better about myself, wouldn't you know it, I met a guy.

You've heard of love at first sight, right? Well, when I met this guy, I felt at home at first sight. We hit it off immediately and dated for a few years. He got along great with my children and was a great role model for them. He showed genuine interest in not only my life but also my children's lives. He taught them lifelong skills—- like how to read and how to tie their shoes. Every time I saw him interact with my children, my heart melted. Needless to say, I locked him down, and after dating for three years, he proposed.

While I was caught up being a love bird, I got the news my uncle had Multiple Myeloma. I was devastated!! My life flashed before my eyes, and I instantly wondered what I would do if he did not survive his diagnosis?

Once he was diagnosed, it seemed like treatment progressed pretty quickly. I remember talking to my aunt, and they were in Chicago at the cancer treatment center, taking the disease head-on with aggressive treatment. I remember being impressed at how quickly they rallied and made a plan of attack, and I admired and respected them even more than I had before.

I wanted to cry, scream, fight, yell; you name it. I didn't know what to do with my emotions. But I knew that the least I could do was be there to support my aunt and uncle in any way that I could. When they left the treatment center and came back to California, I offered to make meals that were safe for him to eat while he was going through his treatments. My soon-to-be-husband made it a point to be there for me and would accompany me on visits to see my uncle while he was sick.

At one of his worst moments, we all were concerned that he would not make it through the week. Uncle Bernard was weak and underweight. He barely had a voice, and even making him laugh was painful for him. Even he thought he wasn't going to make it at this point.

When I came to visit him, he made sure to give me his last words and what he wanted to leave with me if he left this earth. He told me to be strong. He told me to lean and depend on God because he is the gatekeeper of all of the answers to why we experience painful things like what he was going through. He told me to make sure that I am an example to everyone I encounter, and he told me to try my hardest to love everyone I interact with, no matter the relationship I had with them.

I left that hospital visit feeling very sure that I would never see my uncle alive again. It was too much to take. I was not ready to accept that, and I was upset beyond belief. Despite my grief, I loved seeing my uncle think of his circumstance as an opportunity to help others.

I mean, it's so like him.

Luckily as you know, that wasn't his last day on this earth. He fought for his life and made it through that extremely rough time.

My Wedding

When my fiancé and I decided to get married, we knew that our wedding would have to be small, so we were very selective with our guest list. There were certain people that we knew without a doubt would be invited to watch us celebrate our union. And, of course, Uncle Bernard was on that list. It was pretty important to me that my uncle was there to see me get married. I wanted to show him how far I had come since my first marriage and my ability to plan and pay for a wedding on my own. I wanted him to know that I recognized and appreciated what he did for me the first time around.

But as luck would have it, I found out a week before the wedding that Uncle Bernard might not be able to make it to my wedding. While he was sick, he damaged vital parts of his spine and lost at least 2 inches in height while he was fighting his disease. Let me tell you, for a man that started out at 5'9", he couldn't afford to lose more than two inches for the rest of his life. So understandably, he was looking forward to having his height restored through corrective surgery. He was waiting to receive a date for the surgery that would repair the damage his Multiple Myeloma had inflicted on his spine. If the surgery was successful, it would not only reduce the physical pain of losing his vertebra but restore him to the height he was before his illness and treatment.

Uncle Bernard and Aunt Vanessa called to tell me why they might not make it. I was super disappointed, but I knew this surgery was important to him, and he was looking forward to how it would benefit his life. So, although I was disappointed that he would not be able to come to my wedding, I was happy that he would be able to repair a portion of his body that would return him to something that resembled his lifestyle prior to Multiple Myeloma.

My wedding day was everything it could possibly be from the start. Every part of that day surpassed my expectations from the moment I woke up that morning. Even the time spent preparing for the wedding in my hotel suite was magical. It was everything that I could've imagined and more. I felt happier than I ever had. I had joy. I had peace. I was surrounded by everyone I loved, and the excitement of seeing my future husband was all-consuming.

Despite my happiness, I was still having lingering thoughts of my uncle. I was sad that he wouldn't be there to witness that day. I had more joy in my life than ever — and doggone it, I wanted him to see that! But that moment of sadness only lasted for a short while because I knew that he was missing my ceremony in order to do something that would make his life better.

When the moment came for me to walk down the aisle and meet my groom at the altar, I remember looking at the guests who came to our wedding three hours away from where we lived. I remember appreciating them making an effort to even come a few hours away from home just to celebrate our love. I clung to my father tightly as we walked towards my husband-to-be. I took in every person that I saw, making sure I made eye contact with them as I walked down the aisle.

Because our wedding was so small, we had no bridal party. So we asked our guests to wear all black so that they would coordinate with our wedding color scheme, and they would serve as the bridal party in addition to witnessing our union. As I'm walking down the aisle, I notice everyone in all black, and I'm looking into the faces of all of my loved ones as I approach my soon-to-be husband.

But out of the corner of my eye, I see something that immediately makes me Hella-irritated. I noticed that one of the guests at my wedding was wearing a navy blue and lime green tracksuit!! My lip curled up, and I gave a stank face in my head. How dare somebody come to my wedding not only out of the color scheme but in the most casual outfit possible? On top of that, this distract-suit-wearing tyrant was seated close to the front of the altar! He was sitting on the second row near the center aisle! I was instantly flamed, thinking of how this tacky person was going to ruin my wedding photos by being completely irreverent of the dress code. I mean the audacity!

I wasn't gonna let this ruin my experience, but I made a mental note to check whoever was wearing this outfit at the reception. I'll be d@%*ed if you think you can come up to my wedding wearing whatever you feel like! All I knew was somebody was overdue for being put in their place. And then I thought, *Did one of my family members bring a tacky guest?* I wouldn't be surprised. But you picked the wrong day to bring one of your weirdo friends to my event!

As I walked toward my future husband, still clinging to my father's arm, I looked into the eyes of each guest, and it wasn't just a glance. I wanted them to know that I really saw them and appreciated them being there. As I got closer to the tracksuit guy, I started to realize that I recognized him even from behind. And with almost perfect timing, the tracksuit guy turned his head to look at me walk down the aisle.

At that moment I realized it was my Uncle Bernard!

At that moment, I completely lost it. I was instantly filled with a host of emotions that I couldn't hold back if I wanted to. I'm not a big crier, especially in front of other people. But this was one of those moments where most everyone else faded from existence in the room. I literally could only see my Uncle Bernard, my Aunt Vanessa, my cousin Talia, and my soon-to-be husband. I had prepared myself to enjoy my wedding day without my uncle. But what I didn't prepare myself for was the slim chance that he would surprise me and actually show up!

When I locked eyes with Uncle Bernard, my knees started to buckle, and the tears flowed uncontrollably. My dad had to hold me up to make sure that I did not ruin all the effort I put into making my day special. I really wanted to stop walking down the aisle and run over and hug him and thank him for making the effort to do something that I knew was very hard and painful for him to do. It was yet just another example of the amount of love that he has for me. Locking eyes with Uncle Bernard made me know more than ever that I am loved and supported no matter what I choose to do.

While Uncle Bernard had shown over and over throughout my life how supporting and loving he could be, that one moment spoke volumes. It reminded me why I am who I am: A strong black woman who is also compassionate, hard-working, loving, and encouraging to her own children because of the example that I've seen from my uncle.

Seeing how strong he was, despite having just checked out of the hospital that same day after having spinal surgery a few days before, because his being at my wedding was important to him, meant the world to me. It also taught me that love knows no boundaries and will enable a person to do anything to reach someone when they really care. **"**

Vanessa, Talia, and I were able to stay and attend the reception. I was surprised that I wasn't feeling much pain or discomfort. I started getting tired after the cake-cutting ceremony. Once we ate some cake, we left shortly after the dancing had begun. We still had a two-hour trip ahead of us.

On the way back home, I reclined in my seat and thought about the events of the day. I started the day in the hospital and ended the day at a wedding reception 100 miles away. I thanked God that I was able to see my niece get married. I thanked Him again for performing another miracle on my cancer journey.

Sometime around midnight, I discovered why I had not felt any pain during the day. I did not realize that I was receiving pain medication intravenously continuously while I was in the hospital.

Sometime around midnight, the pain medication wore off. I felt a dull, throbbing pain along my back. It was not intense but strong enough to wake me from my sleep. When I figured out what was going on, I thanked God that the medication had not worn off earlier and prevented me from attending the wedding.

I was at a point where I was able to count it as a joy when I encountered this particular trial. The scriptures say,

> *My brethren, count it all joy when you fall into various trials, knowing that the testing of your faith produces patience.*
> — James 1:2-3, New King James Version

Q: How did you feel about me being able to attend Stefany's wedding?

IRA: Your attendance at Stefany's wedding was an awesome surprise. I was blessed by your attendance. If I wanted any person in my family to be present for her wedding, it was you. You have a special place in Stefany's heart. She was honored by your presence.

Q: What were you feeling when you saw me at Stefany's wedding?

CRIS: I was pleasantly surprised, and when Stefany saw you, I broke out in happy tears at her reaction.

Q: Did my cancer journey affect your perspective on my attending Stefany's wedding?

TALIA: Yes, at first, it was determined you would not attend. I was so happy for her to have you there. I am proud that it was within your capacity to do, AND you did it.

Q: Did you have any thoughts about me going to my niece's wedding in Santa Barbara after surgery?

NORMAN: Yes, I know I did, although they are pretty fuzzy at this point. If you were to ask me for what else I thought besides kind of nuts, I could not tell you today.

RUTH: Yes. I thought it might be too soon for this weekend trip/event and that you might be pushing yourself too fast. On the other hand, it was a way for you to see family and be part of a family celebration!

From Zion to a City of Hope: A Journey of Faith

May 22, 2016

TODAY I WOKE UP A LITTLE SORE FROM THE SURGERY BUT HAPPY TO BE HOME. Being home is my personal confirmation that the major milestones of this journey have been reached—no more life-saving procedures, no more high-risk procedures.

What comes next is the clinical trial. That will start this week. I am optimistic about what is yet to come.

 Vanessa Foster-Dotson
May 22, 2016

*** Update for Friday, 05/20/16 - Sunday, 05/22/16 ***

It is well! Henry has been progressing positively. He was transferred to a regular post-op room at City of Hope on Friday, 05/20/16, and has been increasing his movement ever since. Yesterday he was able to do one lap around the entire west and east wing, approximately 1/8th of a mile.

Since being moved, Henry has experienced problems with digestion as well as a low-grade fever. Both of these are considered "normal" after receiving the type of surgery that Henry received. The staff is still monitoring him, and yesterday his fever even broke for most of the day.

Overall, the doctors and nurses continue to say that Henry is progressing VERY well. As a result, the current plan is to transfer him to acute rehab at a different facility one or two days early. Yes! At this point, visitors are definitely welcome and desired at either location. I will send an update when I know the details regarding the acute rehab move.

Meanwhile, please keep my dear friend Rosalind in prayer. On the same day that Henry was undergoing surgery, she was told that her Ovarian cancer had returned She and her husband George are also preparing to send their triplets...our godchildren...off to college in the fall. Definitely a crazy time. However, they are all children of God, and ALL WILL BE WELL!!!

Please also pray for my sister-friend, Johnette's godmother, who is experiencing very serious medical challenges.

Thank you once again, and God Bless! Your prayers are helping to keep us strong and continue to renew my faith as I watch the blessings flow. We greatly appreciate each one of you and ask that you pray for everyone who is reading this update.

👍 39   Seen by 38   22 Comments

WL: We agree that the same GOD through JESUS CHRIST is the SAME YESTERDAY, TODAY, and FOREVER. May God CONTINUE to TOUCH your Family and Friends.

JW: We know that our God is a Healing God and his Grace and Mercy teach us all every day. Thank you, my sister-friend, for your prayers for me during my godmother's illness. You are always thinking of others when you are going through your own journey with Henry—keeping your friend Rosalind in prayer. I really don't know how people get through storms in life without knowing God and what He can and has done already. Love you.

KI: My prayers go out to both of you. Henry, you're a fighter and in God's hands! Love you!

ML: Henry and Vanessa, just wanted to share with you – we've had nine days of prayer at my church which is a novena in the Catholic tradition. Everyone is invited to come together for collective prayer for one hour. This is in addition to the many prayer groups and ministries we have.

The theme was praying for the undoing of "knots" in our lives – illness, financial burdens, relationships, stresses, etc. I asked our group to pray last Tuesday before your surgery on Wednesday morning and for the family's continued strength.

I was overjoyed and thankful to receive your updates on how well the surgery went and that you were up the next day! Thank you, Lord, for hearing our prayers! I will ask tonight for the family members and friends mentioned!

Vanessa Foster-Dotson
May 25, 2016

**** Update for Monday, 05/23/16 - Wednesday, 05/25/16 ***

A true blessing from God!!! This will be a quick note because I need to get back to work. I just want to let everyone know that Henry is back HOME! Not only was he released two days earlier than expected, but the surgeon also said that Henry was doing so well that he could go straight home instead of going to acute rehab for two weeks as per the original plan.

Henry still has back pain and digestion challenges, but overall, he is doing well, the best recovery that the surgeon has ever experienced! More to come later...

THE POWER OF PRAYER!!!

👍 44   Seen by 57   24 Comments

JH — I am actually not surprised. Henry's attitude going in was so positive when I talked with him last week, and his faith and will have brought him to a quicker recovery. Go, Henry!!!

DM — Look at God. I have come to know that God is truly able. I continue to pray healing for Henry and strength for you both.

WL — Amen to the GREAT I AM, THAT I AM. May God continue to give both of you strength and health as you continue to give him PRAISE for ALL that he has done for and through you.

JB — Nothing less than expected! This is God's 'M.O.'! A SHORT RECOVERY, AND A MAGNIFICENT PROGNOSIS, in indeed the prayer I prayed. Nothing less than his best!

LL — God is soooooo awesome!!!

DR — Praise God for providing and delivering once again. For coming through in GOD STYLE!

That's our God, and He is faithful!!!

BM — Amen! Thank you, Jesus!

Going On Trial

"Consider it all joy, my brethren, when you encounter various trials, knowing that the testing of your faith produces endurance. And let endurance have its perfect result, so that you may be perfect and complete, lacking in nothing."
— James 1:2-4, New American Standard

New Meds For An Old Foe
Pasadena, CA
May 26, 2016

IT IS TIME FOR ME TO RESUME MY CHEMOTHERAPY NOW THAT I HAVE RECOVERED FROM BACK SURGERY. I have not had any chemotherapy since November of last year. I stopped to prepare to collect stem cells. I stayed off of chemotherapy in preparation for back surgery. Dr. Chen wanted to be sure I was as healthy as possible before surgery and minimize the time needed for recovery.

My oncologist told me that I would not resume the chemotherapy I had before surgery. Before the surgery, we had discussed the possibility that I could be eligible to participate in a new clinical trial.

Well, he told me today I was approved to be part of that clinical trial, which meant switching to a drug called "Ixazomib."

I did not try to pronounce it; I just remembered its commercial name, "Ninlaro."

Ninlaro will replace the Velcade I was receiving once a week intravenously. Ninlaro is essentially Velcade in pill form. It will be less invasive to my daily routine because I will not have to go to City of Hope once a week to receive treatment. My new treatment plan will consist of Ninlaro, Revlimid, and Dexamethasone, all in pill form that I can take at home.

This is a significant change in the positive direction. It means when I feel up to it, I can resume working without having to schedule so many hospital appointments. My work requires me to travel domestically during the week when on assignment and twice a year internationally when doing standards development work.

I look forward to returning to work because I will remove some of Vanessa's stress. After all, she is taking care of everything.

At this point, I took the time to thank God for making a way for me to return to work. I knew my actual return to work date was unknown and quite a while in the future, but knowing that I can receive my medication without going to the hospital gave me great hope and inspiration to work harder to reach that day as soon as possible.

God always makes a way. That does not mean He only makes one way. It does not mean all other ways close before He provides another way. Sometimes He provides us more than one way.

In this instance, I had choices. I did not have to agree to participate in the clinical trial, but it was better from a logistical perspective. The only unknown was what the side effects of the Ninlaro would be. I was willing to face that unknown because I believed that God had provided this other way.

I stepped out on faith to try new meds for an old foe.

> *"So, my old foe, we meet on the battlefield once again."*
> — Jabberwocky, *Alice in Wonderland,* Lewis Carroll

Putting In The Work

"The only place where success comes before work is in the dictionary."
— Vidal Sassoon

Select Physical Therapy, Pasadena, CA
June 16, 2016

IN ADDITION TO CHEMOTHERAPY MEDICATION, I NEED TO DO A LOT OF REHABILITATION WORK. It has been a couple of weeks since the staples were removed from my back, so my neurologist has given his approval for me to start physical therapy. Rehabilitation will help keep me from getting keloid scars along the nine-inch incision line on my spine. I also need to develop overall muscle tone.

"Movement can replace many drugs, but no drug can ever replace movement."
— Avicenna

I have chosen to return to Select Physical Therapy, which helped me when I returned from Zion. I developed a good rapport with my physical therapist Edgar, and I want to pick up where we left off.

Returning to Select Physical Therapy felt good because I was returning to something familiar. The same location on Lake Street. The same front-office staff. My same physical therapist and many other familiar physical therapists. The same initial assessment to determine my starting condition.

There were, however, some changes. In the six months since I had my last session, a few people were no longer there. There were some new team members. There were some new clients. They had also started using a new scheduling system that allowed clients to make appointments online—just enough of a change to notice but not enough to feel unfamiliar.

Edgar was glad to see me. He asked why I was back and what I was looking to do.

"I'm here because I need to rehab from back surgery."

"Okay, what type of back surgery did you have?"

"They replaced my T7 vertebra. I now have a titanium T7 vertebra."

"Really! No way! I've never had a client that has had that type of surgery. Take off your shirt so I can have a look."

I removed my shirt and lay down on the treatment table.

"Oh wow, you had a really long incision! But they did a good job closing it up. I see very little scarring."

"Yes, I had 36 staples in my back to hold it all together. My crushed T7 vertebra resulted in me being three inches shorter."

"No kidding? That much loss of height? That's amazing."

"Well, we will massage your back when you come in to reduce the chances of you developing keloids."

"Hey, do you mind if some of the interns come over and take a look at your back? I'm sure none of them have seen anything like this before."

"Sure, no problem," I said.

Select Physical Therapy is big on preparing the next generation of physical therapists. Edgar is an alumna of USC, so there are a lot of USC students who work there as interns. There were always at least three or four interns working whenever I came in for my appointments.

Edgar called over the interns to have a look. It felt a little odd being the center of attraction due to the novelty of my prosthetic. On the other hand, I felt like I was a small part of something that would positively impact the next generation of physical therapists. They all had good bedside manners and showed respect during my objectification, so I was okay with their examination.

Once the assessment was complete, Edgar and I discussed what my physical therapy would consist of.

"We need to first work on strengthening the muscles that provide your stability," he began. "The muscles in your body perform two basic functions; stability and mobility. Stability has to do with your balance and posture. Since you've spent a lot of time off your feet in bed, the muscles that provide stability are weak due to lack of use."

"Okay," I replied, to show I was following what he was saying.

"I will set up some simple exercises to work on your stability. Some you will do lying down; some you will do standing up. There are no weights involved, just elastic bands with different tensions."

"Next, we want to work on your stamina. You need to do aerobic exercises to get your heart rate up for at least 15 minutes. You don't want to get it up too high, so I will tell you how hard you should push yourself, and I will monitor you to make sure you know how to exercise safely."

"My oncologist said I could only do zero-impact exercises because of the Multiple Myeloma. Multiple myeloma takes calcium out of the bones, so they are more prone to lesions (small stress fractures)."

"Yes, so you will use the stationary bikes and elliptical machines for your aerobic exercises. No running, treadmill work, jumping jacks, or jump rope."

"Uh-huh," I said halfheartedly.

The only thing I will truly miss is jumping rope. That was my aerobic exercise of choice. It was part of my exercise routine before diagnosis. I would jump rope every other day for 20 minutes to warm up on weight training days and for an entire hour on aerobic days.

My mind drifted off to when the kids were in elementary school, and I was a volunteer parent. I would sometimes help with yard duty at lunchtime and jump rope. Bart and Talia would bring their friends over and say, "I bet my dad can jump rope better than you!" I would get a jump rope and jump fast or do crisscross jumps, jump rope while jogging, and all sorts of combination jumps. It was a great way to stay in shape.

"Next, we will do some strength work."

My mind snapped back to the present at the sound of Edgar's voice.

"We will start with bands and light weights. Gradually, we will work up to the heavier weights."

"My oncologist also said I should not lift more than 15 pounds over my head. It might cause too much compression on my spine and damage more vertebrae."

"That's good to know. I will set up a program that does not include any exercises that will cause additional compression along your spine. No weights directly over your head. Also, you will do exercises that will "take your back out of the equation." That means exercises in the prone (face down) or supine (face up) position."

"That sounds good to me."

When I was in high school, I did a fair amount of weight training in preparation for each gymnastics season. Our coach was also the line coach for our football team, so we did circuit training to get into shape during the gymnastics off-season. We had our own kind of "Hell Week" where we were run through the circuit many times in each training session.

"Lastly, we will work on your flexibility. You will do stretching exercises to start and end your workout and some throughout your workout. Staying limber will not only keep you from hurting yourself while you are working out, but it will also help you stay safe just going about your everyday activity."

"That's great," I said. I always liked to stretch. It felt good, and it was essential to have good flexibility while doing gymnastics. Some of the strength moves are not difficult if you are flexible.

So, I had my work cut out for me. I knew what Edgar had in mind for my rehabilitation. But there was one question that I really wanted him to answer.

"You've seen the kind of shape I'm in, and you know what my limitations are in terms of the types of exercises I can do safely," I began.

"In all honesty, what chance do I have of returning to the fitness level I had before

Multiple Myeloma, and what is a realistic amount of time it would take to get there?"

Edgar did not hesitate in his response.

"I think there is a very good chance that you can get 90 percent of your fitness level back, maybe even a little more. Our goal is to first get you back into a regular gym so you can resume a regular exercise program, not a rehabilitation program."

"If you work hard and are consistent, you could reach your goal in three to four months. Since you were involved in sports, you understand what it takes mentally to accomplish your fitness goals."

> *"Your body can stand almost anything. It's your mind you have to convince."* — Unknown

"The main thing is not to push it too hard. You have to listen to your body. After your workout, you should be sore. But you want to feel that good kind of soreness. The soreness that tells you that you did your best, that you did not slack off. Not the soreness that causes so much pain that it keeps you from working out the next day. That's when you've gone too far."

"Thanks for giving me a straight answer. I want to know what is a reasonable expectation, based on expert opinion, and not my own."

"You're welcome. We'll get started when you come back for your next appointment."

I was glad to hear that my restoration to fitness was not deemed impossible or improbable in the natural realm. It let me know there was quite a bit I could do to help make it a reality. But my biblical worldview informs me that I can do all things through Christ who strengthens me. So, I have faith that my restoration will happen either naturally or supernaturally.

Either way, my healing and restoration will be a blessing from God.

Staying On Track

"Not that I have already obtained all this, or have already been made perfect, but I press on to take hold of that for which Christ Jesus took hold of me." — Philippians 3:12, Berean Study Bible

---

Select Physical Therapy, Pasadena, CA

WORKING HARD TO ACHIEVE A GOAL IS SOMETHING I LEARNED FROM MY FATHER. I remember him putting in a tremendous amount of time and effort as the president of the Southwest branch of the NAACP in the mid to late sixties. He was one of the foot soldiers in the civil rights movement in Los Angeles.

Even when he did not hold the office of president, he spent a lot of time working for the cause. I remember him calling my brother, sister, and me into the dining room to help him stuff envelopes for some underway campaign. I don't know if it was internal or public politics, but I remember it was a Get-Out-The-Vote campaign.

I developed this approach to facing challenges through my participation in competitive sports in high school. I was on the gymnastics team all three years of high school and was one of the team captains in my senior year. I learned how to compete in a team sport based on its members performing as individuals, similar to diving, track, and field.

It is from this perspective I embraced my challenge. The biggest obstacles that I had to face were going at it, either too hard or not giving it my total effort: one extreme or the other.

There were a lot of clients at Select Physical Therapy that were athletes rehabbing from sports-related injuries. They were eager to return to competition and worked hard to get back into shape as soon as possible. That type of environment, coupled with my work ethic and goal-driven personality, gave Edgar reasons to caution me more than once.

"I know that you are driven and like to push yourself. You're like a beast sometimes when you really get into it. Whenever I give you a set of exercises to do, you always do at least one more repetition or add just a little more time or weight to it. I want you to discipline yourself to only do three sets of each exercise and ten repetitions in each set."

It was not that I was doing anything fast. I was just overly persistent; you might even say a little relentless.

"Okay, Edgar, I will back off a little bit."

On the other extreme, there were days when I did not feel up to going to work out. I didn't know if it was because I overdid it at the last workout session or because of my last chemotherapy infusion or some negative thought trying to influence my behavior.

I can probably count on one hand the number of times I did not go work out. What got me out despite what was going on was in my mind or body was a quote I remembered:

> *"You can never expect to succeed if you only put in work on the days you feel like it."* — Unknown

On those days, I would drag myself up out of bed (my appointments would set for 6, 6:30, or 7 in the morning) and make my way to the gym. When I arrived, I would slowly get into it. On those days, Edgar would not admonish me to be more disciplined.

Even on those days, I felt better after the workout was over. It was a combination of things, but I think it mainly was a sense of accomplishment because I was able to push past the temptation to not go.

I also felt like I had used my mustard seed faith to do it.

> *"Movement is a medicine for creating change in a person's physical, emotional and mental state."* — Carol Welch

> *"My steps have held to your paths; my feet have not stumbled."* — Psalm 17:5, New International Version Bible

A CITY OF HOPE

Happy Anniversary!

"We are not the same persons this year as last; nor are those we love. It is a happy chance if we, changing, continue to love a changed person."
— W. Somerset Maugham

Pasadena, CA
July 16, 2016

ONE YEAR AGO TODAY, I WAS DIAGNOSED WITH MULTIPLE MYELOMA AT CANCER TREATMENT CENTERS OF AMERICA CHICAGO. This past year has had so many highs and lows that it will take me longer than usual to complete the reflection I customarily do on occasions such as this.

What I can say right now is I know I am a better person today because of this journey, and I believe I will be an even better person when this journey ends than I am today.

More to come!

Pasadena, CA
August 1, 2016

 Vanessa Foster-Dotson
August 1, 2016

**** Update for Thursday, 05/26/16 - Monday, 08/01/16 ***

Happy Anniversary! It was a year ago last month that Henry was diagnosed with Multiple Myeloma (MM). On July 8th, 2015, his primary-care doctor said that she thought that Henry had MM. On July 16th, his condition was confirmed, and he began fighting for his life.

His journey started with an unexpected trip to the Cancer Treatment Centers of America in Chicago. The images of trying to get Henry on the plane, in the car, to the bathroom, in the bed, etc., are still quite fresh in my mind. He was SO sick. And it all happened so quickly.

After 90% of Henry's blood being cancerous, over 30 days in Chicago, subsequent hospital stays once we returned to Pasadena, chemo, three attempts at stem cell harvesting, a Stem Cell Transplant and then back surgery, it has been amazing to watch how Henry has fought,

continued

and how God has shown up. Henry has always been very positive and inspiring. I am convinced that his positive attitude played a significant role in his recovery.

But your prayers and God's response sealed the deal. As we have begun to get out of the house more, we have learned that people were praying that we were not even aware of. How awesome is that! We are so blessed!

Unfortunately, there is still no human cure for MM today. However, it is treatable. The current plan is that Henry will be taking some form of chemo for the rest of his life.

Henry is on his second four-week round of chemo since his back surgery. The only side-effects that he has experienced are occasional hiccups, and he still has a bit of neuropathy. Other than that, he has not lost any hair, he has regained his weight, and his lab results are all good. He has lost an inch or so in height. He has titanium in his back now and has to rest sometimes but in general...MY HENRY IS BACK!!!

As I look back over the year, I have really learned to appreciate life. I am still task-oriented and focused on forging ahead. But I have found that I stop more frequently to just realize that God didn't have to do it, but He did! And that we need to STOP and LISTEN to people, especially our loved ones. And that I really need to call people more often (I'm still working on this.). And that although I still get upset with Henry at times, I am so fortunate that he is here. So, sometimes I just need to get over it...sometimes (smile).

Yes, it has been a crazy year. I am not exactly sure as yet why we had to take this journey, and I know that we are still marching down the path called life. Thank you so much for being with us. Thank you for your prayers, support, EVERYTHING!

And as I close, please pray for Henry's continued recovery. Please also pray for complete healing for my mother, Annie Foster, as well as Rosalind, Uncle Alfred, Aunt Jettie, Aunt Karen, Sharon, Johnette, and family and others.

Please say a special prayer for everyone reading this update. Please also pray for this nation and the world. We are in unbelievable times.

Lastly, please be sure to vote and encourage everyone that you know to vote and encourage them to encourage others. I am not a political fanatic, but I feel that EVERYONE's vote this year is critical!

God Bless and much love! Happy Anniversary indeed!

👍 40   Seen by 47   30 Comments

LW — Vanessa, I'm so glad you are my childhood friend's lifemate. It is wonderful to see how God showed up and showed out in Bernard's recovery. But it has also been soul-stirring seeing you be by his side in the midst of grueling and challenging times. Each day I say a little prayer for you to continue to be strong in your faith in God and strong in your commitment to each other. Hugs and love to you both.

CP — Vanessa, it has been extremely a time of test and trials, and yet God has manifested himself to you both. I praise God for the faith walk you continue to take with Henry knowing it was the powerful corporate prayers of the righteous that availeth much. We love you both to life and continue to lift you up. Stay strong and encouraged. God has you.

LD — Continued prayers for Henry and the names you listed. May God continue to bless you.

PJ — Thank you for reminding me just how great God has been in our lives! I thank God for you, Vanessa! You were there when a lot of women would have left. My brother would not have made it without your love, care, concern. I love you, Nessa! I don't know what it's like to have a natural sister, but in my book, you're my sister – naturally!!

SB — Life is not the same anymore. You have been updated, you have the path of God simulated, and He is yet to change the course. Yet you continue to listen and obey His directions! Hallelujah!!!!

PH — Hallelujah! I thank God for bringing you both through! You're examples of trusting Him and using wisdom despite the incredible and painful circumstances. The just live by faith because, without it, it's impossible to please God. I'm inspired by you both and blessed to be your friends and neighbors. My prayers for complete healing continue.

And I will be voting!

LD — So glad he is doing well. God will certainly use your journey to encourage others facing similar situations. Thanks for sharing so we can continue to pray. God bless you!

When the challenges of LIFE come to our DOOR, we must realize that we HAVE THE VICTORY. Fight, fight and fight some more. You have given the devil two black eyes, a busted lip, and a swollen lip.

He forgot that when you called on your savior, he did not leave or forsake you. He forgot that the keys that JESUS took from him give us healing, deliverance, and restoration. He forgot that the same POWER (TNT, DYNAMITE, H-BOMB) THAT RAISED CHRIST FROM THE DEAD, QUICKENS (MAKES ALIVE, WHOLE) OUR MORTAL BODY.

 Continued blessings to my brother and sister in Christ! You both are blessed and fearless warriors. To God be the Glory!

One Year Into The Journey

Pasadena, CA
August 20, 2016

JULY 16TH WAS THE ONE-YEAR ANNIVERSARY OF MY MULTIPLE MYELOMA DIAGNOSIS AT CTCA. I took some time to reflect on what had transpired that year. Usually, I complete my reflections the same day. This time, I was unable to do so. There simply was too much to process.

While I was working through my reflections of this anniversary, another anniversary came and went. August 17th was the one-year anniversary of my return to California from CTCA. That anniversary triggered even more reflection.

At that point, I realized I had to bring this reflective period to a close. I was teetering on a fine line between reflection and living in the past. I gave myself a deadline to stop reflecting and start writing. It has taken me until now to be able to put my hands on the keyboard to capture my thoughts. I shared some of these thoughts with my Facebook friends.

 Henry B. Dotson III
August 20, 2016

Greetings all,

I am one year into my cancer journey, and I want to take the time to share with you some of my thoughts.

Giving Thanks

First, all glory and honor go to God for His goodness and His mercies that He bestows on me every day. I am nothing without His son Jesus Christ.

I am thankfu l for all of you who have supported me and continue to do so through the good and the bad.

I am thankful for my family, both immediate and extended. They encourage me with just the sound of their voices, no matter what we talk about. The times we are able to spend together face to face are precious to me.

Finally, to the flesh of my flesh and bone of my bone, I thank Vanessa. I thank God for putting you into my life, and I look forward to whatever may come my way because I know you will be by my side.

continued

Reflections

I remember hearing a sermon many years ago where a guest pastor said,

> "While I don't know you all personally, I know where each of you are in your lives – You are either about to enter a storm, in a storm, or just getting through a storm." (Paraphrased).

Most of you know I am very intentional about maintaining a positive attitude, and I see the glass as half full instead of half empty. So, I find it interesting that my reflections of this past year are couched in this seemingly less than uplifting quote. Nonetheless, I have found my inspiration here, so I put my "glass half full" lenses on to express my reflections, with this quote in mind.

The quote caused me to focus my lenses and to realize that the pastor had left out another possible state of being – living in the relative calm that exists between storms. The place you find yourself after "just getting through a storm" and before "about to enter a storm." That is where I found myself earlier this year.

My first storm was surviving cancer in Zion and the life-threatening infections upon my return to California. My "just getting through a storm" was enduring the treatments I received to knock down the percentage of myeloma cells in my marrow. The "about to enter a storm" started when Vanessa and I were confronted with the decision of staying at City of Hope or returning to CTCA to receive the care I needed.

The calm between storms came when I was able to celebrate my last birthday. It lasted until I embraced the decision to stay at City of Hope. That decision ended my Middle Passage and prepared me for the second storm.

The second storm was the Stem Cell Transplant followed by vertebra replacement surgery. I was motivated to recover as quickly as possible from back surgery because I wanted to see my niece walk down the aisle at her wedding if at all possible.

During that period of calm, I realized there were still considerable challenges to be faced, but they were all for repair instead of simply for survival. As I reflect on this calm, I realize that much of my motivation to take on these challenges was based on my belief that God has more for me to do; that I am still here because I have not yet fulfilled my purpose. I also realize that part of my motivation comes from the love of my family.

My second "just getting through a storm" was my recovery from

continued

surgery. The calm after the storm came when I was able to attend my niece's wedding. Now I am part of a clinical trial and looking forward to getting into remission. I do not know how long this calm will last or when the next storm will come.

Conclusions

With times of trouble, times of calm, and times of celebration, we do not know how long they each will last. But my God says in His Word that: in everything, there is a season; trouble will not last long; be not afraid; all things work for good to those who love God and are called according to His purpose; count it all joy, and He will never leave you or forsake you. So, now I am in this season of a clinical trial. I look forward to seeing what God will do in my life. I look forward to being used and useful to the kingdom.

Grace and Peace to you all.

- Henry

 66   Seen by 75   21 Comments

MW Henry, so touching and inspiring. Certainly an example of that half-full Glass. God is truly demonstrating His magnificence through you, and may He continue to bless you always!

FK Thank you, Henry! It is good to be reminded of what is truly important in life. You continue to be a blessing to us in many ways.

RJ Thanks, Henry and Vanessa. From afar, we prayed, we believed, and we trusted God that you would be well in His time and season. We always checked in to see how well you were doing, looking for Vanessa's 'Good Report,' and knowing that you would be here today to share your reflections. We thank you for the inspiration you bring to our lives. Bless the both of you.

PJ You are an amazing brother. You've always inspired me with your love, your wisdom, and your laughter. Why God blessed me with a brother like you, I'll never know. I'm just glad He did!! Vanessa, my sister from another mister, your undying love and faithfulness to my brother astounds me. I'm so glad it's You! Love you both, forever!!

Lovely thoughts, Henry. And let me add that as much as I knew you back in the day, I would expect no less love in your life or blessings, as you were always one of the good guys. I wish you all the best and each day be joyful.

City of Hope has lived up to its name, motto, and credo. It is indeed a place of hope. The staff is concerned about the spiritual health of their patients. And yes, it is a place of medical miracles.

The battle is not over, but we have the upper hand. I have put my hope in God's word, and He has not disappointed me. I will be a living testimony of what He has done for me.

> *"You are my refuge and my shield; I have put my hope in your word."*
> — Psalm 119:114, New International Version

> *"As for me, I will always have hope; I will praise you more and more. My mouth will tell of your righteous deeds, of your saving acts all day long - though I know not how to relate them all."*
> — Psalm 71:14-15, New International Version

PART FIVE:
DAWN OF A NEW DAY
August 27, 2016 – November 24, 2016

"However long the night, the dawn will break."

— African Proverb

"One of these days at dawn you will rise from within like a sun."

— Jalaluddin Rumi

Celebrate Good Times Come On!

A GOOD COLLEGE FRIEND (HENRY) AND HIS WIFE (LINDA) DECIDED TO HOST A CELEBRATION FOR VANESSA AND ME. They wanted to bring together other college friends that also wanted to see me. They wanted to show their appreciation of our friendship over the years and celebrate the progress I have made in my fight against Multiple Myeloma.

Henry and Linda were inspired to host a celebration when they read Vanessa's post celebrating the first anniversary of my Multiple Myeloma diagnosis. Henry called me the day after the post. He told me what he and Linda wanted to do, and he wanted to know when would be a good date for the event.

I was excited about seeing many of my college friends all together once again. I asked Vanessa what date she thought would be good for the celebration. After checking the calendar, we decided on September 3rd, the Saturday of the Labor Day weekend.

With a date chosen, Henry went to work getting the word out. He solicited the help of a friend of his to help promote the event. Together, they posted announcements on the Facebook Prayer Team page to encourage and invite team members to come to the celebration. They also set up an Eventbrite event.

Henry Lindsey
August 2, 2016

JUST ANNOUNCED!!

An Appreciation event for Henry and Vanessa Dotson.

Pool Party, Dance, and Dinner!!!

Henry Lindsey
August 2, 2016

September 3rd. Rancho Cucamonga. Please watch your emails for further details.

You are being notified first because we expect an amazing turnout. We want to ensure your attendance.

Blessings, Henry and Linda Lindsey

Henry Lindsey
August 9, 2016

Please check your e-mails!!

The Celebration for Henry and Vanessa Dotson has been announced. September 3rd, 2016.

Sharon Young
August 9, 2016

Hi Prayer Warriors, My name is Sharon Young, I haven't met most of you, but I hope to do so at the upcoming event to Celebrate Henry and Vanessa Dotson, taking place on September 3rd at Linda and Henry Lindsey's home!

Please feel free to share on social media with your friends!

This a great way to celebrate a wonderful couple. I wish it coincided with a visit to see my Cali family. The timing is off to come from Detroit.

Henry Lindsey
August 21, 2016

September 3rd is fast approaching!!!! I am getting so excited to see Mr. Dotson. I've prayed every day that the Lord allows the Dotson's once again to visit my home. Please join my family and business group in celebrating this special event.

> *Hey Folks,*
>
> *We would like to express our appreciation for all of the support we have received and continue to receive as I go through this journey. Let's celebrate life and the meaningful relationships we have nurtured along the way. I want to spend this time we are together to fellowship and continue to build on the relationships we have.*
>
> *We look forward to what is yet to come.*
>
> *With our love and heartfelt gratitude, Henry and Vanessa Dotson!*

continued

Join us for good food, music, a no-host bar, and a silent auction. We are going to celebrate and have a good time. A financial gift of $25 or more is optional for Henry and Vanessa Dotson. We hope you can make it!

Cheers,

We Want More Group

Henry and I had spoken about the cost of medication and my concerns about not knowing what the out-of-pocket costs would be. Still, I felt uncomfortable when I saw that his post made mention of an optional financial gift. Just as before, I did not want people to think fundraising was the real motive behind the gathering.

I was so concerned that I posted a message on the page to re-emphasize the event's purpose was to celebrate and express my appreciation for their support.

 Henry B. Dotson III
August 27, 2016

Greetings all,

I pray all is well with you. I am ever thankful and humbled by your continual prayers for my complete healing. It has been a little more than a year since I was first diagnosed and close to a year since I was released from City of Hope after returning from Chicago.

What a difference a year makes! I am looking forward to seeing as many of you as possible next weekend at the Lindseys' home to tell you firsthand about this past year's journey. You have all been so much a part of it, and I would like to see you face to face so we can celebrate together what God has done so far toward my complete restoration.

Stay Blessed and be well!

- Henry B. Dotson III

 22   Seen by 21   11 Comments

 JB   Looking forward to seeing you.

 DM   I pray the Lord's blessing on you both.

DS Belief is faith in first gear.

VS We look forward to seeing you!

VW God is good! Still praying for ya!

CS Remarkable.

BC Awesome... Praise God!

A Dotson Celebration

Rancho Cucamonga, CA
September 3, 2016

THE DAY OF CELEBRATION HAD FINALLY ARRIVED. I was so excited! I was so looking forward to seeing my college friends! The event was called "An Affair to Remember." I spent most of the 45-minute drive thinking about who was going to show up. This was one of the few times I didn't have much to say on the way to a fun event.

Vanessa broke the silence by telling me when some people thought the event was a memorial. They misread the name of the event and thought it was in remembrance of me. She said a couple of people called her in tears when they told her they would be there.

I felt sorry for their momentary pain, but I was glad that Vanessa could give them the good news. It was also touching to know my friends cared so deeply about me.

When we arrived at the Lindsey's house, we were shocked at what we saw. Henry had a giant blue banner with white letters draped across the front of the second story of his house. It simply read: "Dotson Celebration." It was so large that it almost looked too big for the house.

The gesture humbled me.

We were immediately greeted by hugs and cheers when we entered the house. It was a little overwhelming. There were a lot of familiar faces and many people I did not know. They were friends and business associates of Henry. They just wanted to be amongst the well-wishers.

In addition to those I've mentioned, my friend Jim showed up, and so did a childhood friend that I've known since we were five years old. Even though she didn't expect to know anyone there except Vanessa and me, she drove a long way to be there. I was blessed by their presence.

I was so excited seeing everyone that I bounced from table-to-table, meeting and greeting. There was good food, good music, and good conversation. Being around many of my longtime friends was food for my soul. I even felt better physically.

I was given the opportunity to say a few words and shared them from my heart. I included some of those words in my September 6th post on the Facebook page. By the time we left the celebration, I was on cloud nine.

After our initial welcome, Vanessa spent some time saying hello to the few people she knew. This was definitely my crowd. So Vanessa, being an introvert, settled in a comfortable spot and mostly went into observer mode. A couple of people she did know came and sat with her to talk as I socialized.

Dinner was served buffet-style. Some people ate while sitting in the family room or standing in the kitchen, while others ate at tables outside the pool. Vanessa and I got our plates and sat outside.

"Are you enjoying yourself?" Vanessa asked.

"Oh, this is great," I said, beaming. "I haven't seen some of these people in years!"

"That's good. I'm glad you're having a good time."

Another one of my friends that I hadn't seen in more than 20 years arrived about that time. I popped up and went over to get a hug. We talked in line while she got her food. We walked over to my table, and I introduced her to Vanessa. There was no room at our table, so she sat at another table.

I was still engrossed in our conversation, so I picked up my plate and sat at her table to continue the conversation. Soon, other new arrivals came and sat at the same table. I struck up conversations with them also. Those conversations continued for some time.

At some point, I looked over at Vanessa. She was sitting at her table alone, looking at me. There was an empty chair at the table where I was sitting, so I looked at it and looked back at Vanessa. She did not react, and I did nothing further to suggest she come over. I was too busy trying to make the most of my time with my old friends.

On the way back home from the affair, Vanessa told me she felt abandoned. She said she was sitting all alone, surrounded by many people she did not know. Being an introvert, Vanessa is not one to carry a conversation. She will participate, but she typically will not lead. She says after a short time, she runs out of things to say.

That was not the first time this has happened. With me being an extrovert, I easily get caught up in what I'm doing with others. Over the years, Vanessa and I had to develop signals she would give me when she wanted me to know it was time to go. She would either touch my leg or tap my foot with hers under the table. If we were not close enough for physical contact, she would emit a short dry cough.

Usually, when she told me that I had left her alone at some social event, I would sincerely apologize and vow to do better. I've gotten better over the years, but on the whole, there is still much room for improvement.

This time was different. This time I felt remorse. This time it grieved me to know that I had abandoned Vanessa. I knew it was difficult for her to share with me her feelings on this occasion. She did not want to bring me down, but she just had to say something because of how bad she felt. It took courage for her to speak up instead of suffering in silence.

This time I saw that my self-centeredness was still alive and well within me, and I felt ashamed. This time I did not just sincerely apologize to Vanessa. This time I asked for her forgiveness. Mercifully, she did forgive me, and I knew I simply had to do much, much better.

I would like to say that since then, I've gotten much better, but that is not for me to say. Vanessa is the only one who has a say that matters. I have not asked her how I am doing. Instead, I pray for more sensitivity and awareness.

In my September 6th post on the Prayer Team Facebook page, I expressed my heartfelt gratitude for Vanessa. I did not write the words because it was expected. I wrote them because they spoke my truth.

I wrote them to Vanessa.

Some Words of Thanks

Pasadena, CA
September 6, 2016

 Henry B. Dotson III
September 6, 2016

Some Words of Thanks

I want to share some of my thoughts on last Saturday's event. The occasion was called "An Affair to Remember." We discovered the name of the event was a little confusing for some. A few thought I was being remembered instead of the affair being what would be remembered. As a matter of fact, Vanessa shared with me that a couple of people cried when they got the announcement for the event. Sorry for the misunderstanding – rumors of my transition to glory were premature and greatly exaggerated.

With more than 80 people in attendance throughout the afternoon and evening, the size of the gathering was a bit overwhelming. It was humbling to see the number of people impacted by my journey that showed up on a holiday weekend, not to mention those who responded but declined the invitation. This was truly a once-in-a-lifetime event! I was honored blessed by their presence.

I would like to first thank the We Want More Group for brainstorming and planning the event. I did not know this group existed until Henry informed me that they wanted to do something on my behalf. No group outside of my family and close friends has ever done anything like this. Within my circle, the events have been the typical celebrations and gatherings everyone is used to attending. No one has ever planned an event on my behalf to recognize me for being me. In particular, I would like to thank Sharon Young, who I met face to face for the first time that day, for all her efforts in making this happen.

She was my point of contact with the group and had a lot to do with what went on and for publicizing the event online. Thank you, Sharon. I must next thank Henry and Linda for hosting the "Affair to Remember." They graciously opened their home so we could all celebrate and fellowship with each other in comfort and style. They

continued

even prepared a place for me to lie down in case I needed to rest before the event was over. It was Henry that brought the idea for this event to the We Want More Group in the first place. So I thank you, Henry, not only for you and Linda's hospitality on this occasion but for your friendship over the years. Your desire to reconnect in person after more than a year in such a special way touches me deeply. Thank you, Henry!

I want to thank those of you who attended that have been following our journey online and have supported us with your thoughts, prayers, words of encouragement, acts of kindness, and resources. Your support has truly been a blessing to Vanessa and me. To those of you who came by to see me in person or to help Vanessa with errands and chores, you made such a difference by lightening the load we had to carry. We are forever grateful to you for sacrificing your time in our time of need. Thank you all.

Lastly, I must acknowledge and thank Vanessa. Not enough can be said to convey what she means to me. We have journeyed together these past 14 months through very trying times and circumstances. Her love and commitment to me and our marriage never wavered. The Bible says, "He who finds a wife finds a good thing."

Vanessa is my "good thing." The journey is not over, but this was a time for celebration and recognition that our most difficult days are behind us. I love you, Vanessa Ann.

Comments

SM What a blessing that must have been. So sorry I missed it, but prayerfully I'll get to see you this weekend while I'm there. Tell Vanessa to inbox your number so we can hook up if you're up to it. Ok??

PH Awesome! We are lamenting that we missed it, though. Still, we're so happy to acknowledge you and all that God is doing through you!

CC Love you both, again sorry we could not attend.

GT I'm so happy for you both and for being a part of this journey. It's given me encouragement also.

JH It was a great night, and thanks to the Lindseys for hosting.

CS You're a very lucky couple.

CW Awesome!

Pasadena, CA
September 6, 2016

Cecily came down to Southern California to visit family and friends. She lives in Northern California with her husband, and they have two adult daughters. Vanessa and I met her for dinner in San Dimas, near her parents' house. It was the first time we had seen Cecily since my diagnosis.

We had a great time catching up and getting some much-needed hugs. I was glad Vanessa had a chance to thank Cecily in person for helping with all the medical jargon and issues she faced when we were at CTCA.

It is important to take the time to be with the people you care about and let them know they are appreciated.

> **Q: How did you feel about our get-together for dinner in San Dimas?**
> **CECILY:** We do not see each other that often because of our distance from one another. But there is a connection we have had since 1976. We have been there for one another through all the events in life: graduation, marriage, divorce, children, remarriage.
>
> You looked like yourself at dinner in San Dimas. I have faith, but not like yours, and I knew the Lord had touched you. I witnessed your strong faith.

FROM ZION TO A CITY OF HOPE: A JOURNEY OF FAITH

I Got the Victory

"For whatever is born of God overcomes the world; and this is the victory that has overcome the world – our faith."
— 1 John 5:4, New American Standard Bible

Pasadena, CA
September 25, 2016

SUNDAY PRAISE REPORT

 Henry B. Dotson III
September 25, 2016

SUNDAY PRAISE REPORT

Greetings Prayer Team, Today, I have good news to share! I saw my oncologist and clinical research nurse last week. I was surprised to be informed that I am officially in remission! My lab results came back with no indication of Multiple Myeloma (MM)! May God be given all glory and honor! Thank you all for your constant prayers, words of encouragement, and support.

This is a major victory, but the battle is not over...

Although I am in remission, I still have MM cells in my body. I am still taking chemotherapy and will continue to do so for quite some time. "No indication of Multiple Myeloma" means the normal test used to detect MM is no longer useful because the amount of MM in my body is too low for it to detect. There is another, more precise test that will tell how much "residual" disease I have. The doctors say there is always some residual disease. That is why they say Multiple Myeloma is not curable, only treatable. They cannot get rid of it entirely with the therapies currently available.

My recovery to this point is indeed a miracle. The fact that I was even diagnosed with having Multiple Myeloma before it was too late was a miracle. The fact that I recovered from kidney failure during the early treatment phase of my disease is a miracle. The fact that I recovered from two different lethal infections I contracted while in the hospital is a miracle. The speed of my recovery is a miracle. Miracles happen every day. I see them every time I go to City of Hope for my care.

continued

Every cancer survivor is a miracle and has their own miraculous story to tell.

But, I sense that there is something more happening in my situation. This journey I am on is not one that I make alone. All of you have been on this journey with me through your prayers and support. I believe part of the reason for this journey is for God to prove Himself faithful not only to me but to all of you. If you ever doubted the power of prayer or ever doubted the power of your prayers, this journey we are on together should remove all doubt! The Bible says there is healing power in the prayers of those who believe James 5:14-16. I believe in my spirit that this is not the end of the journey. The story is not complete.

I believe in the total and complete restoration of my body according to the promises of God. I sense that in order to achieve that complete restoration, I will need even more power from your prayers. The doctors may not be able to get rid of the disease, but I know a Master Physician who can!

I believe if we press in and focus our prayers on complete and total healing, God will answer in a mighty way. This has been an amazing prayer team. I truly believe I would not be here today if it were not for your prayers. I am now calling on those of you who want to be prayer warriors to join me as I add fasting to my prayers. I believe the healing I desire requires prayer and fasting. I will be tested to see how much minimal residual disease I have at the end of October. This test will measure residual Multiple Myeloma cells down to parts per million. I believe if we offer up our prayers along with fasting, the doctors will not find any residual disease! This has never happened before, and it would be an even more miraculous thing for me to be able to say, "I am cured of Multiple Myeloma!"

For those who want to be a part of this, choose how you will fast during the month of October in whatever way works for you. I am excited to see what God is about to do! May God continue to bless you all!

Henry B. Dotson III

Comments

 Praise God from whom all blessings flow. My pastor just preached a series on miracles which I will send.

GA Amen. Henry, I was thinking and going to touch base with Vanessa and you. What an Awesome God we have! You and Vanessa will continue to be in my thoughts and Prayers.

LJ AGREEMENT-Fasting and Praying with y'all. God is truly awesome, and I admire y'all (Henry/Vanessa) tenaciously living such a testament to God's miraculous healing power, love, grace, and togetherness. Love you both, and I look to see you soon in Cali.çç

RN Hallelujah Hallelujah!!! Praise be unto God!! We shall believe the report of the Lord! So excited and happy for you, Henry Dotson and Vanessa Foster-Dotson!!!!!! My sister is rejoicing for you from heaven, and I wanna cut a praise dance!!

SR Henry, this is good news, and I love that you are so insightful and real about your situation.

I will do some form of fasting this month in honor of you and will pray that your birthday that comes at the end of this month brings you more good news.

SB Yes, a very important thing is the friendship established with everyone who takes on the opportunity to pray daily for those who suffer and what joy it is when there is healing!

LW I am so happy for you, Bernard. And will continue praying for miracles for all of us. May you and Vanessa continue to be blessed.

WL Praise God for his HEALING. May every ATOM in your body reject every atom called MM. It is a JOY BEYOND MEASURE to see what GOD has done in YOUR life. The Langleys are in agreement with prayer and fasting with you.

RH Thank you, God. Such wonderful news, Henry. I will continue to pray and will fast with you. I wish you all of God's grace. Love you!

PH I'm in! Praying and fasting specifically for the miracle! To God Be the Glory!

DH   Amen. Henry, I was thinking and going to touch base with Vanessa and you. What an Awesome God we have! You and Vanessa will continue to be in my thoughts and Prayers.

JB   We serve a mighty God. Thank you for being a faithful example of trusting and taking God at his literal word. You are letting the power that works in you produce a light that shines brightly for all to see. How Great is Our God!

PJ   On Wednesday, October 5, Garden of Praise Apostolic Church will be fasting and praying for three days. Not only for our needs but also for you, Bernard, and we will also be including Mrs. Foster for a complete restoration in her body!! To God be the glory!! We love you both!!!

DC   Henry, I love this post!! And won't our master physician always do it!! You are amazing!! So glad you are now one of my buddies!! Sending you lots of love.

JR   God delivers. Praise God.

LD   To God be the glory!!!!!!! They can't get rid of the residual MM cells, but God is the healer!!!

CP   To God be all the Glory! We lift your name up.

Q: How did you feel when you learned i was in remission?

BART: I felt proud of you for living through the journey and thankful to the Lord that you were in remission.

CHARITY: I was overjoyed! What a miracle and answer to prayer!

TALIA: Proud!! PARTY TIME!!!

IRA: I was elated to hear that you were in remission! As I stated earlier, God showed me that you would survive this illness. Even though I had confidence regarding your recovery, it was exciting to hear your doctor's assessment.

CRIS: All I could do was to praise the Lord for the things He had done (and is still doing).

PAT: My heart was overjoyed to hear that my brother was in remission! God did it! I shared the news with my congregation, and we had a time!! So much rejoicing, so much Thanksgiving, so much relief was expressed that day! What a mighty God we serve!!

BERYL: I was elated to hear that you were in remission and clearly in awe of the God who healed you. This was the Lord's work, and it was marvelous in our eyes! What a testimony to all whom you came in contact with!

You and Vanessa allowed us to share this journey with you, but I knew that God had a greater purpose in mind. At the time, I was not sure what it was, but I knew that nothing is wasted in the kingdom (Romans 8:28-29).

KATHY: I was cautiously relieved. There are lots of remissions and returns, so I was cautious in my exuberance.

SANDRA: When you were in remission, I felt ecstatic and thankful to hear about your remission.

NORMAN: Happy. Relieved. We have a lot of Rallye miles behind us. In that vein, it is like getting out of the nauseating mountain driving and heading out to the desert on the nearly arrow-straight road.

A whole lot easier. What I do wonder is if this Rallye is done, or if this was just a leg? We both know what it felt like between, say, legs six and seven at 6 a.m., a beautiful sunrise coupled with sheer exhaustion.

RUTH: Amazed and ecstatic.

CECILY: Ecstatic, but again you had the strongest faith I knew, and that would be your outcome.

JEFF AND CHARALE: We remember the unspeakable joy when we heard the news that you were in remission and how our faith was lifted in hearing good report after good report (even in the midst of some minor setback or delays along the way, i.e., stem cell counts not being quite where they needed them to be, etc.).

LOIS: I felt so grateful to God for His grace and mercy toward you.

MARGARET: Elated! I thanked the Lord and told everyone in the prayer chains that we had been successful! However, I also knew that remission does not mean it is over and that you, like me, would continue to undergo tests and treatments. That has proven to be true, but it is also something that we both have been able to live with without difficulty. For that, I thank the Lord every day.

JIM: Hearing that you were in remission was great news for me. It was a validation of your spirit and faith, and a testament to the many who joined in prayer for you.

Q: Did you participate in the fast? If yes, how did the experience affect you?

BART: Yes. I felt very confident that there could be a miracle in your life and that you could receive complete healing.

PAT: Not only I, but my congregation as well participated in the fast.

As we prayed for your healing, I truly felt a connection with all the other participants in the fast. I didn't know who, I didn't know how many, but I knew that we were all praying and fasting with the same goal in mind.

As I look back over the events surrounding your illness, I see the mighty hand of God being true to his word. 'Ask anything in My Name, believing, you will receive it.' Okay, I may not have a quote going on, but Ð GOD DID IT!!!

BERYL: Yes, I participated in the fast. I had others participate in the fast with me.

Fasting allows me to commune with God more intimately. Because there were many of us fasting, I felt I was part of a powerful community of believers on one accord praying on your behalf.

When I fast, it is not uncommon for me to be reminded of my illusion that I am in control. It was during this time of fasting that I found myself enjoying God's presence.

I started focusing more on God moments; like how you wouldn't have gone to the doctor if you had not injured your back helping others; how, if you had waited for your second opinion appointment in Cali, you might not have been here; how others had an opportunity to give back to you through Go Fund Me; how you ministered to the CTCA staff (you even were put in a bigger room with more sunshine, because of the Son shining in your heart); how the price of the medication was reduced; on and on and on.

How great is our God!

I think this particular fast caused me to appreciate even more God's mercy and grace. God owes us nothing, yet He freely bestows these gifts to us because of Who He is.

SANDRA: I did not participate in the fast, but I did pray heavily and asked for prayer requests at my local church.

I was affected in the following ways: spiritually, I felt like anything was possible through God as long as we had faith; emotionally, I felt broken; and physically, I felt drained.

NORMAN: By default, Yom Kippur started the evening of the 11th and ended the evening of the 12th.

Very different context for me. It is our day of atonement. It is the day I ask the Lord for forgiveness. It is the day that, according to custom, by fate for the Jewish year is sealed.

It is also the time of year at which you ask anyone you offended to forgive you. We can, and I do, ask for blessings for others. Last year, one was for you.

Sometimes I feel connected or spiritual, sometimes not. It always ends with a headache. No food or fluid for 25 hours does that.

RUTH: Only on Yom Kippur, so that probably doesn't count as I would be fasting and spiritually-focused, per custom.

JEFF AND CHARALE: Yes.

We felt that no matter what "death sentence" the enemy tries to send our way, that with the power of faith, prayer, fasting, community, and agreement, that nothing is impossible for God and for us who truly believe.

A Father's Blessing

"Your Father's blessings are greater than the blessings of the ancient mountains, than the bounty of the age-old hills."
— Genesis 49:26, New International Version Bible

"The father of a righteous man has great joy; he who has a wise son delights in him."
— Proverbs 23:24, New International Version Bible

Tempe, AZ
October 25, 2016

VANESSA AND I ATTENDED BART AND CHARITY'S WEDDING TODAY. It was held outdoors in a country setting in Chandler, Arizona. It was a small wedding. There were just eight in the bridal party, including the bride, groom, flower girl, and ring bearer. Immediate family members and grandparents made up the attendees; about ten altogether.

The wedding was an extraordinary moment for me in three ways. The first is being alive to witness my son's wedding. Second, my bout with cancer was the catalyst for their relationship changing from friendship to closer. Third, I was able to see the fulfillment of my blessing over my son.

I felt so blessed that God allowed me to be here. My life was saved in Zion, and I had the strength to endure the wear and tear of air travel. Witnessing my son marry the person God chose for him filled me with joy. I am a proud papa! I am confident that Charity will live up to her wedding vows just as Vanessa has.

Bart told me that his relationship with Charity turned serious after he returned from Zion. He confided in her and shared how he felt about me having cancer. She was there to comfort and support him through this difficult time in his life. I was amazed to see how God used something that appeared to be a bad thing for a good thing.

Rites of Passage

When Bart was 12 years old, I decided to set up Rites of Passage ceremonies to help him transition from boyhood to authentic manhood. Our society does not have any formal ceremonies for this transition. Many boys wind up learning from what they observe in their environment, or what the media says is a "real man."

That is not what I wanted for my son. I looked for reference material on the subject. I found a book entitled *Raising a Modern-Day Knight* by pastor Robert Lewis. It is biblically based, and I shared the same values it promotes. I used it as a model for my Rites of Passage ceremonies.

Here is the definition of a "real man" from the book:

A REAL MAN...

Rejects Passivity

Don't copy the behavior and customs of this world, but let God transform you into a new person by changing the way you think. Then you will learn to know God's will for you, which is good and pleasing and perfect.

Accepts Responsibility

Be on your guard, stand firm in the faith; be men of courage, be strong.

Leads Courageously

But as for me and my family, we will serve the Lord.

Expects the Greater Reward

Behold, I am coming soon! My reward is with me, and I will give to everyone according to what he has done.

I created four Rites of Passage ceremonies for Bart: one for when he became a teenager; one for when he graduated from high school; one for when he graduated from college; and one for when he got married.

Bart called me in mid-September to let me know he and Charity planned to get married. Vanessa and I were surprised. We knew about their relationship, but he had not let on that it had reached that point. When I asked him had they set a wedding date, he said they were getting married on October 25th.

I scrambled to organize the final ceremony. I called up my friends who had participated in his previous ceremonies and set the date and location of the ceremony. The previous ceremonies were held out of town in a recreational setting. With such short notice, this ceremony was held in Redondo Beach, California, October 7 – 9, 2016. Bart flew in from Arizona for the ceremony.

At the end of the last ceremony, I gave my blessing over him as his father. I commemorated the event by giving him a written copy of my blessing. It read:

Henry Bernard Dotson, III's Blessing
On
Henry Bernard Dotson, IV
October 9, 2016

Henry, today I want to impart a father's blessing to you as a father myself and as a representative of your Heavenly Father.

I bless your life Henry. The life God gave you. Psalms 139 says He knew you before He created the world; that He created your innermost being. He formed you in your mother's womb to be exactly who you are, to look as you do, to have the personality and character you have. You are fearfully and wonderfully made. There were no surprises. All the days ordained for you were written by God even before you were born. You were uniquely crafted and specifically designed for God's purpose. He rejoiced when you were created, celebrated and boasted when you were born and has been with you every day and year that has passed. He loves you and wants you to know the height, depth and breadth of His Love for you - not for what you do or have done, but for who you are.

I bless your personal faith in Jesus Christ that you may not only believe what He has said, but receive what He has promised for your life. I bless you in your walk with God that you may be a faithful follower of Jesus Christ with your mind bound to His thoughts, your hands bound to His work, and your feet bound to His path for your life.

I bless the day you were born, the perfect timing of your birth, and the destiny that God pre-planned for your life. All the days of your life were ordained before one of them came to be. May you discover the sheer joy of walking in the steps that God has ordered for your life.

I bless your gender as a cherished man of God created in God's perfect design. I bless your birth order. May the timing of your arrival and your relationship with your sister be used by God to perfect you according to His will.

I bless your emotional life that you may understand deep in your heart that God will always provide a safe place for you, a place of refuge in this earth from the forces that set themselves against you. May God's perfect love displace any fears in your life.

I bless your marriage to Charity. What God has joined together, may no one ever separate. May you always be one with Charity and know the leading of the Lord to support, encourage and love her in all things. I bless you with sexual purity, marital fidelity, and many children of your own.

I bless you as a father and I bless your offspring, that the generational blessing upon you and your family line would be passed on to them. May each of your beautiful children provide breadth and depth to your life experience and may each of them share your values in life and experience a personal walk with God.

I bless the work of your hands, that whatever roles you find yourself in at Backbone Communications, or any other Organization be fulfilling to you and glorifying to God.

I bless your finances, that you may always know the abundance of God's supply, that you will always discern and obey the requirements for financial blessing and live securely without need or fear of want.

I bless and release you into the destiny and purpose God has for you and the anointing over your life. You demonstrate gifting in the areas of intellect, teaching, critical thinking, writing, and encouragement. May you continue to grow in these areas of gifting and any others God has for you.

I bless you with God's everlasting love, wisdom, peace, and joy. May God continue to keep His hand of favor and prosper you in all that you do, and may you serve our Lord Jesus Christ all the days of your life.

Henry, know this day that you are a blessed son of the most-High God with the same inheritance as that of His Son Jesus Christ. In Whose name and authority, I pronounce this blessing on you today. Amen.

The ceremony was moving for all of us. We knew that our collective commitment to these ceremonies had come to an end. Bart said he was very grateful for all of the rites of passage ceremonies.

I felt as if I had fulfilled one of my purposes in life. I had raised my son in the way that he should go to the best of my abilities. I had the same feeling when Bart and Talia accepted Jesus Christ as their Lord and Savior and were baptized in 1997.

Q: How do you think my cancer journey has affected your relationship with Charity?

BART: The visit to Chicago affected my relationship with Charity in many ways. Initially, it served as a bonding experience since Charity had experienced near-fatal physical illness and subsequent prolonged hospitalization of her sister. Charity helped me to identify a flight out to Chicago. After I returned, we had many conversations about health, relationships, and God. I know that Charity felt that my opening up to her really showed how much I trusted and cared about her.

Q: How do you think my cancer journey has affected your relationship with Henry?

CHARITY: It brought Bart and me closer together, probably faster than we would have under "normal" circumstances. It gave us an opportunity to really relate to each other and for me to share my personal experience with my sister having a cardiac arrest.

We started relating on a deeper level, and in the months to come the diagnosis gave us something to continue to relate over. As I wrote in something I gave to Henry while we were dating, your cancer diagnosis gave us "an opportunity to be vulnerable with each other, and show support and God's love to each other in our friendship, which is really the foundation we still operate on today.

In some ways, I'm thankful for the cancer diagnosis because it really shaped our relationship in a positive way. As for my relationship with you, when I finally got to meet you, the drama gave us a deeper connecting point from the start since I had experienced multiple traumas with my younger sister.

Q: Did my cancer journey affect your perspective on sharing your engagement plans with me?

BART: No, your cancer journey didn't affect me sharing my engagement plans with you.

Q: Did my cancer journey change your perspective on your Rites of Passage Ceremony?

BART: I hadn't considered how your cancer journey affected my perspective on the Rites of Passage ceremony. However, I can't imagine what it would have been like not to have had the blessing of that event and your wise words.

Q: Did my cancer journey change your perspective on Bart's Rites of Passage Ceremony?

NORMAN: I cannot tell which event you are referring to specifically. I know I attended two. I preferred the second one for various reasons.

I would prefer to think of the first rite of passage ceremony as a pole vault; there is usually only one on the field; it changed my perspective. Especially given the way the discussions progressed.

The second rite of passage ceremony was to educate Bart, to make him aware of a responsible adult's life and values. And, bag the macho, man of the house crap.

It was for Bart to understand that he has entered a partnership. Partners have responsibilities to each other, to look out for each other, to counsel each other, to share wisdom and values.

I am not sure about your cancer journey.

It would be interesting to learn if your cancer pole vault changed his perspective and the value of a father sharing those things mentioned above with him. My dad sure did not. And, the lack of partnership or the 50/60s mentality is causing my mom a lot of grief now because she doesn't know jack.

RUTH: I thought your cancer journey made Bart's rite of passage ceremony even more essential, in the essential sense of the word, as well as more poignant. You were getting to the heart, soul, and mind of what is most important to you and your lifelong friends, and how to share/teach some of those life lessons/wisdom with your son on the eve of his marriage.

Q: Did my cancer journey affect your perspective on my attending your wedding?

BART: Before cancer, of course, I had never considered that you wouldn't attend my wedding. The wedding wouldn't have been complete without you there.

CHARITY: I was so thankful you were able to attend the wedding! We actually had all immediate family members healthy at the time of our wedding, which felt like a success considering in the last two years there had been a cardiac arrest, a very serious cancer diagnosis and successful battle, and two collapsed lungs!

I don't think we wouldn't have had a wedding if you were unable to attend safely. It was very important to us to have our family there, and while I was disappointed Talia couldn't be there, I was very thankful my father-in-law was there and healthy!

A father's blessing is significant to me. It is an integral part of the approval a son is looking for from his father. I never received one from my father, but I knew he was proud of me. He would make one or two comments from time to time, but that was about it. We did have one serious heart-to-heart conversation while I was going through my divorce that was very encouraging.

That being said, there was one father's blessing I was determined to ask for. That was Vanessa's father's blessing before I asked her to marry me.

Monrovia, CA
November, 1997

ONCE I DECIDED TO MARRY VANESSA, I KNEW I HAD TO GET HER FATHER'S BLESSING BEFORE ASKING HER FOR HER HAND. In the week following my birthday party, I called Vanessa's parents in New Jersey. Her mother answered the phone.

"Hello?"

"Hello, Mrs. Foster, this is Henry. How are you?"

"I'm fine; how are you?"

"I'm good, thanks. Can Mr. Foster pick up the phone? I want to talk to you both."

"Okay, hang on. Shep! Pick up the phone. Henry wants to talk to us."

"Okay. Hi Henry."

"Hi Mr. Foster, I want to know if I have your permission to ask Vanessa to marry me." I did not hesitate; I wanted to get straight to the point. I was a little nervous, and I thought this was no time for small talk.

(There was a short pause.)

"Well, sure!"

"Oh, that's wonderful!" Mrs. Foster said. "When do you plan to ask her?"

"I'm not sure. I would like to do it when we are back East so she will have family nearby."

Vanessa did not go home for Christmas last year. She made that sacrifice to be with the children and me at Christmas time. That was her first time away from home at Christmas, and she said that was the last time she would not go home for Christmas. She told me:

> "I don't know where you will be next Christmas, but I am going to be home. I don't like the cold, but I want to see snow on the ground on Christmas day. It's not natural to not see snow on Christmas day."

I agreed to go along with her since she had sacrificed for me. This would be the first time I would be on the East Coast in December. My Christmas holidays had all been spent in Southern California.

"Well, every year, the whole family gets together for Christmas dinner. This year it will be at our house. You could ask her here after dinner."

"That sounds good, Mrs. Foster. And I would like it to be a surprise."

"Well, we can help. Vanna (Vanessa's sister) can help run errands, and she can call people."

"Vanessa has mentioned the names of some of her friends that she wants me to meet. Maybe they can help too."

"I'll see if I have her friends' phone numbers, and Vanna can get in touch with the ones I don't have."

"This is going to be a big Christmas day," I said. "Thank you, Mr. Foster!"

"You're welcome."

"Goodbye. I will be talking with you all soon."

"Goodbye, Henry."

I was elated when Vanessa's father consented. I don't know if he prayed over Vanessa regularly. But to me, it meant he was willing to hand over to me the responsibility to provide the spiritual covering over his daughter. At the very least, it meant he was in favor of me being Vanessa's husband.

I felt like I was doing things decently and in order, God's way.

Beverly Hills, CA
October 30, 2016

TONIGHT, WE CELEBRATED MY BROTHER'S 60TH BIRTHDAY. Since we enjoyed ourselves so much at our joint birthday last year, my brother, sister, and I decided to celebrate each of our 60th birthdays together. My brother is the oldest, so his birthday is this year. I will follow next year, and my sister's birthday celebration will be in 2018.

We were a small party of guests at a fancy restaurant Ira selected. Our party consisted of Ira, Cris, their daughter Stefany, Vanessa, Pat, and me.

It felt good to be with my siblings at a time of celebration instead of a time of sorrow. My cancer journey had made me more appreciative of these moments together.

Q: How do you feel about me being able to attend your 60th birthday celebration?

IRA: If I wanted any relative to be present at my 60th birthday, it was you. I am not sure if our relatives or friends understand our friendship. When we were growing up, I always thought that we were good friends in addition to being brothers.

There was the normal competition that brothers have, but it never seemed to affect our friendship. I think you are one of the few people that understand me. Also, you are one of the few people that I can have meaningful conversations with about several subjects.

To answer your question simply is yes, your attendance was important to me.

Q: How do you feel about me being able to attend Ira's 60th birthday celebration?

CRIS: I felt happy, and I was thankful that you were able to attend.

PAT: Oh happy day!! I was so thrilled that I really can't even explain my emotions sitting across from my brother, who had been through so much! There he was talking, laughing, telling his same stale jokes; it was fantastic!! I know we were there to celebrate my older brother's 60th milestone; however, I was sitting in front of my miracle!

From Zion to a City of Hope: A Journey of Faith

Under The Microscope

"In general, all cancers have been traditionally characterized by the way they appear under the microscope and the organs in which they arise."

— Harold E. Varmus

Pasadena, CA
November 2, 2016

MRD Test

Henry B. Dotson III
November 2, 2016

full MRD Test

Greetings All,

This post is to keep you updated on my condition. First of all, thank you all for your prayers and fasting for the month of October as we look to God for supernatural healing. I am certain God heard your prayers. I had my bone marrow biopsy procedure on 26 Oct. I believe I will get the results on 16 Nov. That is when I will be informed how much "Minimal Residual Disease" (MRD) is present in my system. That is when God will reveal what He has done. The biopsy procedure involves inserting a needle into my pelvis bone through to the marrow to extract the sample (my apologies if this makes you squeamish).

The first time this procedure was performed on me was in Chicago when I was first diagnosed with MM. I do not remember the procedure because I was (as Vanessa puts it) "delirious." Vanessa told me the doctor said pushing the needle through my bone was "like going through butter." This is not a good thing.

When the procedure was done on 26 Oct, the physician's assistant who was performing the procedure said she was hurting her hand because the bone was so hard. I asked her if that was a good thing, and she said, "Most definitely, we want you to have hard bones."

She also said there was plenty of marrow to collect from. The last time she performed the procedure on me (about four months ago), she said she was having difficulty collecting a good amount of

continued

marrow. Both of these indicators (hard bones and a large amount of marrow) are very good signs.

This is a dramatic turnaround from the first procedure. While it does not give a clear indication of what the results of the MRD test will be, it does show that my bones have been restored! To God be the glory! I am looking forward to seeing what the next report from the doctor will be.

Please continue to keep us in your prayers. We truly appreciate you rising to the occasion and adding the power of your prayers.

Stay Blessed,
- Henry

   Comments

AR Thank you for keeping us updated and showing us that prayer is powerful. The Lord is great and greatly to be praised!

BM Such good news to hear, Henry! Yes, God deserves all the Glory! Thank you Jesus. Keep all of us "mini-survivors" in your hands and continue to bless us abundantly! In Your Precious Name. Amen!

BC Thanks for your steadfast Faith, brother, and weathering the storms of life. I will continue to keep your family in my prayers!

GT I've had that procedure recently. It sounded scary at first, but it was over before I knew it.

CC Claiming a good report for healing, in the name of JESUS!!!

DS God knows your anatomy best.

PM Thank God for his grace and favor. He's a way maker!

Walk For Hope

Duarte, CA
November 6, 2016

TODAY, I PARTICIPATED IN CITY OF HOPE'S ANNUAL WALK FOR HOPE. They have put on this event for the past 20 years to raise money and awareness for women's cancers and honor women who have fought and will fight these diseases. Vanessa's sorority alumnae chapter has participated in the past as part of their community service activities, and today, I was part of their team.

It was important for me to participate for three reasons: I wanted to do something to support the work of City of Hope; I wanted to support Vanessa in her community service work. And I wanted to test my physical condition by doing a 5K walk.

I was able to complete the 5K walk without any difficulty. The effort I put in during physical therapy paid off today. All of those laps around those nurses' stations and wings of hospitals also contributed to my strength and stamina.

The Walk for Hope was a win-win-win situation. For the first time in quite a while, I could do something for others by showing up to lend my support. It was nice being the giver instead of the receiver. I felt like I was living up to my wedding vows by supporting Vanessa. It also felt so good to be able to do something positive for others through physical exertion. The last time I was able to do so was when I helped Jezreel move.

I once heard a preacher say, "If you water the grass, the hose will get wet." He was using this example to teach a concept to the congregation. That is, if you focus on doing something solely to bless others, you too will be blessed as a result.

Participating in today's event and thinking about what the pastor said has unexpectedly helped me. It has helped me become more comfortable accepting financial blessings sent in response to posts about this cancer journey. I had been concerned about people thinking part of our motivation to communicate was to raise money.

Being on the giving side of the Walk For Hope has reminded me of what a blessing it is to give. I now feel better knowing my receiving a financial blessing allowed the giver to receive a blessing. I also realize if people thought our motivation was to raise money, they probably would not have given anything anyway.

I thank God for letting me be the hose.

Go Tell It On The Mountain

"Oh give thanks to the LORD, call upon His name;
Make known His deeds among the peoples.
Sing to Him, sing praises to Him;
Speak of all His wonders.
Glory in His holy name;
Let the heart of those who seek the LORD be glad."
— Psalm 105:1-2, New American Standard

Pasadena, CA
November 19, 2016

VANESSA AND I RECEIVED A PHONE CALL TODAY FROM MY ONCOLOGIST WITH THE RESULTS OF THE MRD TEST. When I saw "City of Hope" as the caller ID on the phone, I knew it was the call we had been waiting for.

"Vanessa, get on the phone. It's City of Hope."

"Okay, hang on. I'm coming."

I answered the phone as Vanessa entered the bedroom and picked up another phone to listen in.

"Hello," I said.

"Hello, Mr. Dotson. We have the results of the MRD test."

It was my oncologist. Hearing his voice on the other end of the phone was a bit of a surprise. We usually spoke with him in person at City of Hope, so this seemed a bit unnatural.

"What do the results say?" I asked. I took a deep breath and blew it out slowly as my doctor answered.

"The test results show no measurable disease can be found. This is the best possible result we could hope for."

"That's great news!" I said. "Does this mean I am cured?"

"Well, we still classify Multiple Myeloma as a chronic illness, so there is no real cure. There are always immature myeloma clonal cells in bone marrow, and with myeloma patients, there is a greater risk that they could become active."

"But you cannot see any sign of those cells in the test results down to parts per million, correct?" I asked.

"That is correct. As I said, this is the best possible result we could hope for."

"Well, thank you very much for your call."

"You're welcome, Mr. Dotson. Have a good rest of the weekend."

"Goodbye."

"Goodbye."

After we hung up the phone, Vanessa shouted, "Yes Lord!!, Thank you Jesus." I shouted, "Hallelujah!! Thank you, Lord Jesus!"

In my mind, I thought, *If you cannot find a trace of the disease anywhere, then I am going to claim the victory in Jesus' name.*

Vanessa and I continued to lift up praises to God and Jesus for a few more minutes. Then we stopped and held hands and said a prayer of thanksgiving for what God had done.

I was so excited that I immediately asked Vanessa if she would let me post on the Facebook page to share the good news.

"Of course," she said. "This needs to come from you."

So I set about crafting my post. It took a little while to collect my thoughts and to get them organized. The adrenaline was flowing, but I wanted the message to be tempered by the Holy Spirit.

After a little while, Vanessa asked, "Have you posted your message?"

"I'm still working on it," I replied.

"Oh, okay. I'm just checking."

I knew from her comments that she thought I would have posted the message by then. I did not feel rushed or pressured. I just wanted to "get it right." I knew this was the news that everyone had been waiting for and praying for. This was the moment I really wanted to be spirit-led. I said a little prayer and asked the Lord to use me, to speak through me to the Facebook Prayer Team.

I also felt as though Vanessa and I had come to the end of this journey. I wanted to communicate a message that encouraged the prayer team to use this journey as the catalyst to do even greater things through the power of prayer.

> *"Let no one deceive himself. If any of you thinks he is wise in this age, he should become a fool, so that he may become wise."*
> — 1 Corinthians 3:18, Berean Study Bible

> *"No human wisdom or understanding or plan can stand against the LORD."*
> — Proverbs 21:30, New Living Translation

The spirit-led words came to me, and I crafted the message. Here is my post:

I've Been Restored

Pasadena, CA
November 19, 2016

 Henry B. Dotson III
November 19, 2016

I'VE BEEN RESTORED

Greetings Facebook Prayer Team,

The test results are in! There is no sign of myeloma cells!! No measurable disease can be found! While not conceding that I am completely cured, my doctor said, "This is the best possible result we could hope for." I am taking it on faith in what my Bible says that God has performed my complete healing. Your prayers and fasting have helped to bring about this victory. I am forever thankful that you all responded to my call to action in my time of need. What a mighty God we serve!

I have now entered the Maintenance Phase of my treatment. In this phase, I will take a low dose of chemotherapy medication in pill form indefinitely. This is to prevent the "immature myeloma clonal cells" from maturing and becoming active. This is precautionary and will be part of my "new normal" routine.

God has brought me a long way. From near-death to complete healing of this life-threatening disease. This healing is not without the signs of battle. The chemotherapy treatments have left me with a mild case of neuropathy – a slight tingling in my toes and a couple of fingers. I have lost three inches in height from my crushed T7 vertebra.

I occasionally get a slight tingling in my left thigh from lesions in my L2 vertebrae. I was told I should not run or jump because I have a weakened spine. I was also advised not to lift more than fifteen pounds above my head. Lastly, there may be some mild side effects from the ongoing chemotherapy medication I will take in the Maintenance Phase.

These afflictions are truly minor compared to the miracles God has done. I am reminded of Apostle Paul when he wrote his second letter to the church in Corinth. He said:

continued

> *"... I will not boast about myself, except in my weaknesses. Even if I wanted to boast, I would not be a fool, because I would be speaking the truth. But I refrain, so no one will credit me with more than he sees in me or hears from me, or with these surpassingly great revelations. So, to keep me from becoming conceited, I was given a thorn in my flesh, a messenger of Satan, to torment me. Three times I pleaded with the Lord to take it away from me. But He said to me, "My grace is sufficient for you, for My power is perfected in weakness." Therefore, I will boast all the more gladly in my weaknesses, so that the power of Christ may rest on me."*
> — 2 Corinthians 12:5 - 9, Berean Study Bible

God's grace is sufficient for me; His power is perfected in my weakness. I will boast about God's miraculous healing of my body more gladly in my weakness so that the power of Christ may rest on me. I am nothing without Christ, and I do not want anyone to credit me with any part of the miracles that have taken place. I am a sinner saved by grace and have been blessed to be used by God to fulfill His purpose in my trials and tribulation. To God be the Glory!

When I take the time to reflect on the events of my life, I often envision myself as being on a journey. I see myself walking down a path that takes me through the many different experiences of life. In my spirit, I feel the part of my journey that began in early July of 2015 with the diagnosis of Multiple Myeloma (MM) has come to an end with the complete restoration of my bone marrow, as indicated by my test results.

While on this part of my journey, I was blessed to have you all come alongside me to provide your love, comfort, and support. We all walk our individual paths in life, but there are times when our paths meet, and we walk gether for a time. This has been the case on this part of my journey.

I've discovered through your comments that our walk together has not just supported me in my time of need, but it has provided you with encouragement, reassurance of what God can do, and confirmation of the power of your prayers. We have all become witnesses to the miracles God performed in our walk together. I believe we've all grown spiritually as a result of this experience. We all have a testimony about what God has done in our lives as we traveled our individual paths, bound together by our collective journey through my bout with cancer.

continued

As I stated earlier, I feel this part of my journey has come to an end. It is time to look forward to what God has in store for me beyond MM. I also feel as though we have reached a point where our individual paths, while still moving forward in parallel, are taking us each in our own new direction. I believe it is time for all of us to see what God has in store for us individually, beyond my MM.

Ecclesiastes 3:1 says, *"For everything there is a season, and a time for every purpose under heaven...."* I believe the time for the Facebook Prayer Team for Henry "Bernard" Dotson, III has reached the end of its season; that it has served its purpose under heaven. With this in mind, this will be my last planned entry on this "secret" group page (I still find it hard to imagine something being a "secret" with over 200 people being in on the secret). Vanessa will also make a last entry to give her final thoughts on this remarkable journey. The group page will remain open for a time to allow you all time to reflect and make any final comments. We will let you know beforehand when the page will be closed and archived.

Again, I want to thank you all for your love, comfort, and support. You have been a blessing to Vanessa and to me in our time of trial and tribulation. We will never forget what you have done for us. To God be all the glory for the things He has done!!

Be well and prosper in the Lord,

- Henry

    Comments

RH   Henry, thank you for sharing the wonderful news. Our prayers have been with you along the journey and will continue. Sending well wishes and steadfast prayer. Peace and Love!

WL   You continue to give hope to many who would have given up. May God continue to touch you from the top of your head to the soles of your feet. As you continue to trust God, he will give you strength and grace for tomorrow.

BC   Praise God for his work in you and through you... God needs your wonderful testimony, brother. Continued prayer for you and your family.

DC — Henry, I met you before I knew you. I know that sounds weird, but it's so true! I received an email about Soror V going with you to Chicago for treatment. That day I emailed her and sent my love. I noted in that email that I would be praying for you! And that's just what I did! And continued to do! I will never forget my first selfie with V or that email because that's the real day our paths crossed. I typically like everyone, but it's different when you really love folks, and you connect with them in a way that makes you wonder have we met before!? God is so amazing!! I am so grateful that he placed you in our lives! I just read this post to William, and he said God is good! Henry's a real cool dude!! We gotta kick it with Henry and Vanessa! Lol, so we're going to be kicking it! Let's hope we don't get you in any trouble!! But I imagine by your dance skills you might get us in trouble! You got moves!! We indeed serve a faithful GOD! We love you Henry!!

LJ — Glory to God! I am so blessed by the testimony of you two as a couple walking this miracle out, one day, one moment at a time. Blessings, love y'all.

MH — God is so good! Thank you for sharing your journey and allowing us to partner with God in your faith walk and healing! The encouragement, as you so well stated, was for all of us! With that report, what a wonderful way to start the holidays!

AC — I am reminded of this song in light of your testimony. Praise God from who all blessings flow...Praise Him all creatures here below, Praise Him above the Heavenly Hosts, Praise Father, Son, and Holy Ghost...Amen To God be the glory, and may He continue to bless you Henry B. Dotson III

PJ — What a Mighty God we serve!!! (MM) must bow down to the Name of Jesus!! There is nothing Our God CAN'T do!! Bernard, it has been a journey. The Lord said we would walk "through" the valley of the shadow of death. What an example you have been to walk through with complete faith and a positive attitude! I thank God for you, brother, for your life, love, and laughter. God bless you as God takes you higher in Him. I love you.

Q: How did you feel when you learned no multiple myeloma cells could be seen?

BART: I felt even more convinced that the Lord was at work in making your journey a miracle story.

CHARITY: Again, I was overjoyed and so thankful to God!

TALIA: Very, very proud of you. Grateful and more mindful of the words you shared with us during the time you were in Chicago.

IRA: Your November report was another confirmation of your recovery. I did not realize that your form of cancer would remain in your body for the rest of your life. Also, I did understand that you would have a chemo regimen for the rest of your life.

However, your illness was far worse than I first thought. As we talked later about the degree of your illness, it became apparent how serious your situation was. When you arrived in Chicago, you told me that your blood was 90% cancerous. Your kidneys had stopped functioning due to the calcium chips that had blocked blood from entering through your kidneys. In many ways, your odds of survival were slim.

But here, you were cancer-free. I believe you were aware of all the people praying for you around the country. It was not simply good wishes. It was the power of prayer and supplication that carried you through this experience.

CRIS: Hallelujah! Thank you, Jesus! God is good all the time!

PAT: I was elated yet not surprised to hear that no Multiple Myeloma could be found in your body! What God had done in your life over this short period of time; there was nothing too hard for God!!

BERYL: I was overjoyed to the point of tears. God did it. He heard our cry. I knew God was able, but I did not know if it was His Will for you to be cancer-free. Having known others, including my sister, who had gone home to be with the Lord, I was not sure what the outcome would be. When I heard the news, I kept repeating, "Thank you, Lord." I also knew that God does not do things capriciously, but however He does it, it is for our good and His glory. I went from crying to smiling when the thought hit me, "God is up to something."

KATHY: Now, I let myself feel exuberance. I was in awe of the journey, the miracle, the blessing.

SANDRA: I felt relieved after learning you had no multiple myeloma cells in your system.

NORMAN: A mixed bag answer. Again, happy. The other part, though, I think you will remember, I asked down to what level. I know that cancer lurks unless it is caught early and excised entirely. The big question is, can it be kept in the corner, boxed in, unable to express itself again. God willing, this will be your experience.

RUTH: I am amazed, grateful. Mindful of your remarkable internal strength, drive, and perseverance, and Vanessa's sheer love, faith, and persistence.

CECILY: Unbelievable! No, not really. But I Rejoiced. Again, your faith was my guide.

LOIS: Again, I was in awe and grateful to God's mercy and love!

MARGARET: I thought it was a miracle, and I still do. God works miracles every day, and we have both been fortunate to receive two of His best ones!

JIM: A couple of years ago, I went through treatment for Hepatitis C. This was the third time I had gone through treatment. The first two were trials, and while they temporarily reduced the viral count, they ultimately were not successful. The third time was the charm, as my viral count went to zero and has stayed that way.

Hearing that your count was at zero was definitely a déjà vu experience for me. I know what it is like to wait for the numbers to come in and how it feels when the outcome is positive, so I really felt that we had a common bond from that perspective, and I could relate to how you felt.

Happy Thanksgiving

Pasadena, CA
November 24, 2016

WE CELEBRATED THANKSGIVING SATURDAY WITH OUR EXTENDED FAMILY. This family tradition returned to normal after last year's limited celebration. It was great because Bart and Charity were able to attend. It was the first time the rest of the family got to meet Charity. Everyone welcomed Charity into the family. "There's a new addition to the Dotson clan," my uncle Alfred said.

Part of our extended family tradition is to gather in the living room and have everyone say what they are thankful for. That includes the children who can talk. Vanessa and I are the last to speak. Our remarks bring the planned activities to an end, and then we close in prayer.

This year I did not want to overstate the obvious, so I did my best to keep my remarks brief. The main thing I said was this Thanksgiving celebration was much sweeter than all the rest. My cancer journey was freshly behind me, and I had an even greater appreciation for what this celebration is all about.

Being consistently thankful is now a conscious everyday sense of being for me. Many people use the acronym "TGIF" (Thank God It's Friday). Now I use a different acronym; "TGIAD," – Thank God It's Any Day. Any day above ground is a day to be thankful for. Not a single one is promised, so each day is a blessing.

Thanksgiving Day is every day for me.

Jezreel and her two boys showed up for the gathering. They are regulars at this event but were not invited last year because of doctor's orders to limit the number of attendees. I hugged her for a long time and thought about Valenda.

Jezreel, Vanessa, and I went upstairs and had our heart-to-heart talk as usual, but this time was different. Jezreel said she was doing okay, but she was more concerned about me. I assured her I was doing well, and I thanked her for helping save my life. She did not think she had done much. I sent her a questionnaire for her point of view on my journey.

Q: When did you hear about my diagnosis?

JEZ: I don't recall the month. I know that I had not heard from you or Vanessa for a while. I spoke to Vanessa, and I learned that you had hurt your back, and you were in the hospital for kidney failure. I do not remember the diagnosis of cancer until later. I remember you were getting back therapy. Cancer was not mentioned when I initially spoke to Vanessa.

When I learned of the back scans and kidney failure, I remembered thinking that you looked sick, and I told her as much. You had yellow eyes in Saugus, California, and you seemed sick when you came to move me. Your eyes were yellow, and I almost didn't want you to help because I felt something was not right.

Q: How did you hear about my diagnosis?

JEZ: Auntie Vanessa told me everything. I felt so bad because you left my house looking like you were in bad shape. The next thing I know is you are thanking me, and that's when I was told about the diagnosis. Around the same time, I began to pay attention to the Facebook post calling all to prayer.

Q: Had you heard of multiple myeloma before hearing of my diagnosis?

JEZ: No, I never heard of it. I was told you had bone cancer.

Q: How did you feel when you learned of my diagnosis?

JEZ: When I learned of bone cancer, I immediately thought of my mother. I was concerned, and I felt like I knew something really was not right. My suspicions were confirmed.

I felt awful because I thought I was on the verge of losing yet another person in my life that was about positivity and encouragement, and support.

I took it upon myself to fast in secret for a week. I prayed all day and begged God not to take you out of this life.

Q: When did you understand how serious my condition was?

JEZ: I began to read the notices on Facebook, but I knew from intuition that it was serious.

Q: Did you ever seriously question my survival?

JEZ: The report was grim, no doubt. I didn't want to allow my thoughts to think of you being taken out by bone cancer like it did my mom. I knew her diagnosis was grim, and I had zero faith in her survival.

I learned to think differently. I am a believer that we suffer ailments from weaknesses in our soul's base. I thought that you might have been keeping secrets that were eating at your foundations (your bones). Cancer is a deep dark secret that eats at us and becomes overgrown by multiple cell replication.

I was shocked because I thought you would be the type to have it all together spiritually. I learned of your frailty and prayed, according to that, more about the physical effects of cancer. I prayed towards your spirit getting stronger in the way it needed to.

Q: How did you feel when you first saw me after my diagnosis?

JEZ: I felt guilty for not speaking up when I saw you, and I felt that I did not save your life. I felt guilty for needing as much help as I did to allow you to help me move. I remember after the move, you just sat. I felt like I half-killed you.

Q: Was it difficult for you to see me in my physical condition?

JEZ: I knew that I did all that I could do to help your condition. After fasting and reading the positive updates on Facebook, I knew you would beat cancer.

The most difficult part was that my mom was gone, and she did not have so many in prayer for her survival. A twinge of bitterness set in for her lack of support. But ultimately, I was grateful and knew you were winning the war on cancer. I had zero doubts about your survival.

Q: How did you feel when you learned i was going to undergo a stem cell transplant?

JEZ: I felt that it is important to be financially stable. I became more driven to be financially stable and more connected to my community. I learned that money was why you could get stem cell surgery. Being connected to the gospel type of community is, and was, equally important.

Q: How did you feel when you learned i was going to undergo Vertebrae Replacement surgery?

JEZ: All of the procedures seemed like science fiction, and I was in awe at all that was available. It didn't seem to be available for my mom.

Q: What were your thoughts about the Dotson Celebration in Rancho Cucamonga?

JEZ: The celebration was amazing to me; it is something I wish that I could have had. I wish all of these people could have been gathered around for my Mom's funeral. It was nice to see them gathered for a saved and healed life.

Q: How did you feel when you learned i was in remission?

JEZ: I was not surprised; it was expected.

Q: Did you participate in the fast during the month of October 2016?

JEZ: I did not participate in a group fast; I did not know about it.

I fast regularly every Wednesday, and I learned that it was very powerful. I started the fasting chapter in my life to help save your life. It was like in the biblical days of the Ninevites, when even the cattle had to fast for consecration.

Q: How did you feel when you learned no multiple myeloma cells could be seen in november 2016?

JEZ: None of this was a shock; we had so many in agreement for your healing.

Vanessa Foster-Dotson
November 23, 2016

Happy Thanksgiving!!! I have so much to be thankful for. The first thing that I want to say thank you for is for each of you! Thank you for praying for, and supporting Henry and me, as we have journeyed down the Multiple Myeloma path.

This has been an unknown and windy path with bumps along the way. Henry has always stated that he is at peace because no matter what happens, he knows that he will be alright because he knows that God has his back. I also have faith, and I definitely believe that God has our backs.

However, this journey has still been a scary one for me. Finding myself in the suburbs of Chicago with an extremely sick husband and no family or friends anywhere around was very uncomfortable. Having to make life or death medical decisions was scary. Watching Henry suffer and literally fight for every second of his life was difficult, to say the least. Going through the numerous medical appointments and procedures was a bit nerve-racking.

All the while, making sure that the lights stayed on, food was on the table, and the bills got paid. It was an unfamiliar juggling act. I guess that I could go on and on. But my point is, through it all, God was with us, and so were you.

I will never forget that God takes care of His children and has a plan for our lives, and Henry and I are His children. I know that our Multiple Myeloma journey did not take God by surprise. However, I was definitely surprised.

So, thank you so much for your prayers, fasting, and all forms of support. You will never know how much it meant to me. You provided me with the strength to move forward when I was weary. You were my voice when I was weak.

So, at this point, all I can do is say thank you, and please know that each of you is greatly appreciated. The prayer group was a lifeline for me in many ways.

If you were able to read the last post, Henry's recent diagnosis is a huge blessing. From 90% cancerous blood to no trace of cancer! ABSOLUTELY AWESOME!!! I am so thankful that God has decided to keep Henry in my life.

continued

You know, sometimes when you are married, you may slightly take your spouse for granted. It's not intentional. It just happens. You may let the busyness of life rob precious time. Although that I am far from perfect, I am trying hard to spend every moment that I can to engage with Henry. I cannot imagine a life without him.

A few years ago, I gave him a 50th birthday party, and I did not take the opportunity to videotape him dancing with our children. Well, thanks to his recovery, I got a second chance. Look at him dancing below at our son's wedding reception. What would my life be like without Henry's positive spirit? I am so thankful for having Henry in my life.

I am also thankful to have my mother and Rosalind still in my life. Rosalind's cancer has stabilized. She is not "out of the woods," but she is doing so much better. She is eating, keeping up her weight, and sounds strong on the phone.

My mother is still struggling. The doctors are saying that there isn't anything that they can do to reverse her cancer. Needless to say, this is extremely difficult to accept. I just want the cancer to go away. I have to rest in my faith that this again is not a surprise to God, and He is following the plan for my mother's life. I must find comfort in knowing that she is still here, being her fun-loving self. I can't wait to see her and make new memories.

I am also thankful for my sister, Leavanna Parker, her husband Jarvis, and their kids. I am just thankful for who they are and what they do.

I am thankful for our children, Talia and Henry IV. As they continue to grow and learn how to navigate their own paths and their bumps, I am proud of the people that they are becoming.

Well, as you may be able to tell, I am thankful for so many things. I have a blessed life. I am thankful for your agreeing to be a part of Henry's prayer group and for allowing us to communicate his status in this format. You have reinforced my belief in the power of prayer.

As per the last post by Henry, now that there aren't any traces of cancer in his blood, we are entering a new phase of our lives. So, it saddens me to say that this is my last planned post. But before I go, I want to take a moment to revisit some of my past prayer requests one more time. God has answered many of our prayers!

May you and your family have a blessed and wonderful Thanksgiving!

continued

Status Updates and Prayer Requests:

- My mother, Annie Foster (Rare Breast Cancer): See above. Please pray for a full recovery and no pain.
- Rosalind (Ovarian Cancer): See above. Please pray for a full recovery and continued strength and appetite.
- Margaret (Ovarian Cancer): Continues to do well and is still in remission. Please pray for continued remission.
- Mr. C (Multiple Myeloma): Continues to do well. Had the same test as Henry and only had a very small trace of MM in his blood. Please pray for a full recovery—no traces of MM.
- Mr. Z (Multiple Myeloma): Continues to do well. He has some pains. Please pray for a full recovery—no traces of MM.
- Uncle Alfred Dotson (Multiple Myeloma): Continues to improve. Please pray for a full recovery—no traces of MM.

Prayer Requests:

1. Complete healing for Henry. No permanent back damage, no fevers.
2. Please say a special prayer for Lewis's father, who was diagnosed with pancreatic cancer.
3. General prayer for all of the family members and friends of anyone that is reading this update and has recently been diagnosed, or is suffering from, cancer or some other life-threatening health challenge.

Prayers Answered for Henry:

1. Healthy kidneys - no dialysis
2. Healthy eyes
3. Increased platelet count
4. Clarity of thoughts and words
5. Exponential blood count level increase
6. Renewed spirit
7. Release from CTCA and return home
8. Easy transition to being in CA
9. Stabilized blood counts...all counts being positive
10. Stabilized kidney counts

continued

> 11. No long-term anemia
> 12. Increased appetite and weight
> 13. Continued improved strength and movement
> 14. Total favor in regard to all aspects of Henry's back surgery that took place on May 18th, as well as a speedy and full recovery.
> 15. Complete healing – body, mind, soul, and spirit. (no cancer, no pain, no infections, etc.).
>
> 👍 23   Seen by 23   5 Comments
>
> **BC:** I am sending prayers for everything on your list and more! God is amazing!!!
>
> **DW:** I am always praying for you all. God, heal Henry, Lord Jesus, and comfort the entire family. Amen.
>
> **VP:** Always in my prayers.
>
> **GA:** I will continue to keep you two in my thoughts and prayers.

Q: How did you feel about the Thanksgiving 2016 celebration in terms of my health condition?

CHARITY: I was so grateful to be a part of the celebration both for a holiday and for your health. It was great to see you up and around the house, and even cooking your famous salmon I had heard so much about. I know you hadn't been able to cook it the year before. It seemed like you were really doing better than even the times I had seen you previously that year.

What's Left

"One never notices what has been done; one can only see what remains to be done."
— Marie Curie

Pasadena, CA
November 26, 2016

A WEEK AFTER THE GREAT NEWS OF MY HEALING, I FOUND MYSELF IN UNFAMILIAR TERRITORY. I spoke with my oncologist to find out what was left to do before I would begin what would be the "new normal."

The takeaways from the conversation were that: 1) I would continue to have annual bone marrow biopsies in late October as long as I was on the clinical trial with Ninlaro; 2) I will receive maintenance doses of chemotherapy indefinitely, or until there is a cure for Multiple Myeloma, and 3) I would need to get my childhood vaccinations two years after the Stem Cell Transplant. That means sometime after February 25, 2018.

I asked my oncologist when I would be able to get back to work, which includes domestic and international travel. He advised me to take it slow. Continue with physical therapy and regular exercise to build up my strength and endurance. As far as travel goes, start with short personal trips to see how that works out. Then, try longer domestic trips, eventually working up to an international trip.

I shared what my oncologist said with Vanessa. She was okay with the medical treatments that remain, but not the work travel. We will have to cross that bridge when we get to it.

So, what's left? More physical therapy. Baby steps in terms of travel. I will have to go with the flow instead of setting a date for reaching the "new normal." It will come when it comes. Fortunately, I have learned to persevere with a good attitude because the Bible says:

"Let perseverance finish its work so that you may be mature and complete, not lacking anything."
— James 1:4, New International Version

> *"So do not throw away your confidence; it holds a great reward. You need to persevere, so that after you have done the will of God, you will receive what He has promised."*
> — Hebrews 10:35-36, Berean Study Bible

> *"...we have gained access by faith into this grace in which we stand. And we rejoice in the hope of the glory of God. Not only that, but we also rejoice in our sufferings, because we know that suffering produces perseverance; perseverance, character; and character, hope. And hope does not disappoint us, because God has poured out His love into our hearts through the Holy Spirit, whom He has given us."*
> — Romans 5:3-5, Berean Study Bible

From faith to grace, from grace to joy, to joy in perseverance, from perseverance to character, and from character to hope. Hope in receiving what God has promised. This is truly the dawn of a new day!

PART SIX:
EPILOGUE

"A true epilogue is removed from the story in time or space. That's the reason it is called an 'Epilogue'; the label serves to alert the reader that the story itself is over, but we are going to now see a distant result or consequence of that story."

— Nancy Kress

Pasadena, CA
December 2020

IT HAS BEEN A LITTLE MORE THAN FOUR YEARS SINCE I ACHIEVED REMISSION, WITH NO SIGN OF MYELOMA SEEN IN MY BODY. Since that time, many things have happened that are a consequence of the journey. I present them here organized by topic.

The Genesis of this Book

The most significant consequence of this story is the writing of this book. Shortly after I made what I thought would be my last post to the secret Facebook page in November 2016, God planted a seed in my mind. It was an urging to start a preface to a book I never intended to write. In obedience, I wrote the first draft of the preface of this book in December of 2016, just weeks after receiving the results of the MRD test. I struggled to do so because I had to ask myself the initial hard questions you find in the preface. The first draft was only four paragraphs long; the first four paragraphs of the final version of the preface. After completing the first draft, I set it aside, thinking I had been obedient to God, and I was done.

Friday Late-Night Prayer Meeting

Our church holds Friday late-night prayer meetings on the last Friday of every month. We gather to participate in corporate prayer around 7:00 p.m. and respond to prayer requests until midnight. Sometimes during these meetings, someone will give a testimony about how their prayers were answered.

Vanessa and I received a call from our pastor asking if we would give our testimony about my cancer journey at the January 2017 late-night prayer meeting. We agreed, thinking we would just come up to the front of the congregation and share for five to ten minutes. Nothing could have been further from the truth.

Two high chairs and a regular-size living room chair replaced the furnishings that normally decorated the front of the church. There were also three microphones set up. The pastor called Vanessa and me up to the front and conducted a one-hour interview about our journey. It took us by surprise, but we handled it. I thought if our testimony could help someone going through a challenge in their life, then I was willing to share it. An audio recording was made of the interview and copied onto CDs.

On Sunday, our pastor encouraged those who attended the two church services to get a copy of our testimony. After the service we attended, a worker from the bookstore came to me and said, "Henry, your CDs are selling like hotcakes!" (Our church sells copies of the recorded messages for $2 to recover the cost of the blank CDs). I thought that was good because our testimony could help more people than those who attended the late-night prayer meeting.

Praise Reports

In the following weeks, I began to get phone calls and text messages from people who had listened to the CD. Some just wanted to thank us for our testimony. Many said it was just what they needed to hear, and it ministered to them. Others shared praise reports about how they had sent a copy of the CD to people in their sphere of influence, and those people were greatly encouraged. Still, others called asking me to speak to them or someone else who was dealing with cancer.

"You ought to write a book. It would be very helpful," was the response repeated with greater and greater frequency.

A Word From God

At first, I would respond to the remark by saying something like, "I've never really seriously thought about doing that." But as time went on, I found myself continuing to have to reply to the same remark. My response gradually changed to, *"I've thought about it, but I'm not sure if that is something I want to do."* I was reluctant. In part because I wanted to get back to work, and partly because I knew it would take a lot of time and effort to do it right, based on how I had struggled to write the first draft of the preface.

Finally, in late April of 2017, while in a light afternoon sleep, I heard God's still voice say to me:

> "Henry, one of the reasons I spared your life was for you to tell your story of miraculous healing. You will bless many with your testimony because it will be an encouragement to them and a reminder that I am the living God and I am still in the miracle-making business.
>
> I have been speaking to you through others when they were saying to you, 'You ought to write a book.' I am speaking to you now as confirmation of what they have been saying.

I know you desire to return to work, to return to being self-employed doing something you are passionate about. To that, I say to you, 'Seek ye first My kingdom and My righteousness, and all these things will be added unto you.

I know you are concerned about how long it might take; and that you want to do it right. To that, I say to be anxious about nothing. It will take as long as it takes. You will know it is done when it is done. You will do it right as long as you allow your writing to be led by the Holy Spirit. This is your story, but it also My story.

I am not a man that I should lie, or a son of man, that I should change My mind. I am the same yesterday, today, and forever."

I woke from my sleep feeling well-rested and at peace. It was the same peace I felt when I rose from my sofa after being in despair the first three days of my divorce journey. I immediately got up and began to do more work on the preface and write the book outline.

While writing this book, I had the opportunity to go back to CTCA in Zion, IL, and personally thank my two lead doctors and several of my caregivers for working so hard to help save my life. It was a little surreal to go back to that place where so much of my healing took place. I thanked my healthcare providers, and I took a moment to thank God again for all He had done for me.

> "God gave you a gift of 86,400 seconds today. Have you used one to say thank you?"
> — William A. Ward

Time with the Community

At the end of 2016, I was still attending two cancer support groups. One was the original group I joined at CSCP. The other was the San Gabriel Valley Multiple Myeloma Support Group. In March 2017, I recognized that I was not getting much out of the original group.

I spoke with Wendy, the program director, about it. She said another group focuses on living with cancer instead of the early stages of a cancer diagnosis. I asked her when I should change groups. She said it varies from individual to individual. Typically, after about a year or a year and a half, people make the change. She added, "You will know when it's time to leave the group."

That time came later that month. I felt like I was still contributing, but I was not leaving with my needs met. CSCP assigned a new facilitator to the group around that same time. That made my departure easier for me.

I did not, however, join a new group. I did not feel as though I needed support when it came to living with cancer. I felt the Multiple Myeloma support group sufficiently met my need for community support. Vanessa and I continue to attend those meetings today.

Return to Work

I returned to work in early 2017; around 18 months from when I was diagnosed with Multiple Myeloma in Zion. God was true to his Word. I did not miss a beat upon my return. I returned to work and was twice as busy as I was when I had to stop because of the diagnosis. I was blessed more than I could have possibly imagined.

Not only was I able to return to work, but I was also able to resume my participation as a member of a U.S. technical advisory group that works to develop international standards for the utility industry. I was even able to take on more responsibility with the standards development body. As an active member, I have traveled internationally and domestically to attend face-to-face meetings with no limitations due to my health.

I became busier when I returned to work than I was before I left. I was traveling two weeks out of the month for a year. I managed my chemotherapy treatments while on travel because I was taking Ninlaro in pill form. That meant I did not have to go to City of Hope as often.

When it comes to international travel, Vanessa and I have decided how best to handle it with the appropriate safety precautions. From now on, I do not travel abroad without Vanessa coming along. She has the flexibility to work from anywhere as long as she has internet connectivity. I also get medivac insurance in case something happens while on travel, and I need to get back to City of Hope quickly.

I wondered how Job felt when God restored to him everything in abundance. I am thankful that God is the same yesterday, today, and tomorrow. He did it for Job, and He's done it for me.

Health Challenges

I have experienced some additional health challenges since the end of the story. Some minor and one in particular that again took a miracle from God to save my life.

A Compromised Immune System

Once I was in remission, my active treatment plan changed to a maintenance treatment plan. My maintenance treatment plan consists of a significantly reduced amount of chemotherapy medication to keep the Multiple Myeloma cells from becoming active again. One of the side effects of the medication is a decrease in my white blood cell count, which makes my immune system weaker than the average person's. The medical terminology is a "compromised immune system."

Having a compromised immune system means I need to contact City of Hope whenever my vital signs stray from the "normal" range. If my pressure goes up, or I have a fever, or if my pulse quickens, my body is trying to fight some bacterial or viral infection. I oftentimes am instructed to come to City of Hope to be examined to determine what my body is fighting. Once they identify what the specific bacteria or virus is, they administer the appropriate antibiotic or anti-viral medication to help my immune system fight the invader.

If I get to City of Hope right away, these visits can last from 4 hours to 3 days, depending on how long it takes for my vital signs to return to the normal range. In these cases, I experience minimal discomfort, and my health condition is slightly affected. If I do not get to City of Hope (or some other hospital) promptly, the infection has the opportunity to grow untreated and will most likely overwhelm my immune system. Since I have been in remission, I had one occasion when I did not get to a hospital promptly, and it almost cost me my life.

One More Miracle

Vanessa and I visited Bart's family in Arizona during the Christmas Holidays in December 2017. While attending a gathering on Christmas evening, I had a visceral response to some infection that attacked my body. The feeling was so strong that I told Vanessa I wanted to go back to the hotel and lie down. We stopped by a retail pharmacy on the way back to the hotel and picked up some over-the-counter cold and flu medication.

Things did not go well after we returned to the hotel. My condition continued to deteriorate. Ultimately, I was admitted to a hospital in Arizona. Once again, Vanessa called upon the prayer team for their support. And once again, they did not disappoint.

Epilogue

Tempe, AZ
December 31, 2017

 Vanessa Foster-Dotson
December 31, 2017

Hello Dear Prayer Team!

I was hoping that I would not need to come to you again, at least not so soon. But my dear Henry needs prayer. We have been in AZ to visit our son, daughter-in-love, and new grandson since Friday, December 22nd. We were due to return Friday, 12/29, but we are still in AZ. Henry had been coughing for a while prior to our visit, but his coughing actually got significantly better during the week before we departed. We thought that he was over whatever he had. Doctors said that the coughing was going around, typically lasts for several weeks, and that it was nothing to worry about...just take some over-the-counter meds, and all should be good.

Well, on Christmas evening, Henry's coughing started to get much worse. He stayed in bed all day Tuesday, didn't eat, his walking was labored, and he had a fever. We went to the emergency room on Wednesday, 12/27. Henry had a high fever, like 104, his kidneys were in bad condition because he was dehydrated, and the coughing was horrible...a deep, persistent, dry cough with nothing coming up.

Henry was immediately given a lot of fluids, and his kidneys responded positively. After several tests, it was determined that Henry has RSV, a respiratory virus.

Treatment began for the RSV. Henry's initial temperature still stayed around 104, spiked at 106, and got as low as 98.6. It is now around 101. In an effort to get his fever down, he is sleeping on a cooling blanket, which is set to about 44 degrees. He is extremely uncomfortable. The doctors believe that he also has some type of bacterial infection, but they have not been able to determine what it is as yet. Meanwhile, I am also showing cold symptoms and have stayed at the hotel on a couple of occasions.

Bottom line, please pray for my baby once again. Initially, I thought that maybe Henry just had a bad cough, and that he needed to get some type of serious medicine. But it is much more. We thought that his immune system was somewhat back to normal, but we have learned over the last few days that as long as he is taking chemo, his immune system is compromised. So we vowed to take better care of

continued

ourselves going forward...like SERIOUSLY!!! But for now, please pray that:

1. Henry's temperature goes back down to normal and stays there without having to use a cooling blanket.
2. The doctors are able to identify the bacterial infection that is affecting Henry's body and treat it quickly.
3. Henry is able to cough up any mucus that is in his chest.
4. Henry does not have any negative side effects from the medicines that he is being given...physically, mentally, emotionally, etc.
5. Henry is returned to complete health quickly.
6. We are able to be consistent in taking better care of ourselves going forward.

Thank you all once again for participating in this corporate prayer. I was trying to hold things down, but this is getting bigger than me. I am not sure why we are experiencing these things, or what God has in store for us. But we know whose we are, and we know that God is always faithful.

I will do my best to keep you updated on Henry's progress.

Thank you once again, and God Bless!

👍 33   Seen by 91   Comments

TB We cover both of you with the blood of Jesus and our confession of faith. We know that Jesus heals and is an advocate for his children. We curse every disease at its root. We stand together on one accord putting these diseases to flight. EXPECTING ANOTHER MIRACLE, my dear cousins.

AR God is faithful. If he did it before, he can do it again! I'll pray for your specific requests.

CS I pray that God has given you both strong bodies and that this bad virus leaves your body today—praying that Henry returns to his healthy state.

WL I am praying for Henry that he is healed from the top of his head to the soles of his feet. Lord touch the coughing that it cease in the name of Jesus.

Epilogue

Thank God that he has you, Vanessa. As his prayer warriors, we also stand in agreement with each issue that you stated and that they are addressed and healed. Please give Henry my love.

You have submitted your petition, Nessa. I am standing in agreement with you and thanking God for not only hearing but answering your prayers! The prayers of a righteous man availeth much! Heal Lord as only you can in the name of Jesus!!

My condition got worse before it got better. I had contracted two different infections: one bacterial and one viral. I experience total failure (not collapse) of my right lung. At one point, my doctor told Vanessa in my presence, "If this treatment doesn't work, we may have to put him on life support." That got my attention. Again, I did not feel as bad as I imagined I would if I were that close to death.

Once again, God heard the corporate prayers that went up on my behalf. After a twelve-day stay in the hospital, I recovered and was never placed on life support. When I returned to California, my oncologist ordered chest x-rays and other respiratory tests. When the results came in, he said, "Your lungs are in better shape than they were when you left to go to Arizona. That was the best possible outcome we could have received." I knew it was another miracle from God.

Once again, Vanessa gave me the opportunity to submit a post to the secret Facebook page to express my gratitude.

Tempe, AZ
January 10, 2018
Great Is Thy Faithfulness

Henry B. Dotson III
January 10, 2018

GREAT IS THY FAITHFULNESS

Happy Belated New Year and Greetings to all my FB Prayer Group family! Once again, I humbly come before you to thank you all for all of your prayers and support during my last health challenge. Words cannot express how much my soul and body were strengthened by your prayers, well wishes, and words of encouragement. I want to especially thank Jackie, Alexa, Annette, and the pastors from Bart's church for taking the time to come to visit me in the hospital. Jackie, thank you so much for spending time with Vanessa, as caregivers

continued

need attention just as much as the ones receiving care. You are truly sisters in Christ, and we are blessed to have you in our lives.

Special thanks go out to one of my brothers in my community of authentic men. Larry came out from CA to visit me while in the hospital. While we ran across each other sporadically growing up in South LA, we cemented our friendship in college. I could not ask for a finer friend. When I hurt, he hurts. When I rejoice, he rejoices. We celebrate the good and the bad, and he was there for me, as usual. What more could one want or ask?

I was also encouraged by my best friend, Norman. While he could not come out to visit, he was always checking up with me by text or by phone. There is something unspoken between the two of us that gives me a sense of peace and being cared about that is hard to describe. I do not try to figure it out; I am just glad to claim him as part of my tribe.

Family is chicken soup for the soul. Nothing warmed my heart more than to have Talia come out from CA to just be there with me in my hospital room. No words needed to be said. Just knowing she was there did wonders for me. Bart came by as often as he could, during lunch breaks and after work. Hugging my son, or just the touch of his hand on my shoulder, meant the world to me.

Vanessa is my rock, my bride, my gift from God. Continually living up to her marriage vows to be with me through it all...my Proverbs 31 woman. I count it all joy.

For the rest of you who offered up your prayers and were not able to be there in person, I have a word for you. Whether you know it or not, you are all prayer warriors! Some of you may not quite know what I mean, so let me try to explain. You individually committed yourselves to collectively offer up your prayers to intervene on my behalf for God to provide my divine healing. By doing so, you stepped out in faith that God would hear your collective prayers and that I would be healed. That is huge! Your faith mixed with His faithfulness overcomes he that is in the world looking to steal, kill, and destroy.

The LORD'S loving kindnesses indeed never cease, For His compassions never fail. They are new every morning; Great is Your faithfulness. *"The LORD is my portion,"* says my soul, *"Therefore I have hope in Him."* — Lamentations 3:22-24.

It is because of His faithfulness that we have the power of corporate prayer. So, if you ever doubted the power of prayer or just the power

continued

of your prayers, you have no reason to doubt it any longer. Through your corporate prayer and His faithfulness, you are your own living witness and testimony to what can be done as a prayer warrior! I am healed in the name above every name!

The refrain from the hymn, "Great Is Thy Faithfulness," by William Runyan is so appropriate that I have included it for your consideration:

> *Great Is Thy faithfulness!*
> *Great Is Thy faithfulness!*
> *Morning by morning new mercies I see.*
> *All I have needed Thy hand hath provided.*
> *Great is Thy Faithfulness, Lord unto me!*

Lastly, I want to remind you all that while corporate prayer is one of the most powerful weapons we have, everything shall be done according to the Sovereign Will of God.

> *"There is an appointed time for everything. And there is a time for every event under heaven – A time to give birth and a time to die."* — Ecclesiastes 3:1-2

My dear friend Steve passed away from complications due to his battle with MM a few days ago. We were reacquainted through divine appointment at City of Hope as we both prepared for Stem Cell Transplants. We kept in touch regularly, discussing the procedures and treatments we were receiving as only cancer patients can. More importantly, we visited each other by phone, text, and in the hospital, talking about the goodness of God and His mercy. Please add Steve's family to your list of those in need of corporate prayer as they grieve the loss of their loved one and celebrate his life.

This is a reminder to me that we all have a set number of days to fulfill our purpose on the earth. When we have each run our race, it will be time to return to the God of our fathers according to His divine Wisdom. So let us not get weary in well-doing. Let us all continue to use our days to leave this place better than when we found it. Let us be that light upon a hill that cannot be hidden. Always be prepared to give an account to everyone who asks you to give the reason for the hope that lives in you, but be sure to respond with gentleness and respect. Let us pray for the next generation of saints that will take our place in the fulfillment of God's purpose on the earth.

continued

Please continue to pray for us and to pray for one another. God has given us all two precious gifts; a portion of time and a portion of health and strength. Let us use them wisely and stay close to the Lord.

Be Well and God Bless

- Henry

Comments

PO — Henry, you are always in my prayers. My husband and I are a part of the worship team at our church and guess what hymn we sang just this past Sunday....You guessed it...Great is Thy Faithfulness! How fitting is that??? Stay strong, my friend, stay strong. God is good!

LW — Bernard, thank you for posting this. It just warms my soul to see God at work in your healing AND your relationship with Vanessa. My prayers and thoughts continue to be with you in this season of healing: much love, your other little sister, Lori.

JD — Amen, Amen, and very well said, my friend - my brother!! My love for you and Vanessa goes beyond words!! I am continually praying for you. Be well, and looking forward to seeing you soon in Pasadena.

PM — My beloved Henry and Vanessa, the two of you, are the most special people in my world. I love your testimony, and I love the way you two love each other. You are a powerful example of what prayer can do. Thank God for allowing you to go through this challenge of life-threatening illness again and conquering it once more. I also thank him for your victory of healing and faithfulness. God bless you and keep you!!!

LD — Awesome words, Henry. Our prayer line was just praying for you this morning, as well as me praying for you daily. Be very blessed!

CL — Powerful thank you letter. It is filled with love, wisdom, and revelation knowledge, Henry.

Epilogue

By now, I am sure that you, the reader, know that I do not miss an opportunity to reflect on significant events in my life. My second near-death experience was no exception. After some reflection, I again made a post to the secret Facebook page.

Pasadena, CA
January 21, 2018
One More Thing

Henry B. Dotson III
January 21, 2018

ONE MORE THING

Greetings Prayer Team,

In my quiet time with the Lord, I asked Him was there any other lessons He was trying to teach us when He miraculously brought us through another life-threatening trial. He answered me in the spirit and said, "There's one more thing…"

They say confession is good for the soul but bad for the reputation. This may be true, but I am not as much concerned about my reputation before men as I am concerned about my integrity and walking in the Will of God. I believe if I strive to be a man of integrity, a good reputation before men will follow, despite the truths revealed during confession. I know if I am in the Will of God, all things will work for my good.

So, in a moment of transparency and confession, but also in obedience to the Will of God, let me tell you One More Thing. But first, my confession.

My falling deathly ill in Arizona was my fault. I did not follow the instructions I was given at City of Hope about the precautions I need to take as a patient that has taken and continues to take chemotherapeutic medication.

I was told more than a year ago that as a chemo patient, I am "immuno-compromised." What that means is because I take chemo, my immune system is not as strong or as effective as someone who has not taken chemo. So I was told whenever I have symptoms of any kind (a persistent cough, runny nose, chills, headache, etc.), I need to immediately check my vital signs (temperature, blood pressure, heart rate). If any of my vital signs are not normal, I need to proceed immediately to the hospital.

continued

Abnormal vital signs are an indication that a virus or some kind of bug (bacteria) is attacking my body and my immune system is fighting back. My immune system needs help to fight off these attackers. So by going immediately to the hospital, they can find out as soon as possible what foreign invader I am dealing with. Once they know that, they have plenty of medications to supplement my immune system and help kill off the attackers. This fast action minimizes the damage caused by the attackers.

I fell ill Christmas evening. My symptoms were a sudden weakness and an overall bad feeling. I did not immediately check my vital signs. Instead, I went to bed at the hotel. The next day I started to run a fever. I did not need to check my vital signs at that point. I already knew my temperature was out of the normal range. I did not go immediately to the hospital. Instead, I spent the day and night in bed, taking NyQuil and putting a cold washcloth on my head and neck.

It wasn't until the next day, December 27th, two days after I fell under attack, and at Vanessa's insistence, that I went to the hospital. By then, my immune system was overwhelmed, and my body was under serious, life-threatening attack.

I confess that it was I that brought this on myself.

So, what is the One More Thing God wants us to learn from this? It is that He will never leave us or forsake us, even if we are the cause of our own misery, suffering, trials, tribulations, and distress.

In John 10:11-14, Jesus says that He is the "Good Shepherd," and the Good Shepherd lays down His life for His sheep, especially when the wolf pounces and scatters the flock. In Luke 15:4-6, Jesus tells the Parable of The Lost Sheep where He says,

> *"What man among you, if he has one hundred sheep and loses one of them, does not leave the ninety-nine in the pasture and go after the one that is lost until he finds it? And when he finds it, he joyfully puts it on his shoulders, comes home, and calls together his friends and neighbors to tell them, 'Rejoice with me, for I have found my lost sheep!'"*

In my situation, I was the lost sheep. I was lost because I was not obedient to God's words spoken to me through the health care providers at City of Hope about how I should take care of myself. But because there is a Good Shepherd, who laid down His life for me on the Cross, who would not leave me nor forsake me, He came after me

continued

with all His healing power, restored my health, and brought me back to safety. Safety from the wolf that was trying to destroy me in my moment of physical weakness.

Again, to God be the glory for the things He has done!

- Henry

　　　　　　　　　　　　　　　　　　　　　　　　Comments

RH Amen. Praise God for His goodness and grace! Thank you for this message. I know I need to obey in order to succeed and overcome in life. Thank you for the reminder.!

JW Henry, Our God, is Good. We all make mistakes or not-so-good decisions. All of us, but it was His Grace that brought you through again. You are a faithful servant and blessed. May God continue to bless you and my friend and sister Vanessa.

TC I'm so glad you are Human...that's why you are Loved sooo very much!

PH I am inspired by God's Word flowing through you. In my best Heavy D voice, I got nothing but love for ya'!

CC Love and blessings to you. Pray about wearing a mask when out in public. This latest flu bug is treacherous.

COVID-19

When the COVID-19 pandemic hit, Vanessa immediately put me on lockdown. As a cancer patient, I am in one of the high-risk categories due to my compromised immune system. Vanessa said we'd been through too much to take any chances. She never wanted to go through that again.

As a result, the only place I go is to City of Hope once a week for my maintenance chemotherapy treatment. It has not been a difficult adjustment. Although a couple of times, I stopped at our pharmacy on the way home from City of Hope to buy some Reese's peanut butter cups.

Vanessa found out when she saw the wrappers in the trash can and read me the riot act. She also played the guilt card, saying I had betrayed her trust. I apologized and asked for her forgiveness. I was in the dog house for a few days, but she graciously commuted my sentence. I have been on the straight and narrow ever since. It became much easier once I discovered I could buy Reese's peanut butter cups at the gift store at City of Hope, and Vanessa started bringing home the Family Size package when she went shopping.

The major difference is that I no longer travel for work. But most of my clients are working from home, and Zoom meetings replace face-to-face meetings.

The only real challenge is not getting together with family and friends like we used to. We have had dinner with one couple at a time in our backyard. We maintained social distancing and were still able to enjoy the company.

Epilogue

HomeGoings

"If we deny love that is given to us, if we refuse to give love because we fear pain or loss, then our lives will be empty, our loss greater."
— Margaret Weiss

On Thursday, December 22, 2016, Vanessa's mother, Annie R. Foster, transitioned from this side of eternity to be with her Lord and Savior. We were in New Jersey for the Christmas holidays when her condition started to deteriorate. Vanessa and I, along with her sister's family, were with her when she took her last breath. It was a privilege to be there to let her know she was loved and to witness her transition. For me, the only thing that compares with witnessing a transition due to natural causes is witnessing the birth of a child.

On Saturday, July 1, 2017, we received the news that Vanessa's best friend for the last 30 years, Rosalind Gardner, transitioned to be with her Lord and Savior. We attended her homegoing service in Delaware. It was a very, very difficult time for Vanessa. She was still going through the grieving process over the loss of her mother when we received the news. Here are her thoughts about her BFF:

> "Gone too soon! I had moved from the east coast and arrived at my new job. You greeted me with "Hi! My name is Rosalind. Nice to meet you." Thus began our BFF bond.
>
> We went to grad school together; we were roommates, we bought a house together, we shared, we talked, we laughed, we cried, and we were so different but yet so much alike.
>
> I learned many things from you, my dear Rozzy. You were my big sister, always sharing life lessons.
>
> You provided strength as I struggled to support Henry during his cancer battle.
>
> You did not want to tell me that your cancer had returned. Finally, you told me. We prayed, and I believed that you would get better just like Henry was getting better.

> *I will never forget the morning that you called and said that you were going into hospice. You asked, "Vanessa, does this mean that I am going to die?"*
>
> *I think about you all of the time. I miss you! Your spirit is in this book. Thank you for being such an important part of my life."*

I saw God comfort her as only He can. We serve a mighty God!

As mentioned before, in January 2018, my friend Steve, who also had Multiple Myeloma, and received a Stem Cell Transplant at City of Hope, transitioned to be with the Lord. It was a reminder that this disease continues to be the cause of death, and the grace of God saved me.

October 10, 2018, Vanessa's aunt, her mother's youngest sister, Edna Walton, transitioned to be with the Lord. On March 26, 2019, Vanessa's aunt, her mother's only surviving sister, Lucy Smith, transitioned to be with the Lord. Vanessa's mother has one surviving sibling, her brother George.

On January 12, 2020, we received news that our friend Linda, who hosted our Dotson Celebration with her husband Henry, transitioned to be with the Lord. At the time of this writing, the Facebook Prayer Team is still praying for the family.

> *"Blessed are those who mourn, for they will be comforted"*
> — Matthew 5:4, English Standard Version

> *"In My Father's house are many rooms. If it were not so, would I have told you that I am going there to prepare a place for you?"*
> — John 14:2, Berean Study Bible

Epilogue

New Additions

"Children are indeed a heritage from the Lord, and the fruit of the womb is His reward. Like arrows in the hand of a warrior, so are the children born in one's youth. Blessed is the man whose quiver is full of them." — Psalm 127:3-5, Berean Study Bible

Our son and daughter-in-law have been blessed with three new additions to the family since the end of the story: Adam Henry Dotson was born September 28, 2017; Daisy Joy Dotson was born June 18, 2019; and Benjamin Kelly Dotson was born September 12, 2020.

Adam has experienced significant health challenges due to a bacterial infection he contracted at five months old. He has experienced brain trauma as a result of the infection, and he requires special care. We continue to lift him up in prayer and give thanks to God in anticipation of Adam's ultimate healing.

Vanessa and I have been able to travel to Arizona to see Adam and Daisy. We have not been able to see Benjamin due to COVID-19 imposed travel restrictions.

"Every child born into the world is a new thought of God, an ever-fresh and radiant possibility." — Kate Douglas Wiggin

Celebrations

"We turn not older with years, but newer every day."
— Emily Dickinson

60th Birthday

Twenty years after Vanessa planned my first "surprise" birthday party (the one where I heard from God), She gave me a "surprise" 60th birthday party in October 2017. This celebration was all the sweeter because there was a time when we were not sure that I would see my 60th birthday.

It was not a surprise that she had planned something "big" for this milestone birthday. It was obvious we had reason to celebrate. What was a surprise was the venue and the number of people who attended the celebration.

The celebration took place at the clubhouse of the golf course next to the Rose Bowl in Pasadena. It was a catered event, and there was a DJ. 150 "close" family and friends were there, including east coast relatives. Vanessa told me she had invited a little over 300, so I only saw one-half of the invitees who wanted to be there.

It was humbling and gratifying to see so many people there celebrating with me. I've never really thought about how many people are special to me. I just know that I am exceedingly blessed to have many people I can say are true friends when many people do not have a single true friend.

I was a little overwhelmed because I have never seen so many at the same time! As much as they said I was a blessing to them, I know that I am the one blessed more abundantly than they could ever know because they are a part of my life. I thank God for them all.

At this celebration, I am happy to report that I did not abandon Vanessa like before. I am still a work in progress, but there was no work to be done on this occasion. I am getting better at making her a part of what I do as an extrovert in social settings. God is not through with me yet!

One of the highlights of the evening was when those in attendance were given the opportunity to say a few words to me. Each one had touching kind words to say, and I enjoyed every word.

Jezreel came forward and shared her thoughts about me and the joy she felt just being there to celebrate. As she spoke, I thought about Valenda and what she said at my 40th birthday party. I felt her presence, and I felt as if our relationship had come full circle.

All things had worked together for my good.

Epilogue

20th Wedding Anniversary

On September 4, 2018, Vanessa and I celebrated our 20th wedding anniversary. We celebrated by taking a 10-day Western Mediterranean cruise. We went with a group that included two couples with whom we celebrated our 10th wedding anniversary on a 10-day Alaskan cruise. We had a wonderful time.

I did catch some type of bug while on the trip. I had a low-grade fever and was a little tired. Once aware, Vanessa again jumped into action. She made sure to go to a pharmacy and get some medication at every port, even though she did not speak Italian, French, or Spanish. She nursed me back to health!

I thought about the goodness of God and how he saved me by putting Vanessa in my life.

Franklinville, NJ
December 25, 1997

EVERYTHING WAS GOING ACCORDING TO PLAN. Vanessa and I flew into Washington, DC, a little more than a week before Christmas. Our itinerary included stops from Washington, DC to Vanessa's parent's house in Franklinville, New Jersey. Vanessa wanted to visit friends and introduce me to them.

Little did she know that I had already met them by phone a few weeks before, and they were all in on the surprise. Vanessa would introduce me to a friend at every stop, and we would act as if it was the first time we had spoken to one another. When Vanessa was not around, we would talk about how things were going with their part of the plan.

It was now Christmas evening at the Foster home. Most of Vanessa's aunts, uncles, and cousins on her mother's side of the family were there. Vanessa's best friend from high school had also come by. Dinner was over, and most of the family was settling down to watch TV, talk, and finish their second helping of dessert.

Vanessa was in the dining room helping to clear the table. It was the right time to set the proposal in motion. Vanessa's sister and I had come up with a signal beforehand to let everyone know I was about to begin. She would start playing our favorite song, You Went and Saved the Best for Last, by Vanessa Williams. I motioned for Vanna to start playing the song. She turned on the stereo, and the music began to play.

The volume on the TV was making it was hard to hear the song. Vanna started turning down the volume on the TV. One of Vanessa's aunts began to complain. The Chicago Bulls game was on, and she was a die-hard Michael Jordan fan.

"What's going on?!" she exclaimed. "I can't hear anything! I want to hear the game. I want to hear what Michael has to say!"

Someone close to her whispered something in her ear. She quieted down after that.

I went over to Vanessa and asked her if she heard the music playing.

"Yes, I hear it playing," Vanessa said. She remained focused on clearing the table and not paying any attention to the music.

"Do you recognize the song?" I asked.

"What?" she replied impatiently. Her focus was on getting the table cleared, and I was beginning to annoy her. She stopped to listen for a moment and said, "Yes, it's Vanessa Williams," and went back to work.

I took her hand and said, "That's our song, Vanessa."

The look on her face told me she was really annoyed. She was about to say something to me, but she saw everyone looking at us when she looked up. One of her cousins had a video camera pointed in our direction.

It finally dawned on her what was going on, and she was shocked. "Oh no!" she exclaimed. She ran from the dining room and locked herself in the bathroom. It took her sister 10 minutes to coax her out. Once out, Vanna led her by the hand back to the dining room where I was waiting.

I started my well-rehearsed speech. All the while, Vanessa looked like a deer in the headlights. She stood frozen, embarrassed by the onlookers. She does not like to be the center of attention.

When I got to the point where I was about to pop the question, her cousin with the video camera shouted out, "No!" I stopped, and we all looked at her. She said, "Get down on one knee!" I responded as any professional actor would when given direction in a scene. Once I was in place, her cousin said, "Okay, go ahead."

When I presented Vanessa with the ring and asked her if she would marry me, she did not answer. Instead, she grabbed the ring and ran to her mother. She said, "Look, look, Mom! Look at the ring! Look at the ring!!"

To complete the surprise, I presented Vanessa with another Christmas gift. It was a white T-shirt with red-letter printing on the front and back. On the front, it read:

You Went
And Saved
The Best...
...For Last
HBD3   VFD

On the back, it read:

> *December 25, 1997*
> *A*
> *Christmas*
> *To*
> *Remember*

I never did get a "Yes" from Vanessa, but it was evident that God was fulfilling His promise to me.

On Friday, September 4, 1998, God fulfilled His promise. Vanessa and I married in New Hope, Pennsylvania.

Multiple Myeloma Milestones

February 25, 2021, I celebrated my fifth Stem Cell Transplant birthday.

July 16, 2021, was the sixth anniversary of my Multiple Myeloma diagnosis in Zion. November 19, 2020, was the fourth anniversary of my miraculous healing at City of Hope. On those days, I reflected on all of the miracles to allow me to reach those milestones.

To God Be The Glory!!!

> *"There are only two ways to live your life. One is as though nothing is a miracle. The other is as though everything is a miracle."*
> — Albert Einstein

The Facebook Prayer Team

> *"Is anyone among you sick? Then he must call for the elders of the church and they are to pray over him, anointing him with oil in the name of the LORD; and the prayer offered in faith will restore the one who is sick, and the LORD will raise him up, and if he has committed sins, they will be forgiven him. Therefore, confess your sins to one another, and pray for one another so that you may be healed. The effective prayer of a righteous man can accomplish much."*
> — James 5:14-16, New American Standard

At the end of November 2016, Vanessa and I posted what I thought would be our last posts on the secret Facebook page. I thought it was time for all of us to move on and see what God had in store for us in our separate journeys.

There is a Yiddish saying – *"Der mentsh trakht un got lakht"* ("Man plans and God laughs"). God's plans are always higher than my plans. Since November 2016, Vanessa and I have reached out to the prayer team with posts on the Facebook page on several occasions.

We reached out to the prayer team through all our health challenges, home goings, new additions, and celebrations shared in this epilogue. We continue to ask for prayers for our grandson Adam.

Each time, the prayer team has heeded our call, and God has used the team to continue ministering to us through corporate prayer.

Additionally, I received feedback from some prayer team members about their own prayer groups and was inspired to write the following post:

Pasadena, CA
March 16, 2018
Be Not Discouraged

 Henry B. Dotson III
March 16, 2018

BE NOT DISCOURAGED

Greetings All,

I pray this posting finds you well. I have received feedback from several of you about your own prayer groups or about people that have been brought to the attention of this prayer group. The reports have been very encouraging, and those doing the reporting have been very much encouraged about the power of their own prayers and their prayer groups.

In the midst of all these encouraging reports, I am compelled by the Holy Spirit to write this post.

The power of prayer is undeniable. Scripture tells us there is power in prayer. Our own personal experiences confirm the power of prayer in our hearts, minds, and spirits. That being said, there will be times when our petitions will not be answered in the way that we would like them to be. It is for those times that I say,

"Be not discouraged."

When we come together in corporate prayer, we pray to God about a specific situation, and we make our petition known for a certain outcome. We express the desires of our heart - the desired outcome - and pray that God hears our prayer and will bring about that outcome.

We must keep in mind God's Will has two aspects. His Sovereign Will - which is what He ultimately brings about to happen, and His Permissive Will - in which He gives us our freedom of choice.

Prayer works best when our will is aligned with God's Will. If what we pray for is perfectly aligned with God's Will, we tend to see that exact outcome manifest sooner than later. If what we pray for is not perfectly aligned with His Will, the outcome seems to be either "Not yet," or "I have something better planned for this situation. Something greater and better than you can imagine!"

When we get the "Not yet," or the "Something greater" answer, it calls upon us to be patient to see what God will do and what He has in store for us. We must not allow ourselves to listen to the enemy or doubt the power of prayer. We must recall what He has done for us in the past and meditate on the Word when it says,

> *"Brothers and sisters, as an example of patience in the face of suffering, take the prophets who spoke in the name of the Lord. As you know, we count as blessed those who have persevered."* — James 5:10-11

So, I say be not discouraged, persevere, and God will answer your prayers in the way best suited for the situation. Maybe not your way, but definitely His way, and that is always the best way! And you, too, will be counted as blessed because you persevered.

Stay blessed!!

- Henry

                                                                Comments

PART SEVEN:
A JOURNEY OF FAITH

"Nothing whatever, whether great or small, can happen to a believer, without God's ordering and permission. There is no such thing as 'chance,' 'luck' or 'accident' in the Christian's journey through this world. All is arranged and appointed by God. And all things are 'working together' for the believer's good."

— John Charles Ryle

"Follow boldly in your Master's steps, for He has made this rough journey before you. Better a brief warfare and eternal rest than false peace and everlasting torment."

— Charles Spurgeon

"Now faith is the assurance of what we hope for and the certainty of what we do not see."

— Hebrews 11:1, Berean Study Bible

From Zion to a City of Hope: A Journey of Faith

A Journey of Faith

I VIEW MY STORY AS A JOURNEY OF FAITH. I do so for two reasons. Firstly, because a journey is an act of traveling from one place to another, and I traveled from a place of near-death to the place of restored health. Secondly, because I believe my faith in the Word of God guided me along the journey and was itself moved from one level to another, higher, level through the course of the journey.

I have a biblical worldview. The term worldview may sound abstract, but it simply explains how one "views" the world. Its basis is what one believes to be true about the world. My biblical worldview is the lens through which I view the world and tell my story.

Throughout my journey, I rested my mustard-seed-sized-faith on one life-sustaining scripture that is a promise from God:

> *"And we know that all things work together for good to them that love God, to them who are the called according to his purpose."*
> — Romans 8:28, King James Version

I know that many of the promises God makes to us in scripture are conditional, and this one is no exception. When I focused on the latter part of the scripture, I saw the conditions, and there are two of them. It says the promise is for them that love God, and it is to them who are called according to His purpose. So, if I did not love God, I would not receive the promise of things working out for my good. Also, if I were not called according to His purpose, which means if my behavior were not in response to His call on my life to help fulfill His purpose in the earth, I would not receive the promise of things working out for my good.

I knew I loved God, so I do not spend any time contemplating whether or not I satisfied the first condition of His promise. However, I had to check myself to make sure what I was doing was in response to His call on my life.

I believe that God speaks to us all the time, but we are not listening most of the time.

Many think God mostly speaks to us supernaturally. And the Bible has many stories about God speaking to man in miraculous ways to support that point of view. Examples include hearing a voice from heaven, a burning bush, a finger writing on a wall, even speaking through the jawbone of an ass. We read about these supernatural occurrences. They make us want to see a bolt of lightning, hear the clap of thunder, and have some translucent vision appear before us with oracle-like words of wisdom that answer the big questions of life. Because this would make it very easy for us to know the message indeed was from God. And for some, it is the only way to convince them that it is God speaking.

But God can speak to us in many ways. Sometimes it is a thought that comes into your mind yet resonates in your spirit. Or you may stumble upon an answer to a question you had asked God in prayer. Or it could be a stray thought that motivates you to act in a slightly different way – like going out to lunch instead of eating at your desk as you usually do only to find out when you return that there has been an automobile accident and one of the cars crashed through the front of your building and came to rest on top of your desk. Sometimes it's that still small voice you hear in your head when you are thinking about something that matters very deeply to you. It feels like a candid conversation you would have with a friend that knows you very well. Sometimes it's a clear, seemingly audible voice that is telling you words you need to hear right away – explicit instructions or the reply to something you have been contemplating for a long while and are just now ready to receive the message.

Sometimes God uses miracles – amazing good things that are highly unlikely to occur but do – to speak to us. Miracles happen every day. Most people attribute miracles to chance or good fortune, not to God. But what is chance? Chance is a statistical probability, the odds of something happening. It is a mathematical calculation. Miracles entail something actually happening, some force in action. Chance is not a force. It cannot make things happen.

And what is good fortune or good luck? Many will say it is a matter of being in the right place at the right time. If that be the case, I would ask, "How does one come to be at the right place at the right time?" From my biblical worldview, I believe God navigates the circumstances of our lives to be at the right place at the right time.

While He can speak to us supernaturally or miraculously, he speaks to us through other people more often than not. Oftentimes God uses the hands, feet, voices, and resources of others to minister to His people. You may hear a word from someone that confirms what you should do about something that has been on your mind. It could be a suggestion, an act of kindness, words of encouragement, anything. It could be someone showing up and saying, "For some unknown reason, I am motivated to give you this." Other Christians might be more aware of His hand in matters and tell you directly, "God told me to... (fill in the blank) for/to you."

That is how God typically ministers to us... through other people. We just need to be listening and to recognize it is Him.

That is how I traveled on my journey of faith – listening for God's call on my life to make sure I was helping to fulfill His purposes on the earth – and having the faith-based assurance that all the things I was experiencing would work out for my good.

Looking Back

"It's so difficult, isn't it? To see what's going on when you're in the absolute middle of something? It's only with hindsight we can see things for what they are." — S.J. Watson, Before I Go to Sleep

Pasadena, CA
December 2016

WHEN I MADE THE LAST POST CONCERNING MY HEALING ON THE "SECRET" FACEBOOK PAGE, I understood in my spirit that this miraculous leg of my life's journey was complete. Several weeks have passed since that post, and I know that I am transitioning into another season; another leg of my life's journey is about to begin.

It is my custom to take time to look back at the experiences I had in that season to understand better what has happened. It is my way of elevating my perspective to have a better picture in my mind's eye of the forest than the one I had when amongst the trees.

I present my observations here to you, the reader, in chronological order, grouped according to where the experiences appear in the preceding parts of the book. You can think of it as my way of bringing this journey into sharper focus through the lens of my biblical worldview.

Providential Beginnings

BEGINNINGS ARE NOT ALWAYS EASILY RECOGNIZED as such, especially when not planned. But planned or not, they all share one thing in common; they all require faith (in something or someone) to move forward. The beginning of this journey was no different. It called forth my faith in the providence of God rather than reasoning or my intellect or wisdom.

I did not recognize that I was beginning an unplanned journey when Vanessa and I went to see my family doctor about a series of unusual tests for an already diagnosed injury. Nonetheless, I found myself entering into a health crisis that (as all crises do) immediately challenged my faith.

Through the providence of God, my faith was and still is, rooted in His wisdom and the knowledge of the truth that God's plans for me are for my welfare and not for my calamity; but rather to give me a future and a hope.

The foundational scripture for me concerning my providential beginnings is Romans 8:28:

> *"And we know that all things work together for good to them that love God, to them who are the called according to his purpose."*

When I look back at the providential beginnings of my Multiple Myeloma journey, I can see how God was moving in my life to prepare me and my circumstances for what lay ahead.

My crushing blows were painful ends to very close relationships. My divorce shook me, and the loss of my friend Valenda left an ache in my heart that only God could heal.

> *"Don't get lost in your pain, know that one day your pain will become your cure."*
> — Jalaluddin Rumi

> *"Every new beginning comes from some other beginning's end."*
> — Seneca

Upon closer examination in hindsight, I can see that there was much more to my preparation than just the jarring, crushing blows. I formed my Christian worldview from an early age because of the crushing blows in my parents' lives. The pain of their separate experiences drew them closer to God, and He, in turn, navigated the paths of their lives to bring about a new family unit that believed in Him.

Through the pain of my divorce, I experienced tremendous growth, both emotionally and spiritually. There was a deepening of my relationships with others who became my support system in my time of need. I discovered who my true friends were and who my fair-weather friends were.

I see where God took this painful experience in my life and used it to show Vanessa my true character and the kind of man I had grown to become through adversity.

> *"All the adversity I've had in my life, all my troubles and obstacles, have strengthened me... You may not realize it when it happens, but a kick in the teeth may be the best thing in the world for you."*
> — Walt Disney

He navigated the circumstances of our lives so that she became my closest and most trusted friend during this trial in my life.

She was there from the beginning to see the pain, sadness, despair, and anguish.

She was there to see my loneliness and responded by keeping company with me and seeing that I got out from time to time with others. She was there to see how I remained committed to my children and did all I could to be in their lives and to meet their needs as their father. She was there to see me come from a low, destabilized place to a higher, stable place.

He knew the desires of her heart, and He knew she needed a humble husband and one that she could respect.

As a result of my trials, I had (unbeknownst to me) earned her respect.

God also knew the desires of my heart, so He used this painful experience to draw me closer to Him, so I could better hear His still small voice and know to put my trust in it.

So, because of my first crushing blow, when He spoke to me in that still small voice and told me Vanessa was the one He brought to me to be my new wife, I heard Him, I listened to Him, and I took action!

In hindsight, I can also see how He knew Vanessa was precisely the one I would need by my side during my cancer journey.

How my second crushing blow, the death of my dear friend Valenda, prepared me for my cancer journey did not become apparent until the day of my diagnosis, eight and a half years later.

When the admitting oncologist at CTCA first informed Vanessa and me that they had positively diagnosed me with Multiple Myeloma, I was stunned. Still, I was also relieved to finally get a correct diagnosis.

In the short time from when the admitting oncologist said I was a very sick man, that it was a miracle that I survived the trip to CTCA until I was delirious from heavy doses of chemotherapy, I had a revelation from God.

As I was processing the news while being transported from the doctor's office to a hospital bed for treatment, I asked myself, "How did I get here?" Unexpectantly, God answered in His still small voice and said,

> "You got here in a miraculous way."

I recognized His voice, but at first, I did not understand His answer. I was stuck on the word "miraculous." I thought of the miracles in the Bible. I had not experienced anything close to what came to mind.

But when I looked back on the sequence of events that had occurred to get me to CTCA at that very moment, it suddenly became crystal clear:

> *God performed this miracle through the people He had put into my life at the right time and place to prepare me for a time such as this.*

I thought about the people God had used to get me to CTCA: Jezreel, Dr. Mahmoud, Margaret, and (of course) Vanessa. When I thought about Jezreel, I realized that God had also used Valenda to help me get to CTCA. That revelation made me aware of how He used His impeccable timing and navigation of the circumstances in my life to get me to CTCA.

God placed Valenda in my life so we would develop a close friendship. Through this friendship, I developed a strong bond; with Valenda and her children. God strengthened my bond and commitment to Valenda's children through the pain of her passing. This bond assured my relationship with Valenda's daughter Jezreel would continue to grow through the years.

"New beginnings are often disguised as painful endings." — Lao Tzu

God navigated the circumstances of my life so that I was motivated to help Jezreel in her time of need eight and a half years after Valenda's passing.

Had I not helped Jezreel move her belongings from Los Angeles to Costa Mesa, I would not have pulled the muscles in my back.

Had I not pulled the muscles in my back, I would not have sought medical attention for my injury.

God placed Dr. Mahmoud in my life by navigating my circumstances and Dr. Mattai's, so I could not schedule an appointment with her anytime soon.

Had Dr. Mattai been available, I would not have seen Dr. Mahmoud. God knew Dr. Mahmoud was the right doctor for me at that time. Another doctor may not have ordered x-rays for a soft tissue injury (something not always done).

Had Dr. Mahmoud not ordered the x-rays, she would not have seen the problem with my spine. Had Dr. Mahmoud not only seen the problem with my spine but correctly diagnosed it as a side effect of Multiple Myeloma, Vanessa and I would not have sought an oncologist as soon as we did.

God navigated the circumstances of my life so that there was no oncologist available at City of Hope to take me on as a patient in a timely fashion. I then listened to God's small voice when he said to me:

"You don't have time to wait for an oncologist at City of Hope."

Had I not listened and waited for an oncologist to become available at City of Hope, I would have died from kidney failure.

I had to put my trust in God to direct me to where I should go for treatment. I had to put my mustard seed's worth of faith into God, making a way out of no way, the same way I did when I received the news from my first wife that she was planning on leaving me.

God placed Margaret in my life three years earlier as a colleague who became a mentor and a friend. He used her – this daughter of a missionary – to direct my path to CTCA Chicago.

Had I not put my trust in Him, I would not have been waiting to hear from Him for an answer. Had I not waited to hear from God through Margaret and recognized it was Him speaking to me, I probably would not have sought treatment at CTCA Chicago. I probably would have sought treatment somewhere else in the greater Los Angeles area.

Had I not trusted that I had indeed heard from God instructing me to go to CTCA Chicago, I would not have been persistent when told I did not qualify for the CTCA program. God honored my persistence and did make a way out of no way. He changed the mind of the person we spoke to from no to yes.

God protected me when the enemy attacked me at LAX on the way to CTCA Chicago. The devil did not win that day. That day, I made it to my appointed place of rest. God, and God alone, pushed back my adversaries and trampled down the devil and his legion that rose against me that day!

Cancer Treatment Centers of America, Zion, IL
July 16, 2015

When we entered the elevator, I looked up at Vanessa from my wheelchair. Her face was pensive. She stared straight ahead and did not say anything. The other occupants of the elevator were also silent. I could feel the heaviness in that small space.

Although it was a tense moment, I found comfort in Vanessa being by my side. It was then I realized that God had placed Vanessa in my life 27 years beforehand in part so that she would be here right now.

God knew I would need a helpmate to stand by me as I embarked on this journey. He had again navigated the circumstances of my life and Vanessa's life to prepare us for what lay ahead.

When realizing all God had done, I felt that familiar peace that passes all understanding wash over me. Just as before, I did not know how this would all work out, but I knew it would be for my good.

Whether I lived or died really did not matter to me. I was only looking forward to seeing what God was going to do next.

When I got settled in my mind, I heard God say:

> *"I have navigated the circumstances of your life from the beginning such that you are here in Zion, where you will receive your healing."*

God prepared me in those scant 15 minutes, in the midst of my struggling to come to grips with the reality of my circumstances, to begin this most unexpected journey.

Looking back, I can plainly see that providence, God's timely preparation for future eventualities, was most assuredly there at the beginning of my Multiple Myeloma journey. He was there in the beginning (Genesis 1:1) and will always be there at all of our beginnings.

Zion

Many miracles filled my stay in Zion, not just the miracle of pulling me back from the brink of death. I saw God moving in the lives of everyone involved in my care. There was an aura of God's presence around the entire campus of CTCA Chicago.

> *"Then you will know that I, the Lord your God, dwell in Zion, my holy hill."* — Joel 3:1, New International Version Bible

Early on in my Multiple Myeloma journey, I knew that I was not in control at all. I knew that I had to trust in God for whatever was to come. In Zion, it became crystal clear that I would have to rely totally on God and my care providers at CTCA.

My situation was literally out of my hands. In the beginning, I received no assurances from my doctors, only that they knew what to do and that they would do their best.

In addition to the doctors using their God-given skills to administer His healing of my body, God also used a night nurse to ward off a spiritual attack of Satan. At the time, it never occurred to me to inquire about the nurse, find out who she was, or thank her.

Looking back, I sense that it was part of God's plan for me not to know more about her. Lack of more information served to emphasize the fact that this was a miracle. It reminded me of the story in the Bible when Jesus restored the sight of a blind man, and the Pharisees questioned him about who Jesus was.

> *"So the Pharisees also asked him how he had received his sight. The man answered, 'He put mud on my eyes, and I washed, and now I can see.'"* — John 9:15, Berean Study Bible

> "So a second time they called for the man who had been blind and said, 'Give glory to God! We know that this man is a sinner.' He answered, 'Whether He is a sinner I do not know. There is one thing I do know: I was blind, but now I see!'"
> — John 9:24-25, Berean Study Bible

Whether or not she was an angel in human form, I do not know. There is one thing I do know: I was under spiritual attack, she laid hands on me, and I was delivered the spiritual victory!

As a result of my total dependence on God, and trust in what only He alone can do, I experienced His healing power through faith. In Zion, I became as Zion. My faith in God was not moved because He delivered me according to His word.

> "Those who trust, lean on and confidently hope in the Lord are as Mount Zion, which cannot be moved, but abides and stands fast forever. As the mountains are round about Jerusalem, so the Lord is round about His people from this time forth and forever."
> — Psalm 125:1-2, Amplified Bible

When I stop to think about my experience in Zion, if I were able, I would dance like David danced (2 Samuel 6:4).

Middle Passage

I believe the concept of a Middle Passage resonates with anyone who has suffered "crushing blows" or has survived life-threatening experiences. The ones we experience today most certainly are nowhere near as horrific as those inflicted on generations of Africans by European slave traders, nor are they as singularly unique as Arthur Ashe's journey in the elite world of professional tennis.

Nonetheless, I believe all Middle Passages share a common thread. We journey from what is known into the unknown under extraordinarily difficult circumstances, with no certainty of where our journey will take us or in what condition we will find ourselves after the Middle Passage is over.

In the natural, my Middle Passage appears focused on making a critical decision about my treatment to move forward. Vanessa and I had to identify the questions needing to be answered by my City of Hope doctor to make that decision.

The implications and consequences of this decision would not only impact my care, but it would also impact the lifestyle Vanessa and I would experience moving forward.

In addition to the cancer treatments, I discovered I needed other types of support. I found I needed support to help me transition from being a nominally healthy, non-cancer patient to becoming a cancer patient with physical challenges brought on by the side effects of treatment.

I needed emotional support, and I needed a sense of community, both from individuals diagnosed with cancer. I did not know this when I started attending support group meetings, but I quickly found this to be the case.

Community was a vital waypoint during my Middle Passage. Being part of a community helped me heal and changed the course of my journey. It was in a community where I charted my course toward my ultimate healing at City of Hope.

> *"Healing is impossible in loneliness; it is the opposite of loneliness. Conviviality is healing. To be healed we must come with all the other creatures to the feast of Creation."* — Wendell Berry

With all the weight of the decision at hand, there was something much more to my Middle Passage than the logistics of travel, the level of care I would receive, and our future lifestyle. My faith was severely tested because I had to find peace in my spirit, in the middle of tremendous uncertainty, about the Middle Passage of my journey, regardless of what decision I made.

> *"Faith is not merely a journey for the feet, but it is a journey for the heart."* — Aiden Wilson Tozer

I was being called upon once again to put my trust in God, no matter where my journey took me next, even though I was unsure of where that would be. God prepared me for this moment with my experience in Zion and other events in my life. I knew He would never leave me, no matter what I decided to do.

> *"I am learning to trust the journey even when I do not understand it."* — Mila Bron

Our faith is a matter of the heart, not the body, not the mind. My faith in God caused me to trust Him even when I did not understand my journey. Because of my trust, I did not second guess my choices when I had peace in my spirit. It was a peace that passed all understanding and abided in me in the midst of the chaos that surrounded me.

My Middle Passage was the complex emotional and spiritual part of my journey. I had to leave the familiar, life-saving, safe, and spiritually comforting place of Zion and transfer my treatment to City Of Hope – a place I knew little about. I had to follow where God led me, despite my concerns about leaving the Mother Standard® of Care at CTCA.

I concluded my Middle Passage when I placed my trust in God, loosened my emotional ties to Zion, and brought my faith with me to City of Hope. In God's infinite wisdom, the physical manifestation of my healing took place where He wanted it to, and my spiritual growth continued along with my relationship with the Father.

A City Of Hope

Just as God had planned, the miracles involved in restoring my health continued at City of Hope until I was in remission and my life was whole again.

It has been said you cannot truly appreciate the view from the mountain top unless you've spent time in its deepest valley. A good portion of my climb up the mountain from the deepest valley took place at City of Hope. God did not remove the mountain; He enabled me to make the climb up the mountain with help from City of Hope.

Looking back, I see City of Hope as the place and time in my journey, where my hope in the promises of God came to bear fruit. My faith in the Word of God laid the foundation for the hope that I had within me.

Hope rests in the will. Hope in the promises of God is what enabled me to be strong in spirit, to suffer and endure adversity. Hope gave me the will to fight against Multiple Myeloma, my weakness, and my impatience. My hope in the promises of God enabled me to wait for the day when they would come to be, even in the midst of my trials.

"Once you choose hope, anything's possible." — Christopher Reeve

Dawn of a New Day

I reached the summit of this journey with my health restored and my faith firmly planted in God. I will not be the person I once was physically, but I am a better person in so many other ways because of the journey. It was indeed the dawn of a new day.

"Weeping may endure for the night, but joy comes in the morning."
— Psalm 30:5, New King James Version

This new day brought confirmation of my healing. All of us on the journey celebrated what God had done.

More important than celebrating was giving testimony to the goodness of God. We take so many things for granted that we do not appreciate most of them. The journey gave me a new perspective on life and the many blessings we receive daily from God. Just the fact that we wake up in the morning is a blessing.

> *"When you arise in the morning, think of what a precious privilege it is to be alive - to breathe, to think, to enjoy, to love."*
> — Marcus Aurelius

Looking back, I realize that the journey brought me to a place where I am ready to face the next season in my life. God has something more in store for me, and I needed to travel this path to prepare for what is to come. I must seize the day that comes with the dawn and listen for God's still voice to tell me what He would have me do.

> *"For our light and momentary troubles are achieving for us an eternal glory that far outweighs them all. So we fix our eyes not on what is seen, but on what is unseen. For what is seen is temporary, but what is unseen is eternal."*
> — 2 Corinthians 4:17-18 New International Version Bible

In Retrospect

"Life will often test you. How you respond shows your character and your character determines your destiny."   — Jon Gordon

"The mark of a good action is that it appears inevitable in retrospect."
— Robert Louis Stevenson

Pasadena, CA
January 2017

LOOKING BACK ALLOWS US TO SEE THE THINGS THAT HAVE HAPPENED FROM A MORE COMPREHENSIVE POINT OF VIEW. Retrospection is more about lessons learned. Retrospection enables us not just to see things better; it also helps us to make sense of it all.

When many people view their lives retrospectively, they say what happened was chance, luck (good or bad), or destiny, without really putting much thought into it.

My Christian worldview informs me that destiny is controlled by God, not by a human being or something else. For me, destiny is about God's Sovereign Will, in which things come to pass in my life and the lives of everyone else as He sees fit. I believe what happens in our lives ultimately fulfills His purposes on the earth.

I meditated on all that happened on my Multiple Myeloma journey and what lessons I have come away with through this lens. I share those lessons with you now, in retrospect.

Seek Help From Others

Cancer is not something you should ever try to face alone. Isolating yourself is arguably the worst thing you can possibly do. Do not let fear or not wanting to ask for help keep you from receiving the support you need. The Bible says,

> *"For God has not given us a spirit of fear, but of power, love, and self-control."*   — 2 Timothy 1:7, Berean Study Bible

> *"Pride precedes destruction; an arrogant spirit appears before a fall."*
> — Proverbs 16:18, New International Version Bible

Seek help not only from healthcare providers and caregivers but from a community of people. The Facebook Prayer Team, Cancer Support Community Pasadena, and a host of others helped me along my cancer journey. I was healed because of them through the power of the Holy Spirit.

Do Not Be Afraid to Help

I believe many want to help someone facing a major crisis in their lives but are afraid to help because they don't know what to do other than to pray.

Cancer Support Community provided me with a resource they created that I believe applies not only to those who want to help cancer patients but also applies to those who want to help anyone facing a major crisis in their lives. I have included the text of the resource here for your consideration:

The Do's & Don'ts of "How to be a Good Friend to a Person with Cancer"

DO	DON'T
• Offer your presence often, be a good listener when they are ready to talk.	• Tell them that everything's going to be all right because you don't know.
• Talk about things other than their cancer.	• Tell them you know how they feel because you probably don't.
• Say, "I love you" and be yourself.	• Be afraid to admit that you don't know what to say when you are at a loss for words.
• Ask what you can do to help – be sincere and specific so that they know you mean it. If they can't come up with anything, ask again in another week or so.	• Be afraid to touch them, but don't force it either.
• Use disposable dishware when delivering food to reduce the stress of returning them.	• Hesitate to call them or leave them a message to let them know you're thinking of them.
• Arrange a phone chain to update friends on their condition, treatment, etc. (Be sure to get approval first!)	• Avoid the subject of cancer if that's what they want to talk about.
• Offer to help by driving them to appointments, taking their kids to childcare, and doing housecleaning, gardening, cooking, shopping, yard work, or babysitting.	• Be afraid to talk about your life. Just because they're sick, it doesn't always mean they are not interested in hearing about you.
• Respect how they choose to deal with their cancer.	• Discount the real feelings they may be having by telling them not to feel that way, not to worry, not to be scared, or not to cry.
• Tell them about the support, education, and hope they can find at Cancer Support Community!	• Share advice unless asked.
	• Be afraid to talk about difficult subjects. Ask them how they're feeling.

God's In Control

When I fully comprehended what was about to happen due to my diagnosis, I instinctively knew that I was **not** in control.

I experienced what I already knew to be true in my head and my heart through my journey. That God has been, and will always be, in control, because of His Sovereign Will. I learned that my faith in that simple truth was all that I needed to hold on to to reach this point in my Multiple Myeloma journey on this side of eternity.

> "When you have faith in God, you don't have to worry about the future. You just know it's all in His hands. You just go to and do your best." — Elder Bryan Mathison

Mustard Seed Faith

> "... Truly I tell you, if you have faith as small as a mustard seed, you can say to this mountain, 'Move from here to there,' and it will move. Nothing will be impossible for you." — Matthew 17:20, New International Version Bible

The next lesson I learned is even when you have faith as small as a mustard seed, which, according to His Word, can move a mountain, your faith is most likely going to be used by God to move **you** instead of the mountain. There was no clap of thunder because of my faith that made me instantly whole and removed the need for me to go through cancer treatment. Instead, there was a peace and confidence instilled in me by my faith that got me through it all.

> "My faith didn't remove the pain, but it got me through the pain. Trusting in God didn't diminish or vanquish the anguish, but it enabled me to endure it." — Robert Rogers

There were difficult days without a doubt. Each day I experienced some level of pain. As Jim Rohn said:

> "There are two types of Pain in this world: Pain that hurts you, and Pain that changes you!"

Each day I had a choice. Each day by faith, I chose to allow pain to change me, and I endured it.

Follow By Faith

The next lesson I learned about God being in control is when I submit my will to the Lord's Sovereign Will; He will affirm His truth in my heart and give me what is best for me. I set my heart on God's heavenly outcomes and released my self-serving attachment to the Cancer Treatment Centers of America in Zion, Illinois. According to both His Sovereign and Permissive Will, God was then able to use City of Hope to manifest my healing. And that is the best I could ever possibly hope for.

> *"Faith is confidence in Christ; a total trust in His character and His claim to be God. Once you settle this, submit your will to the Lord's will. Surrender your right to know what's right and take the next right step. Your choice to do God's will does not guarantee instant revelation, but it does mean you move forward under the Spirit's guidance. Follow by faith, even if you don't feel a spiritual sensation. Obedience to what you know, may eventually answer what you don't know. Choose God's will and He will affirm His truth in your heart. You are a confidant of His will."*
> — Boyd Bailey

Stay In Line With God's Will

> *"...For You are my help; I will sing for joy in the shadow of Your wings. My soul clings to You; Your right hand upholds me."*
> — Psalm 63:7-8, Berean Study Bible

In retrospect, it is abundantly clear to me that the very best place to be is as close to God as possible at all times, not just when going through trials and tribulation.

I remained prayerful throughout the day, meditating on His Word and always anticipating Him speaking to me in His many different ways. In so doing, I was spirit-led and in line with God's will.

There is no better place to be than with the One who gave you life.

> *"Stick with the one that brought you to the party."*
> — Bishop Edward A. Smith

It's Not About Me

God's grace saved me through faith. A faith that in itself was a gift from God. In retrospect, my healing is more about being a living testimony for the benefit of others than it is about me not succumbing to Multiple Myeloma after a near-death discovery of the disease.

This story is not just my story; it's not about me. My journey affected the people around me, even people I have not met. It has direct implications for everyone around me. It is our story. All of us have become part of this miracle from God. It has been part of God's plan from the beginning of time.

> *"For it is by his grace that we have been saved through faith, and this faith was not from you, but it is the gift of God, not of works, lest anyone should boast."*
> — Ephesians 2:8 - 9, Aramaic Bible in Plain English

This story is about Vanessa and me holding on to God's promises that he made to us in His Word.

This story is about my Prayer Team that faithfully lifted us up in prayer every day and witnessed the power of corporate prayer.

This story is about the support team that encouraged me and helped me get to and from the hospital. They visited me and comforted me with their presence. They gave of their time and endured the emotional toll of seeing me deteriorated because of the strong chemotherapy medication.

I asked members of my family and my support team questions about the journey in retrospect. Here are some of their responses in their own words:

Q: How did you feel when you learned you helped save my life?

JEZ: In my mind, saving your life would have been to speak up sooner. I saw that you did not look right on our two meetings. I even told my grandmother that your eyes were yellow. I knew something was not right. I never said anything, and even the second time, I remember asking if you felt okay. When I walked up to the car during our second meeting, you seemed to be coughing and did not look well.

What is the proper way to say, "Dag, you don't look so good," after a reunion? My lesson was to speak up. My lesson is to not doubt my gifts.

MARGARET: I am still humbled by that thought. I am not sure I did it – I was just God's instrument. I didn't think about it at the time – I just knew you had to get to CTCA. I knew it in my soul. I think God puts the correct person in your life at the correct time to complete his plan and fulfill his will. I think I was that person, and I am very glad that I was there for you and for Him to use.

Q: Have you ever been part of a miracle before?

BART: Nothing on this scale before!

CHARITY: Yes, with my sister's cardiac arrest, and when both of her lungs collapsed, as well as when we lived in Oklahoma City during a very devastating F5 tornado. But each time is so different from the last, and this was no exception.

TALIA: Yes – My life.

IRA: Yes, I have been a participant in a number of miracles. The first miracle I can remember was when I prayed over one of our church members. He came up asking for prayer. He said it was something serious, but he did not disclose that it was cancer.

The following week he came back to church to share his testimony. He said his first exam revealed numerous tumors in a particular area of his body. When he went back for his second exam, all of the tumors had disappeared.

There have been more than ten times when I have laid hands on people with short limbs. Almost all of them were short legs. As I laid hands on them and prayed, their legs grew out to the proper proportion. After these experiences, it has never been old when I see the power of God move.

As far as your healing is concerned, I expected you to be healed. I did not know how or how long, but the Lord responded to our prayer in such a demonstrative fashion, I knew you would survive. I think it was a miracle that you survived.

Again, I did not find out the details of your illness until approximately 15 months after your original diagnosis. But based on your accounts, as well as Vanessa's descriptions, you were at the brink of death.

For everyone that knew your situation and that it could be fatal, this was a testimony to the power of God. There were some people besides our family that knew you were close to death. They heard your faith confession, and then they saw God honor your faith. It was a miracle.

PAT: Not only have I been part of a miracle, but I have also been the recipient of miracles myself. It was no surprise, yet surprising when God performed his miracle on my brother. It's one thing to know God can do it, but to actually see it happen is still amazing to me. And it surprises me every time!

BERYL: I have been part of a miracle before, but not as intimately as I was as I shared this journey with you and those on the journey with you.

JEZ: I feel like my life is a miracle. The unexplained and impossible are my daily life. To the point that I might seem crazy to others if I spoke upon how many unexplainable things happen.

NORMAN: Trick question. I would say no, but I know that you consider your recovery a miracle. And that puts me in a tough spot.

Religion is a weird thing for me. Its value is clear for me – it provides an orientation, a compass, a set of values, beliefs.

The major religions of the world – Christianity, Islam, and Judaism – share important common values – help the poor, tend to the sick, do unto others, etc. It's a common compass, although the maps might be a bit different, as the endpoint is different between them.

The question of a God, and miracles, and prayer...that's difficult.

At my core, I am very analytical. Religion, prayer, etc., and science, are kind of like a square peg/round hole thing. It either doesn't fit at all, or there are not insignificant gaps. Clearly, religion and prayer influence the mind and body. Asking for a blessing for a sick friend is an example.

Maybe there is a God, and it helps. Maybe it helps the sick to know folks are looking out for them. Maybe it just makes the requester feel better. Maybe all or some of the above.

So how do I determine if it is a miracle, medicine plus mind/body, personal strength? I can't. Maybe God gives people hurdles, challenges, and the plan is to see if you have the will to overcome them. Victim or responder?

RUTH: Yes, I believe I have.

LOIS: Yes, but not with someone so close to me nor with a condition so serious.

CECILY: Maybe I have in the past, but none as obvious, real, and part of from beginning to end—a miracle.

MARGARET: Yes, but remember, I am a Missionary's Kid – I saw many miracles on the mission field, and I also was part of a miracle with my own journey with cancer.

Perhaps that is why I was so confident that He could do it and WOULD do it. Our Lord is a living being that is part of us and our everyday lives.

I think my Faith, and yours, made the difference in both our journeys. Prayer without Faith is hollow and just words. But when you put Faith in the mix, it allows God to unleash his power and will.

I think seeing and believing in miracles helps strengthen our Faith, and that makes the prayer even more powerful. It is a winning cycle – the more the prayers are answered and miracles happen, the easier it is to have faith and stay in prayer.

JIM: I know it sounds somewhat trite, but it depends on your definition of a miracle. I think miracles occur all the time and are all around us. Having gotten that out of the way, I have not been part of a miracle that was of the nature of yours.

Q: How have you been affected by being part of the miracles that took place on this journey?

BART: Personally, it was a miracle that I was able to make it out to visit you in the midst of the radical changes that were happening in my life.

Friends and family enabled me to make it to you. Watching the miracles that happened along the way definitely strengthened my faith. While I knew God healed and had seen minor healings, I had never been part of something so big, so dire, and so personal. I feel as though I can believe in God for big things in terms of health and healing.

CHARITY: It's been encouraging in my walk with the Lord to witness this journey.

TALIA: I feel that my spiritual intuition is something that I should trust. I also recognize that we as a family are blessed and highly favored, but the choices that we make with our blessings affect us as well.

IRA: I was affected in subtle ways. Again, I had already considered you completely healed. Every other outcome that followed was what I expected. This was the first time someone close to me had terminal cancer and survived. However, it was expected.

CRIS: I'm thankful I could be a part of witnessing with my own eyes that nothing is impossible with God.

PAT: It's one thing to know God can do it, but to actually see it happen is still amazing to me. And it surprises me every time!

So, each day, whether I tell them or not, I LOVE MY BROTHERS! And appreciate every day that they are part of my life.

BERYL: I have come to appreciate even more how miracles are done by God, but how He often uses people to be His instruments.

I experienced the miraculous power of a loving, supportive community! We are the Body of Christ! We need one another, and everyone is a valued member.

You had the right to and could have chosen to go it alone or allow only a limited number of people to share this journey with you. But you shared and continue to share with others.

As a person on the journey, I gained strength from God and from those comrades on the journey with us. When I sometimes felt depressed, I would read one of Vanessa's emails or sense someone was interceding for you and those of us on the journey with you.

I also got an opportunity to witness what it is like for someone to be loved "in sickness" and in health. I am sure she had her moments, but Vanessa demonstrated a steadfastness that I personally got to experience as I read her emails. I still marvel at the strength God gave Vanessa to care for you, make decisions, and communicate with us.

I hope that I will have a "Vanessa" in my life should I ever face a similar journey. Better still, I hope that I will be a "Vanessa" should the need arise to help someone else.

JEZ: I have to be stronger in intentional thought and words.

SANDRA: The miracles have affected me tremendously.

NORMAN: It certainly has demonstrated the value of faith and how faith can help someone overcome the odds against them. The question for me becomes, "How does the mechanism of faith change the outcome?" Intervention by God or increased personal strength?

I do not know, and maybe it doesn't matter other than knowing it helps.

RUTH: I was reminded that one could not predict or control what will happen. But one can take steps, step after step, as you and Vanessa did. For my part, and Norman's, just to "be there" with the people involved in an open, honest, simple, and loving way is what is both essential and most meaningful and rewarding.

CECILY: It confirms my belief that God is real and robust faith matters.

You did not waiver; you just were steadfast. You knew from the beginning you would live, and this was amazing to me. I have doubts about myself at times and of my faith when tested. But you were honest, open, and faithful from the beginning. You knew you would be cured.

LOIS: It has left me in awe of the goodness of God and how strong you were at standing steadfast in the knowledge that "God's Got Me no matter what."

MARGARET: I think anytime you are part of one of God's miracles, it touches you and changes you forever. I know both our journeys (separately and together) have given me new perspectives that I would never have had before. I guess it is because we faced death and came through, but also because we saw the power of God and what can be done if we pray and have faith.

JIM: I think what affected me most was the strength and faith that you demonstrated during the journey. I suspect that, in some ways, you provided more strength to others than they provided to you. I am sure you had your moments of doubt and shared them with those closest to you, but for the rest of us, what we saw was Henry the Optimist.

Q: What blessing have you received as a result of being part of this journey?

BART: The biggest blessing I have received is the continued presence of my father in my life. This has manifested itself in many ways – notably, your presence at one of the most significant days of my life, my marriage, and the continued blessing of having you be a part of my life, family, and see the family grow with the upcoming birth of my son, Adam Henry Dotson.

CHARITY: I've been blessed to get to know a great family and see how someone else responds to difficulty. I've been blessed to see such a miraculous recovery and so many answers to prayer. It's amazing to see God's goodness and glory in this way.

TALIA: Inspiration, an excellent example, AND my Daddy came back from the shadow of death!

IRA: This may seem trite, but I believe the greatest blessing I have received is your survival. I am not sure how life would have been if you were to leave at such a young age. Things would never have been the same.

CRIS: The blessing I have received is God's faithfulness and love, especially when times seem difficult.

PAT: I am blessed to still have my brother Bernard! As I said before, I could not begin to imagine my life without him here.

BERYL: Same as my answer to how I have been affected by being part of the miracles that took place on this journey.

JEZ: I have learned to be more confident in the power of prayer and my own gifts of discernment and intuition.

SANDRA: I've been blessed with a better love for and understanding of life. Also, I've become much happier and content with my health, friends, and family.

LOIS: It has left me in awe of the goodness of God and how strong Henry was at standing steadfast in the knowledge that "God's Got Me, no matter what."

CECILY: I have been blessed by restoration and an increase in my faith. With you being my great long-time friend, I was blessed to witness your strength and faith in the Lord.

JEFF AND CHARALE: We are both the better for having shared in your journey through the ups and the downs and the potential tragedy that turned to triumph.

MARGARET: My blessings are many, and it is difficult to put them into words. In some ways, it has given me power over my own frailties and made me understand life in a different way. Many of my fears are gone, and I am able to grow in my faith like never before. I think when you have to face death and live to see the other side, the blessings include happiness and contentment with life as it comes.

JIM: Certainly, one blessing was simply getting to know you better in a context other than work. Being able to help you in whatever small way I could was also a blessing.

Q: How did our conversations during the journey impact you?

BERYL: Hearing your voice and your confidence in God and in those whom He used to minister to you was invaluable. Bernard, I never heard you speak of fear, regret, anger, or depression. I remember your saying to me once when you heard of your diagnosis, the question was not "Why me?" but "Why not me?"

You also said that you had friends and family who you knew would support you. You also gained friends as you participated and ministered to others in the support groups. I also think about the amount of detail that you shared with me regarding Multiple Myeloma and the different procedures. I loved the fact that you were an active participant in your treatment.

As I think of your responses, I am reminded of a quote by Chuck Swindoll:

> *We cannot change the inevitable. The only thing we can do is play on the one string we have, and that is our attitude. I am convinced that life is 10% what happens to me and 90% of how I react to it.*

And so it is with you.

Q: Did my cancer journey affect your perspective on how you should care for me?

TALIA: Yes. I can't rough you up anymore.

Q: Did my cancer journey affect your perspective on our Sunday time before going to work?

TALIA: Yes. I took extra pleasure in the moments we got to spend together and the information that you shared with me. It became extremely important to me.

Q: Have you ever been part of a prayer group/team before? If yes, how was this experience different than yours with other groups?

BART: Yes. I've never seen such a high degree of engagement, support, or consistency in a prayer group as I have seen with the group for you.

CHARITY: I guess I haven't been part of a prayer group/ team before. Usually, my family (myself included) is on the receiving end of the prayer group.

IRA: I have been a member of prayer teams, fasting, and prayer teams over the last forty years.

Generally, I do not disclose this because I do not want to appear as if I am exalting myself. My experiences are not so much my own designs. As a member of a domestic missionary organization, we have had numerous seasons of prayer and fasting. Again, it is not the design of my own volition; it is just a result of belonging to an organization that has been called to this lifestyle.

Unlike my other experiences, this was joining hands with people I did not know. I was impressed by their perseverance in prayer behind you. It was cool seeing other members of the Body respond with so much love.

CRIS: Yes. I don't know if it's been different per se, other than maybe having the amount of support.

PAT: Yes, but I had never been in a prayer group that went worldwide or on social media.

BERYL: Yes, I have been a part of a prayer group at my church and at Christian organizations where I worked. We met face-to-face or prayed via phone.

What made this experience different was, I was praying with people, most of whom I had never met. I did not hear prayers or see faces because we did not physically meet. But through the use of social media, we were able to connect because we loved you and wanted you healed.

I also think what made this experience different was that I was different. I felt so powerless when I first heard of your diagnosis. I couldn't fix the situation, so I found myself crying out to the Lord. I participate in a Bible study on Monday nights, and we often discuss who God is. During this journey, I was reminded of God's sovereignty. He is in absolute control of all things, even when all things seem out of my control.

SANDRA: Yes. This experience was different from others because I felt more close and intimate with God.

JEZ: This was my first prayer team, but at the time, I was reading about the power of prayer and fasting.

LOIS: Yes. It was more consistent and persistent, which other prayer groups are not necessarily.

CECILY: Your circle of friends and support people were amazing. The people who posted shared a solid system of faithful beliefs. I could feel their love for the Lord, their faith, their strength to assist in prayer and healing. I witnessed the path of a miracle. Amazing.

Your faithful friends seem more real in faith. More convicted. Felt a more trusting relationship and strong belief in the Lord.

JEFF AND CHARALE: We have never experienced a group that was that connected through the journey, and made everyone feel as though they were walking it through with you.

Vanessa was very transparent in her posts and shared triumphs as well as struggles.

MARGARET: Yes – most of my life, even before I was a Christian because I lived in a home where our center was God's word, and prayer was a major part of it.

Not really, but I have been a part of some very powerful prayer groups and seen some fantastic results from prayer.

Q: Has this journey affected your faith?

BART: This journey has helped me to believe more for healing, to see God as a miraculous healer and loving father, and to see how God uses circumstances to bring people together and make His name great on the earth.

CHARITY: It's been strengthening to see God answer prayers the way He has in this journey. In a very dark/ difficult time in my life (due to other health issues going on with family, etc.), this was a contrast and an encouragement to witness God's goodness in action.

TALIA: It strengthened it.

IRA: It has been an experience that demonstrated God's faithfulness to those who serve Him. You have been a person that has sacrificed your time, energy, and gifts to alter the future for several African countries. I do not know anyone else that has such a commitment to the continent of Africa like you. You have honored Him with your life, and He has more He wants to do with you.

CRIS: It has caused me to be more in faith regarding the various physical ailments I go through.

PAT: In my walk of faith, many times, God has plainly said no. Why some people are chosen to stay, and others are not, I don't know. But what I do know is that when God does His things straight up in your face, you become a bold-faced believer that GOD CAN DO ANYTHING...Until the next challenge. (I'm just being real!).

BERYL: We used to sing a song when I worked at a missionary organization. The words are:

> "Faith, mighty faith, the promise sees and looks to God alone.
> Laughs at impossibilities And cries it shall be done.
> And cries it shall, it shall be done, And cries it shall be done.
> Laughs at impossibilities, And cries it shall be done."

Bernard, honestly, many people whom I have prayed for who had a life-threatening illness have transitioned home to be with God or continue to suffer to some degree here on earth. Admittedly, I am glad the Lord allowed you to remain here on earth miraculously healed, but as I went through this journey with you, I realized that my faith in God has to include faith in His work and His ways. Even though I don't understand many things in life, I have come to appreciate more the promise of Romans 8:28:

> "And we know that all things work together for good to those who love God, to those who are the called according to His purpose."

KATHY: This journey, though not mine personally, has reaffirmed my faith and the power of prayer. Whenever I feel lacking, I can look at this and know again that hope is always available, and blessings are always there – small and large.

SANDRA: This journey has affected my faith greatly. It showed me how God orchestrates and plans our lives and the purpose he has for all of us.

NORMAN: At times, I would say it increased my sense of spirituality, of faith, of the possibility of God helping those that know how to ask and use what they receive.

RUTH: This journey is a reminder of not only the power of faith but also how one's internal beliefs are at the core of driving external behaviors.

LOIS: More assurance and confidence in my Lord and savior.

CECILY: This journey has contributed to my beliefs. I come from a Christian family and was baptized as a believer, but I have to say I was part of witnessing a miracle.

Another main factor was your courage and Vanessa's strength and commitment to her husband. Her love for you came out in her beautiful health updates. Her writings were like reading a descriptive excerpt from a book.

MARGARET: Every new experience in my life's journey enhances and strengthens my faith, and this one did as well.

Q: Do you consider yourself better for having gone through this journey? If so, how?

BART: I consider myself blessed and fortunate to be a part of this journey. If I am better, it is a result of seeing God's faithfulness, which builds my faith in who He is, and the might of His hand.

CHARITY: Yes, I would say so. As I've mentioned already, there were multiple health issues going on with family around the same time as the Multiple Myeloma. And while God worked miracles and provided for my family as well, it was very discouraging to continue to face difficulty after difficulty. Then, my uncle passed away after battling lung cancer in the midst of all the other issues.

So, it was a beacon of light to hear and experience a story like this one while these other circumstances were going on. Knowing the people (the Dotson's) but not being in the middle of it gives a person a unique perspective, unlike what I had experienced with the health difficulties of my sister, dad, and so on.

It helped balance things out a bit. And in the end, I think I'm better for having gone through all of it. For facing the darkness, the difficulties, the tough questions of life and faith, and coming out stronger on the other side because of stories like this one and those of my immediate family.

TALIA: I hope so. I hope that I value the people in my life and show them more. I hope that I carry on the legacy of being a testimony to God's greatness.

IRA: This journey has reinforced principles that I had already acknowledged and embraced. I saw someone I love near death. Their professional and personal accomplishments were irrelevant to the medical crisis they were facing. This was a true trial. What was in your heart in abundance was going to come to the surface.

You always expressed confidence in God. You never asked, "Why did this happen to me?" or "What did I do wrong?" or "Why did I deserve this?" You never questioned God's wisdom or His resolution of this crisis. Many people do not do that. They blame God, or they sink into a depression over their current state.

If you walk with God for any length of time, He will begin to test your personal commitment to Him. He will allow situations, obstacles, and challenges to present themselves in our lives. The test is always the same. Will you continue to love God despite what is happening in your life? Will you continue to obey God during this crisis? "Will you complain, or will you praise God for the coming victory?

In my opinion, you passed all three tests. Once you proved to the devil and all the angelic hosts that you would not compromise your love for God nor question His love for you, it opened the door for Him to restore your body to health. There is a saying about tests. It goes like this, "If you do not have a test, then you will never have a testimony." It is true that this is a play on words. Sometimes these sayings have a resonance of truth. This is one of those sayings.

CRIS: Yes, better because I feel that it has caused my faith in God to grow and be stronger.

PAT: I am so much better for having gone through this journey because it helped me appreciate my brothers more. They have just kinda always been there. Especially Bernard. He, up until this challenge, had never really been sick to my knowledge. So, the thought of him not being in my life was incomprehensible! Although I knew I wouldn't live forever, crazy as it sounds, it never crossed my mind that my brothers wouldn't either! Go figure! So, each day, whether I tell them or not, I LOVE MY BROTHERS! And appreciate every day that they are part of my life.

BERYL: I consider that I am better because I have experienced God and His presence in one of the most difficult situations that I have found myself in. Like the psalmist in Psalm 139, there is nowhere I can go that God's presence is not with me. I have become more aware of my constant need for God. I am learning to let go of my need to be in control. His presence makes all the difference.

KATHY: Yes. Watching others' depth of faith strengthens my own.

JEZ: I am more confident in the promise of God in the agreement we set in prayer and affirmation.

SANDRA: After this journey, I do consider myself bettered because it showed me how fast people can go from being healthy to being on the verge of death in a split second. The journey also changed my thought process, and appreciation for life, along with a new perspective on God's love for us.

NORMAN: Like a personal improvement...Not really. Did I learn stuff along the way? Yes.

RUTH: Not better per se. But very glad I could, along with Norman, be able to have genuinely warm and positive visits, bringing you some homemade food, and my own comfort in being able to be with both you and Vanessa during these periods of uncertainty, wear and tear.

LOIS: Oh yes. I believe God uses every occurrence in my life to reveal Himself, His character, and modus operandi!

CECILY: I feel a closer bond between you and me, but definitely a newly developed closeness with Vanessa that is definitely more of a bond than before. I respect her strength, fragility, and communication skills. I respect her honesty and ability to speak the truth.

JEFF AND CHARALE: We are both the better for having shared in your journey through the ups and the downs, the potential tragedy that turned to triumph.

MARGARET: Any experience that contributes to affirming my faith is a good one, even if it is hard to live through. I think without trouble and trials, we do not grow, so I am thankful for all my experiences, and this one is part of that reaffirmation.

JIM: I believe that any time I can be of service to others, no matter how big or small, that it makes me a better person or perhaps is just a reflection of the person that I am, or that I am capable of being.

Q: Did my cancer journey affect your perspective on your cancer journey?

MARGARET: It made me feel lucky and stronger. I know my cancer was bad, but yours was much worse, and you were actually in a more dangerous condition than I was. When I saw you making it back, it gave me encouragement that I could too.

Every cancer patient needs encouragement – we all get down and wonder if we can continue, and watching you gave me the strength to go on as well.

Q: How did our conversations as cancer patients impact you?

MARGARET: Each conversation helped me with understanding the disease and how to cope with it. I actually looked forward to them. Cancer can be a very lonely condition, and I think only someone that has it or has had it can understand that. The support I received from you and other cancer patients really helped me then and now.

Q: Did my cancer journey change your perspective on our relationship? If so, how?

NORMAN: I would not say it changed the perspective. We have had a long and close relationship. It has certainly increased the frequency with which we speak with each other.

I now think about where we are in our lives, and it has caused me to start pondering what I will do with the rest of my life. It has caused me to ponder how much life I have left, albeit an unanswerable question at this time.

RUTH: To appreciate its depth and how it goes to emotional honesty and emotional comfort—the essence of a blessed friendship!

CECILY: It did not really change it as I always have known You are a ROCK, and you also do ROCK!!!!

I love you more. Respect you more. I am so grateful to God for you crossing my path in 1976 at Cal Poly Pomona and us just hanging out.

There are few people who you do not need to see that often, but it is one of your strongest relationships. I have a unique relationship and closeness with you as you are part of my family, my brother, one of my besties. I know you are always there for me, and I have always respected you as a great human being.

MARGARET: Not really - I always knew you were a fighter. What I learned was that your faith was strong and could help support mine even more. This fellowship is important, and I don't believe we would have that connection if we had not both gone through this trial.

JIM: Your journey brought us together in a way that was certainly different than what it had been while we were at SCE and how it had evolved since those times. I would say it made our relationship much more personal as opposed to professional.

Q: Were you encouraged by the comments of others on the facebook page? If so, please elaborate.

BART: I was incredibly encouraged by the comments of support and prayer on your Facebook group. I remember frequently having my Facebook notifications overrun with responses once Vanessa posted something.

Honestly, I never would have known that people could care so much and be such a meaningful part of such a personal journey before seeing that.

CRIS: Yes. It was just a blessing to see how many people were standing in faith with you throughout.

JEZ: I was encouraged and jealous of the comments. My spiritual side is encouraged; my flesh side doesn't really know that I have that much earthly support. My Mom did not, but I learned why we all need each other, and I am better for that.

SANDRA: Yes, I was encouraged by the comments on the Facebook page. It was just uplifting to see so many people being positive.

LOIS: Yes, of course! It showed how people were standing together praying and believing, no matter what things looked like.

CECILY: You had one of the strongest and richest prayer groups I have ever been involved in. You could feel the faith. Feel the love of the Lord. Feel the love for you.

JEFF AND CHARALE: The risk of being so public with the journey is in having to navigate through well-meaning people who are not necessarily "faith folks" that may share comments that could potentially, albeit unintentionally, undermine the faith environment. We would chew on the meat and spit out the bones, so to speak, and prayed that Vanessa would be able to do likewise.

JIM: The support you received on the Facebook page was tremendous. Their faith, the support for you, and the love made it seem like a real team effort, not just you out there on your own.

This story is about you, the reader. You are now part of the journey because you have been impacted by reading this book. I do not know what impact it has had on you, but I know that it has done its part according to God's plan.

In retrospect, I have learned the best thing you can do is to stay obedient to His Word, call on His name in times of trouble, and watch Him work! It's not about me, but about He who lives in me.

> *"Whoever keeps His commandments remains in God, and God in him. And by this we know that He remains in us: by the Spirit He has given us."* — 1 John 3:24, Berean Study Bible

This story is about all of us in the final analysis, but it is not all about us. It is about God and His glory. His glory is manifested in us and through us, for His pleasure. In that way, we can all be a living testimony about the goodness of God.

> *"God does not exist to make a big deal out of us. We exist to make a big deal out of him. It's not about you. It's not about me. It's all about him."* — Max Lucado

Being a living testimony about the reality and goodness of God is only part of why God healed me. God has sustained my life for other reasons. God's plan for my life is still unfolding. My biblical worldview informs me that God is working out a divine purpose in my life that is part of His divine purpose in this world.

I am here for the pleasure of God and to fulfill my purpose on the earth. Therefore, I do not worry about how long I will be here on this side of glory. God knows the number of hairs on my head and the number of days I will inhabit the earth.

In contemporary culture, we talk about "untimely death" or "premature death." We say things like "She died too young," or "He died too soon." We probably will not ever know why a person has fewer days than we expected them to have.

But in God's economy, there is no such thing.

What I do know is, as long as I am here, I am here for a reason. God will not call for me sooner than my allotted time has passed, and I will not stay a second longer, despite what I or others think.

Retrospection ultimately leads me back to God. I always come back to the point where I recognize: All things I think about in retrospect are on my mind because God has moved in my life in some way for my good.

It does not matter if I am thinking about a celebration, a feeling of sorrow, or anything in between. God has used it for my good. It is the ultimate fulfillment of His promise in Romans 8:28.

"I will think about all that you have done; I will meditate on all your mighty acts." — Psalm 77:12, Good News Translation Bible

Moving Forward

"It is for us to pray not for tasks equal to our powers, but for powers equal to our tasks, to go forward with a great desire forever beating at the door of our hearts as we travel toward our distant goal."

— Helen Keller

ONE OF THE MOST IMPORTANT ASPECTS OF EACH LEG OF YOUR JOURNEY IN LIFE IS TO PREPARE YOU FOR THE NEXT LEG OF YOUR JOURNEY. Once I took time to look back and reflect in retrospect, I knew it was time to look ahead and move forward. I do so with strong convictions.

Oftentimes, people do not move forward sooner because they were stuck where they were. I was momentarily stuck because I was in a battle for my life. My body was under attack, and some of my bones were fractured and crushed in that battle.

I also had to contend with the side effects of the cancer treatments I received to combat Multiple Myeloma, along with back surgery to repair some of the damage caused by Multiple Myeloma.

Now that my battle is over and I have had the appropriate amount of physical, mental, and spiritual recovery, it is time for me to move forward.

To move forward, you must prepare to do so. That means bringing along the things needed to get to your destination. It also means not bringing along the things that will only slow you down. They may have been useful before, but now it is time to let them go. Then, using the lessons learned from the past, you can more easily decide what you need to carry forward and what you need to leave behind.

> *"Once your life has been broken into pieces, when it is time to move on, you only pick up the pieces that you need."* — Lynda Varada

> *"If all that we see are the scattered pieces of 'what was,' the story of 'what is yet to be' will never be told. If, however, we are able to envision the pieces as what they are now freed to be, the story of 'what is yet to be' will stand among the greatest ever told."*
> — Craig D. Lounsbrough

The first part of moving forward is a living testimony about this journey. I believe this is the first step in moving forward for all of us who were a part of this journey.

"There will come a time when you believe everything is finished. That will be the beginning." — Louis L'Amour

"Take the first step in faith. You don't have to see the whole staircase, just take the first step." — Martin Luther King, Jr.

I asked my support team members if they have moved forward by sharing lessons learned and giving a testimony about their experiences. Here is how they responded to the questions I asked:

Q: What advice would you give to someone who found themselves in a situation similar to yours?

BART: If I had a friend that suddenly found out that his or her father was diagnosed with Stage 4 cancer, I would tell them three things:

First, prayer works miracles, and there are people out there who will support you in your journey.

Second, make it a point to spend as much time with your parent as you can (especially if you live in their town), no matter how painful it is.

Third, don't neglect what you're feeling on the inside. This will be a journey and a fight – make sure to have grace with yourself, your emotions, your thoughts, and your responses to each thing that happens along the way.

CHARITY: After facing many health difficulties with loved ones from multiple angles and perspectives, I would tell someone else that God really is the only way to get through the stress, pain, and hardship.

I know that can sound like a cliché, but when worry, or stress, or anxiety, or circumstances are far bigger than yourself, find their way into your life, you have two options: You can crumble and fall apart from either not knowing what to do or from trying to do everything on your own; Or you can realize you can't do this by yourself, seek and accept help, and most of all, believe prayer is the most powerful thing we can do, and allow the Lord to guide and direct your steps as He promises in His word (Psalm 32:8)."

TALIA: Don't ask why; just follow through. Whatever you can do, do that.

IRA: First, I would want to know if they are a Christian. If they were not a Christian, I would extend them the opportunity to become a Christian. Without God, your future destiny is so horrifying that you would want an opportunity to return to Earth and repent.

If they were not are a Christian, I would share how God healed my brother from cancer, final stage cancer. I would encourage them to remain committed to God regardless of the circumstances. I would want to know if they had a Bible-believing pastor that can assist in shepherding them through this crisis. I would share God's promises regarding healing.

Finally, I would ask if I could pray for them and continue to pray for God's solution in their lives.

CRIS: I would tell them that God is not a respecter of persons. What He's done for others, He'll do for them.

PAT: I would encourage them to TRUST GOD!! I would encourage them to believe in the power of corporate prayer. Nothing is too hard for the Lord!!

BERYL: Ask yourself the question, not why has this happened, but Who is in absolute control of all things?

Know that you, too, have been chosen by God to be on this journey. Submit to the process. Be open to what God is teaching you.

Ask God to guide you on how to best support the person directly going through this situation and follow His lead.

Find out what the individual/family would want from you. Honor their wishes.

If individual/family permits, come together as a community to engage in prayer, support, encouragement, and spiritual warfare. Share updates, and provide tangible support, i.e., food, money, time.

Look for God to show up in some unexpected places, unexpected ways. Reflect upon who He is, His Word, His ways.

Journal your experience.

Share with others the lessons that you are learning without violating confidentiality unless you have individual/family's approval.

KATHY: I would tell people to never give up hope, pray even if they're not sure, and prepare for an outcome different than you'd like. Offer support in whatever way you can, even if it is just to listen with no solution.

JEZ: I would say, be encouraged and seek solutions.

SANDRA: If I found someone in a similar situation, I would advise that they don't lose hope.

NORMAN: There is an intersection here with my religion. We offer to bring a meal, and we offer to listen. We are supposed to help the sick in the ways we can. When Vanessa asked if folks could bring a meal to help lighten her burden, we did. We spoke more frequently.

I think I would suggest similar things to someone in the same situation.

Help where and when you can help. Even the cheesecake was a way I thought I could help by making you desire food (Okay, so that did not work so well).

RUTH: To take whatever steps you can, and allow others to help and do as they can. One cannot know the future, but you can do the best of your ability, even as that ability may have good days and bad days. Pursue all avenues of information, a wide range of resources, and confer/consult with select others about the right next steps for you to take, even if the odds are small.

MICHAEL: Use the Word of God.

LOIS: Believe God, stand with the person ill, especially if they can't. Be the one in the gap; be open to assist wherever the family needs you if at all possible. Send words of encouragement.

CECILY: Not sure how to answer this. It is who I am to assist people through the health process with the best information I have. If I do not know, I usually will find out.

JEFF AND CHARALE: We would counsel anyone who finds themselves in a similar situation where a loved one has been given a proverbial "death sentence" to be there for them in every way. Pray with them, pray for them, do what you can in the natural realm to support them. Lift them up with phone calls, texts, visits to the extent that it is feasible and practical without allowing your support to be a burden that they would need to manage. Love on them as the Holy Spirit leads, and keep hoping for the best, and believing for the best, and expecting to see the best outcome – total healing as He promised in his Word.

MARGARET: PRAY – and act!! FIGHT, don't give up – get help, and don't listen to anything negative. Find the right doctor, medical team, and treatment for you and stick with it. Mostly, pray and get the prayer chains going. Get your support team in place and make sure they stay with you all the way.

JIM: The advice I would give would be to determine what kind of support they could provide and then do so. That will be different depending on factors such as geographic proximity and others. I believe the consistency of the support, not just a one-time thing, regardless of what the support is, is important.

Q: Have you already shared my story with others? If so, how has it impacted their lives?

BART: Yes, I have shared your story with all of my close friends, as well as my church.

My church leaders, in particular, have been very receptive to hearing what God has done in your life. With my close friends, it has actually opened up conversations about deeper issues: faith, parents, and death.

CHARITY: I have mentioned or briefly shared your story with others.

I'm not sure of the impact on their lives, but I'm sure it was encouraging in some way. It's a story I look forward to telling more of in the future as well.

TALIA: Yes. I try to encourage others to always do their best and do what they know is right. I can't speak for others, but that is always what I am illustrating when I tell your story.

I've been meeting more and more people going through some form of cancer treatment. Sharing your story offers them encouragement and inspiration while allowing them to express the difficult feelings and emotions of this process. Many people state that it is difficult for them to talk to those who have not been through it, and they feel a sense of comfort and acceptance when speaking and interacting with me. I am able to encourage and support others in my community.

IRA: I have shared your testimony with a few people. Some of my friends knew what you were going through, so they rejoiced when I told them of your healing.

It seemed like it encouraged them regarding relatives facing a similar situation. As we age, illnesses have begun to crop up with our friends and family. At times like these, it is important to have people around you that will aid your recovery.

PAT: Yes. People are amazed to hear of God's healing power. Also, when they hear of your attitude through it all ("why not me?"), they leave encouraged.

BERYL: Yes, I have shared your story with people in my support system who were praying for you as well as with people whom I have met only once.

I have had several people tell me that they have family/friends dealing with major life issues. Your story has encouraged my contacts to not lose heart or allow their emotions to get the best of them. One person whom I do not know well came up to me and said thank you. Just hearing how you responded to your diagnosis and seeing your story unfold was a blessing. I plan to give the book to several of them.

KATHY: Yes. I believe I have encouraged others by sharing your story, those living with MM and those not. I have also been equally encouraged by their experiences.

JEZ: I have shared your story.

I do not know that it has changed their lives, but I know I could candidly speak of how I felt responsible for my mom's demise, as I am learning of my power, the power God has given me.

In my immaturity, I fed my mother every negative outcome instead of affirming her with the power of the word. I knew that her diet had changed, by orders of the doctor, to animal-based, for iron. I got good information and never gave it to her. I never prayed.

This taught me to be different. I sought after God for your survival. I did not tell a soul of my fasting. I took it as my personal responsibility for your and my healing. I prayed that your children would not have to lose their dad. I prayed they would not know this loss this soon. I prayed for your wife because she did not deserve to have such a great believer and lose him this soon.

SANDRA: Yes. I have shared your story with others. I'm not sure how your story may have impacted their lives, but it has certainly changed and impacted mine tremendously.

NORMAN: Yes. Folks you know - my family, Barry, Carol, Rachel - and folks you don't know.

I do not know how it has impacted their lives. There is a woman I work with occasionally up in Corvallis, Oregon. She has cancer. She has been through at least one round of chemo. I suspect more unless her hair never grew back. She is off for round N+1.

I did mention your situation briefly to her so that she knows you can outrun cancer for some unknown period of time. I hope she has your faith, luck, skilled doctors, strength.

RUTH: Yes. I was mostly remarking on what a remarkable person of strength and faith you are, to have survived the various rounds of treatment for each step along the way, and to come through it all with your deep sense of gratitude and positivity, as well as truly embracing Life.

I don't know how it has impacted their lives.

LOIS: Of course, I did; they were in awe at the time – I don't know beyond that.

CECILY: Yes. I feel your cancer journey was a testimony to the strongest faith in the Lord for healing I have ever witnessed. You remained steadfast through it all. Not questioning why me, but acceptance, and looking forward not behind.

These are the steps I needed to take. And now, as you had predicted, there is no sign of MM. You have been healed. Through it all, You stayed very cool.

Which reminds me of another flashback; one of my favorites: Sitting in my dorm room visiting, You grabbed my sunglasses and put them on and proceeded to imitate Stevie Wonder as he sang a song on the radio.

It cracked me up! You are so spontaneous; So funny; So cool. When I shared your story, they admired you and your grace.

My fondest memory of you: You were in front of our dorms at Cal Poly Pomona. We were just standing out front, and from a standing position, you decided to do a backflip.

I was amazed, as I would have to do a round-off backflip. I was never able to get that POWER and height.

There is my analogy about your testimony.

JEFF AND CHARALE: After you shared your testimony at late night prayer, we shared your story of faith and victory with a number of people who were going through a major health challenge. We have purchased and distributed a number of the CDs of that testimony.

I know they were inspired, and their faith was strengthened by hearing your testimony. One person, in particular, comes to mind, whose daughter was going through a bout with a form of cancer. Her battle has been ongoing over the past couple of years, but she is seeing the signs of victory in her battle as we write this. As the Bible says in the book of Revelation, "we overcome by the blood of the lamb and the word of our testimony."

MARGARET: Yes – I have shared both our stories with at least three other cancer patients that had given up, and they are still kicking!!! I tell both our stories every chance I get. I think it is important for everyone to know cancer can be beaten, and we can win if it is God's will.

I think it did impact their lives, but most people do not tell you if that is the case. I think they are very busy just holding it together.

JIM: I kept others who knew you from SCE up to date on your journey, as well as others who are involved in similar journeys.

For the most part, people wanted to know how you were doing and were glad to hear of your remission and recovery.

The New Normal

new normal [**noo-nawr**-m*uh*l]
noun
1. What replaces the expected, usual, typical state after an event occurs.
2. The current state of being after some dramatic change has transpired.
The new normal encourages one to deal with current situations rather than lamenting what could have been.

— urbandictionary.com

There are two definitions of the term "new normal." One is that which has replaced what used to be considered normal. The other is a state of being. One is about the current situation and how a person deals with it; the other is about the person. One is external; the other is internal.

Throughout this journey, Vanessa and I wondered about and were in pursuit of the new normal. It is evident in my recollections and Vanessa's posts. Our focus was on the second definition of the term. We were waiting to get our lives back in order, to get organized in the normal routines of life.

I am now in remission, and no sign of myeloma cells can be seen in my body. We have arrived at that point in time we've talked about. We have begun to make decisions about what the new normal will be for us.

Before I share with you what the new normal looks like for us, I want to share with you an observation I think is important to note.

During our journey, several very significant events occurred. After each one, we found our situation had changed significantly. We were, in effect, in a short-term new normal state. So, we went through several mini, "new normal" states along the way.

In the midst of it all, however, we did not see these incremental changes as our "new normal" for the time being. We were waiting to get to where we are now. It was as if our lives were on hold. What we did not realize was that our lives were never on hold.

> *"For a long time it had seemed to me that life was about to begin – real life. But there was always some obstacle in the way. Something to be got through first, some unfinished business, time still to be served, a debt to be paid. Then life would begin. At last it dawned on me that these obstacles were my life."* — Fr. Alfred D'Souza

We were living out the life we had by continuing to seek God for help and for strength to overcome the current obstacle we were facing at the time. All of those other things that needed to be taken care of, the things we wanted to do in an organized manner, were still being taken care of somehow, sometimes in miraculous ways.

What we did not realize at the time was that God was fulfilling a promise He made to us in scripture:

> *"You have armed me with strength for battle; You have subdued my foes beneath me."* — Psalm 18:39, Berean Study Bible

Vanessa would sometimes recognize the miracles (money showing up exactly when we needed it, for example), but not that they were associated with this promise. So again, it goes to show how God makes good on His word, whether we know it or not.

Vanessa and I considered the different aspects of our lives and what the new normal situation is shaping up to be in each area. For each area, we have made some decisions about the routines we will establish as the usual way we live our lives. We looked at my healthcare, home life, family life, social life, work-life, and church life. Our analytical personality traits have kicked in.

As far as my healthcare goes, I will transition to maintenance mode chemotherapy and remain on the clinical trial. That means weekly visits to City of Hope for lab work, infusion, and annual bone marrow biopsies. Having a compromised immune system means I need to contact City of Hope whenever my vital signs stray from the "normal" range. I may, on occasion, go to City of Hope to determine what my body is fighting.

Vanessa and I will divide the household chores in our home life pretty much the way we used to as my strength returns. There are some things that I cannot do due to restrictions my doctors have placed on me. Most of them have to do with heavy lifting and the types of exercise I can do.

If there is something that I can no longer do, I will seek help from others. Sometimes that other person may be Vanessa. For example, one of the things I can no longer do is climb up into the attic. That is something I will have to get someone other than Vanessa to do.

When traveling alone, I will not take carry-on items on planes that will not fit under my seat. I will not attempt to put something in the overhead storage compartment because I should not lift more than fifteen pounds over my head. If it cannot fit under my seat, I will check the bag at the ticket counter.

In our family life, most things will return to what they were before my diagnosis. We will get together with local family members as usual, and we will travel back east to be with Vanessa's family as usual. That means typically visiting two or three times a year. In addition, we will go see Bart and Charity periodically once they settle into married life.

I will ask for help when it comes time for clean-up after our annual Dotson Thanksgiving gathering. In the past, I would do all of the remaining clean-up after the family members left. Vanessa and I had come to that decision a while ago. She would do the cooking, and I would do the cleaning. The only thing I am on the hook to prepare is the smoked salmon.

In our social life, most things will pretty much return to what they were before my diagnosis. The one thing that will be different is Vanessa and I will continue to attend meetings of the San Gabriel Valley Multiple Myeloma Support Group.

In our work lives, things will return to what they were before my diagnosis for Vanessa. She will be more available for work travel because she will not have to be a caregiver for me. When I return to work, I will not travel as much as before. I will seek opportunities to work from home most of the time and limit travel to about one week per month.

In our church life, we will return to most of the activities we participated in before being diagnosed. We will return to attending our local life group meetings and our regular church services. Some Sundays, I would find it difficult to make the 27-mile trip to church and back. On those Sundays, we will watch the service online or visit a local church to be amongst the saints.

What will change is our participation in mission trips. My oncologist has advised that I not participate in such demanding activities in a foreign country.

I remember when Vanessa and I would lead mission trips, and we would have potential team members complete the medical questionnaire. If I were to complete that questionnaire now, I probably would not qualify to be a team member.

So, I have had to realize that my season of being a short-term missionary has come to an end. I have no regrets. I feel as though I completed my divine assignment in that area, and I will continue to support missionary work in other ways.

I thank God that the new normal is not that much different from normal before my diagnosis.

> *"I have seen his ways, and will heal him; I will lead him also, and restore comforts unto him and his mourners. I create the fruit of the lips; Peace, peace to him that is far off and to him that is near, saith the Lord; and I will heal him."*
> — Isaiah 57:18-19, King James Version Bible

As I stated before, there are two definitions of the term "new normal." I have just shared with you our new normal in terms of the first definition. But, additionally, I also have a "new normal" in terms of the second definition. It is the new normal for my state of being.

I have a new normal in my physical, mental, and spiritual being.

The changes that make up the new normal in my physical being include:

- A skeletal system that is prone to lesions if made subjected to too much stress;
- A compromised immune system for as long as I take chemotherapy medication;
- A slight case of neuropathy in my toes and fingers;
- Loss of feeling along parts of my spine due to the cutting of peripheral nerves during back surgery;
- Minor tingling sensation to the touch on my abdomen and back;
- Occasional late night muscle cramps in my lower legs and feet;
- Abdominal muscle cramps when I flex those muscles.

All of these changes are minor afflictions that serve as a tangible reminder of the journey. I see them as being my "thorn in the flesh," similar to the one carried by Apostle Paul. God's grace is sufficient, and that His power is perfected in my weakness.

The new normal in my mental being includes:

- <u>Having greater mental toughness.</u> Here is the definition of mental toughness I refer to:

    mental toughness [**men**-t*uh*l **tuhf**-nuhs]

    noun

    The ability to resist, manage and overcome doubts, worries, concerns and circumstances that prevent you from succeeding, or excelling at a task or towards an objective or a performance outcome that you set out to achieve.

    — Mental Toughness Inc.

Staying focused on God, and being willing to give Him praise no matter what I was going through, helped me develop more mental toughness.

- <u>Having a different perspective on death and dying.</u> Facing the possibility of my death, and watching others do the same in my cancer support communities, has changed how I view dying.

    Wrestling with the prospects of your imminent death is more about coming to terms with how you have lived your life and how short life really is.

I believe that is why those who have survived talk about making sure their lives matter moving forward, telling others they love them, and how every day is a blessing or a gift.

My perspective on death has changed because of my involvement with my cancer support communities. Death is more commonplace in support communities. As a result, the fear and stigma of death are not as prevalent there as they are in society. Instead, it is more of a reminder that we are dealing with serious illnesses, and death is a part of life.

I have attended several funerals for support group members. For me, their deaths became more of a way to honor them and celebrate their lives. In addition, I got to know another side of people who had shared very private and personal information with me by hearing their lives told by their loved ones.

I have become more aware that death is how we transition from finite life to everlasting life with God and Jesus or eternal torment and damnation without them. Death is a comma, not a period. It is a weigh station, not the last stop. We continue to exist. It is more than just suffering the loss of a loved one. It makes me more thankful for the God in me that gives me hope.

The new normal in my spiritual being is very different than the other new normals for my physical and mental being. The effects of Multiple Myeloma caused those. My spiritual new normal is one that I was called to by God to step into.

God called me to this new normal because I have grown in faith and have a deeper connection with Him. This new spiritual normal causes me to view what used to be mountains as molehills. This new spiritual normal is a greater expectation of what is possible because I have experienced what was once impossible.

I am indeed a better person for having gone on this journey.

I have one last comment about the new normal. I do not expect the new normal to remain the new normal for an extended period. Over time, that which is normal changes. We oftentimes think of a new normal as change due to some significant event (like the birth of a child) or a major crisis.

But in reality, we are constantly evolving into the next version of ourselves.

> *"Everything is in the process of becoming something else. It's the law of change."* — C.J. Roberts

I've Got More To Do

"... But one thing I do: Forgetting what is behind and straining toward what is ahead, I press on toward the goal to win the prize of God's heavenly calling in Christ Jesus."
— Philippians 3:12-14, Berean Study Bible

Vanessa and I have given our testimony about this journey to our church family. We are continuing to share our story by writing and publishing this book. But there is more to do besides sharing our story.

I feel in my spirit that my more to do is moving from success to significance.

Success and significance are not the same. Success is about achieving goals you have set for yourself for your benefit. Significance is about making a difference in the world, leaving the world a better place because you were here, leaving a legacy that has left a positive impact on others outside of your immediate family.

At this stage in my life, I have reached some level of success. I have achieved some personal goals, and I have reached some professional goals; I have found and married my life partner; we have raised children and sent them to college; we have some material possessions. Of course, I have not achieved all of my personal goals, but I can say I have reached some level of success by all accounts.

For those of you who have read this story and are in the same season of life that I am, you have probably come to realize that your success is not enough. There is something inside you that is not satisfied despite what you have accomplished.

It begs the question, "Is this all that life is about?" There has got to be something more. It leads you to one of life's big questions, "Why Am I Here?" If you know what I'm talking about, if this resonates deeply with you, you have reached the point where you want to transition from success to significance.

I realize that I am transitioning into a season that will be more about significance than it is about success. Not that success will not be a part of it (and failures too, for that matter), but significance will play a more prominent role in what I decide to do and invest my resources, with time being my most precious resource.

With God's leading, I sense that I will be moving ever forward to fulfilling my purpose on the earth and discovering why I am still here and not on the other side of the dirt. I will bring forward into this new season those things that will help me be significant and leave behind those things that will hinder me from being significant.

"If what you did yesterday still looks big to you, you haven't done much today."
— Lou Holtz

I anticipate this new season will take me places I have not imagined as I continue to have faith in God's Word. I believe the Apostle Paul's prayer for the Ephesians applies to me:

> *"I ask that out of the riches of His glory He may strengthen you with power through His Spirit in your inner being, so that Christ may dwell in your hearts through faith.*
>
> *Then you, being rooted and grounded in love, will have power, together with all the saints, to comprehend the length and width and height and depth of the love of Christ, and to know this love that surpasses knowledge, that you may be filled with all the fullness of God.*
>
> *Now to Him who is able to do so much more than all we ask or imagine, according to His power that is at work within us, to Him be the glory in the church and in Christ Jesus throughout all generations, forever and ever. Amen."* — Ephesians 3:16-20, Berean Study Bible

I say this because my cancer journey has already caused some of this to happen. I never imagined being in Zion, Illinois. I did not know it even existed. I never imagined meeting so many new people along the way; my healthcare providers at CTCA and City of Hope, the cancer support communities I have become a member of, and those who have reached out to me because they heard about my journey.

I believe all of these places and people have been put into my life for me to make a significant difference in their lives, just as they have and will make a significant difference in mine.

All this to the glory of God.

> *"The highest calling is less about where you are called, but all about Who called you and what you are called to do among the people you encounter."* — Bishop Edward A. Smith

I will no longer be so presumptuous as to assume I know what the future holds for the Facebook Prayer Team, nor anything else. I will instead keep reminding myself of the answer to the question I posed at the beginning of this book. "How did I (now we) get here?" We got here by faith. The Facebook Prayer Team is, and always will be, a journey of faith.

> *"For we walk by faith, not by sight."*
> — 2 Corinthians 5:7, New King James Version Bible

Final Thoughts

I found much comfort in Bible scriptures and inspirational quotations throughout the course of this journey. After my bout with Multiple Myeloma, I gained a new appreciation for all the verses of the Serenity Prayer by Reinhold Niebuhr:

> *God grant me the Serenity to accept the things I cannot change,*
> *Courage to change the things I can, and*
> *Wisdom to know the difference.*
> *Living one day at a time, enjoying each moment at a time.*
> *Accepting hardship as the pathway to peace.*
> *Taking, as He did, this sinful world as it is, not as I would have it.*
> *Trusting that He will make all things right if I surrender to His will.*
> *That I may be reasonably happy in this life.*
> *And supremely happy with Him forever in the next.*
> *Amen*

I also experienced the following scripture on this side of eternity, and will experience it again when I am promoted to glory:

> *"Blessed is the man who perseveres under trial because when he has stood the test, he will receive the crown of life that God has promised to those who love Him."* — James 1:12, New King James Version

Lastly, as a result of this journey, I am inspired by this quotation:

> *"In the story of life, the prologue and epilogue are written by God. Yet the plot has been given to us; therefore we should write the best prose we can."* — James D. Maxon

Appendices

About Zion

Zion, Israel

Zion is a place name often used as a synonym for Jerusalem. It commonly refers to a specific mountain near Jerusalem (Mount Zion), where a Jebusite fortress of the same name stood. King David of Israel conquered it and renamed it David's City. He is the same David in the Bible that slew Goliath, the Philistine giant, by hitting him in the head with a stone David threw from his slingshot when David was a young boy.

For Christians, the Bible tells us that Zion is the place on earth where God lived amongst the Jewish people after King David's conquest. It was a holy place where the people sought spiritual refuge and received many blessings from God.

Zion, IL

Zion, Illinois, was founded July 15, 1901, by the Reverend Dr. John Alexander Dowie (1847-1907), a Scottish-born minister with extraordinary healing powers. Many testimonies of these healings were presented in Superior Court in Chicago during this time on his behalf. That included healings of prominent citizens of the time, such as Amanda Hicks, a first cousin of Abraham Lincoln, and Miss Jean Harrison, a niece of U.S. President Benjamin Harrison, and Sadie Cody, the niece of Buffalo Bill.

Dr. Dowie printed a weekly publication known as The Leaves of Healing. This publication contained reports of sermons, testimonies, and other points of interest to his congregation. But, most importantly, it reported a vast number of remarkable miracles of healing. "Salvation, Healing, and Holy Living" was the trademark theme of his sermons. These reports circulated throughout the world, and people began to come from great distances for healing.

After the organization of the Christian Catholic Church in Zion, Dr. Dowie dreamed of a city where his congregation would be free from the evils of the world, a city where God would be the ruler. He first looked for land south of Chicago in the Blue Island area, but the land was not suitable, so he searched north of the city. In the fall of 1899, Dr. Dowie visited the land north of Waukegan and envisioned what he would come to name "Zion City."

Zion, IL, is about 45 miles north of the heart of the city of Chicago. Zion is a mile and a half west of Lake Michigan and approximately three miles south of the Wisconsin border.

After successfully securing options on approximately 6,600 acres of land, he unveiled his plan for Zion City at the Watchnight Service on the eve of the New Year 1900. It would be a city where his congregation could worship, work, and play free from the temptations of the world. Zion City was the only city besides Washington D.C. that had plans completed before the first spade of dirt was turned.

There would be places of employment—he imported a lace mill from England—schools and recreational facilities, all controlled by Dr. Dowie. The land would be leased to the people, with definite restrictions, for 1100 years. Dr. Dowie reasoned that Christ's return was to be within 100 years and then the millennium, after which there would be no need for leases. People would share in the profits of the industries in Zion City, and the profits, tithes, and offerings would be sufficient to support the Christian Catholic Church in Zion.

On July 14, 1900, hundreds of people came to what would become Zion City for an all-day affair that culminated in the City's dedication to God. The following year Dr. Dowie's team surveyed the city, laying out all the lots, planning for the utilities, and preparing for the City's opening to the people.

July 15, 1901, was the date that the City lots were made available to the public. The first house was built shortly after that, in August 1901. Dr. Dowie and his family came to Zion City from Chicago in July 1902 and moved into Shiloh House, his newly constructed home. Within two years, nearly 10,000 people came to this new city.

Reverend Anton Darms, an Overseer in the Christian Catholic Church of Zion who knew Dr. Dowie personally, later wrote,

> "The City of Zion was, therefore, to be a city free, so far as it could be made free, by imperfect man, from evil and the contaminating influences generally prevalent in the ungodly cities of the world. It was to be a great object lesson to the world, in which the doctrines of Christianity could be worked out without being hampered by the

ungodly influences of the world, and where the Rule of God would be first in the lives of all the inhabitants."

When I decided to go, I did not know exactly where the hospital was located other than Chicago. It certainly was not the Regional Medical Center located closest to my home in California. I did not choose the Midwest Regional Medical Center because its location had a tangential biblical reference. Instead, I desperately looked for something with "spiritual overtones" to guide me. I chose to go to the CTCA center in Chicago because I felt in my spirit this is where I was to go.

I believe that God speaks to us in ways that, from a human point of view, seem to be coincidental circumstances at best and are typically viewed as having no significance whatsoever. But the Bible says,

> *"The natural man does not accept the things that come from the Spirit of God. For they are foolishness to him, and he cannot understand them, because they are spiritually discerned."* — 1 Corinthians 2:14

I believe that God, through the unction of the Holy Spirit, led me to Zion.

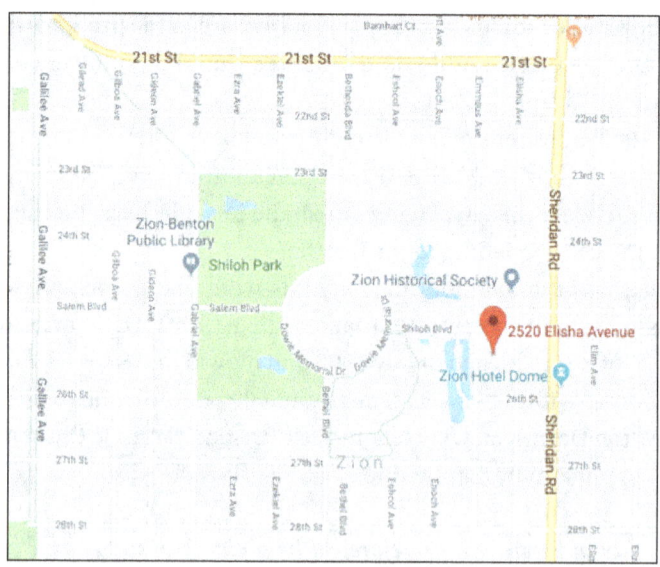

Zion, IL

2520 Elisha Avenue, Zion IL is the street address of Cancer Treatment Centers of America, Chicago.

APPENDICES

Shiloh House, Zion, IL – Home of the Reverend Dr. John Alexander Dowie

Shiloh Park, Zion, IL – West of CTCA Chicago

About CTCA, Chicago

In the early 1950s, Dr. Kalom came to Zion and established a family medicine practice. Dr. Kalom recognized the need for a hospital in town to serve the medical needs of the residents. With the help of William Bicket and others, Dr. Kalom broke ground in 1953. In 1958 construction of the 50-bed hospital was completed. In 1963, a group of community leaders bought the hospital and changed the hospital's name to Zion-Benton hospital. In 1975, the hospital was sold to Capital Investment Company and headed by attorney Richard J. Stephenson as Chairman of the Board.

Capital Investment Company changed the name to American International Hospital. Its cancer program was one of the first in the country to offer a wide range of treatment services—surgery, chemotherapy, radiation therapy, immunotherapy, hyperthermia, tumor biology, nutrition, psycho-social intervention, and spiritual support. Throughout the United States and around the world, patients discovered American International Hospital and traveled hundreds and thousands of miles for care.

Cancer Treatment Centers of America® (CTCA) was founded in 1988 by Stephenson in honor of his mother, who lost her battle with cancer in 1982. To keep his mother's spirit alive, Stephenson embarked on a mission to change the face of cancer care. As a result, CTCA implemented the Mother Standard® of Care where "Stakeholders treat patients, caregivers and each other as if they were members of their own family." The CTCA in Suburban Chicago broke ground on September 25, 1991. Renovations and expansion have taken place since 1998, completing in 2016.

When I arrived in July 2015, construction was underway of the new inpatient tower. At the time of this writing, CTCA's medical staff comprises more than 100 physicians specializing in oncology, emergency medicine, cardiology, internal medicine, family practice, gastroenterology, orthopedics, surgery, podiatric medicine, and nearly 20 other medical areas.

CTCA, Zion, IL; Expansion Project in 2016

Main Entrance - CTCA, Zion, IL, 2016

Northwest entrance to CTCA - Zion, IL

About City of Hope

City of Hope originally started in 1912 as the Los Angeles Sanatorium. A small tuberculosis sanatorium located near Los Angeles operated by the Jewish Consumptive Relief Association (JCRA). It was incorporated in the State of California in May 1913.

In 1914, the JCRA bought ten acres of land in Duarte, California, after Los Angeles required all consumption facilities to be located outside the city limits.

In 1926, Samuel H. Golter became the sanatorium superintendent. In 1932, faced with the Great Depression and a large institutional debt, Golter took on the Executive Director's job to revitalize the sanatorium. He was able not only to save the institution, but to expand it during the 1930s and 1940s. As a result, it was nicknamed "The City of Hope." The use of "City of Hope" first appears in a 1916 report.

By the end of World War II, tuberculosis vaccines were beginning to significantly decrease the prevalence of tuberculosis, and the need for sanatoriums was lessening. In 1946, Golter proposed that the sanatorium become a comprehensive medical center.

The board and delegates to the JCRA's biennial convention approved a campaign to build a new medical building and facilities to treat cancer and tuberculosis. Golter partnered with the UCLA Medical School to create the new Medical Research Institute, City of Hope National Medical Center. In 1952 it was called the City of Hope Cancer Research Institute. The program was sponsored jointly by the City of Hope and UCLA.

The humanitarian principles underlying the sanatorium were deeply important to Golter. His motto, "There is no profit in curing the body, if in the process, we destroy the soul," appears on the Golter Gate in the International Garden of Meditation (the Rose Garden) at City of Hope, emphasizing this patient-centered philosophy. Regarding the sanatorium, he stated:

> *"I felt more than ever that in enlarging the scope of our services we could satisfy both of the entities within man – the spiritual as well as the physical. Our functional program which was dedicated to the saving and prolonging of human life would serve man's physical self, and personal participation in furthering that humanitarian objective would fortify and strengthen his spiritual self."*

I was comforted when I learned about the principles City of Hope was founded on because they touched upon three things that I value: hope, soul, and miracles.

City of Hope - Duarte Road Entrance

City of Hope - Main Medical Entrance

City of Hope - Helford Hospital

The Main Medical building is where I received much of my treatments when my Multiple Myeloma was active and continue to go for low dose chemotherapy maintenance treatments.

Helford Hospital is where I received my Stem Cell Transplant.

About Cancer Support Community Pasadena

The mission of Cancer Support Community is to ensure that all people impacted by cancer are EMPOWERED by knowledge, STRENGTHENED by action, and SUSTAINED by community.

Cancer Support Community is the largest cancer support provider worldwide, with 42 affiliates across the country – including Cancer Support Community Pasadena – and in Canada, Israel, and Japan. Cancer Support Community Pasadena ("CSCP") was the third CSC affiliate established in 1990.

Widely recognized as the "gold standard" among providers of cancer support services, Cancer Support Community Pasadena ("CSCP") has been providing free, professionally-led support, education, and hope to families facing cancer for over 30 years.

Offering 14 weekly and monthly support groups and over 100 monthly educational workshops and healthy lifestyle classes, CSCP has long been a beacon of hope for the greater San Gabriel Valley, opening its doors to patients, caregivers, children, survivors, and those who are bereaved. Additional services include one-on-one counseling sessions and social activities for the entire family.

All of CSCP's programs are grounded in evidence-based research that validates effectiveness in diminishing distress and improving the quality of life for people impacted by cancer. Located on the second floor of the Pasadena Humane building, CSCP provides a lifeline for families at perhaps the most challenging time in their lives.

Cancer Support Community Pasadena Offices

I highly recommend CSCP for anyone living in its service area. The staff and volunteers have a passion for what they do, and many of them are cancer survivors themselves or have a close loved one they have cared for with cancer. They really know how to support the cancer community with psycho-social services.

The best part of CSCP is that all of its services are free!

Citations

Afghan Proverb. (n.d.). Retrieved from Worldofproverbs.com Website: http://www.worldofproverbs.com/2017/05/a-real-friend-is-one-who-takes-hand-of.html

African Proverb. (n.d.). Retrieved from Quotes.net Website: https://www.quotes.net/quote/41889

Angel, Criss. (n.d.). Quote. BrainyQuote.com. Retrieved from BrainyQuote.com Web site: https://www.brainyquote.com/quotes/criss_angel_511782

Angelou, Maya. (1993) Wouldn't Take Nothing for My Journey Now. Penguin Random House. Retrieved from Goodreads.com Web site: https://www.goodreads.com/quotes/284542-when-we-give-cheerfully-and-accept-gratefully-everyone-is-blessed

Angelou, Maya. (n.d.) Quote. Retrieved from Quotespedia.info Web site: http://www.quotespedia.info/quotes-about-human-long-as-does-every-human-being-to-be-at-home-wherever-find-myself-a-5477.html

Ashe, Arthur. (2011). Days of Grace: A Memoir. Ballantine Books. Retrieved from Brainyquote.com Web site: https://www.brainyquote.com/quotes/arthur_ashe_371540

Atkinson, Gordon. (2018). Crocodile Hunter. Gordonatkinson.net/rlp-archive/crocodile-hunter. Retrieved from Quotationspage.com Web site: http://www.quotationspage.com/quote/31375.html

Bailey, Boyd. (2014). God's Permissive Will. Wisdomhunters.com. Retrieved from Wisdomhunters.com Web site: https://www.wisdomhunters.com/gods-permissive-will/

Baum, Frank L. (1900). The Wonderful Wizard of Oz. G.M. Hill Company. Retrieved from Pinterest Web site: https://www.pinterest.co.uk/pin/141652350749904436/

Baxter, John. (2005). A Pound of Paper: Confessions of a Book Addict. Thomas Dunne Books. Retrieved from Goodreads.com Web site: https://www.goodreads.com/quotes/7361988-the-whole-point-of-collecting-is-the-thrill-of-acquisition

Beecher, Henry Ward. (n.d.). Quotation #5212 from Cole's Quotables. Retrieved from Quotationspage.com Web site: http://www.quotationspage.com/quote/5212.html

Berry, Wendell. (1943). The Loss of the Future. Harvard University Press. Retrieved from Quotemaster.org Web site: https://www.quotemaster.org/q10a256a24a47f482da6c9b14da83cb81

Berry, Wendell. (1967). A Place on Earth. Avon. Retrieved from AZQuotes.com Web site: https://www.azquotes.com/citation/quote/410550,

Birthday.Kim. (2020). Count not the candles///see the lights they give. Birthday. Kim. Retrieved from Birthday.Kim Web site: https://www.birthday.kim/count-not-the-candlessee-the-lights-they-give/3382/

Borland, Hal. (1964). Sundial of the Seasons. Echo Point Books & Media, LLC. Retrieved from Brainyquote.com. Web site: https://www.brainyquote.com/quotes/hal_borland_151983

Bron, Mila. (n.d.). Quote Retrieved from Pinterest.com Web site: https://www.pinterest.com/pin/313774299017100180/

Burgunder, Brittany. (2021) Hiding the Need for Help blog. Brittanyburgunder.com. Retrieved from Goodreads.com Web site: https://www.goodreads.com/quotes/10529391-needing-help-doesn-t-have-a-look-but-asking-for-it

Butcher, Jim. (2007). Proven Guilty (The Dresden Files, Book 8). Roc. Retrieved from AZQuotes.com. Web site: https://www.azquotes.com/citation/quote/522753

Carnegie, Dale. (1944). How to Stop Worrying and Start Living. Gallery Books. Retrieved from Goodreads Web site: https://www.goodreads.com/book/show/4866.How_to_Stop_Worrying_and_Start_Living

Carroll, Lewis. (1865). Alice in Wonderland. Macmillan. Retrieved from Villainquoteoftheday.tmblr.com Web site: https://villainquoteoftheday.tumblr.com/post/121337882834/jabberwocky-so-my-old-foe-we-meet-on-the

Coolidge, Calvin. (n.d.). Quote. Quotespedia.info. Retrieved from Quotespedia.info Web site: http://www.quotespedia.info/quotes-about-work-all-growth-depends-upon-activity-a-6487.html

Curie, Marie. (1894). Letter to Jozef Sklodowski (her brother). Retrieved from Brainyquote.com Web site: https://www.brainyquote.com/quotes/marie_curie_131944

Dickinson, Emily. (1894). Letters of Emily Dickinson. Roberts Brothers. Retrieved from Quoteinvestigatior.com Web site: https://quoteinvestigator.com/2018/06/07/not-older/

Disney, Walt. (n.d.). Quote. BrainyQuote.com. Retrieved from BrainyQuote.com Web site: https://www.brainyquote.com/quotes/walt_disney_130929

D'Souza, Fr. Alfred. (n.d.). Passiton.com. Retrieved from Passiton.com Web site: https://www.passiton.com/inspirational-quotes/5094-for-a-long-time-it-had-seemed-to-me-that-life

Einstein, Albert. (n.d.). Quote. Retrieved from Quotefancy.com Web site: https://quotefancy.com/quote/47/Albert-Einstein-There-are-only-two-ways-to-live-your-life-One-is-as-though-nothing-is-a

Gandhi, Mahatma. (n.d.). Quote. Retrieved from Quotespedia.info Web site: http://www.quotespedia.info/quotes-about-time-if-patience-is-worth-anything-a-5343.html

Geisel, Theodor Seuss. (n.d.). Horton Hears a Who. Goodreads.com. Retrieved from Goodreads.com Web site: https://www.goodreads.com/quotes/44212-i-meant-what-i-said-and-i-said-what-i

Golter, Samuel H. (n.d.). Quote. Goodreads.com. Retrieved from Goodreads.com Web site: https://careers.myana.org/profile/city-of-hope/1486483/

Golter, Samuel H. (n.d.). Quote. Goodreads.com. Retrieved from Goodreads.com Web site: https://careers.myana.org/profile/city-of-hope/1486483/

Gordon, Jon. (2018). Quote, Twitter Post. Retrieved from Flickr.com Web site: https://www.flickr.com/photos/pictoquotes/43221913374

Harold E. Varmus. (n.d.). National Center for Biotechnology Information. Brainyquote.com. Retrieved from Brainyquote.com Web site: https://www.brainyquote.com/quotes/harold_e_varmus_688491

Hayes, Alan. (2005). Buddha: Kapilavastu. New York, NY: Vertical. Retrieved from Quotespedia.info Web site: http://www.quotespedia.info/quotes-about-death-without-health-life-is-not-life-a-5241.html

Hollis, James. (1993). The Middle Passage: From Misery to Meaning in Midlife. Inner City Books. Retrieved from AZQuotes.com Web site: https://www.azquotes.com/quote/1184809

Hosaka, Arisa, Ikkaku, Takayuki, Kawabata, Toshihiro. (2005). Animal Crossing: Wild World. Nintendo. Retrieved from Quotationspage.com Web site: http://www.quotationspage.com/quote/40191.html

Howard, Jane. (1998). Families. Taylor and Francis Group LLC (Books) US. Retrieved from Goodreads.com Web site: https://www.goodreads.com/quotes/58361-call-it-a-clan-call-it-a-network-call-it

Howitt, Mary. (1917). Forty Thousand Quotations: Prose and Poetical: Choice Extracts on History, Science, Philosophy, Religion, Literature, etc., compiled by

Charles North Douglas. Children, Quote #137. Halcyon House. Retrieved from Quotes.net Web site: https://www.quotes.net/quote/44492

Hugo, Victor. (1831). The Hunchback of Notre Dame. Gosselin. Retrieved from AZQuotes.com Web site: https://www.azquotes.com/citation/quote/1149040

Jalaluddin Rumi, Maulana. (1926). The Mathnawi of Jalaluddin Rumi. Reynold A. Nicholson. Retrieved from Pinterest.com Web site: https://www.pinterest.com/pin/571464640210716116/

Jefferson, Thomas. (ca. 1773). Thomas Jefferson to John Minor, 30 August 1814, including Thomas Jefferson to Bernard Moore, [ca. 1773?], retrieved from "Founders Online, National Archives, https://founders.archives.gov/documents/Jefferson/03-07-02-0455.

Keller, Helen. (n.d.). Quote. Retrieved from Goodreads.com Web site: https://www.goodreads.com/quotes/472118-on-power-it-is-for-us-to-pray-not-for

King, Jr., Martin Luther. (1960). Quote. Retrieved from Quoteinvestigator.com Web site: https://quoteinvestigator.com/2019/04/18/staircase/

Lou Holtz Quotes. (n.d.). BrainyQuote.com. Retrieved from BrainyQuote.com Web site: https://www.brainyquote.com/quotes/lou_holtz_383816

Lounsbrough, Craig D. (2019). Quote, Facebook.com. Retrieved from Facebook.com Web site: https://www.facebook.com/craiglpc/posts/if-all-that-we-see-are-the-scattered-pieces-of-what-was-the-story-of-what-is-yet/2891570777543414/

Lucado, Max. (2011). It's Not About Me: Rescue From the Life We Thought Would Make Us Happy. Nelson, Thomas, Inc. Retrieved from Goodreads.com Web site: https://www.goodreads.com/quotes/979509-god-does-not-exist-to-make-a-big-deal-out

Marcus Aurelius, Emperor of Rome. (121-180). Quote. Retrieved from Goodreads.com Web site: https://www.goodreads.com/quotes/715167-when-you-arise-in-the-morning-think-of-what-a

Mathison, Elder Bryan. (n.d.). Southern Living Quote #3. Retrieved from Southernliving.com Web site: https://www.southernliving.com/culture/faith-quotes

Maxon, James D. (2011). Traphis: A Wizard's Tale. Easthaven Publishing. Retrieved from Morefamousquotes.com Web site: http://www.morefamousquotes.com/topics/best-prose-quotes/

Nancy Kress. (2015). Anybody Can Write a Novel 2.0. Diviant Art. Retrieved from Quote.org Web site: https://quote.org/quote/a-true-epilogue-is-removed-from-the-325750

National Health Service. (n.d.). Removing stem cells from blood. NHS.uk. Retrieved from NHS.uk Web site: https://www.nhs.uk/conditions/stem-cell-transplant/what-happens/

Niebuhr, Reinhold. (1932). Prayers for a Busy Day, Serenity Prayer. YWCA. Retrieved from Prayerfoundation.org Web site: https://www.prayerfoundation.org/dailyoffice/serenity_prayer_full_version.htm

Parsons, Bob. (n.d.). Quote, Parsons' Rules – Rule #10. Bobparsons.com. Retrieved from Bobparsons.com Web site: https://bobparsons.com/16-rules/

Payne, John Howard. (1880). Home Sweet Home. Lee and Shepard. Retrieved from Olemiss.edu Web site: https://home.olemiss.edu/~mudws/texts/SweetHome.txt

Pickens, T. Boone. (n.d.). Quote. Retrieved from Boonepickens.com Web site: https://boonepickens.com/?page_id=1283

Pilgrim, Peace. (1981). Steps Toward Inner Peace. Friends of Peace Pilgrim. Retrieved from Quotefancy.com Web site: https://quotefancy.com/quote/1367453/Peace-Pilgrim-The-purpose-of-problems-is-to-push-you-toward-obedience-to-God-s-laws-which

Reeve, Christopher. (2002). Nothing Is Impossible. Ballantine Books. Retrieved from Goodreads.com Web site: https://www.goodreads.com/quotes/263437-once-you-choose-hope-anything-s-possible

Roberts, C.J. (2013.). Epilogue (The Dark Duet: Book 3). CreateSpace. Retrieved from Goodreads.com Web site: https://www.goodreads.com/quotes/752064-everything-is-in-the-process-of-becoming-something-else-it-s

Rogers, Robert. (2007). Into the Deep. Focus on the Family. Retrieved from Inspiringlifedreams.com Web site: https://www.inspiringlifedreams.com/quotes-about-faith/#44

Rohn, Jim Quote. (n.d.). Two Types of Pain. Retrieved from Creativecomons.org Web site: https://search.creativecommons.org/search?q=getting%20hurt%20quote&license_type=commercial

Ryle, John Charles. (1860). Expository Thoughts on the Gospels: St. Luke. R. Carter & Brothers. Retrieved from Christianquotes.info Web site: https://www.christianquotes.info/quotes-by-author/j-c-ryle-quotes/

Seneca. (n.d.). Quote. Quotespedia.info.com. Retrieved from Quotespedia.info Web site: http://www.quotespedia.info/quotes-about-philosophy-every-new-beginning-comes-from-some-other-beginning-end-a-4008.html

Shakespeare, William. (1597). Romeo and Juliet. Cuthbert Burby. Retrieved from AZQuotes.com Web site: https://www.azquotes.com/citation/quote/267276

Shakespeare, William. (1623). Antony and Cleopatra. First Folio. Retrieved from AZQuotes.com Web site: https://www.azquotes.com/citation/quote/946384

Smith, Edward A. (n.d.). Stay Close to God. Sermon. Zoe Christian Fellowship Church.

Smith, Edward A. (n.d.). The Highest Calling. Sermon. Zoe Christian Fellowship Church.

Snyder, Paul. (2018). LOVE – In Search of a Reason for Living. CLiP. Retrieved from Google.com Web site: https://www.google.com/books/edition/LOVE_In_Search_of_a_Reason_for_Living/Ek-6Jy1moiMC?hl=en&gbpv=0

Spurgeon, Charles. (1869). Morning and Evening Daily Readings. Passmore and Alabaster. Retrieved from Truth for Life Web site: https://www.truthforlife.org/resources/daily-devotionals/12/28/0/

Stevenson, Robert Louis. (1905). Letters and Miscellanies of Robert Louis Stevenson. Scribner. Retrieved from Brainyquote.com Web site: https://www.brainyquote.com/quotes/robert_louis_stevenson_155194

Stowe, Harriet Beecher. (1869). Oldtown Folks. Fields, Osgood, and Co. Retrieved from Goodreads.com Web site: https://www.goodreads.com/quotes/2571-when-you-get-into-a-tight-place-and-everything-goes

Swedish Proverb. (n.d.). Retrieved from Worldofproverbs.com Web site: http://www.worldofproverbs.com/2012/03/being-away-is-fine-being-home-is-best.html

Swigert, John L. (1969). Nasa.gov. Retrieved from Nasa.gov Web site: https://www.nasa.gov/feature/50-years-ago-houston-we-ve-had-a-problem

Thurman, Howard. (2014). Meditations of the Heart. Beacon Press. Retrieved from Goodreads.com Web site: https://www.goodreads.com/work/quotes/201497-meditations-of-the-heart

Tozer, Aiden Wilson. (n.d.). Christian Publications, Inc. Retrieved from Pinterest.ca Web site: https://www.pinterest.ca/pin/134545107590727394/

Tzu, Lao. (n.d.). Quote. Retrieved from Goodreads.com Web site: https://www.goodreads.com/quotes/854071-new-beginnings-are-often-disguised-as-painful-endings

Unknown. (n.d.). Quote. Brainyquote.com. Retrieved from Brainyquote.com Web site: https://www.brainyquote.com/quotes/erma_bombeck_136506

Unknown. (n.d.). Quote. Dgreetings.com. Retrieved from Dgreetings.com Web site: https://www.dgreetings.com/couple_cards/wedding/quotes-cards.html

Unknown. (n.d.). Quote. Quotespedia.org. Retrieved from Quotespedia.org Web site: https://www.quotespedia.org/authors/u/unknown/sometimes-you-have-to-stop-thinking-so-much-and-just-go-where-your-heart-takes-you-unknown/

Vanier, Jean. (n.d.). Quote. Goodreads.com. Retrieved from Goodreads.com Web site: https://www.goodreads.com/quotes/254298-i-am-struck-by-how-sharing-our-weakness-and-difficulties

Voltaire. (1880). Extracts from a Manuscript in the Hand of M. de Voltaire, Complete Works of Voltaire. Retrieved from Brainyquote.com Web site: https://www.brainyquote.com/quotes/voltaire_134077

Ward, William A. (n.d.). Quote. Retrieved from Brainyquote.com Web site: https://www.brainyquote.com/quotes/william_arthur_ward_105497

Warner, Ann. (2007). Dreams for Stones. Samhain Publishing. Retrieved from Slideshare.net Web site: https://www.slideshare.net/Hanifahindria23/vita-vidia-class3, Slide 5

Watson, Steve J. (2011). Before I Go to Sleep. Text Publishing company. Retrieved from Goodreads.com Web site: https://www.goodreads.com/quotes/549230-it-s-so-difficult-isn-t-it-to-see-what-s-going-on

Weiss, Margaret. (2000). Dragons of Winter Night. Wizards of the Coast. Retrieved from Yourquote.in Web site: https://quotefancy.com/quote/1826582/Margaret-Weis-If-we-deny-love-that-is-given-to-us-if-we-refuse-to-give-love-because-we

Wiggin, Kate Douglas. (1898). The Village Watch-Tower. Houghton, Mifflin and Company. Retrieved from Treasurequotes.com Web site: https://www.treasurequotes.com/quotes/every-child-born-into-the-world-is-a-new-thoug

Winfrey, Oprah. (2015). Quote. Quotespedia.info. Retrieved from Quotespedia.info Web site: http://www.quotespedia.info/quotes-about-time-the-greatest-discovery-of-all-time-is-that-person-a-7582.html

APPENDICES

Topical Index

Aunt Z . . . . See Aunt Zenobia
Aunt Zenobia
   Attendance at Eunice's funeral. 97
   Introduction. 63
Bart
   Bart and Charity's Wedding 435
   Bart introduces Charity to family. . . . 367
   Henry's Blessing 437
   Hopsital visit in Zion 146
   Introduction. 61
   Marriage plans. 436
   Questionnaire Responses . . 62, 147, 148, 149, 164, 165, 197, 231, 244, 282, 367, 378, 388, 432, 433, 439, 440, 453, 510, 512, 514, 516, 517, 519, 523, 527, 530
   Rites of Passage 435
Beryl
   Introduction. 63
   Questionnaire Responses . . . 64, 65, 282, 378, 432, 433, 453, 510, 512, 514, 515, 516, 518, 520, 528, 530
Bibles
   Aramaic Bible in Plain English. 509
   Berean Study Bible 13, 42, 46, 77, 80, 100, 103, 123, 178, 180, 201, 214, 240, 249, 265, 325, 360, 372, 407, 482, 483, 491, 500, 501, 505, 508, 524, 534, 538, 539
   Christian Standard Bible 15
   English Standard Version 13, 17, 84, 158, 258, 482
   Good News Translation Bible. 525
   King James Version 4, 15, 18, 493, 535
   New American Standard 5, 9, 13, 54, 85, 86, 87, 100, 175, 250, 428, 447, 487
   New International Version 17, 22, 28, 82, 87, 100, 115, 131, 176, 179, 204, 210, 227, 320, 326, 331, 350, 408, 416, 435, 463, 500, 504, 505, 507
   New King James Version 14, 353, 397, 503, 540
   New Living Translation 4, 117, 345
Breaking the news
   Telling Bart. 61
   Telling Beryl. 63
   Telling Cecily 75
   Telling Ira and Cris 57
   Telling Jeff and Charale 150
   Telling Jim. 254
   Telling Kathy 66
   Telling Lois and Michael 73
   Telling Margaret 47
   Telling Norman and Ruth 67
   Telling Pat. 59
   Telling Sandra 225
   Telling Talia 62
Cancer Support Community
   Open to Options Program 316
   The Do's and Don'ts of How to Help . 506
Cancer Support Community Pasadena
   About Cancer Support Community Pasadena. 551
   First visit 285
   Support groups 292
Cancer Treatment Centers of America
   About CTCA Chicago 546
   First Encounter 53
   Check-in 90
   Bone marrow biopsy. 105
   Cancer diagnosis. 92
   Chemo Brain 110
   Discharge 184
   Hospitalization 93

Kidney triage 95
Kidneys restored 112
Multiple Myeloma triage 95
Neuropathy. 125
Night Angel. 179
Patient registration 90
PET Scan 113
Physical Therapy 123, 128, 141, 143, 158, 164, 185, 187, 192, 195, 202
Standard chemotherapy treatment . . 116

Caregiver
Definition 85
Henry's part time caregiver. 269

Cecily
Dinner with Henry and Vanessa 427
Introduction. 75
Questionnaire Responses . . . 75, 76, 169, 170, 171, 283, 379, 427, 432, 454, 511, 513, 514, 517, 519, 521, 522, 523, 529, 531

Charity
Bart and Charity's Wedding 435
Introduction. 165
Questionnaire Responses 165, 166, 368, 378, 432, 439, 440, 453, 462, 510, 512, 514, 516, 517, 519, 527, 530
Thanksgiving 2016
  Family Celebration. 455

City of Hope
About City of Hope 548
Admission for back surgery. 381
Discharge after back surgery 390
Discharge after infection
  hospitalization 249
Discharge after Stem Cell
  Transplant 367
First chemotherapy treatment 219
Henry meets an old friend. 347
Hospitalization for residual
  infections 227

Patient registration 215
Radiation treatments 232, 238, 242, 254, 258, 262
Recovery from back surgery 383
Slogan 325
Transesophageal Echocardiogram
  procedure. 235
Walk for Hope 446

Cris
Introduction. 57
Questionnaire Responses 57, 58, 59, 282, 297, 331, 367, 378, 388, 397, 432, 443, 453, 512, 514, 516, 518, 520, 523, 528

CSCP
See Cancer Support Community Pasadena

CTCA
See Cancer Treatment Centers of America

Eunice W. Dotson
Colonoscopy 39
Crushing Blow 19
Dialysis 40
Home Going Celebration. 96
Passing. 95

Henry
60th birthday celeration 484
Christmas 2017 visit to Arizona 470
Colonoscopy exam 40
Henry visits friend in hospital 353

Henry and Vanessa
First Meeting 100
Henry asks Vanessa's father
  for her hand. 441
Henry decides to propose 306
Henry proposes 485
Vanessa reveals her feelings 134
Vanessa's support through
  Henry's divorce. 120

APPENDICES

Henry B. Dotson, Jr.
   Automobile accident 30
   Crushing Blow 18
   Home Going Celebration. 32
   Passing. 31
   Stroke. 31

Henry's Facebook Posts
   Be Not Discouraged 488
   Great is Thy Faithfulness 473
   Happy Birthday to Me!. 298
   Happy New Birthday to Me! 361
   I've Been Restored 449
   MRD Test 444
   One More Thing. 477
   One Year Into the Journey 413
   Pre-Op Prayer Request. 380
   Some Words of Thanks. 425
   Sunday Praise Report 428

Ira
   Introduction. 57
   Questionnaire Responses   57, 58, 207, 208, 209, 281, 297, 330, 378, 397, 432, 443, 453, 510, 512, 514, 516, 517, 519, 527, 530

Jeff & Charale
   Hospital visit in Zion 149
   Introduction. 149
   Questionnaire Responses   149, 150, 151, 282, 379, 432, 434, 514, 517, 521, 523, 529, 532

Jez. . . . . See Jezreel

Jezreel
   Introduction. 28
   Questionnaire Responses 455, 456, 457, 458, 509, 510, 513, 514, 517, 520, 523, 528, 531
   Thanksgiving 2016 Family Celebration 455

Jim
   Introduction. 254
   Questionnaire Responses 254, 255, 283, 379, 433, 454, 512, 513, 515, 521, 522, 523, 529, 532

Kathy
   Introduction. 66
   Questionnaire Responses . . . 66, 67, 169, 282, 378, 432, 453, 518, 520, 528, 531

Lois
   Introduction. 73
   Questionnaire Responses 74, 222, 261, 266, 281, 283, 379, 433, 454, 511, 513, 514, 517, 519, 521, 523, 529, 531

Margaret
   CTCA recommendation. 47
   Hopsital visit in Zion 146
   Introduction. 48
   Questionnaire Responses . . 51, 146, 147, 283, 379, 433, 454, 509, 511, 513, 515, 517, 519, 521, 522, 529, 532

Medical Terminology
   C.R.A.B. Symptoms of
      Multiple Myeloma 41
   Description of a bone marrow biopsy . 106
   Description of a Trans
      Esophageal Echocardiogram 235
   Description of Chemo Brain. 110
   Description of Creatinine 98
   Description of Hyper CVAD 111
   Description of Multiple Myeloma . . . 108
   Description of the acronym ANC. . . . 171
   Description of the acronym VRD. . . . 116
   Multiple Myeloma and kidney failure . 112
   Neuropathy caused by chemotherapy. 125
   PET Scan description 113

Michael
   Introduction. 73
   Questionnaire Responses 74, 75, 529

Multiple Myeloma
   C.R.A.B. Symptoms of
      Multiple Myeloma 41
   Description. 108
   Multiple Myeloma and kidney failure . 112

Preliminary Diagnosis 12

Norman

Henry and Norman's car rallying..... 70
Henry and Norman's deep friendship 67
Henry's groomsman 72
Introduction...................... 67
Norman's support through Henry's divorce........................... 69
Questionnaire Responses 72, 73, 142, 282, 283, 340, 378, 397, 432, 434, 440, 453, 511, 513, 518, 521, 522, 528, 531

Pat

Introduction...................... 59
Questionnaire Responses ... 60, 61, 169, 282, 297, 378, 388, 432, 433, 443, 453, 510, 512, 514, 516, 518, 520, 528, 530

Ruth

Introduction...................... 67
Questionnaire Responses ... 72, 73, 142, 282, 340, 378, 397, 432, 434, 440, 454, 511, 513, 519, 521, 522, 529, 531

San Gabriel Valley Multiple Myeloma Support Group

About 291
First meeting 291

Sandra

Introduction..................... 225
Questionnaire Responses 225, 226, 282, 378, 432, 434, 453, 513, 514, 517, 518, 521, 523, 528, 531

Stefany

Growing up with Uncle Bernard 391
Henry at Stefany's wedding......... 394
Introduction...................... 390

Stem Cell Transplant

Description of the collection process 338
Discharge after Stem Cell Transplant 267
Stem cell collection....... 335, 338, 341, 344, 347, 350, 353, 356, 358
Stem cell infusion 360

Talia

Hospital visit in Zion 146
Introduction...................... 62
Questionnaire Responses ... 62, 63, 147, 148, 149, 164, 165, 197, 231, 244, 282, 330, 367, 378, 388, 397, 432, 453, 510, 512, 514, 515, 516, 517, 519, 527, 530

Valenda

Cancer Diagnosis 25
Introduction...................... 24
Memorial Service 26

Visits from home

Visit from Bart in Zion 146
Visit from Jeff & Charale in Zion 150
Visit from Talia in Zion............ 146

Zion

About Zion 542
An outpatient in Zion.............. 184
Arrival in Zion 85
Discovery of CTCA's location 86

APPENDICES

Scripture Index

1 Chronicles 12:33 94	Isaiah 40 131
1 Corinthians 2:14 544	Isaiah 42:16 86
1 Corinthians 14:5, 13 177	Isaiah 43:2 . . . . 354, 355
1 Corinthians 3:18 448	Isaiah 57:18-19 535
1 John 3:24 524	James 1:12 540
1 John 5:4 428	James 1:2 13
1 Peter 5:8 174	James 1:2-3 397
1 Peter 5:9 77	James 1:2-4 . . . . 350, 401
2 Corinthians 4:16-17 227	James 1:4 463
2 Corinthians 4:17-18 504	James 5:10-11 489
2 Corinthians 5:7 540	James 5:11 265
2 Corinthians 12:5-9 450	James 5:14-16 . . . . 429, 487
2 Corinthians 12:9 137	Jeremiah 17:14 209
2 Kings 20:6 54	Jeremiah 29:11-12 9
2 Timothy 1:7 505	Jeremiah 29:11 13
2 Timothy 4:17 175	Jeremiah 31:16 117
Acts 27:23 178	Joel 3:1 500
Ephesians 2:8 – 9 509	Joel 3:17 87
Ephesians 3:16-20 539	John 3:16 2
Ephesians 6:10-12 . . . . 123, 232, 249	John 9:15 500
Ephesians 6:12 157	John 9:24-25 501
Ephesians 6:13 77	John 10:10 80
Ephesians 6:16 372	John 10:14 . . . . 46, 478
Ephesians 6:18 372	John 11:43 22
Exodus 23:25 177	John 14:2 . . . . 131, 482
Exodus 33:14 320	John 14:27 229
Ezekiel 37:3-5 360	John 16:33 229
Galatians 6:9-10 28	Joshua 24:15 250
Genesis 12:2 4	Judges 3:27 117
Genesis 2:21-23 100	Luke 1:37 137
Genesis 49:26 435	Luke 11:8-10 103
Hebrews 11:1 491	Luke 15:4-6 478
Hebrews 12:22-23 87	Mark 10:7-8 100
Hebrews 3:6 233	Mark 5:19 203
Hebrews 4:16 353	Matthew 10:29-30 259
Hebrews 10:35-36 464	Matthew 11:28 82

Matthew 17:18 131	Psalm 37:34. 328
Matthew 17:20 . . . . 5, 507	Psalm 44:4-8 115
Matthew 5:4 . . . . 369, 482	Psalm 44:5-6 83
Matthew 5:45 13	Psalm 46 131
Matthew 6:27-28 258	Psalm 63:7-8 508
Matthew 7:7-8 353	Psalm 71:14-15 416
Matthew 8:24-26 214	Psalm 77:12 525
Philippians 3:12 407	Psalm 84:5 84
Philippians 3:12-14 538	Psalm 91:14-15 200
Philippians 4:6 42	Psalm 91:16 2
Philippians 4:6-7 13	Psalm 92:1 331
Philippians 4:7 15	Psalm 94:19 13
Proverbs 16:18 505	Psalm 105:1-2 447
Proverbs 18:22 . . . . 14, 49	Psalm 105:4 229
Proverbs 20:30 17	Psalm 107:6-7 214
Proverbs 21:30 448	Psalm 118:1 326
Proverbs 23:24 435	Psalm 118:16 246
Proverbs 31:10 49	Psalm 119:114 416
Proverbs 31:10-12,28-29 100	Psalm 125:1-2 501
Psalm 5:11 202	Psalm 127:3-5 483
Psalm 17:5 408	Psalm 130:5 325
Psalm 18:3 240	Psalm 139:13-16 17
Psalm 18:20-21 85	Romans 5:3-5 464
Psalm 18:39 534	Romans 8:11 131
Psalm 20:1-2 179	Romans 8:18 233
Psalm 30:5 503	Romans 8:28 . . . . 4, 18, 233, 493, 496, 518
Psalm 37:23-24 345	Zechariah 8:13 5

APPENDICES

Quotation Index

Afghan Proverb 67	Jalaluddin Rumi. 417, 496
African Proverb 417	James D. Maxon. 540
Aiden Wilson Tozer. 502	James Hollis 323
Albert Einstein. 487	Jane Howard. 63
Ann Warner 316	Jean Vanier 292
Arisa Hosaka. 55	Jim Butcher. 153
Arthur Ashe 211	Jim Rohn 17, 507
Audre Lorde 371	John Baxter 358
Avicenna 403	John Charles Ryle 491
Birthday.Kim 298	John L. Swigert. 89
Bishop Edward A. Smith 508, 539	Jon Gordon 505
Bob Parsons 113	Kate Douglas Wiggin. 483
Boyd Bailey. 508	Katherine Mansfield 146
Brittany Burgunder. 269	Lao Tzu 498
Buddha 278	Lewis Carroll 402
C.J. Roberts. 537	Lou Holtz. 538
Calvin Coolidge 262	Louis L'Amour 527
Carol Welch 408	Lynda Varada 526
Charles Spurgeon 491	Mahatma Gandhi 369
Christopher Reeve. 503	Marcus Aurelius. 504
Craig D. Lounsbrough 526	Margaret Weiss. 481
Criss Angel 37	Marie Curie. 463
Dale Carnegie. 311	Martin Luther King, Jr. 527
Dorothy Gale 110	Mary Howitt 61
Elder Bryan Mathison. 507	Max Lucado 524
Emily Dickinson 484	Maya Angelou 269
Fr. Alfred D'Souza 533	Mila Bron 502
Frances Ryan 371	Nancy Kress 465
Gordon Atkinson. 67	National Health Service 332
Hal Borland xi	Oprah Winfrey 373
Harold E. Varmus 444	Paul Snyder. 294
Harriet Beecher Stowe 241	Peace Pilgrim 116
Helen Keller 526	Reinhold Niebuhr 540
Henry B. Dotson, Sr. 370	Robert Louis Stevenson 505
Henry Ward Beecher. 61	Robert Rogers. 507
Howard Thurman 319	S.J. Watson 495

Samuel H. Golter 325, 326	Victor Hugo 55
Seneca 496	Vidal Sassoon 403
Swedish Proverb 201	Voltaire 298
T. Boone Pickens 311	W. Somerset Maugham 409
Takayuki Ikkaku 55	Walt Disney 496
Thomas Jefferson 107	Wendell Berry 284, 293, 502
Toshihiro Kawabata 55	William A. Ward 468
Unknown 183, 320, 390, 406, 408	William Shakespeare 55, 87

Permissions and Acknowledgements

Permission has been granted to reprint previously published copyrighted material or print intellectual property from the following:

Ann Warner: Excerpt from *Dreams for Stones* by Ann Warner, copyright ©2015 by Gordon Atkinson. Reprinted by permission of Ann Warner.

Arthur Ashe: Excerpt(s) from *DAYS OF GRACE: A MEMOIR* by Arthur Ashe and Arnold Rampersad, copyright ©1993 by Jeanne Moutoussamy-Ashe and Arnold Rampersad. Used by permission of Alfred A. Knopf, an imprint of the Knopf Doubleday Publishing Group, a division of Penguin Random House LLC. All rights reserved.

Boyd Bailey: Excerpt from *God's Permissive Will*, https://www.widsomhunters.com/gods-permissive-will/ by Boyd Bailey, copyright ©2014 by Boyd Bailey. Reprinted by permission of Boyd Bailey.

Brittany Burgunder: Excerpt from *Hiding the Need for Help* blog, https://brittanyburgunder.com/2021/05/03/hiding-the-need-for-help// by Brittany Burgunder, copyright ©2021 by Brittany Burgunder. Reprinted by permission of Brittany Burgunder.

Cancer Support Community: "The Do's and Don'ts of "How to be a good friend to a person with cancer," The Cancer Support Community. Reprinted with permission of Cancer Support Community Pasadena.

Cancer Support Community Pasadena: Logo, The Cancer Support Community Pasadena. Reprinted with permission of Cancer Support Community Pasadena.

Christopher & Dana Reeve Foundation: Quotation from Christopher Reeve, copyright ©2002 by Ballantine Books. Reprinted with permission of the Christopher & Dana Reeve Foundation.

Craig D. Lounsbrough: Excerpt from Craig D. Lounsbrough Facebook post, copyright ©2019. Reprinted by permission of Craig D. Lounsbrough.

C. J. Roberts: Excerpt from *Epilogue (The Dark Duet: Book 3)*, copyright ©2013 by CreateSpace. Reprinted with permission of the C. J. Roberts.

Hal Borland: Excerpt from *Sundial of the Seasons* by Hal Borland, copyright ©1964 and copyright © renewed 2020 by Echo Point Books & Media, LLC. Reprinted by permission of Echo Point Books & Media, LLC, publisher.

Edward A. Smith: Quotations. Printed by permission of Edward A. Smith.

Gordon Atkinson: Excerpt from *Real Live Preacher Archive, Crocodile Hunter* by Gordon Atkinson, copyright ©2018 by Gordon Atkinson. Reprinted by permission of Gordon Atkinson.

James D. Maxon: Excerpt from *Traphis: A Wizard's Tale* by James D. Maxon, copyright ©2011 by James D. Maxon. Reprinted by permission of James D. Maxon.

Jim Butcher: Excerpt(s) from *PROVEN GUILTY* by Jim Butcher, copyright ©2006 by Jim Butcher. Used by permission of ROC, an imprint of Penguin Publishing Group, a division of Penguin Random House LLC. All rights reserved.

John Baxter: Excerpt from *A Pound of Paper: Confessions of Book Addict* by John Baxter, copyright ©2002 by John Baxter. Reprinted by permission of John Baxter.

Lynda Varada: Quotation. Printed by permission of Lynda Varada.

Nancy Kress: Quotation. Printed by permission of Nancy Kress.

Paul Snyder: Excerpt from *LOVE - In Search of a Reason for Living* by Paul Snyder, copyright ©2018 by Paul Snyder. Reprinted by permission of Paul Snyder.

Dr. Seuss: Excerpts from *Horton Hatches the Egg* by Dr. Seuss, copyright ©1940 by Dr. Seuss. Used by permission of Random House, an imprint and division of Penguin Random House LLC (printed versions only, not for eBook versions). All rights reserved.

Maya Angelou: Excerpts from *Wouldn't Take Nothing for My Journey Now* by Maya Angelou, copyright ©1993 by Maya Angelou. Used by permission of Random House, an imprint and division of Penguin Random House LLC. All rights reserved.

Wendell Berry: Excerpts from *Loss of the Future* by Wendell Berry, copyright ©1968 by Religious Humanism and *The Art of the Commonplace: The Agrarian Essays of Wendell Berry* by Wendell Berry, copyright ©2003 by Counterpoint. Reprinted by permission of Permissions Company, LLC.

Stefany: Stefany's story of her relationship with Henry and her wedding day is printed with her permission.

Taylor and Francis Group: Excerpt from *Families* by Jane Howard copyright ©1978 by Simon and Schuster and copyright © renewed 1998 by Rutledge. Reproduced with permission of the Licensor through PLSclear.

The Estate of Howard Thurman: Excerpt from *Meditations of the Heart* by Howard Thurman copyright ©2014 by Beacon Press Reprinted with permission of The Estate of Howard Thurman.

Martin Luther King, Jr.: Excerpt from *Mother Jones Magazine,* Vol 16, No. 3, p.77 by Martin Luther King, Jr. copyright ©1960. Reprinted by arrangement with The Heirs to the Estate of Martin Luther King, Jr., c/o Writers House as agent for the proprietor New York, N.Y.

Copyright ©1986 by Dr. Martin Luther King, Jr. Renewed ©2014 by Coretta Scott King.

The VanBern Group: Excerpts from Multiple Myeloma Journey Questionnaire responses by Bart, Beryl, Cecily, Charale, Charity, Cris, Ira, Jeff, Jezreel, Jim, Kathy, Lois, Margaret, Michael, Norman, Pat, Ruth, Sandra, and Talia, copyright ©2017 by The VanBern Group, Inc.

All other quotations in the book are in the public domain or are covered under Fair Use, Section 107 of the Copyright Law of the United States (title 17), Appendix A: The Copyright Act of 1976.

Acknowledgements

Many writers compare the authoring process to giving birth – the mental, emotional, and spiritual labor it demands and the overwhelming love one has for the precious child who comes forth as a result. With this book being my first, I think I understand at last why the comparison is made. As a male, I will not personally ever give birth to a child, but I can appreciate how much energy is expended pushing out the product of one's labor.

As in most cases of childbirth in the United States, the authoring process is also not performed alone. There were several key individuals involved aside from those who contributed directly to the content of the manuscript.

I wish to thank all of the people that read the advance review copy of the manuscript and provided feedback. They found more typos and grammatical errors than was humanly possible for our editors and proofreaders in the time allotted.

I wish to thank Alfred Haymond for taking our pictures that appear on the back cover. We learned photo sessions are no more glamorous and exciting than business travel is for road warriors. I have gained a greater respect for fashion models and photographers.

I wish to thank Hazel Clayton Harris and Angela Clayton for proofreading the manuscript. They were both very accommodating and worked with our very busy schedule. Hazel also provided very encouraging words that helped to make the process enjoyable. Something I did not expect.

I wish to thank Laura Seiler for lending her expertise as a technical editor. She graciously fit me in to her very busy schedule, and mentored me on how to view my work from the perspective of a technical editor and the reader. I am a better writer as a result.

I wish to thank Vincent Williams for his work as the book cover designer. His patience and creativity made the task much easier for those of us who often say, "I'll know it when I see it." Working with this type of client can be very frustrating and draining when you are an artist or moving furniture.

I am forever grateful to Julie Davey, who mentored and guided me through the entire writing process. There is a Chinese saying, "When the student is ready, the teacher appears." The Bible says, "Seek, and ye shall find." I believe God orchestrated a divine appointment where we would meet.

Julie is a seasoned author with many years of experience as a journalist and professor of writing at the post-secondary level. She loves everything about writing and encourages everyone to write. She developed and conducted a class entitled, "Writing for Wellness" for cancer patients and others dealing with major trauma.

Her enthusiasm and encouragement were very inspirational.

She took on the difficult task of line editor which involved reviewing the first draft of the manuscript. She said she does not use red ink because it might be discouraging for first time authors. I found a note containing words of encouragement with every section returned to me with her mark ups.

She also put me in contact with Vincent and Laura, checked up on me when she had not heard from me in a while, and always took my calls. I know our working together was a "God thing."

Lastly, I wish to thank our Facebook Prayer Team. Thank you so much for staying engaged online and providing your comments. They helped to shape the book by providing readers with a glimpse of what you were experiencing as you came along side us on the journey.

We salute you by giving you honorable mention by first name and last initial. May God continue to bless you and keep you as you travel along your journeys of life in the future.

Henry B. Dotson, III
August, 2021

From Zion to a City of Hope: A Journey of Faith

Our Facebook Prayer Team

Aaron W. • Abraham M. • Alexa A. • Alfred D. • Amalaye O. • Ameer E. • Angela C. Angela W. • Annette C. • Annette Y. • Annie R. • Archelle F. • Arnold C. Ashley W. • Aubrey S. • Ava D. • Aziza W. • Barbara W • Beryl M. • Bill G. • Edward S. Bobbi M. • Brad C. • Brian W • Brian D. • Carol P. • Carolijn C. • Cash S. • Cathrine J. Cecily S. • Cedric D. • Charale B. • Charity D. • Desire W. • Clifford W. • Sandra C. Courtney P. • Craig C. • Cris D. • Cynthia L. • Daizy L. • Daphne W. • DaRacia M. Darlene C. • David L. • De M. • Debora R. • Deborah P. • Delaine A. • Delisa K. Denise H. • Derrick M. • Diana B. • Don Costa S. • Doralyn S. • Dorri R. • Joycelyn J. Earnest P. • Elaine T. • Eva G. • Evelyn C. • Felicia W. • Felicia H. • Frances K. Frank R. • Frederick D. • Gary G. • Geniverteria T. • George G. • Geriece H. Germaine A. • Gordon B. • Greg G. • Gretchen B. • Hayley D. • Heidi W. Homer C. • Howard R. • Hubert C. • Ira D. • Jackie Dr. • Jackie Du • Jackie Lo Jacqueline S. • Jamelle P. • James C. • James Ma • James Mc • James W. • Janice R. Jeffrey B. • Jeremy D. • Jettie D. • Jezreel S. • Jim H. • Jo-Ann H. • Joan R. • Joeann S. Johnette W. • Jonathan G. • Josie M. • Joslyn G. • Joyce D. • Joyce We. Joyce W. • Kadesh D. • Karen I. • Kathy G. • Kathy F. • Keith C. • Kelly B. • Kelly R. Kelsey T. • Kenny J. • Kevin I. • LaFaye B. • Lashae P. • LaTanya J. • LaTima J. LaVerne H. • Lawrence H. • Lawrence L. • Leavanna P • Leslie B. • Levell D. Lewis G. • Lois D. • Lori W. • Louise E. • Lynda M. • Lynette K. • Lynn B. Mamta S. • Marc C. • Mark C. • Mary P. • Maude H. • Maurice R. • Melanie H. Melodie C. • Mihloti M. • Mikateko S. • Millicent G. • Monica S. • Monica L. Monique S. • Murphy P. • Nicole G. • Om M. • Omega W. • P Ray J. • Paige H. Pamela H. • Patricia J. • Patricia M. • Patti O. • Paula G. • Phaenicia M. Prophetess B. • Randy W. • Ray W. • Regina H. • Regina Z. • Rhonda W. Romeka D. • Robert M. • Roberta M. • Robin B. • Rosalind G. • Rose N. • Roslyn H. Roslyn S. • Ryan B. • Sadie T. • Salome B. • Samana T. • Samuel D. • Sandra C. Saundra M. • Saundra M. • Shareen R. • Sheila A. • Shelia R. • Shelia W. • Shyrea M. Stanton L. • Stefanie G. • Stefany D. • Stephen G. • Steve C. • Susan P. • Susan Z. Sweet S. • Sydney G. • Talia D. • Taliba C. • Terena W. • Terence W. • Terri G. Theresa B. • Thomas M. • Tiffany L. • Tim B. • Tina L. • Tone Tone • Tony D. Tony M. • Tonya B. • Tonya G. • Troy W. • TyAnne E. • Valerie P. • Vanessa D. Vanessa P. • Vanessa H. • Verbon O. • Verneal B. • Veronica W. • Vicky R. • Victor W. Vincent W. • Wendy H. • William L. • Willie M. • Winfred D. • Winifred Y • Zephran H.

www.ingramcontent.com/pod-product-compliance
Lightning Source LLC
Chambersburg PA
CBHW071800080526
44589CB00012B/623